THE RACES OF MAN

D1876588

Owing to the antiquity and rarity of this book, certain pages are regrettably absent, and readability is compromised due to the blurring of the original text. If you possess any insights regarding the availability of these missing sections, kindly inform us. Your assistance is crucial in ensuring the completion of this significant work for the benefit of future generations.

THE RACES OF MAN

AN OUTLINE OF ANTHROPOLOGY AND ETHNOGRAPHY

JOSEPH DENIKER

GYAN

Published by

Gyan Publishing House
5, Ansari Road
Daryaganj, New Delhi-110002
Phone: 011-47034999, 9811692060
E-mail: books@gyanbooks.com

Distribution Network
gyanbooks.com
India, USA, Canada, UK, Australia

© Publisher

All rights reserved. No part of this work may be reproduced, stored, adapted, or transmitted in any form or by any means, electronic, mechanical, photocopying, micro-filming, recording or otherwise, or translated in any language, without the prior written permission of the copyright owner and the publisher.

ISBN: 978-93-7316-006-1 (PB)

First Published, 1900

2nd Impression 2025

Printed at: Gyan Press, Delhi.

The book is sold subject to the condition that it shall not, by way of trade or otherwise, be lent, resold, hired out, or otherwise circulated without the prior publisher's written consent.

THE RACES OF MAN
Arthur: JOSEPH DENIKER

THE CONTEMPORARY SCIENCE SERIES.

EDITED BY HAVELOCK ELLIS.

THE RACES OF MAN.

Naga of Manipur in gala costume, with caudiform appendage.
(*Phot. lent by Miss Godden.*)

THE RACES OF MAN:

AN OUTLINE OF ANTHROPOLOGY AND ETHNOGRAPHY

BY

J. DENIKER, Sc.D. (Paris),

Chief Librarian of the Museum of Natural History, Paris; Honorary Fellow of the Anthropological Institute of Great Britain; Corresponding Member of the Italian Anthropological, Netherland Geographical, and Moscow Natural Science Societies, etc.

WITH 176 ILLUSTRATIONS AND 2 MAPS.

LONDON
WALTER SCOTT, LIMITED
PATERNOSTER SQUARE
1900

PREFACE.

My object in the present work has been to give in a condensed form the essential facts of the twin sciences of anthropology and ethnography. The very nature of such an undertaking condemns the author to be brief, and at the same time somewhat dogmatic; inevitable gaps occur, and numerous inequalities in the treatment. To obviate, partly at least, such defects, I have endeavoured not merely to present the actual facts of the subject, but also to summarise, with as much fidelity as possible, the explanations of these facts, in so far as such may be deduced from theories among which there is often sufficient perplexity of choice. In many cases I have ventured, however, to give my personal opinion on different questions, as, for instance, on the signification of the laryngeal sacs among anthropoid apes, on many questions of anthropometry in general, on the classing of "states of civilisation," on fixed and transportable habitations, on the classification of races, on the races of Europe, on the Palæ-American race, etc.

My book is designed for all those who desire to obtain rapidly a general notion of ethnographic and anthropological

CONTENTS.

INTRODUCTION.

CHAPTER I.

CHAPTER II.

CHAPTER III.

CHAPTER IV.

CHAPTER IV.—(*continued*).

CHAPTER V.

CHAPTER VI.

CHAPTER VII.

CHAPTER VIII.

CHAPTER IX.

CHAPTER X.

CHAPTER XI.

CHAPTER XI.—(*continued*).

CHAPTER XII.

CHAPTER XIII.

CHAPTER XIII.—(*continued*).

LIST OF ILLUSTRATIONS.

THE RACES OF MAN.

INTRODUCTION.

ETHNIC GROUPS AND ZOOLOGICAL SPECIES.

Difficulties in applying to Man the terms of zoological nomenclature—Criterion of species—Terms to give to the "Somatological Units" constituting the genus *Homo*—Monogenesis and Polygenesis—The "Ethnic Groups" are constituted by the different combinations of the "Somatological Units" or "Races"—Somatic characters and ethnic characters.

THE innumerable groups of mankind, massed together or scattered, according to the varying nature of the earth's surface, are far from presenting a homogeneous picture. Every country has its own variety of physical type, language, manners, and customs. Thus, in order to exhibit a systematic view of all the peoples of the earth, it is necessary to observe a certain order in the study of these varieties, and to define carefully what is meant by such and such a descriptive term, having reference either to the physical type or to the social life of men. This we shall do in the subsequent chapters as we proceed to develop this slight sketch of the chief general facts of the physical and psychical life of man, and of the most striking social phenomena of the groups of mankind.

But there are some general terms which are of more importance than others, and their meaning should be clearly understood from the first. I refer to expressions like "people," "nation," "tribe," "race," "species," in short, all the designations of the different groupings, real or theoretic, of human beings. Having defined them, we shall by so doing define the object of our studies.

Since ethnography and anthropology began to exist as sciences, an attempt has been made to determine and establish the great groups amongst which humanity might be divided. A considerable diversity of opinion, however, exists among leading scientific men not only as to the number of these groups, of these "primordial divisions" of the human race, but, above all, as to the very nature of these groups. Their significance, most frequently, is very vaguely indicated.

In zoology, when we proceed to classify, we have to do with beings which, in spite of slight individual differences, are easily grouped around a certain number of types, with well-defined characters, called "species." An animal can always be found which will represent the "type" of its species. In all the great zoological collections there exist these "species-types," to which individuals may be compared in order to decide if they belong to the supposed species. We have then in zoology a real substratum for the determination of species, those primordial units which are grouped afterwards in genera, families, orders, etc.

Is it the same for man? Whilst knowing that the zoological genus *Homo* really exists quite distinct from the other genera of the animal kingdom, there still arises the question as to where the substratum is on which we must begin operations in order to determine the "species" of which this genus is composed. The only definite facts before us are these groups of mankind, dispersed over the whole habitable surface of the globe, to which are commonly given the names of peoples, nations, clans, tribes, etc We have presented to us Arabs, Swiss, Australians, Bushmen, English, Siouan Indians, Negroes, etc., without knowing if each of these groups is on an equal footing from the point of view of classification.

Do these real and palpable groupings represent unions of individuals which, in spite of some slight dissimilarities, are capable of forming what zoologists call "species," "subspecies," "varieties," in the case of wild animals, or "races" in the case of domestic animals? One need not be a professional anthropologist to reply negatively to this question. They are *ethnic groups* formed by virtue of community of language, religion, social institutions, etc., which have the power of uniting human beings of one or several species, races, or varieties,[1] and are by no means zoological species; they may include human beings of one or of many species, races, or varieties.

Here, then, is the first distinction to make: the social groups that we are to describe in this work under the names of clans, tribes, nations, populations, and peoples, according to their numerical importance and the degree of complication of their social life, are formed for us by the union of individuals belonging usually to two, three, or a greater number of "somatological units." These units are "theoretic types" formed of an aggregation of physical characters combined in a certain way. The separate existence of these units may be established by a minute analysis of the physical characters of a great number of individuals taken haphazard in any given "ethnic group." Here are, then, entities, theoretic conceptions exactly like "species" in zoology; only instead of having within our reach the "types" of these species as in zoological collections, we are obliged to rest content with approximations thereto, for it is a very rare occurrence to meet with an individual representing the type of the somatological unit to which he belongs. Most frequently we have to do with subjects whose forms are altered by blendings and crossings, and in whom, setting aside two or three typical traits, we find only a confused mixture of characters presenting nothing striking. Ordinarily, the more peoples are civilised the more

[1] In these ethnic groups there may further be distinguished several subdivisions due to the diversity of manners, customs, etc.; or, in the groups with a more complicated social organisation, yet other social groups—priests, magistrates, miners, peasants, having each his particular "social type."

they are intermixed within certain territorial limits. Thus the number of "somatological units" is so much the greater when the "ethnic groups" are more civilised, and it is only among entirely primitive peoples that one may hope to find coincidence between the two terms. In reality, those peoples are almost undiscoverable who represent "somatological units" comparable to the "species" of zoology.

But, it may be asked, do you believe that your "somatological units" are comparable with "species"? Are they not simple "varieties" or "races"?

Without wishing to enter into a discussion of details, it seems to me that where the genus *Homo* is concerned, one can neither speak of the "species," the "variety," nor the "race" in the sense that is usually attributed to these words in zoology or in zootechnics.

In effect, in these two sciences, the terms "species" and "variety" are applied to wild animals living solely under the influence of nature; whilst the term "race" is given in a general way to the groups of domestic animals living under artificial conditions created by an alien will, that of man, for a well-defined object.

Let us see to which of these two categories man, considered as an animal, may be assimilated.

By this single fact, that even at the very bottom of the scale of civilisation man possesses articulate speech, fashions tools, and forms himself into rudimentary societies, he is emancipated from a great number of influences which Nature exerts over the wild animal; he lives, up to a certain point, in an artificial environment created by himself. On the other hand, precisely because these artificial conditions of life are not imposed upon him by a will existing outside himself, because his evolution is not directed by a "breeder" or a "domesticator," man cannot be compared with domestic animals as regards the modifications of his corporeal structure.

The data relating to the formation of varieties, species, and races can therefore be applied to the morphological study of man only with certain reservations.

This being established, let us bear in mind that even the distinction between the species, the variety (geographical or otherwise), and the race is anything but clearly marked. Besides, this is a question that belongs to the domain of general biology, and it is no more settled in botany or in zoology than in anthropology. The celebrated botanist, Naegeli, has even proposed to suppress this distinction, and definitely show the identical nature of all these divisions by instituting his *great* and *small species*.[1]

The idea of "species" must rest on the knowledge of two orders of facts, the morphological resemblances of beings and the lineal transmission of their distinctive characters. Here, in fact, the formula of Cuvier is still in force to-day in science. "The species is the union of individuals *descending one from the other or from common parents*, and of those who resemble them as much as they resemble each other."[2] (I have italicised the passage relating to descent.) It is necessary then that beings, in order to form a species, should be like each other, but it is obvious that this resemblance cannot be absolute, for there are not two plants or two animals in nature which do not differ from each other by some detail of structure; the likeness or unlikeness is then purely relative; it is bound to vary within certain limits.

But what are these limits? Here we are on the verge of the arbitrary, for there exists no fixed rule determining the point to which individual unlikeness may go in order to be considered as characteristic of a species. A difference which entitles one zoologist to create a species hardly suffices, according to another, to constitute a "variety," a "sub-species," or a "race." As to the second criterion of species drawn from the

[1] Naegeli, *Mechanisch-Physiol. Theorie der Abstammungslehre*, Munich, 1883.

[2] The most recent definitions of species given by Wallace and Romanes approximate closely to that of Cuvier. Eimer has suggested another, based solely on the physiological criterion. His definition has the advantage of covering cases of *polymorphism*, in which the female gives birth to two or several individuals so unlike that we should not hesitate to classify them in two species if guided only by morphology.

transmission and the descent of characters, it is theoretic rather than practical. Without dwelling on the numerous examples of "varieties" as fertile among themselves as "species,"[1] let us ask ourselves how many zoologists or botanists have verified experimentally the fertility of the species which they have created. In the large majority of cases, the species of plants and animals have been established solely from morphological characters, very often from the examination of dead specimens, and without any guarantee that the beings in question proceeded from common parents and that when crossed they would be fertile or not.

In the case of man, as in that of the majority of plants and animals, fertility or non-fertility among the different groups has not been experimentally proved, to enable us to decide if they should be called "races" or "species." To a dozen facts in favour of one of the solutions, and to general theories in regard to half-breeds, can be opposed an equal number of facts, and the idea, not less general, of reversion to the primitive type.[2] And again, almost all the facts in question are borrowed from cross-breeding between the Whites and other races. No one has ever tried cross-breeding between the Australians and the Lapps, or between the Bushmen and the Patagonians, for example. If certain races are indefinitely fertile among themselves (which has not yet been clearly shown), it may be there are others which are not so.[3] A criterion of descent being unobtainable, the question of the rank to be assigned to the genus *Homo* is confined to a morphological criterion, to the differences in physical type.

[1] See on this point, Y. Delage, *L'Hérédité*, pp. 252 *et seq.* Paris, 1895.

[2] The question is summed up by Darwin, *Descent of Man*, vol. i., p. 264, 2nd edition. London, 1888.

[3] In questions of hybridity, it must be observed, we often confound the notions of "race" and "people," or "social class," and we have to be on our guard against information drawn from statistics. Thus in Central America we consider "hybrids" all those descendants of the Spaniards and the Indians who have adopted the semi-European manner of life and the Catholic religion, without inquiring whether or not this physical type has reverted to that of one of the ancestors—a not infrequent occurrence.

According to some, these differences are sufficiently pronounced for each group to form a "species"; according to others they are of such a nature as only to form racial distinctions. Thus it is left to the personal taste of each investigator what name be given to these.

We cannot do better than cite upon this point the opinion of a writer of admitted authority. "It is almost a matter of indifference," says Darwin, "whether the so-called races of man are thus designated, or ranked as 'species' or 'sub-species,' but the latter term appears the most appropriate."[1] The word "race" having been almost universally adopted nowadays to designate the different physical types of mankind, I shall retain it in preference to that of "sub-species," while reiterating that there is no essential difference between these two words and the word "species."

From what has just been said, the question whether humanity forms a single species divided into varieties or races, or whether it forms several species, loses much of its importance.

The whole of this ancient controversy between monogenists and polygenists seems to be somewhat scholastic, and completely sterile and futile; the same few and badly established facts are always reappearing, interpreted in such and such a fashion by each disputant according to the necessities of his thesis, sometimes led by considerations which are extra-scientific. Perhaps in the more or less near future, when we shall have a better knowledge of present and extinct races of man, as well as of living and of fossil animal species most nearly related to man, we shall be able to discuss the question of origin. At the present time we are confined to hypothesis without a single positive fact for the solution of the problem. We have merely to note how widely the opinions of the learned differ in regard to the origin of race of certain domestic animals, such as the dog, the ox, or the horse, to get at once an idea of the difficulty of the problem. And yet, in these

[1] Darwin, *loc. cit.*, vol. i., p. 280.

cases, we are dealing with questions much less complicated and much more carefully studied.

Moreover, whether we admit variety, unity or plurality of species in the genus *Homo* we shall always be obliged to recognise the positive fact of the existence in mankind of several somatological units having each a character of its own, the combinations and the intermingling of which constitute the different ethnic groups. Thus the monogenists, even the most intractable, as soon as they have established hypothetically a single species of man, or of his "precursor," quickly cause the species to evolve, under the influence of environment, into three or four or a greater number of primitive "stocks," or "types," or "races,"—in a word, into somatological units which, intermingling, form "peoples," and so forth.

We can sum up what has just been said in a few propositions. On examining attentively the different "ethnic groups" commonly called "peoples," "nations," "tribes," etc., we ascertain that they are distinguished from each other especially by their language, their mode of life, and their manners; and we ascertain besides that the same traits of physical type are met with in two, three, or several groups, sometimes considerably removed the one from the other in point of habitat. On the other hand, we almost always see in these groups some variations of type so striking that we are led to admit the hypothesis of the formation of such groups by the blending of several distinct somatological units.

It is to these units that we give the name "races," using the word in a very broad sense, different from that given to it in zoology and zootechnics. It is a sum-total of somatological characteristics once met with in a real union of individuals, now scattered in fragments of varying proportions among several "ethnic groups," from which it can no longer be differentiated except by a process of delicate analysis.

The differences between "races" are shown in the somatological characteristics which are the resultant of the continual struggle in the individual of two factors: variability, that is to say, the production of the dissimilar; and heredity, that is to say, the perpetuation of the similar. There are the differences in outer form, in the anatomical structure, and in the physiological functions manifested in individuals. Thus the study of these characters is based on man considered as an *individual* of a zoological group. On the other hand, the differences between the ethnical groups are the product of evolutions subject to other laws than those of biology—laws still very dimly apprehended. They manifest themselves in ethnical, linguistic, or social characteristics. The study of them is based on the grouping of individuals in *societies*.

To study these two categories of characteristics, either in their general aspect as a whole, or in describing successively the different peoples, is to study mankind with the object of trying to assign the limits to the "races" constituting the ethnical groups, and to sketch the reciprocal relations and connections of these groups with each other.

The science which concerns itself more especially with the somatological characteristics of the genus *Homo*, whether considered as a whole in his relation to other animals, or in his varieties, bears the name of *anthropology*; that which deals with the ethnical characteristics is called *ethnography* in some countries and *ethnology* in others.

This latter science should concern itself with human societies under all their aspects; but as history, political economy, etc., have already taken possession of the study of civilised peoples, there only remain for it the peoples without a history, or those who have not been adequately treated by historians. However, there is a convergence of characters in mankind, and we find even to-day the trace of savagery in the most civilised peoples. Ethnical facts must not then be considered separately. We must compare them either among different peoples, or, down the course of the ages, in the same people, without concerning ourselves with the degree of actual civilisation attained.

Certain authors make a distinction between ethnography and ethnology, saying the first aims at describing peoples or the different stages of civilisation, while the second should explain these stages and formulate the general laws which have governed the beginning and the evolution of such stages. Others make a like distinction in anthropology, dividing it theoretically into "special" and "general," the one describing races, and the other dealing with the descent of these races and of mankind as a whole.[1] But these divisions are purely arbitrary, and in practice it is impossible to touch on one without having given at least a summary of the other. The two points of view, descriptive and speculative, cannot be treated separately. A science cannot remain content with a pure and simple description of unconnected facts, phenomena, and objects. It requires at least a classification, explanations, and, afterwards, the deduction of general laws. In the same way, it would be puerile to build up speculative systems without laying a solid foundation drawn from the study of facts. Already the distinction between the somatic and the ethnic sciences is embarrassing; thus psychological and linguistic phenomena refer as much to the individual as to societies. They might, strictly speaking, be the subject of a special group of sciences. In the same way, the facts drawn from the somatic and ethnic studies of extinct races are the subject of a separate science—Palethnography, otherwise Prehistory, or Prehistoric Archæology.

The object of this book being the description of ethnical groups now existing on the earth, and of the races which compose them, the title of "Ethnography" might fitly be given to it in conformity with the classifications which have just been mentioned. Nevertheless, it contains in its early chapters a summary, as it were, of what these classifications style

[1] Such is, for example, the scheme of Topinard, consisting of two double parts (*Elements d'Anthropologie*, p. 216, Paris, 1885), to which corresponds the system newly propounded by Em. Schmidt (*Centralblatt für Anthropologie, etc.*, vol. ii., p. 97, Breslau, 1897). The last-mentioned admits in reality two divisions, Ethnography and Ethnology, in what he calls Ethnic Anthropology; and two others, Phylography and Phylology, in what he names Somatic Anthropology. The two last divisions correspond to the Special Anthropology and the General Anthropology of Topinard.

"General Anthropology and Ethnology," for the descriptions of the several peoples can scarcely be understood if we have not in the first instance given at least a general idea of the somatic as well as the ethnic characters which serve to distinguish them.

CHAPTER I.

SOMATIC CHARACTERS.

DISTINCTIVE CHARACTERS OF MAN AND APES.

Monkeys and anthropoid apes—Erect attitude—Curvature of the spine—Brain—Skull—Teeth—Other characters—Differences less accentuated in the fœtus and the young than in the adult.

DISTINCTIVE MORPHOLOGICAL CHARACTERS OF HUMAN RACES.

Stature: Individual limits—Dwarfs and giants—Average stature of different populations—Influence of environment—Differences according to sex—Reconstitution from the long bones—*Teguments:* Skin—Hair of head and body—Four principal types—Microscopic structure—Correlation between the hair of the head and the pilosity of the body—*Pigmentation:* Colouring of the skin, the eyes, and the hair—Changes in the pigment.

Distinctive Characters of Man and Apes.

THE physical peculiarities distinguishing man from the animals most nearly allied to him in organisation, and those which differentiate human races one from another, are almost never the same. I shall in a few words point out the former, dwelling at greater length on the latter, which have a more direct connection with our subject.

From the purely zoological point of view man is a placental or *Eutherian* mammal, because he has breasts, because he is more or less covered with hair, because his young, nourished in the womb of the mother through the medium of the placenta, come fully formed into the world, without needing to be protected in a pouch or fold of skin, as in the case of the marsupial mammals (implacentals or *Metatherians*), or completing their development in a hatched egg, as in the case of the monotremata or *Prototherians*.

In this sub-class of the placental mammals, man belongs to the order of the *Primates* of Linnæus, in view of certain peculiarities of his physical structure—the pectoral position of the breasts, the form, number, and arrangement of the teeth in the jaw, etc.

The order of the Primates comprises five groups or families: the Marmosets (*Hapalidæ*), the *Cebidæ*, the *Cercopithecidæ*, the anthropoid apes (*Simidæ*), and lastly, the *Hominidæ*.[1] Putting aside the first two groups of Primates, which inhabit the New World, and which are distinguished from the three other groups by several characters, let us concern ourselves with the apes of the Old World and the *Hominians*. Let us at the outset remember that the monkeys and the anthropoid apes exhibit the same arrangement of teeth, or, as it is termed, the same "dental formula," as man. This formula, a character of the first importance in the classification of mammals, is summed up, as we know, in the following manner: four incisors, two canines, four premolars, and six molars in each jaw.

The *Cercopithecidæ* walk on their four paws, and this four-footed attitude is in harmony with the structure of their spine, in which the three curves, cervical, dorsal, and lumbar, so characteristic in man, are hardly indicated; thus the spine seems to form a single arch from the head to the tail. As to this last appendage, it is never wanting in these monkeys, which are also provided with buttock or ischiatic callosities, and often with cheek-pouches.

The *anthropoid apes* form a zoological group of four genera only. Two of these genera, the gorilla and the chimpanzee, inhabit tropical Africa; the two others, the orang-utan and

[1] If we include the Lemurs in the order of Primates, the five families just enumerated are all included in a "sub-order," that of *Anthropoidea*. (See, for further details, Flower and Lydekker, *Introduction to the Study of Mammals Living and Extinct*, London, 1891.)

the gibbon, are confined to the south-east of Asia, or, to be more precise, to Indo-China, and the islands of Sumatra and Borneo. We can even reduce the group in question to three genera only, for many naturalists consider the gibbon as an intermediate form between the anthropoid apes and the monkeys.[1] The anthropoids have a certain number of characters in common which distinguish them from the monkeys. Spending most of their life in trees, they do not walk in the same way as the macaques or the baboons. Always bent (except the gibbon), they move about with difficulty on the ground, supporting themselves not on the palm of the hand, as do the monkeys, but on the back of the bent phalanges. They have no tail like the other apes, nor have they cheek-pouches to serve as provision bags. Finally, they are without those callosities on the posterior part of the body which are met with in a large number of *Cercopithecidæ*, attaining often enormous proportions, as for instance, among the *Cynocephali*. The gibbon alone has the rudiments of ischiatic callosities.

If we compare man with these apes, which certainly of all animals resemble him most, the following principal differences may be noted. Instead of holding himself in a bending position, and walking supported on his arms, man walks in an erect attitude—the truly biped mode of progress. In harmony with this attitude, his vertebral column presents three curves, cervical, dorsal, and lumbar, very definitely indicated, while they are only faintly marked in the anthropoids, and almost absent in the monkeys. This character, moreover, is graduated in man; in civilised man the curvature in question is more marked than among savages. There is no need, however, to see in that any "character of superiority." It is quite simply an acquired formation; it is more marked in civilised man just because it is one of the conditions of the stability of the vertebral column, a stability so essential in sedentary life, while a curvature less marked gives much more flexibility

[1] J. H. Kohlbrugge, "Versuch einer Anatomie . . . Hylobates," *Zoolog. Ergeb. einer Reise in Ned. Ind., von M. Weber*, vols. i. and ii. Leyden, 1891.

to the movements, at once so numerous and varied, of the savage.[1]

But to what does man owe this erect and biped attitude? Professor Ranke has put forward on this subject a very ingenious hypothesis.[2] According to him, the excessive development of the brain, while conducive to enlargement of the skull, would at the same time determine the change of attitude in a being so impêrfectly and primitively biped as was our progenitor. In this way would be assured the perfect equilibrium on the vertebral column of the head, made heavy by the brain. Without wishing to discuss this theory, let me say that several peculiarities in the anatomical structure of man, compared with those of anthropoid apes and other mammals, give it an air of plausibility.

In fact, while with the majority of mammals the equilibrium of the head is assured by very powerful *cervical ligaments*, and with anthropoid apes by very strong muscles, extending from the occiput to the spinous processes of the cervical vertebræ, twice as long as those of man (Figs. 1 and 2, *a*), which prevent the massive muzzle from falling upon the chest and pressing on the organs of respiration,[3] we see nothing of a similar kind in the genus *Homo*—no cervical ligament, and no powerful muscles at the nape of the neck. The very voluminous brain-case of man suffices to counterbalance the weight of the much reduced maxillary part, almost without the aid of muscles or special ligaments, and the head balances itself on the vertebral column (Fig. 2).

This equilibrium being almost perfect, necessitates but very thin and flexible ligaments in the articulation of the two occi-

[1] D. J. Cunningham, "The Lumbar Curve in Man and the Apes," *Cunningham Memoirs of the Royal Irish Academy*, No. II., Dublin, 1886.

[2] J. Ranke, "Ueber die aufrechte Körperhaltung, etc.," *Corr.-Bl. der deutsch. Gesell. f. Anthr.*, 1895, p. 154.

[3] The enormous development of the laryngeal sacs in the orang-utan is perhaps also in harmony with this protective function, as I have shown in a special work. See Deniker and Boulart, "Notes anat. sur . . . orang-outans," *Nouv. Arch. Mus. d'hist. nat. de Paris*, 3rd Series, vol. vii., p. 47, 1895.

pital condyles of the skull on the atlas. The slight muscles to be found behind the articulation are there only to counterbalance the trifling tendency of the head to fall forward.

In connection with this point, we must remember that Broca and several other anthropologists see, on the contrary, in the biped attitude, one of the conditions of the development of the brain, as that attitude alone assures the free use of the hands and extended range of vision. Somewhat analogous

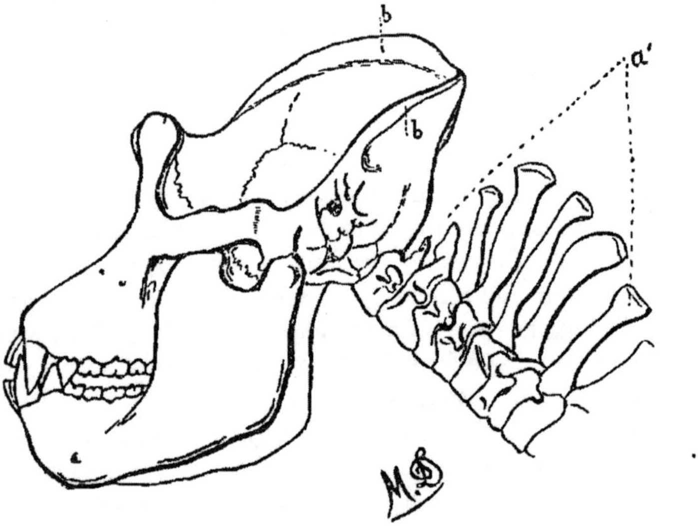

FIG. 1.—Skull of Gorilla, one-fourth actual size.
a, spinous processes of cervical vertebræ; *b*, cranial crests, sagittal and occipital.

ideas have lately been put forward by men of science of the first rank like Munro and Turner.[1]

In any case, let us remember in regard to this point, that at birth man still bears traces of his quadrupedal origin; he has then scarcely any curves in the vertebral column. The cer-

[1] R. Munro, "On Interm. Links, etc.," *Proceed. Roy. Soc. Edinb.*, vol. xxi. (1896-97), No. 4, p. 349, and *Prehistoric Problems*, pp. 87 and 165, Edin.-Lond. 1897; Turner, Pres. Address Brit. Assoc., Toronto Meeting, *Nature*, Sept. 1897.

vical curve only shows itself at the time when the child begins to "hold up its head," in the sitting posture to which it gradually becomes accustomed—that is to say about the third month. On the other hand, as soon as the child begins to walk (the second year), the prevertebral muscles and those of the loins act upon the lower regions of the spine and produce the lumbar curve.

Thus, perhaps, the chief fact which determines the erect

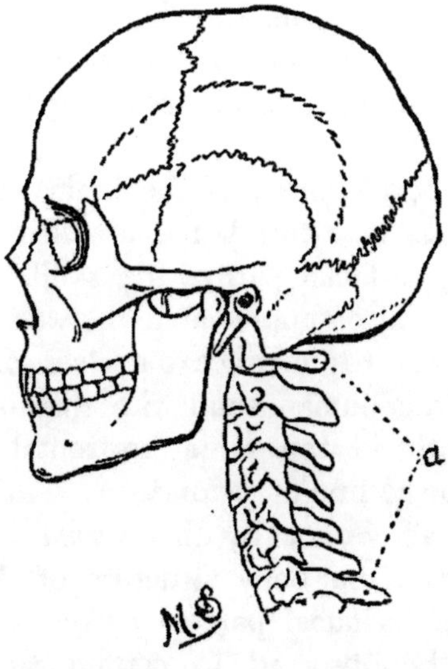

FIG. 2.—Skull of Man, one-fourth natural size. *a*, spinous processes of cervical vertebræ.

attitude so characteristic of man is the excessive development of his brain, and the consequent development of the brain-case.

It is in this excessive development of the brain that the principal difference between man and the anthropoid apes must be sought. We know in fact from the researches of numerous anthropologists (see Chapter II.) that the average weight of a man's brain in European races (the only races sufficiently known in this respect) is 1360 grammes, and that of a woman's is 1211 grammes. These figures may rise to 1675 grammes in certain instances, and fall to 1025 in others.[1] Brains weighing less than 1000 grammes are generally considered as abnormal and pathological.

On the other hand, the brains of the great anthropoid apes (gorilla, chimpanzee, and orang-utan), the only ones comparable to man in regard to weight of body, have an average weight of 360 grammes. This weight may rise to 420 grammes in certain isolated cases, but never exceeds this figure. And even in these cases, with the orang-utan, for example,[2] it only represents one half per cent. of the total weight of the body, while with European man the proportion is that of at least three per cent., according to Boyd and Bischoff.[3]

The excessive development of the brain and of the brain-case which encloses it is correlative, in the case of man, with the reduction of the facial part of the skull. In this respect the difference is also appreciable between him and the animals. In order to convince ourselves of this we have only to compare the human skull with that of any ape whatever, placing both in the same horizontal plane approximately parallel to the line of vision.[4]

Viewed from above, or by the *norma verticalis*, as the anthropologists say, the bony structure of the human head leaves nothing of its facial part to be seen (Fig. 11); at the very most may be observed, in certain rare instances, the lower part of the nasal bones, or the alveolar portion of the upper jaw (Fig. 10). On the other hand, with apes, anthropoid or otherwise, almost all the facial part is visible. Examined in profile (*norma lateralis*), the bony structure of the heads of man and monkeys presents the same differences.

[1] Topinard, *L'homme dans la Nature*, p. 214. Paris, 1891.

[2] Deniker and Boulart, *loc. cit.*, p. 55.

[3] Boyd, "Table of Weights of the Human Body, etc.," *Philos. Trans. Roy. Soc. London*, 1861; Bischoff, *Das Hirngewicht der Menschen*, Bonn, 1880. The difference remains nearly the same if, instead of the weight of the body, we take its surface, as was attempted by E. Dubois (*Bull. Soc. Anthr. Paris*, p. 337, 1897).

[4] For further details about this plane, see p. 59.

With the anthropoid apes, the facial portion forming a veritable muzzle rises, massive and bestial, *in advance* of the skull, while with man, very reduced in size, it is placed *below* the skull. The facial angle, by means of which the degree of protuberance of the muzzle may, to a certain point, be measured, exhibits notable differences when the skulls of man and animals are compared in this particular. On continuing the examination of the profiles of the bony structures of the two heads in question, we notice also the slight development of the facial part of the malar bone in man, as compared with its temporal part, and the contrary in the ape; as well as the difference in the size of the mastoid processes, very strong in man, very much diminished proportionately to the dimensions of the head in the anthropoid apes.

Seen from the front (*norma facialis*), the human skull presents a peculiarity which is not observed in any anthropoid skull, namely, that the top of the nasal opening is always situated higher than the lowest point of the lower edge of the orbits (Fig. 12); while in the anthropoid apes it is always found below this point. Lastly, if the skulls in question, always placed on the horizontal plane, are compared from behind (*norma occipitalis*), it will be noted that on the human skull the occipital foramen is not seen at all; on the skulls of monkeys it is plainly visible, if not wholly, at least partly.[1]

All the other characters which distinguish man from the anthropoid apes are only the consequences of the great enlargement of his brain-case, at the expense of the maxillary part of the face, and of the erect attitude and biped progression.

Let us take, for instance, those enormous crests which give an aspect at once so strange and horrible to the skulls of the adult males of the gorilla and the chimpanzee. These projections are due to the extreme development of the masticatory muscles which move the heavy jaws and of the cervical muscles, ensuring the equilibrium of the head. Not

[1] See on this subject the interesting study of Dr. Török in the *Centralblatt für Anthropologie, etc.*, directed by Buschan, 1st year, 1896, No. 3.

having found sufficient room for their insertion on the too small brain-case, they have, so to speak, compelled the bony tissue in the course of development to deposit itself as an eminence or crest at the point where the two lines of insertion meet on the crown of the head. The best proof of this is that the young have no crests, and that on their skulls the distance between the temporal lines marking the insertion of the temporal muscles is almost as great as it is in man. In the gorillas, it is the same with the enormous spines of the cervical vertebræ, to which are fixed the muscular masses of the nape of the neck. These crests and these processes being less developed in the orang-utan, its head is not so well balanced, and its heavy muzzle falls on its chest. So one may suppose that the laryngeal sacs, considerably larger than those of the gorilla, serve him as air-cushions to lessen the enormous weight of the jaw resting on the trachea. The gibbon, better adapted to biped progression, and having a less heavy jaw, has no skull-crests. Further, with it, the ventricles of Morgagni, that is to say, the little pouches situated behind the vocal cord in the larynx, never develop (except in one species, *Hylobates syndactylus*) into enormous air-sacs as in the orang-utan. In this respect, the gibbon approaches much nearer to man than the other anthropoids, but it is also more distinguished from him than the others by the excessive length of the arms, or, to be more exact, of the pectoral limbs. It holds itself erect and walks almost as well as man, aided by the long arms and hands which touch the ground even when the animal is standing quite upright, and which he uses as a pendulum when walking. In the case of three other anthropoids, which bend forward in walking, the pectoral limb is shorter than in the gibbon but longer than in man.

The first toe, opposable in the anthropoid apes and unopposable in man, the relative length of the toes and fingers generally, etc., only constitute modifications correlative to the erect attitude and biped movement of man, and to his terrestrial habitat as opposed to the arboreal habitat of the anthropoid apes, and to their biped movement necessitating the support of the hands.

The differences in the form and size of the teeth are also the consequence of the inequality of the development of the maxillary part of the face in man, and in the apes in general.

The size of the teeth in proportion to that of the body is less in man than in the apes (Figs. 1 and 2). Putting aside the incisors and the canines, the size of the molars and the premolars of these animals is larger in relation to the length of the facial portion of the skull. The "dental index" of Flower, that is to say the centesimal relation of the total length of the row of molars and premolars to the length of the naso-basilar line (from the nasal spine to the most advanced point of the occipital foramen), is always greater in the anthropoid apes than in man; in the latter it is never above 47.5, while it is 48 in the chimpanzee, 58 in the orang, and 63 in the gorilla.

As to the arrangement of the teeth on the alveolar arch, with man they are in a compact line forming a continuous series without any notable projection of any one tooth above the common level; while in all the apes is observed an interval (*diastema*) between the canines and the lateral incisors of the upper jaw, and between the canines and the first premolars of the lower jaw. These gaps receive in each jaw the projecting part of the opposite canine.

Like the anthropoid apes, man has five tubercles in the lower molars, while the monkeys have in general only four. This rule admits, however, of numerous exceptions: very often the fifth posterior tubercle is wanting in the two last molars in man; on the other hand, it is regularly found in the last molar in certain kinds of monkeys (*Cynocephali*, *Semnopitheci*). As to the wisdom tooth, in certain pithecoid apes (*Cynocephali*, *Semnopitheci*) it is greater in size than the anterior molars; whilst in certain others, like the *Cercopitheci*, it is much less than the two first molars. With the anthropoid apes this tooth is of the same size as the other molars or a little smaller, and it is generally the same with man, though in somewhat frequent cases it is entirely wanting. The dental arch is different as regards form in man and in apes. In man it has a tendency towards the parabolic and elliptical form, whilst in apes it usually takes the form of U.

It should be noted that all the characters that distinguish man from the anthropoid apes have a tendency to become more marked with the development of civilisation and life in a less natural environment, or artificially modified, as we have already seen in regard to the curves of the vertebral column. Thus the absence of the fifth tubercle in the lower molars has been more often noted in European races (29 times out of 51, according to Hamy) than with Negroes and Melanesians. The wisdom tooth seems to be in a state of retrogressive evolution among several populations. Especially in the white races it is nearly always smaller than the other molars; the number of the tubercles is reduced to three instead of four or five; very often in the lower jaw it remains in its alveola and never comes through.

In the same way the little toe tends, in the higher races (perhaps owing to tight boots), to become atrophied and formed of but two phalanges instead of three. Pfitzner has noted this reduction in thirty feet out of a hundred and eleven that he examined.[1]

It is perhaps in similar retrogressive evolutions due to the "social environment" that we must seek the explanation of a great number of characters of "inferiority" and "superiority," so called, of certain races.

The difference between man and the ape in regard to teguments is not so appreciable as might be thought. Man comes into the world covered almost entirely with *lanugo* or short fine hair. This hair is afterwards replaced in early infancy by permanent hair which only occupies certain parts of the body. Primitive man, it may be presumed, was entirely covered with hair, except perhaps on the front part of the trunk, where natural selection in the struggle with parasites (infesting that warm part of the mother's body in contact with the

[1] Pfitzner, "Die kleine Zehe," *Arch. f. Anat. u. Phys.*, 1890.

young when being suckled) would soon cause the disappearance of the hair from that place, as indeed we see in apes.[1] It is curious to observe in this respect that the disposition of the hair of the arms in man is far from recalling that of the anthropoid apes, as Darwin thought, but rather resembles the disposition observed among the monkeys. In fact, instead of being directed upwards towards the bend of the elbow, this hair is turned downwards towards the wrist in the higher half of the arm; and transversely in its lower half. The anthropoid apes being accustomed to cover the head with their arms, or to keep them above their head so as to cling to the branches of the trees on which they spend their life, the hairs may have taken in this case an opposite direction to that of the primitive type of the Primates by the simple effect of gravity.[2]

Space does not permit us to pass in review several other characters distinguishing man from the anthropoid apes: absence of certain muscles (*acromiotrachelian*, etc.) in the former, simplicity of the cerebral folds in the latter, the absence of the lobulation of the liver and that of the penile bone in the former and their presence in some of the anthropoid apes, etc.

Let me say in conclusion that all these distinctions are only very marked when adult individuals are compared, for they become accentuated with age. The fœtus of the gorilla at five months bears a very close resemblance to the human fœtus of the same age. A young gorilla and a young chimpanzee, by their globular skull, by their not very prominent muzzle, and by other traits, remind one of young Negroes. In comparing the skulls of gorillas, from the fœtal state through all the stages of growth to the adult state, we can follow step by step the transformation of a face almost human into a muzzle of the most bestial aspect, as a result of the excessive develop-

[1] Bell, *The Naturalist in Nicaragua*, p. 209, 1874; Shevyref, "Parasites of the Skin, etc.," *Works Soc. of Naturalists*, St. Petersburg, 1891, in Russian.

[2] Walter Kidd, "Certain Vestigial Characters in Man," *Nature*, 1897, vol. lv., p. 237.

ment of the face in front and below in the anthropoid ape, and the growth of the skull upward and behind in man, as if these parts moved in different directions in relation to a central point in the interior of the skull near to the *sella turcica*.[1]

Distinctive Characters of Human Races.

In treatises on anthropology, anatomy, and physiology will be found all the information wished for on the different somatic characters of man, as well as on their variations according to sex, age, and race. It would be exceeding the limits of our subject were I to describe here, one by one, all the anatomical or morphological characters drawn from the bony, muscular, nervous, and other systems of which the human body is composed. We shall only pass in review the characters which possess a real importance in the differentiation of races. These are much less numerous than is generally supposed, and belong for the most part to the category of characters that are observed in the living subject. It is generally believed that the sole concern of anthropology is the description of skulls. This is one of the common errors of which there are so many current among the general public on scientific subjects. To be sure, the skull, and especially the head, of the living subject furnish the principal characters which differentiate races, but there exist several others, without a knowledge of which it is difficult to direct one's steps in the midst of the diversity of forms presented by the human body according to race. We distinguish in general two kinds of somatic characters: (1) those dealing with the form and structure of the body—morphological characters; and (2) those which are connected with its different functions—physiological characters, with which we will include psychological and pathological characters.

We shall first examine the morphological characters,

[1] See for further details Deniker, *Recherches anatom. et embryol. sur les singes anthropoides*, Paris and Poitiers, 1886 (Extr. from *Arch. de Zool. experim.*, 3e ser., vol. iii., supp., 1885-86).

beginning with those furnished to us by the body as a whole—the stature, the nature of the tegument (the skin and hair), and its colouring. We shall afterwards pass to an examination of the morphology of the head, and the different parts of the body, with their bony framework (skull and skeleton). We shall complete this brief account by a glance at the internal organs, muscles, brain, viscera.

Stature.—Of all the physical characters which serve to distinguish races, stature is perhaps that which has hitherto been regarded as eminently variable. It has been said that not only does stature change with age and sex, but that it varies also under the influence of external agencies. These variations are unquestionable, but it must be remarked that they are produced in a similar way in all races, and cannot exceed certain limits imposed by race.

Even from birth stature varies. Setting aside individual variations, the new-born are on an average a little taller, for example, in Paris (499 millim. for boys) than in St. Petersburg (477 millim.). Unfortunately we have hardly any data in regard to this important question for the non-European populations. Here in a tabulated form is the average height of the new-born of different populations, so far as information has been obtainable.

AVERAGE STATURE.

POPULATIONS.	BOYS.		GIRLS.		NAME OF OBSERVER.
	Millim.	Inches.	Millim.	Inches.	
Annamese	474	18.49	464	18.10	Mondière.
Russians of St. Petersburg	477	18.60	473	18.45	Mies.
Germans of Cologne	486	18.95	484	18.88	Mies.
Americans of Boston	490	19.27	482	18.80	Bowditch.
English	496	19.35	491	19.31	C. Roberts.
French of Paris ..	499	19.52	492	19.35	Mies.

According to this table there would also be from the time of birth an inequality of stature of the two sexes; boys exceed girls by a figure which varies from 2 to 10 millim., that is to say on an average half a centim. (less than a quarter of an inch). The data relating to different races are insufficient; it may be remarked, however, that with people very low in stature, like the Annamese (1m. 58, or 5 feet 2 inches), on the average the new-born are also shorter than those of people of greater stature, as, for instance, the English or the inhabitants of the United States. The French (average height 5 feet 5 inches) appear to be an exception to this rule.

We shall examine at greater length in Chapter IV. increase of stature in connection with all the phenomena of growth. Let me for the present say that as regards man, the age of 18 to 25 years, according to race, may be considered as the practical limit of this growth. In order to make a useful comparison of statures of different populations, we should only take, then, adults above these ages.

It must be said on this point that the greater part of the reliable information which we possess concerning stature relates solely to men, and among these, more especially to conscripts or soldiers. And it has often been objected that the figures in documents furnished in connection with the recruiting of armies do not represent the true height of any given population, for the conscripts, being in general from 20 to 21 years of age, have not yet reached the limit of growth.

This is true in certain cases; for example, when we have the measurements of all conscripts, who, in fact, grow from 1 to 2 centimetres during their military service; but when we have only the measurements of those enrolled, that is to say only of men above the standard height (and that is most frequently the case), the question presents a different aspect. The average height of this picked section of the population, higher by 1 to 2 centimetres than that of men of their age in general, may be considered (as I have elsewhere shown[1])

[1] Deniker, "Les Races de l'Europe," *Bull. Soc. Anthr. Paris*, p. 29, 1897.

to represent the average stature of the whole number of adult males of any given population. We may then, while making certain reservations, take the height of those enrolled (but not that of all the conscripts) as representing the height of the adults of any given population.

The individual limits between which the height varies are very wide. It is admitted in general that the limits of height in the normal man may vary from 1m. 25 (4 feet 1 inch) to 1m. 99 (6 feet 6¾ inches). Below 1m. 25 begins a certain abnormal state, often pathological, called Dwarfism. Above 2m. we have another corresponding state called Giantism. Dwarfs may be 38 cent. high (15 inches), like the little feminine dwarf Hilany Agyba of Sinai (Joest), and giants as high as 2m. 83 (9 feet 5 inches), like the Finn Caïanus (Topinard).[1]

Dwarfism may be the result of certain pathological states (microcephaly, rickets, etc.), as it may be equally the result of an exceeding slowness of growth.[2] In the same way giantism is often seen associated with a special disease called acromegaly, but most frequently it is produced by an excessive growth. In any case, exceptional statures, high or low, are abnormal phenomena, the acknowledged sterility of dwarfs and giants being alone sufficient to prove this.

Extreme statures which it is agreed to call normal, those of 1m. 25 and 1m. 99, are very rare. One might say that, in general, statures below 1m. 35 and above 1m. 90 are exceptions. Thus in the extensive American statistics,[3] based on more than 300,000 subjects, but one giant (above 2m.) is met with out of 10,000 subjects examined, and hardly five individuals in 1000 taller than 1m. 90 (75 inches). Again, in the statistics of the Committee of the British Association,[4] which embrace 8,585 subjects, only three individuals in a

[1] Joest, *Verh. Berl. gesell. Anthr.*, p. 450, 1887; Topinard, *Elem. Anthr. gén.*, p. 436.

[2] Manouvrier, *Bull. Soc. Anthr. Paris*, p. 264, 1896.

[3] B. A. Gould, *Investigations in the Milit. and Anthrop. Statistics of American Soldiers.* New York, 1869.

[4] Final Report of the Anthropometric Committee, Brit. Ass., 1883.

thousand have been found taller than 1m. 90. Yet in these two cases, populations of a very high stature (1m. 72 on an average) were being dealt with. If we turn to a population lower in stature, for instance the Italian, we find only one subject 1m. 90 or above in height in 7000 examined, according to the statistics of Pagliani.[1] In the same way, low statures under 1m. 35 (53 inches) are met with only once in every 100,000 cases among the subjects examined by the American Commission, and not once among 8,585 inhabitants of the United Kingdom; even in a population low in stature, like the Italians, only three such in every 1000 subjects examined are to be found. We do not possess a sufficient number of figures to be able to affirm that among all the populations of the globe the instances of all these extreme statures are exceptional, but what we know leads us to suppose that it is so, and that the limits of normal stature in man are between 1m. 35 and 1m. 90.

The figures of individual cases are much less interesting than the averages of the different populations, that is to say the height obtained by dividing the sum of the statures of individuals by the number of subjects measured. On comparing these averages it becomes possible to form a clear idea of the difference existing among the various peoples. But here there is an observation to make.

The data of this kind published up to the present in the majority of books may often lead to error. In fact, as a general rule they give only the average height without stating the number of subjects measured. Very often it is only the rough guess of a traveller who has not even measured at all the populations of which he speaks. In other cases we have averages drawn from the measurements of two, three, or four subjects, which are evidently insufficient for a standard which varies so much in one individual and another, and even in the same individual according to the hour of the day.

We know, in fact, that man measures one or two centimetres more on rising in the morning than on going to bed at night,

[1] Pagliani, *Lo sviluppo umano per età, etc.* Milan, 1879.

when the fibro-cartilaginous discs situated between the vertebræ are compressed, more closely packed, and the vertebral column is more bent. Unscrupulous conscripts whose stature is near the regulation limit know perfectly well that if the day before the official examination they carry heavy loads, they compress their intervertebral discs so that their height is sometimes diminished by three centimetres.

It is necessary then, in order to avoid error, not only to have measurements taken from adult subjects, but also from several series containing a great number of these subjects. Calculation and inference have shown us that it is necessary to have at least a series of one hundred individuals to guarantee the exact figure of the height of a population but slightly blended. Series of 50 to 100 individuals may still furnish occasionally good indications, and series of 25 to 50 individuals an approximation; but with series under 25 individuals doubt begins and the figures are often most deceptive.

I have brought together and grouped in the table at the end of this volume (Appendix I.) average statures calculated in series of twenty-five individuals or more. These series have been based on the collation of hundreds of documents, of which limits of space prevent a full enumeration.

An examination of our table shows that the extreme averages of different populations fluctuate, in round figures, from 1m. 38 (4 ft. 6 in.) with the Negrillo Akkas, to 1m. 79 (5 ft. 10.5 in.) with the Scots of Galloway.[1] But if we set aside the pigmy tribe of the Akka, quite exceptional as regards stature, as well as the Scots of Galloway, and even the Scots of the north in general (1m. 78), who likewise form a group entirely apart, we arrive at the extreme limits of stature, varying from 1465 mm. with

[1] These figures differ from those up to the present given in most works, according to Topinard (*Elem. Anthro. gén.*, p. 462), who fixes the limits between 1m. 44 (Bushmen of the Cape) and 1m. 85 (Patagonians), but the first of these figures is that of a series of six subjects only, measured by Fritsch, and the second the average of ten subjects measured by Lista and Moreno. This is insufficient, and since the publication of Topinard's work we have only been able to add a few isolated observations concerning those interesting populations the actual height of which is still to be determined.

the Aeta or Negritoes of the Philippines, and 1746 mm. with the Scots in general. In round figures, then, we can recognise statures of 1m. 46 (4 feet 9.5 inches) and 1m. 75 (5 feet 9 inches) as the extreme limits of averages in the different populations of the globe. The medium height between these extremes is 1m. 61, but if we put on one side the exceptional group of Negritoes (Akka, Aeta, Andamanese, and Sakai), we shall note that the rest of mankind presents statures which ascend by degrees, almost uninterruptedly, from millimetre to millimetre between 1m. 54 and 1m. 75, which makes the average 1m. 65 (5 feet 5 inches), as Topinard has discovered.[1] Topinard has likewise proposed the division of statures, since universally adopted, into four categories, viz.: short statures, under 1m. 60; statures under the average, between 1m. 60 and 1m. 649; statures above the average, between 1m. 65 and 1m. 699; and lastly, high statures, 1m. 70 and over.

Our table shows conclusively that there are many more populations (almost double the number) whose stature is above or under the average, than populations of a short or high stature.

Short stature is rare in Africa, being found only among the Negrillo pigmies and Bushmen; in South America a few tribes of low stature are also met with; but the true home of low stature populations is Indo-China, Japan, and the Malay Archipelago. In the remaining portion of Asia this low stature is only met with again in Western Siberia, and among the tribes called Kols and Dravidians in India.

Statures under the average predominate in the rest of Asia (with the exception of the populations to the north of India and anterior Asia) and in Eastern and Southern Europe, while statures above the average comprise Irano-Hindu populations, the Afrasian Semites, the inhabitants of Central Europe, as well as the Melanesians and Australians.

Thus high stature is plainly limited to Northern Europe, to North America, to Polynesia, and especially to Africa,

[1] Topinard, *Elem. Anthr. gén.*, p. 463.

where it is met with as well among Negroes as among Ethiopians.

What is the influence of environment on stature? This is one of the most controverted questions. Since the time of Villermé the statement has been repeated in a variety of ways that well-being was favourable to growth and increase in stature, and that hardship stunted growth. There are facts which seem to prove this. In a population supposed to be formed of a mixture of many races, the well-fed upper classes appear to possess a higher stature than the lower classes; thus, while the English of the liberal professions are 69.14 inches (1757m.) in height, the workmen of the same nation are only 65.7 inches (1705m.).[1] But can we not likewise adduce here the influence of race? That predominating in the aristocracy and well-to-do classes does not, perhaps, predominate in the working classes. Beddoe[2] and others have remarked that the stature of miners is lower than that of the population around them; in the same way, workmen in shops and factories are inferior in height to those who labour in the open air, and this in Belgium (Houzé) as well as in England (Beddoe, Roberts) or Russia (Erisman, Anuchin).[3] According to Collignon,[4] the populations of Normandy and Brittany living in the neighbourhood of railways and high-roads are superior in height to those living in out-of-the-way places. He concludes from this that the material conditions of life being improved since the formation of roads, the stature of the population has increased. According to Ammon and Lapouge, the population of the towns in France and Southern Germany are taller in stature than those of the country,

[1] *Final Report Brit. Assoc.*, 1883, p. 17.

[2] Beddoe, *The Stature and Bulk of Man in the Brit. Isles*, pp. 148 *et seq.* London, 1870.

[3] Houzé, *Bull. Soc. Anthr. Bruxelles*, 1887; Roberts, *A Manual of Anthropometry*, London, 1878, and *Jour. Stat. Soc.*, London, 1876; Anuchin, "O geograficheskom, etc.," *Geograph. Distrib. of Stature in Russia*, St. Petersburg, 1889; Erisman, *Arch. f. soz. gesetzgeb.*, Tübingen, 1888.

[4] Collignon, "L'Anthropologie au conseil de révision," *Bull. Soc. Anthr. Paris*, 1890, p. 764.

because of the migration towards urban centres of the tall dolichocephalic fair race which they call *Homo Europeus.* However, Ranke observed just the opposite, and there are other objections to be raised against this theory, based on the data of recruiting. These town-dwellers of high stature are perhaps only conscripts too quickly developed; town life accelerates growth, and town-dwellers have nearly reached the limit of their height while dwellers in villages have not finished growing. This is so true that in countries where statistics have been taken of the civic population, as in England for example, the population of the towns is shorter in stature than that of the country. Beddoe explains this fact by the bad hygienic conditions in towns, the want of exercise and drinking habits of dwellers in cities.[1]

To conclude, the influence of environment cannot be denied in many cases: it may raise or lower stature, especially by stimulating or retarding and even arresting growth; but it is not demonstrated that such a change can be perpetuated by hereditary transmission and become permanent. The primordial characteristics of race seem always to get the upper hand, and the modifications produced by environment can alter the stature of the race only within very restricted limits. Thus miners of a high stature like the Scotch, for example, while shorter than the Scotch of the well-to-do classes, will be still taller than the individuals of the well-to-do classes in, for example, Spain or Italy, and much more so than those of Japan (1m. 59). Stature is truly then a character of race, and a very persistent one.

So far I have spoken only of the height of men. That of women (as regards adult women of seventeen to twenty-three years of age, according to race) is always lower than the height of men, but by how much? Tentatively, Topinard gave the figure 12 centimetres as the general differ-

[1] Ammon, *Die Natur. Auslese beim Menschen*, Jena, 1893; Vacher de Lapouge, *Les selections sociales*, Paris, 1896; Beddoe, *loc. cit.*, p. 180; Ranke, *Der Mensch.*, vol. ii., p. 109, Leipzig, 1887.

ence between the stature of the two sexes in all races. The data for the height of women being very scarce, I have only been able to bring together thirty-five series of measurements of women comprising each more than fifteen individuals, for comparison with series of measurements of men.

It follows from this slight inquiry that in twenty cases out of thirty-five, that is to say, almost two-thirds, the difference in height between the two sexes in any given population hardly varies more than from 7 to 13 centimetres (3 to 5 inches); fourteen times out of thirty-five it only varies from 11 to 13 centimetres (4.5 to 5 inches), so that the figure of 12 centimetres (5 inches) may be accepted as the average. Besides, the difference does not appear to change according to the average stature, more or less high, of the race: it is almost the same for the Tahitians and the Maricopas, who are tall, as it is for the Samoyeds and the Caribs, who are short.[1]

Thus, then, in a general way, the categories of statures—tall, short, etc.—for women will be comprised within the same limits already indicated for man, only reduced by 12 centimetres for each category. Thus, high statures for women will begin at 1m. 58 instead of 1m. 70; short statures under 1m. 48 instead of 1m. 60

The stature of a living man is naturally higher than that of his skeleton, but what the difference is is not exactly known. It can hardly, however, exceed 2 or 3 centimetres, according to Topinard, Rollet, and Manouvrier.

By means of measurements of the long bones of the limbs (femur, humerus, etc.), the height of the skeleton of which they form part may be approximately calculated. For this purpose we make use of Rollet's formula,[2] according to which the length of the femur must be multiplied by 3.66 for the height of man, and by 3.71 for the height of woman, or multiply the length of the humerus by 5.06 or by 5.22, according

[1] Boas (*Zeit. f. Ethnol.*, 1895, p. 375) found, however, in thirty-nine series of Indians the difference greater with tribes of high stature (13.5 centimetres) than with tribes of low stature (9.9 centimetres).

[2] Rollet, *Mensurations des os longs, etc.*, Lyons, 1889 (thesis).

to sex. But this formula is only applicable to subjects whose stature is near the average, 1m. 65. In the generality of cases we must substitute for it more exact calculations by the help of Manouvrier's tables.[1] It is by this means that Rahon[2] has been able to determine approximately the height of the prehistoric populations of France, which will be dealt with in Chapter IX.

Teguments: The Skin.—The human skin is essentially composed of two parts, the corium (Fig. 3, D) and a superficial

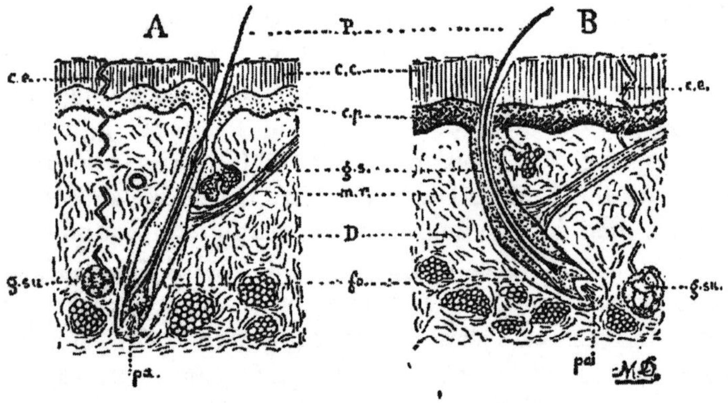

FIG. 3.—Microscopic section (partly schematic) of skin and of hair: A, of a European; B, of a Negro.

c.c. horny layer or cuticle and *c.p.* pigmented layer (rete Malpighii) of the epidermis; D. corium; *g.su.* sweat gland; *c.e.* excretory duct; *pa.* hair papilla, and *fo.* hair follicle; *m. erector pili* muscle; *g.s.* sebaceous gland; *p.* hair.

epidermis; the latter is formed in its turn of two cellular layers, the horny layers (Fig. 3, *c.c.*), the quite shallow cells of which are freely exposed to the air, and Malpighi's layer situated beneath it, with granules of pigment in more or less quantity in its lower range of cells (Fig. 3, *c.p.*). In certain places the epidermis is modified so as to form either a mucous

[1] Manouvrier, *Mem. Soc. Anthro.*, 2nd ser., vol. iv., p. 347, Paris, 1893.
[2] Rahon, *Mem. Soc. Anthro.*, vol. iv., p. 403, Paris, 1893.

FIG. 4.—Mohave Indians of Arizona; smooth hair type. (*Phot. Ten Kate.*)

membrane, as, for instance, on the lips, or a horny substance, sometimes transparent (as the cornea of the eye) and sometimes only translucent and more or less hard (the nails).

There is little to say about the differences in the nature and structure of the skin according to race. Its colouring, of which I shall speak later on (see *Pigmentation*), is more

FIG. 5.—Pure Veddah of Dangala Mountains of Ceylon; wavy hair type. (*Phot. Brothers Sarasin.*)

important. Attention has been drawn to the hardness of the corium and the velvety softness of the skin in the negro; the latter quality is probably due to the profusion and size of the sebaceous glands which accompany the hair. Bischoff has made an interesting observation on the relative rarity of the sweat glands (which are found in the thickness of the corium, Fig. 3, *g.su.*) among the Fuegians,[1] but comparative studies on this subject have not been pursued in regard to other races. The disposition of the papilla ridges on the tips of the fingers, so well studied by Galton,[2] is of great interest as regards the identification of the individual; but from this

Fig. 6.—Same subject as Fig. 5, front view. (*Phot. Brothers Sarasin.*)

fact alone, that it is a good characteristic of the individual, it loses all its value as a characteristic of race.

Hair of the Head and Body.—The most important horny product of the skin, as regards the differentiation of races, is

[1] Bischoff, *Sitzungsber. Mat. Phys. Cl. Bayr. Akad.*, Munich, 1882, pp. 243 and 356.
[2] Galton, *Finger Prints.* London, 1892.

undoubtedly the hair of the head and body. The general structure and number of the hairs (about 260 to each square centimetre) hardly show any difference between race and race; on the other hand, the length of the hair of the head, the relation of this length in one sex to that in the other, the nature of the hair, its consistence, its transverse section, its form, its colour, vary much according to race.

The body hair has its origin in a layer of the epidermis, deeply imbedded in the corium as though it were in a little sac or follicle (Fig. 3, *fo.*); from the bottom of this sac, and covering by its root a little papilla (Fig. 3, *pa.*) filled with vessels designed to nourish it, each hair rises and pushes its way to the outside; it is always accompanied by a little muscle which can move it (Fig. 3, *mr.*), and by a sebaceous gland (Fig. 3, *g*) designed to lubricate it.

Four principal varieties of hair are usually distinguished in anthropology, according to their aspect and their nature—straight, wavy, frizzy, and woolly. It is easy to form a clear idea at first sight of the differences which are presented by these varieties, but the most careful examination shows that the differences are deeper, and can be pursued even into the microscopic structure of the hair.

Straight and smooth hair (*droit* or *lisse* in French, *straff* or *schlicht* in German) is ordinarily rectilinear, and falls heavily in bands on the sides of the head; such is the hair of the Chinese, the Mongols, and of American Indians (Fig. 4). Straight hair is ordinarily stiff and coarse, but it is sometimes found tolerably fine; for example, among the western Finns. It is true that in this case it has a tendency to become wavy. *Wavy hair* (*ondé* in French, *wellig* in German) forms a long curve or imperfect spiral from one end to the other (Figs. 5 and 6). It is called curly when it is rolled up at the extremity (Fig. 7). The whole head of hair when wavy produces a very pleasing effect; I will merely cite as examples certain fair Scotchwomen. The type is very widespread among Europeans, whether dark or fair. The frizzy type (*frisé* in French, *lockig* in German) is that in which the hair is rolled spirally, forming a succession of rings a centimetre or more in diameter (Fig. 8). Such is the hair of the Australians (Figs. 21 and 22), the Nubians, of certain Mulattos, etc. Lastly, the type of woolly hair (*crépu* in French, *kraus* in German) is characterised by spiral curves exceedingly narrow (from 1 millimetre to 9 millimetres as the maximum); the rings of the spiral are

FIG. 7.—Toda woman (India); curly hair type. (*Phot. Thurston.*)

very near together, numerous, well rolled, and often catch hold of each other, forming tufts and balls, the whole result recalling in appearance sheep's wool (Fig. 9). The type admits of two varieties. When the hair is relatively long and the spirals sufficiently broad, the whole head looks like a continuous fleece, as with certain Melanesians (Fig. 153), or the majority of Negroes (Figs. 9 and 47). In his classification of the human races, Haeckel[1] has taken this type as characteristic of the

FIG. 8.—Kurumba man of Nilgiri Hills; frizzy hair type.
(*Phot. Thurston.*)

group of *eriocomes*. But when the hair is short, consisting of

[1] Haeckel, *Natur. Schöpfungsgeschichte*, 4th ed., p. 603. Berlin, 1873.

very small spirals, it has a tendency, when tangled, to form little tufts, the dimensions of which vary from the size of a pea to that of a pepper-corn; these tufts are separated by spaces which appear bald (pepper-corn hair). This type (called *lophocome* by Haeckel) is very widespread among Hottentots and Bushmen, but the majority of Negroes have it in their infancy, and even at adult age, especially towards the temples, on the forehead—briefly, in all the places

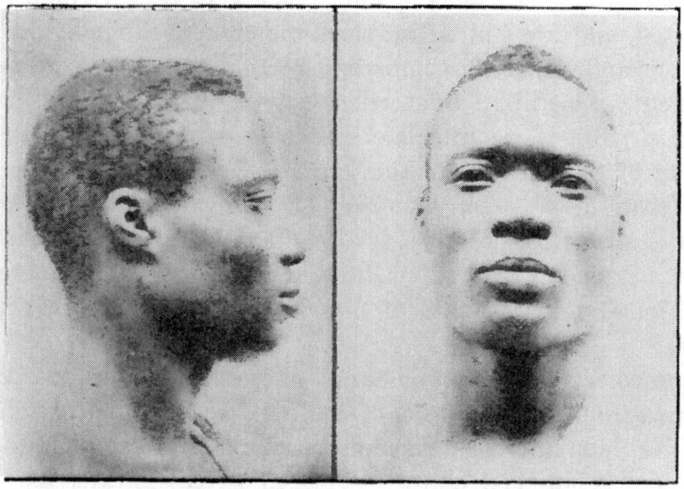

FIG. 9.—Agni Negro of Krinjabo, Western Africa; woolly hair type. (*Photo. Thoman, lent by Collignon.*)

where the hair remains very short (Fig 9). We must not think that the disposition of which I have just spoken is due to the hair being stuck in the skin of the head like the bristles of a brush, for the mode of insertion is the same in all races, with Bushmen as with Europeans or Mongols. At the most it may be noted that the rows of hair in Negroes are more irregular, and are closer together in certain places, leaving in other rows intervals between them of two or three millimetres. Only, as a consequence of the shortness and the excessive twisting, the hair gets entangled and the spirals catch hold of each other, so forming glomerules or tufts.

Does there exist any difference of form between straight, waved, frizzy, or woolly hair? The microscopical examination of transverse sections of the hair allows us to reply affirmatively to this question. This examination, already applied to the hair in 1822 by Heusinger, then successively by Blower (of Philadelphia), Kölliker, Pruner-Bey, Latteux, and Waldeyer,[1] has yielded results which have been vigorously discussed, and are still debatable if we cling to the individual and absolute figures, comparing sections made according to defective methods, or carried out on different levels of the hair. But if we calculate the *index*—that is to say, the relation of the breadth to the length (= 100) of the section (and that in a great number of individual cases)—we obtain satisfactory results, as Topinard and Ranke[2] have shown in general, as also Baelz in the case of the Japanese, and Montano in the case of the races of the Malay Archipelago.[3]

If we consider a great number of microscopical sections, all obtained from the same level of the hair, we note that straight hair gives a circular section, whilst woolly hair gives one in the form of a lengthened ellipse. This ellipse is less extended, a little more filled out, in the sections of wavy hair. If the major axis of the ellipse be supposed to equal 100, the minor axis will be represented by figures varying from 40 to 50 for the woolly hair of the Bushmen and the Hottentots, from 50

[1] Pruner-Bey, "Chevelure comme caracterist. des races hum.," *Mem. Soc. Anthr.*, vol. ii., p. 1, Paris, 1863; Latteux, *Technique microscopique*, p. 239, Paris, 1883; Waldeyer, *Atlas der Menschl. u. Thier Haare*, Lahr, 1894.

[2] Topinard, *Elem. Anthrop. gén.*, p. 265; J. Ranke, *loc. cit.*, vol. ii., p. 172.

[3] Baelz, "Körperl. Eigensch. d. Japaner," *Mitth. Deut. Gesell. Nat. und Völkerk. Ostasiens*, vol. iii., fasc. 28, p. 330, and vol. iv., fasc. 32, p. 39, Yokohama, 1883-85; Montano, *Mission aux îles Philippines*, Paris, 1885 (Extr. from *Arch. Miss. Scient.*, 3rd series, vol. xi.).

to 60 for that of the Negroes, while the straight hair of the Eskimo will have this axis = 77, that of the Thibetans = 80, that of the Japanese = 85, etc. The hair of Europeans represents an elliptical section in which the major axis being = 100, the minor axis will be represented by figures varying from 62 to 72 (Topinard). It can be said to-day with certainty, after the work of Unna,[1] that the woolly hair of Negroes rolls up into a compact spiral precisely because of the flattened shape of this elliptical section, and of the special form of the follicle and papilla. In fact, in the Negro the follicle, instead of being straight, as in the European (Fig. 3, A), is curved inward in the form of a sabre, or even of the arc of a quarter of a circle (Fig. 3, B); further, the papilla is flattened instead of being round. One would say that the hair has encountered in its development so much resistance on the part of the dermis (which is so hard, in fact, among the Negroes), that it would be twisted, as it were, from the first. Emerging from an incurvated mould, it can only continue to roll up outside, given especially its flattened shape; it rolls up into a spiral, the plane of which, at the beginning, is perpendicular to the surface of the skin.[2] As to the thickness of the hair, it appears that in general it is greater in straight hair than in woolly; however, the hair of the western Finns is straight and fine at the same time.

A certain correlation appears to exist between the nature of the hair and its absolute and relative length. Thus straight hair is at the same time the longest—Chinese, Americans, Indians (Fig. 4), while woolly hair is shortest, from 5 to 15 centimetres (Fig. 9); wavy hair occupies an intermediate position. Moreover, the difference between the length of the hair of men and women is almost inappreciable in the two extreme divisions. In certain straight-haired races the hair of the head is as long with men as with women; one need but to

[1] P. S. Unna, "Ueber das Haar als Rassenmerkmal," *Deutsche Med. Zeit.*, 1896, Nos. 82 and 83.

[2] See Stewart, *Microsc. Journ.*, 1873, p. 54; and T. Anderson Stuart, *Journ. Anat. Phys.*, 1881-82, xvi., p. 362.

call to mind the plaits of the Chinese, or the beautiful heads of hair of the Red Indians, which may attain in certain cases a length of even two metres (Catlin). In frizzy-haired races the hair of the head, on the contrary, is equally short in the two sexes; the hair of the head of women among the Bushmen, Hottentots, and even Negroes, is not appreciably longer than among the men. It is only in the categories of wavy and in part of frizzy hair, that the differences are appreciable. With European men the length of the hair rarely exceeds 30 or 40 centimetres, while with the women it averages 65 to 75 centimetres, and may attain in exceptional cases to 2 metres (as in the case of an Englishwoman, according to Dr. D. Watson).

Another fact to be noted is that the general development of the pilose system on the face, as on the rest of the body, seems also to be in relation to the nature of the hair of the head.

Straight-haired races are ordinarily very glabrous, the men have hardly a rudimentary tuft of beard—American Indians (Fig. 4), Mongols (Fig. 20), Malays; while in the wavy or frizzy-haired races, the development of the pilose system is considerable—Australians, Dravidians, Iranians (Fig. 22), Ainus (Fig. 117), etc. The woolly-haired races are not, however, included in this rule; glabrous types (Bushmen, western Negroes) are found side by side with rather hairy types (Melanesians, Akka, Ashanti). There appears to be a certain likeness between the abundance of hair on the head and on the body. Thus, according to Hilgendorf, the Japanese who are glabrous have from 252 to 286 hairs to each square centimetre on the head, whilst the hairy Ainus have only 214. Negroes and white men do not appear, however, to present the same differences (Gould). Even baldness results largely from the nature of the hair. According to Gould, baldness is ten times less frequent among Negroes than among Whites, between 33 years and 44 years, and thirty times less so between 21 and 32. Among Mulattos it is more frequent than among the Negroes, but less than among Whites.

Lastly, among Red Indians it seems to be still more rare than among Negroes. White hair follows almost the same rule.[1]

In the mass, the human races may be divided according to the character of their hair as follows:—

Woolly Hair.—Bushmen, Negro, and Melanesian races.

Frizzy Hair.—Australian, Ethiopian, Beja, Fulbé, etc., and Dravidian.

Wavy Hair.—The white races of Europe, of Northern Africa, and Asia (Melanochroi or the dark-complexioned Whites, and Xanthochroi or pale Whites).

Fine, straight, or lightly-waved Hair.—Turco-Tatars, Finns, Ainus, and Indonesians (Dyaks, Nagas, etc.); lastly,

Coarse straight Hair.—Mongolians and American races, with some exceptions. It must be noted that, in the manifold blendings of races, characteristics of the hair amalgamate. Thus the half-breeds between Negroes and American Indians have, most frequently, the hair frizzy or wavy. But there are also frequent reversions to the primitive type, almost always, however, a little weakened.

There are no races of *hairy men*. Everything that has been said of different "hairy savages" in the interior of Africa or Indo-China resolves itself into the presence of a light down (probably the remains of embryonic lanugo) in the case of the Akkas of the Upper Nile, or to the fortuitous existence of one or two families of hairy men and women from Burma exhibited some years ago in Europe and America. Other "phenomena" have been shown, like the famous Julia Pastrana or the "Dog-men" of Russia. All these subjects are only particular cases of atavism, or of a reversion to the probable primordial condition of man or of his precursor at the period when he was as hairy as, for instance, the anthropoid apes of to-day; they are by no means the representatives of a hairy race.

The beard is, as we know, one of the sexual characteristics of man, although many fine ones are found among certain women, notably among the Europeans of the south, and especially among Spanish women. The more hairy the body, the thicker as a

[1] B. A. Gould, *loc. cit.*, p. 562.

rule is the beard. In the glabrous races (Mongols, Malays, Americans) a few straggling hairs are all that can be seen at the corners of the mouth and on the chin (Figs. 20 and 168); in the very hairy races, like the Ainus, the Iranians, certain Semites, the Todas, the Australians, the Melanesians, the beard is strong and abundant on the lips, the chin, and the cheeks, where it reaches sometimes to the cheek-bones (Fig. 22); in the Negro and Bushmen races neither the moustache nor the beard can attain to great dimensions, because of the curly nature of the hair (Figs. 140 and 143). The eyelashes and the eyebrows are likewise much developed in races having an abundant beard, and this is the case in both sexes; we have only to recall the thick and joined eyebrows of the Persian women. On the other hand, among the Mongolians we note the small development of the eyelashes in relation to the particular structure of their eye (see p. 77).

Pigmentation.—The distribution of the pigment which gives the colouring to the skin, to the hair, to the iris, varies much according to race, and forms, along with the nature of the hair, a good distinctive characteristic. As I have already stated above, the pigment is accumulated principally in the lowest layers of the rete Malpighii (Fig. 3, *c.p*), but it is also met with in small quantities in the horny layer, and even in the dermis.[1] According to race, the microscopic granules of pigment of a uniform brown are very unequally distributed around the nuclei of the cells, to which they give the most varied tones from pale yellow to dark brown, almost black. As the pigment exists in all races, and in all parts of the body, it is to its more or less plentiful accumulation in the cells that the colouring of the skin and its derivatives is due. Further, there must be added, for certain races at least, the combination with the tint of the blood of the vessels, as seen through the skin.

Every one knows that our white races become tanned in the sun; the cause of this is the pigment, developing abundantly

[1] Breul, "Vertheil. d. Hautpigments bei verschied. Menschenrassen," *Morph. Arb.*, directed by G. Schwalbe, vol. vi., part 3. Jena, 1896.

and being deposited in the cells under the combined action of air, heat, and light; the congestion of the vessels has also something to do with it. In the same way, persons living a long time in dense forests or in dark though airy places end by becoming paler, in consequence of the loss of the pigment, but recover colour immediately on re-exposure to the sun. But the modifications produced by the action of air and sun vary even among Europeans according to the colouring peculiar to their race.

Thus among the fair races of Northern Europe the skin, burnt by the sun, becomes red, as if swollen; on the other hand, among the dark-coloured peoples of the Mediterranean, it takes a bronze tint. There are thus between these two races notable differences, if not in the chemical nature of the pigment, which is scarcely likely, at least in regard to its quantity. It is the same with other races generally, and ten principal shades of colour at least can easily be distinguished. In the first place, among Whites, three shades: 1st, pale white; 2nd, florid, or rosy, peculiar to the Scandinavians, English, Dutch, etc.; 3rd, brownish-white, peculiar to Spaniards, Italians, etc. In the races called Yellow, three varieties of colour can likewise be distinguished: 4th, yellowish-white, a sickly hue the colour of wheat, as, for example, among certain Chinese; 5th, olive-yellow, the colour of new portmanteau leather, as among the majority of South American Indians, Polynesians, and Indonesians; 6th, dark yellow-brown, dark olive, or the colour of dead leaves, as among certain Americans, Malays, etc. In the dark-skinned races, four shades at least must be distinguished: 7th, red, copper-coloured, as, for example, among the Bejas, Niam-Niam, Fulbé; 8th, reddish-brown, chocolate, as among the Dravidians, the Australians, certain Negroes and Melanesians; lastly, 9th, sooty black, and 10th, coal-black, for example, among the different Negro populations.

In order to avoid an arbitrary designation of colours, anthropologists make use of chromatic tables, in which examples of the chief variations of colour are marked by numbers. The best table, almost universally adopted, is that of Broca, of thirty-four shades.[1] The Anthropological Institute of Great Britain and Ireland has published a very practical and simplified edition of it,[2] which contains only the ten numbers of principal shades proposed by Topinard, namely, those I have just enumerated.

The pigment is not uniformly distributed, as I have said, through the whole body, and this is so with the Whites as well as with the darkest races. In all of them the parts of the body most deeply coloured are the nape of the neck, the back (as with animals), the back part of the limbs, the arm-pits, the scrotum, and the breasts; the belly (as with animals), the insides of the hands, the soles of the feet, are among the most lightly coloured. The parts covered by garments are less coloured among white and yellow races than the parts uncovered; it is affirmed, but without reliable proofs, that the contrary takes place among the dark and black populations.

In the iris, the pigmentation assumes a particular character. As we know, this perforated diaphragm of the eye is composed, histologically, of three layers: an anterior epithelial one; a middle one, the "stroma," with muscular fibres, designed to enlarge or reduce the pupil; and lastly, a posterior layer, called the pigmental layer. But it must not be thought that this layer is the only repository of the pigment of the iris. It is also found accumulated in the thickness of the stroma, and between the muscular fibres. In both places the granules of the pigment have the same brown colour as in the rest of the body, but the pigment of the posterior or pigmental layer is only seen through the stroma and appears blue or grey, more or less light or dark, according to its quantity, just as the black veins of the blood appear to us blue through the skin. On the contrary, the pigment accumulated in the stroma or between the muscular fibres of the iris exhibits its natural yellow, brown, or almost black colour-

[1] Broca, *Instructions génér. pour les rech. Anthropologiques sur le vivant*, 2nd ed., Paris, 1879.

[2] J. G. Garson and Ch. H. Read, *Notes and Queries on Anthropology*, edit. for the Anthro. Institute, 2nd ed., London, 1892.

ing, according to the quantity of it, under the form of a trail radiating very clearly from the pupil towards the periphery of the eye occupying one-third, two-thirds, or even the whole of the iris.

Seen at a certain distance, irises without pigment in their stroma appear blue or grey; those having the whole or the greater part of this charged with pigment appear brown, dark brown, or almost black, according to the quantity of this pigment. But irises having a blue or grey foundation strewn with yellowish spots of pigment appear green, yellow, yellowish-grey, greenish-grey, etc.

There are thus distinguishable only three fundamental shades of the iris, or, as is commonly said, of the colour of the eyes: light (blue or grey); dark (bright or dull brown or black); and intermediate shades (green, yellow, yellowish-grey, greenish-grey, etc.). This classification is entirely based on the quantity of pigment in the iris.

It is only in fair European races that blue or grey eyes are found, perhaps also in the Turco-Ugrian races; light-brown eyes are met with among some Mongolians. In all the other populations of the earth the eyes are dark-brown or black. It is the same with the colouring of the hair. It varies appreciably among the wavy-haired races, much less so among the straight and frizzy-haired races, and remains always black among the woolly-haired races. Four principal shades can be distinguished in the hair—black, dark-brown, chestnut-brown (*châtain* in French), and fair. In this last shade, golden must be separated from flaxen and dull grey-reddish hair. Red hair of all shades is only an individual anomaly, accompanied besides, almost always, by freckles (*ephelides*) on the face and neck. There are no red-haired races, but light and chestnut hair may have a reddish reflection in it. Red hair is very common in countries where several white-coloured races (brown or fair) are intermixed. In these crossed races there are found heads of hair of all colours—black, brown, fair, reddish-brown, dull-grey, chestnut, etc. This is the natural result of the intermixture of blood. Among a

4

dark-haired people, which has remained free from intermixture, or has only intermingled with dark-haired races, an exceptional red-haired individual constitutes a pathological condition, called "erythrism" by Broca. Erythrism can only manifest itself in certain races; at least, until now no example has been instanced among the Negroes; on the other hand, erythrism is somewhat common among the Jews of Europe, and among such Jews it is most frequently associated with frizzy hair.[1]

The colouring of the hair depends not only on the pigment, but on the more or less quantity of air in the medulla of the hair, which blends the white and grey tones with the general tint given by the pigment. In the air, the hair fades, becomes less highly coloured, duller. Certain acids of the perspiration render the hair reddish-brown, as for instance, under the arm-pit.

At birth pigment is found in the body in less quantity than in the adult state. Every one knows that the hair of children, often light-coloured at birth and in early years, becomes darker as they grow up. Almost all our European children are born with blue eyes, and the pigment only begins to increase in the iris, transforming the eyes into grey, brown, or black at the end of some weeks, or even months after birth. New-born Chinese, Botocudos, Malays, Kalmuks, are much less yellow than the adults of these people, and, lastly, Negroes at birth are of a reddish-chocolate or copper colour, which only becomes darker at the end of three or four days, beginning in certain places, such as the nape, nipples, scrotum, etc.

[1] Fair hair with all its shades is met with especially among the European populations of the North; it is rarer in the South. There are, it is computed, 16 fair-haired individuals to every 100 Scotchmen; 13 to every 100 Englishmen; and 2 only to every 100 Italians (Beddoe). On the other hand, brown hair is met with in 75 cases out of 100 Spaniards, 39 out of 100 Frenchmen, and 16 only of 100 Scandinavians (Gould). The fair variety is rarer among straight-haired races; it is found, however, among the western Finns, among certain Russians, etc.

The presence of temporary spots of pigment noticed among new-born Japanese by Grimm and Baelz, among the Chinese by Matignon, among the Tagals of the Philippines by Collignon, and among the Eskimo by Sören-Hansen,[1] is more puzzling. These are somewhat large blue, grey, or black spots, situated in the sacro-lumbar region and on the buttocks, which disappear about the age of two, three, or five years. The existence of these spots, like that of the ephelides in the European child, would prove rather the migration of pigmental granules to the places selected than a general increase of them. In most races women appear to have clearer skin than men; in that respect, as in many other characters, they have a closer resemblance to children. It is thought by some that the hair of women is lighter than that of men among European races.[2]

Among Negroes the pigment is visible not only on the skin, in the hair, and the iris, but also in the sclerotic, in the mucous membrane of the lips, the mouth, the genital organs, etc.; the internal organs, even, are not free from it; the suprarenal capsules, the mesentery, the liver, the spleen, are often coloured with black spots of pigment, and even the brain contains numerous pigmented points in its envelopes and in its grey matter. Such an abundance of pigment would become a danger to the White, as is proved by certain diseases, melanism, for example, in which the pigment especially invades the viscera, or Addison's disease, in which, on the contrary, there is an over-production of pigment in the skin and the mucous membranes.

The total absence of pigment, which may occur with the Negro as with the White, is termed albinism. This may be accompanied, if complete (that is to say, when, besides the white skin and hair, the iris is also deprived of pigment, and appears red), by somewhat serious affections of the eyesight.

[1] Baelz, *loc. cit.*, vol. iv., p. 40; Matignon, *Bull. Soc. Anthr.*, p. 524, Paris, 1896; Collignon, *ibid.*, p. 528; Sören-Hansen, *Bidrag Vestgrönl. Anthr.*, Copenhagen, 1893; Extr. from *Meddel. om Grönl.*, vol. vii., p. 237.

[2] Havelock Ellis, *Man and Woman*, p. 223. London, 1897.

But, in every respect, albinos are weakly, and probably not fertile amongst themselves.

In considering from all points of view the nature of hair and pigmentation in general, we cannot help noticing a certain correlation between these two characters. In fact, to the white colouring of the skin corresponds, in a general fashion, wavy hair, the colouring of which varies often in accord with the colour of the eyes and the shades of the skin (white, fair, brown races); to the yellow colouring corresponds straight, smooth hair; to the reddish-brown skin, frizzy hair; and to the black, woolly hair.

CHAPTER II.

I. MORPHOLOGICAL CHARACTERS (*continued*).

Cranium or Skull: Cranial measurements—Orbits and orbital index—Nasal bone and nasal index—Prognathism—*Head of the living subject:* Cephalic index—Face—Eyes—Nose and nasal index in the living subject—Lips—*Trunk and Limbs:* The Skeleton—Pelvis and its indices—Shoulder blade—Thoracic limb—Abdominal limb—*Proportions of the body in the living subject*—Trunk and neck—Curve of the back—Steatopygy—*Various Organs:* Genital organs—Brain—Its weight—Convolutions—The neuron—Its importance from the psychical point of view.

HAVING treated of the body in its general aspect, we shall now examine from the morphological point of view its different parts: the head, trunk, limbs, etc., as well as their relations to each other and their reciprocal dimensions, both in the skeleton and the living subject.

Cranium or Skull.—This part of the skeleton forms the object of investigation of a very extended branch of anthropology called craniology.

Craniology must not be confounded with the cranioscopy of the phrenologists, a sham science founded by Gall, who wished to establish a connection between certain bumps or irregularities of the surface of the skull and the parts of the brain in which, as was pretended, were localised the different intellectual functions. It is now demonstrated that the inequalities of the external table of the cranium walls have no relation whatever with the irregularities of the internal table, and still less have they anything in common with the conformation of the various parts of the brain. But if there be no such direct connection as this between the cranium and the brain, there is nevertheless a certain remote relation between them, and the brain has attained such a development in man that the study of everything which concerns it, immediately or remotely, possesses great interest. This would alone suffice to explain the pre-eminent position assigned to craniology in the natural history of man. But there exist still other reasons why the study of the skull is one of the most cultivated branches of anthropology. As in the case of all the other mammals, the skull in man is one of the parts of the skeleton, and even of the entire body, which exhibits the greatest number of well-marked variations. The differences in the form and the dimensions of the skull in correlation with those of the brain and the masticatory organs, serve to distinguish races and species, both in man and other vertebrata. Besides, the teeth, which characterise not only genera but even families and orders of the mammifera, are always attached to the skull, though not forming part of the bony system. We may also observe that the skull, with the other bones of the skeleton, constitutes the only anatomical document of prehistoric man which has come down to us; it is only in studying it that we can connect and compare, from the point of view of physical type, existing with extinct races of mankind.

The characters that may be observed in the skull are very numerous, and may be divided into *descriptive* characters, which give an account of the conformation of the bony structure of the head and its parts, and *craniometrical* characters, which give the dimensions of these parts by exact measurements taken by means of special apparatus or instruments. These two orders of characters are complementary to each other. The cranial characters vary according to race, but within the limits of each race there are other lesser variations according to age and sex.

The general form of the cranium, as also the number, the consistence, and structure of the different parts which compose it are modified as the individual develops and grows older. Formed of a single cartilaginous and membranous substance at the beginning of embryonic life, the cranium is composed in the last fœtal state of a great number of *points of ossification of various texture.* At birth the number of these points has considerably diminished; they have united for the most part to form the different parts of the *bones of the cranium* or *brain case* and the *bones of the face;* as the child grows, these points grow and end by being contiguous; about the age of eighteen or twenty years they form bones separated by *sutures.* There are twenty-one separated bones described in classic treatises on anatomy. Later on these bones begin to unite, the *sutures* which separate them disappear, and in extreme old age the cranium is formed of a bony mass almost as continuous and homogeneous as was the cranial cartilaginous and membranous mass in the embryo. According to the number of the pieces composing the cranium, and also according to their position, structure, and conformation, according to the degree of obliteration of the sutures and the order in which the obliteration of each suture takes place, according to the general form of the forehead, the angle of the lower jaw, according to the volume and dimensions of the skull, and lastly, according to the state of the dentition, etc., the nearly exact age of the individual to whom the skull had belonged may easily be discovered in this cycle of development. Other characters serve to distinguish the sex: the forehead is straight and rounded in woman, retreating in man; the cranial cavity is less in woman than in man in any given race; the orbital edges are sharper in woman, the impress of the muscles less marked, the weight of the skull in general less than that of the masculine skull, etc.[1] Lastly, the characters of race are

[1] These characters, in conjunction with several others—the small development of the lower jaw-bone, the frontal sinuses poorly developed, the much greater development of the cranial vault proportionately to its base, the persistence of the frontal and parietal bumps—make the feminine skull approximate to the infantile form. See the works of Broca, Manouvrier, and also Rabentisch, *Der Weiberschädel, Morpholog. Arb.*, Schwalbe, 1892, vol. ii., p. 207; and H. Ellis, *loc. cit.*, p. 72.

numerous and special. I shall proceed briefly to enumerate some of them. First in order of importance comes *cranial capacity*, or the volume of the cavity of the brain-case, which gives an idea of the volume of the brain, and approximately of its weight.

Cranial capacity may vary to the extent of double the minimum figure (from 1100 cubic centimetres to 2200 cubic centimetres) among normal individuals in the human race. The average capacity for the races of Europe is from 1500 to 1600 cubic centimetres; that of the skulls of Asiatic races appears to be very nearly the same; that of the Negro races and Oceanians a little smaller, perhaps from 1400 to 1500 cubic centimetres on an average That of the Australians, the Bushmen, and the Andamanese is still less, from 1250 to 1350 cubic centimetres. But it must not be forgotten that the volume of the head, as with its other dimensions, has a certain relation to the height of the individual, and, as a matter of fact, Bushmen and Andamanese are very short in stature; Australians, however, are of average height. Partly, too, to their disproportion of height must, probably, be attributed the difference between the volume of the cranium in man and in woman. According to the series examined, this sexual difference may extend from 100 to 200 cubic centimetres, and even beyond, in favour of man. The cranial capacity of woman represents from eighty-five to ninety-five of the cranial capacity of man.[1] The cranial capacity of lunatics, of certain criminals, and especially of celebrated or distinguished men, scholars, artists, statesmen, etc., appears to be slightly superior to the average of their race. We shall revert later to the question of cranial capacity in connection with weight of brain.

The general form of the brain-case is an oval, but this oval may be more or less rounded, quite globular (Fig. 11), or more or less elongated to resemble an ellipse, the major axis of which

[1] H. Ellis, *loc. cit.*, p. 89 and onwards; L. Manouvrier, article "Cerveau" in the *Dict. de Physiol. de Ch. Richet*, vol. ii., part 8, Paris, 1897.

is almost double the minor (Fig. 10). The numerical expression of the cranial form is given in anthropology by what is called the *cephalic index*—that is to say, by the relation of the length of the cranium (ordinarily measured from the glabella to the most prominent point of the occiput (Figs. 10 and 13, A B) to its greatest breadth (Fig. 10, C D, Fig. 12, M N). Reducing uniformly the first of these measurements to 100, we obtain the different figures for the breadth, which expresses the cranial form; thus very round skulls (Fig. 11) have 85, 90,

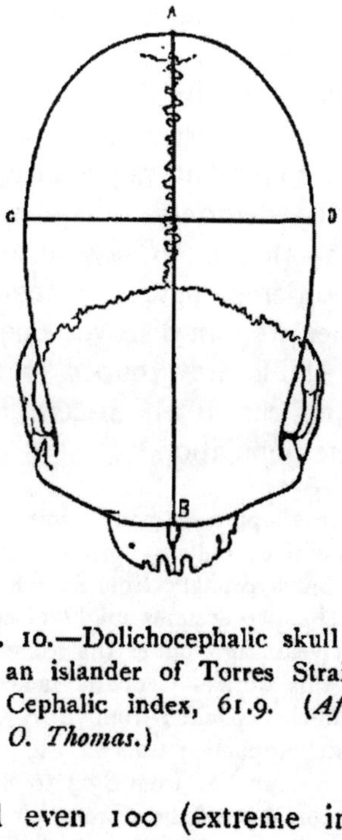

FIG. 10.—Dolichocephalic skull of an islander of Torres Straits. Cephalic index, 61.9. (*After O. Thomas.*)

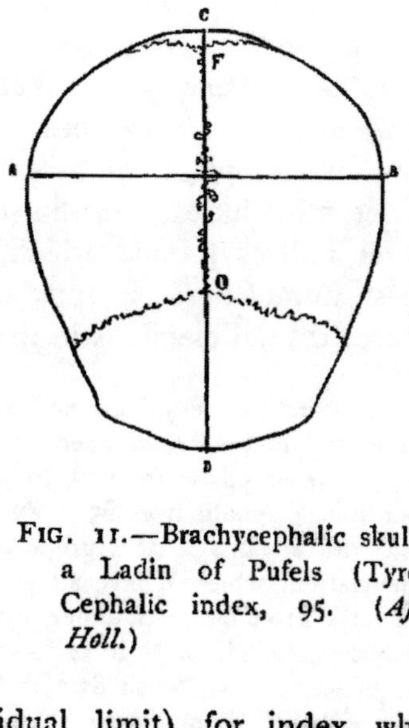

FIG. 11.—Brachycephalic skull of a Ladin of Pufels (Tyrol). Cephalic index, 95. (*After Holl.*)

and even 100 (extreme individual limit) for index, while elongated skulls (Fig. 10) may have an index of 70, of 65, and even of 58 (extreme individual limit). According to Broca's nomenclature, skulls having indices between 77.7 and 80 are mesaticephalic or mesocephalic; those having the indices below this figure are sub-dolichocephalic (up to 75), or dolichocephalic (beyond 75, Fig. 10); those which have the index above 80 are sub-brachycephalic (up to 83.3), or brachycephalic (above 83.3, Fig. 11).[1] Peoples or ethnic groups being formed of various elements, it is in most cases impossible to determine, after the examination of an isolated skull, to which population it belongs; all that can be said is that the skull is brachy- or dolicho-cephalic, orthognathous or prognathous, etc. We must have a certain number of skulls (from ten to thirty at least, according to the homogeneity of the population) to be able to discern the constituent elements of this population as far as they are manifested in the cranial characteristics. The *average* measurements are then deduced from a given number of skulls, by adding the individual measurements and dividing them by the number of skulls examined. But the average of any measurement whatever only gives a very general and somewhat vague idea of the actual dimensions of skulls. To determine it we must *co-ordinate* and *seriate* these skulls—that is to say, arrange them, for example, in an ascending order of figures expressing their cephalic index. In this manner we can discover one or several indices around which the skulls are grouped in the largest number. It is thus that we can often discern two or three cranial elements in the same population.[2]

[1] According to the quinary nomenclature adopted in many countries of Europe, the indices are grouped by series of five: dolichocephalic from 70 to 74.9; mesocephalic from 75 to 79.9; brachycephalic from 80 to 84.9; hyper-brachycephalic from 85 to 89.9. The two systems might be combined with advantage, as I proposed ten years ago, under the following nomenclature, which I have adopted in this work:—Cephalic index of the skull: From 69.9 and under, hyper-dolichocephalic; from 70 to 74.9, dolichocephalic; from 75 to 77.7, sub-dolichocephalic; from 77.7 to 79 9, mesocephalic; from 80 to 83.2, sub-brachycephalic; from 83.3 to 84.9, brachycephalic; from 85 to 85 9, hyper-brachycephalic; from 90 and upwards, ultra-brachycephalic.

[2] Skulls may also be grouped by sections (for instance, ascending to the quinary nomenclature of the cephalic index) to see what is the proportional part of each of these sections. Thus if we take a series of 10 skulls having the following indices, 75, 77, 78, 80, 80, 81, 81, 81, 82, 84, their *average* index will be expressed by the figure 80 (the sum of the indices divided by the number of skulls), while the most frequent *mean* index

If we apply these methods to the study of the cephalic index, we see that generally the crania of Negroes, Melanesians, Eskimo, Ainus, Berbers, the races of Northern Europe, etc., are dolichocephalic, while those of the Turkish peoples, the Malays, certain Slavs, Tyrolese, etc., are brachycephalic; that the dolichocephalic predominate in Great Britain, while the brachycephalic are in a majority in France, etc. (See p. 75, and Appendix II.)

The relation of the height to the breadth or to the length of the skull gives likewise an idea of its general form. It is thus that we recognise low skulls (platycephalic), medium (orthocephalic or metriocephalic), or high (hypsicephalic).

In order more correctly to describe the different peculiarities of the cranium, and to be able to refer the measurements to fixed co-ordinates, it is desirable to place the skull, when being studied, on a horizontal plane. Unfortunately, anthropologists are far from being agreed as to this initial plane. In France, in England, and in many other countries, that adopted is the aveolo-condylean plane of Broca (Fig. 13, L K), which passes through the condyles and the alveolar border of the upper jaw; it is nearly parallel to the horizontal plane passing through the visual axes of the two eyes in the living subject; whilst in Germany the plane still in favour is one passing through the inferior border of the orbit and the centre or top of the contour of the auditory meatus [1] (Fig. 13, N M). The skull once conveniently placed in position according to a horizontal plane, the different views of it are the following: seen from above (*norma verticalis* of Blumenbach, Figs. 10 and 11), from below (*norma basilaris*), from the side or in profile (*norma lateralis*, Fig. 13), from the full face (*norma facialis*, Fig. 12), or from behind (*norma occipitalis*).

will be 81. Further, the series should be considered as not very homogeneous, for it comprises 1 dolichocephalic, 1 sub-dolichocephalic, 1 mesocephalic, 6 sub-brachycephalic, and 1 brachycephalic.

[1] It is rather a line than a plane; the cranium always being asymmetrical, we cannot make a horizontal plane pass exactly through the borders of the two orbits and the two auditory meatus.

In regard to the face, different measurements express its general form; thus the relation of the bi-zigomatic length (Fig. 12, I G) to the total height of the bony structure of the head (Fig. 12, K L), or to its partial height from the glabella to the alveolar border of the upper jaw-bone (Fig. 12, F H), serves to separate skulls into brachy- or dolicho-facial, or, as they are also called, *chamæprosopes* and *leptoprosopes.* Other characters, such as the excessive development of the supraciliary ridges (Fig.

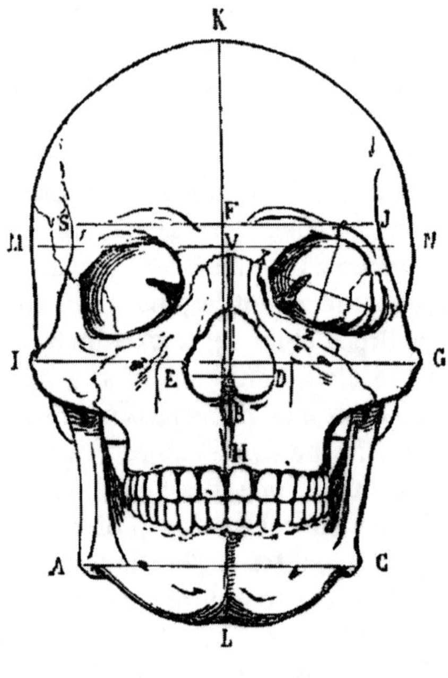

FIG. 12.—Skull of ancient Egyptian exhumed at Thebes, with principal craniometrical lines.

13, A), also give a special physiognomy to the bony structure of the face.

But the parts that deserve particular attention are the orbits and the nasal skeleton. The orbital orifice represents a quadrilateral figure more or less irregular, more or less angular or rounded, the length and breadth of which can be measured. According to Broca,[1] the breadth is measured from the point called dacrion (Fig. 12, X) (situated at the intersection of the fronto-lachrymal suture and the crista lachrymalis) to the most distant point of the opposite edge of the orbit (Fig. 12, Y); the height (Fig. 12, T Z) is also measured perpendicularly to the preceding line. The relation of this height to the breadth = 100, or the orbital index, expresses in figures the form of the more or less shallow quadrilateral of the orbit.

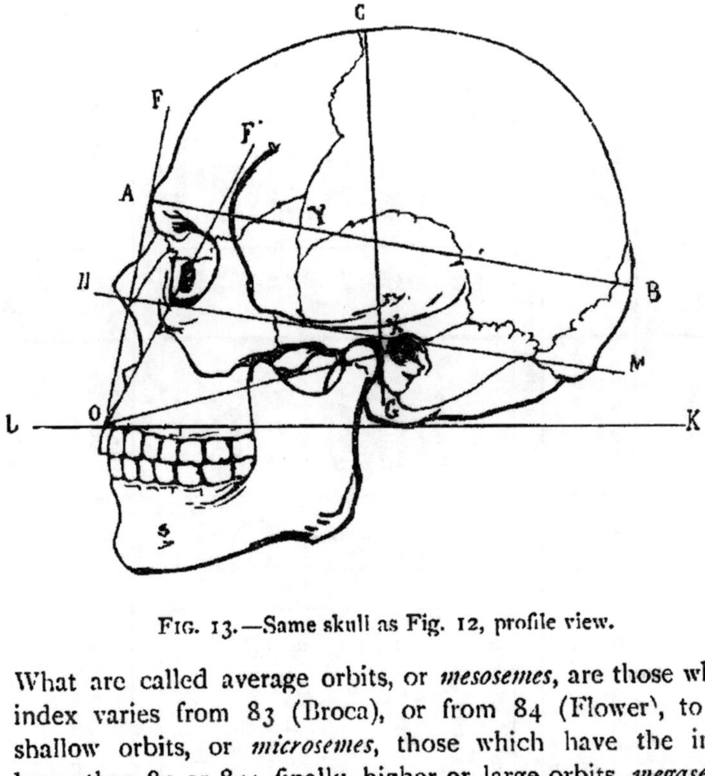

FIG. 13.—Same skull as Fig. 12, profile view.

What are called average orbits, or *mesosemes*, are those whose index varies from 83 (Broca), or from 84 (Flower), to 89; shallow orbits, or *microsemes*, those which have the index lower than 83 or 84; finally, higher or large orbits, *megasemes*, those which have their index from 90 and upwards. The annexed table gives the orbital indices of the principal populations of the globe.

[1] Broca, "Recherches sur l'indice orbitaire," *Rev. Anthro.*, p. 577, Paris, 1875.

TABLE OF ORBITAL INDICES.

(Crania of both Sexes together; series of more than 10 subjects.)

No. of Crania.	Ethnic Groups.	Orbital Index.	Observer.	No. of Crania.	Ethnic Groups.	Orbital Index.	Observer.
			MICROSEMES.				
49	New Caledonians ...	80.6	Broca.	21	Bushmen	83	Turner.
14	Tasmanians	80.8	Flower.	16	Hottentots	83.9	Broca, Hamy
101	Australians	81.5	Fl., Tur., C.E.[1]	53	Spanish Basques of Zarans	83.6	Broca, Hamy
22	Kafirs	83	Broca.				
			MESOSEMES (84-89).				
23	Papuans of the North-west (Rubi) ...	84	C.E.	18	Maori	87	Turner.
20	Ruck Islanders (Carolines)	84.1	Virchow.	208	Various Europeans ...	87	Flower.
11	Croats	84.3	Broca.	48	Fuegians	87.5	Mantegazza, Hya., Den.
20	Papuans in general ...	84.4	Broca.	31	Japanese	88	Baelz.
13	Botocudos	84.7	Rey.	63	Southern Bretons ...	88.1	Broca.
68	Melanesians	85.1	Flower.	19	Eskimo...	88.2	Broca.
132	Ainus	85.2	Koganei.	33	English...	88.4	Flower.
20	Negroes of Kordofan...	85.1	Broca.	43	Veddahs	88.5	Sarasin, Fl.
84	Western Negroes ...	85.4	Broca.	23	Corsicans	88.6	Broca.
96	Papuans of the N. W. (Kordo)	85.8	C.E.	26	Kabyles...	88.9	Broca.
11	Natives of Admiralty Islands	86	Turner.	16	Hindus	89.2	Flower.
43	Negroes	86.3	Flower.	11	Bugis of Mangkassar	89.2	C.E.
80	Auvergnats	86.5	Broca.	28	Berbers...	89.5	C.E.
11	Vitians (Fiji)	87	Flower.	28	Arabs	89.5	Ten Kate.
				11	Dyaks	89.8	C.E.
				19	Javanese	89.5	C.E.
				12	Tatars of the Volga ...	89.5	C.E.
			MEGASEMES (90 AND UPWARDS).				
69	Kalmuks	90.2	Den., Ivanovs	14	Andamanese	91.7	Flower.
26	Indians of N. America	90.8	Broca.	127	Am. Indians in gen. ...	91.7	Broca.
13	Modern Mexicans ...	90.8	Broca.	17	Malays	91.9	C.E.
43	Javanese	91.1	Broca.	30	Peruvians not deformed	92	Broca.
88	Polynesians	91.6	Fl., Broca.	16	Modern Aztecs ...	92.1	C.E.

[1] C.E., an abbreviation which is met with in other tables for *Crania ethnica* of De Quatrefages and Hamy, Paris. 1882.

The capacity of the orbital cavity and its depth are also measured, but, as the researches of L. Weiss have demonstrated, there is no correlation between the form of the skull (dolicho- or brachy-cephalic) and this depth. On the other hand, it appears to have some relation with the form of the face; broad faces (*chamæprosopes*) have deeper orbits than long faces (*leptoprosopes*).[1]

The skeleton of the nose presents numerous variations according to race. The nasal bones may be more or less inclined, one in relation with another, so as to form either an almost flat plane or a sort of prominent roof; their outline may be straight, concave, or convex; their breadth and their length also vary. The form of these bones, together with the nasal opening which is found below, may be expressed by the figures of the nasal index—that is to say, of the relation between the height of the bony mass (from the root of the nose to the anterior nasal spine) and its breadth (lines V B and E D of Fig. 12). According to the greater or lesser breadth of the nasal bones and of the nasal opening, the skull is called *leptorhinian* (long-nosed) or *platyrhinian* (flat-nosed); the intermediate forms bear the name of *mesorhinian.* The form of the nasal opening appears to be transmitted very tenaciously by heredity (Broca).

The following table, in which I have introduced only series of more than ten skulls, gives the distribution of the principal ethnic groups according to their nasal index.

It is easy to see in running the eye over this table, that almost all the populations of the so-called white races are leptorhinians, while all the yellow populations are comprised exclusively in the group of mesorhinians, and Negroes and Bushmen in that of the platyrhinians.

The Polynesians seem to be leptorhinians, the Melanesians with the Australians show a tendency towards platyrhiny.

Prognathism, that is to say the degree of projection of the maxillary portion of the face, is a characteristic trait of certain skulls; however, it does not seem to play so important a part

[1] L. Weiss, *Beitr. Anat. der Orbita*, part 3, p. 25. Tübingen, 1890.

NASAL INDEX OF THE CRANIUM.

(Series of more than 10 Skulls of both Sexes together.)

Number of Skulls.	Ethnic Groups.	Nasal Index.	Observer.
	LEPTORHINIANS (less than 48).		
46	Eskimo	42.2	Broca, Flower
54	Spanish Basques	43.8	Broca
17	Guanches	44.2	Broca
28	Arabs	44.4	C.E.
28	Berbers	46.2	C.E.
32	English	46.0	Flower
83	Auvergnats	46.2	Broca
17	Frisians	46.3	Topinard
122	Parisians	46.7	Broca
12	Tatars of the Volga	47.1	Ten Kate
52	Argentine Araucans	47.1	Ten Kate
127	American Indians in general	47.2	Ten Kate
48	Fuegians	47.5	Mant., Hyad., Den.
15	Botocudos	47.2	Rey., Virch.
18	Maoris	47.5	Turner
88	Polynesians	47.9	Flower, Broca
	MESORHINIANS (48-53).		
11	Natives of the Admiralty Is.	48.0	Flower
72	Italians of Lombardy	48.3	Flower
28	Sardinians	48.6	Flower
66	Kalmuks	49.0	Denik., Ivanovs.
94	Chinese	49.1	T. K., Br., Fl.
31	Japanese	49.5	T. K., Baelz
16	Hindus	50.0	C.E.
11	Bugis of Mangkassar	50.0	C.E.
	MESORHINIANS (48-53)—*Continued.*		
21	Annamese	50.1	Topinard
33	Marvars (India)	50.0	Flower
21	Russians (chiefly of Kazan)	50.3	Malief
14	Andamanese	50.6	Flower
126	Ainus	50.9	Koganei
19	Inhab. of Ruck Isl. (Carolines)	51.2	Virchow
29	Permiaks	51.7	Malief
43	Veddahs	51.8	Saras., Flower
17	Malays	51.9	C.E.
11	Dyaks	51.9	Montano
135	New Caledonians	52.3	C.E.
16	Modern Aztecs	52.1	C.E.
	PLATYRHINIANS (over 53).		
25	Negroes of Fernando Po	53.7	Topinard
11	Negroes of the Sudan, Darfour, etc.	54.2	C.E.
35	Negroes of Senegal	55.1	C.E.
25	Negroes of Upper Guinea	55.2	C.E.
22	Nubians (Bejas)	55.1	Broca
18	Negroes of Kordofan	55.4	Topinard
13	Fijians of Viti-Levu (interior)	56.5	Flower
132	Australians	56.2	Fl., Br., Turner, C.E.
21	Bushmen	58.4	Turner
15	Negroes of Lower Guinea	58.8	C.E.
12	Kafirs	61.7	C.E.

in the classification of races as anthropologists had thought twenty or thirty years ago. It presents too many individual varieties to be taken as a distinctive character of race. The degree of prognathism is measured by means of different *facial angles*, of which that of Cloquet, passing by the forehead, the upper alveolar point (between the two incisors), and the external auditory meatus (Fig. 13, F O K), is one of the best. However, as it expresses the relation of points too far removed from each other, it is better to confine ourselves to the measurement of *alveolar prognathism*, that is to say, of the subnasal projection of the face. This prognathism is measured with the angle determined by the alveolar point, the external auditory meatus, and the nasal spine (Fig. 13, F′ O K).

Among numerous other measurements which give indications for certain characters we must cite: the minimum frontal diameter (Fig. 12, S J); the interorbital line; the length and the breadth of the palate, the relation of which constitutes the *palatal index*, etc. Among the measurements of the curves it is necessary to note the horizontal circumference of the head, the antero-posterior curve with its frontal, parietal, and occipital portions, etc. Besides the facial angles, a great number of others are taken; the more important are the sphenoidal angle and the different occipital angles (of Daubenton, Broca, etc.), which give the inclination of the occipital foramen in relation to a horizontal plane. The measurements of these angles furnish valuable indications on the characters called *seriary*, to which we have recourse in order to compare man with animals which bear the closest resemblance to him.

But all these measurements do not suffice to exhaust the data of the morphology of the skull. There still remain a host of *descriptive* characters: the general form of the skull, pentagonal, oval, elliptical, etc.; the contour of the face more or less angular or rounded, its *canine fossa* more or less deep, its zygomatic arches, and its molar bones more or less projecting, etc. Certain anomalies in the sutures of the bones, as for example the persistence of the medio-frontal suture, the dispositions of the *pterion* (point of union of the sutures between the frontal, the temporal, the sphenoid, and the parietal bones), are only important as seriary characters, but there are others which possess some value in the differentiation of races. The

FIG. 14.—Jenny, Australian woman of Queensland. Height, 1m. 56; cephalic index, 71.2; nasal index, 119. (*Photo. Prince Roland Bonaparte.*)

Wormian bones, or points of ossification inserted between the bones of the skull, are of the number. One of these bones found between the parietal bones and the occipital, has even received the name of the *Inca bone* (Fig. 23, A), on account of its very frequent occurrence among Peruvian crania (deformed or not). In fact, it is met with in an imperfect state

FIG. 15.—Same subject as Fig. 14, seen in profile. Example of nose concave and flattened, of prognathism, and of prominent superciliary arches. (*Photo. Prince Roland Bonaparte.*)

20 times in 100 and perfect 5.4 times in 100 among Peruvians, while in Negro crania it is found only 6 times in 100 imperfect, and 1.5 perfect; among Europeans it is still more rarely

imperfect, and is hardly ever met with perfect (Anuchin). This peculiarity seems to be a special character of the American race, seeing that among the crania of the Indians of the New World (outside Peruvians) the anomaly in question is found 10 times in 100 imperfect and 1.3 times perfect. Among the Indians of Rio Salado, an affluent of the Gila in Arizona, the frequency of this anomaly is still greater than among Peruvians (5.7 perfect cases against 5.4 in Peru).[1] In the same way, the presence of a suture which divides into two, more or less imperfectly, the malar bone (Fig. 23, B) appears to be a special character of Ainu and Japanese crania; Hilgendorf has even proposed to call the lower portion of the malar bone thus formed *os japonicum* (Fig. 23, B, *a*). While the suture is only met with 11 or 12 times in 100 in Mongolian races, and 9 times in 100 in European races according to Ten Kate,[2] it is found from 25 to 40 times in 100 among Japanese according to Doenitz.

It is well understood that in the description of crania the alterations of form produced by all kinds of causes are taken into account. (Such, for example, is the considerable asymmetry or *plagiocephaly* due to a physiological cause, as the hypertrophy of the capacity of the skull, or its atrophy in the pathological cases of *hydrocephaly* or *microcephaly*, and so many other ethnic deformations which will come up for treatment in Chapter V., etc.)

The head of the living subject furnishes more numerous characters than the skull, especially if the face be considered with the play of feature. Sometimes an examination of the face suffices to determine the race of the subject.

The measurements of the head are about fifty in number, but they are not all of equal importance. Very few of them, indeed, are really useful.

The chief of the *angular measurements* is the facial angle; great importance was formerly attached to it when prognathism, or the degree of projection of the maxillary region,

[1] Ten Kate, *L'Anthropologie*, 1894, p. 617.

[2] Ten Kate, *Zur Anthropologie der Mongoloiden*, Berlin, 1882 (thesis).

was considered as a character of inferiority. In spite of the numerous instruments invented (double square, Harmand's instrument, Jacquard's goniometer, etc.), great precision in these measurements is not attainable. The only angle which can be taken with sufficient exactitude, thanks to the facial medium goniometer of Broca, is Cuvier's angle, formed by a line running either from the glabella or the point between the eyebrows to the interval between the incisor teeth, and by another line starting from the external auditory meatus towards this interval. This angle enables us to estimate the *total prognathism* and the *alveolar prognathism*, but the variations which it presents are too slight (3 to 4 degrees), taking race with race, to constitute a distinctive character. Prognathism of the lips, pushed forward to form the prominence of the "muzzle," which gives so characteristic an expression to the profile of certain Negroes or Australians (Fig. 15), is not expressed by this measurement, and ordinarily cannot be measured in any way.

Among the *measurements of the curve of the head* the principal are those of the *horizontal circumference* with its *anterior and posterior portions*, the limits of which are found at the supra-auricular point, that is to say, in the depression which is found immediately in front of the spot where the helix of the pinna of the ear is inserted. The value of this measurement has also been exaggerated, it being said that men of well-developed minds have the circumference greater than men without intellectual culture. The comparative observations of Broca made on house-surgeons and attendants of hospitals seem to bear out the assertion; but they have not been confirmed, and stature appears to have a decided relation with the size of the head.

The measurements in a straight line are more numerous and more important than those of angles and curves. Those which give the antero-posterior diameter or maximum length of the head (from the glabella to the most prominent point of the occiput, as on the cranium) and the transverse maximum diameter, are the first to note. We have already seen (p. 57) that their centesimal relation constitutes what is called the *cephalic index.* Let us note afterwards the *total height of the head* (projection on a vertical plane), the *maximum breadth of the face* (between the zygomatic arches) and the different "lengths" of the face, the relation of which to the breadth

FIG. 16.—Japanese officer (old style), born at Tokio. Example of elongated face. (*Phot. Coll. Mus. Nat. Hist., Paris.*)

constitutes the *facial index.* The latter is far from expressing the form of the face as well as does the cephalic index the form of the head, on account of its irregularity, and the want of agreement between anthropologists with regard to the "facial lengths." Nevertheless we distinguish according to these measurements elongated faces or *leptoprosopic* (Fig. 16), short faces or *chamæprosopic* (Fig. 17), and medium faces, *meso-* or *ortho-prosopic* (Fig. 14).

Other measurements taken are the *frontal minimum diameter* or minimum breadth of the forehead (between the temporal

FIG. 17.—Two men, Nagas of Manipur. Examples of large faces with prominent cheek-bones. (*Phot. Miss Godden.*)

ridges of the frontal bone, which makes a projection under the skin); the *distance between the inner angles* or *canthus* of the eyes is a good measurement, especially if it be compared with the *breadth of the nose*, taken by just touching with the points of the callipers the alæ of the nose. Referred to the length of the nose (between the root of the nose and the point of insertion of the septum) reduced to 100 it gives the *nasal index*, one of the important characters in the classification of races. Among several other measurements may be mentioned the *breadth of the mouth* between the commissure of the lips, the subject being in repose; the *length and the breadth of the ears*, etc. All these measurements are taken either with callipers or with sliding compasses, similar to those used by shoemakers or engineers, or with special instruments.[1]

Measurements taken on the living subject can never be as accurate as those obtained on the cranium; but, on the other hand, they may be much more numerous, and the greater number of observations compensates largely for individual errors due to difficulties of the mode of operation. Further, when measuring heads of living subjects, there is the advantage of knowing sex, approximate age, and exact origin, while in the case of one-half the crania examined, one or more of these particulars may be wanting. All these conditions sufficiently explain why, in these latter days, the attention of anthropologists is directed towards measurements of living subjects, among which those of the head occupy the foremost place.

Do the measurements of the head of the living subject correspond to the measurements of the cranium? Various researches made with the object of elucidating this question leave it still unsettled. It was believed at first, for instance, that the *bregma*, or point of junction between the coronal and the sagittal sutures in the cranium (Fig. 11, o), corresponded in the head with the most prominent point of the line passing from the supra-auricular point to another perpendicularly to the horizontal plane; but the very careful researches of Broca and Ferré have shown that this point is always in front of the bregma by a quantity which varies according to sex and indi-

[1] See P. Broca, *Instruc. gén.*, *etc.*; Garson and Read, *Notes and Queries*, *etc.;* as well as P. Topinard, "Instruc. Anthropometr. pour les voyageurs," *Rev. d'Anthro.*, p. 397, Paris, 1885.

vidual. The correspondence of the *tourbillon* of the hair with the *lambda*, or point of junction on the cranium of the sagittal and occipital sutures (Fig. 11, F), has not either been clearly demonstrated. The principal measurement, the *cephalic index*, does not appear always to correspond on the cranium and on the head of the living subject. *A priori*, the living head should have the index a little higher than the cranium, the muscles of the temporal region being thicker than those of the supra-occipital and frontal region. However, experiments made in connection with this subject are contradictory. According to Broca, two units must be subtracted from the index taken on the living subject in order to obtain the index on the cranium; this is also the opinion of Stieda and Houzé and a great number of anthropologists, while Mantegazza and Weisbach advocate the reduction of the index by three units; and Virchow and Topinard do not admit any. In the face of these divergent opinions, it is best to give the indices on the cranium and the living subject separately as they are, and indicate the rate of reduction or augmentation.

However, in a general way, one may admit, and I admit in this book, the difference of two units between the indices of the cranium and the living subject. In this way the two may be compared by adding these two units to the index of crania and removing them from the index of the living subject. I have given (p. 57) the divisions of the cephalic index of the cranium; those of the living subject are the same with the addition of two units.

We may now proceed to examine a little more closely the principal measurements and the indices on the living subject by beginning precisely with the *cephalic index*, which I believe to be, in spite of the recent criticisms of Sergi[1] and Ehrenreich,[2] one of the good characteristics of race, enabling us to make some secondary partitions in the principal parti-

[1] Sergi, *Congr. internat. d'Archéol. et d'Anthr. préhist.*, 11th sess., Moscow, 1893, vol. ii., p. 296.

[2] Ehrenreich, *Anthr. Stud. Urbewohner Brasiliens*, chap. i., Brunswick, 1897.

tions of the genus *Homo*, based, as we shall see afterwards (Chapter VIII.), on the colour of the skin and the nature of the hair. Assuredly this index cannot express by itself alone the true form of the head or the cranium, but it supplies very clearly a first indication which gives a much better idea than detailed description, useful, to be sure, but rendering the study almost impossible when it is a question of comparing with one another a great number of different types. On the other hand, this index has such a fixity within the limits of any given race, that it is difficult to conceive how it could be dispensed with. The figures given by different authors when they rest on a sufficient number of subjects agree so much among themselves as to the cephalic index, that it is impossible to deny its fixity. The recent researches of Gonner[1] on one hundred children of Basel, far from weakening the assertion, as it would appear, speak in its favour; made on only the new-born or children one month old, they confirm what was already known, that the cephalic index varies with age, and by no means contradict its fixity. Ordinarily, at birth children appear to be more dolichocephalic than the adults of their race, but from the first month the head grows faster in breadth than in length; thus at the end of the first month, according to Gonner, the head is broadened in 52 children in 100, and remains stationary in 9 per 100. My own researches lead me to believe that the heads of children increase at first in breadth, to arrive afterwards gradually at a definite form, which is fixed about the age of ten, twelve, or fifteen years, according to race.

If instead of comparing, as Gonner has done, children of one month old with their parents, he had taken children from ten years upwards, he would have arrived at the same results as Spalikowski, who on forty-eight infants at Rouen found forty-one of which the cranial form corresponded with their parents. The researches of O. Ammon, Johansson and

[1] A. Gonner, "Vererbung der Forme . . . des Schädels," *Zeits. für Geburtshilfe und Gynäkologie*, 1895, vol. xxxiii., p. 1.

Westermarck, Miss Fawcett and Pearson, as well as my own (yet unpublished), lead to the same result.[1]

The differences of the cephalic index according to sex are insignificant. According to my personal researches, this difference hardly exceeds on the average 0.7 in the living subject and 1.5 in the cranium; and even this latter figure is exaggerated. It may, in a general way, be admitted that the difference between the cephalic index of men and women hardly exceeds one unit—that is to say, the degree of personal error in the observation. This difference is, in any case, less than the discrepancies between the different series of a single and homogeneous race.

In the table of the cephalic index which appears at the end of this volume (Appendix II.), however, I have given only the figures relating to men. A few series comprising individuals of both sexes appear there as exceptional cases. I have taken care to mark these with a letter S. In this table will be found side by side with indices taken on the living subjects some taken on crania, but no series contains measurements of crania and heads intermingled. The series of ten to twenty subjects or crania in the table appear there exceptionally, for the only series furnishing figures really exact are those comprising more than twenty individuals.

An inspection of the table shows us that there is a certain regularity in the distribution of the different cranial forms on the surface of the earth.

Dolichocephaly is almost exclusively located in Melanesia, in Australia, in India, and in Africa. Sub-dolichocephaly, diffused in the two extreme regions, North and South, of Europe, forms in Asia a zone round India (Indo-China, Anterior Asia, China, Japan, etc.), but is met with only sporadically in other parts of the world, especially in America. Mesocephaly

[1] Spalikowski, "Études d'anthropologie normande," *Bull. Soc. amis Sciences nat. Rouen*, 1895, Nos. 1 and 2, p. 113; Ammon, *loc. cit.*, p. 143; Johansson, and F. Westermarck, *Skandin. Arch. f. Physiol.*, vol. vii., 1897, p. 341; Miss Fawcett and K. Pearson, *Proc. Roy. Soc. London*, vol. 62, 1898, p. 413.

is frequent in Europe in the regions bordering on the sub-dolichocephalic countries, as well as in different parts of Asia and America. Sub-brachycephaly, much diffused among the Mongolians of Asia and the populations of Eastern Europe, is very rare elsewhere. Lastly, brachycephalic and hyper-brachycephalic heads are almost exclusively limited to Western and Central Europe, to some populations of Asia, Turco-Mongols, Irano-Semites, and Thaï-Malays.

Has the form of the head, so far as the cephalic index can express it, an influence on the volume of the brain, and consequently on its weight, and even perhaps on the mentality? This question is subordinate to another, namely: To what point is the weight of the brain the expression of the psychical value of this organ? We shall see further, on p. 101, that the weight can only be considered as a very rough approximation for the solution of psychological questions. But even in recognising in the weight of the brain the exaggerated importance that too long has been attributed to it, it may be said that it is not in relation with the conformation of the skull. The only investigation made into this matter—that of Calori—restricted to the figures of adults (from 20 to 60 years) by Topinard,[1] shows us that among Italian men the brachycephalic have on an average 27 grammes of brain more than the dolichocephalic, while among Italian women it is the dolichocephalic who have the better of the brachycephalic by 21 grammes. The differences in the two shapes being so very trifling, one may consider one's self equally intelligent whether dolichocephalic or brachycephalic.

Next to the form of the head, that of the face is of great importance in recognising races. It may be more or less long or broad, oval (Fig. 109), ellipsoidal (Fig. 136), or round (Figs. 119, 164, and 169), with soft contours or very angular, and then it may be found as an elongated rectangle (Fig. 121) or a square (Fig. 124); it may approximate also to the pentagonal form (Fig. 17), etc.

The *forehead* may be broad or narrow, low or high, retreating

[1] *Elem. Anthro. gén.*, p. 567.

(oblique, Fig. 21) or straight (Figs. 24 and 90), it may present a medium protuberance, as for instance, among many Negro tribes (Fig. 140), etc. The *superciliary arches* may be absent (Mongolian races) or very prominent, overhanging the eyes (Australians, Fig. 15; Veddahs, Fig. 5).

The *cheek-bones* may be little developed (Europeans) or very prominent (Mongolians, Figs. 17 and 20; Bushmen, Fig. 24, etc.), but cheek-bones projecting forward must be distinguished from those developed laterally. The *chin* may be pointed, rounded, square, projecting, retreating (Fig. 15), but these variations are of little importance, and may be found in conjunction with the most diverse forms of the face, while giving to it its own character. The posterior angles of the lower jaw may be more or less wide, and thus help to produce the angular contour of the face; quadrangular in the case of the square chin (Fig. 121), or with pentagonal contour in the case of the pointed chin (Fig. 118).

The *eyes* furnish also some differences of form. We distinguish the ordinary eye, as in our countries, and the *oblique* or *narrowed Mongolian eye*. The latter presented in its most perfect form is characterised as follows. It is placed obliquely, so that its external angle is higher than its inner angle (Fig. 121). This disposition is due to the too high attachment of the external palpebral ligament to the skull, as Regalia has shown.[1] Its palpebral aperture is much narrower than in the ordinary eye, and instead of having the form of an almond, it has rather that of a scalene triangle (Figs. 18 and 118) or of a little fish whose head corresponds to the inner angle (Fig. 119). But these peculiarities are not the most important, and may be met with, though rarely, in ordinary eyes. The essential characters of the Mongolian eye consist, as Metchnikof[2] has shown, in a puffiness of the upper eyelid, which turns down at the inner angle of the narrowed eye, and, instead of being free, as in the ordinary eye, is folded towards

[1] Regalia, "Orbita ed obliquità dell' occhio Mongolico," *Archivio p. Antr.*, vol. xviii., p. 1, Florence, 1888.

[2] E. Metchnikof, *Zeitsch. f. Ethnol.*, p. 153, Berlin, 1874.

the eyeball, forming a fixed fold in front of the movable ciliary edge; this last becomes invisible and the eyelashes are scarcely seen. Moreover, towards the inner angle of the eye, the eyelid forms a fold covering more or less the caruncula, and sometimes extending more or less far below (Fig. 18). These peculiarities, which can be met with quite often among the children of all races as a transitory characteristic, may be explained up to a certain point by the very small development of the pilous system in general in people among whom they persist. For among Europeans, for instance, the inversion of the eyelid (*entropion*) may become a cause of disease (*trichiasis*) precisely on account of the growth of the eyelashes.[1]

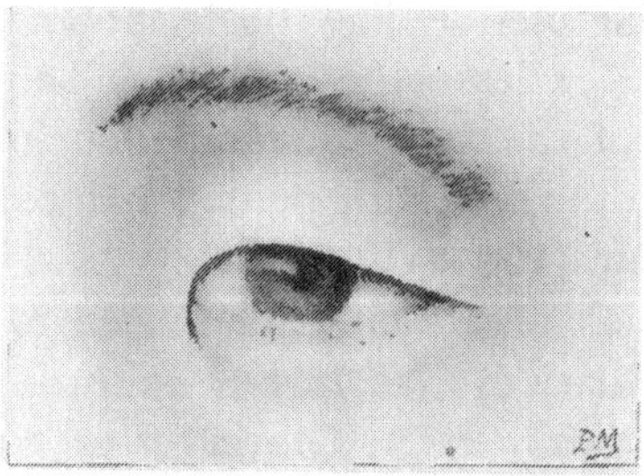

FIG. 18.—Eye of a young Kalmuk girl of Astrakhan. Example of Mongoloid eye (*from nature*).

Sometimes this puffiness only extends to the outer part of the eyelid; we have thus a variety of the Mongolian eye, with a palpebral triangular opening, very frequent among the eastern Finns (Fig. 106) and the Turco-Tatar populations.

The *nose*, by the variety and the fixity of its forms, presents one of the best characters for distinguishing races. We can express by means of the nasal index of Broca its width (measured by just touching the alæ of the nose) in relation to its length (from the root to the sub-nasal spine) supposed = 100. This index varies in the proportion of one to three

[1] J. Deniker, "L'Étude sur les Kalmouks," *Revue d'Anthropologie*, 2nd series, vol. vi., p. 696, Paris, 1883.

(from 40 to 120), according to race. Among the platyrhinians, the breadth of the nose exceeds 85 (Fig. 14); among the leptorhinians, this breadth is less than 70 (Fig. 16); lastly, among the mesorhinians, it oscillates between 70 and 85,

FIG. 19.—Welsh type of Montgomeryshire. Eyes and hair dark. (*Photo. and particulars, Beddoe.*)

according to the nomenclature of R. Collignon.[1] I give in Appendix III. a table of the nasal indices of the principal populations; I have only introduced into it series of

[1] Collignon, "La nomenclature quinaire de l'indice nasal," *Rev. d'Anthropol.*, 3rd series, t. ii., p. 8, Paris, 1887.

more than ten individuals, whose measurements have been taken according to the Broca-Collignon method, explained above.[1]

Besides the general form of the nose given by the nasal index, there remain a host of descriptive characters which may be observed in this organ. It may be more or less flattened (examples: Negroes, Melanesians, Mongolians), or more or less prominent (Europeans, Jews, Arabs). Its profile may be: (1) straight and sometimes sinuous (examples: Turco-Tatars, Europeans, Fig. 19); (2) concave (certain Finns, Bushmen, Lapps, Australians, Fig. 15); (3) convex and sometimes arched (American Indians, Semites, Fig. 21). Each of these forms may be in combination with a fine, thick, or medium tip, and with a plane of the nostrils directed upwards, downwards, or horizontally. A. Bertillon[2] admits at least fifteen varieties of the forms of the nose. In the majority of cases concave noses have the extremity thick, and the plane of the nostrils directed upward (Figs. 9, 14, and 15); convex noses, on the contrary, have most frequently the tip fine, and the plane of the nostrils directed downward (Figs. 21, 102, 103, and 134). But there are also convex noses with very thick tips, for instance, among the Jews and the Iranians of the Assyroid type (Fig. 22), or again, among the Papuans and the Melanesians (Fig. 53), as well as concave noses with fine tips, for instance, among certain European races (Figs. 97, 104, and 105). Broad noses are most frequently flattened (Figs. 14, 15, and 24), but the flattening may also extend to narrow noses, as for example among the Mongols (Fig. 20). The sunken, very depressed root of the nose is almost always associated with a considerable prominence on the supraciliary

[1] German anthropologists take the measurement of the breadth of the nose, not level with the nostrils, but behind, at the point of their attachment to the maxillary bone, compressing the soft parts; the nasal indices thus obtained are much too low, and not comparable to those which result from the measurements taken according to the Broca-Collignon method.

[2] A. Bertillon, "Morphologie du Nez," *Rev d'Anthro.*, 3rd series, vol. ii., 1887.

arches: examples, Australians, Fuegians, etc. (Figs. 14, 15, and 48).

In a general way, as may be seen from the table, the lepto-

FIG. 20.—Kalmuk of Astrakhan. Example of convex and flattened nose. (*Phot. S. Sommier.*)

rhinians, who have for the most part the convex and straight noses, with fine, straight, or turned-down tips, are met with almost exclusively among Europeans, Eurasians, Armenians,

Caucasians, and Eurafricans (Arabo-Berbers), as well as among the inhabitants of anterior Asia. The mesorhinians, among whom the form of the profile of the nose varies much, include different populations of India, some American, Turco-Tatar, and Mongol peoples. And lastly, the platyrhinians, having most frequently the profile convex and the tip turned up,

FIG. 21.—Jew of Algiers. Example of convex and prominent nose. (*Phot. Coll. Mus. Hist. Nat., Paris.*)

comprise the whole of the black populations of Africa, Oceania, and India.

At birth and during early infancy the nose is most frequently concave, with the tip turned up (Fig. 130); it only becomes straight or convex in the adult; in old age it has a tendency to become convex with the tip turned down (Bertillon, Hoyer). In the dead body it always takes the arched form. According to Broca and Houzé, the nasal index has a tendency to get lower—that is to say, the nose becomes relatively thinner as the individual advances in age; according to Hoyer,[1] the contrary takes place.

The ears present few characteristic traits for distinguishing races,[2] but the same cannot be said of the lips. They are thin in the so-called white races and among Mongols; very thick and protruding among the Negroes; somewhat thick among Malays, Melanesians, etc. Their form contributes

FIG. 22.—Persian Hadjemi. Example of Assyroid nose. (*Author's Phot. Coll.*)

much towards hiding or accentuating dental or alveolar prognathism.

Skeleton of the Trunk and Limbs.—The parts of the skeleton other than the head furnish but few materials for characterising

[1] P. Broca, "Recher. sur l'ind. nas.," *Rev. d'Anthro.*, vol. i., Paris, 1872; Houzé, "L'ind. nas. des Flamands et des Wallons," *Bull. Soc. Anthr.*, Bruxelles, vol. vii., 1888-89; O. Hovorka, *Die aussere Nase*, Wien, 1893; Hoyer, "Beitr. zur Anthr. der Nase," Schwalbe's *Morph. Arb.*, vol. iv., p. 151, 1894.

[2] Schwalbe, "R. Virchow's Feftschrift," 1891; E. Wilhelm, *Rev. Biol. du nord de la France*, Lille, 1892, No. 6.

races. We have already seen (p. 14) that the differences of curvature in the *vertebral column* according to race may be explained by the mode of life. As to the other peculiarities of the spine,—spinous processes split in the cervical vertebræ,[1] narrow sacrum, etc.,—all that can be said about them is that they are more frequent among Negroes, and perhaps among Melanesians, than among Whites.

The *pelvis* has more importance on account of its function from the obstetrical point of view, and of its influence on the general form of the body. Unfortunately this part of the skeleton has only been studied in very inadequate series among a dozen populations. Subjoined is given:—1st, the table of *pelvic index*—that is to say, the centesimal relation between the maximum breadth of the pelvis (between the iliac crests) and its height (from the top of the iliac crest to the lowest point of the ischion), taking for our unit sometimes the first of these measurements following Turner, sometimes the second following Broca; 2nd, the table of the index of the inlet (*pelvic or brim index* of English authors)—that is to say, the relation of the antero-posterior diameter of this aperture (from the middle of the promontory of the sacrum to the pubic symphysis) to its maximum transverse diameter, which, let us suppose, = 100.[2] It will be remarked that the tables, formed of series of five subjects at least, are given in separate parts for men and for women, as the sexual differences are very appreciable in the pelvis of all races. In a general way the pelvis is broader and less high, its slope more pronounced, in woman than in man. The iliac fossa are wider in the former than in the latter; the *superior inlet* or *brim* is elliptical or reniform in woman, in the form

[1] See the summing up of the question in Cunningham, "The Neural Spine," *Journal of Anat. and Physiol.*, vol. xx., p. 637.

[2] See, for further details, Verneau, *Le bassin dans les sexes*, etc., Paris, 1875; Turner, "Report Hum. Skelet.," *Rep. of Challenger: Zoology*, part 47; J. Garson, "Pelvimetry," *Journ. Anat. Physiol.*, vol. xvi., London, October, 1881; Henning, "Rassenbecken," *Arch. für Anthr.*, 1885, and *Sitzungsb. Naturforsch. Gesell.*, Leipzig, 1890-91, p. 1; Marri, *Archivio per l'Antr.*, 1892, p. 17.

of a playing-card heart in man, etc. But, as may be seen by our table, if these differences are very appreciable in certain races, notably among Whites and Negroes, they become less and less among Melanesians, among whom the pelves of the two sexes approximate nearly to the masculine type.

Has the form of the pelvis, and especially that of the inlet, any relation to the form of the head of the fœtus and of the child? Exact data for solving this question are wanting. However, comparing from our tables the index of the superior inlet and that of the cephalic index, it may be observed that, in a general way, pelves with a large aperture are met with in brachycephalic races, and pelves with a narrow aperture in dolichocephalic races. But there are numerous exceptions: I note at least four (English, Russian, Swedish mesocephal and Malay women) in the meagre list of 12 series of women that, with much difficulty, I have been able to draw up.

The form of the *shoulder-blade* varies little with race. The *scapular index*—that is to say, the centesimal relation between the breadth of the shoulder-blade and its length (measured on the vertebral edge and taken as the unit of comparison)—oscillates between 64.9 (Australians) and 70.2 (Andamanese). In a list of 14 series of from 10 to 462 shoulder-blades that I have drawn up from the works of Broca, Livon, Turner, Topinard, Garson, Martin, Hyades, Sarasin, Hamy, Koganei, and my own measurements, the populations are arranged as follows: index from 64.9 to 66.6, Australians, Europeans, Fuegians, Bushmen, Ainus, Peruvians, Polynesians; indices from 67.2 to 70.2, Japanese, Veddahs, Hindu-Sikhs, Malays, Negroes, Melanesians, Andamanese. This classification suffices to show that the greater or less breadth of the shoulder-blade has almost no value as a seriate character or as a character of race. It is the same with the *sub-spinal index*, which it has been proposed to add to the foregoing in order to judge of the form of the shoulder-blade.[1]

[1] On the index of the shoulder-blade see Broca, *Bull. Soc. Anthr.*, 1878, p. 66; Livon, *De L'omoplate* (thesis), Paris, 1879; Garson, *Journ. Anat. Physiol.*, vol. xiv., 1879-80, p. 13; Turner, *loc. cit.*

MEN.				WOMEN.			
Number of Pelves.	Ethnic Groups.	Index.	Observer.	Number of Pelves.	Ethnic Groups.	Index.	Observer.
1a.—INDEX OF HEIGHT (TURNER).[1]							
7	Fuegians	77	Garson, Martin.	28	Europeans	74.3	Garson, Verneau.
7	Australians	77	Garson, Turn., Vern.	7	Australians	76.6	Gars., Turn., Vern.
46	Europeans	79	Verneau, Turner.	8	Andamanese... ...	76	Gars., Turn.
1b.—PELVIC INDEX OR INDEX OF WIDTH-HEIGHT (BROCA).							
17	Negroes in general ...	121.3	Garson, Verneau.	13	Andamanese... ...	125.5	Garson.
11	Melanesians	122.7	Verneau.	10	Melanesians	129	Garson, Verneau.
46	Europeans	126.6	Garson, Verneau.	5	Australians	130.4	Garson, Verneau.
5	Fuegians	129.8	Hyades, Deniker.	10	Negresses	134.2	Garson, Verneau.
				28	Europeans	134.9	Garson, Verneau.
2.—INDEX OF THE SUPERIOR INLET.							
63	Europeans Princ. French	80	Verneau, Flower.	33	Europeans Princ. Engl.	77.6	Garson.
8	Europeans ,, Italians	82	Marri.	49	Europeans ,, French	79	Verneau.
17	Fuegians	85.1	Deniker, Hyades, Martin, Garson.	14	Japanese	82.8	Dönitz, Werner.
				5	Hawaiians	83	Turner.
12	New Caledonians ...	91	Verneau.	13	Fuegians	83	Deniker, Hyades, Sergi, Martin.
38	Negroes	92.3	Turner, Henning, Verneau, Vrolik.	50	Russians	84.8	Filatof.
24	Australians	96.6	Flower, Turner, Vern., Ecker, etc.	9	Italians	86.7	Marri.
				32	Negresses	88.4	Turner, Verneau.
14	Andamanese... ...	98.7	Turner, Fritsch.	8	Australians	88.5	Turn., Vern., Garson.
5	Bushmen	99.5	Gar., Turn., Flow.	8	Bushmen	91.6	Muller, Hux., Ver., Fl.
				16	Andamanese... ...	91.7	Henning.
				20	Malays	94.8	Garson, Flow., Turn.

[1] Transformed into terms of the pelvic index of Broca these figures, according to the formula: ind. Turn.: 100=100: x, we have the figures: Fuegians, 129.8; Australians, 129.8; Europeans, 126.5; European women, 134.6; Australian women, 130.5; Andamanese women, 131.5.

As to the skeleton of the limbs, here is a summary of what can be said about it from the point of view which specially concerns us now. In the *thoracic limb* the *humerus* presents an interesting peculiarity: the perforations of the *olecranon cavity* (which receives the extremity of the ulna) are very frequent in prehistoric bones in Europe (10 to 27 times in 100), as well as in America (31 times).[1]

This perforation is met with more often among men than women, perhaps because it is more especially connected with the extent and frequent repetition of the movements of flexion and extension. Here is its growing frequency in the races from a list which I have drawn up with series varying from 20 to 249 humeri: white population of the United States (3.8 times in a hundred), French, Fuegians, Ainus, Basques, Melanesians, Japanese, Negroes, Polynesians, Mongolians, and American Indians (36.2 times in a hundred). The *torsion of the humerus*—that is to say, the degree of rotation of the lower part of this bone in relation to its upper part, is a character of a certain seriate value; but it is of no use in the differentiation of races. Besides, the degree of torsion varies too much in the same race: it is greater in woman than in man, in short than in long humeri (Manouvrier, Martin, etc.). This torsion is measured by the *angle of torsion*, which is taken either according to Broca's method or Gegenbaur's. This is how the different peoples are arranged according to the decreasing figures of this angle (series of 10 humeri): according to Broca's system:—Melanesians (angle of 141°), Guanches, Arabs or at least Kabyles, Polynesians, Negroes, Peruvians, Californians, Europeans, French (164°); according to Gegenbaur's system:—Ainus (149.5°), Fuegians, Veddahs, Japanese, Swiss, Germans

[1] It has been thought that this frequency was due to the facility with which the thin lamella in question forming the bottom of the cavity can be destroyed after prolonged interment. However, there are prehistoric burial-places, as, for example, certain long barrows of Great Britain, in which not a single perforated humerus in a series of from ten to thirty bones has been found.

(168°). Until further discoveries are made, a single fact becomes prominent from the examination of this character—that is, that the torsion appears to be greater in white races than in black and yellow. In the ulna Collignon has noted a special incurvation in certain prehistoric bones.

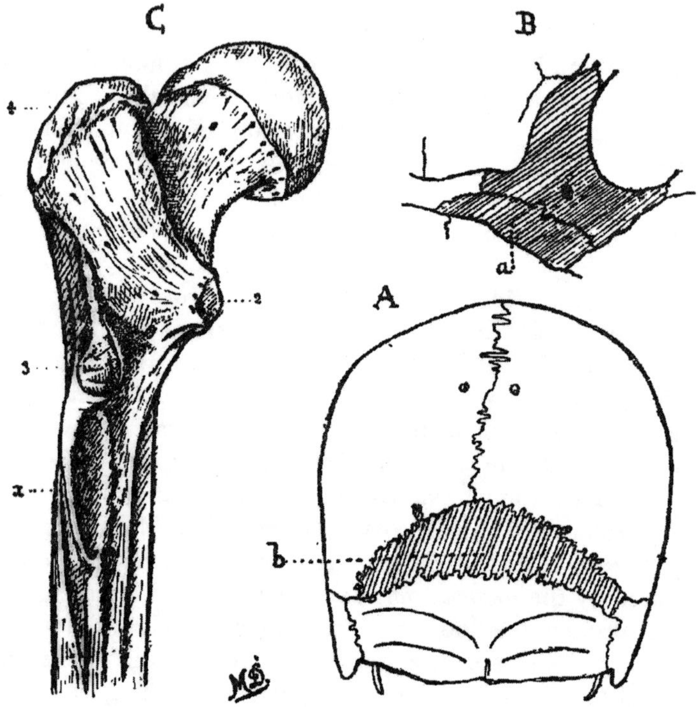

FIG. 23.—A, Skull with Inca Bone, *b*; B, Malar Bone divided in two (*a*, *os Japonicum*); C, superior part of femur with third trochanter (3), and the hypo-trochanteric fossa (*x*); 1 and 2, normal trochanters.

In the *femur* one peculiarity has especially attracted the attention of anthropologists in recent times; it is the more or less frequent presence of the *third trochanter* (Fig. 23, C 3), or tuberosity situated between the great (*ibid.*, 1) and the lesser (*ibid.*, 2) trochanter on the offshoot from the *linea aspera* which furnishes a point of attachment to the lower part of the *gluteus maximus*. This projection, pointed out and studied for the first time by Houzé,[1] appears in infancy as a special centre of ossification analogous to those of the other diaphyses (Török, Deniker, Dixon), and so does not seem to depend on the greater or less development of the *gluteus maximus* (Bertaux).[2] The third trochanter is almost always accompanied by a *hypotrochanteric fossa* (Fig. 23, C).

Here is the frequency with which the third trochanter occurs according to a list which I have compiled :—

Number of Femurs.	Populations.	Frequency per 100 of the 3rd trochanter.	Observers.
42	Belgians and French of the Reindeer Period	13	Houzé
28	Negroes	21	Houzé, Costa
68	Ainus	26.5	Koganei
73	Japanese	28.8	Koganei
67	Inhabitants of Brussels	30 2	Houzé
102	Italians	30.4	Costa
54	Hungarians	36.1	Török
110	Belgians and French of the Polished Stone Period	38	Houzé
76	Fuegians	64.3	Hyad., Denik., Martin, Costa

Two points will be observed in this table, the rarity of the third trochanter among Negroes, and its excessive frequency among the Fuegians. The women of the latter have also the hypochanteric fossa 80 times in a 100 (out of 76 femurs examined); it almost forms then, like the third trochanter, a character of race.

[1] Houzé, "Le 3e trochanter," *Bull. Soc. Anthr.*, Brussels, 1883.

[2] See the summary of the question by Dwight in *Journ. of Anat. Physiol.*, vol. xxiv., pt. i., London, 1889, p. 61; also that by Costa, in *Archivio per l'Antr.*, vol. xx., 1890, p. 280; and by Poirier in his *Traité d'Anatomie*, vol. i., p. 221, Paris, 1890.

In the *tibia* attention has been called to *platycnemia*—that is to say, the transversal flattening in the upper third of the diaphysis of the bone, so that its posterior side becomes transformed into a border. It has been supposed that this form is a reversion towards the simian type, but Manouvrier[1] has shown that platycnemia never attains in the anthropoid apes the degree which it presents in the human race, where it is due especially to the development of the *tibialis posticus* muscle which plays a great part in the maintenance of the upright position, and in the movements of walking and running. The degree of platycnemia may thus vary according to the more or less sedentary or wandering habits of the different populations.

The retroversion of the head of the tibia—that is to say, the slope of the articular surface of it behind—pointed out and described for the first time by Collignon in prehistoric tibias, is also not a simian character. According to Manouvrier,[2] it is often met with among Parisians in a degree superior to that exhibited by anthropoid apes. This retroversion, generally associated with platycnemia, is connected with the half-bending attitude of the lower limb in the manner of walking which is called the *bending gait*, common among peasants, and especially mountaineers. The retroversion is more marked in the tibia of the new-born child than in that of the adult, and this appears to have a connection with the permanent bending of the knee during intra-uterine life.

The length of the bones of the pelvic and thoracic limbs varies according to race, but it is difficult to establish the degree of these variations, owing to the small number of observations made. Besides, we can more profitably substitute for measurements of limbs on the skeleton those of the living subject; in the latter case we can at least relate all the measurements to the true height of the subject, whilst the height is never exactly known from the skeleton.

However, the measurements of the long bones have their

[1] Manouvrier, *Mémoires Soc. Anthr.*, 2nd ser., vol. iii., Paris, 1888.

[2] *Ibid.*, vol. iv., 1890.

importance, for they permit us to *reconstitute* approximately, as we have already seen (p. 33), *the height* of subjects of which we have only the bones, as is the case of all populations that have preceded us.

It is for this reason that I give the following figures derived from nine series of from five to seventy-two skeletons. The length of the humerus represents from 19.5 (Polynesians) to 20.7 per cent. (Europeans) of the height of the skeleton; that of the radius from 14.3 (Europeans) to 15.7 (Negroes); that of the femur from 26.9 (South Americans) to 27.9 (New Caledonians); lastly, the length of the tibia represents from 21.5 (Esthonians) to 23.8 per cent. (New Caledonians) of the height of the skeleton. Thus the differences are insignificant, and the variations between race and race do not extend beyond the limits of a unit and a half for each of the bones.

The length of the radius in relation to the humerus (= 100) exhibits variations a little more appreciable. It is 72.5 among Europeans, 76 among New Caledonians, 79 among Negroes, 79.7 among Veddahs, 80.6 among Fuegians, 81.7 among Andamanese. Let us note that the forearm, relatively to the arm, is much longer in the fœtus in the first stages of development and in early infancy than in the adult;[1] it is shortened in proportion to the height as the fœtus and the infant grow.

Proportions of the Body in the Living Subject.—In spite of the quantity of material accumulated, we have not been able up to the present to make any use of the differences which these proportions exhibit according to race. The reason is that these differences are very trifling. In order to understand this proposition better I will give by way of illustration the proportions which we may consider as nearly normal in a European of average stature (1m. 65, or 5 ft. 5 ins.). Topinard established thus the principal proportions of the European,[2] assuming the height = 100.

[1] Hamy, *Rev. d'Anthrop.*, 1872, p. 79.

[2] Topinard, *L'homme dans la Nature*, p. 126.

Head	13
Trunk and neck	35
(32.7 without neck.)	
Thoracic limb	45
Arm	19.5
Forearm	14
Hand	11.5
Abdominal limb	47.5
(from the ischiatic plane to the ground.)	
Foot	15
Span of arms (middle finger of one hand to middle finger of the other) . . .	104.4

The proportions in the different populations of the earth oscillate round these figures without diverging from them more than three units, or five at most. Thus, for example, the proportions of the height of the head vary between 11.4 and 15, according to Rojdestvensky;[1] the proportions of the trunk without the neck from 32.6 to 32.8, according to Topinard, etc.

The length of the thoracic limb scarcely varies more than between 42.6 and 47.6, according to the lists of sixteen and twenty-seven series published by Ivanovsky and Topinard,[2] and according to a third list of twenty-four series that I have drawn up. We can count on the fingers the populations in which the proportion for the hand exceeds the figure 11 with its decimals or sinks below it; it is the same in regard to the foot, of which the figure 15 with its decimals is rarely exceeded or is not reached.[3] The variations of length for the abdominal limb do not extend further than from 45.1 to 49.2 (Topinard), etc.

The thoracic perimeter exceeds half the height in all adult populations of the world, except perhaps some groups

[1] Rojdestvensky, "Proportions of the Head," *Bull. Soc. Friends of Nat. Sc.*, vol. xc., part 1, Moscow, 1895 (in Russian).

[2] Ivanovsky, "Mongols, etc.," *Bull. Soc. Friends of Nat. Sc.*, vol. lxxi., Moscow, 1893 (in Russian); Topinard, *Elem. Anthro. générale*, p. 1076.

[3] See Ivanovsky, *loc. cit.*, p. 257; Topinard, *loc. cit.*, p. 1089.

of Georgian Svanes and Jews, or other populations which happen to be in bad hygienic conditions.

Thus proportions of the limbs are not good characters of race. Besides, certain dimensions (length of limbs, of the head) are always dependent on height. Thus individuals and races of high stature have the face and abdominal limb a little more elongated than individuals and races of short stature. On the other hand, individuals and races of short stature have in general the head larger, the trunk shorter, and the thoracic perimeter relatively more considerable than individuals and races of high stature, but the differences are very trifling as a general rule.

Trunk and Limbs of the Living.—To complete our study on the living subject, let us again note some peculiarities. The *neck* is ordinarily long and thin among Negroes, Ethiopians (Figs. 9 and 138), and on the contrary short among the majority of the American Indians (Figs. 163 and 169); the shoulders are very broad among the women of the latter (Fig. 165), and very narrow among the Chechen and Lesghi women. Usually the long neck is associated with a form of trunk like an inverted pyramid and a high stature, while the short neck surmounts a cylindrical trunk and is associated with a low stature. *Ensellure*—that is to say, the strongly marked curve of the dorso-lumbo-sacral region—is especially marked among Spanish women whose lumbar incurvation is such, and the movements of the lumbar vertebræ so extensive, that they are able to throw themselves backwards so as even to touch the ground (Duchenne of Boulogne). Ensellure is also more marked among Negroes than among Whites. It must be noted that it may also be merely a consequence of abdominal obesity, pregnancy, or *steatopygia.*

By the last-mentioned term is designated excessive projection of the buttocks due to the accumulation of subcutaneous fat (Fig. 24); these are physiological fatty tumours proceeding from the hypertrophy of the adipose tissue more or less abundant in these regions among all races, and analogous to the fatty tumours of the cheeks of the orang-utan, which are simply

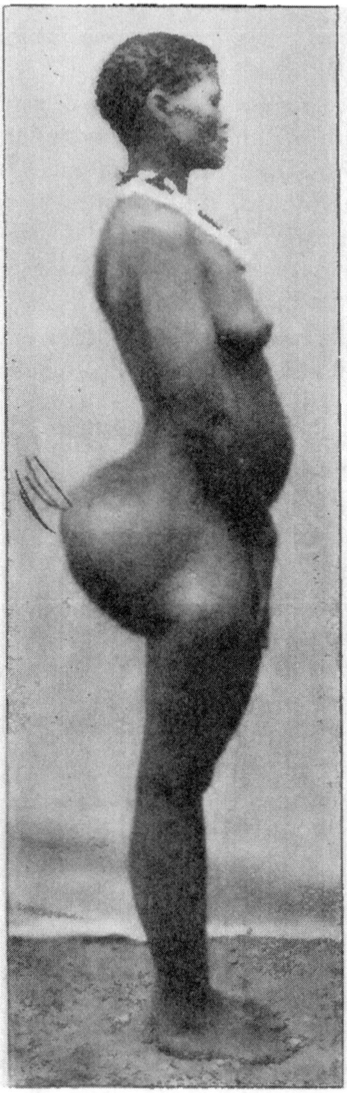

FIG. 24.—Hottentot woman of Griqualand (Cape Colony): 35 years; height, 4 ft. 8 ins.; cephalic index, 76.4. Example of steatopygia. (*Photo. Prince Roland Bonaparte.*)

Bichat's fatty balls existing among men and among the anthropoids,[1] only excessively developed. As in those tumours, the fat of the steatopygous masses does not even disappear after disease which has emaciated the rest of the body. Steatopygia is characteristic of the Bushman race; it is only met with in all its characters (alteration of form on the lateral and anterior sides of the thighs; persistence even in emaciation, etc.) among populations into the composition of which enters the Bushman element: Hottentots (Fig. 24), Nama, etc. The cases of steatopygia observed among other Wolof or Somali women, for example, are only the exaggeration of adipose deposit among the muscular fibres, as with Europeans, not of the subcutaneous adipose layer. Steatopygia is especially marked in the Bushman woman, in whom it commences to develop only from the age of puberty; but it exists also, though in a less degree, in the male of that race (Fig. 143).

We cannot enlarge on other exterior characters: on the form of the trunk and of the limbs; on the leg with poorly de-

[1] Deniker and Boulart, *loc. cit.*, p. 53.

veloped calf, and the foot with the prominent heel which is observed among certain Negroes (but not among all); on the more or less diverging big toe which is remarked among the majority of the peoples of India, Indo-China, and the insular world dependent on Asia, from Sumatra to Japan, etc.

Two words, however, on the subject of the pretended existence of races of *men with tails.* We must relegate to the domain of fable the cases of this kind which are announced from time to time in publications for the popularisation of science so called. The costumes of certain populations have given rise to the fable of men with tails (see frontispiece). Isolated cases of men having as an anomaly a caudal excrescence more or less long, free, or united to the trunk, are known to science, and numbers have been described, but no single serious description has ever been given of populations with tails.[1] Quite recently, again, Lartschneider has demonstrated that the ilio-coccygian and pubio-coccygian muscles in mammifera have lost in man their character of symmetrical and paired skeleton muscles, and are driven back towards the interior of the pelvis as single unpaired muscle plates (fibres of the *levator ani*). Primitive man has never had a caudal appendage since he acquired the biped attitude; the disappearance of the tail is even one of the indispensable conditions of that attitude.[2]

The different internal or external organs of man afford also some special characters, though not very numerous, for differentiating race.

The *muscular system*, little known outside white races, has, up to the present, not given any important indication on this point. At the very outside, we can say, thanks to the works of Chudzinsky, Le Double, Macalister, Popovsky, Testut, Turner, etc., and the Committee of the Anatomical Society of Great Britain and Ireland, that certain muscular anomalies are more frequent in the Negro than in the White, and that the muscles

[1] M. Bartels, *Arch. f. Anthr.*, vol. xiii., 1880, p. 1.

[2] Lartschneider, "Die Steissbeinmuskeln, etc.," *Denkschr. K. Akad. Wiss. Wien. mat. nat. Kl.*, vol. lxii., 1895.

of the face are less differentiated in the former than in the latter.[1] In the splanchnic system some differences have also been observed between the White and the Negro, notably the excessive volume of the liver, the spleen, the suprarenal-capsules, and, in general, the hypertrophy of all the organs of excretion in the latter compared with the former. The venous system appears also to be more developed in the Negro than in the White. Somewhat notable differences must certainly be observable in the structure and general conformation of the organs of the voice and of speech—tongue, larynx, lungs. But our knowledge on this subject is still very imperfect. Attention has been drawn to the feeble development of the anterior fibres of the stylo-glossal muscle of the tongue, the greater development of the Wrisberg cartilage of the larynx with the muscles stronger in the Negro than in the White,[2] but nothing is known about the larynx of other races.

There is nothing, even to the bony parts of the vocal apparatus, which does not undergo ethnic variations. Thus the larger cornua of the *hyoid bone* are not attached to the body of it in 75 to 95 per cent. of cases observed among the Indians of America, whilst the same anomaly is met with in only 25 to 35 per cent. of cases among Europeans, and only in 30 per cent. among Negroes, which probably harmonises with the differences in the production of sounds in the language of each of these peoples.[3]

The *genital organs* also present some differences according to race, but rather in the dimensions of the various parts than in their form. The only peculiarity worth notice is the exaggerated development of the labia minora among the Bushman women, known under the name of "apron." This peculiarity, which appears from infancy, is met with only

[1] See on this subject, Le Double, *Traité des variations du Syst. musc. de l'homme*, 2 vols, Paris, 1897; and Testut, *Anomalies muscul.*, Paris, 1884.

[2] Hovelacque and Hervé, *Précis d'Anthro.*, p. 301. Paris, 1887.

[3] Ten Kate, "Sur quelques points d'ostéologie ethnique," *Revista del Museo de La Plata*, vol. vii, 1896, p. 263.

among the Bushman race and the people into whose composition enters the Bushman element—Hottentots, Nama, Griqua, etc.[1]

The breasts of women may also present variations of form. Ploss[2] classes them under four heads according to their height, which is inferior, equal, or more or less superior to the diameter of their base; we have thus mammæ like a bowl or the segment of a globe, hemispherical, conical, and pyriform. These forms may be found in combination with a more or less extended and prominent areola, and with a nipple which may be discoidal, hemispherical, digitiform, etc. It is especially among Negresses that we meet with conical and pyriform mammæ, and digitiform nipples, while mammæ shaped like the segment of a sphere predominate among Mongolian and European women of the fair race; women of the south-east of Europe and hither Asia have for the most part hemispherical breasts.

Among the internal organs, the *brain*, or better, the *encephalon*, deserves a little more attention. I have already said with regard to cranial capacity (p. 56) that appreciable differences have been observed in the volume of the brain-case according to age, sex, and race. This difference is in harmony with irregularity in the volume and consequently in the weight of the brain. At birth, European boys have 334 grammes of brain on an average, girls 287 grammes. This quantity increases rapidly up to 20 years of age, remains almost stationary between 20 and 40 or 45, then begins to decrease, slowly at first, until 60 years, then more rapidly.

Let me also add that the weight of the encephalon varies enormously according to individuals. Topinard[3] in a series of 519 Europeans, men of the lower and middle classes, found that variations in weight extended from 1025 grammes to 1675

[1] R. Blanchard, "Observations sur le tablier . . . d'après Peron et Lesueur," *Bull. Soc. Zool. de France*, 1883, with Figs.

[2] H. Ploss, *Das Weib*, 5th edit., by Max Bartels, vol. i. Leipzig, 1897.

[3] Topinard, *L'homme dans la Nature*, p. 215.

7

grammes. The average weight of the brain among adult Europeans (20 to 60 years) has been fixed by Topinard, from an examination of 11,000 specimens weighed, at 1361 grammes for man, 1290 grammes for woman. It has been asserted that the other races have a lighter brain, but the fact has not been established by a sufficient number of examples. In reality all that can be put against the 11,000 brain-weighings mentioned above concerning the cerebral weights of non-European races, amounts to nothing, or almost nothing. The fullest series that Topinard[1] has succeeded in making, that of Negroes, comprises only 190 brains; that of Annamese, which comes immediately after, contains only 18 brains. And what do the figures of these series teach us? The first series, dealing with Negroes, gives a mean weight not much different from that of Europeans—1316 grammes for adult males of from 20 to 60 years; and the second, dealing with the Annamese, a mean weight of 1341 grammes, almost identical with that of Europeans. For other populations we have only the weight of isolated brains, or of series of three, four, or at most eleven specimens, absolutely insufficient for any conclusions whatever to be drawn, seeing that individual variations are as great in exotic races as among Europeans, to judge by Negroes (1013 to 1587 grammes) and by Annamese (from 1145 to 1450 grammes). Even in the great series of Europeans, surprises await us in comparing the figures. Thus Peacock found an average of 1388 grammes for the English from a series of 28 brains, whilst Boyd finds 1354 grammes from a series of 425 brains. The difference (34 grammes) is greater here than between the brains of Annamese and Europeans, and hardly less than that which we have just found between Negroes and Europeans (45 grammes). For the French the figures are more in agreement. Broca found from the weights of 167 brains an average of 1359 grammes, and Bischoff[2] from 50 brains an average of 1381 grammes; difference, 22 grammes.

[1] Topinard, *Elem. d'Anthrop. génér.*, p. 571.

[2] According to the same author, the average weight of the brain of 364 Bavarians is 1372 grammes.

Not having at our disposal sufficient data for the weight, let us see if the cranial capacity could not supply them, for we know, since the investigations of Manouvrier,[1] that we have just to multiply by the co-efficient 0.87 the capacity of the cranial cavity to get with reasonable exactitude the weight of the brain which it contained. This is what we learn from the figures of cranial capacity brought together by Topinard,[2] after the necessary corrections, and reduction to cubic measurement by the system of Broca: among Europeans the measurement is 1565 c.c. on an average for men, varying from 1530 c.c. (22 Dutch) to 1601 c.c. (43 Finns). We have in various series the following succession of cranial capacities for the populations of the other parts of the world: the greatest is contained in a series of 26 Eskimo (1583 c.c.), the least that of 36 Australians (1349 c.c.) and of 11 Andamanese (1310 c.c.). Between these two extremes the other populations would be thus arranged in a decreasing order of capacity: 36 Polynesians (1525 c.c.), 18 Javanese (1500 c.c.), 32 Mongols (1504 c.c.), 23 Melanesians (1460 c.c.), 74 Negroes (1441 c.c.), and 17 Dravidians of Southern India (1353 c.c.).

The difference between the highest and lowest of these figures is 255 c.c., a little greater than that which is shown between man and woman in all races. On the other hand, Manouvrier[3] gives the following weights, deduced from cranial capacities: 187 modern Parisians, 1357 grammes; 61 Basques, 1360 grammes; 31 Negroes, 1238 grammes; 23 New Caledonians, 1270 grammes; 110 Polynesians, 1380 grammes; and 50 Bengalis, 1184 grammes; the difference of the two extremes is 196 grammes. Must we then see in these differences the influence of stature and bulk of body, as

[1] Manouvrier, "De la quantité dans l'encéphale," *Mém. Soc. Anthr.*, 2nd ser., vol. iii., p. 162. Paris, 1888.

[2] *Elem. Anthr. gén.*, pp. 611 *et seq.* The figures are drawn from the series of Broca and Flower, the latter being augmented by 64 c.c. (the mean difference established by Topinard and Garson between the two systems of determining cranial capacity).

[3] Article "Cerveau," in the *Dict. de Physiol.* of Ch. Richet, vol. ii., part 3, p. 687. Paris, 1897.

appears unquestionable in the sexual difference? We are tempted to believe it when we see that the mean weight of the largest brain in Europe has been found among the Scotch (1417 grammes, an average obtained by Reid and Peacock from 157 brains), whose stature is the highest of the human family, and that the mean weight of the Italians, whose average stature is rather small, is only 1308 grammes (from 244 cases weighed by Calori). The Polynesians and the Caucasians,[1] peoples of high stature, also outweigh the Andamanese and the Javanese, of very low stature. However, we see (from weights and cranial capacity) that Negro populations of very high stature, also Australians and New Caledonians of medium stature, have the cerebral weight much smaller than the Eskimo and certain Asiatics of low stature, like the Javanese.

There is here a double influence, that of stature and that of race. We might have introduced a third element—the weight of the body, but it represents too many different things, and may vary according to the degree of stoutness of the individual, the dietary, regimen, etc. C. Voit found, when operating on two dogs of nearly equal bulk, that the weight of the brain of the well-fed dog represented 1.1 per cent. of the weight of its body, whilst the brain of the dog which had fasted for twenty-two days represented 1.7 per cent. of the weight of the body.[2] At all events, we cannot deny the influence of the bulk of the active parts of the body on the volume of the brain.[3] But then a new question arises. Is

1 "11 Osseles, 1465 grammes; 15 Ingush-Chechen, 1454 grammes; 11 Georgians, 1350 grammes; but 12 Amenians of medium height of 1634 mm. give 1369 grammes for the brain."—Gilchenko, *Congr. Intern. Arch. préhis.*, vol. i., p. 183, Moscow, 1892.

2 C. Voit, "Gewichte d. Organe," *Zeitsch. für Biologie*, 1894, p. 510.

3 Manouvrier has demonstrated (*Dict. Phys.*, p. 688), working on three series of from 54 to 58 Frenchmen, that individuals of low stature have a lighter brain (1329 grammes) than those of high stature (1398 grammes); two series of women (23 and 27 individuals) yielded a similar result (1198 grammes for the low-statured, and 1218 for the tall). A series of 44 distinguished men of *all* nations and *all* statures gave a mean weight of

the increase of the volume of the brain made at the cost of the white substance formed solely of conducting-fibres, or of the grey substance formed principally of cells with their prolongations (neurons), that is to say, of the part which is exclusively affected by the psychic processes? This question still waits its solution. It is not the gross weight of the brain, but really the weight of the cortical layer which should be compared in the different races and subjects, in order to judge of the quantity of substance devoted to the psychic functions in each particular case.[1] Before the very delicate weighings of this kind are made, we have a roundabout method of ascertaining the quantity of that substance by the superficial area which it occupies. The cerebral cortex, composed of the grey substance, forms on the surface of the brain sinuous folds called *cerebral convolutions.* Now, in brains of equal volume, the greater the surface of the cortex, the more numerous, sinuous, and complicated will be these folds. As the thickness of the grey layer is very much the same in all brains, it is evident that the complexity in the structure of the convolutions corresponds to the increase of the grey substance, and consequently of the psychic force. Now, the little that is known of the cerebral

1430 grammes—that is to say, exceeding that of the French of high stature and the Scotch. From this may be drawn the conclusion that *intelligence* causes an increase in the weight of the brain independently of the stature. Here, by way of documents, are several data of this interesting series. The minimum of this series belongs to the anatomist Döllinger, who died at the age of seventy-one (1207 grammes), the maximum to the novelist Thackeray, who died at the age of fifty-three (1644 grammes). Between these two extremes are inserted, Harless (1238 grammes), Gambetta (1294 grammes), Liebig (1352 grammes), Bischoff (1452 grammes), Broca (1485 grammes), Gauss (1492 grammes), Agassiz (1512 grammes), and De Morny (1520 grammes), to mention only the best known names ranging between these extremes. M. Manouvrier has excluded from this series exceptionally heavy brains, like those of Schiller (1781 grammes), of Cuvier (1829 grammes), of Tourgenieff (2012 grammes), and lastly of Byron (2238 grammes).

[1] According to Danilevsky and Dr. Regibus, the weight of the grey substance represents 37 or 38 per cent. of the total weight of the brain.

convolutions in different races, and of various subjects in the same race, appears to conform to this deduction. The brains of idiots, of the weak-minded, present very simple convolutions, almost comparable to those of the anthropoid apes, whose brain is like a simplified diagram of the human brain. On the other hand, distinguished personages, great scholars, orators, men of action, exhibit a complexity, sometimes truly remarkable, of *certain* convolutions. I say expressly certain

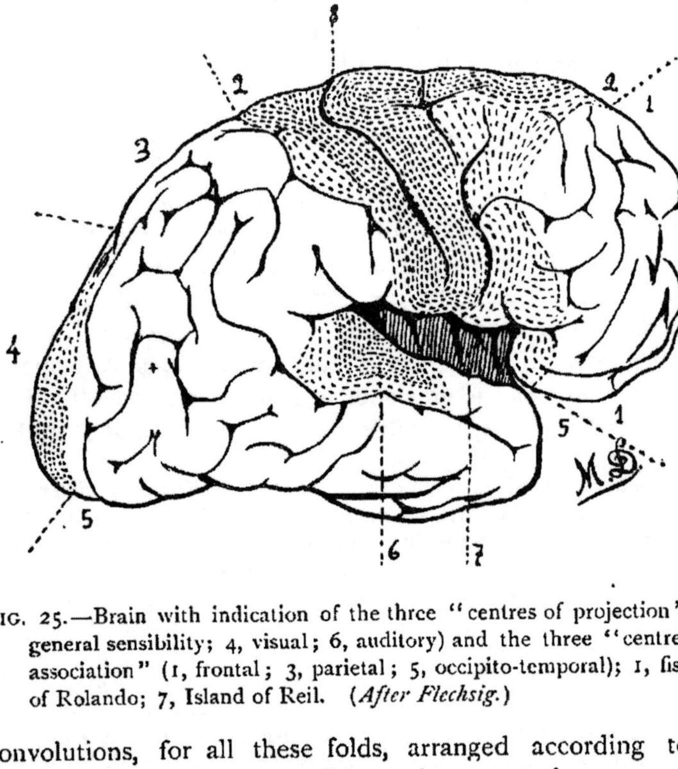

FIG. 25.—Brain with indication of the three "centres of projection" (2, general sensibility; 4, visual; 6, auditory) and the three "centres of association" (1, frontal; 3, parietal; 5, occipito-temporal); 1, fissure of Rolando; 7, Island of Reil. (*After Flechsig.*)

convolutions, for all these folds, arranged according to a certain plan, common to all men, have not the same value from the physiological point of view. In the grey layer of certain of them are the centres of motor impulses, and of the general sensibility of the body (for example, those which are arranged around the fissure of Rolando,

Fig. 25, 2, 2), and only regulate the voluntary movements of the limbs, the trunk and the head; others are connected with different forms of sensibility—visual (Fig. 25, 4), auditory (Fig. 25, 6), gustatory, olfactory, etc. But there are, between the different motor or sensorial regions (*centres of projection*) which take nearly a third of the grey substance of the brain, a great many more convolutions the grey substance of which is connected with no special function (white spots in Fig. 25). What is their purpose? Basing his opinion on the tardy *myelinisation*[1] of the nerve-fibres which terminate in it, subsequent to the birth of the individual and to the myelinisation of the fibres of the sensory and motor centres, Flechsig[2] supposes that these convolutions were designed to enable the different cerebral centres to communicate with each other and to render us conscious of this communication; therefore he has named their grey substance "*centres of association*" (Fig. 25, 1, 3, 5). Without the convolutions, the other centres would remain isolated and condemned to a very restricted activity. Now, as the eminent anatomist Turner[3] has shown so clearly, it is found that the convolutions of the sensory and motor centres do not present any great differences in the brain of a child, a monkey, a Bushman, or of a European man of science, like Gauss; what differentiates these brains is the degree of complexity of the convolutions concerned with association. There, then, is the part of the brain which we want to utilise for the purpose of comparison, reduced by almost a third. But let us suppose that differences of volume and weight are found in these two-thirds of the grey substance. Have we more reason to think that we are approaching the solution of the problem?

[1] Every nerve-fibre of the adult is composed of an axis-cylinder which communicates with the nerve-cells and with a myeline sheath formed around it. In the course of the development of the embryo this sheath appears after the formation of the axis-cylinder.

[2] Flechsig, *Gehirn und Seele*, 2nd ed., Leipzig, 1896; *Die Localization der geistigen Vorgänge*, Leipzig, 1896.

[3] Sir W. Turner, Opening Address at the British Association, Toronto, 1897, *Nature*, 2nd Sept. 1897.

It is believed that certain cells of the grey substance only, the great and the little pyramidal-shaped cells, are associated with the psychical functions, and that each of these, forming with its axis-cylinder, dendrons and other branching prolongations what is called a *neuron*, is not in constant connection with, and does not occupy a fixed position once for all in regard to, other similar *neurons*, but may by means of its prolongations place itself alternately in contact with a great number of these.[1] Hence the complexity of the nervous currents resulting from these continual changes of contact. Thus the cerebral activity might not merely be measured by the quantity and the size of the cells of the grey substance, but also by the number and the variety of the habitual contacts which are probably established after an education, a training of the cells. As from the same number of keys of a piano the tyro can produce only a few dissimilar sounds, while an artist elicits varied melodies, so from cerebral cells practically equal in number a savage is only able to extract vague and rudimentary ideas, while a thinker brings out of them intellectual treasures. How far are we, then, from the true appreciation of cerebral work with our rude weighings of an organ in which, with one part that would assuredly help us to the solution of the problem, we weigh at least three other parts having nothing or almost nothing to do with it! And even if we succeeded in finding the number, the weight, and the volume of the neurons, how are we to estimate the innumerable combinations of which they are capable? The problem appears almost insoluble. However, in science we must never lose hope, and—who knows?—perhaps some day the solution of the question will be found, and it will then appear as simple as to-day it appears a matter of course to see through the body with radioscopical apparatus.

[1] See the summary of the question in Ramon y Cajal, *Nouv. idées struct. syst. nerveux*, French trans., Paris, 1894; also Donaldson, *Growth of the Brain*, ch. vii., 1895.

CHAPTER III.

2.—PHYSIOLOGICAL CHARACTERS.

Functions of nutrition and assimilation: Digestion, alimentation, growth, temperature of the body, etc.—*Respiration and circulation:* Pulse, composition of the blood, etc.—Special odour—*Functions of communication:* Expression of the emotions, acuteness of the senses, etc.—*Functions of reproduction:* Menstruation, menopause, increase in the number of conceptions according to season, etc.—*Influence of environment:* Acclimatation—Cosmopolitanism of the genus *Homo* and the races of mankind—Cross-breeding.

3.—PSYCHOLOGICAL AND PATHOLOGICAL CHARACTERS.

Difficulties of studying them—Immunities—Nervous diseases of uncivilised peoples.

2.—PHYSIOLOGICAL CHARACTERS.

THE differences observable in the fulfilment of the organic functions—nutrition, respiration, circulation of the blood, reproduction, etc.—according to race are unquestionable; but they are still too little studied for us to be able to speak with as much certainty of them as of morphological differences. Further, these functions exhibit so many individual variations that it will always be difficult to rely on averages; besides, the latter present as far as we know a great uniformity.

The functions of nutrition and assimilation scarcely present any varieties according to race. Indigent populations living from hand to mouth by hunting, fishing, the gathering of fruit, etc., exposed to the alternations of famine and plenty, surprise us by their faculty of absorbing a great quantity of food; thus the Eskimo and the Fuegians feed for several days running on a stranded whale. The tendency to obesity is observed in certain races more than in others; very frequent among the Kirghiz, it is rare among their neighbours the Kalmuks, etc. The early obesity of Jewish women, which is besides artificially fostered in Africa and in the East, is also to be noted. Growth in different races would prove of some interest, but investigations into this subject have been made only in Europe and America.[1] Great difficulties stand in the way of these inquiries among uncivilised peoples, as it is almost impossible to ascertain the exact age of individuals. In a general way stature and weight increase with age somewhat irregularly, and as if by fits and starts; almost always a period of rapid growth in height succeeds a period of calm, during which the dimensions of the body increase in width (shoulders, pelvis, etc.). It has also been remarked that growth in height is especially rapid from the month of April to July and August, that it diminishes from November to March; and that, lastly, weight increases especially from August-September to the end of November. Sexual differences make themselves felt from birth. We have already seen (p. 26) that at birth the stature of boys exceeds that of girls by a figure which varies from two to eight millimetres (.08 to .32 of an inch), let us say of half a centimetre (less than the quarter of an inch) on an average. During the first year stature increases very rapidly: the child a year old is one and a half times as tall as at birth. The increase is less rapid until the fourth year, when the height is double what it was at birth. From the fourth year the growth is a little slower till the age of puberty, when there is a fresh start, and when the sexual differences are especially marked; girls grow more rapidly than boys between ten and fifteen years of age, but after fifteen boys take the lead and grow at first quickly, then slowly till their twenty-third year, at which age they have almost attained

[1] See the works of Bowditch on 2,500 American children of both sexes, *Eighth Ann. Rep. State Board of Massachusetts* (1877); of Pagliani on the Italians (*Archivio per l'Antr.*, 1876, vol. vi.); of Axel Key on 1,800 Swedish children (*Intern. Congr. Med.*, Berlin, 1887); of Schmidt on 10,000 German children, etc.

the limit of their stature; while women seem to stop growing at twenty.

The size of most of the organs increases pretty regularly; the heart in girls at the age of puberty and the brain in the two sexes are the only exceptions to this rule. The weight of the brain is $2\frac{1}{2}$ times greater at one year than at birth, $3\frac{1}{3}$ at five years, 3.7 at ten, and 3.9 at fifteen; later its growth diminishes, to reach its maximum before the age of twenty, 4 times its initial weight, and to decline slightly after forty or forty-five years.

At birth the brain represents 12.4 per cent. of the total weight of the body, at a year old 10.9 per cent., at five 8.4, at fifteen 3.8, and at twenty-five 2.3 per cent. only.[1] Unfortunately we have hardly any parallel observations on non-European populations. The only observations of this kind based on a sufficient number of subjects (several thousands) relate to the Japanese. According to Baelz, the stature of the Japanese increases after the age of puberty only 8 per cent., whilst it increases 13 per cent. among Europeans. On the other hand, Drs. Hamada and Sasaki say that growth diminishes greatly among Japanese men from sixteen or eighteen, and is found to be completely arrested at the age of twenty-two.[2] There is abundance of evidence that Negroes, Melanesians, and Malays attain their maximum height between eighteen and twenty-one. Dietary regimen and comfortable circumstances have a great influence on growth, as I have already said when speaking of stature (p. 31).

The activity of transformations in the system certainly presents differences according to climate, but not according to race. Thus the alimentary supply is conditioned solely by the heat required.[3] The *temperature of the body* hardly varies two

[1] H. Vierordt, "Das Massen-wachsthum, etc.," *Arch. für Anatom. u. Phys.; Anatom. Division*, 1890, supplem. volume, p. 62.

[2] Baelz, "Die Körperlichen Eigenschaften der Japaner," *Mittheil. Deutsch. Gesell. Ost. Asi.*, 1882, vol. iii., p. 348; Hamada and Sasaki in *Seii-Kwai* (*Japanese Med. Journ. of Tokio*), February No., 1890.

[3] Lapicque, *Rev. Mens. École. Anthr.*, 1897, No. 12.

or three tenths of a degree, for instance, among two peoples so different as regards type and mode of life as the French of the north and the Fuegians. In fact, the temperature taken in the mouth is from 37.1° to 37.2° C. among the former and 37.4° among the latter.[1] Besides, among Europeans the individual variations range between 37.1° and 37.5° C. Among Negroes the temperature appears to be, on the contrary, a little lower than that of Europeans.

Let us pass on to the *respiratory functions.* The vital capacity or the quantity of air in the expanded lungs, which is 3.7 cubic metres among the English according to Hutchinson, and from 3 to 4 cubic metres among Europeans in general, falls to 3 metres among the Whites and the Indians of the United States (Gould), and even to 2.7 among the Negroes of this latter country. The difference is very trifling; however, it has to be taken into consideration, seeing that among Europeans persons of high stature have an absolute capacity superior to that of people of low stature. Frequency of respiration seems to be greater among uncivilised peoples than with Europeans (14 to 18 respirations per minute); it is from 16 to 20 respirations among the Fuegians, 18 to 20 among the Mongol-Torgootes, 19 among the Kirghiz, and 18 among the Afghans.[2]

For the *circulation of the blood* here are a few scattered data. The pulse is the same among the Fuegians (72 beats per second) and the Tarantchi of Chinese Turkestan (72.9 beats) as among Europeans (71 to 72); it is a little faster among the Whites and the Negroes of the United States (74.8 and 74 beats), and much faster among the Indians of America and the Mulattos (76.3 and 77 beats), among the Torgootes

[1] Hyades and Deniker, *loc. cit.*, p. 181.

[2] These figures, as well as those relating to the pulse, are borrowed for the Fuegians from Hyades and Deniker, *loc. cit.*, p. 182; for the American populations from Gould, *loc. cit.*; for the Europeans from the work of H. Vierordt, *Anatomische Daten und Tabellen*, 1893; and for the rest from the memoir (in Russian) of Ivanovsky, "The Mongol-Torgootes," already quoted.

(76.6), and among the Kirghiz (77.7). The number of red globules in the blood varies but little according to race: Europeans have on an average five millions of them to the cubic millimetre, Hindus and Negroes seem to have half a million less, and the Fuegians half a million more.[1] But these differences are insignificant when we think that the number of these elements of the blood may vary by a million in the same subject according to the state of his health, nutrition, etc.

Certain travellers (Erman, Huc) have asserted that they could recognise a population by its *odour*. Without going so far as this, it must be admitted that some ethnic groups and, more particularly, the Negroes and the Chinese have their specific odour, which gets fainter with scrupulous cleanliness, but, it is said, never disappears. In the case of the Negro this odour is due especially to the abundance of the secretion of his very voluminous and numerous sebaceous glands. It was on this property that the planters relied for putting their dogs on the scent of the fugitive Negro. The Blacks themselves are perfectly aware of it, it appears, and those of the West Indies have even framed this proverb—

> "The Lord He loves the nigger well,
> He knows His nigger by the smell."

The odour of musk exhaled by the Chinese is attested by a great amount of evidence; that of the Australians and New Caledonians appears to be also duly reported. We must not confound these odours *sui generis* with those which certain peoples contract from the food they eat, as, for instance, the odour of garlic among the populations of Southern Europe and the Jews.[2]

With regard to *muscular force*, the data furnished by the

[1] Maurel, *Bull. Soc. Anth. Paris*, 1883, p. 699; Hyades and Deniker, p. 183.

[2] R. Andree, *Ethnol. Parallele*, Neue Folge, Leipzig, 1889.

dynamometer are deceptive, and cannot teach us anything; besides, the individual differences are enormous.

Functions of Relation.—A whole chapter could be written on the muscles and gestures serving for the *expression of the emotions*, and on their differences according to race.[1] Let us content ourselves with a single example connected with astonishment and surprise. These feelings are expressed almost everywhere by the raising of the eyebrows and the opening of the mouth; several peoples (Eskimo, Tlinkits, Andamanese, Indians of Brazil) accompany this play of feature by a slap on the hips; the Ainus and the Shin-Wans of Formosa give themselves a light tap on the nose or the mouth, whilst the Thibetans pinch their cheek. The Negro Bantus have the habit of moving the hand before the mouth as a sign of astonishment, and the Australians, as well as the western Negroes, protrude their lips as if to whistle (Fig. 141). In a general way the play of physiognomy is more complicated the more the people is civilised. Certain peoples execute movements of facial muscles difficult to imitate, such as the protrusion of the upper lip alone, which the Malays execute with the same facility and grace as a chimpanzee (Hagen). I shall speak in Chapter IV. of conventional gestures. The *attitudes of the body* in repose also vary with the different peoples: the kneeling attitude is common to Negroes (Figs. 135 and 142); the squatting position is frequently used by them and the peoples of the East, and also by the Americans; the upright position on one foot, the other being bent and the sole supported on the knee of the former, is met with as well in Oceania as among the Bejas, Negroes, etc.[2]

The *acuteness of the senses* is superior to ours among uncultured and half-civilised peoples. The Andamanese can discover certain fruits in the forests a long way off, being guided solely by the sense of smell. Taking as a unit the normal visual

[1] Darwin, *Expression of the Emotions*, London, 1872; Mantegazza, *Physiognomy and Expression* (English trans.), London, 1895; M. Duval, *Anatomie artistique*, p. 285, Paris, 1881.

[2] See *Globus*, 1897, vol. xxi., No. 7.

acuteness calculated according to the formula of Snellen, we shall have the following figures for different populations:—1.1 for the Germans; 1.4 for the Russians; 1.6 for the Georgians; 2.7 for the Ossetes and Kalmuks; 3 for the Nubian Bejas; and 5 for the Indians of the Andes. It is in a Kalmuk that the individual maximum of visual acuteness (6.7) has been noted.[1] An interesting fact has been observed by Dr. Herzenstein from the study of 39,805 Russian soldiers, viz., that visual acuteness is greater as the pigment of the iris and the hair is more developed. In fact, we only find among the fair-haired 72.4 per cent. of individuals whose visual acuteness is stronger than the normal, and 2.7 per cent. whose acuteness is weaker, whilst among the dark-haired the corresponding figures are 84.1 and 1.7; they see then, other things being equal, better than the fair-haired.[2]

The functions of reproduction are so difficult to study, even among civilised peoples, that it is almost impossible to say anything positive about them when dealing with savage peoples. Thus, for example, we can scarcely draw up an exact table of the first appearance of menstruation. This period varies from the age of ten (Negresses of Sierra Leone) to that of eighteen (Lapps). The influence of climate is unquestionable; authors as competent as Tilt in England, Krieger in Germany, Dubois and Pajot in France, are agreed on this point. They state that the first indication of the period of puberty appears between eleven and fourteen in warm countries, between thirteen and sixteen in temperate countries, and between fifteen and eighteen in cold countries. But they are also obliged to admit the influence of other factors—race, occupation, dietary regimen, etc. Thus in Austria, with the same climate and in the same social conditions, Jewish girls menstruate at fourteen to fifteen, Hungarian girls at fifteen to sixteen, and Slovak girls at fourteen to sixteen (Joachim); on the other hand, it is known that

[1] Kotelmann, "Die Augen, etc.," *Zeit. f. Ethn.*, 1884, Verh., p. 77.

[2] Dr. Herzenstein, *Izviestia*, etc., of *Friends of Science*, Moscow, vol. xlix, part 4, p. 347 (in Russian).

dwelling in a town, indolent life, premature sexual excitations, accelerate the appearance of the menses. Alimentation has also its share of influence in the matter. Thus among the badly-fed girls of the despised caste of Illuvar (Southern India) their periods appear at about sixteen, while the girls of India in general menstruate at eleven, twelve, or thirteen.[1] It must not be thought that in all countries the appearance of the menses is also indicative of the period when sexual relations begin. Among the majority of the peoples of India, among the Turks, the Mongols, the Persians, among the Polynesians, the Malays, and the Negroes, young girls enter into sexual relations much before the appearance of the menses—at eleven, ten, and even nine years of age. The time when marriage takes place is also not an indication; it is a matter of social convention, among the savage as among the half-civilised. Thus among the Mongol Torgootes girls begin to have sexual relations at fourteen on an average, and marry at eighteen; for boys the corresponding figures are fourteen and a half and nineteen (Ivanovsky).

The time of the *appearance of the critical age* is subject to so many fluctuations that even for European populations it is scarcely possible to establish averages, but most of the figures oscillate around the ages of forty-five to fifty. It is known that in woman ovulation goes on regularly throughout the year without those accelerations or exasperations of the genesic functions in certain seasons which are observed among animals in heat. In this respect the human female differs totally from wild animals (except the apes, among whom menstruation has been noted), and approximates closely to the female of domestic animals. And yet certain facts seem to indicate that it has not always been so. These facts have reference to the greater frequency of conceptions during certain periods of the year.

The Swedish physician Wargentin was the first to point out in 1767 this frequency in his own country. Since then, several statisticians, doctors, and naturalists have confirmed it:

[1] See for further details, Ploss, *loc. cit.*, vol. i., p. 288.

Quetelet for Belgium and Holland (maximum of births in February, the maximum of conceptions in May); Wappæus for Central Europe (two maxima of conception, in winter, and at the end of spring or the beginning of summer); Villermé (same periods) for different countries, including those of the southern hemisphere; Sormani for Italy (conceptions in July); Mayr for Germany (conceptions in December); Beukemann for the different provinces of the German empire (maximum of conceptions in December in the north, in spring in the south); Hill for India (maximum of conceptions, December-January); lastly, different authors for Russia (maximum of conceptions in winter).

The explanations which have been put forward up to the present of this phenomenon are of different kinds. According to certain authors, the maxima observed in many countries in the spring are owing to the fact of there being in this season "plenty of everything," better nourishment, in short, something which compels the genesic instinct of man, like that of most animals, to participate in the "awakening of nature." To this it is replied by other observers that in certain countries the maxima are reported in the winter months, that is to say in the season when the temperature and the relative absence of the good things of life do not seem to be *a priori* favourable to generation; these scientists look for the cause in the social organisation. They notice that in countries of the north it is in the month of December that, after having finished their work in the fields, the inhabitants give themselves up to festivities and rejoicings, and that it is in this month the greatest number of unions are contracted; on the other hand, in the south the most popular festivals are those of the spring at the awakening of nature. Others, again, assert that these differences are owing as much to religion as to latitude.

All these explanations are somewhat unscientific, and have never been verified by figures or experience. According to Rosenstadt,[1] cosmic and social influences do not count at

[1] B. Rosenstadt, "Ursachen welche die Zahl der Conceptionen, etc.," *Mitth. Embryol. Instit. Univers. Wien*, 2nd series, part 4, Vienna, 1890.

all in the question, for often the periods during which recrudescence of conceptions occurs are the same for countries differing entirely in climate, religion, and manners (Italy, Russia, Sweden). These influences may, at the most, create conditions favourable to the bringing about of the phenomenon, may prepare the ground for it. But as to the phenomenon itself it would be, according to Rosenstadt, merely the remains in man of his animal nature, a "physiological custom" inherited from the animals, his ancestors.

Primitive man would inherit from his ancestors the habit of procreating by preference at particular times. On the arrival of this period of sexual excitement fecundations would take place wholesale. With the development of civilisation man has sexual relations all the year round, but the "physiological custom" of procreating at a certain period does not entirely disappear; it remains as a survival of the animal state, and manifests itself in the recrudescence of the number of conceptions during certain months of the year. This conclusion is corroborated by the fact that among certain savage tribes copulation seems to take place at certain periods of the year; for example, among the Australians at the time of the yam harvest (see Chap. VII., *Marriage*, etc.).[1]

It is perhaps as a survival of these habits that we must regard the annual festivals followed by wholesale marriages among the Sonthals, and the wholesale marriages still practised to-day in Brittany on the eve of Lent. Thus in the little market-town of Plougastel-Daoulas (Finistère), containing only 7000 inhabitants, thirty-four marriages were celebrated at once on the 5th of February 1896, and the preceding year, before Lent, forty-eight couples had been united on the same day in this locality.[2] The famous "Bharzwad Jang," or "Marriage of the Shepherds," a ceremony practised by certain tribes (*Mer*, *Shir*, *Rabai*) of Western Kathiawar (India), is also perhaps a survival of this custom. It consists in the

[1] Fr. Müller, *Allgem. Ethnographie*, 2nd ed., p. 212, Vienna, 1879; Kulischer, *Zeit. f. Ethn.*, vol. viii. (Verh., p. 152), Berlin, 1876.

[2] Correspondence of the *Temps* of the 6th of February 1896.

celebration of marriage on the same day, but at stated intervals (of about twenty-four years), of all the bachelors of the tribe. At the last ceremony of this kind, which took place from the 28th of April to the 3rd of May 1895, 775 couples were thus married at once.[1]

The question of the *fertility* of women in different populations is one of great interest as regards the future of these populations, but it is scarcely more than outlined yet. If we know in a general way that the birth-rate is very low in France and somewhat low in the non-immigrant part of the population of the United States, that it is very high in Russia and among the Jews, etc., we know almost nothing about the subject in connection with uncivilised peoples; in their case, as in our own, we must take into account the different elements of the problem—social conditions, voluntary limitation (Australians), infanticide (Polynesia), etc.

Influence of Environment.—I can scarcely treat here as fully as I could wish such interesting questions as the influence of external circumstance, of acclimatation and crossings or hybridisation, inasmuch as they are still very little and imperfectly studied. The direct influence of environment has rarely been observed with all the scientific exactness to be wished. Ordinarily we have to rest satisfied with phrases which do not mean a great deal.[2] Even the influence of con-

[1] J. M. Campbell, *Journ. Anthr. Soc. Bombay*, vol. iv., 1895, No. 1.

[2] I cannot refute here all the erroneous assertions in regard to the assumed influence of environment, referring the reader to the works of Pallas (*Acta of the Acad. of St. Petersburg*, 1780, part ii., p. 69) and of Darwin (especially to *The Descent of Man*). It is enough to give some examples. Negroes are not black because they inhabit tropical countries, seeing that the Indians of South America, who live in the same latitudes, are yellow; Norwegians and Great Russians, who are fair and tall, live side by side with the Laplanders and the Samoyeds, who are dark and of very low stature. It has been said and repeated frequently that the Jews who immigrated to Cochin (India), after the destruction of Jerusalem by Titus, became as black as the indigenous Tamils among whom they live. This is so little true that in this country the name of "white Jews" is given to the descendants of true Jews (who really are white), to dis-

ditions so abnormal as the complete absence of light and solar heat, those sources of everything living, during several months, has only been observed incidentally. Nossiloff,[1] however, has noted day by day the influence of the polar night on an ordinary population (not hardened and picked, like the crews of polar expeditions) and proved its depressing action, manifesting itself in general apathy of body and mind, in a tendency to drowsiness, and in diminution of the height and the thoracic perimeter; this action is especially noticeable in children, who visibly pine away during this period. Unfortunately the observations of Nossiloff are limited to a small number of subjects.

It is more than probable that all the modifications which the organism undergoes as a result of the influence of environment are mostly of a chemical nature, and have only a remote effect on the human frame. According to W. Kochs,[2] the whole question of acclimatation in tropical countries resolves itself into the quantity of water in the organism. He bases his deductions principally on the difference found to exist in the quantity of water contained in the flesh of oxen of the Argentine Republic in comparison with that

tinguish them from the "black Jews" or Tamils converted to Judaism. Further, it has been pretended, according to an assertion of Khanikof, reproduced by Darwin (*Descent of Man*, p. 304), and repeated by so many others, that the Wurtemburgers of blond type, who emigrated to the Caucasus in 1816, had become dark. This statement is no truer than the preceding one. Radde, who has studied these settlers, says expressly (*Zeit. f. Ethnol.*, vol. ix., Verh., p. 12) that they are as fair as their compatriots who have remained in Germany. According to Pantioukhof (*Anth. Observ. in the Caucasus*, p. 25, Tiflis, 1893, in Russian), 25 out of 51 of the settlers, or 55 per cent., have light eyes, while in Wurtemburg the proportion of light eyes *among children* is 65 per cent. (*Arch. f. Anthr.*, 1886, p. 412), which reduces the figure to about 56 per cent. or 58 per cent. for the adults,—a figure very near to the preceding one.

[1] S. Russkikh, "Influence of the Polar Night on the Human Organism," *Zapiski of the Ourtian Friends of Nat. Sc. Soc.*, Ekaterinburg, 1895 (in Russian).

[2] W. Kochs, "Eine wichtige Veränderung, etc.," *Biol. Centralbl.*, p. 289, 1891.

found among cattle of Northern Germany. The former have from 80 to 83 per cent. of water, while the latter have from 72 to 75 per cent. only. If it is the same with man, as Kochs supposes, he would have from 7 to 8 per cent. less solid matter to burn in his body in the tropics than in temperate countries, and the vital energy would be affected accordingly. Thus only the organism that had acquired the quantity of water necessary for supporting the heat of the tropics would be acclimatised; this is so true that Whites acclimatised in tropical countries suffer more from the cold in Europe than their compatriots who have never left Europe.[1] Besides, the Negroes of Senegal begin to suffer from cold when the thermometer falls below 20° C. (68° Fahr.), whilst the Fuegians who are not more warmly clad bear very well the cold of 0° to –4° C. (32° to 25° Fahr.).

Taken as a whole, the genus *Homo* is *cosmopolitan*. In fact, man inhabits the whole earth from the icy regions of Greenland (in the neighbourhood of the eightieth degree of N. latitude) to the torrid zone which stretches between the tropic of Cancer and the Equator. He is found in countries situated at 75 or 200 metres below the level of the sea (Caspian depression, depression of Louktchin in Eastern Turkestan), as well as on table-lands at an elevation of more than 5000 metres (Thibet). But if we consider the numerous sub-divisions of the genus *Homo* which are called species, sub-species, or races, the question of cosmopolitanism becomes more complicated as at the same time the positive data for its solution are less numerous.

Apart from the European and Negro races, peoples have never changed their habitat abruptly—have not transported themselves in a body into climates very different from their native country, though slow migrations, advancing from place to neighbouring place, have been numerous at all times and among all peoples; these have been followed by acclimatation, the sole criterion of cosmopolitanism. It must also be remarked that civilised peoples withstand better than

[1] Davy, *Philos. Transac. Roy. Soc. London*, 1850, p. 437.

savages changes of every kind. In this respect the former bear a stronger resemblance than the latter to domestic animals, which rarely become sterile outside of their native country. According to Darwin,[1] this results from the fact that civilised peoples, as well as domestic animals, have been subjected in the course of their evolution to more numerous variations, more frequent changes of place, and also more important crossings.

The question whether each race of mankind can live and reproduce itself—that is to say, become acclimatised—on any point of the globe will, evidently, only be resolved when attempts of this kind are undertaken by each race and pursued during several generations. Now there are no exact data on this subject except for the so-called white race and in some measure for Negroes. Without reckoning cosmopolitan peoples like the Jews and the Gypsies, it is certain that the majority of European peoples can as a race get acclimatised in the most diverse regions, in Canada (English and French) as in Brazil (Portuguese and Germans), Mexico (Spaniards), Australia (English), Southern Africa (Dutch Boers). The assumed failures of acclimatation are connected with countries where there has never been any European *colonisation* (India, Java), and where it is known that there are isolated cases of the collective acclimatation of several families.

According to Clements Markham and Elisée Reclus, the Englishman not only as an individual but as a race is able to live in the Cisgangetic peninsula.[2] Many generations of Englishmen have flourished in various parts of India. Numerous examples could be cited of children being acclimatised without detriment to their strength or health. According to Francis Galton, the mortality in 1877 of European soldiers in India (12.7 per 1000) was less than that of native soldiers (13.4) and Hindus in general (35). In the Dutch Indies the Dutch have kept themselves in good health for several genera-

[1] Darwin, *Descent of Man*, 3rd ed., p. 208.

[2] Cl. Markham, *Travels in India and Peru*, London, 1869; Elisée Reclus, *Géographie universelle*, vol. viii., p. 630, Paris, 1883.

tions.[1] We must leave out of the question certain unhealthy regions (like Lower Senegal) where the natives suffer almost as much as Europeans. On the whole, the so-called white race appears to have the aptitude of acclimatation in all countries, provided, of course, that it makes the necessary sacrifices for several generations.

If it be said of certain regions that they are not colonisable by Europeans, it is thereby implied that the sacrifices entailed by acclimatation are out of all proportion to the advantages to be gained by colonisation. As to Negroes, they thrive in temperate countries like the United States, where they multiply at the same rate as the Whites. By a strange anomaly they do not seem to thrive as well in Mexico, in the Antilles, and in Guiana—that is to say in the same isothermal zone (26°-28° C., or 70°-82° Fahr.) as their native country; nevertheless they live and reproduce there.

Upon the whole, if we consider (1) that the most mixed and most civilised races are those which are soonest acclimatised, (2) that the tendency of races to intermingle, and of civilisation to develop, goes on increasing every day in every part of the world, we may affirm without being accused of exaggeration that the cosmopolitanism of mankind, if it does not yet exist to-day in all races (which seems somewhat improbable), will develop as a necessary consequence of the facility of acclimatation. For it to become general is only a matter of time.

As to the fertility of acclimatised families, it has been established outside of hybridisation. Thus it has been possible to trace back certain English families in the Barbadoes for six generations.[2] As much may be said of the French in the islands of Mauritius and Réunion. In the Brazilian province of Rio Grande do Sul, between 25°-30° S. latitude—that is, in a sub-tropical region—it has been ascertained that there are three or four generations of German colonists,

[1] Rosenberg, *Malayshe Archip.*, Leipzig, 1878, Preface.

[2] Huxley, *Evidence as to Man's Place in Nature*, London, 1863.

whose children enjoy very good health.[1] Lastly, in Matabeleland there are already two or three generations of Dutch.[2] It must be said that certain European races are more capable than others of becoming acclimatised in tropical countries. Thus it is universally acknowledged that people of the south of Europe —Spaniards, Italians, Provençals—become sooner acclimatised in Africa and equatorial America than the English and the Germans of the north.

But in spite of the facility of acclimatation, race-characters hardly seem to change in the new environment; the chemical constituents of the tissues having changed, the body adapts itself without change either in outward form or even colour.

The German colonists of Brazil and the Steppes of the Volga bear a perfect resemblance to each other after more than a century of separation from their race-brothers of Swabia or Franconia. It is the same after two or three centuries with the English of the Barbadoes, the French of Réunion, the Dutch of the Transvaal, etc.

The phenomena of *hybridity* are even less studied than those of the influence of environment; I shall speak of some of these in regard to different populations, but the facts are too isolated and disputed for any general conclusions to be drawn.

In reality, all that we know is that a great number of races produce half-breeds by crossing, but whether these half-breeds in so crossing produce a new race or revert to one of the ancestral types has not been demonstrated. Humanity appears to move in a confused medley of the most diverse and composite forms, without any one of them being able to persist; for the means of persistence, artificial selection or sexual selection, are wanting. The only selection which may have a decided influence on the predominance of the characters of a race in its interminglings is that which proceeds from the *number* of individuals of each of the races concerned in

[1] Hettner, *Zeits. Gesel. Erdk.*, vol. xxvi, 1891, p. 137.

[2] *Proceedings Geogr. Soc. London*, 1891, p. 34.

the blending and their respective fecundity, but this selection has hardly begun to be studied.

3.—PSYCHOLOGICAL AND PATHOLOGICAL CHARACTERS.

It remains to speak of *psychological characters*—that is to say, of temperament and the different manifestations of mind, feeling, and affections. But it must be admitted that it is almost impossible to treat these in the face of many contradictory facts. Speaking generally, it may be said that the American and Mongoloid races are grave, meditative, a little obtuse, melancholic; and that, on the contrary, the Negro races and Melanesians are playful, laughing, lively, and superficial as children. But there are many exceptions to such general rules. Each traveller, each observer, tends to judge in his own way a given people according to the nature of the relations (pacific, hostile, etc.) which he has had with it. We are unable to affirm anything when we have once made up our minds to escape from the commonplace generalities that savages are wanting in foresight and general ideas, that they are cruel, that their imitative faculties are highly developed, etc.

Pathological characters are better known, as for example, in regard to immunities. It is a proved fact that Negroes, for instance, are proof against the contagion of yellow fever; that they resist much better than Europeans the terrible intermittent fevers which prevail on the coasts of Africa. But if savage peoples enjoy certain immunities, they are, on the contrary, very susceptible to the infectious diseases which civilised peoples introduce among them; whole tribes have been exterminated by syphilis, measles, and consumption in South America, Polynesia, and Siberia.[1] There are also diseases peculiar to certain populations, such, for example, as the *sleeping sickness* among the Wolofs and Songhaï, which manifests itself in an invincible tendency to sleep.[2] It has

[1] For details see Bordier, *Géogr. Médicale*, Paris, 1883, with atlas.

[2] *Bull. Géogr. histor. et descript.*, p. 53, Paris, 1889.

long been asserted that savage peoples are not afflicted by nervous and mental diseases. Nothing of the kind. The genuine "great hysteria" of Charcot has been observed among Negresses of Senegal, among Hottentot women and Kafirs, as well as in Abyssinia and Madagascar.[1] Other nervous diseases have been noticed among Hurons and Iroquois,[2] and in New Zealand. Some forms of neurosis appear to be limited to certain ethnic groups. Such is the "Amok" of the Malays—a sort of furious and imitative madness perhaps provoked at the same time by suggestion. Developed especially among the Malays, it is also met with among the Indians of North America, where it has been called "jumping" by the Whites. The "Myriachit" of the Ostiaks and other natives of Siberia, the "Malimali" of the Tagals of the Philippines, the "Bakchis" of the Siamese, are similar diseases. Under the name of "Latah" are designated among the Malays all sorts of nervous diseases, but more particularly the imitative madness which impels women to undress before men, to throw children up in the air in imitation of a game of ball, etc. Besides, the name Latah is also given to a mental state in which the patient is afraid of certain words (tiger, crocodile), and which is met with somewhat frequently not only among the Malays, but also among the Tagals and the Sikhs of India.[3]

[1] G. de la Tourette, *Journal de Médecine*, February, 1893.

[2] Brinton, *Science*, 16th Dec. 1892; and *Globus*, 1893, 1st half-year, p. 148.

[3] See Logan's *Journal of the Indian Archipelago*, vol. iii., Calcutta, 1849, pp. 457, 464, and 530; H. O. O'Brien, "The Latah," *Journ. of the Straits Branch of the R. Asiat. Soc.*, Singapore, June 1883, p. 144; Metzger, "Amok und Mataglap," *Globus*, vol. lii., 1882, No. 7; Rasch, *Neurolog. Centralbl.*, 1894, No. 15; 1895, No. 19.

CHAPTER IV.

ETHNIC CHARACTERS.

Various stages of social groups and essential characters of human societies: Progress.—Conditions of Progress: Innovating initiative, and tradition—Classification of "states of civilisation."

I.—LINGUISTIC CHARACTERS.

Methods of exchanging ideas within a short distance—Gesture and speech—Divisions of language according to structure—Jargons—*Communications at a relatively remote distance:* optic and acoustic signals—*Transmission of ideas at any distance and time whatever*—Handwriting—Mnemotechnic objects—Pictography—Ideography—Alphabets—Direction of the lines of handwriting.

So far we have considered man as an isolated being, apart from the groupings which he forms with his fellows. But in order to get a correct idea of the sum-total of the manifestations of his physical life, and especially of his psychical life, we must further consider him in his social environment.

Nowhere on the earth has there been found a race of men the members of which lived completely alone and isolated as the majority of animals are seen to do. It is in fact but very rarely that the latter combine into societies; they form a family group only temporarily during the period of raising the young, etc. Man, on the contrary, becomes almost helpless apart from society, incapable of maintaining the struggle for existence without the help of his fellow-men. The development of all the manifestations of "sociality" is then the measure of progress of human societies. The more man is "socialised," if I may thus express it, the less he depends on nature.

This dependence on nature has long served as a criterion in ethnography for dividing peoples into two groups—the "civilised" and the "savage." The name given by the Germans to "savages," *Naturvölker* (peoples in a state of nature), explains sufficiently this way of looking at things. According to their greater or less dependence on nature, peoples were divided into hunters, shepherds or nomads, and tillers of the soil or settlers, without, however, characterising in a very precise way each of these states. Morgan was the first to bring a little definiteness into this nomenclature, and at the same time he has shown the necessity of introducing another criterion into the estimate of states of civilisation. In fact, to establish the three forms of socialisation—*savage*, *barbarous*, and *civilised*—he has accepted as a distinctive mark between the second and the third the existence of handwriting—that is to say, of the material means used by the two forces necessary to the inception and maintenance of progress: innovating initiative, and conservation of what has been acquired.[1] He has not made as much of this classification as, in my opinion, he might have done. In fact, the ethnic groups of the earth only differ among themselves from the social point of view by the *degree* of culture—its essence being always and everywhere the same: pursuit of more and more easy means of satisfying wants and desires. Now, if the form assumed by this species of activity, in a word, if *production*, subject to the influence of climate, geographical position, etc., is the basis of all social development, as Grosse has so well shown,[2] the nature and evolution of the needs and desires themselves depend up to a certain point on the "temperament" of the

[1] L. Morgan, *Proc. Am. Assoc. Acad. Sc.*, Detroit Session, 1875, p. 266, and *Journal Anthro. Inst.*, vol. vi., 1878, p. 114. The distinction between the first and the second form lies, according to Morgan, in the knowledge of pottery—a somewhat unreliable and narrow criterion, which, however, does not directly interest us here.

[2] Grosse, *Die Formen der Wirtschaft*, etc., Leipzig, 1896.

race, which must likewise be taken into consideration. The nature and amount of psychic force in any given society, the evolution of which is effected by its mode of production, may in its turn, having attained a certain degree of development, re-act on the economic state, and modify it. We see nothing like this in the animal communities. Bees and ants arrange their hives and manage the affairs of their community to-day as they did a thousand insect-generations ago. It is very probable that race has something to do with psychic force, but up to the present time the fact has not been scientifically demonstrated. However that may be, in order to form a correct opinion as to the degree of civilisation of any people, we should have to take into consideration not only its material culture, but also its *état d'âme*, its psychology, to realise the psychical resources which it has at its command. Thus certain peoples (Australians, Bushmen), though at the bottom of the scale as regards material culture, are nevertheless well endowed from the artistic point of view; in the same way the Polynesians of a hundred years ago, who were inferior in knowledge of pottery and metallurgy to the Negroes, were superior to them in general intelligence and the richness of their mythology.

But progress is only possible if, side by side with individual power of initiating change, there exists in the social aggregate what may be called the power of conservation. There may be produced among savage peoples, as Ratzel[1] has so well pointed out, persons of exceptional natural talent, men of genius; but the activity of these will almost always be sterile. Even if they succeed in ameliorating the material condition, in raising the moral or intellectual level of the members of their tribe or of their class, the result of their activity has only an ephemeral existence, their efforts are not continued, and after their death, for want of the conservative power, everything falls back into the primitive condition. The secret of civilisation lies not so much in efforts of isolated individuals as in accumulation of these efforts, in the transmission from one generation to

[1] Ratzel, *History of Mankind*, vol. i., p. 24. London, 1896.

another of the acquired result, of a sum-total of knowledge which enables each generation to go further without beginning everything over again *ab ovo*. In this way progress is unlimited by the very conditions of its origin, and civilisation is only the sum of all the acquisitions of the human mind at any given period.

The conservative and transmittive power become really established in a society only when the means of communicating thought are sufficiently developed, when language has taken a definite form, and an easy method is devised of fixing it by conventional signs more or less indelible and transmissible to future generations. Thus, to estimate different states of civilisation we must have recourse to linguistic characters, understanding by such everything which concerns the means of communicating ideas in time and space—that is to say, spoken or mimetic language and its graphic representation. But before passing rapidly in review the linguistic characters, I owe the reader a few words of explanation of the terms which I am about to use in designating "states of civilisation."

In these latter days a classification of these states nearly in accordance with the desiderata which were formulated at the beginning of this chapter has been proposed by Vierkandt.[1] This classification takes material culture into account, but the primordial division which is adopted in it, between peoples in a state of nature (or better, uncivilised) and civilised peoples, is based on the development of certain psychical traits denoting a greater or less development of individuality, of the spirit of free investigation, etc. Savage peoples, without any true civilisation, are divided in this classification into semi-civilised and uncivilised properly so-called, with sub-divisions into nomads and tillers of the soil for the former, and hunters and wanderers for the latter.

Admitting the criterion of the existence or non-existence of writing and the relative value of the two elements of progress

[1] Vierkandt, *Naturvölker und Kulturvölker*, Leipzig, 1896; and *Geogr. Zeitschr.*, vol. iii., pp. 256 and 315, 2 maps, Leipzig, 1897.

mentioned above, I arrive at a classification of "states of civilisation" which recalls somewhat that of Vierkandt, but which differs from it on several points. It may be summarised as follows:—

(1) *Savage peoples*, progressing exceedingly slowly, without writing, sometimes possessing a pictographic method; living in little groups of some hundreds or thousands of individuals. They are divided into two categories: *hunters*[1] (examples: Bushmen, Australians, Fuegians) and *tillers of the soil* (examples: Indians of North America, Melanesians, the majority of Negroes).

(2) *Semi-civilised peoples*, making an appreciable but slow progress, in which the conservative power predominates, forming authoritative societies or states of several thousands or millions of individuals; having an ideographic or phonetic writing, but a rudimentary literature. They are divided likewise into two categories: *tillers of the soil* (examples: Chinese, Siamese, Abyssinians, Malays, Ancient Egyptians, and Peruvians) and *nomads* (examples: Mongols, Arabs).

(3) *Civilised peoples*, making rapid progress, in which the initiating and innovating power predominates, forming states based on individual liberty, and consisting of several millions of individuals; having a phonetic writing and a developed literature. Their economic state is especially characterised by *industrialism* and *cosmopolitan commercialism* (examples: the majority of the peoples of Europe and North America).

Having said this much, we shall begin the study of ethnic characters with those which we may consider the indispensable condition of all associability, that is to say the linguistic characters.

I.—LINGUISTIC CHARACTERS.

Without pursuing the inquiry whether language is born of inarticulate cries, of onomatopæias or otherwise, whether it has a single or a multiple origin, we may content ourselves

[1] That is to say, engaged in the pursuit of land animals (hunting), or of aquatic (fishing); or gathering plants or fruits.

with stating the fact, that language does not constitute the only means by which men may understand each other and communicate ideas. There are several others. They may be arranged in three groups:—means of communicating near at hand: gestures and words; means of communicating at a relatively remote distance: various signals; means of communicating at any distance and time whatever: writing.

Gestures.—Many gestures are natural and common to all men. All who have had to ask for anything to eat or drink in a foreign country without knowing the language, must have appreciated this means of international communication. However, the same gestures do not always and everywhere signify the same thing. Let us take, for example, the simplest ideas, negation and affirmation. In Central and Northern Europe these ideas are expressed, as every one knows, by a bending of the head forward and by lateral movements of the head. But there are few exotic peoples (Andamanese, Ainus, certain Hindus) who make use of the same gestures. Most of them, on the contrary, affirm by shaking the head laterally (Arabs, Botocudos, certain Negroes) and deny by raising it; most frequently this latter gesture is accompanied by an uplifting of the eyebrows (Abyssinians) or a particular smacking of the tongue (Syro-Arabs, Naya-Kurumbas, etc.). The natives of the Admiralty Islands express negation by a tap on the nose.[1] In Italy and generally in Mediterranean Europe, the signs of negation, with many other feelings besides, are expressed by gestures of the hands; thus to say "no," the hand is moved sharply before the breast, the fingers being closed except the forefinger, which is held up vertically. Perhaps the practice of carrying burdens on the head, thus preventing the movements of this part of the body, has had something to do with the abundant development of gestures with the arms by which the European of the south may be recognised. An almost analogous sign, but consisting in a slow movement outward and downward, signifies "yes" among the Indians of North America. These last have pushed to the utmost limits the use of the language

[1] Andree, *Anthropologische Parallele*, p. 52.

of gesture. G. Mallery has collected the treasures of this language, which is being lost to-day, and has drawn up a vocabulary of it.[1] At the period when this language flourished, the Indians were able to express by gestures not only common and proper nouns, but also verbs, pronouns, particles, etc.; they made elaborate speeches by combining the gestures of the body, the head, and the arms. They introduced abbreviations exactly as that is done in pictographic writing. Here is an example of how a Dakota Indian (Fig. 26) says by

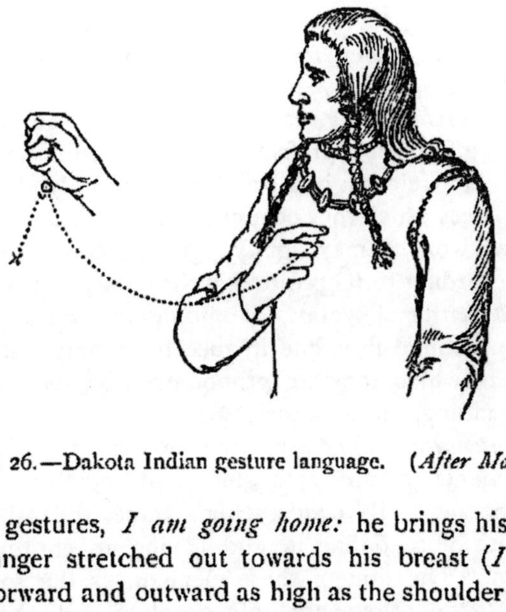

FIG. 26.—Dakota Indian gesture language. (*After Mallery.*)

means of gestures, *I am going home:* he brings his hand with the forefinger stretched out towards his breast (*I*), then extends it forward and outward as high as the shoulder (*am going*), and, closing the fist, he lets it drop abruptly (*home*). It is supposed that extreme diversity of dialects has been the chief cause of the development of this strange sign-language; it would serve as a bond between tribes which could not converse with one another.

Speech.—Setting aside the almost unique example of the North American Indians, gestures are generally only the

[1] G. Mallery, "Sign Language," *First Annual Report Bur. of Ethnol.*, 1879-80, p. 269. Washington, 1881.

auxiliaries of *speech*. The latter, which is the exclusive appanage of the genus *Homo*, while it is formed of a somewhat limited number of articulate sounds, nevertheless presents such a mass of varied combinations of these sounds that at first one would expect to be lost in the multitude of languages, dialects, idioms, vernacular forms, etc. Fortunately, linguists have been able to establish the fact that, in spite of their apparent diversity, dialects are capable of being grouped into languages, and the latter into linguistic families, which, in their turn, have been reduced, according to their morphological structure, to three principal groups: *monosyllabic* or isolating languages, *agglutinative* languages, and *inflectional* languages.

In the *monosyllabic languages* all the words are *roots*, there are neither suffixes nor prefixes nor any modification of the words, and their relation in a proposition is only given by the respective places which they occupy in it. Thus in the Chinese language the word *ta* may signify "great, greatness, greatly, to enlarge," according to its position in the phrase. The grammar is entirely a matter of syntax. Homophonous words of various signification abound in it, and in speech are only distinguished by the way in which they are pronounced, by the *tones*, high, low, rising, falling, interrogatory, etc.

In *agglutinative languages* the words are formed of several elements, adhering, agglutinated together, of which one only possesses its own peculiar value, the others being coupled with it to define it, and having an entirely relative signification. The first of these elements is the root of the word, whilst the others are only obsolete roots, having lost their own signification, and are reduced to the rank of determinative particles or *affixes* with a definite meaning. The affixes may be placed before the root (as in the Bantu languages), and then they bear the name of prefixes, or at the end (as in Turkish and Mongolian), and then they are called suffixes. Thus the suffix *lar* or *liar* in Turkish gives the signification of the plural of the word to which it is joined (ex. *arkan*, the rope; *arkanlar*, the ropes); the suffix *tchi* designates the person concerned with something, etc., for instance, *arkantchi*, rope-maker; the suffix *ly* indicates possession (ex. *arkanly*, with a cord, attached). Other suffixes, *la*, *lyk*, denote action, quality (*arkanla*, to attach with a cord; *arkanlyk*, the best kind of cord).[1]

Among the agglutinative languages we distinguish a special group called *polysynthetic* or *incorporating languages;* this group is formed exclusively of American idioms. It is characterised by the phenomenon of incorporation, by syncope or by ellipsis, of nouns to the verb, so as to form but one word of the whole proposition; for instance, in Algonkin, the phrase-word *nadholiniu*, "bring us the canoe," is formed of the elided words *naten* bring, *amochol* canoe, *i* euphonic, and *niu* to us. A similar incorporation takes place when in Italian they say, for instance, *dicendo-ci-lo*, "in telling it to us."

The *inflectional languages* differ from the agglutinative to this extent, that the root may modify its form to express its relations with another root. But this change is not indispensable; sometimes the inflection may be attained by the modification of prefix or suffix. Thus, in Hebrew, the root *mlch* gives, when modified, *malach* he reigned, *malchu* they reigned, *melechu* the king, *melachim* kings, etc.

With the exception of the Chinese, the peoples of Indo-China, and the Thibetans, who speak monosyllabic languages, and also the Indo-Europeans and the Semito-Hamites, who use inflectional languages, all the rest of mankind belongs, by its mode of speech, to the division of agglutinative language. It must not be thought, however, that the difference is very marked in the three categories which I have just mentioned. We have already seen, for example, that the inflectional languages, like Italian, may have agglutinative forms; the Arab, the Frenchman, the Provençal have also recourse occasionally to agglutination; on the other hand, most of the isolating languages of Indo-China and Thibet exhibit several agglutinative characteristics, and even in

[1] See for the details Fr. Müller, *Grundr. d. Sprachwissensch.*, vol. i., Vienna, 1876; Hovelacque, *Linguistique*, Paris, 1877.

Chinese, that pre-eminently monosyllabic language, there may be distinguished "*full*" *roots* having their signification, and "*empty*" *roots* playing the part of affixes.

It was thought until quite recently that originally all the languages of the earth were monosyllabic, that by a process of evolution they became transformed into agglutinative languages, passing thence into the final and most perfect form, the inflectional. But the immense disproportion between the number of peoples speaking the agglutinative languages and that of the other two categories; the presence of the agglutinative forms in monosyllabic languages; the unequivocal tendency of several inflected languages, like English, towards monosyllabism; lastly, the recent researches of Terrien de Lacouperie into the ancient pronunciation of Thibetan and Chinese words, have appreciably shaken this belief: one is rather led to see in agglutination the most primitive form of language. From it would be derived monosyllabism, polysyntheticism, and inflection; the two latter forms would tend in their turn towards monosyllabism.[1] I shall mention with regard to each of the principal ethnic groups, the peculiarities of the languages which they speak, and in Chapter VIII. I shall say a few words about linguistic classifications and the relation between "peoples" and "languages." For the moment it is enough to point out that besides morphological structure, there are other characters: vocabulary, grammatical and phonetic forms, which enable us to group the allied idioms into linguistic families. Let me add that side by side with the thousands of languages and principal dialects distributed among the populations of the earth, there exist *jargons*, that is to say, semi-artificial languages, originating especially in the necessities of commerce.[2]

[1] For *resumé* of the question see A. Keane, *Ethnology*, p. 206. London, 1896.

[2] Such are the *lingua franca* and the *sabir*, a medley of French, English, Italian, and Turkish spread over all the Asiatic and African coast-lines of the Mediterranean, and particularly among the Levantines. Such also is the Pigeon (or *Pidjin*) English, a mixture of Chinese, English, and

Let us not forget either that the different sexes and certain castes or classes, especially of sorcerers and priests, have often a special language, sacred or otherwise, but always unknown to persons of the other sex or of other castes, and kept secret. Language varies also among certain peoples (for example, among the Javanese) according as a superior speaks to an inferior, or *vice versâ*.

Signals.—To communicate at a distance relatively remote, all peoples make use of optic or acoustic signals. *Optic signals* are at first amplified gestures; thus the various tribes of Red Indians recognised each other at a distance by making conventional signs with the arms and the body. An arm raised high with two fingers uplifted and the others closed, signified "Who are you?" etc. Signals by means of lighted fires, to announce the tidings of a beast killed, the approach of the enemy, etc., still remain in use among the Indians of America, not only in the north, but also in the south of the continent as far as Cape Horn. Signalling by means of objects visible from afar, of a more complicated kind, is in everyday use even among civilised peoples, forming the basis of optic telegraphy; and there exists for sailors of all nations a truly international language, by means of flags of different colours, the code and the dictionary of which are found on board of every ship bound on a long voyage.

Among *acoustic signals,* apart from conventional cries and sounds of instruments, we must note two kinds of language of a quite special character. There is, firstly, the *whistle language,* which by means of whistles more or less loud, succeeding in a certain order and produced simply by the mouth, sometimes by introducing into it two fingers, enables a conversation to be held at a distance.

This language has attained a high degree of perfection in

Portuguese, employed in the ports of the Far East; the "whalers' language," a mixture of Hawaiian, Chinese, English, Chukchi, Japanese, etc., which is heard in the north of the Pacific Ocean; the *Foky-Foky* of Guiana, etc.

the Canary Islands,[1] but is also known in other parts of the globe (among the Berbers of Tunis, for instance). This language, however, must not be confounded with conventional signals, always the same, given by the whistle for commands in the navy, for example. The other mode of communicating at a distance, a highly developed one, is the *drum language* of the Dualas and other Bantu Negroes of the Cameroons, the Gallas, the Papuans, etc. With simply a drum they succeed, by varying the number and the order of the beats, in forming a veritable language of two hundred to three hundred words, very complicated and difficult to learn.[2]

Writing.—The idea of communicating his thought graphically, in time and in space, to his fellow, must have come to man from the origin of civilisation; but through what stages must it have passed before becoming embodied in a system at once so simple and ingenious as that of alphabetic writing! Before inventing phonetic writing in general, man must have passed through the period of ideographic writing, and this is already an advance on another and prior method of representing and communicating thought, a method much more simple, which may be called in a general way *the use of symbolic objects and mnemonic marks.* As typical of this use of symbolic objects we may mention the messages of the Malays of Sumatra, which are formed of packets containing different objects: small quantities of salt, pepper, betel, etc., having respectively the signification of love, hate, jealousy, etc. According to the quantity and arrangement of the objects in the packet the message serves to express such or such a feeling. This system attains its perfection in the *Wampums* of the Red Indians. These are either chaplets of beads of different colours fashioned from shells (Fig. 83, 7), also used as money, or embroideries made with the same beads on long ribbons forming kinds of belts, which have

[1] Lajard, *Bull. Soc. Anthr. Paris*, 1891, p. 469, and 1892, p. 23.

[2] M. Buchner, *Kamerun*, Leipzig, 1887; Andree, *Verh. Berl. Ges. Anthr.*, 1888, p. 411; Betz, *Mitth. Forschungsreisenden deut. Schutzgeb.*, vol. xi., part 1, 1898.

the value of diplomatic documents to the Indians.[1] The staff-messages in use among the Melanesians, the Niam-Niams, the Ashantis, and the peasants of Lusatia and Silesia, etc., have the same signification. This is often a sort of passport or a summons; the form of the staff, as well as the particular marks which it bears, are so many signs to make known the commands of the chief, or of the mayor, the order of the day for the assembly, etc.

The notches which these staffs sometimes bear form a connecting link with the mnemonic marks which the less civilised peoples have the habit of making on trees, on bits of bark, or pieces of wood. It is the first step towards writing properly so called. Little horn tablets bearing notches have been found in the sepulchral caverns of the quaternary period at Aurignac (Dordogne). Even still the Eskimo, the Yakuts, the Ostiaks, the Macusis of Guiana, the Negroes of the west coast of Africa, the Laotians, the Melanesians, the Micronesians, commonly make use of them to keep their accounts, or note simple facts; they even continue in use among Europeans, as a survival of the old practice under the form of "baker's tallies," or words to denote letters (*Buchstabe*, little staff of "beechwood," in German), etc. Here, for instance, is the translation of what was conveyed by a notched tablet found by Harmand in a Laotian village attacked by a cholera epidemic (Fig. 27): Twelve days from now (12 notches to the right) every man who shall venture to penetrate into our enclosure will remain a prisoner, or pay us four buffaloes (4 notches lower down) or twelve ticals (pieces of money) as ransom (12 notches). On the other side, but doubtful, is the number of men (8), women (9), and children (11) of the village.[2]

An analogous mnemotechnical object is the *knotted cord*,

[1] See for details, H. Hale, "Four Huron Wampum Records," *Journ. Anthr. Inst.*, vol. xxvi., No. 3 (1887), and the interesting note of E. B. Tylor at the end of this paper. Hamy, *Galerie Americ. du Mus. Trocadéro*, Paris, 1897, Pl. I.

[2] Harmand, *Mém. Soc. Anthro.*, Paris, 2nd ser., vol. ii., 1875-85, p. 339.

which is met with among a great number of peoples, Ostiaks, Angola and Loango Negroes, Malagasi, Alfurus of the Celebes, etc. According to the number and colour of the cords, and the number of the knots which they bear, events past or to come are brought to mind, accounts of a bartering transaction kept, etc. Among the Micronesians of the Pelew Islands, when two individuals make an appointment with one another for a certain date, each makes on a cord as many knots as there remain days to run. Undoing a knot each day and coming to the last knot at the date of the appointment, they of necessity recall it. According to Chinese tradition, the first inhabitants of the banks of the Hoang-ho, before the invention of writing properly so called, also made use of little cords knotted to notched staffs as mnemonic instruments. Besides, is not our practice of tying a knot in our handkerchief to remember something a simple survival of these customs? The method of expressing certain events and certain ideas by means of knots made in different ways and variously arranged has been carried to the last degree of perfection in the case of the *quipus* of the ancient Peruvians. The *quipus* are cord rings to which are attached various little cords of different colours. On each of these little cords are found two or more knots variously formed. The Peruvian and Bolivian shepherds again make use of similar *quipus*, but much less complicated, to keep accounts. Let us also note in the same order of ideas the different marks of ownership, of family relationship, of tribeship (the *Totems* of the Red Indians, the *Tamgas* of the Kirghiz, etc.), which it is the custom to put on weapons, dwellings, animals, and even the bodies of the

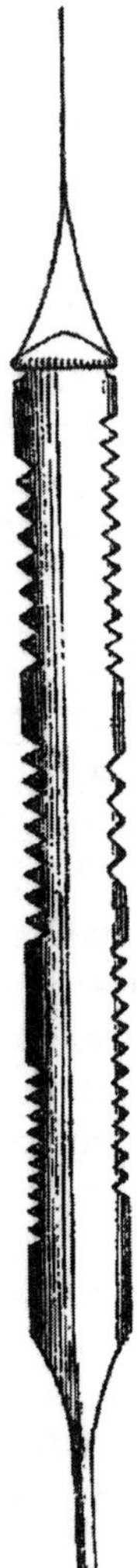

FIG. 27.—Writing by notches of the Laotians. (*After Harmand, Engraving of the Soc. Anthrop. Paris.*)

men (New Zealand). Hence are derived trade-marks and armorial bearings.

Lastly, are not the pebbles bearing strokes printed in red, the number of which varies from one to nine, and several other signs (Fig. 28), found by M. Piette[1] in the palæolithic stations of the south of France, at Mas-d'Azil (Ariège), also mnemonic objects? It has been asserted that they were playing dice, but the size of the pebbles is against this view.

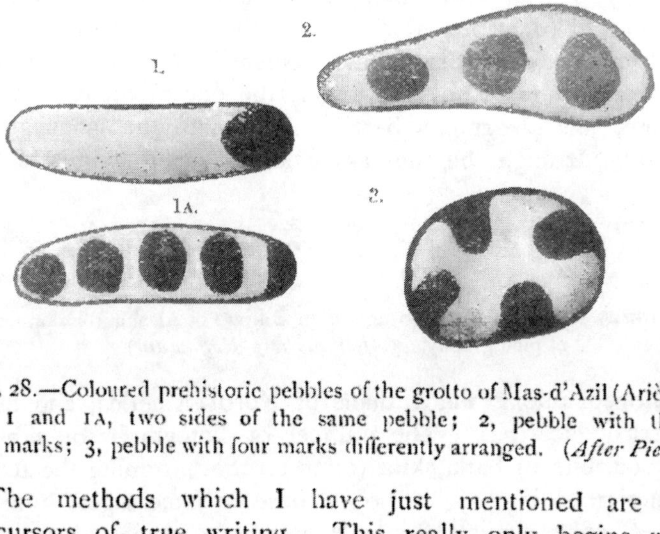

FIG. 28.—Coloured prehistoric pebbles of the grotto of Mas-d'Azil (Ariège). 1 and 1A, two sides of the same pebble; 2, pebble with three marks; 3, pebble with four marks differently arranged. (*After Piette.*)

The methods which I have just mentioned are the precursors of true writing. This really only begins with drawings expressing a sequence of ideas, with *pictography*. Imperfect attempts at pictography are found in the drawings of the Melanesians, representing different events of their life; in certain rock-pictures of the Bushmen (Fig. 64) and Australians. But already among the Eskimo, side by side with the simple representation of objects, certain figures are seen to appear denoting action or relations between objects: this is the beginning of ideographic writing. Here, for example, is the gist of a hunting story engraved by an Eskimo of Alaska on

[1] Piette, "Étude d'ethnogr. préhist.," *L'Anthropologie*, 1896, No. 4, p. 385. Article accompanied by an excellent folio atlas.

an ivory whip (Fig. 29). The first figure (1) represents the story-teller himself, his right hand making the gesture which indicates "I," and his left, turned in the direction in which he is going, means "go." Continuing our translation, we read the subsequent figures as follows:—(2) "in a boat" (paddle raised); (3) "sleep" (hand on the head) "*one* night" (the left hand shows a finger); (4) "(on) an island with a hut in the middle" (the little point); (5) "I going (farther);" (6) "(arrive at) an (other) isle inhabited" (without a point); (7) "spend (there) *two* nights;" (8) "hunt with harpoon;" (9) "a seal;" (10) "hunt with bow;" (11) "return in canoe with another person" (*two* oars directed *backward*); (12) "(to) the hut of the encampment." As is evident, this ideography bears a relation to the language of gesture. It might be thus assumed *a priori* that it is highly

FIG. 29.—Journal of the voyage of an Eskimo of Alaska. Example of pictography. (*After Mallery-Hoffmann.*)

developed among the Indians of North America, and as a matter of fact it is. The number of pictographs on tablets of wood, bits of bark, skins (often on those forming the tent), is enormous in every tribe. These are messages, hunting stories, songs, veritable annals embracing cycles of seventy, a hundred and more years (the latter bear the picturesque name of "winter tales").[1] We may judge of the degree of development of this art among the Indians by the following example of a petition (Fig. 30) presented in 1849 to the President of the United States by the Chippeway chiefs asking for the possession of certain small lakes (8) situated in the neighbourhood of Lake Superior (10), towards which

[1] S. Mallery, "Pictographs of the North American Indians," *Fourth Rep. Bur. Ethn.*, 1882-83, Washington, 1884. By the same, "Picture Writing of the American Indians," 1888-89, *Tenth Rep. Bur. Ethn.*, 1893.

leads a certain road (11). The petition is painted in symbolic colours (blue for water, white for the road, etc.) on a piece of bark. Figure 1 represents the principal petitioning chief, the totem of whose clan is an emblematic and ancestral animal (see Chapter VII.), the *crane;* the animals which follow are the totems of his co-petitioners. Their eyes are all connected with his to express unity of view (6), their hearts with his to express unity of feeling. The eye of the crane, symbol of the principal chief, is moreover the point of departure of two lines: one directed towards the President (claim) and the other towards the lakes (object of

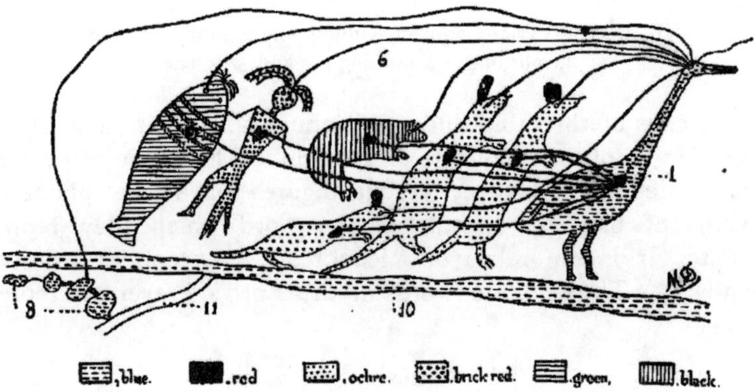

FIG. 30.—Petition of Chippeway Indians to the President of the United States. Example of pictography. (*After Schoolcraft.*)

claim). In the other pictographs the symbolism is carried yet further by the reproduction either of parts of the object for the object itself (head or footmarks for the whole animal, etc.), or by conventional objects for very complicated ideas. Thus the Dakotas indicate "a fight" by the simple drawing of two arrows directed against each other (Fig. 31, 1); the Ojibways represent morning by the rising sun (2), "nothing" by the gesture of a man stretching out his arms despairingly (3), and "to eat" by the gesture of the hand carried to the mouth (4), exactly as the ancient Mexicans and Egyptians have drawn it in their hieroglyphics, or again, the natives of Easter Island (Fig. 31, 5) in their rude attempt at ideographic writing on their "speech tablets."[1] The writing of these tablets is but a series of mnemonic signs which succeed each other in *boustrophedon* arrangement (see p. 142), being used for sacred and profane songs, or for magical rites.

From a similar pictographic method is derived the figurative writing in hieroglyphics of the Egyptians, the Chinese, the

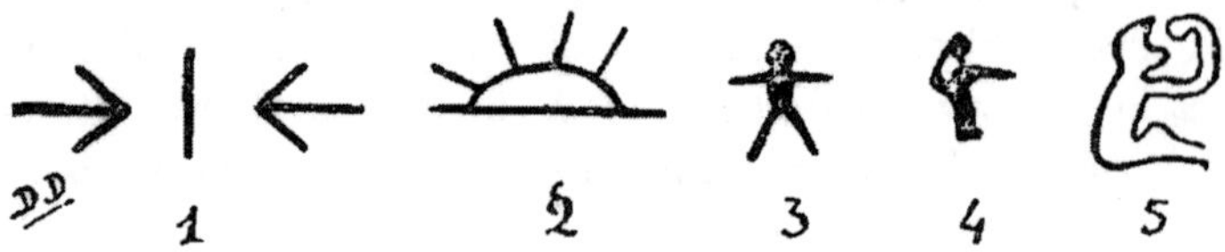

FIG. 31.—Various signs of symbolic pictography: 1, war; 2, morning; 3, nothing; 4 and 5, to eat.

Mexicans of the table-land of Anahuoc and their neighbours the Mayas of the peninsula of Yucatan. This mode of writing is a step in advance; certain figures have the phonetic value of the first syllable of the word which they represent. It is the rebus or "iconomatic" system, as Brinton calls it. Thus the first words of the Lord's Prayer are repre-

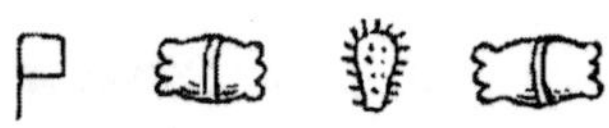

FIG. 32.—Paternoster in Mexican hieroglyphics.

sented in the Mexican code by the figures of a flag (Fig. 32) (*pantli*), a stone (*tetl*), the fruit of the Indian fig (*nochtli*), and another stone (*tetl*), the first syllables of which form pa-te-noch-te (Pater-noster).[2] The drawings not representing more than sounds, in this species of writing there is a tendency to simplify them, and thus we see the primitive figure being transformed into a conventional sign representing a sound, a

[1] Among the present natives of Easter Island there are only one or two who can decipher these tablets —W. Thomson Smith's *Rep. U.S. Nat. Mus.*, 1889, p. 513.

[2] Aubin, *Revue orientale et Americaine*, vol iii., p. 255.

syllable. This transformation may be traced in the Egyptian hieroglyphics as well as in the cuneiform writing of the ancient Assyrians. In Chinese writing the same phenomenon has taken place, as is evident from Fig. 33, which represents the ancient hieroglyphics side by side with the modern—morning, 1; the moon, 2; a mountain, 3; tree, 4; dog, 5; horse, 6; man, 7. These characters, though simplified, have kept their first signification corresponding to the figure. The association of these figures with the purely phonetic signs constitutes one of the principal resources of Chinese writing, which enables homophonic words,[1] etc., to be distinguished.

Chinese characters have been adopted by only one people with an agglutinative language, the Japanese, who along with

Fig. 33.—Ancient Chinese hieroglyphics (top line), Modern (bottom line).

these characters (*Mana*) use another method of writing (*Kana*), which is syllabic. The Egyptians, speaking an inflectional language, had, on the contrary, to abandon hieroglyphic writing at an early period in order to pass on to syllabic

[1] The two hundred and fourteen "keys" or hieroglyphics comparable with the hieratic characters of Egypt—that is to say, ideograms representing categories of objects or symbolising general ideas—joined to a thousand phonetic signs, suffice by their combinations to convey a definite sense to the series of homophonous hieroglyphics forming the forty-four thousand characters of Chinese handwriting. Thus the word or syllable *pa* signifies banana, war-chariot, scar, cry, etc. To distinguish the various acceptations of the word, there must be joined to the phonetic sign *pa* (derived from a word the proper sense of which has long been obliterated) the key of plants, or that of iron, of diseases, of the mouth, according to the sense which it is desired to give to it. The monosyllabic structure of Chinese lends itself admirably to this hieroglyphic writing.

writing and running characters (hieratic and demotic). It is supposed that from the Egyptian (hieroglyphic and hieratic) writing was derived the alphabet styled the Phœnician, the prototype of most of the alphabets of the world.[1]

The *direction* of the lines in writing is especially determined by the nature of the materials written upon. As long as it is a question of tracing on rocks, monuments, etc., there is no dominant direction, and the signs are disposed, as in the pictograph, at hazard, in any direction whatever. Even the ancient Greeks wrote sometimes from right to left, sometimes from left to right, sometimes in "boustrophedon"—that is to say, alternately, in both directions, as oxen walk during ploughing.

But from the time people began to write on palm leaves, on bits of bark, on tablets, papyrus, paper, it has been found necessary to choose a uniform direction.

The brush of the Chinese determined the direction downwards and from right to left, as for painting. The ancient Syriac *estranghelo* was also written in the same way, but from left to right; this direction still persists in Mongol writing, which is derived from it, while Arabic had transformed it into horizontal writing from right to left. And to-day certain peoples, for instance the Somalis, yet write Arabic downwards, and read it from right to left, turning over the leaf at 90°. Writing from right to left may have been favoured by the sacred custom of the Arabs placing themselves with their face to the east, the light coming from the right; besides, contrary to what takes place with us, in Arabic writing the paper must be made to move from left to right with the left hand, while the right hand, which writes, remains motionless.[2]

[1] The discovery by A. J. Evans of a special syllabic writing in the island of Crete leads one to conjecture, on the contrary, that it was from this unfortunate island that the first alphabet set out. This writing, more ancient than the Phœnician characters, is a direct derivative of pictography; it is found again at Cyprus and in Asia Minor at the epoch of the Ægean civilisation.—A. J. Evans, *Rep. Brit. Ass.*, 1896, p. 914.

[2] C. Vogt, "L'Écriture, etc.," *Rev. Scient.*, 2nd half-year, p. 1221. Paris, 1880.

The propagation of the different methods of ancient and modern writing and their adoption by different peoples, are closely bound up with the religion and progress in civilisation of these peoples. Thus the Mussulman world has adopted the Arabic writing; the Buddhists of the north, without distinction of race, hold in great esteem the sacred Thibetan characters, whilst those of the south venerate the Pali writing. The Mongol and Manchu alphabets are remains of the Uighuro-Nestorian influence and of the Syriac writing in Central Asia, as the Javanese alphabet is the remains of the civilising domination of the Hindus in Java. With the expansion of European colonisation the characters of the Latin alphabet become more and more prevalent; in Europe even, they tend to relegate to the second place the other characters (gothic, cyrilic, etc.). At the same time, new modes of writing are coming to the front, the telegraphic alphabet, stenography, precursors of a writing of the future, universal, international, simple, and rapid.

CHAPTER V.

II.—SOCIOLOGICAL CHARACTERS.

I. MATERIAL LIFE: *Alimentation:* Geophagy—Anthropophagy—Preparation of foods—Fire—Pottery—Grinding of corn—Stimulants and narcotics—*Habitation:* Two primitive types of dwellings—Permanent dwelling (hut)—Removable dwelling (tent)—Difference of origin of the materials employed in the two types—Villages—Furniture—Heating and lighting—*Clothing:* Nakedness and modesty—Ornament precedes dress—Head-dress—Ethnic mutilations—Tattooing—Girdle, necklace, and garland the origin of all dress—Manufacture of garments—Spinning and weaving—*Means of existence:* tools of primitive industry—Hunting—Fishing—Agriculture—Domestication and rearing of animals

I. MATERIAL LIFE.

Alimentation.—The first and most imperious preoccupation of man at all times is the search for food. It is therefore natural that we should begin our brief account of sociological characters with those relating to this preoccupation.

In tropical countries man finds in nature without effort edible plants in sufficient quantity for his support. It is said that in the island of Ceram a single sago-tree will yield what will nourish a man for a whole year.

In temperate countries there are also not wanting vegetable species which, with only slight effort on man's part, produce nutritive substances. The animal world also supplies everywhere a great variety of species suitable for food. These, for the most part, belong to the division of vertebrates or molluscs; however, certain of the arthropods (crustaceans, inseets, etc.), echinoderms (sea-urchins), nay, even worms (large earthworms of China, Tonkin, and Melanesia), also furnish their contingent to human gluttony.

The mineral kingdom contributes only salt, which, however, is unknown to certain tribes, as, for example, the Veddahs (Sarazin), the Somalis (Lapicque), etc. Besides, according to Bunge,[1] peoples whose food is almost exclusively animal (as is the case of the Veddahs, Eskimo, etc.) never eat salt, while those whose chief food is of vegetable origin experience an irresistible need for this condiment, probably because of the insufficiency of mineral substances in plants.

Perhaps also to this need of supplying the deficiency of mineral substances (calcareous or alkaline salts) is due the habit of eating certain earthy substances—kaolin, clay, limestone. *Geophagy* has, in fact, been observed in all parts of the world: in Senegal (the earth called "konak"), in Persia (argillaceous earth from Nichapur and the saline steppes of Kirman, composed of carbonate of magnesia and chalk),[2] and especially in the Asiatic archipelago, in India, and South America. In the markets of Java are sold little squares or figures in baked clay ("ampo" in Javanese) which are much valued, especially by pregnant women.[3] In Calcutta are sold similar products, and in several towns of Peru hawkers offer for sale little figures in edible earth. The Indians of Bolivia eat a white clay, a kind of kaolin called "pasa."[4] The Whites settled in South America are likewise addicted to geophagy. Women assert that the eating of earth gives a delicate complexion to the face. The same custom has also been pointed out among women in several countries of Europe, more especially in Spain, where the sandy clay which is

[1] Bunge, *Lehrbuch physiol. Chemie*, 2nd ed., p. 110, Leipzig, 1896.

[2] Goebel, *Bull. Ac. Sc. St. Petersb.*, vol. v. (1861), p. 397, and Schmidt, *ibid.*, vol. xvi. (1871), p. 203.

[3] Wilken, *Vergelijk. Volkenk. v. Ned Ind.*, p. 89, Leyden, 1893; *Science et Nature*, Paris, 1885, 1st half-year, p. 393.

[4] T. Gautier, "Sur une certaine argile blanche, etc.," *Actes de la Soc. Scient. du Chili*, vol. v. (1895), pt. 1 to 3, Santiago, 1895.

used for making the "alcarrazas" is especially in vogue as an edible earth.[1]

We must now pass on to speak of another food—human flesh. *Anthropophagy* is much less general than is usually believed. Many peoples have been wrongly accused of this crime against humanity by travellers who have had neither the time nor the means necessary to verify the fact, and by writers who here formed a hasty generalisation from isolated facts.[2]

Cannibalism has also been too hastily inferred from the observation of facts like "head-hunting," or the practice of adorning houses with human skulls and bones. As with human sacrifices, these are perhaps survivals of ancient cannibalism, but not proofs of its existence at the present time.

Besides, it must be noted that most of the statements of authors have reference to bygone times, which would lead us to suppose that anthropophagy is a custom tending to disappear among all peoples, even among those who have not been converted to one of the religions whose dogmas condemn this practice (Christianity, Buddhism, worship of Riamba in Africa,[3] Islamism, etc.).

It appears from the very conscientious work of P. Bergemann,[4] that actually the only regions of the world where anthropophagy has been really proved to exist are Oceania (including the Asiatic Archipelago), Central Africa, and Southern America.

The Battas of Sumatra, the natives of the Solomon Islands, of New Britain, and of certain islands of the New Hebrides, as well as a large number of Australian tribes, are known as

[1] Hellwald, *Ethnogr. Rosselsprünge*, p. 168, Leipzig, 1891.

[2] Thus, merely from a phrase heard from the lips of a Fuegian boy by Byron, and reproduced in the *Voyage of the Beagle* by Darwin, the Fuegians have until the present time been accused of cannibalism, and yet no observer living months and years among these savages has been able to verify the existence of this custom, in spite of all efforts to discover it.

[3] Wissmann, *Im Inneren Afrikas*, p. 152, Leipzig, 1888.

[4] P. Bergemann, *Verbreitung d. Anthropoph.*, Breslau, 1893.

incorrigible cannibals. We can speak less confidently as to the other inhabitants of Oceania. Dyaks, Fijians, New Caledonians, Karons of New Guinea, seem to have abandoned cannibalism. In South America positive facts abound concerning the anthropophagy of the Arovaques and certain Indians of Columbia, the Botocudos and some other Brazilian tribes; but for the rest of the continent they resolve themselves into the statements of ancient travellers or to the report of survivals. On the other hand, Central Africa appears to be the chief seat of anthropophagy. It is of frequent occurrence among the Niam-Niams, the Monbuttus, the Bandziris, and other tribes of the River Ubangi, as well as among the tribes of the Congo basin, the Basangos, the Manyuema, the tribes of Kassai, etc. We have likewise genuine proofs enough for the Fans of French Congo and certain tribes of the Benguelas. In general, cannibalism appears to be unknown in Africa beyond the tenth degree of latitude to the north and south of the Equator.

Cannibalism is practised for three reasons: necessity, gluttony, superstition.

Necessary Anthropophagy may take place in consequence of the want of animal food, as in Australia, or in consequence of accidental circumstances (shipwreck, famine), as it may occur even among civilised peoples; but this kind of cannibalism is as rare as that which is attributable to *gluttony*. It is said, however, that the Melanesians of the Solomon Islands, the New Hebrides, and New Britain hunt man merely to satisfy their taste for human flesh. The Niam-Niams pursue the same kind of sport not only for the flesh, but for the human fat which they utilise for lighting purposes. Various tribes of the Ubangi buy slaves or capture men separated from their fellows in order to fatten them up and eat them afterwards; sometimes, to improve the flavour of this kind of meat, the carcasses are left to soak in water; similar facts have been observed among the Manyuema. However that may be, the majority of cases of cannibalism may be explained by *superstitious beliefs*. There is especially a belief in the possibility of appropriating the virtues and the qualities of a man by eating the whole or certain portions of his body—the heart, the eyes, the liver. Sometimes drinking the blood of the victim is regarded as sufficient.[1]

Of the three causes which I have just enumerated the first two are probably the remains of downright anthropophagy—that is to say, of the habit of eating one's relatives and especially one's offspring just the same as any other flesh, as it exists among many animals. The Australians, for example, are known to eat their children which they have killed for other reasons (restriction of progeny).

R. S. Steinmetz[2] has thought it possible to bring together all these cases of anthropophagy under the name of "endocannibalism," or the practice of eating parents and relatives. He mentions a great number of tribes in which this practice exists alone or combined with "exocannibalism," that is to say the habit of eating the flesh of strangers. This second sort of cannibalism, much more widely diffused, however, than endocannibalism, is alone amenable to moral, religious, or social ideas, while endocannibalism is but the remains of a natural state of primitive man, the residue of instincts which still stirred his soul at the period when he wandered solitary through the virgin forests without realising the possibility of forming any social group whatever.[3]

Ritual anthropophagy persists for a considerable length of time, and may accord with a relatively developed civilisation. The Battas, the Monbuttus, the Niam-Niams, are tribes

[1] Among the Kalebus of Central Africa (between Lomami and Lukassi, 6° lat. S.) the whole of the body is eaten with the exception of the fingers, which are left untouched from a fear of disease "which retires to them as the last place of refuge" (Wissmann).

[2] R. S. Steinmetz, "Endocannibalismus," *Mittheilungen der Anthropol. Gesel. in Wien*, vol. xxvi. (xvi.), pt. 1-2, 1896.

[3] It seems to me that Steinmetz's theory encounters a great difficulty in the fact that anthropophagous peoples (for example, certain Australian tribes) avoid eating relatives, with the exception of infants; the clans exchange one with another the bodies of their dead in order that each may only eat individuals unrelated to it.

almost half civilised; one has a well-developed method of writing and a style of ornament, the others have a fairly advanced social organisation. As a survival, anthropophagy manifests itself not only in the practice of cutting off the heads (Dyaks) in human sacrifices, but also in a multitude of religious or superstitious practices among a great number of even civilised peoples. The belief in the supposed curative properties of human flesh, especially that of executed criminals, is still in full force in China,[1] and was so in Europe in ancient times and in the Middle Ages; the Salic law forbade the magical practices associated with anthropophagy. To drink from the skull of an enemy was a very widespread custom in Asia and Europe, and even until the beginning of this century the remains of the skull of a hanged criminal figured among the remedies in the pharmacopœias of Central Europe.

Preparation of Foods.—There is no people on earth which eats all its food quite raw, without having subjected it to previous *preparation.* Some few northern tribes, the Eskimo, the Chukchi, eat, it is true, reindeer's flesh and fish quite raw, but they cut these up, prepare dried provisions from them, and moreover they cook their vegetable food.

Food is prepared by cutting it into pieces, subjecting it to a fermentation, moistening it, triturating it, and especially by exposing it to the action of fire.

No tribe exists, even at the bottom of the scale of civilisation, which is not to-day acquainted with the *use of fire*, and as far back as we can go into prehistoric times we find material traces of the employment of fire (cinders, charcoal, pieces of worn-out pyrites, cracked flint, etc.). However, the *preservation* of fire produced by the natural forces (conflagrations, lightning, volcanoes, etc.) must have preceded the *production* of fire (Broca, Von den Steinen). Most of the forces of nature transformable into heat—light, electricity, motion, and chemical affinity—have been turned to account by man in the production of fire with more or less success. Kindling flame by concentrat-

[1] Schlegel, "Festgabe Bastians" (suppl. No. to vol. ix. of *Interna'. Archiv. für Ethnogr.*, 1896).

ing the solar light with bi-convex glasses and mirrors, mentioned from the remotest antiquity, could never have become general. It is the same with electricity. On the other hand, motion and chemical affinity have been at all times, and still are, pre-eminently the two productive forces of fire. Motion is utilised in three different ways: by the friction of two pieces of wood, by the striking together of two pieces of certain mineral substances, or by pneumatic compression. The last method is little used; it has been observed among the Dyaks of Borneo and in Burma. It is based on the principle of the *pneumatic tinder-box* of our scientific demonstration rooms. But the two other modes of utilising motion are still in general use among all savage peoples.[1]

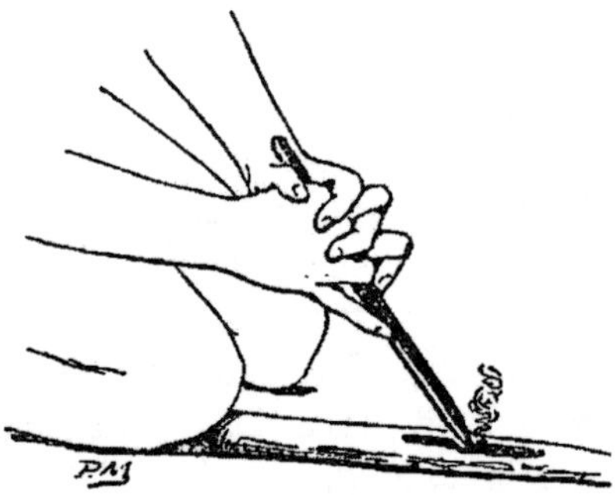

FIG. 34.—Method of fire-making by rubbing. (*After Hough.*)

A little red-hot ember capable of setting fire to certain substances (tinder, down, dry grass, etc.) may be obtained either by rubbing together two pieces of wood, or by sawing one across the other, or by turning the end of one in a little hole made in the other. Hence, three ways of making fire by friction, each having a well-defined geographical area. The first way (simple rubbing), the most primitive and the least easy, is employed especially in Oceania. It consists in rubbing a little stick of hard wood, bending it downward, against a log of soft wood held between the knees (Fig. 34). A little channel is thus hollowed out of the log, and in the end the operator succeeds in obtaining incandescent particles of pulverised wood, which gather at the bottom of the channel. He has only to throw in a little dry grass or tinder and to blow upon it to obtain the flame.

[1] W. Hough, "The Methods of Fire-making," *Report of the U.S. National Museum for 1890*, p. 95. Washington, 1891.

The *sawing* method (Fig. 35) is employed by the Malays and by some Australian tribes, as well as in Burma and India. A piece of bamboo split longitudinally is sawn with the cutting edge of another piece of bamboo until the sawdust becomes hot and sets fire to the tinder on which it falls.

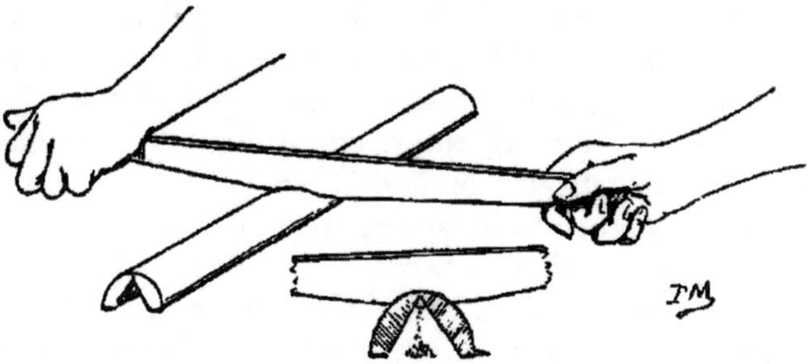

FIG. 35.—Method of fire-making by sawing. (*After Hough.*)

The *twirling* or *rotatory* method (Fig. 36), which consists in turning the end of a fragment of wood supported on the surface of another fragment, is the most generally used. It is met with among Negroes, the Indians of North and South America, the Chukchi, in certain regions of India, etc. The most primitive apparatus consists of a log or board of soft wood, held horizontally with the feet, on which is placed the blunted point of a cylindrical stick of hard wood. Twirling the stick rapidly between the hands in both directions, a little hole is hollowed and the dust of the wood which gathers around the point becomes incandescent. It is thus that some tribes of Zulus and of Australians, the Ainus, etc., make fire.

FIG. 36.—Method of fire-making by twirling among the Kafirs. (*After Wood.*)

But to this primitive apparatus important improvements are made among other populations, especially among the Redskins and the Eskimo. The hole in a horizontal board is hollowed out beforehand, then a communication is made between this hole and one of the vertical faces of the board by a channel through which escapes to the outside the woody powder produced by rubbing, in the form of little incandescent cylinders, which falls on the tinder. As to the upright stick, different contrivances are fitted to it to render its motion more rapid and more regular. Thus the Eskimo wind round it a cord which is drawn alternately in both directions;[1] in this case the upper end of the stick is held by an assistant or by the operator himself. They apply also to these apparatus a mouth-drill, etc.

The second method of obtaining fire, that of *striking together* two pieces of iron pyrites or two pieces of flint, or flint against pyrites, must, like the first, have been known from the most remote period. To-day it is only employed by some few backward tribes—Fuegians, Eskimo, Aleuts. With the knowledge of iron, which replaced pyrites, the true "flint and steel" was invented; it very quickly superseded in Europe and Asia the production of fire by friction, as, in its turn, it has been superseded by apparatus utilising the chemical affinity of different bodies (matches).

But the old processes survive in traditions, in religion. Thus the present Brahmins of India obtain fire for religious ceremonies by the friction of two sticks, in front of shops where English matches are sold; it is still by friction that the Indians of America, amply provided with matches, procure fire for the sacred festivals. Even in Europe, in Great Britain, and in Sweden, at the beginning of this century the fire intended for superstitious uses (to preserve animals and people against contagious diseases) was kindled by rubbing together two pieces of wood. This practice was forbidden by a decree, dating from the end of last century, in the same district of Jönköping whence to-day are sent forth by millions the famous Swedish matches.[2]

[1] An apparatus of this sort was in use half a century ago among Polish peasants (*Globus*, vol. lix., 1891, p. 388).

[2] Tylor, *Anthropology*, p. 262.

The long and difficult processes of obtaining fire compel savage tribes to preserve it as one of the most precious things. Almost everywhere it is to women that the care is committed. Among the Australians, women who let the fire go out are punished almost as severely as were the Roman vestals of old. The Papuans of Astrolabe Bay (New Guinea) prefer to go several leagues in search of fire to a neighbouring tribe than to light another (Miklukho-Maclay). The preparation of "new fire" among a great number of tribes, especially in America and Oceania, is celebrated with festivals and religious ceremonies.[1]

Cooking.—Fire, once discovered, heat, light, and at the same time the means of rendering a great variety of foods more digestible, were artificially assured to man. But it is somewhat difficult to roast a piece of meat in the fire, especially when there is not a metal skewer at hand, as was the case with primitive man. So, at an early stage, he tried to find some method of cooking his food, especially fruits. He heated stones in the open fire, and with these stones he cooked his meat and vegetables. The process is still in use to-day among tribes unacquainted with pottery. Thus the Polynesians before their "civilisation" by Europeans proceeded in the following way to cook their food. Stones heated in the fire were put at the bottom of a hole dug in the ground; upon these stones was spread a layer of leaves, on which were placed the fruit of the bread-tree, then a fresh layer of leaves and other heated stones; care being taken to cover the whole with leaves and earth. In half-an-hour a delicious dish was drawn out of the hole.[2]

Among most savage Indonesians food is cooked in bamboo vessels filled with water, in which heated stones have been previously plunged. This method of cooking with stones is also in use at the two extreme points of America, among the

[1] A certain moderation must nevertheless be observed in the explanation of myths and practices in which fire is concerned. See on this subject an intelligent though somewhat exaggerated critique by E. Veckenstedt, "Das wilde, heilige und Gebrauchsfeuer," *Zeitschr. für Naturwiss.*, vol. lxvi., p. 191, Leipzig, 1893.

[2] O. Mason, *Origins of Invention*, p. 158, London, 1895

Indians of Alaska and the Fuegians. It is even used in Europe among the Serbian and Albanian mountaineers.

Pottery.—But real cooking, even of the simplest sort, is only possible with the existence of *pottery*, the manufacture of which must have followed closely on the discovery of a method of obtaining fire, for no example is known of unbaked pottery.

There are still peoples unacquainted with this art, such as the Australians and the Fuegians, but the absence of it is not always the sign of an inferior degree of civilisation, as we may see in the Polynesians before the arrival of Europeans, and also

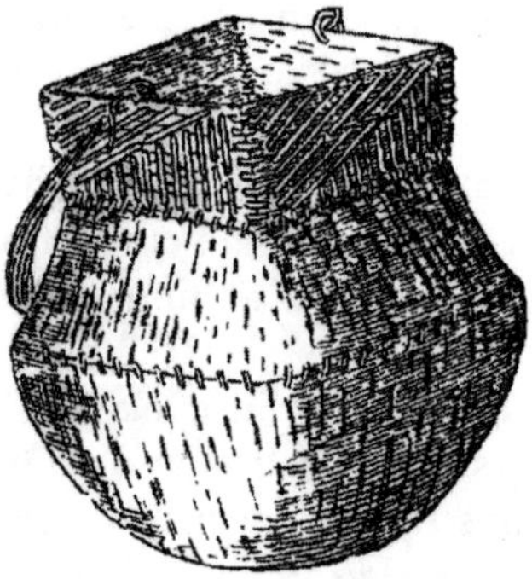

FIG. 37.—Bark vessel, used by Iroquois Indians. (*After Cushing.*)

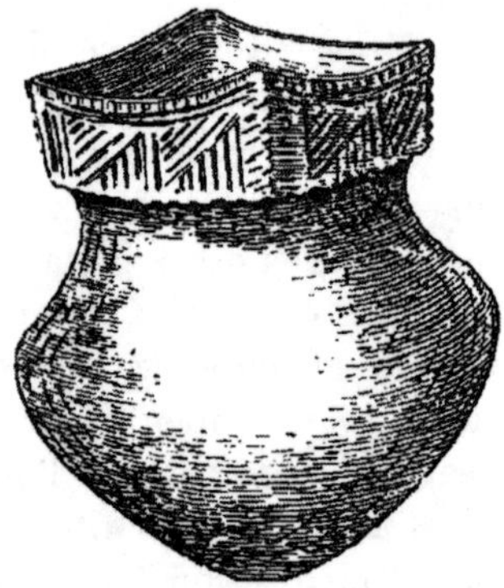

FIG. 38.—Type of Iroquois earthen vessel, moulded on the bark vase of Fig. 37. (*After Cushing.*)

the present Mongols, whose cooking utensils consist of iron, wooden, and leather vessels, for pottery which easily breaks would be an encumbrance in nomadic life.

The most primitive pottery is made without the potter's wheel. In its manufacture we may admit, with Otis Mason,[1] three special methods of working. *Modelling* by hand; *moulding* to an exterior or interior mould, usually a basket or other object of wicker-work, which burns away afterwards in the baking (Figs. 37 and 38); and lastly, a method of proceeding which may be called *coiling* in clay. Long strings of clay are

[1] Otis Mason, *loc. cit.*, p. 158.

taken and rolled so as to form a cone or a cylinder, or any other form of the future pot, then the sides are made even.

The Zuñi Indians of New Mexico begin this work in a little basket-dish (Fig. 39), which shows the connection of this method with that of moulding, whilst the Wolofs, whom I have seen working in the same way, as well as the Kafirs (Fig. 135, to the left), have only as a base to work upon a clay disc or a wooden porringer, moulding being unknown to them. But in both cases this mode of manufacture is already a step towards pottery formed by the wheel, only instead of the clay it is the hand of the workman which turns, naturally much more

FIG. 39.—Making of pottery without wheel by the Zuñi Indians (coiling method). (*After Cushing.*)

slowly. Besides, the primitive wheel, that is to say, a disc or a board set in motion by the hand, sometimes without a pivot, as still seen in China, does not revolve with the dizzy speed of the true wheel, the construction of which is an adaptation of the general processes of the transmission of forces by means of levers and wheels.

In regard to pottery it must be noted that its manufacture is left almost exclusively to women among most of the tribes of America, while it is entrusted without distinction to men and women in Africa.

Grinding of Corn.—We need not dwell on the means of

preparing food independently of the action of fire (milk and its products, pemmican, etc.); they vary infinitely. Let us deal briefly, however, with the method of preparing grain. Many peoples are unacquainted with flour: they eat the grain

FIG. 40.—Primitive harvest, the women (Shoshones) gathering wild grain. (*After Powell.*)

either roasted or cooked, as we do still the most anciently known perhaps of the graminaceæ, rice and millet. In the primitive state of agriculture certain tribes of North America combined in one single operation the threshing, winnowing, and roasting of grain. After being triturated between the hands, the grain is thrown into a basket-dish (Fig. 40) in which are red-hot stones; the straw burns, the husk comes off and partly burns too, whilst the grain is being roasted.

From the time when some intelligent man perceived when crushing a grain of corn, perhaps by chance, between two stones, that flour might supply a more delicate food than roasted grain, the art of the miller was discovered. There are three ways of preparing flour: pounding in a mortar, trituration on a flat surface, and true grinding by means of a mill turned by the hand or other motor power—animals, water, wind, steam.

The mortar, used by a great number of savage or half-civilised tribes to crush not only grain but also the roots of starchy plants, cassava, yam, etc., must have been known for a very long time. Its most primitive form is met with among the Indians of North America—a block of granite or sandstone in which a cavity has been made, with a piece of porous rock, almost cylindrical, for the pestle. In Africa and Oceania the mortar and pestle are of wood. Almost everywhere the pounding is done by women. The rudest hand-mills, such as are met with among the Arabs, the Kabyles, the Bushmen, are made of a round stone pierced in the centre, turned on another stone by means of a handle passing through the hole. Incisions on the triturating surface of the millstone is not found as yet in these primitive machines.

The preservation of food is known to a great number of savage and half-civilised tribes. The Eskimo preserve their meat by means of cold, many fisher peoples resort to salting, the art of preparing true pemmican by enclosing the food in a mass of grease or honey is known to the Veddahs of Ceylon, to Negroes, etc.

Stimulants.—Among most savage peoples special *fermented beverages* are found: "koumiss," or fermented mare's milk, among the Turco-Mongols; bamboo beer among the Moïs of French Indo-China; millet or eleusine beer among the Negroes; sago-juice wine among the populations of the coast of the Indian Ocean—Dravidians (Fig. 81), Indonesians, Malays; "pulque," derived from the juice of the agave, among the Mexicans of the high table-lands. I must lastly mention "kava," the national beverage of the Polynesians, concocted from the juice of the leaves of a pepper-plant (*Piper methysticum*), which is made to ferment by means of the ptyalin of the saliva, these leaves being previously chewed in company, each spitting out his "quid" into the common dish.

The distillation of fermented liquids for the purpose of obtaining alcohol is known to most semi-civilised peoples. We need but instance the "arka" of the Turco-Mongols derived from "koumiss," the arrack of the Chinese and Japanese, etc.

Among the stimulants, tonics, narcotics, drugs, etc., other than fermented beverages, and tea, coffee, and chocolate of international fame, must be mentioned the kola nut used as a stimulant on a large scale in the whole of Western Africa; the "maté" (*Ilex paraguayensis*) taking the place of tea in a large portion of South America; different roots and certain fish (like the *Fistularia serrata* of Java)[1] used by way of aphrodisiacs; lastly, the "coca" of the Peruvians and Bolivians (*Erithroxylon coca*), the leaves of which taken as an infusion plunge you, says Mantegazza, in the most delicious dreams, while pulverised and chewed with lime they only act as a stimulant. It is possible that the chewing of *betel* or *siri*, that is to say, areca palm nut mixed with shell lime and wrapped in a leaf of betel (*Chavica betle*), produce the same effect; but this habit appears to be induced by hygienic considerations in regard to the mouth. However that may be, the chewing of betel nut, inseparable from Malaysian civilisation, always has a tendency to blacken the teeth of peoples addicted to it.[2]

[1] *Internation. Arch. für Ethnographie*, vol. ix., pt. 3, Leyden, 1896.

[2] *Revue scientifique*, 1892, 1st half-year, p. 145. It is also from hygienic considerations in regard to the mouth that many peoples of India and the Negroes of Senegal chew continually the dried roots of different plants reputed antiseptic. In Siberia and in the east of Russia the chewing of pine resin ("séra") has probably the same origin. The habit of chewing tobacco is only common among European sailors and among the Javanese and Chukchi.

The practice of tobacco smoking, universal at the present day, only spread into Europe in the sixteenth century. In the primitive home of this plant, America, the Indians smoke moderately, although the pipe with them plays a ceremonial part ("the calumet of peace," etc.). The pipe, which in Europe is yielding place to the cigar, is still held in great honour throughout the whole of Asia, where ethnographers point out more than 150 ethnic varieties of this object, without counting the numerous forms of "narghile." The cigarette appears to be of Malay origin.[1] The habit of smoking opium, which so speedily becomes an invincible passion, tends at the present day to spread wherever Chinese influence penetrates: in Corea, Indo-China, etc.

The practice of smoking haschish, a product of Indian hemp (*Cannabis Indica*), is localised in Persia and Asia Minor; but it is found also among the Baluba Negroes of the Congo basin, who attach to it a great importance from the politico-religious point of view.

Not satisfied with eating, drinking, inhaling by the mouth, and chewing stimulants, man absorbs them too by the nose. The habit of taking a pinch of snuff, formerly the fashion in the best society of Europe, seems now to be relegated to the lower classes. But among several of the Bantu Negroes of Uganda, of the Cameroons, and the east coast of Africa, snuff-taking (introduced by Europeans?) is still in great honour, and Kafirs in high positions carry coquettishly very small snuff-boxes in the lobe of their ears. Instead of snuff, the Mura Indians of the Lower Amazon take "parica," a very stimulating powder, which is derived from the dry seeds of a vegetable called "Inga." The stuff is taken by two persons together, during the festival of the ripening of the Inga. One of these Indian braves puts the parica into a tube and puffs it into the nose of his companion.[2]

As Letourneau[3] judiciously observes, the chief motive for

[1] Hellwald, *Rosselsprünge*, etc., p. 206.

[2] H. Bates, *Naturalist on . . . Amazons*, vol. i., p. 331, London, 1863.

[3] Letourneau, *Sociologie*, p. 44, Paris, 1880.

the use of various drugs and stimulants all over the earth is the desire experienced by every human being to emancipate himself, if even for a moment, from the ordinary conditions of existence. He is only too happy to be able to find at pleasure, in the midst of the fatigues, the annoyances, and the miseries of daily life, a moment of forgetfulness, the semblance of refuge.

Habitation.—The natural shelters—caverns, overhanging rocks, holes in the ground, thick foliage, hollow trunks of trees, etc.—must have been utilised by primitive man as places of abode. But which of these shelters served as a model for the first artificial dwellings? Not the cavern, for even now it is made use of just as it is by civilised populations in China, Tunisia, Afghanistan, and even France, in the valley of the Cher. Besides, with the exception, perhaps, of the huts of the Eskimo, half underground and covered with a dome of ice blocks, constructions in mineral substances are scarcely found among savage peoples.[1] Substances of vegetable origin were those first utilised for fixed habitations (hut, etc.), and substances derived from animals for dwellings which could be carried.[2]

The *hut*, which is the prototype of the *fixed habitation*, is derived probably from the *screen* formed of a series of branches stuck in the ground, as one sees it still among the Australians. Sometimes this screen is constructed of large palm-leaves resting against crossed branches, as for example among the Veddahs of Ceylon, Andamanese, the Botocudos, and other Indians of Brazil. The leafy branches of these screens had but to be arranged in the form of a circle or in two parallel rows, their tops joined together, the interstices

[1] The beaten-earth and sun-dried clay structures of the Sudan, of Turkestan, and Mexico are of "secondary formation"; they are derived probably from the straw huts, as we shall see further on.

[2] We call every habitation "fixed" which has not been constructed with the view of being removed, however light and imperfect it be. Thus, the rude hut which the Fuegian abandons so readily is nevertheless a fixed habitation, whilst the tent of the Kirghiz, a much more complicated structure, and far more comfortable, must nevertheless be classed among movable habitations.

stopped up with grasses, moss, and bark, in order that the frail shelter might be transformed into a stronger dwelling, a better protection against the inclemencies of the weather. The form which this primitive dwelling was thus obliged to take depended then, before everything else, on the arrangement of the branches of the screen: if put in the form of a circle the hut became conical provided the branches used in its construction were rigid and but little spread out (Fuegians); hemispherical, cupola-shaped, if they were flexible and leafy

FIG. 41.—Hemispherical hut in straw of Zulu Kafirs. (*After Wood and other sources.*)

(Australians); if they were placed in two parallel rows the hut ook the form of a two-sided roof, flat (Indians of the Amazon), or convex (Todas), according to the materials.

Trying to secure themselves still better from the rain, the vind, and the sun, the first architects must have dug out the oil beneath the hut, as the Ainus, the Chukchi, the Kamthadales still do at the present time, and this may have uggested the idea, as Tylor says,[1] of extending the vertical

[1] E. B. Tylor, *Anthropology*, p. 281.

walls above the ground. The rushes, the little twigs, and the clods of potter's clay or grass which were used at first to stop

Fig. 42.—Hut and granary of the Ovampos (South Africa). *(After Wood.)*

up the holes, eventually formed the walls, and the ancient hut thus raised was transformed into a dwelling a little more comfortable, having *roof* and *walls*. This was probably the origin of the hive-shaped huts of the Zulu Kafirs (Fig. 41), and the cylindrical, conical-roofed huts of the Ovampos (Fig. 42), and the Gauls of the time of Cæsar. Straw entering into the composition of the roof, and sometimes even the body of these dwellings, they may be styled *straw huts* or *thatched huts*. As to the quadrangular huts, they are transformed in the same manner into those little houses so characteristic of the Muchikongos, of French Congo and the coast of Guinea.[1] Among the peoples inhabiting the shores of the Pacific and Indian Oceans, from the Kamtchadales and the Indians of the north-west of America to the Maoris and the natives of Madagascar, the quadrangular houses are erected on poles even when they are far from water. The materials of which they are constructed are bamboos, reeds, and palm-leaves.[2]

In order to give solidity to the straw and reed-built walls, it must have been necessary at an early period to plaster them over with potter's earth (Senegal, palafittes of the bronze age in Europe). In very dry countries it was seen that lumps of clay were able of themselves to form sufficiently solid walls, and this observation has led naturally enough to the making of sun-dried bricks, which were known to the Babylonians, to the Egyptians, and are still used to-day in the Sudan, in Turkestan, and Mexico.

Movable Habitations.—From the moment when the tired hunter of primitive times fell asleep beneath the skin of a wild beast spread out on two or three poles, and folded it up on the morrow to carry it away with him in his wanderings, the *tent* was invented. Skins continued to be the best material for its construction until the invention of felt and stuffs, plaited or woven of a sufficient breadth. Bark has only been used

[1] L. Hösel, "Die Rechteckige Schrägdachhütte Mittelafrikas," *Globus*, 1894, vol. xxvi., pp. 341, 360, and 378, with map.

[2] There are many other types of dwellings peculiar to different regions: he reed-built houses of Lob Nor (Eastern Turkestan), the Finnish houses lerived from semi-underground structures, the dwellings of the Caucasian nountaineers, etc.

exceptionally, in Siberia for example, and for summer tents only (Fig. 43). Like the hut, the tent may be circular, conical (Indians of North America), cupola-shaped (Kafirs), or quadrangular in the form of a prismatic roof (Thibetans, Gypsies). The last-mentioned of these forms has not been improved on, and the Arab tent of the present day, which is derived

FIG. 43.—Summer tent of Tunguz-Manegres, of birch-tree bark (exceptional type).

from it, differs from its prototype only in its dimensions and the awning set up at the entrance. On the other hand, the two circular forms have been improved on by the use of pieces of wattling instead of poles, and felt instead of skins. The tent has thus become a comfortable dwelling, the best suited to the life of half-civilised nomads, a real house with a roof, conical in the "Gher" of the Mongols (Fig. 44), almost hemispherical

FIG. 44.—"Gher" or tent of the Kalmuks of Astrakan, part being raised in order to show framework and interior. (*Photo. S. Sommier.*)

in the "Yourte" of the Kirghiz.[1] This dwelling of the nomads has even served as a model for the permanent wooden habitations of the tribes of the Yenisei or Altai. Their wooden house has a ground-plan of hexagonal or octagonal form, imitating the circular yourte or felt tent (Fig. 45), and it is only little by

FIG. 45.—Hexagonal house of non-roving Altaians, constructed in imitation of the felt tent of the nomads. (*After Yadrintsev.*)

little, under Russian influence, that it is transformed into a four-sided house.[2] The "mazankis" of the Teleuts of Siberia

[1] This tent has never, as a general rule, been placed among the Turco-Mongols on a waggon, to be carried from place to place, as authors have been pleased to affirm, from Rubruquis to our own day. The habit in question has only existed in some Nogaï tribes, and has only been practised in special circumstances (marriage, conveyance of women), the survival of which is found among the Tatars of Koundrov, near Astrakhan.

[2] Kharouzin, *Istoria*, etc. (*History of the Development of the Habitation among Turco-Mongol Nomads of Russia*), Moscow, 1896 (in Russian).

and the Little Russians with their walls of fascines plastered with clay and lime, are only imitations of wattled tents.

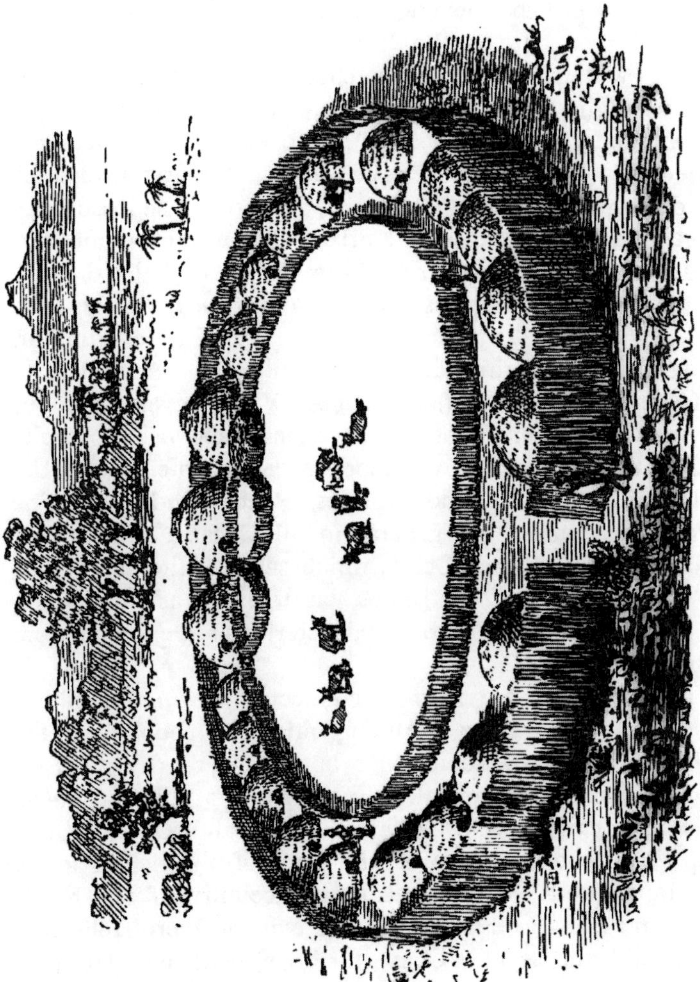

FIG. 46.—Kraal, or Kafir village, with defensive enclosure. (*Partly after Wood.*)

As social life becomes more complicated, there appear, side by side with the dwelling properly so called, other structures: granaries and storehouses, ordinarily built on wooden pillars (among the Malays and the Ainus), or on a clay stand (among the Negroes of the Sudan) or a wooden support (Fig. 42), to protect them against the attacks of wild beasts. Access to them, as to the houses on poles, is gained by primitive ladders, a series of notches in a tree-trunk. Other structures, light straw huts on trees, serve as refuges in case of attack and as posts of observation to watch the movements of enemies. The idea of defence was also the first motive for the grouping of houses into villages. In non-civilised countries almost always the villages and urban agglomerations are surrounded with palisades (Kraal of the Kafirs, Fig. 46), ditches, sometimes filled with traps and prickles (Laos), lastly, with walls. Watch-towers replace the airy posts of observation on trees (example: Lesghi village of the Caucasus). According to the forms of propriety (see Chapter VII.), several families may inhabit enormous houses in which each has a special apartment adjoining the common space in which dwell the non-married people (Nagas, Mossos, Pueblo Indians). The "communal houses," so general in all Oceania and among certain peoples of Indo-China, which serve at the same time as "bachelor's dens," as "clubs," as temples, as inns, represent the common rooms of phalansteries as separated from the private parts.

With habitations are naturally connected *furniture*, methods of *heating* and *lighting*. Among primitive peoples all the furniture consists of some skins and straw or dry grass for bed and seat. Mats are already a sign of a fairly advanced civilisation; carpets, seats, and beds come after (Figs. 44 and 120). The wooden pillow in the form of a bench is found from Japan and New Guinea to the country of the Niam-Niams and the Eastern Sudan, where it must probably have penetrated from Egypt. Chests for linen, plate, etc., are quite late inventions.

For heating purposes a fire in the middle of the hut was used in the first instance. The Fuegians burn enormous trees, which project from the hut and are brought forward into the fire as the end is consumed. The smoke issues by the open extremity of the hut. The Altaians, the Kamtchadales, the Tunguses, the Kalmuks, are content with a similar fire kept in the middle of the tent or wooden house (Figs. 44 and 45). Among the Russian peasants one may meet with houses, "koornaïa izba," having a stove, but not a chimney; the smoke issues by the windows and by an orifice in the roof. In Corea the smoke of the stove is carried under the planks; in China under a sort of clay bed (Kang). The mantelpiece, raised above the hearth, appears to be a European invention which preceded that of the true chimney, which latter appeared in the eleventh century. Among the Eskimo the seal oil, which burns in great lamps of earth dried in the sun, serves to give warmth and light at the same time.

Very finely made lamps have been described as existing among the Indians of North America. The Polynesians burn coco-nut oil in a half of the shell of the coco-nut itself, using the fibres which cover the fruit by way of wick. In Egypt, in Babylon, in Europe, lamps have been known from the earliest times.[1] But most primitive peoples are still content to burn fat pine-knots or resinous torches for lighting purposes. The Moïs-Lays of French Indo-China obtain light by means of little pieces of fir-wood burning aloft on a chandelier formed of a double metal fork.[2] This description may be applied word for word to the "loocheena" of the Russian peasants, the use of which has not disappeared at the present time. Moreover, the torch was much used in the whole of Europe side by side with closed and open lamps before the invention of the candle, the light of which grows dim to-day before the petroleum lamp even in China and Turkestan, and before the electric light among us.

[1] It is possible that in Western Europe a hard leaf of some plant folded in a certain way has served as a model for the lamps with wicks called Roman, to judge from certain actual forms.—Letourneau and Papillault, *Bull. Soc. Anthr. Paris*, 1896, p. 348. Vinchon, *ibid.*, p. 615.

[2] Neis, *Excursions et Reconnaissances*, Saigon, vol. x., p. 33, 1881.

Dress and Ornament.—To say that primitive man went about quite naked is almost a commonplace, but to say that nudity is not synonymous with savagery would appear a paradox to many. And yet nothing is more true. Among the peoples who know nothing of dress there are some quite savage, like the Fuegians, the Australians, the Botocudos, and others who have attained a certain degree of civilisation, like the Polynesians (before the arrival of Europeans) and the Niam-Niams. Let us remember, moreover, that the Greeks of classic antiquity only half covered their nakedness. It does not necessarily follow that the less clothes a people wears the more savage it is. It is a question of climate and social convention, entirely like the emotion of modesty, which is not at all something natural and innate in man. It is not met with among animals, and one could mention dozens of cases of peoples among whom the sentiment is entirely lacking. On the contrary, the fashion of covering the female genital organs, for example among different tribes of the Amazon,[1] and the male organs among the New Caledonians[2] or the New Hebrideans, is such as rather to attract attention to these parts than to hide them. The same thing may equally be said of the little ornamented aprons barely covering the genital organs which are worn by the Kafir women (Fig. 47), etc. Certain authors (Darwin, Westermarck) even think that ornament in general, that of the region of the abdomen in particular, was one of the most powerful means of sexual selection, by attracting attention to the genital organs. It is, rather, the garment which gives birth to the sentiment of modesty, and not modesty which gives birth to the garment. Among a people as civilised as the Japanese, men and women bathe together quite naked without any one being shocked. It was the same in Russia during the last century.

And yet, to prove how conventional all this sentiment of modesty is, it is only necessary to say that the Japanese

[1] Von den Steinen, *Unter d. Naturvölk, Zent. Brazil*, Berlin, 1894, p. 190.

[2] Glaumont, "Usages, etc.," *Rev. d'Ethnogr.*, Paris, 1888, p. 101.

FIG. 47.—Zulu girl with the three types of ornament: head dress, necklace, and belt; also leather chastity apron decorated with pearls. (*Phot. lent by Miss Werner.*)

are shocked to see the nude in works of art;[1] that it is as indecent for a Chinese woman to show her foot as for a European woman to expose the most intimate parts of her

FIG. 48.—Ufhtaradeka, typical Fuegian with primitive mantle of seal-skin; height, 1 m. 56; ceph. ind., 79.1. (*Phot. of the Scientific Miss. of Cape Horn, Coll. Mus. Nat. Hist., Paris.*)

body; that a Mussulman woman surprised in the bath by indiscreet eyes hastens before anything else to hide her face, the rest of the body being exposed to view without any great

[1] C. Davidson, "Das Nackte, etc.," *Globus*, vol. lxx., 1896, No. 18.

shock to modesty; that a European woman could never uncover her breast in the street and does it in a ball-room, etc.

Starting from the primordial nudity of mankind, we are led to inquire what was the motive which prompted men to clothe themselves. In countries with a rigorous climate it was the necessity of protecting themselves from cold and damp, but in the other parts of the world this has not been the case. The sentiment of vanity, the desire of being different from others, of pleasing, of inspiring with horror, begot ornaments which became transformed little by little into dress.

Adornment of the Body.—Strange as it may appear at the outset, the fact that ornament preceded dress is well established in ethnography. It is, moreover, often difficult to draw the boundary-line between the two. Thus the *first* and most primitive *mode of personal adornment* is certainly that in which the body itself is adorned without the putting on of any extraneous objects whatsoever. And the most simple of these primitive adornments, the daubing of the body with colouring matter, may also be considered as one of the first garments. Almost all peoples who go naked practise this mode of adornment (Figs. 59 and 124), but it is held in special esteem on the American continent. The colours most used are red, yellow, white, and black, yielded by such substances as ochre, the juice of certain plants, chalk, lime, and charcoal. Certain tribes of the Amazon basin fix a covering of feathers on their body, daubed with a sticky substance. The painting of the face (Figs. 158 and 159) is colouring only of a modified form. Thibetan women coat their face over with a thick layer of paste or starch, which with a refinement of coquetry they inlay with certain seeds arranged so as to form designs more or less artistic, without interfering with the red spots on the cheeks made with the juice of certain berries. Chinese women only put a thin coating of rice-starch without seeds, and the Javanese women, like our ladies of fashion, are content with rice powder. The red spots on the cheeks of Mongolian and Thibetan women are the prototypes of the paint which spoils so unnecessarily the fresh complexion and the faces, naturally so beautiful, of the women of Southern Europe (Spain, Serbia, Roumania).

The custom of applying lac to the teeth, in vogue among the Malays, the Chinese, and the Annamese; the colouring of the lips so generally practised from Japan to Europe; the dyeing of the nails and the hair with "henna" (*Lawsonia*

FIG. 49.—Ainu woman tattooed round the lips.

inermis) in Persia and Asia Minor; lastly, the painting of the eyebrows and eyelashes in the east, the dyeing of the hair in the west, are various manifestations of this same mode of primitive adornment.

Side by side with colouring must be placed tattooing, which leaves more indelible marks. There exists an infinite number of varieties of it, which, however, may be reduced to two principal categories: *tattooing by incision*, in which the design is produced by a series of scars or gashes, and *tattooing by puncture*, in which the design is formed by the introduction under the skin of a black powder by means of a needle. The first method is practised by dark-skinned peoples, Negroes, Melanesians, Australians (Figs. 14, 15, 149, and 150). In this case the incision having injured the non-pigmented dermic layer the scars are less coloured than the surrounding skin. Tattooing by puncture is only possible among clear-skinned peoples; among the latter may be instanced the New Zealanders, the Dyaks, and the Laotians, called "green-bellies."

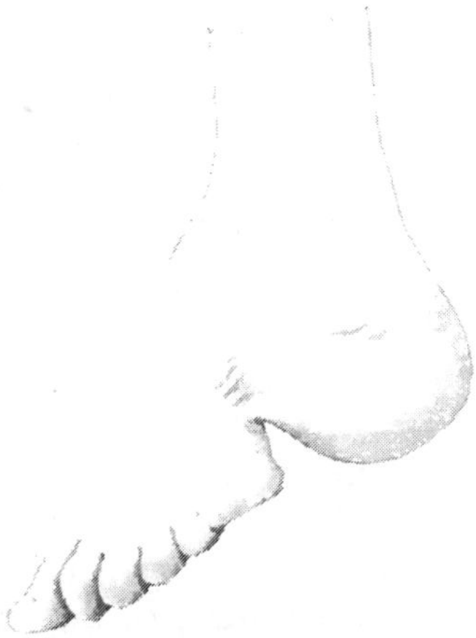

FIG. 50.—Foot of Chinese woman artificially deformed. (*After photograph.*)

In the case of a great number of peoples, tattooing is restricted to one sex only, chiefly to women (Ainus, Fig. 49, Chukchi), or else to certain categories of persons (postilions and drawers of carriages in Japan; sailors, criminals, and prostitutes in Europe).

Tattooing may be already considered as an *ethnic mutilation;* but there exist many others of a less anodyne character which are also connected with ornamentation. Chinese women deform their feet by means of tight bandages, and end by transforming them into horrible stumps (Figs. 50 and 51), which only

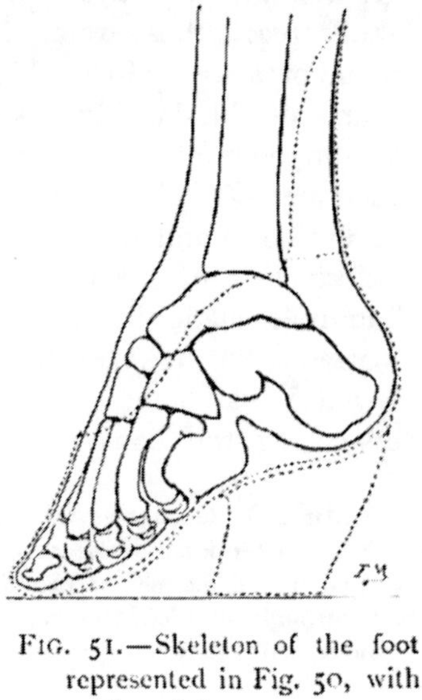

FIG. 51.—Skeleton of the foot represented in Fig. 50, with outline of shoe.

allow them to walk by holding on to surrounding objects. European and other "civilised" women compress themselves in corsets to such an extent that they bring on digestive troubles, and even displacement of the kidneys.[1] The Australians draw out the teeth of young men on their reaching the age of puberty; Negroes of the western coast of Africa break the teeth and transform them into little points; the Malays file them into the form of a half-circle, a saw, etc. As to cranial deformations, a whole chapter would not suffice to describe them all. Topinard distinguishes four principal types of such, without counting the various special forms (trilobate skull of the islanders of Sacrificios, etc.). In general the skulls are lengthened by this practice into a sort of sugar-loaf, the top of which points more or less upward and backward. It is chiefly by compression, by means of bandages, boards, or various caps and head-dresses, that the desired form of the head is obtained.[2]

Intentional deformation is practised by the Chinooks and other Indian tribes of the Pacific slope of the United States; by the Aymaras of Bolivia; in the New Hebrides; among a great number of tribes of Asia Minor, where the deformed skulls recall those which Herodotus had described under the name of *macrocephali*. In Europe the custom of altering the shape of the head has spread a little everywhere; the best known deformation is that which Broca had described under the name of "Toulousaine," and which is still practised both in the north and south of France (Fig. 52). What effect may deformation of the head have on intellectual development? Inquiries made in this direction afford no positive information; but it may be presumed that without being as harmful as some people believe, the deformation, by displacing the convolutions of the brain, may favour the

[1] Mme. Dr. Gaches-Sarraute, *L'Hygiène du Corset*, Paris, 1896.

[2] This intentional deformation must be distinguished from that which is caused by the manner of placing the child in the cradle. This is always less strongly marked, and may pass unnoticed in the head of the living subject, but it may always be recognised in the skull.

outbreak of cerebral diseases in persons predisposed to them.[1]

Adornment with Objects attached to the Body.—The perforation of the ear, the nose, and the lips is made with the view of placing in the hole an ornament of some kind or other.

FIG. 52.—Native of the Department of Haute-Garonne whose head has undergone the deformation called "Toulousaine." (*Phot. Delisle; engraving belonging to the Paris Anthro. Society.*)

Thus this species of mutilation may be considered as a natural step towards the *second manner of adornment*, which consists in placing or suspending gauds on the body. When people have few garments or none at all they are compelled to hook

[1] See for the details, L. A. Gosse, *Essai déform. artif. crâne*, Paris, 1885; Broca, *Instr. craniol.*, 1875; P. Topinard, *Revue Anthro.*, 1879, p. 497, and *Elem. Anthro*, p. 744; Delisle, *Déform. du crâne*, Paris, 1880, and *Congr. Américaniste*, Paris, 1892, p. 300; Ambialet, *L'Anthropologie*, 1893, p. 11.

these objects to the body itself. The Botocudo perforates the lobes of the ears and the lower lip to insert into them heavy wooden plugs; other Indians of South America perforate the cheeks to stick feathers therein; the Papuans and the Australians the nasal septum, that it may hold a bone or stick (Figs. 53 and 149); the Caribs and the Negroes of the Ubangi the lower lip, for the insertion of crystal, bone, or metal rods, or simply pins. Similar customs persist, moreover, among peoples more amply clothed. The nose-rings among the Dravidians or among Tatar women; the ear-pendants of the American Indians (Figs. 158, 159, 160, and 161); the bone plugs placed in the cheeks among the Eskimo; the metal plates or precious stones inlaid in the teeth among the Malays of Sumatra, exist to prove this point. And the ear-rings of our civilised European women are the last vestige of a savage form of adornment which requires the mutilation of an organ.

The hair also is used to attach ornaments: flowers, jewels, ribbons, chips, feathers (Figs. 47, 117, 154, 158, 159, and frontispiece). As to the arrangement of the hair, it depends a great deal on its nature. The Negroes, with their short and woolly hair, are enabled to have a complicated head-dress (Figs. 47 and 141). Peoples with smooth hair are content to leave it floating behind (Americans, Fig. 160, Indonesians), or to gather it up into a chignon (Annamese, Coreans, Eskimo), in one or several plaits (Chinese), or in several rolls or bands, stuck together and disposed in various ways (Mongols, Japanese, Fig. 120, Chinese). But it is among peoples with frizzy and slightly woolly hair that the head-dress attains a high degree of perfection. We have but to mention the capillary structures of the Bejas (Fig. 138), the Fulbés (Fig. 139), the Papuans and some Melanesians, whose mops of hair with a six-toothed comb coquettishly planted at the top are so characteristic (Figs. 152 and 153).

The custom of shaving the hair of the head and the beard, as well as the habit of plucking out the hairs, are more general among peoples whose pilous system is little developed than

FIG. 53.—Dancing costume of natives of Murray Islands (Torres Straits). Type of Papuan (in the centre), Melanesian (on the right), and mixed race (on the left). (*Phot. Haddon.*)

among hairy peoples. All the Mongolians, all the Indians of America, and almost all the Oceanians shave or pluck out the hair. Amongst them the razor, sometimes a fragment of obsidian or glass, is used in conjunction with depilatory tweezers. The wearing of the beard or long hair is often a matter of fashion or social convention. From the time of the patriarchs the beard has been honoured in the East, while in the West the fluctuations of fashion or opinion have made of its presence or absence a sign of opposition (Protestant clergy before the eighteenth century in Germany, Republicans of the middle of this century in France), or a distinctive mark of certain classes (Catholic clergy, servants, actors, soldiers in many states). Several superstitious ideas are connected with human hair. From at least the ninth century to the end of the Middle Ages, the Slavs and the Germans shaved the crown of their children's heads, believing that it facilitated teething.

It would take too long to enumerate all the peoples among whom the cutting of the hair is a stigma of slavery or degradation; certain peoples cut their hair as a sign of mourning (Dakota Indians, etc.), others, on the contrary, let it grow very long for the same reason. On the other hand, the habit of letting the nails grow to a length of several centimetres, so general among the wealthy classes in Indo-China and Malaysia, is inspired chiefly by vanity; the object being to show that they have no need to resort to manual labour in order to live.

The Girdle, Necklace, and Garland.—Ornaments fixed to the body without mutilating it (the *second stage in the evolution of ornament*) are very varied. Originally strips of hide, sinews of animals, or herbaceous twigs, sometimes plaited, were fastened around the head or parts of the body where there was a depressed surface, above a bony projection or a muscular protuberance—the neck, the waist, the wrists, the ankles, as is still seen among the Fuegians (Fig. 174), Melanesians, Bushmen, and Australians. According to the parts of the body thus adorned, four classes of ornaments may be recognised: garlands, collars, belts (Fig. 47), and bracelets (on the arms and legs). To these simple bands men began at first to attach all sorts of secondary ornaments: bright shells (frontispiece and Figs. 53 and 151), seeds and gay-coloured insects, beads of bone and shell-fish (Figs. 151, 159, and 160), claws of wild beasts, teeth and knuckle bones of animals and human beings (Figs. 158 and 159), bristles and hoofs of the Suidæ, pieces of fur, feathers of birds, leaves and flowers. And it is to these superadded ornaments that we may trace the origin of the garment proper. The thong of the head, over and above its utilitarian purpose as a quiver (the Bushmen push their arrows into it), becomes transformed into the crown of feathers so well known among the American Indians and Melanesians (Fig. 53), into a wreath of flowers among the Polynesians, into all kinds of head-covering among other tribes (Figs. 22, 40, 107, 108, 109, 115, 134, 145, etc.).

To the thong of the neck or collar may be suspended a beast's skin, and you have it then transformed into a mantle. Among the Fuegians this piece of skin is so scanty that they are obliged to turn it about according to the direction of the wind in order to protect the body effectually (Fig. 48). The thong of the waist, the girdle, was likewise laden with different appendages, and became transformed into a skirt. The leafy branches which the Veddahs push under their belt, the pieces of bark upheld by the belt among the Niam-Niams, the Indo-Malayan "sarong" (Figs. 126 and 146), which combines the functions of a skirt and a belt,—these are all merely the prototype of the skirt.

Space fails us to show in detail how the other ornaments and garments have sprung from these humble beginnings. How from the bracelet proceeded the ring; how the stone, the twisted tooth, the perforated shell (Figs. 53 and 152) replaced the thongs in this class of ornament; how, when once metals became known, gold and silver plates, hollow and solid rings in gold, silver, copper, or iron (Figs. 112 and 158), brass wire rolled several times around the neck and the limbs, were substituted for thongs of skin, blades of grass, and shell beads. The inlaying of precious stones has transformed ornament. The wearing of massive metal becomes uncomfortable even in the climate of the tropics; in certain countries of Africa, rich ladies of fashion have slaves specially employed in emptying pots of water over the spiral-shaped bracelets which coil around the whole arm or leg and become excessively hot in the sun (J. G. Wood).

It is necessary, however, to say a few words about the *fabrication of stuffs* and the *making of garments*.

The skins of animals—ox, sheep, reindeer, horse, seal, dog, eland, etc.—were used at first just as they were. Then men began to strip off the hair when there was no necessity to protect themselves from cold, soaking the skin in water, to which they added sometimes cinders or other alkaline substances. This is still the method adopted by the Indians of the far west to obtain the very coarse and hard ox-hide for their tents. But if they wish to utilise it for garments, or if they have to deal with the skin of the deer, they scrape it afterwards with stone or metal scrapers, cut it into half the thickness and work it with bone polishers to render it more supple.[1] Tanning comes much later among half-civilised peoples (like the ancient Egyptians, etc.). Apart from the mammals, few animals have furnished materials for the dress of man;[2] the famous mantles and hats of birds' feathers so artistically worked by the Hawaiians and the ancient Mexicans were only state garments, reserved for chiefs; clothes of salmon skin, prepared in a certain way, have not passed beyond the territory of a single tribe, the Goldes of Amoor; the fish-bladder waterproofs of the Chukchi are only fishing garments. On the other hand, the number of plants from which garments may be made is very great. Several sorts of wood supply the material of which boots are made (the sabot in France and Holland). The bark of the birch is utilised also for plaited boots ("lapti" of the Russians and Finns), the bark of several tropical

[1] O. Mason, *loc. cit.*, p. 274.

[2] Note also that almost everywhere foot-gear and often head-gear are made from materials obtained from the mammals: leather, fur, and felt.

trees, almost in its natural state or scarcely beaten, is employed as a garment by the Monbuttus, the Niam-Niams, the tribes of the Uganda, and is characteristic of Zandeh peoples in general; this kind of garment is also found in America (among the Warraus of Guiana and the Andesic tribes). In Oceania the preparation of stuffs from the beaten bark of paper mulberry (*Brusonnetia papyrifera*) has attained a high degree of perfection, and the "Tapa" of Tahiti with its coloured and printed patterns, the "Kapa" of Hawaii, might enter into competition with woven stuffs.[1]

The latter have been known since remote antiquity. Woven stuffs are found in the pile-dwellings of the bronze age in Europe and in the pyramids of Egypt. But it seems that the *plaiting* of vegetable fibres and grasses, as it is still practised to-day with esparto grass, must have preceded true weaving. The Polynesians still manufactured, at the beginning of this century, robes plaited with the stems of certain grasses, and plaited straw hats are made by Malays, Indians of North-west America, etc. On the whole, weaving is only plaiting of a finer substance, yarn, which itself is only very thin cord or twine. The process of spinning cord or thread is always the same. In its most primitive form it consists simply in rolling between the palms of both hands, or with one hand on the thigh, the fibres of some textile substance. This is how the Australian proceeds to make a line with his wife's hair, or the New Zealander when he transforms a handful of native flax, inch by inch, into a perfect cord. The Australian had only to transform into a spindle the little staff with two cross-pieces, on which he rolls up his precious line, to effect a great improvement in his art.[2] In fact, the spindle is a device so well adapted for its purpose that it has come down from the most remote Egyptian antiquity into our steam spinning factories almost without alteration in form. Primitive weaving must have been done at first with the needle, like tapestry or modern embroidery,

[1] See for details W. Brigham, "Hawaiian Kapa-making," *Hawaiian Alman. and Annual*, p. 76. Honolulu, 1896.

[2] Tylor, *Anthropology*, p. 246.

but soon this wearisome process was replaced by the following arrangement: two series of threads stretched between two staffs which may be alternately raised and lowered half (*warp*) by means of vertical head-threads attached to wooden sleys; between the gaps of the threads passes the shuttle carrying the woof, which is thus laid successively above and below each thread of the warp. This is the simplest weaving-loom.

The dyeing of thread and stuffs by an application of mordants (kaolin especially) is known to all peoples acquainted with weaving. Nature supplies colours such as indigo, turmeric, litmus, purple, madder, etc., which are subjected to transformations by being left to steep with certain herbs. The Polynesians were acquainted even with printing on textures by means of fern-fronds or Hibiscus flowers, which they steeped in colour and applied to their "tapa."

The primitive "tailors" cut their hides or stuffs with flint knives, sewing the pieces together in shoemaker fashion; they made holes with a bone or horn awl and passed through them a thread made of the sinews of some animal, or of woven grass, etc. Sewing with needles is less common among uncultured peoples, but it has been found in Europe from the neolithic period.

Means of Existence.—To procure food and the necessary raw materials for the construction of a shelter and the making of clothes, man had to resort at an early stage to various tools, arms, and instruments, which rendered his hunting, fishing, and fruit-gathering expeditions more productive.[1]

We will glance rapidly, in the first place, at *tools of a general character* needed for all kinds of work. Among most uncultured peoples the raw materials used for making tools were, and are, stone, wood, bone, shell, horn. The metals—copper, bronze, iron, steel—only came later on. This does not mean that the knowledge of the use of metals is necessarily connected with a superior stage of civilisation. Thus most Negroes of Central Africa are excellent black-

[1] For details see G. de Mortillet, *Origines de la chasse, de la pêche*, etc.; O. Mason, *loc. cit.*; Tylor, *Anthrop.*; Holmes, *Fifteenth Rep. Bur. Ethnol.*

smiths (Fig. 135), though otherwise less advanced than certain peoples unacquainted with metals, like the New Zealanders or the Incas of Peru, for example (before the arrival of the Europeans).

We cannot dwell on the methods of working each of the materials from which tools may be made. It is enough to say that there are two principal methods of working stone—cutting and polishing. The chips are removed from a stone either by percussion with another stone (Fig. 54), or by pressure with the end of a bone or piece of pointed wood (Fig. 55). It

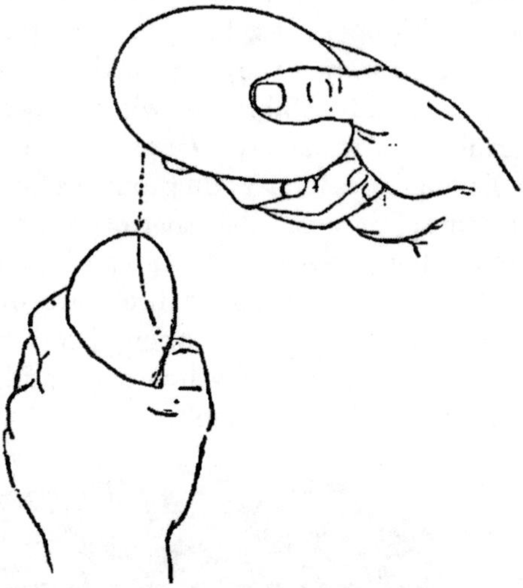

FIG. 54.—Method of making stone tools by *percussion;* the first blow. (*After Holmes.*)

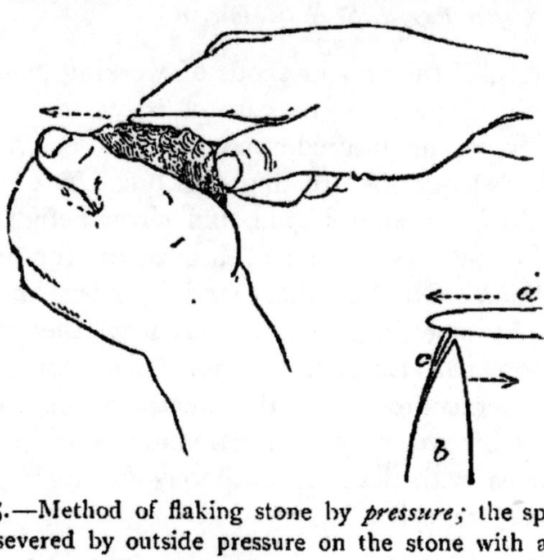

FIG. 55.—Method of flaking stone by *pressure;* the splinter (*c*) is severed by outside pressure on the stone with a pointed bone (*a*). (*After Holmes.*)

was thus that the Europeans of the post-tertiary period obtained their flint tools (Fig. 84), and to-day the same process may still be seen in operation, less and less frequently it is true, among the Eskimo when they are making their knives, and among the Fuegians and Californians when they are preparing their spear-heads or arrows, etc. (Figs. 56 and 73). The process of polishing takes longer and produces finer tools (Figs. 71 and 112). In Europe it succeeded that of stone-cutting, and it flourished among the peoples of Oceania and America before the arrival of Europeans. Polished tools are obtained by rubbing for a long time a chipped or unchipped stone against another stone with the addition of water and sand, or the dust of the same rock from which the tool is made.

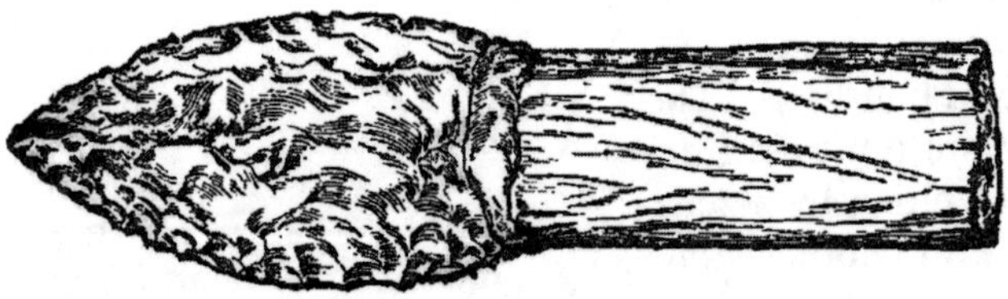

FIG. 56.—Knife of chipped flint of the Hupa Indians; it is mounted on a wood handle with pitch. Attached to a longer handle it becomes a spear. (*After Ray, U.S. Nat. Museum.*)

As to metals, of the two methods of working them, *forging*, which can be adopted in the case of native metals, is more general amongst uncultured peoples than *casting*, which implies a knowledge of treating the ore. The Indians of America could forge copper, gold, and silver before the arrival of Columbus, but the casting of bronze or iron-ore was unknown to them. On the other hand, Negroes know how to obtain iron by smelting the ore, and from the very earliest times the peoples of Europe, Anterior Asia, China, and Indo-China were acquainted with the treatment of copper ore,[1] and obtained bronze by the amalgamation of copper with tin, and sometimes with lead or antimony (in Egypt, Armenia, the Caucasus, Transylvania).

[1] Weeren, "Analyse, etc.," *Verh. Berl. Ges. Anthr.*, June-Oct. 1895.

In the early stages of material progress the objects manufactured were not differentiated; the weapon of to-day became the tool of to-morrow, the agricultural implement of the day after. However, there are savages who have sometimes special instruments for cutting or chopping (axes, knives, saws of stone or shell), saws for scraping or planing (scrapers and raspers of stone, bone, shell, etc.), for piercing (awls of bone or horn, stone bits), for hammering and driving in (stone hammers), etc. As to the fastenings which keep together the different parts of the tools, these are chiefly *bands* (sinews, strips of hide or bark, plaited or spun cords) and the sticky preparations of various gums and resins. An axe or a knife is fixed to its handle by means of cords of plaited coco-nut fibres in Polynesia (Fig. 71) and very rarely among Negroes (Fig. 74), by resin in Australia and among the Hupa Indians of the Oregon (Fig. 56), and by sinews or strips of sealskin among the Chukchi and the Indians of California (Fig. 73).

The invention of primitive "machines" followed that of tools. Alternate rotatory motion must have been utilised in the first instance as being the easiest to obtain. Example: the flint-pointed drill of the Indians of the north-west of America, the apparatus for making fire (see Fig. 36), or the turning-lathe of the Kalmuks (Fig. 57), the Egyptians and the Hindus, moved by the palms of the hand at first, with a cord afterwards, and later again with a bow.[1] The transformation of this alternating motion into a continuous circular one must probably have resulted from the use of the spindle furnished with its wheel. In this instrument, so simple in appearance, is found the first application of the important discovery that rotatory movement once produced may be maintained during a certain time by a heavy weight performing the function of a fly-wheel.

The potter's wheel (p. 55) is a second application of the same principle; rollers for the conveyance of heavy objects are a third (see Chap. VII., *Transports*). The screw and the nut

[1] Reuleaux, *Hist. du développ. des machines dans l'humanité* (translated from the German), Paris, 1876 (extr. from the section *Cinématique*).

appear to be a comparatively recent invention, presupposing a degree of superior development. Certain authors see in the use of twisted cords, and the cassava-squeezer of the Caribs of Guiana,[1] the first steps towards that invention. The principle of the single pulley is frequently applied by savages, and the compound pulley or tackle-block is known to the Eskimo, who make use of it to land huge cetaceans (Fig. 58).

We may divide the activity displayed by uncivilised and even half-civilised peoples in procuring the necessaries of life

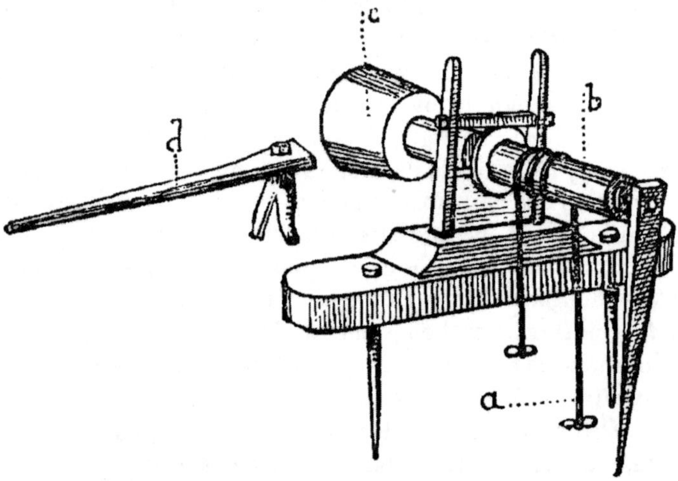

FIG. 57.—Kalmuk turning lathe with alternating rotatory movement obtained by means of a strap (*a*); (*c*) block of wood to make a porringer; (*d*) bench for the workman. (*After Reuleaux.*)

into four great categories: hunting, fishing, agriculture with fruit-gathering, and cattle-breeding.

Hunting is almost the only resource of uncivilised peoples; it is still a powerful auxiliary means of livelihood with nomads and primitive tillers of the soil, and it is only among civilised peoples that it assumes the character of a sport. Originally,

[1] This is a long woven bag in which the tough warp and woof run spirally and diagonally, so that when the two ends are forced together the cylinder becomes short and wide, and when pulled apart, it becomes long and slender.

man was obliged to hunt without weapons, as certain tribes still sometimes do. On dark nights, when the cormorants are asleep, the Fuegian hunter, hanging by a thong of seal-skin, glides along the cliffs, holding on to jutting points of rock; when near a bird he seizes it with both hands and crushes its head between his teeth, without giving it time to utter a cry or make a movement. He then passes on to another, and so continues until some noise puts the cormorants to flight.

But more frequently the inventive faculty is brought into play to construct all kinds of weapons for facilitating the capture of prey. As most of these contrivances are at the same time weapons of war, we shall glance at them in Chapter VII. Moreover, the multiplicity of weapons has not prevented primitive man from using all sorts of stratagems for capturing animals. Any one who has dipped into the old books on venery, or even into catalogues of modern gunsmiths, is able to realise this, for most of the traps, snares, and pitfalls represented are also found among savages. Bow-traps are especially favoured, but the springe for birds and the pitfalls for large animals are not despised. To these we may add the use of bait, poisoning, the smoking of bees in order to take their honey, the imitation of the song of birds to allure them to the gin, disguise by means of the skin of a beast the better to approach it, and the artifices devised by man in his war with animals are not yet exhausted. There is still the most treacherous of all: having degraded certain animals by domestication (falcon, dog, cat, etc.), man makes them hunt their untamed kind (see *Domestication*).

In *fishing* there is the same display of artifice. The simple gathering of shells, sea-urchins, and crustaceans at low tide, mostly left to the women, supplements but little the means of subsistence of fishing populations. The bulk of fish and animals of aquatic habits are taken by means of suitable weapons, and still more often by means of traps, weirs, poisoned waters, etc.

The weapons most used in fishing are pikes with one or several teeth (tridents, fish-spears), that the Melanesians, the

Fuegians, the Indians of Brazil, and so many other savages handle with the utmost dexterity, never missing the fish for which they lie in wait sometimes for hours at a time. The bow is also sometimes employed to shoot the fish (Andamanese),

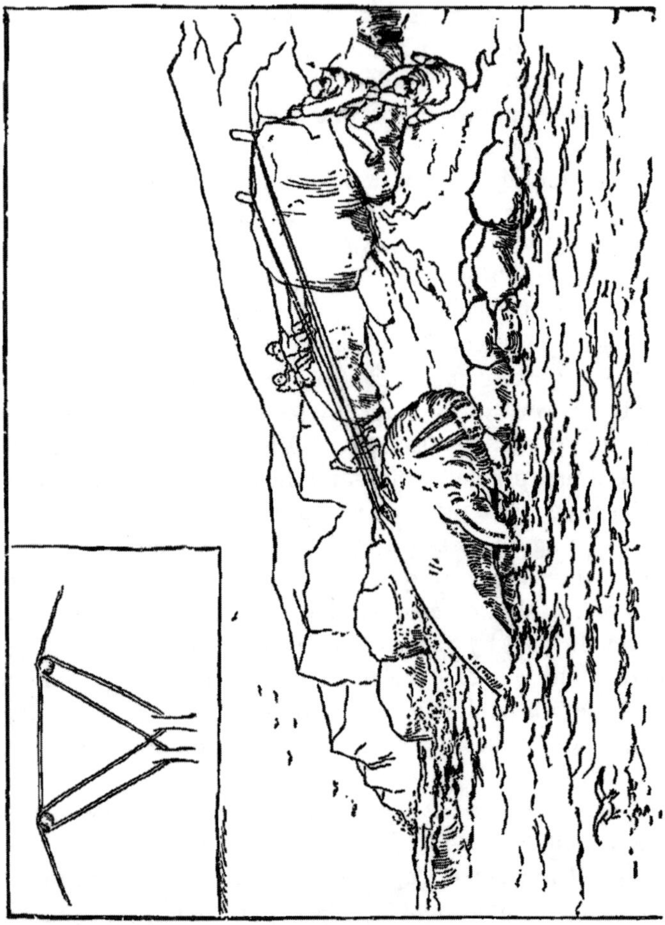

FIG. 58.—Principle of tackle utilised by Eskimo, landing a walrus. Above, on left, detail of the arrangement of the rope round stakes. (*After Elliot.*)

but the special missile used in fishing is the *harpoon*, the wood or bone head of which usually takes the form of a fork or pike with one or several barbs.

The Fuegians simply throw their harpoons like a javelin, the

Eskimo make use of instruments to hurl them (see Chap. VII.). In many harpoons the head is only fitted to the shaft and attached to it by a long cord; immediately the animal is wounded the shaft separates itself from the head and acts as a float, indicating the spot where the victim has plunged, for it will not be long before he comes again to the surface to breathe, and other wounds are then inflicted. The Eskimo of Asia and the Chukchi also attach bladders to the shaft as floats. But all these weapons are chiefly employed against marine mammals (seals, sea-lions, walruses, whales, etc.); for catching fish recourse is had to other means. Poisoning the water appears to be one of the most primitive. It is constantly practised by Australians, Indonesians, and Melanesians. We have next to refer to the various devices for catching fish, which, according to O. Mason, may be grouped into two categories—(1) those intended to bring the fish, quietly following its way, into a place or trap from which it cannot afterwards get out, and (2) those which consist in getting it to swallow a hook hidden under some form of bait.

Among the former of these devices, bow-nets and sweep-nets in bamboo and rattan are very widely used among the Dyaks, Micronesians, etc. Cast-nets are less common among uncivilised peoples; they are met with, however, in Polynesia. Fish-hooks other than those in metal are made of bone, the thorns of certain trees, of wood, and especially of mother-of-pearl. For *fishing-boats*, see Chapter VII. (*Navigation*).

Agriculture.—It is constantly stated that man has passed successively through three stages—that in the first he was a hunter, in the second a nomadic shepherd, and in the third a tiller of the soil. This is only true if we consider agriculture as it is understood at the present day in Europe, that is to say as closely connected with the existence of certain domestic animals (horses, oxen, etc.) which supply man with motive power and at the same time with manure. But there are numerous peoples, without these domestic animals, who nevertheless are acquainted with agriculture, only it is a special kind of agriculture which is related rather to our ornamental and market gardening, at least by the method of cultivation.[1] Hahn has proposed to call this species of cultivation after the principal, and almost the only, tool which is used—"Hoe-culture" (Hackbau in German); while cultivation by means of a plough drawn by animals might be called true agriculture (Ackerbau).

It is evident that in the development of mankind the most primitive hoe-culture, such as is practised by certain tribes of Africa and South America, may well have sprung from the gathering of plants and roots. The Australians, the Papuans (Fig. 152), and the Indians of California even yet make use of pointed staves, hardened in the fire, to unearth natural roots; certain Negroes and Bushmen join to the staff a stone whorl which makes the work easier. These "digging sticks" are the first agricultural implements; they perhaps preceded the hoe. The habit that many Australian tribes have of returning periodically to the same places for the gathering of fruits and roots, giving these time to grow, is one of the first steps towards the cultivation of the ground; it proves a comprehension of the development of a plant from a sown seed. Hoe-culture prevails at the present time in vast regions of tropical Africa and in South America. The tubers, maniocs, yams, and sweet potatoes play a prominent part there, but the graminaceæ also are represented by the maize introduced from America and rice from Asia, and it is among the two peoples who have adopted these cereals as the staple of their food, the Incas of Peru and the Chinese, that hoe-culture has been improved by the introduction of manure. Carried to a still greater degree of perfection by the employment of artificial manure, it has been transformed by civilised peoples into "plantations" (sugar-cane, coffee, etc.) in tropical countries and into "horticulture" in all climates.

True agriculture could only have originated where the ox, the horse, the buffalo, and other animals used in ploughing were first domesticated—that is to say, in Eurasia, and perhaps more particularly in Mesopotamia, where the art of irrigation was known at a period when in other countries there was not even any agriculture at all. As far

[1] Hahn, *Die Hausthiere*, etc., Leipzig, 1896, in 8vo, with map.

back as the historic Chaldean monuments can take us we find agriculture existing in this part of Asia. In Europe it has appeared since the neolithic age, after the quaternary period. Domestic animals having most probably been introduced into Egypt from Asia, it may be supposed that before their introduction the country of the Pharaohs was cultivated by the hoe, like the kingdom of the Incas of old, or that of the "sons of Heaven" of the present day. Besides, in Asia, as in Europe, hoe-culture existed thus early, and the favourite plant cultivated was millet (*Panicum miliaceum*, L.), consumed but little to-day, but universally known, which attests its importance in antiquity.[1]

The system of laying lands fallow and raising crops in rotation could only have been established with the development of agriculture. Hoe-culture was satisfied with the total exhaustion of the soil, even if it had to seek out new ground cleared by a conflagration of the forests, the ashes of which were the first and only manure.

The plough, that implement so characteristic of true agriculture, has evolved, as regards its form, from the double-handled hoe of Portuguese Africa (Livingstone), which bears so close a resemblance to that of the Egyptian monuments, to the "sokha" of the Russian peasants, and even to the steam plough of the modern farmer, not to mention the heavy ploughs, all of wood except the share and the coulter, still in use in many rural districts of Central Europe. Reaping in both systems of cultivation is accomplished with knives or special implements, bill-hooks, examples of which, almost as perfect as those of to-day, are found as far back as the days of ancient Egypt and the bronze age in Europe; the scythe, known to the ancient Greeks, appears to be a later improvement.

The threshing of wheat, which often constitutes but a single

[1] This opinion of Hahn's appears to be corroborated by this fact, that millet is still the "national cereal" of the Turkish peoples, who, like all other nomad shepherds, beginning with hoe-culture, have arrived at their present state through having preferred to breed animals other than those used in ploughing—that is to say, the camel, sheep, and later, the horse.

operation with winnowing and the preparation of food (see p. 156) in hoe-culture, is accomplished in true agriculture with the aid of domestic animals, either by making thèm tread on the threshing-floor, or draw over the cut corn a heavy plank strewn with fragments of flint (the *tribulum* of the Romans, the *mowrej* of the Arabs and the Berbers, in Syria, Tunisia, and Egypt). For grinding, see p. 156.

The use of granaries for storing the crop is known to most semi-civilised peoples (see p. 168); almost always the granaries are arranged on poles (example: Ainus), or on clay stands (example: Negroes). "Silos," or holes in the ground for hiding the crop in, exist among the Kabyles of Algeria, the Laotians (Neïs), the Mongols of Zaidam (Prjevalsky), etc.

Domestic Animals.—The breeding of domestic animals should be considered, as I have already said, an occupation denoting a social state superior to that in which hoe-culture is prevalent. But before concerning himself specially with the *breeding* of cattle, man knew how to *domesticate* certain animals. I emphasise this term, for domestication presupposes a radical change, by means of selection, in the habits of the animal, which becomes capable of reproducing its species in captivity; this is not the case with animals simply *tamed.*

One of the first animals tamed, then domesticated, by man was probably *the dog.* The most uncultured tribes—Fuegians and Australians—possess domesticated dogs, trained for hunting. Europeans of neolithic times bred several species of them: the *Canis familiaris palustris,* of small size; a large dog (*C. f. Inostrantzewi*), the remains of which have been found in the prehistoric settlements of Lake Ladoga and Lake Neuchâtel, and which would be nearly allied to the Siberian sledge-dogs; lastly, the *Canis familiaris Lesneri,* of very slender form, with skull somewhat resembling that of the Scotch greyhound (deer-hound), which gave birth in the bronze age to two races: the shepherd dog (*Canis familiaris matris opitimæ*) and the hunting dog (*Canis familiaris intermedius*). It is from these three species of Arctic origin that most of the canine races of Europe and Central and Northern Asia are descended; those of Southern

Asia, of Oceania, and Africa would be derived from a different type, represented to-day by the *Dingo* of Australia.[1] We may lay stress on these differences of canine races because often the races of domestic animals vary according to the human races which breed them. Thus, it has been observed in the Tyrol that the geographical d stribution of races of oxen corresponds with that of varieties of the human race.

After dogs, several other carnivorous animals have been tamed with a view to the chase: tiger, ferret, civet cat, wild cat, leopard, and falcon; but man has only been able to domesticate two: the ferret and the cat. The Chinese have succeeded in domesticating the cormorant and utilising it for fishing, placing, however, a ring on its neck, so that it cannot give way to its wild instinct to swallow the fish which it catches.

Many animals have been domesticated by peoples acquainted only with hoe-culture; such as the pig and the hen in Africa and Oceania; the she-goat in Africa; the turkey, the duck (*Anas moschata*), the guinea-pig, and the llama in America. But true agriculture begins only with the domestication of the bovine races, the she-goat, and the ass; and true breeding of cattle with the domestication of the camel and the sheep among nomads. The horse and the mule do not appear until a little later among nomads, as among sedentary peoples.

Among the domesticated bovidæ other than the ox must be mentioned the yak in Thibet and around Thibet; the gayal of Assam and Upper Burma; the banteng (*Bos sondaicus*) of Malaysia; and the buffalo, which is found everywhere where rice is planted. In mentioning, besides the animals just referred to, the reindeer of hyperborean peoples (Laplanders, Samoyeds, Tunguses, Chukchi), we shall have exhausted the list of nineteen domesticated mammals actually known to the different peoples, according to Hahn. As to birds, out of thirteen, we have named only

[1] Th. Studer, "Beiträge zur Geschichte unserer Hunderassen," *Naturwissench. Wochenschrift*, 1897, No. 28. See also *Mem. Soc. Hélvétique sciences naturelles*, 1896.

four: cormorant, duck, hen, and turkey; to these must be added the goose, the swan, the Guinea-fowl, the peacock, the pheasant, the canary, the parrot, the ostrich, and, lastly, the pigeon, which perhaps of all the winged race is the easiest to tame. The other classes of animals have furnished few useful helpers of man. Among insects there are the bee and the silk-worm; among fishes we can mention only three: carp, gold-fish, and *Macropus viridiauratus*, Lacep., chiefly bred for amusement by the Chinese.

CHAPTER VI.

II. SOCIOLOGICAL CHARACTERS—*continued.*

2. PSYCHIC LIFE: *Games and Recreations*—Their importance—Games of children and adults—Sports and public spectacles—Masks—*Fine Arts*—Graphic arts—Ornamentation—Drawing—Sculpture—Dancing—Its importance among uncultured peoples—Pantomime and dramatic art—Vocal and instrumental music—Instruments of music—Poetry—*Religion*—Animism—Its two elements: belief in the soul, and belief in spirits—Fetichism—Polytheism—Rites and ceremonies—Priesthood—International religions—*Myths*—*Science*—Art of counting—Geometry—Calculation of time—Clocks and calendars—Geography and cartography—Medicine and surgery.

2. PSYCHIC LIFE.

Games and Recreations.—In two works based on carefully observed facts, Groos has shown that animals do not expend all their muscular and psychic energy in procuring the means of material existence, but, further, expend this energy in games, which are really a process of training, of education. In a greater degree is this the case with man, that animal whose psychical life has expanded so enormously.[1] In fact, games are the first manifestations of the psychical life not only of man individually but of mankind as a whole.

It is necessary to distinguish between the *games of children* and those of adults. The former are above all imitation, while the latter aim at either gaining an advantage or demonstrating muscular or mental strength and skill.

The boys of "savages" handle tiny bows and lassoes made by themselves, and hunt toy guancos, birds, and turtles made of clay and wood, in imitation of their fathers; while the little

[1] K. Groos, *Die Spiele der Thiere*, 1896; *Die Spiele der Menschen*, 1899.

girls treat their rag dolls as actual children, repeating the gestures and words of their mothers. It is the imitative game of the young.

But if the object of the game is to exercise the strength and skill, it becomes common to children and adults. It is such with the game of hand-ball, known to all peoples with the exception perhaps of the Negroes; and stilts, which are met with in Europe, China, Eastern Africa, and Polynesia. Side by side with these games in which muscular skill plays the principal part, there are others in which attention and quickness of the senses are put to the test. To guess in which hand some object is hidden is a recreation among the Tlinkits, as among Europeans. Among the Hottentots this game is complicated, inasmuch as it is necessary to point out by a special position of the fingers the hand of the partner which is supposed to conceal the object, thus recalling the very ancient game known to the Egyptians, and called by the Romans *mirare digitis*, which survives at the present time under the name of "Morra" in Italy.

This is how it is played:—Simultaneously each partner, putting out his hand, shows whatever number of fingers he may think fit, bending the others, and at the same moment mentioning a number; he whose figure equals the sum of the fingers stretched out by the two partners wins the game. It is evident that this game, known in absolutely the same form in China, is already a game of chance. It is the same with most games played with dice, whether the latter be represented by true dice (China, prehistoric Europe), or by otter's teeth, seeds, etc., variously marked or coloured (Indians of North America), or by sheep's astragali (Central Asia, Persia, etc.). *Lotto* is known to the Chinese, the Siamese, etc., and it was the Celestials who introduced roulette or the thirty-four animal games into Indo-China.[1]

[1] Roulette flourished among the Eskimo of Greenland in the eighteenth century; it is known under the name of "Chombino" among the Assiniboines and Blackfeet Indians.—H. Egede and Wied, cited by Andree, *Ethnogr. Paral.*, p. 104 (Neue Folge).

The chief intellectual game is chess, invented in India; varieties of chess are the game of draughts, known wherever European civilisation penetrates, and the game of *Uri* or *Mugole*, spread by the Arabs throughout the whole of Africa from Madagascar to Senegal. The object used in this latter game is a block of wood with 16, 24, or 32 little cups disposed in two or four rows, in which the aim is to place in a certain way a certain number of little stones or seeds. A third variety of the game of chess, backgammon, holds a middle place between *Uri* and the game of dice, and in consequence is half a game of chance. It is known under the name of *Tob* in Egypt and Palestine, of *Pachisi* in India, and of *Patolitzli* in ancient Mexico.[1]

Sports and Spectacles.—Hand-to-hand contests soprized by the Japanese and the Mongols, horse-races esteemed by all nomads, the superb nautical sports practised of old by the Hawaiians, in which, standing upright or astraddle on a canoe, they descended cataracts several metres in height,[2] and so many other sports still form, as it were, a link between games properly so called, giving pleasure to those taking part in them, and *spectacles*, which give pleasure to others. Most spectacles are composed of the dance, pantomime, scenic representations, music and song, of which I shall presently treat. Outside the manifestation of these arts, public spectacles are confined almost everywhere to the different ceremonies, festivals, and processions connected with various rites or customs (initiation, common marriages, worship of the dead, etc.), or to jugglery, exhibition of animals, acrobatic performances, sleight-of-hand tricks, etc., most of which have originated in India. To these we must add combats between men and animals or between animals themselves, the best known of which are the bull-fights so dear to the Hispano-Portuguese of Europe and America, and the cock-fights which have had ardent supporters not only in England and

[1] See the interesting study on this game by Tylor, *Journ. Anthr. Inst.*, vol. viii., p. 116, and in *Internationales Archiv. Ethnog.*, suppl. vol. ix. (Festg. Bastian), Leyden, 1896.

[2] "Hawaiian Surf-Riding," *Haw. Alman.*, p. 106, Honolulu, 1896.

Fig. 59.—Dance of Australians during the Corroboree or ceremony of initiation. (*Drawn by P. Moulet, partly after Brough Smyth and Sam Kent.*)

the United States, but also in Spanish America, all over the Malay Archipelago, etc. In China and Siam people are less blood-thirsty; they are content to look at contests between crickets, grasshoppers, and fishes.

Masks play an important part in festivals, ceremonies, and spectacles, as in so many other manifestations of the social life of uncivilised and half-civilised peoples (religion, war, justice). Let us merely mention the fantastic masks used in dances and processions among the Javanese and the Dyaks, and especially those of the Melanesians; certain of them are made of cocoa-nuts, with an imitation of the beard and moustache in the fibres of this fruit, others have the human skull as a groundwork. The Papuans are very skilful in making masks with tortoise shells, etc.[1]

FIG. 60. — Anthropomorph ornamental design of the Papuans of New Guinea. (*After Haddon.*)

The Arts.—Artistic manifestations are distinguished from games by this fact, that their object is not only to afford pleasure to the artist himself during the execution of his work, but also to cause this pleasure to be shared by the greatest possible number of his fellow-beings. These manifestations are called forth then by the sentiment of human sociability, and the more they are developed in an ethnic group the higher this group is from the point of view of social organisation.

The Graphic Arts.—It is often among the less advanced and

[1] See, for more details, the excellent article of Andree on "Masks" in his *Ethnographische Parallele*, Neue Folge, p. 107.

more uncultured peoples that we find very skilful draughtsmen. And here it is necessary to make a distinction between design properly so called, whether it be on the flat surface, in bas-relief, engraved, etc., and what is generally called *ornamental* or *decorative art.* The latter exists among almost all peoples (except perhaps the Fuegians), and does not always spring from artistic feeling. Sometimes vanity, the desire to possess the most ornate object, inspires the hand of the artist, who almost always, among the uncivilised, is not a professional. The characteristic trait of the decorative art of primitive peoples is that every leading idea is inspired by real objects; there are no lines purely and voluntarily ornamental, and still less are there geometric figures, as was thought until recent times. All the supposed figures of this class are simplified drawings of animals, inanimate objects, etc.[1] The most frequent ideas are inspired by animals (zoomorphs), men (anthropomorphs), and manufactured objects (skeuomorphs); those which are drawn from plants (phyllomorphs) are excessively rare (Haddon).

FIG. 61.—Zoomorph ornamental design on a club (New Guinea). (*After Haddon.*)

FIG. 62.—Zoomorph ornamental design on a spatula (New Guinea). (*After Haddon.*)

Fig. 60 shows us, for example, in an engraving on a bark belt executed by a Papuan, the human face transformed into an ornamental motive. At the extremity of the object is still plainly seen a face with both eyes, and a mouth widely opened showing a fine set of teeth; lower down, perpendicularly to this,

[1] In this connection see E. Grosse, *Die Anfänge der Kunst*, Freib. and Leip., 1894; Haddon, *Evolution in Art*, London, 1895; H. Stolpe, *Studies i Amerikansk Ornamentik*, Stockholm, 1896.

we see two faces with only the mouth and a single eye left, its companion having strayed into the intervening space between the two faces. Another example: the head of the frigate bird, a favourite ornamental *motif* of the half-Melanesian populations

FIG. 63.—Conventional representation of an alligator; ancient pottery of Chiriqui, Isthmus of Panama. (*After Holmes.*)

of the south-east extremity of New Guinea, is plainly visible in the middle of the second row, and throughout the fourth row of ornaments on a club (Fig. 61), but it is transformed into arabesques on the other rows. Overlapping in a certain order,

FIG. 64 —Ornamental motive derived from the preceding design (Chiriqui pottery). (*After Holmes.*)

this head is transformed into spiral ornaments (Fig. 62). In the same way, among the ancient inhabitants of Chiriqui (Isthmus of Panama) the already somewhat diagrammatic figure of the alligator (Fig. 63) is transformed into ornament (Fig. 64) in which it would be difficult, without the presence of intermediate forms, to find a resemblance to the reptile in question. Among the Karayas of Central Brazil ornaments like those reproduced here (Fig. 65) are simplified forms of lizards (A), bats (B), of the skin of a rattle-snake (C), and of another snake (D).[1] Imitations of manufactured objects, drawing of cords, arrangement of fibres in a tissue, etc., are often suggested by the mode of manufacture of the decorated object—for example, in pottery by the impress of the woven basket which has served as a mould in the manufacture of the pot, etc. (see p. 154). Often the entire object is transformed into ornament and becomes unsuitable for the use to which it was intended, such as the double fish-hooks in mother-of-pearl of the islanders of the Torres Straits,[2] and the ornamental and symbolic axes of the Polynesians of the Hervey Islands or Cook's Archipelago (Fig. 67).

FIG. 65.—Decorative designs of the Karayas (Central Brazil)—A, lizards (engraved on a tomb); B, flying bats; C, rattle-snake; D, other snake (plaiting on a club). (*After Von den Steinen.*)

It is interesting to note that the more a people loves ornament, the less it is capable of producing drawings properly so called. Thus the Polynesians, the Malays, the Indians of North-west America, are past-masters in ornamentation, but they draw badly; while the Australians, whose ornaments are rudimentary, paint on the polished surfaces of rocks and grottos, in white, red, and yellow, large pictures representing hunting scenes, "corroborees," also human faces with a sort of aureole around them (hair?), but almost always without a mouth. The Bushmen, whose tools and arms bear no ornament, have also their great rock-pictures. We can form an idea of them by the annexed reproduction of a picture drawn

[1] Von den Steinen, *Unt. Naturvolk. Zent. Braz.*, Berlin, 1894.

[2] See the plate at p. 77 of Haddon's work, already quoted.

FIG. 66.—Bushman painting, representing the battle going in favour of the Bechuana, who are trying to recover their stolen cattle. (*After R. Andree.*)

on the wall of a cave near Hermon, and published by Andree.[1] It represents Bushmen, who have carried off the cattle of the Bechuanas, engaged in a struggle with the latter, who are pursuing them. All the details of the picture are well observed, even to the form and coats of the oxen, the respective colours, stature, and arms of the combatants (the little yellow Bushmen armed with bows, and the tall, black Bechuanas armed with assagais). The Melanesians are as skilful in ornamentation as in drawing, their drawing having a tendency to become transformed into pictography; pictography has almost entirely swallowed up drawing among the Indians of North America, but it reappears among the Hyperboreans (Eskimo, Chukchi, Yakuts, Tlinkits). What all these primitive drawings lack is perspective and relief; we should also look in vain for it in the art of half-civilised peoples like the Chinese, the Hindus, the Persians, the Cambodians.

Sculpture, which like drawing is met with even among the remains of quaternary man in Europe (Fig. 85), attains little development among uncultured peoples in general. The carved wooden articles of the Melanesians and Negroes, the gigantic statues of the Polynesians of Easter Island, the figures in low relief of the monuments of the ancient Peruvians, Mexicans, and Khmers, the numerous little figures in wood or potter's clay of the Malays, Negroes, etc., are not superior to the stage of development of Egyptian and Greek art earlier than the fifth century B.C., in which the median or sagittal plan of the human body is always straight, vertical, and never distorted. Even if there is an assemblage of two or more figures, their lines are always either parallel or perpendicular to each other.[2] Needless to say that among many peoples "national art" has been profoundly modified by an adopted religion, which has introduced or created an art of its own (prohibition against representations of human figures by Islam, conventional postures in Buddhist drawings, etc.).

[1] Andree, *Eth. Paral.*, N.F., p. 67.

[2] See on this subject I. Lang, *Billedkunst. Fremstell.*, etc.; *Vidensk. Selsk. Shrif.*, 5th series; *Hist. Philos.*, vol. v., No. 4, Copenhagen, 1892 (with French Summary).

Dancing.—The productions of the graphic arts charm the eye after completion; those of the musical arts are enjoyed only while being performed. But there is an art which combines these two modes of æsthetic enjoyment: it is *dancing*. Its plastic attitudes are so many pictures, and its movements have a rhythm like music.

FIG. 67.—Symbolic adze of Mangaia Island (Hervey Islands or Cook's Archipelago, Polynesia), Museum of Copenhagen. (*After Haddon.*)

This art, sunk among civilised peoples to the level of a simple amusement, plays a large part in the life of uncultured peoples. Thus the great nocturnal festivals of the Australians, the "Corroborees" (Fig. 59), celebrated in connection with important events, are only a succession of very varied dances, strictly regulated, and executed by young men trained a long time beforehand by the elders of the tribe for these choregraphic exercises. Men alone take part in them, as in all serious affairs; women are only there as spectators or musicians. It is by dancing alone that, among uncultured peoples, joy in common is expressed in regard to a happy event which affects the whole tribe. Let us also note that these dances are executed by a gathering of individuals who have given proof of their solidarity, having sacrificed part of their liberty by submitting to the discipline of the elders in order to afford pleasure to the people of their tribe. The joy, moreover, is mutual, for the performers "feel" the dance without seeing it, and the spectators witness it without experiencing the immediate effects of movement.

Dancing is then a great school of "solidarity" in primitive societies; more than any other act, it brings into prominence the benefits of sociality. But this favourable result is only possible in the smaller groupings, in which at least half of the society may take part in the dance; this condition no longer exists in civilised societies, numbering millions on millions of members: thus in these societies the choregraphic art is in a complete state of decay.

Dances of the character of "corroborees" are a step towards the *ritual dances* which play so great a part in most religions. I may instance the epileptic dances of the Siberian and American Shamans, or the Negro fetich-worshippers, the gyrations of the Dervishes, the masked ballets performed by the Buddhist-Lamaite priests, the sacred dances of the Levites among the ancient Jews, etc. Christianity retained the dance in its rites even until the eighth century, and one may still see the partial survival of it in what takes place in Seville Cathedral during the Easter festival. Dancing assumed a sacred character by being conjoined with a symbolic mimicry, especially as connected with offerings, with sacrifices, or with religious ecstasy.

But it has also evolved in another direction by having associated with it two other species of mimicry, one recalling strife and battles, the other love. Hence come *warlike dances* and *lascivious dances*. The latter have this characteristic, that they are performed either solely by women—as, for example, the "Hula-Hula" of the Hawaiians—or by both sexes (Eskimo), and very seldom by men alone (the "Kaoro" of the Australians, performed at the advent of the marriage season, or the time of the yam harvest). Moreover, it may be presumed that the alternating dances of men and women were, at the beginning of societies, a powerful aid to sexual selection.

The movements performed during the dance vary with every people, and also according to the nature of the dance. The

Australians leap, advance suddenly, then fall back with threatening or lascivious gestures, as the case may be (Fig. 59); Negroes add to the steps and innuendoes movements of the head and pelvis. Among most Asiatics (Chinese, Japanese, Malays) men do not dance, and in the case of women, the choregraphic art degenerates into a series of rhythmical movements of the arms and trunk, without change of position. It is to mimicry, that is to say, the first step towards pantomime, that dances imitating the movements of animals (Eskimo, Araucans) owe their origin. The pantomime of the uncultured, like their dancing, is always accompanied by music and song, sometimes by masks and disguises. We have but to develop the share of song and recitation, to render the music less dependent on the rhythm, in order to transform these exercises into real *dramatic representations.*[1]

Vocal and instrumental *music* are the common property of mankind as a whole. There is no people that does not know at least how to hum an air of a few notes; and rare are those who have no instrument of music (Fuegians, certain Micronesians, Veddahs). The music of uncivilised peoples is most frequently reduced to one only of its elements, rhythm, —better understood when we bear in mind that the greater part of the time it forms only the accompaniment of dancing. Melody and harmony are reduced to their simplest expressions.[2] And yet in the opinion even of specialists it is very difficult to note the airs of "savages," and three-fourths of the notations published in different works are incorrect. That is the result of these airs having been written down according to our scale, which is heptatonic. Now this scale, although existing even among many uncivilised peoples, is not the only one which is used.

We find them using certain successions of sounds with fixed intervals, that is to say, true scales of two, three, and even six sounds. Most frequently "natural tones" (tonic,

[1] Wallaschek, *Primitive Music*, chap. viii., London, 1893.

[2] Grosse, *Anf. d. Kunst*, chap. iii.

third, fifth) form the scale (Bushmen). The airs of uncivilised peoples are often in the *minor* tone, for example, the following Fuegian air, transcribed by Carfort:—[1]

In fine, the scale being merely a convention based on the construction of instruments, the most perfect of which, like our violin, can only give half-tones or, exceptionally, quarter or third tones, there can be no such thing as a "natural scale." It is the musical instruments of a people that determine the scale it uses; thus the study of these instruments should precede that of singing.[2]

As the most primitive music may be reduced to rhythm alone, the earliest musical instruments were objects serving to beat time; pieces of wood clapped together, as still seen to-day among the Annamese, or rude drums like those which the Australian women use during the corroborees—a cloak of opossum skin stretched between the thighs, on which they tap with a stick (Fig. 59). But, like castanets, the triangle, etc., these, properly speaking, are not instruments of music producing a scale, or at any rate a series of varying sounds. Three kinds of true musical instruments may be distinguished—wind instruments, string instruments, and percussion instruments. Of wind instruments the most ancient is probably the flute or the shepherd's pipe of cane, bamboo, animal or human bone, etc., as seen among the Botocudos and the Yurunas of Xingu

[1] *Miss. Scientif. Cap Horn*; vol. i. *Hist. d. Voy.* by Martial, p. 210, Paris, 1888.

[2] Tylor, *Anthropology*, p. 292; Wallaschek, *loc. cit.*, pp. 151, 155, and *Mitth. Anthr. Ges. Wien.*, 1897, vol. xxiii., Sitzungsb., p. 11. According to the investigations of Weber, the ear can distinguish sounds which vary $\frac{1}{64}$th of a semitone.

(Brazil).[1] The bow was the first corded instrument; the Kafirs and Negroes of Angola "play on the bow" by attaching to it a gourd and tightening at will by means of a sliding ring the cord which they play (Fig. 135). As to instruments of percussion: the most generally used among the Negroes are the Sansá, a sort of musical box (Fig. 68), and the xylophone, a kind of piano (Fig. 69). The most uncivilised peoples, however, have composite instruments; as, for instance, the "gora" of the Bushmen (Figs. 70 and 71).[2]

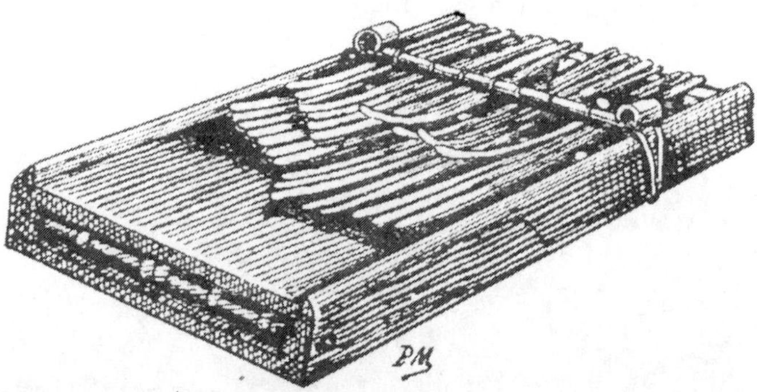

FIG. 68.—"Sansá" or "Zimba," a musical box of the Negroes, placed on or in a calabash; played with the fingers. (*After Wood.*)

The harp of the Kafirs and the gora give forth only feeble sounds, and serve chiefly to satisfy the musical taste of the performer; they are scarcely heard by the others. This fact,

[1] According to Wallaschek (*loc. cit.*, p. 155), the heptatonic scale (diatonic) owes its origin to the construction of the primitive flute, which had at most six to eight holes. To have had more would have been useless, as the instrument could not have been held without more fingers. Facility in making this instrument is due to the fact that, holes simply being pierced at regular intervals along the tube, a series of the most harmonious sounds can be obtained.

[2] Here is a description of it: a quill split and cut into the form of a leaf is attached to the end of a bow (Fig. 71); it is held to the mouth and set vibrating; it is then a reed and a stringed instrument combined. But it gives forth such feeble sounds that the artist is obliged to stuff one of his fingers in his nose and the other in his ear so as better to hear the music; it serves thus as a sort of microphone.

like others, proves that music is a less powerful means of socialisation than dancing; it affords joys more intimate, more individual, except when it is reduced to what is its least musical element so to speak—rhythm; then the part it plays is a considerable one, especially in warlike manifestations. No army has been able to do without music.

Poetry.—Singing and poetry are indistinguishable during the early stages of civilisation. The poetic productions of uncultured peoples have as yet been very little studied,[1] but from what is known about them it appears that the earliest

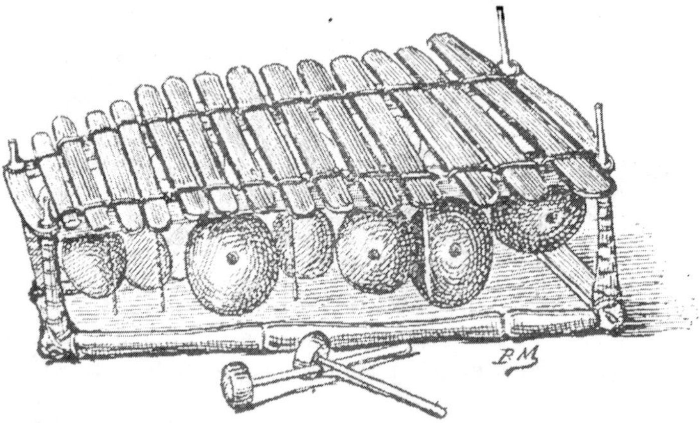

FIG. 69.—"Marimba," the Negro xylophone. (*After Wood.*)

creations of this kind are repeated rhythmical phrases, expressing the most common sensations, and concerned chiefly with the digestive functions: complaint in regard to hunger, the pleasure experienced after feasting, or a desire for certain articles of food as expressed in this song of the Australian—

> "The peas that the white men eat are good—
> I should like some, I should like some."

Afterwards come the emotions of hunting: the jubilation at

[1] The only all-round study that I know is the chapter "Poetry" in Grosse's work, *Die Anf. d. Kunst*, from which I borrow my account and some selected examples, which he gives from Eyre, Spencer, and Grey.

having killed an animal, recitatives after the manner of the following :—

"The Kangaroo ran very fast,
But I ran faster still.
How fat he was,
How plump he was!
What a fine roast he made!
O Kangaroo, O Kangaroo."

FIG. 70.—Bushman playing on the "gora." (*Partly after Wood.*)

War-songs are not unknown to Australian savages, but the beauties of nature and the feelings of love are subjects only occasionally met with in the poetry of uncivilised hunters. They begin to appear among the Eskimo, and are highly developed among half-civilised nomads, contemplators of nature, whose lyric poetry is sometimes inspired by very elevated feelings, as is shown, for example, by Kalmuk songs.[1] As to epic poetry, it is met with only among half-civilised peoples who possess a history.

Religion.—For a considerable time now the question has been discussed by ethnographers, theologians, and moralists, whether or not there exist peoples without a religion. The answer to this question depends entirely on the meaning we give to religion. If by this word is meant an acknowledged revealed doctrine, accompanied by a well-ordered ritual and a strongly organised priesthood, as implied in current speech, or even if it simply means the belief in "beings superior to man" and in "a future beyond the tomb," as Quatrefages would use it,[2] there are certainly peoples who

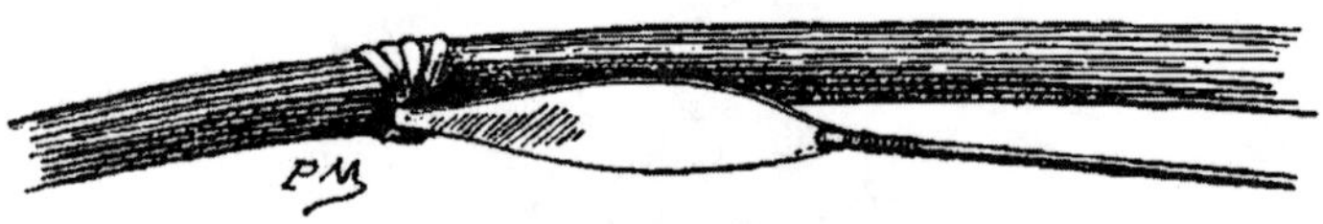

FIG. 71.—Detail of construction of the "gora." (*After Wood.*)

have nothing of this kind. If, on the contrary, we content ourselves with the *minimum definition* of religion, given by E. B. Tylor,[3] "belief in spiritual beings," it is difficult to find a tribe on the earth which has not this belief. I should like to modify a little this definition of Tylor's by substituting "imaginary beings" for "spiritual," to indicate clearly their psychological origin, for it is in beings entirely created out of their imagination that savages believe.

This belief originates chiefly in the fear of unusual or extraordinary events, and especially of disease and death. Sometimes the idea of a "spiritual being" is so inseparable from the sensation of fear that it only presents itself when the latter occurs. Thus the Fuegian Yahgan have no clear idea of "spirits," and it is only at dusk under the influence

1 Deniker, "Les Kalmouks," *Rev. d'Anthr.*, 1884, p. 671.
2 De Quatrefages, *L'espèce humaine*, 2nd ed., p. 356, Paris, 1890.
3 E. B. Tylor, *Primitive Culture*, vol. i.

of fear that they imagine themselves to be attacked by the "savages of the west," by the "Walapatu," which some of them regard as ghosts, and others quite simply as individuals of a neighbouring tribe, that of the Alakalufs.[1]

But cases of this kind are rare, and most uncivilised peoples have the rudiments of natural religion a little more developed, a belief in spirits less vague. We may, with the eminent ethnologist Tylor, give the name of "Animism" to this primitive religion.

Animism in the most primitive forms consists in believing that the body of a man contains another more subtle being, a "soul," capable of being temporarily separated from its envelope, and admitting further that everything that exists, beasts, plants, stones, down to objects fashioned by hand, have equally a soul which is endowed with corresponding qualities. Thus the Shans of the Kieng-Tung (upper Burma) believe that the soul leaves the body of a man asleep in the form of an iridescent butterfly;[2] the Malays have the same ideas, and take care on that account not to awaken a man asleep. His observation of the shadow which exactly repeats every movement of a man, of reflections in the water, may confirm a savage in his animistic beliefs, but what especially establishes them are the dreams and visions during which he lives another life and is "another man." Death is considered as a separation of man from his shadow or his soul, something like the separation which is effected during sleep. Most frequently it is the breath, the air breathed

[1] These Yahgans give the name of "Kachpik" vaguely to: 1, very wicked imaginary beings living in the depth of the forests, and, 2, every person who has a strange or wicked character. They give the name of "Hanuch" to: 1, imaginary beings with an eye at the back of the head and no hair, and, 2, to madmen or individuals living alone in the forests. It is the belief in these three or four imaginary beings to which all religious manifestations of the Yahgans may be reduced. (Hyades and Deniker, *loc. cit.*, p. 253.)

[2] R. Woodthorpe, *Journ. Anthr. Inst.*, vol. xxvi., No 1, August 1896. In Yorkshire the country people call the night butterfly (sphinx) "soul," and in Ireland butterflies are the souls of ancestors (L. Gomme, *Ethnology in Folklore* ,

out, which represents the immaterial being that forsakes the body. Thus, among the natives of Nias Island, the one to become chief is he who succeeds, sometimes not without a desperate struggle with his rivals, in swallowing the last breath of the dying chief.[1] Besides, for the most part uncivilised people think that death is only a prolonged sleep, and it is on that account that some are accustomed to keep the corpse as long as possible, sometimes until putrefaction sets in, in their huts or in the immediate neighbourhood (see p. 243). They imagine that the soul seeks to re-enter the body, and if it does not find it, wanders restlessly around the dwellings, and is angry with the living who have hidden the body from it. Cases of lethargy, of hypnotic sleep, of fainting-fits, which strike the imagination the more forcibly because more rare than ordinary sleep, confirm the belief in the separation of man and his double. In fine, the mind of a savage does not regard death as a natural phenomenon, but as a violent and very prolonged separation of man and his soul.

But what is the cause of this separation? Here comes in the second element of animism, the belief in "spirits," imaginary beings who take the most diverse forms, like the soul itself. Sometimes the "soul" of a dead man is also a "spirit"; there are here no subtle distinctions. However, what especially differentiates "spirits" from "souls" is this, that the former are more active, that they constantly take part in human affairs, so that the whole life of a savage is passed in compromises or continual struggles with spirits. Every disease, every misfortune, every death, comes from the angry "spirit." Happily, side by side with wicked spirits, who are legion, there are encountered from time to time benevolent ones, who become protectors, or "patrons" of men. Most frequently these are the "souls" of the old men of the tribe, of the "ancestors." As these old men have

[1] Modigliani, *Un Viaggio a Nias*, p. 277, Milan, 1890. Besides, the Nias admit, like many other peoples, three souls in man; that which manifests itself by the breath is comparable to the "double" of the ancient Egyptians.

ordinarily endowed the tribe or the family with some material advantage by giving during life counsels dictated by their long experience, they are laid under contribution after death. Their memory is recalled in times of misfortune, and advice is asked of them. This is the origin of ancestor worship.

The number of spirits is infinite, there is a whole world of them. Every object, sometimes every category of objects, has its spirit, and as objects may be made so spirits may be created, or at least may be made to communicate to objects a portion of their power. This circumstance gives birth to *fetichism*,[1] which is only one of the sides of animism, one of the grossest forms. Fetichistic peoples consider certain objects called *fetiches*, *gris-gris*, etc., as beings endowed with an inherent will and power. Every object, a piece of wood, a bundle of grass, a stone, a nail, a claw, a lock of hair, a horn, a rag, a bit of string, may become fetiches; the material value of the object bears no relation to its power as a fetich; the most insignificant things may be the greatest fetiches.[2] As to the relations which exist between spirits and objects, they are of a twofold character: either the fetich is regarded as an animated being, as the material envelope of a spirit,

[1] The word "fetichism" is a corruption of the Portuguese term *feitiço*, "charm," derived probably from the Latin *factitius*, in the sense "full of magical artifices," which the first navigators on the coast of Guinea applied to the fetiches venerated by the Negroes. Des Brosses was the first to introduce, in 1760, the term "fetichism" to denote the belief in fetiches. Auguste Comte gave a much more extended meaning to the word, to denote a religious state opposed to polytheism and monotheism. To-day the fetichism of Auguste Comte is the *animism* of English ethnographers, of which true fetichism forms only a part. (E. Tylor, *Prim. Cult.*, vol. ii., p. 143.)

[2] In certain cases, fetiches are supposed to be animated with power of movement; thus the staffs which negro sorcerers put into the hands of men in convulsions, caused by wild dances, are reputed to draw these men in their mad career, and to direct them in the search of persons accused of crime. Similarly, the two staffs which the Siberian Shamans hold in their hands during their exorcisms are supposed to draw them, like horses driven at full gallop, towards regions inhabited by spirits.

or it is only an instrument by which the existence of the spirit is manifested, a vehicle in some way of part of its power. It must be remarked, however, that the two forms of connection between the spirit and the material object are frequently interblended, and a fetich to which sacrifices are offered as to a living being, may become a simple amulet preserving its possessor from wounds or any other misfortune. Fetichism is the first step towards *idolatry*, but it is essentially distinguished from it in that idols are only *images, representations* of certain supernatural beings, whilst fetiches are these beings themselves, or at least the direct vehicles of a portion of their power. The boundary line between idolatry and fetichism is, however, often difficult to define exactly.

Animism with its variants, more or less developed, is the religion of all uncivilised peoples untouched by international or universal religions: Buddhism, Christianity, Mahomedanism, etc., and even among those who have accepted one of these religions, animistic ideas persist with great obstinacy.

How many Christian peasants there are who believe as firmly in spirits, in ghosts, in guardian genii of cattle and crops, as in the various saints of the church with whom they sometimes confound them! Besides, spirits, such as angels and demons, are admitted by most Christian churches. Fetichistic practices also form part of the outer worship of Lamaite Buddhism and Taoism, and they are not only tolerated but prescribed by other universal religions. I need but mention the amulets, talismans, scapularies, miracle-working relics, etc., among Mahomedans (Figs. 139 and 140) and Christians (Fig. 161).

Worship of Natural Objects and Phenomena.—It is impossible to review even the principal forms which animism assumes. As society grows and develops, the notion of the soul and of spirits is transferred from the more immediate objects surrounding man to objects more remote and the phenomena of nature. The latter, by reason of their greatness or violence, are regarded as spirits much higher and more powerful than the others. They become superior divinities entitled to "worship." Thus we have the worship of water (sacred rivers, Ganges, Nile), worship of plants and especially trees (sacred forests of the Gauls, the Germans, the Finns, the Papuans), the worship of animals and more especially birds (the eagle of the Aztecs and the Peruvians, the ibis of the Egyptians), and serpent-worship (prevalent everywhere, but principally in India and Western Africa).

The worship of the elements varies according to the kind of life led by a people; the succession of climates, the rain which gives life to the seed, the sun which burns the grasses, etc., are incarnations of so many divinities for agricultural peoples, while they have no importance for peoples living by the chase. Fire is considered as a divinity by several peoples (see p. 153). The adoration of fire was the ancient religion of the Persians, and is still preserved to-day among certain Parsees of India: we pass over the god Xiuhtecutli, "lord of fire," of the ancient Mexicans, the goddess Vesta of the Romans, etc. Often the worship of the sun was combined with that of fire, and the ancient solar festivals sung by Ovid have become the midsummer eve bonfires, which the clergy still bless every year in several places in Lower Brittany. I can only mention the legends relating to the divine origin of fire, which all resemble more or less that of Prometheus (the *Mahonika* of the Polynesians, the *Tleps* of the Circassians, etc.). The difference between the great spirits which animate the phenomena of nature and the little spirits concerned with the trivial facts of man's daily life once admitted, there is established a hierarchy in the world of spirits entirely modelled on the hierarchy of human society. Above gnomes, elves, demons, sprites, and so many common spirits, we find among the Khonds[1] the six great gods (of rain, first-fruits, procreation, hunting, war, and boundaries), who in their turn are governed by the sun-god and his wife, the powerful goddess of the earth. The religion of the Khonds is already *polytheism*, and this may end either in the dualism of two contrary prin-

[1] Macpherson, quoted by Tylor, *Primitive Culture*, vol. ii., p. 325.

ciples (the germs of which are seen in the example quoted above, and which are impersonated by Ormuzd and Ahriman of the religion of Zoroaster) or in *pantheism* or *monotheism*.

Religion and Morality.—Animistic religion is destitute of the moral element which many persons consider inseparable from religion. Its code of morals has nothing to do with religion; it is based on public opinion and social conventions independent of beliefs. It is only in the more developed forms of polytheistic or monotheistic religions, and especially in those whose ministers sought to have an effective influence on the people, that the moral element was introduced little by little and placed beside the dogmatic and ritual element.[1] If the survival of the soul and the after-life form part of the beliefs of a great number of uncultured peoples, as shown especially by funereal rites, the life beyond the tomb is for them only the continuation of real life; the country of the dead resembles the country of the living, the same customs flourish there, the same usages, the same kind of life; the Eskimo continue their fishing feats, and may even die there a second time; the Polynesians give themselves up there to the same pleasures as they enjoyed on earth, etc. The other world is only a duplicate of this world, and no idea of justice is connected with it; the evil and the good in it have the same destiny.[2]

Rites and Ceremonies.—What is the nature of the relations of man and spirits in primitive religion? Sometimes an attempt is made to combat the spirits. The Fuegians barricade themselves in their huts and keep themselves armed, in readiness to ward off blows, the whole night long, when they fancy they hear the "walapatu";[3] the Austrālians hold

[1] E. Tylor, *Primitive Culture*, vol. i., p. 427.

[2] Put forward by Tylor (*Prim. Cult.*, vol. ii., chaps. xii. and xvii.), the ideas which I here formulate have been developed by L. Marillier ("Survivance de l'âme:" Paris, 1894, *Pub. École prat. Hautes Études, sect. Sc. relig.*), and combated by Steinmetz (*Arch. für Anthro.*, vol. xxiv., p. 577), but the arguments of the latter do not seem to me convincing. He compares, for example, the difference of the destiny of the noble and the common Polynesians in the other world to distributive justice.

[3] Hyades and Deniker, *loc. cit.*, p. 254.

an annual celebration for the purpose of getting rid of all the ghosts of the last year's dead; the Negroes of the Gold Coast assemble together in arms from time to time to drive the evil spirits from their village; rushing about in all directions, with frantic howling, they return home and assert that they sleep more easily, and for a while afterwards enjoy better health.[1] But these contests with spirits are rare, and it is usually found preferable to employ craft against them (hence exorcism, incantation, the use of symbols, etc.), or gentleness (prayer, offerings, sacrifices). The last method, which is most frequently used, develops into an outward cult; the "fetich-house," like that seen in Dahomey and other Negro countries, becomes transformed into a temple; the place of sacrifice into an altar, and instead of real animals or plants, images of them in paper, butter, clay, etc., are sacrificed, or finer offerings such as grass, flowers, perfumes, etc.

Priesthood.—In the earliest stages of religion man put himself into communication with spirits at his own risk and peril; but as he soon perceived that he was frequently unsuccessful in obtaining what he wished, and could not prevent them laying their spells on him, he was compelled to have recourse to intermediaries. He observed that certain individuals are better fitted to deal with spirits; that they can fall into a trance and remain in this death-like condition long enough to be able to treat with demons, and he came to the conclusion that they were appointed to intercede with spirits for simple mortals and to direct propitiatory ceremonies, offerings, and prayers. It was thus that the priesthood arose, under the form of fetich-men or shamans, who play so important a part in the life of Negroes, the Tunguse peoples and Mongols, and the Indians of North America. All the functions of life, marriage, pregnancy, the entering upon the age of puberty, birth, death, hunting or warlike expeditions, require the offices of the sorcerer, of the shaman, who is usually at the same time a doctor (see below). As society develops, numerically and in civilisation, there is

[1] E. Tylor, *loc. cit.*, vol. ii., p. 199.

formed a sacerdotal class, which sometimes holds both the temporal power and the civil (as is still the case to-day in certain regions of Africa, and in Thibet). Often side by side with the regular priesthood thus constituted the ancient sorcerers continue to live and to wield great authority over the people; in most of the Lama-Buddhist temples the presence of a sorcerer is admitted for oracles, propitiations, etc.

International Religions.—This is not the place to speak of universal or international religions like *Brahmanism*, spread over India and the Asiatic archipelago; the once flourishing *Buddhism* of the south, based on the doctrine of the "little vehicle" (Hinâyâna), the last remains of which are to be found in Siam and the Island of Ceylon; the Buddhism of the north, or Lamaism, based on the doctrine of the "great vehicle" (Mâhāyāna), which rules the Thibetan and Mongol world, nor of the other more or less altered forms of this religion, Chinese Foïsm, Japanese and Annamese Buddhism, Indian Jainism, etc. And we must take for granted as better known the other universal religions, *Judaism* with its sects which do not acknowledge the *Talmud* (like the *Karaites* of the Crimea); *Mahomedanism*, with its two principal divisions, the sect of *Shiahs* (Persians) and that of the *Sunis* (other Mahomedan peoples); *Christianity*, with its great divisions and numerous sects (Copts, Nestorians, etc.). And we must notice finally the "national religions"—*Taoism* in China, *Shintoism* in Japan, *Confucianism* in both these countries, etc.

Myths.—Myths occupy an intermediate position between science, poetry, and religion, for they try to explain all phenomena while leaving a great deal to the imagination. The infinite variety of myths is only apparent. They all may be reduced to a very limited number of ideas or fancies, which are the same among all peoples. They are all explanations, more or less simple and childish, of the origin of plants, animals, men, the earth, the stars, etc., founded on the idea of animism. The details change according to the nature of the country, but the substance remains always the same. It is a vegetation of fancy more or less luxuriant and beautiful on the common ground of animism. Thus religion and myths are often one and the same thing, since they are derived from a common source, from that habit which primitive men share with children of giving a personality to every object they contemplate, from the sun to a knife, from a blade of grass to the ocean. We cannot dwell longer on this subject, which would require developing at considerable length;[1] I will merely say that on carefully studying myths we find in them psychological data relating to the mode of thinking of a people, rather than indications of the relations and affinity of one people with another, for borrowed details in myths are innumerable among all peoples.[2]

Sciences.—It is only with the rudiments of the sciences that we have to deal in the case of uncivilised and even half-civilised peoples.

The *knowledge of numbers* exists more or less among all the peoples of the earth. We often say, "Such a people can only count up to three, because it has no special word to denote a higher number." This reasoning is not always just, for, by adopting it, we might accuse the French of scarcely being able to count beyond sixty, since they have no special words for, say, seventy-five or eighty, and to express these fall back on words already employed in counting—sixty and fifteen or four score. Many savages employ a similar method. Thus the Yahgan Fuegians have only words for the number one (*Kaueli*), two (*Kombaï*), and three (*Maten*); but they make use of the words *Akokombaï* (literally "the other two," or "another time two") to denote four, and *Akomaten* (the other three) to indicate six.[3]

Certain Australians proceed in a similar manner.[4] If these

[1] See A Lang, *Culture and Myth;* and his *Modern Mythology*, London, 1897.

[2] Legends, traditional tales, proverbs, etc., are simplified myths, with the poetic element predominating. The study of them forms a special branch of ethnology called "Folk-lore."

[3] Hyades and Deniker, *loc. cit.*, p. 316.

[4] Brough Smyth, *The Aborigines of Victoria*, vol. ii., p. 3, London, 1878; Curr, *The Australian Race*, Melbourne-London, 1886-87, 4 vols. *passim*.

tribes had been able to continue the same process beyond this point they would have arrived at the duodecimal system; what they lacked for that were objects which should always be within their reach to assist them in this mode of calculation. Peoples who thought of distinguishing by special words the first five figures had at once, in their fingers, an aid to enable them to set up a decimal system. Many South American Indians, Caribs, Tupis, and Tamanacas of the Orinoco count by the fingers, hands, and feet, employing thus the decimal system; instead of five they say "a hand"; instead of ten, "two hands"; instead of twelve, "two hands and two fingers"; instead of fifteen, "two hands and one foot"; instead of twenty, "a man"; and so forth. With the development of civilisation the fingers of the hand are replaced by objects, by little stones, seeds or shells, which are arranged in boxes representing units, tens, etc. From these were derived the abaci of the Chinese and Russians.

Geometry—Calculation of Time.—Measures of distances, surfaces, etc., which gave birth to geometry, are found again among certain uncivilised peoples. The Indians of Veragua find the height of a tree by measuring the distance from which they see it, turning their back and bending the body in such a way that the head is between the outstretched legs; the ancient Egyptians measured the surfaces of their lands empirically by means of geometric figures, etc. The measurement of time by the movement of the stars exists among all peoples, the succession of day and night, and the phases of the moon, being the things easiest to observe. Thus days and months or "moons" are nearly everywhere equal. But it is not the same with regard to the year. It is the succession of vegetation or seasons which determines periods longer than months. Thus the Andamanese count by successions of three seasons (cold, dry, and wet); the Papuans by successions of two seasons (corresponding to the prevailing monsoons), but the epochs at which these seasons arrive do not coincide exactly with lunar divisions, and tallying computation becomes more difficult. Thus, as soon as writing was invented, the more intelligent of the nomadic tribes, especially, turned their attention towards noting coincidences of the position of the sun in relation to the constellations, according to the seasons, for the principal constellations, especially the Great Bear, Orion, the Southern Cross, are known by almost all the peoples of the earth, who have emerged from the state of savages dependent on the chase.

The verification of the time when the year begins (coinciding generally with some commemorative festival) became later the business of State astronomers (Egypt, India), who were at the same time astrologers or magicians.

Calendars and Clocks.—There are yet in China astronomers who periodically harmonise the lunar with the solar year, though, for the ordinary purposes of life, other peoples make use of the solar year calculated either from a reign (as in ancient Egypt), or day by day in a cycle of sixty years, formed by the combination of ten *kou* (stock) and twelve *tchi* (branches), as in the Hindu calendar. A similar calendar is found among the ancient Mexicans.[1] In regard to the divisions of the days into hours, they are somewhat uncertain among the Andamanese and Australians, and they begin to assume a definite character only with the introduction of the sundial, as for example among the Zuñi Indians, who have before nearly every cabin a pillar, the shadow of which serves to indicate the hours. In China and in Corea the use of the candle which burns a certain time is a remnant of the mode of calculating time according to the duration of the fire.[2] The running of water and sand has been utilised, as we know, in the construction of clepsydras and other primitive clocks of classic antiquity and of the Middle Ages.

Geography and Cartography.—We can only indicate summarily what primitive navigators and half-civilised nomads know of geography. Orientation according to the cardinal points is known even to peoples as primitive as the Fuegians

[1] R. Schramm, "Jahrform, etc.," *Mittheil der Geogr. Gesell.*, vol. xxvii., 1884, p. 481, Vienna.

[2] O. Mason, *Origins of Invention*, pp. 71 and 116.

and the Andamanese, but cartography is only developed among those who draw. The Australians can draw maps on the sand very accurately, except as regards distances; we have even maps drawn on weapons, like that of figure 79, F, representing a lagoon and an arm of Broken River, between which is situated the territory of the tribe to which the owner of the weapon belonged.[1] The Micronesians of the Marshall Islands construct with bamboo rods geographical maps in which these rods represent the direction of the currents, and the shells or seeds attached to their intersections, the different islands [2]

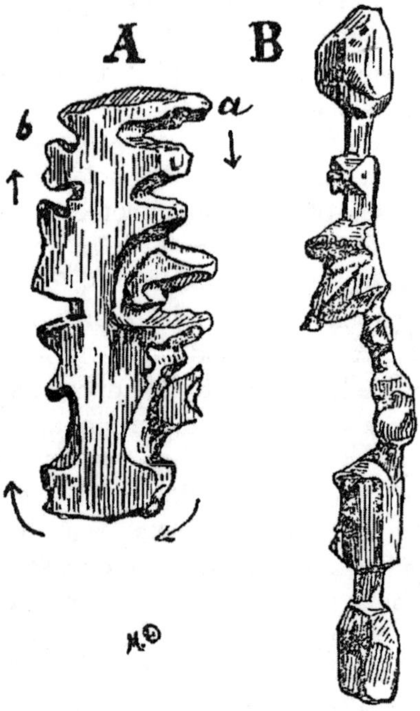

FIG. 72.—Eskimo geographical map. (*After Holm.*)

But it is the Eskimo who excel in the cartographic art, as may be seen from the specimen which I reproduce from S. Holm.[3] This consists of two wooden tablets (Fig. 72). One of them (A) represents all the fiords, bays, and capes of that part of the coast of Eastern Greenland comprised between Kangerdenarsikajik (*a*) and Sicralik (*b*); we must read the names of these places in the direction of the arrow. The second tablet (B) represents the islands off the coast, situated opposite to different bays. By bringing it near to, or removing it from the first, we have the

[1] Brough Smyth, *loc. cit.*, vol. i., p. 284.

[2] Schmeltz and Krause, "Museum Godeffroy," Hamburg, 1881, p. 271 and plate xxxii.

[3] S. Holm, *Meddelels. om Groenl.*, p. 101, Copenhagen, 1887.

distance between the coast and each of the islands. The ancient Mexicans had topographical maps, marine charts, and even cadastral plans, much more perfect than those of the ancient Egyptians. The Chinese maps still further surpass these models, and remind one already of our coasting pilot books in their use of orientation by means of the compass.[1]

I should take up the whole chapter if I were to give an account, even in an abridged form, of everything concerning *primitive medicine.*[2] I will merely point out that, according to their animistic conception of the world, "savages" have no other idea of disease than as a malevolent manifestation of a spirit who enters into the man, of a demon who "possesses" him. Thus, fetich-men and shamans are the first doctors. They know how to "drive" from the body of the patient the evil spirit who torments him, to "draw out" the disease in the form of a pebble, or some other object deftly concealed before the operation. Moreover, the bones, mummified portions of the body of sick persons, or of fetich-men themselves, may become after their death relics possessing miraculous healing power, etc. For the matter of that, even among civilised peoples diseases are often attributed to the "evil eye," to "spells" (France), to "Jettatura" (Italy), etc. Among the Indians of North America there are also special healers (medicine-men) who are held in great esteem, and who sometimes form a corporation (*Mide*), into which admission can only be gained after a professional examination in the "doctors' cabin" (Schoolcraft, Hoffmann). Along with incantations and magical proceedings, with dancing and music, the principal remedies of the Australian healers and the American medicine-men are scarifications, blood-letting, and blood-sucking. Negroes show a preference for cupping-glasses. The processes of advanced surgery among certain peoples go as far as ovariotomy (Australians), laparotomy and the cæsarian operation (Negroes of Uganda); but not as far as the amputation of limbs, the fingers excepted. Trepanning, known from

[1] See for the details, Andree, *Ethn. Paral.*, p. 197.

[2] See Max Bartels, *Medecin der Naturvölker*, Leipzig, 1893.

the quaternary period in Europe, is also employed among Negroes, Persians, New Hebridians, etc., for nervous diseases, epilepsy, etc. The clyster, the great remedy of our ancestors, is hardly used, except by the Dakota Indians and the Negroes of the west coast of Africa, where also the doctor squirts the drug into the sick person from his mouth through the medium of a calabash (Monnier).[1] Attenuation of virus is even practised by, for example, the Bushmen, who use it to cure the bite of scorpions and serpents.[2]

[1] M. Monnier, *La France Noire*, p. 110, Paris, 1894.

[2] H. Schintz, *Deutsch Süd-west Africa*, p. 396, Oldenburg, 1894.

CHAPTER VII.

SOCIOLOGICAL CHARACTERS—*conclusion.*

3.—FAMILY LIFE.—Relations of the two sexes before marriage—*Marriage and family*—Theory of promiscuity—Group marriage—Exogamy and endogamy—Matriarchate—Degrees of relationship and filiation—Polyandry—Levirate—Polygamy and monogamy—Patriarchate—Rape and purchase of the bride—Duration of conjugal union—*Children*—Birth—Nurture—Name of the child and of adults—Initiation, circumcision, etc.—*Old men and their fate*—*Funereal rites*—Mourning.

4.—SOCIAL LIFE.—(*a*) *Home life of a people*—*Economic organisation*—The forms of property depend on production—Common property and family property—Village community—Individual property—*Social organisation*—Totemism—Clan rule—Family rule—Territorial rule—Caste and class rule—Democratic rule—Social morals—Right and justice—Taboo—Retaliation, vendetta, and ordeals—Secret societies—Extra legal judges—Formulæ of politeness—(*b*) *International life of peoples*—Absence of sympathetic relations—Hostile relations—*War*—Arms of offence—Bow and arrows—Arms of defence—Neutral relations—*Commerce*—Money—Cowry—Transports and means of communication—Primitive vehicles—Navigation.

THE subjects about to be treated are so vast and complicated that it is almost impossible to give an idea of them in a few words and without going into details. So our account will of necessity be somewhat dogmatic, and will only touch on some salient facts of family and social life.

3.—FAMILY LIFE.

The relations of the two sexes are somewhat free among uncivilised and half-civilised peoples so long as there is no formal marriage or birth of a child. In the whole of Oceania,

Malaysia, among the Samoyeds, Mongols, and certain Negroes, sexual intercourse between the young people of both sexes is by no means prohibited.[1] Sometimes even, as among the Bavenda for example, the young men and women give themselves up to obscene "games."[2] Uncivilised peoples among whom the loss of virginity would be considered dishonouring to a girl are somewhat rare (Nias islanders, Igorrotes, Malays of Menangkabau). Most of them treat it with indifference, and among some of them defloration is obligatory before marriage; it is effected artificially or naturally by the parents (Bataks, Pelew islanders), by the matrons (Bissayas of the Philippines), by the priests (Cambodia), and even, it is said, by persons paid for this kind of work.[3] It would be possible to give instances of many other customs which shock our ideas about chastity and marriage. Thus in the Algerian Arab tribe of the Ouled-Naïl, no young girl will find a husband if she has not previously acquired a dowry by regular prostitution. On the other hand, it must not be forgotten that the prostitution of girls before marriage was required by certain cults of antiquity (cult of Aphrodite at Abydos, Ephesus, etc., cult of Mylitta in Babylonia, etc.).

Marriage and Family.—But marriage once contracted, the woman, among almost all uncivilised and half-civilised peoples, is no longer free. From this moment either the husband, the family on the mother's or father's side, or the clan, see strictly to the observation of the marriage rules which are in vogue, and the laws, written or unwritten, punish every slip of the woman who was so free before marriage. It is the contrary to what one often sees in our civilised societies. In fine, *marriage* is above all a social convention, and the form which it takes in different ethnic groups is intimately connected with the social and economic constitution of these groups.

[1] S. Wilken, *Verglijk. Volkenkunde van Nederl. Ind.*, p. 293, Leyden, 1893; Ivanowsky, *loc. cit.*, p. 19 of the original impression; Post, *Grundz. ethnol. Jurisprud.*, vol. i., Oldenb.-Leipzig, 1894.

[2] Bartels, "Reife-Unsitten, etc.," *Zeit. f. Ethn.*, 1896 (Verh., p. 363).

[3] Giraud-Teulon, *Origines du mariage et de la famille*, p. 33, note, Paris, 1884; Wilken, *loc. cit.*, p. 294.

The position of woman in society, ideas on conjugal obligations, etc., are entirely subordinated to the ideas which prevail about property and the social organism.

Theory of Promiscuity.—We often hear it said that marriage has sprung from a "state of promiscuity" in which mankind primitively lived; every man could then couple with every woman, "like the animals," people sometimes add, forgetting that among animals the most akin to man this state of promiscuity is rather exceptional, and that the polygamous and even monogamous family exist among a great number of birds and mammals.[1]

The theory of promiscuity or "communal marriage," so well summed up some time ago by Lubbock,[2] has few defenders at the present day. We know that actually there does not exist on the earth any population practising an "irregular promiscuity," and the evidence of history is reduced to three or four texts of Herodotus, Strabo, and Solinus, the interpretation of which is far from easy.[3]

Group Marriage.—What has been often taken for promiscuity is only a form of marriage, different from our individual marriage, which, nevertheless, represents the first attempt to regulate sexual relations and to define

[1] See for further details, Letourneau, *The Evolution of Marriage, etc.*, chap. i., London; and Westermarck, *History of Human Marriage*, chaps. iv. to vi., London, 1891.

[2] Lubbock, *Origin of Civilisation*, chap. iii., 1875.

[3] The long list of peoples practising promiscuity given by Lubbock dwindles as we become better acquainted with the different populations in question. Certain peoples, like the Fuegians (Hyades and Deniker, *loc. cit.*), the Bushmen, the Polynesians (Westermarck, *loc. cit.*), the Irulas (Thurston, *Bull. Madras Mus.*, vol. ii., No. 1, 1897), the Teehurs of Oude (W. Crooke, *Tribes and Castes N. W. Province, etc.*, vol. i., p. clxxxiii., Calcutta, 1896), should be mercilessly struck out of this list, since they all have individual marriage to the exclusion of other forms. Others, like the Australians, the Todas, the Nairs, have been entered in it because they practise "group marriage" or certain forms of polyandry, which is not the same thing as promiscuity. There remains of the list but two or three tribes about whom we have no exact general information at all (example, the Olo-Ot of Borneo).

ties of kinship in order to ensure the existence and bringing up of children. This form of marriage, admirably studied by Howitt and Fison[1] among the Australians, has received from them the name of "group marriage." Its essential feature is that men and women, by the fact of belonging to such and such a group or clan are not marriageable one with another, and are obliged by the fact of their birth to contract unions with members of other groups of the tribe.

Marriage by groups is met with in its most pronounced form among the Australians and some tribes of India (Nairs, Todas). Among the Australians this custom co-exists with individual exogamous marriage (the "Noa" of the Dieri of Central Australia), and exhibits itself in its simplest form in the example of the Wotjoballuk Australians of the north-west of Victoria. This tribe is divided into two classes or clans, the Gamutch and the Krokitch. The men of the Gamutch clan are by right the husbands of all the women of the Krokitch tribe, and *vice-versâ*. But it is only a virtual right. In practice, during the great festivals of *initiation* (see p. 241), the old men of the tribe, assembled in council, distribute among the bachelors of a clan the unappropriated girls of the other clan. This marriage, called "Pirauru" among the Dieri, and known under the name of "Paramour custom" by the colonials, gives the right to the man of the Gamutch clan, for example, to contract a marriage with the woman of the Krokitch clan thus allotted to him when the occasion shall present itself; he may also take with him one or more of these women and make her or them live with his wife of the individual marriage. However, as the same woman may be allotted in the successive festivals to several men, there are certain rules of precedence to observe in the fulfilment of the conjugal duties, if chance puts two men before their "common" wife:

[1] A. W. Howitt, "Australian Group Relations," *Smithsonian Rep.*, Washington, 1883; A. W. Howitt and L. Fison, "Kamilaroi and Kurnai," Melbourne-Sydney, 1880, and *Journ. Anthr. Inst.*, vol. xii., p. 30, 1882.

the elder brother takes precedence of the younger, the man up in years of the youth.[1]

Exogamy and Endogamy.—Group marriage is closely connected with what is called *exogamy* or *exogeny*, that is to say, marriage outside the clan, as opposed to *endogamy* or *endogeny*, marriage within the clan. It must be said, however, that exogamy is as often met in the individual form of marriage, and that sometimes endogamy, interdicted within the limits of a clan, is, on the contrary, practised within the limits of the tribe of which these clans are the components. There is in this case exogamy in relation to the clan and endogamy in relation to the tribe.

Matriarchate.—But how are matters of filiation and family to be decided with such a system of marriage, for it is impossible to settle the question of paternity in this case? To Bachofen and McLennan[2] we must attribute the honour of having discovered a complete system of filiation, in vogue among many uncivilised peoples, and the exact opposite to that which we are accustomed to in our societies: filiation by the mother, or *matriarchate*. Thus in our example of the Australians of Wotjoballuk (p. 232), the posterity of a man of the Gamutch clan married to a woman of the Krokitch clan will belong to the Krokitch clan; if, on the contrary, the father is a Krokitch and the mother a Gamutch, the children will belong to the Gamutch clan. This filiation establishes the uterine relationship and, united to exogamy, prevents marriage between nearest relatives. In fact, the son of the first couple being of the Krokitch clan, will not be able to marry

[1] A. W. Howitt, "Dieri, etc.," *Journ. Anthr. Inst.*, vol. xx., 1890, p. 53. Among the Nairs of the coast of Malabar things are done in exactly the same way. The main point in both cases is the prohibition of marriage in the clan itself (L. Fison, "Classificat. Relationship," *Journ. Anthr. Inst.*, vol. xxv., 1895, p. 369). Among the Todas of Nilgiri the groups are limited in this sense, that the men who cohabit with a woman must be brothers, and at the same time can only marry with the sisters of this woman.

[2] Bachofen, *Das Mutterrecht*, Stuttgart, 1861; J. F. McLennan, *Studies in Ancient History*, London, 1876.

his uterine sister, since she is of the same clan as he is, but only an alien woman, or a relative, according to our conventions, of the Gamutch clan, for example, the sister of his father. Theoretically, a father of the Gamutch clan would be able to marry his daughter, since she belongs to the Krokitch clan; but in practice these cases are forbidden by custom, for example among the Australian Dieri,[1] or they are avoided by the existence not of two, but of four or a greater number of classes in the tribe, with prohibitions against the marriage of people of certain of these classes.[2]

However, peoples who practise group marriage and exogamy have not to regard incest very seriously, for *degrees of relationship* are not fixed with them as with us. To fix relationship, they make use of a system called by Morgan, who discovered it (among the American Indians first), and described it admirably,[3] the "*classificatory system.*" In its simplest form, such as it is met with, for example, among the Micronesians and the Maoris, it may be thus summed up. All persons allied by consanguinity are divided into five groups. The first is formed of *myself* and my brothers, sisters, and cousins; we all bear the same name, which is that of the whole group. The second group is formed of my father and mother with their brothers and sisters, as well as their cousins, all likewise bearing the same name; the third group comprises my grandparents, with their brothers, sisters, etc.; the fourth, the cousins of my children, whom I

[1] L. Fison, *loc. cit.*, *Journ. Anthr. Inst.*, vol. xxiv., 1895, p. 36.

[2] Thus, if there are four clans, A, B, C, and D, as among the Kamilaroi, for example, the children sprung from the parents of the clans A and B may not intermarry; they belong to the clan C, the members of which may only marry with the members of the clan D. It is their children only who will be able to contract marriages in the groups A and B. In this way incest is only possible between the grandfather and the granddaughter, that is to say, reduced practically to zero.

[3] L. Morgan, "Syst. of Consanguinity, etc.," *Smithson. Contrib. Knowl.*, vol. xvii., Washington, 1871; and *Ancient Society*, London, 1877. See also the very clear statement of the system in Lubbock, *loc. cit.*, and its extension to the Australians and the Melanesians of the Fiji Islands in Howitt and Fison, *loc. cit.*

consider as my sons and daughters; lastly, the fifth group is composed of the grandchildren of my brothers and sisters, whom I consider as my grandchildren. A similar system of nomenclature is very common among certain peoples of India, and sometimes causes much embarrassment to English judges newly landed. To give an example: A witness said that his father was at home at such and such an hour; then, a few minutes after, he affirmed that his father was in the fields. The judge is perplexed until, by a series of questions, he elicits the fact that the witness means his "little" father, equivalent to our term uncle.[1] Westermarck has tried to interpret the classificatory system differently; he sees in it only an artifice of speech, a way of addressing persons of different ages; but as Fison judiciously observes, if it be held that this system has no reference to degrees of relationship we should have to deny any idea whatever of this subject to certain peoples who have no other expressions to denote degrees of relationship.[2]

Polyandry, that is to say, marriage in which the woman possesses several husbands, is considered by the majority of authors as a form derived from group marriage. With the exception of two doubtful examples (Khasias and Saporogian Cossacks), polyandry always assumes the fraternal form; that is to say, the husbands of the woman are brothers. The classic country of polyandry is Thibet. There each of the brothers cohabits in turn with their common wife, a certain period being allotted. Among the ancient Arabs, according to Strabo, matters were arranged less systematically, and the first comer on his arrival at the woman's house asserted his marital rights, after having taken care, however, to place his staff across the door, as is still done in the case of temporary marriages in Persia and among the Todas, who leave the cloak as well as the staff. Polyandry is practised by several peoples living on the borders of Thibet (Miris, Dophlas, Abors,

[1] Tylor, *Journ. Anthr. Inst.*, vol. xviii., 1888-89, p. 262.

[2] Westermarck, *loc. cit.*, p. 82; L Fison, *loc. cit.* ("Classific. System"), p. 369.

Khasias, Ladakhis, etc.), but appears to be but rarely met with elsewhere, and almost never outside of India. It is explained by the scarcity of women in these countries (a statement not confirmed by statistics in regard to certain of them), and by the necessities of the pastoral life of these peoples.

Levirate, or compulsory marriage with a dead brother's widow, a very widespread custom in India (where it is called *niyoga*), among the Iroquois and other American Indians, the Melanesians, the Negroes, as well as the ancient Egyptians and Jews, is considered as a survival of polyandry. However, Maine, Westermarck, and others see in it only a custom established with a view to securing the protection of orphan children.[1] With polyandry is also connected, on not very good grounds it seems to me, *parental marriage*. In this form of union the father or uncle or some other relative really cohabits with the nominal wife of his son or nephew during the minority of the latter. This custom, according to Shortt, prevails in India among the Reddies or Naickers, and according to Haxthausen among the peasantry in Russia, where a modification of this kind of relation, strongly reprehended, however, is still known at the present day under the name "Snokhachestvo."[2]

Polygamy and Monogamy.—Individual marriage, which may, as we have seen in Australia, co-exist with group marriage, assumes two different forms—*polygamy* and *monogamy*. The latter does not necessarily proceed from the former. Many savage tribes, like the Veddahs and the Andamanese, are monogamous, as are also a certain number of mammals and birds. Among others (Fuegians, Bushmen) polygamy is exceptional. In reality it only takes root in societies a little more advanced, in which, especially, the idea of individual property is already more

[1] Maine, *Ancient Law*, p. 241, London, 1885; Westermarck, *loc. cit.*, p. 510.

[2] Shortt, *Transact. Ethn. Soc.*, London, N.S., vol. vii., p. 264; Haxthausen, *Transcaucasia*, p. 403, London, 1854. Leroy-Beaulieu (*L'Empire des Tzars*, vol. vi., chap. 5, p. 488, Paris, 1885-89) attributes this custom to the over-exercise of paternal authority.

or less firmly planted. Woman is then considered very much as a slave, from whom pleasure and labour may be obtained; she is treated like any other property; the more wives a man has, the richer and more esteemed is he. Polygamy is widely diffused over the world, either in its pure form (Mahomedans, Australians, American Indians, Negroes, etc.) or in its modified forms: lawful concubinage (all over the East), or unlawful (Europe), and temporary marriage (Persia, Japan).

It is only with the development of society that *monogamy*, nominal or real, develops, and with it a little respect for woman. She enjoys more liberty, as do also the children who have passed a certain age. Thus is constituted the family of to-day, in which, however, the patriarchal spirit is still dominant.

Patriarchate.—Individual polygamous marriage is most frequently allied to a new form of affiliation, that of kinship through males, which, in its turn, is rooted in the constitution of property and the subordination of woman to man. In the matriarchate the natural protector of the child and the family is the mother's brother; in the patriarchate his place is taken by the father, who extends the right of property not only to include the mother, but also the children; he may sell them, hire them out, etc. The patriarchate is the *régime* under which live most half-civilised peoples and a great number of uncivilised.

Several *matrimonial customs* may be explained by the primitive forms of marriage. Thus the practice of showing hospitality to a stranger by lending him one's wife, so common among savages and half-civilised nomads, may be explained as a relic of group marriage, in which, as we have seen, the exchange and the lending of women are practised.[1] Similarly, the custom, very prevalent, especially in Malaysia, which requires a husband to live in his wife's family, is considered by most authors as a relic of the matriarchate. Another

[1] The Torgoot Mongols, who practise this custom, explain it by the general rules of hospitality (Ivanovski, *loc. cit.*); in this respect they are in agreement with Westermarck, *loc. cit.*, chap. vi.

custom, nearly always allied to the first, but which is also met with as a survival in the cases where the woman goes to live with her husband's family, is that prohibiting newly-married couples from speaking to their fathers and mothers-in-law (*avoidance*). The best known form, widely diffused from the Kafirs to the Mongols, is the forbidding of the husband not only to speak to, but even to see his mother-in-law; if by chance he should meet her, he is obliged to take to flight, or, at any rate, to turn aside out of the way. Among several peoples of the Caucasus and certain North American Indians this custom is observed only until the birth of the first child. This custom, in a general way, is considered as a relic either of exogamy (Tylor) or of anti-incest customs (Westermarck).[1]

Among the most widely diffused practices having a connection with marriage, we must mention the abduction of the wife, whether real (Arabs, Turco-Mongols, Caribs, Patagonians, Burmese, Australians, etc.) or simulated and symbolic, and often forming part of the marriage ceremonies (among a host of peoples). Ethnologists are not agreed as to the origin of this custom; some see in it the last vestiges of exogamy, others the relic of the slavery of women, etc.

Side by side with simulated abduction there is almost always the purchase of the wife from her parents (the "Kalym" of the Turco-Tatars, etc.), which proves that marriage by purchase took the place of marriage by capture in the

[1] It must be observed on this point that, according to Westermarck, the horror of incest is not an instinctive sentiment (animals do not have it), but rather a social habit springing from sexual repulsion for persons, even unrelated to the family, with whom one has been brought up from infancy. Thus we often see marriages prohibited between one village and another (ancient Peru), or between god-parents, who superintend the baptism of a child, and are in no way allied to each other by blood (Russia). The learned Helsingfors professor, who believes in the omnipotence of sexual selection, explains the frequency of the aversion to incest by the survival of individuals who did not contract consanguineous marriages, always mischievous in his opinion. However, he admits that the bad effects of consanguineous marriages may be mitigated by material well-being, as is the case in Europe.

exogamous relations between tribes, and contributed to their social cohesion, preventing quarrels and wars (Tylor). The *marriage portion* is only found in societies having a relatively high organisation. It is, as it were, a payment for the guardianship which the husband assumes over the wife and her children under the patriarchal system. The institution of the marriage portion is probably derived from the practice still in vogue among many peoples, according to which the parents offer presents in exchange for the money or the service given as the purchase-price of their daughter.

The duration of the conjugal union varies so much among different peoples that no general rule can be laid down regarding it. From unions of a night (under the *régime* of group marriage, in temporary or trial marriages) to the indissolubility prescribed by the Christian religions, there is quite a scale of conjugal relations more or less durable. Most frequently the husband may discard the wife when she has ceased to please him; sometimes *divorce* is hedged round with certain formalities of established custom.

Children.—In all societies, as in the animal world, the family is principally established for the bringing up of *children.* But it is far from true that the arrival of children is everywhere accepted with joy. The voluntary limitation of progeny is not an invention of advanced civilisation. Savages could teach us much on this point. The Australians with this object practise ovariotomy on women, the operation "mika" (artificial hypospadias) on men, or simply kill off the superfluous infants. Infanticide on a large scale was practised by the Polynesians before their "Europeanisation"; it exists still here and there in Thibet, so far as girls are concerned. Some would even see in this custom the origin of polyandry.

Birth.—But having once decided to let a child live, the uncivilised look well after it. One could write a volume, if one wished to enumerate all the hygienic and at the same time superstitious customs attendant on the pregnancy, parturition, and recovery of the woman among different peoples. The act of generation is considered by nearly all the uncivilised as something at once mysterious and impure. The pregnant woman is kept quiet and rubbed; she has to occupy a hut apart before, during, or after the birth of the child, according to the custom of the different countries. Rarely is the woman allowed to be confined alone; the examples quoted have reference for the most part to isolated cases, such as may happen even among the civilised. She is often assisted at the time of the confinement by one or more women, and sometimes by men.[1]

Among the customs which accompany birth, the most curious is that of the "couvade" practised by the Basques, the Indians of Brazil and Guiana, and other peoples. According to this custom, the husband, after the coming into the world of the child, behaves exactly as if it were he who had been confined; he betakes himself to bed, receives congratulations, sometimes looks after the baby. E. B. Tylor sees in this custom a survival of the matriarchate in a society with a patriarchal *régime.* It would be the ransom paid by the husband for the right, which formerly belonged to the mother, to be called the head of the house.[2]

As to the child, from the moment of his entrance into the world, every effort is made to keep away from him the spirits which might harm him; the Laotians, in the vicinity of the house which shelters him, hang bells, rattles, and cloth-bands, so that, shaken by the wind, they may make a noise and keep away evil spirits (Harmand, Neis). The Malays and the Nias Islanders for this purpose prepare special fetiches (Modigliani).

The *name* which is given to a child is also the result of much care and forethought. Fetichers, shamans, sorcerers, and priests are consulted. The name chosen is sometimes determined by the locality or house of the birth. Thus the Kalmuks who were exhibited at Paris in 1882 gave the name of "Paris" to the child which one of their number brought into the world. The Negroes of Senegal, under similar

[1] See Ploss, *Das Weib*, 5th ed., vol. ii., 1897, Leipzig.

[2] E. Tylor, *Journ. Anthr. Inst.*, vol. xviii., p. 248.

circumstances in 1895, called one of their new-born "The Frenchman." But most frequently the name given is of a plant or animal (Red Indians, Mongols, etc.). It must be said, however, that among many peoples the name given at birth is not borne throughout life. It may be changed more than once. The most frequent cause for doing this is the fear of spirits; the Dyaks and the Mongols change the name of sick persons to "deceive the spirit" who has caused the disease; among the Fuegians, the Indians of North America, the Polynesians, and the Malays, the name of a dead man is not allowed to be uttered, and all his namesakes are obliged to change their name. Often, too, the name is changed because their "trade" requires it; the Okanda healers bear another name when they practise their art; and among civilised peoples changes of name are bound up with certain social conditions (monks, actors, prostitutes, etc.).

Education of Children.—Suckling ordinarily lasts a very long time among uncivilised peoples, till the child is two, three, four, and five years old, sometimes even older.[1] Children are treated kindly by uncivilised peoples, and rarely are they chastised as they are in Europe, though a certain "discipline" appears among the half-civilised, with the necessity of making the child learn many more things. At the age of puberty, among most uncivilised peoples, the ceremony of *initiation* takes place. This is a sort of higher education with certain tests, followed by a ceremony, after which the individual is declared adult. It is met with among the Australians, as also among the American Indians, Negroes, etc., with the same essential features. The young men of the tribe are led into a place apart, where the sorcerers, the fetichers, or the "old men," teach them during a varying period all that a "man" should know about social and sexual life. The candidates are then put tests, sometimes very cruel, to make sure of their power

[1] Ploss (*loc. cit.*) mentions Australian, Eskimo, and North American Indian tribes among whom the child is suckled till the age of fourteen or fifteen.

to resist thirst, hunger, and physical pain. Those who emerge victorious from these tests are brought back triumphantly into the villages, and feasted during several days.[1]

Among the operations to which young men are subjected during initiation, we must specially notice *circumcision*, generally practised all over Oceania, among the American Indians and other peoples, without taking into account the Israelite and Mussulman world, in which this custom has now but a religious symbolic signification. Moreover, several religions have kept the custom of initiation, giving to it very varied forms (shaving of the forelock among Buddhists, first communion among Catholics, etc.).

The lot of the old men is not an enviable one in primitive societies. They are not cared for, and often when they become infirm they are left to die of hunger. The voluntary suicide of the old men, which is committed amid great pomp among the Chukchi[2] and some other peoples, may be explained as much by the miseries of existence as by the belief in a better life beyond the tomb, which is the basis of *funereal rites*.[3] Among nearly all peoples it is customary to put into the grave objects which the dead had used in their ordinary occupations, but only such as constituted private property: weapons by the side of a warrior, pottery near to a woman, etc.[4] These objects are usually broken to signify that they also are dead, and that their "soul" goes to accompany their owner into the other life. It is also with this idea that a warrior's favourite horse is sacrificed on his grave (Red Indians, Altaians), or a symbolic ceremony suffices, the animal being led in the funeral procession, a custom

[1] For an illustration of this see the "Description of Australian Initiation" (Bura), by R. Mathews, *Journ. Anthr. Inst.*, vol. xxv., 1896, No. 4.

[2] Deniker, "Le peuple Tchouktch, etc." (from Avgustinovich), *Rev. d'Anthr.*, 1882, p. 323, and De Windt, *Globus*, 1897, vol. lxxi., p. 300.

[3] Tylor, *loc. cit.* (*Anthr.*), pp. 346, 420.

[4] In various countries in Europe these objects give place to a piece of money put into the mouth or the hand of the dead; as one never knows what may happen, it is always well to have a little money at one's service.

still practised all over Europe at the interments of superior officers. In India women are sacrificed, slaves in Dahomey and among the Dyaks, etc., in order that the dead may not be deprived of anything in the other world.[1]

Funeral ceremonies and the practice of going into mourning give place to feasts of diverse character. Among the Dualas of the Cameroons (Western Africa), the "feast of the dead" lasts nine days, the time required for his soul to make the journey to *Bela*, the place of eternal rest. Among the Battas of Sumatra, we find these funeral feasts accompanied by dances and a special kind of game, the *Topingha*. The exhumation of the bones of the dead person at the end of a certain time, practised by several Indonesian, Melanesian, and American tribes, is the occasion of orgies; I may also mention the habit of visiting the cemetery at stated periods, and taking food either on the grave or by the side of it, which is very general in Europe.

Among the feasts organised in honour of the dead let us mention the *Bung* of the Japanese, at the end of which miniature skiffs in straw are thrown into the sea, supposed to transport the souls of the dead who have been present at the feast back to their dwelling-place.

The modes of sepulture, although very varied,—interment, incineration, exposure to the air (natural mummification), embalming, pure and simple abandonment on the earth or to the waves,—have not a great importance from the ethnical point of view; often two or three modes may co-exist among the same people (examples, Mongols, Papuans).

Mourning.—Outward manifestations of grief caused by the death of a near relative exist among all peoples of the world, even the most uncivilised. These are, first, cries, lamentations, and tears (Bushmen, Bechuana, ancient Egyp-

[1] Many practices in relation to the dead are explained by the belief that they are sleeping for a greater or less time (see p. 216). Thus, among the Micronesians of the Gilbert Islands, the woman sleeps by the side of her dead husband, and covers her body with the putrid matter which oozes from the corpse.

tians, Caribs of Guiana, Italians, Russians). Then succeed material signs displayed on the body, some of which are the consequence of cruel practices which seem to suggest the idea of sacrifice for the purpose of removing the anger of "the dead man's soul," which wanders about the survivors. We need only mention the cutting off of the finger-joints among the Bushmen, of the toes among the Fijians, the drawing out of teeth in Eastern Polynesia, the laceration of the skin among the Australians, the burnings among the New Caledonians. Under a milder form the same idea of sacrifice manifests itself in the custom of plucking out the hair of the beard (Australians, Fijians), of cutting or shaving off a part or the whole of the hair (Jews and Egyptians in ancient times, Huns, Albanians, Hovas, Malays, American Indians, Basutos, Gallas). Certain signs of mourning on the body seem to be caused by the desire not to be recognised by the "spirit" of the dead person; such is the custom of daubing the face or the whole body, practised by the Negroes of Central Africa, the Australians, the Polynesians, etc. Among peoples who are more clothed, the mode of dress is altered. General negligence in dress is a sign of grief among the Bechuana and the Malays; tearing of the garments is practised among the American Indians; the Manganya of Southern Africa wrap the body in palm-leaves, which they wear until they fall withered to the ground. The conventional colour of the clothes, white among the Chinese, black among Europeans, is a sign of the same kind.

4.—SOCIAL LIFE.

Social life may be studied both as limited to a given people (inner life) and in the relations of one people with another (international life).

The inner life of a given ethnical group comprises economic or property organisation, and social organisation properly so called (administration and politics). Ideas of morals, right, and justice depend much on the forms which these organisations have taken, as well as on usages and customs; and the latter in their turn are derived principally from family organisation and religious ideas.

The international life of peoples manifests itself in three different ways: either in hostile relations (war), in pacific neutral relations (commerce), or in sympathetic relations (exchange of ideas and feelings, feasts, congresses, etc.).

Inner Life of a People—Economic Organisation.—The system by which property is held depends on the mode of production, for the distribution and consumption of wealth are in intimate relation with the mode of procuring it. Among savage hunters it is often necessary for several to combine to catch big game; thus Australians hunt the kangaroo in bands of several dozen individuals; the Eskimo gather quite a flotilla of kayaks for whale-fishing. The captured kangaroos, the whale brought to shore, are considered common property; each eats of the spoil according to his hunger. The territory of each tribe among the Australians and Red Indians is considered collective property; every one hunts on it in his own way, on condition that he does not encroach on the territory of neighbouring tribes. But in the midst of this common property certain objects used solely by the individual, his garments, his weapons, etc., are considered personal property, while the tent with its furniture, etc., belongs to the family; as the canoe which is used for whale fishing, holding five or six persons, belongs to these persons in common.

Thus in the same society three sorts of property, collective, family, and individual, may exist simultaneously side by side. What decides its category is the character of the labour expended, the mode of *production*. I have made a flint implement with my own hands, it is mine; with the assistance of my wife and children I have built the hut, it belongs to the family; I have hunted with the people of my tribe, the beasts slain belong to us all in common. The animals which I have killed by myself on the territory of the tribe are mine, and if by chance the animal wounded by me escapes and is killed by another, it belongs to both of us and the skin is his who gave the finishing stroke. For this reason each arrow bears the mark of its owner.

It is thus that matters are arranged among the Tunguses and North American Indians. Among the latter, rules have been strictly laid down in regard to bison-hunting from the point of view of individual property.[1]

But since the introduction of fire-arms, the balls bearing no distinctive marks, the slain bisons are divided equally; they are considered as common property. This example shows plainly how closely are related production and the system by which property is held. Common and private property do not lead among savages to monopoly, for the products of the chase cannot be kept for long without getting spoilt; so after having taken what he wants for himself, the hunter gives the remainder to his relatives, his family, or the tribe. It is this which partly explains the carelessness of savages and the absence among them of the spirit of thrift and thought for the future.

Family Property.—With the introduction of agriculture, most of the objects of personal property become family property; the transformation frequently coincides with the appearance of the patriarchal form of family life; the land still remains for some time common property, but soon it likewise becomes family property. The members of the same family group enjoy in common the products of the soil, which common labour has fertilised. This mode of property existed in Russia before the sixteenth century, that is to say, before the establishment of the communal ownership of the soil still in vogue to-day. It is found in England from the thirteenth to the fourteenth century (Seebohm), and in certain parts of France (in the Nivernais, according to the statement of Guy Coquille) in the form of "porçonneries" having "pot and fire" in common, working in the same fields and accumulating their savings in the

[1] Even in the cases where several arrows have pierced the animal their reciprocal positions decided to whom belonged such or such part of the slain animal; the skin, for instance, was his whose arrow had penetrated nearest to the heart.

same box.[1] With the growth of population, this family joint-ownership developed into an agricultural commune, the true "village community" of English authors, with the alienation of holdings and the admission of strangers into its midst, with periodic distributions of the various strips of land. The best type of this kind of community is the Russian "mir." In India it is met with side by side with the family commune among the Dravidian and Aryan peoples, and in Western Europe numerous traces of it are found.[2] But these are only traces and survivals, for communal property has been destroyed here as in the Mussulman world, often by means of force, with the establishment of the feudal system, which gave birth to the different modes of land tenure which we find to-day. In Russia and in India the dissolution of the communal system is still taking place under our eyes, but from intrinsically different causes, especially the rapid increase of population and diminution of the size of holdings.

Social Organisation.—The constitution of society is modelled on that of property. In the simplest cases the family organisation is at the same time the social organisation. Under the *régime* of group marriage, and even after its partial replacement by individual marriage, tribes are divided into a certain number of clans, each of which, with the majority of peoples, has its *totem.* The totem is a class of material objects (never an isolated object, thus differing from the fetish) for which uncivilised man professes a superstitious veneration, believing in a sort of mysterious connection between himself and each representative of the class of objects. Most frequently the totem is some species of animal or vegetable which the members of the clan regard as their ancestor, and also as the patron and protector of the whole clan. The Iroquoian legends relate circumstantially how the tortoise, their totem and ancestor, got rid of its shell and gradually developed

[1] Kovalewsky, *Tableau des origines de la famille, etc.*, pp. 59 and 91, Stockholm, 1890; Maine, *Early History of Institutions*, London, 1875.

[2] G. L. Gomme, *The Village Community*, London, 1890; and Kovalewsky, *loc. cit.* Baden-Powell, *Indian Village Com.*, London, 1896.

into man. The totem is represented on different objects belonging to the clan. Our blazons and armorial bearings are derived from the totem, as well as marks of ownership. The totemistic divisions are independent of the territorial divisions of the tribe; the connection is, rather, a moral one. The inhabitants of a territorial district may belong to several clans, and, on the other hand, the members of one and the same "totem" may inhabit places distant from each other.

Nearly always the totem is subject to taboo[1] (page 252). The social organisation of *clans* and "phratries" (groups of clans of which the members are intermarriable) joined to totemism is widespread among North American Indians, Australians, Melanesians of the Solomon Islands, the Tshi-speaking tribes of the Gold Coast, etc. It exists side by side with other social organisations among the Kirghis, the Kevsurs of the Caucasus (Kovalewsky), the Mandingoes (Binger), etc. Under this primitive *régime* there are no permanent chiefs, but intermittent councils, formed of the "old men" in each clan. If several clans are united into a tribe, an elective chief sometimes appears, but always invested with only a temporary and very limited power.

Family Organisation.—With the change from the hunting to the agricultural mode of life, with the establishment of affiliation by blood and the patriarchal family, with the constitution of family ownership, the social organisation is also transformed. All the members of the family gathered under the same roof (often in the literal sense of the word; for example, among the Indonesians and the Pueblo Indians) constitute the social unit. Such is the origin of the commune in China and Japan, of the "fine" in Ireland, etc. The chief of the race, the living "ancestor," becomes the chief of the society, and his power tends to become hereditary.[2]

[1] J. G. Frazer, *Totemism*, London, 1887 (expanded from his article in vol. xxiii. of the *Encyclopædia Britannica*); E. Smith, *Second Ann. Rep. Bur. of Ethnol.*, 1880-81, p. 77, Washington, 1883.

[2] This family *régime* of society is closely allied to the worship of ancestors and the "hearth," as the names given to the communities show ("feu" in France, "pechtchiché" in the Ukraine).

Territorial Organisation.—When family ownership is replaced by communal ownership, the social organisation takes the *territorial* form. All the people inhabiting a given territory, whether related by blood or not, form the social unit. The Russian "Volost," the Annamese commune, the Japanese "Mura," the "Calpulli" of the ancient Toltecs, are examples of this kind of grouping.[1] Sometimes these territorial organisations form by themselves independent states, governed by an elected chief, assisted by the delegates of each commune (Moqui in North America, Krumen and Vakamba in Africa, Samoans in Oceania), or controlled by popular assemblies (New Hebrideans, most of the peoples of Western Africa and the Congo basin). Sometimes also they form part of vaster confederations at the head of which is an elected chief, a council, etc. (Rejangs of Sumatra with their "Pangherans," or princes, Afghans with their "Khans," etc.).

Organisation of Castes and Classes.—We may find already in the territorial organisation of society the rudiments of the formation of classes, shown by the development of private property and wealth, and also by the authority of the chiefs and powerful persons who become the "protectors" of the weak. This differentiation of classes is also marked by the appearance of *slavery*, the result of wars and the right of private property (enslavement for debt). It takes definite form in the class organisation which presupposes the existence of two groups of citizens at least—the lords and nobles, the aristocracy or directing class, and the "people," the plebeian or directed class. The relations between these classes may extend from the complete servitude of the one and the exercise of the right of life and death by the other, to an almost absolute equality of the two.

There is similarly a perfect gradation for non-free people, as opposed to citizens divided into two or more classes. At

[1] Laveleye, *Propriété primitive*, p. 9, Paris, 1891; Kovalewsky, *loc. cit.*, *passim;* Sakuya Yoshida, *Geschichtl. Entwickl. d. Staats-Verfass. in Japan*, p. 46, Hague, 1890; Bancroft, *Native Races of Pacific States*, vol. ii., p. 226, San Francisco, 1882.

the foot of the ladder are "slaves," in the strict sense of the word, not regarded even as men; while at the top are found those who by birth are not free, but who by fortune or otherwise may come to occupy a position almost equal to that of free citizens of the highest class.

What are the qualifications required in order to become *chief* in primitive social organisations? Most often, by election, those become chief who are bravest in war, strongest, most skilful in the chase (American Indians, Congolese), or the chiefs are the richest (Indians, Polynesians, Negroes), or simply they are the biggest, the best fed (Athapascans, according to Bancroft). But whatever may be the ground on which they are chosen, the power of these chiefs is often most precarious, and it may disappear with the cause of its origin (war, hunting expedition). Chiefs elected for a stated period are invested with more real power. Sometimes they are elected for life; this is a step towards hereditary power which may degenerate into the purest absolutism (ancient Dahomey). The outward ensigns of authority are of various sorts: clubs and commander's staffs (Oceania and Europe), parasols (Asia, Africa),[1] etc. In the same way as the clan is responsible for the misdeeds of each of its members, so the absolute monarch, king, sultan, khan, prince, etc., is responsible for the acts committed by his subjects. The corollary of the conception that kings or other potentates represent the most skilful, influential, and bravest men is that of forfeiture of power when the holder becomes aged or infirm, or when he shows himself incapable of reigning (Quechuas, Masai); in certain absolute States the right of revolt against an incapable holder of royal power is expressly recognised (China), at least in theory.[2]

Feudal and Democratic Organisation.—It would be out of place here to dwell on the development of the feudal system and the theocracy which result from the *régime* of classes. Let us

[1] See Andree, *Ethnolog. Parallele*, p. 250.

[2] See for further details, Post, *.. cit.*, *Grundriss der ethnol. Jurisprud.*, vol. i.

merely say that almost all half-civilised peoples are still in the midst of the feudal *régime* or are just emerging from it. The recognition of individual liberty forms the first step towards the organisations of modern European states, constitutional monarchies or republics, in which the aim is to reduce to a minimum governmental action and the differences of classes, especially before the law,—to establish, in a word, a *democratic régime*.

Social morality, or the basis of conduct imposed on the members of society, is a convention recognised by the laws and by public opinion. This is to say that it changes from one people to another, according to the degree of culture, surrounding circumstances, etc. In the most uncivilised tribes life has a relative security, owing to certain rules of conduct to which each member submits from fear of punishment or the disapprobation of public opinion. The right of the strongest is not applied in all its brutal logic even among savages.

Their rules of morality are of course not always in accordance with ours. Among the uncivilised, it is not a question of absolute right, of absolute morality; everything is reduced to a very restricted altruism, not extending beyond kin and immediate neighbours. It is wrong to kill a man of one's own clan, or to steal something from the collective property of the clan; but it is, on the contrary, very praiseworthy to strike down with a well-directed arrow a stranger to the clan, or to carry off something from a neighbouring clan. Gradually the moral sentiment extends to people of the same tribe, of the same class or caste, of the same religion, but such extension is slow. Among the civilised the moral code sometimes varies as it is applied on this or that side of political or social boundaries.

Besides, in a general way, a number of acts regarded as culpable by the codes of all civilised states, are yet tolerated, and even extolled, in certain particular circumstances; such as the taking of life, for example, in legitimate defence, in a duel, during war, or as capital punishment. Thus in recalling examples of this kind, we shall be less severe on a Dyak who cuts off a man's head solely that he may carry this trophy to his bride; for if he did otherwise he would be repulsed by all, and would not be able to marry. Among the uncivilised, morality is purely utilitarian; it encourages acts of utility to the clan, to the tribe (hospitality, protection of children, respect for common property, etc.), it reprobates those which are not advantageous (support of the old people, compassion for slaves, etc.).

Right and Justice.—At the origin of societies morals and the action of justice are indistinguishable, public opinion constitutes "common law," often respected even by the legislations of the civilised. I cannot undertake to speak here of morals based on religious ideas, nor of ethnical jurisprudence.[1] Let it suffice to give some examples of customs which bring into prominence some of the ideas of right and justice of uncivilised peoples.

Taboo is one of the customs which show in the clearest way the power of public opinion in primitive societies. This custom, common in Australia, Melanesia, and especially in Polynesia, may be briefly defined as an interdiction, by the authority of the council of old men, chiefs, priests, etc., to in any way use a certain object or living thing. Thus, young Australians are forbidden to eat the flesh of the emu before reaching the age when they undergo "initiation" (see p. 241); taboo in this case has a utilitarian purpose, as also in Polynesia, where chickens, bananas, and yams are tabooed when there is a scarcity. Sometimes taboo is only to be observed by women or children, etc. Whoever infringes this law runs the risk of punishment by death.

Another example of judicial and social custom is the *vendetta.* At the beginnings of socialisation, in groups organised in clans, every offensive act had to be personally "avenged" by the victim. The vengeance assumes then the form of a *judicial combat* (prototype of European *duel*). In the case of murder, it is the near relatives who take upon themselves the duty of avenging it, but as the search for the

[1] See for more details, Ch. Letourneau, *L'évolution de la Morale,* Paris, 1887, and A. Post, *loc. cit.*, 2nd vol., Leipzig, 1895.

true culprit is sometimes difficult, the whole clan is held responsible for the act committed by one of its members, and it becomes lawful to kill any one belonging to this clan to avenge the murder. The law of retaliation also implies that the misdeed should be avenged in nearly the same form in which it was committed. Gradually, however, vengeance passes into the hands of the representatives of society (judges, magistrates), and the penal code is established.

Ordeals represent one of the most widespread methods of judicial procedure of non-civilised peoples. Most frequently the carrying out of these trials is entrusted to magicians believed to have the faculty of discovering the guilty person. Needless to say that the presents offered by interested parties had a considerable influence on the decision of these umpires.[1]

The *taking of an oath* is the last remnant of this mode of procedure; it is a moral test which, among many peoples, is associated with the obligation of swallowing certain special beverages (the rust of a sword in wine in Malaysia, blood among the Chinese, etc.).

Secret Societies—Extra-legal Judges.—In every social organisation which is imperfect or powerless to give satisfaction to the just claims of its members, secret societies are formed which undertake the redressing of wrongs and the re-establishment of justice. Such, for example, are the societies of the "Duk-Duk" of New Britain, usually formed of a confidant of the chief of the tribe, and of young men who have entered the "club" on payment of a somewhat large sum. Each Duk-Duk is on occasion a justiciary; clad in his particular dress and wearing a horrible mask, he runs howling through the village, and all those who are not in the secret run away terrified. He goes to the hut of the native against whom a complaint had been

[1] The most common ordeals are the trial by water (swimming across a river, remaining some time under water, etc.) and that by fire. In the latter case the accused is made to run on hot coals, as in India, among the Somalis, in Siam; to lick red-hot iron, as among the Dyaks, the Khonds, the Negroes of Sierra-Leone; or again, to dip the hands in molten lead, as in Burma among the Jakuns of Malacca, or the Alfurus of Buru, etc.

lodged or who is suspected of a crime, and inflicts punishment which may vary from a simple fine to death. No one dare resist him, for sooner or later a violent end would be the fate of him who had raised his hand against the Duk-Duk. The members of this secret society, who recognise each other by certain signs, meet together in places to which the profane are forbidden to approach under pain of death. They give themselves up in these places to songs, dances, and copious feasting, in which human flesh often forms the chief dish. They are also sorcerers and healers.[1]

Similar societies exist among the Yoruba Negroes of Guinea, and the traces of like institutions are found in Europe, as, for example, the famous "Oat-field procedure" (*Haberfeld treiben*), an ancient custom which is kept up in the region of upper Bavaria situated between the Inn and the Isar. It is a sort of trial by a secret tribunal of misdemeanours which are not reached by the ordinary penal law. The court of Munich had in 1896 to deal with one of these procedures, which have now become very rare.[2]

Rules of Politeness.—Departments of social life which depend on mutual sympathy or the feeling of solidarity are not numerous. We must include in this category associations formed for the chase or for agricultural work like harvest, assistance in the reconstruction of a house destroyed by fire, etc. This kind of labour in common is chiefly known in societies in which the commune is the basis of social life, among Southern Slavs and Russians. The custom of "exchanging blood," or drinking in the same cup, widely spread among these Slavs, as among the Malays, the Indonesians, and the Negroes, is also one of the expressions of sincere mutual sympathy, while *rules of politeness* are the manifestations, frequently hypocritical, of feelings of sociability. They vary infinitely. Thus *salutations* present a great diversity, but

[1] Schmeltz and Krause, *Ethnogr.-Anthr. Abt. Mus. Godeffroy*, p. 17, Hamburg, 1881; W. Powell, *Wanderings amongst Cannibals of New Britain*, London, 1883; Graf von Pfeil, "Duk-Duk, etc.," *Journ. Anthr. Institute*, 1897, p. 197.

[2] G. Schultheiss, *Globus*, 1896, vol. lxx., No. 22.

the origin of them all is the desire to show inferiority to the person saluted, and to express sympathy and devotion. The expression of inferiority is a posture which puts you lower than the person saluted. This posture varies from prostration to the ground (Negroes, Cambodians) to simple inclination of the head (Europeans), passing through a series of intermediate forms: touching the ground with the forehead (Chinese), simple genuflexion, and the "curtsey" of our mothers. As to manifestations of sympathy, they are almost always expressed by an embrace or kiss. In the case of the most humble submission, the kiss is given to the soil trodden by the feet of the person saluted, while in that of friendship between equals it is bestowed on the cheek or lips; intermediate forms are not wanting here either, and the various habits of kissing the foot, the garments, the hand, etc., are universally known. To these two principal manifestations of politeness several others may be added. A person meeting a friend or even a casual acquaintance uncovers the whole or a part of the body, the breast (certain Negroes), the arm or head (Europeans); each rubs the other with oil or with earth, nose is brought into contact with nose, and each "sniffs" the other's health (Lapps, Eskimo, Malays, Polynesians);[1] each shakes the other's hands, places the hand on the forehead (Hindus) or on the breast (Mussulmans), or draws out the tongue while scratching at the same time the ear (Thibetans, etc.).[2]

b. International Life of Peoples.—The relations of ethnical groups one with another may be of three sorts—hostile, neutral, or sympathetic. The relations of the last category are only just indicated among civilised peoples in the form

[1] The custom of applying the nose to the cheek and drawing a breath, with closed eyes and a smacking of the lips, exists among the Southern Chinese, but only as an act of love. According to P. D'Enjoy, it is an olfactory gesture derived from the sensations of nutrition, as the European kiss on the lips is derived from the lascivious bite. (*Bull. Soc. Anthr.*, Paris, 1897, pt. 2.)

[2] See for details Ling Roth, *Journ. Anthr. Inst.*, vol. xix., 1889, p. 164; Andree, *Eth. Paral.*, N.F., p. 225; Hellwald, *Rosselsp.*, p. 1.

of international festivals, exhibitions, and congresses; international scientific, charitable, and professional gatherings, etc. Inter-gatherings are non-existent, or reduced to a few feasts and rejoicings among the uncivilised and half-civilised; on the other hand, hostile relations (or war) exist among all peoples, from the most savage to the most refined. Neutral relations (commerce) are but little developed among the uncivilised, and only begin really to assume any importance among the half-civilised; they attain a high degree of development among the civilised.

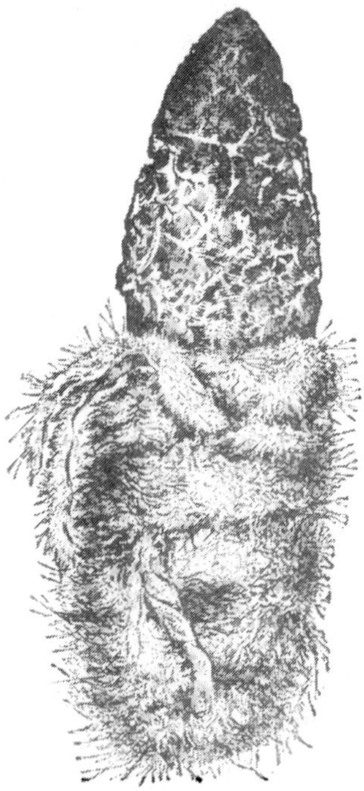

FIG. 73.—Chipped flint dagger of the Californian Indians, with otter-skin wrapping for grip. (*From O. Mason.*)

War is made on various pretexts among the uncivilised, who have no special armies, each member having to fight in conjunction with the other members of his clan, tribe, or people, as the case may be, either to procure for himself provisions, slaves, wives, or cattle, or to avenge defeat, murder, or robbery on the individuals of a "foreign," and consequently hostile (*Hostis* of the Romans) clan, tribe, or people. The conflicts are not very deadly at this stage of civilisation; frequently the hostilities are reduced to mutual insults, to manœuvres in which efforts are made to frighten the enemy by cries, by warlike dances, by disguises and masks of horrible aspect. Sometimes also the fate of the battle is decided by single combat between two chiefs or two braves selected from each of the adverse camps. Ambushes, traps, and surprises are more common than pitched battles.

On the whole, war in primitive societies is only a species of *man-hunt*. Thus the offensive weapons are nearly always the same for hunting and war. It is only among the half-civilised that, with more or less permanent armies, weapons specially designed for war make their appearance, as well as works of a defensive character—fortresses, palisades, protective moats, and caltrops.

I can give here but a very brief description of offensive and defensive weapons.[1]

Offensive weapons may be divided into two categories—weapons held firmly in the hand and missile weapons; each of these categories comprises striking, cutting, and piercing weapons.

Among the *weapons held firmly in the hand*, the *striking* or *blunt* ones play an important part among the uncivilised, for these are derived directly from the staff, pre-eminently the weapon of primitive peoples. The most common is the *club*, only just distinguished from a staff by its terminal swelling in

[1] The difference between offensive and defensive weapons is often not very marked even in our civilisation; thus the sword and the sabre serve as much for giving as warding off blows; the same is true among savages in regard to the staff, the club, etc. Frequently, too, objects which originally have nothing in common with war, become offensive or defensive weapons. Thus the bracelet is sometimes a defensive weapon. Among several Negroes (Ashantis, Kafirs, Vakambas), and in Melanesia, warriors put on their legs and arms bracelets formed of the long hair of different animals (goat, boar, zebra) which almost completely cover the limbs and protect them effectually against the blows of club and spear. The bracelets of wire rolled in numerous spirals around the fore-arm or the leg, which are met with among the Dyaks, the Mois of Indo-China, the Niam-Niams, and the Baghirmis of Central Africa, are veritable protective armour; they are the prototypes of the vantbrace and greaves.

In certain rarer cases the bracelet is an offensive weapon. Among the Jurs, a negro tribe of the upper Nile, bracelets are found provided with two points or spurs, four inches long, and very dangerous. The bracelet of the Irengas (to the east of the upper Nile), as well as that of the Jibba (living on the banks of the Jibba, a left-hand tributary of the Sabba), is a great disc, with an opening in the middle through which to pass the arm. A portion of the disc is removed in order to give it more elasticity, and its outer edge, exceedingly sharp, forms a kind of circular sabre. In order not to wound himself, the wearer covers the edge with a circular case which he only removes for battle.

Australia; it takes the most varied forms in Oceania, where almost every island or group of islands has its particular forms of club. The sharp-ended clubs of the New Hebrides are the connecting-link with *pointed weapons*, of which the spear, the lance, the assagai, the fork, are the best known forms. The point of these weapons is sometimes of flint (as among

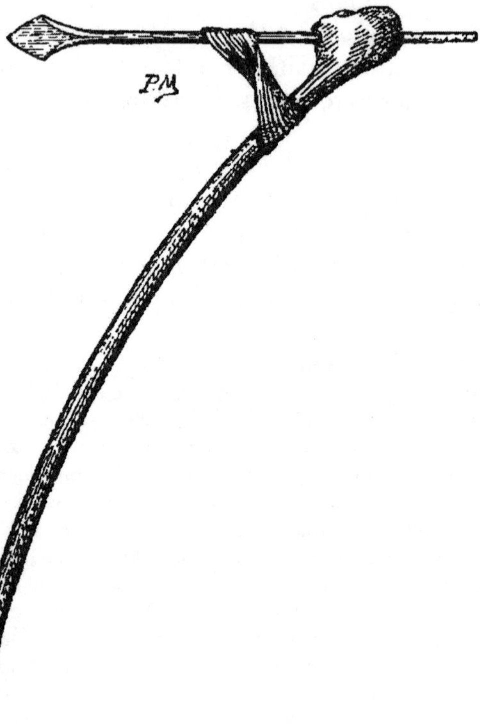

FIG. 74.—Axe of the Banyai (Matabeleland), employed in hunting elephants; special hafting, partly by means of bands. (*After Wood.*)

Melanesians of the Admiralty Islands), sometimes of bone, wood, shark's teeth (natives of the Gilbert or Kingsmill Islands), sometimes of bronze (prehistoric Europe, China), of iron (Negroes), steel (Europeans). *Cutting weapons*, with the exception of the axe, the form of which varies infinitely (Figs. 66, 74, 114, 158), are generally piercing weapons as well. The simplest is the knife, whether it be of flint (Fig. 56), bronze, or iron (Fig. 146); from it is derived the sabre; and the flint poignard or dagger, which gradually became transformed into the steel sword.[1]

Missile Weapons.—The readiest missile weapon to throw at the quarry or the enemy is the weapon carried in the hand; this is what must have happened many times to primitive man in the excitement of the combat or chase.

But to throw a staff, a stone, or any weapon whatever so adroitly as to wound an animal or a man was a difficult thing to do. It became necessary to increase the force of the propulsion, which could be done only in two ways: either by giving a special form to the projectile, or by discharging it by means of a special apparatus constructed for the purpose.

The first of these methods did not produce very brilliant results. The Zandeh peoples and their congeners of Central Africa considerably modified the knife to make use of it as a weapon to throw with the hand (*trumbache*); the Franks had the missile battle-axe called "francisque," and the Romans javelins of all sorts. But the use of these weapons was very restricted in all times. Clubs are still used as missile-weapons either by reducing their size (the kerri-kerri of the Bantu Negroes) or by changing their form (the boomerang of the Australians). The boomerang (Fig. 75) is a wooden blade, the form of which varies from a very gentle curve to that of a square; its surface is always slightly curved. Thrown into the air, certain kinds of boomerang have a secondary movement of gyration and return to the foot of the thrower, as a hoop returns to the child when he throws it before him, having given it first a rotatory motion. Similar weapons (*singa*) exist among the Khonds of Orissa (India); they existed also in ancient Egypt, and have served perhaps as models for the "trumbaches" of the Zandeh of the present day. Let us add to the boomerang the "bolas" of the Patagonians

[1] See for details and series of forms, Lane-Fox (now Pitt Rivers), *Cat. Anthr. Collection in the Bethnal Green Museum*, London, 1877, with illustrations. (The remarkable collection in question is now at Oxford.)

(which must not be confounded with the *lasso*) and the balls of bone united by little cords which the Eskimo use for killing birds, and we shall have exhausted the list of weapons thrown directly by the hand, which, moreover, are not very effective. The true improvements in missile-weapons have

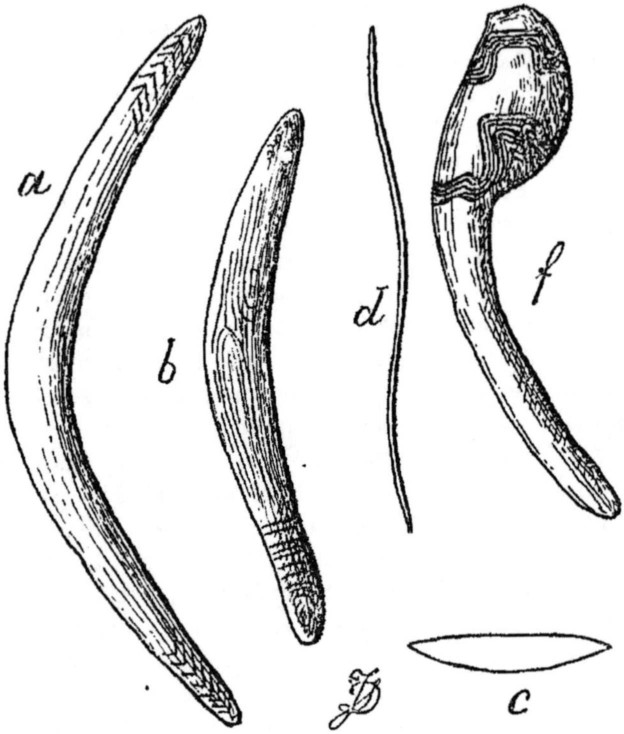

FIG. 75.—Missile arms of the Australians: *a*, *b*, boomerangs; *c*, transverse section of a boomerang; *f*, *Lil-lil*, a kind of boomerang, with geographical map representing the environs of Broken River; *d*, the same seen sideways. (*After Br. Smyth.*)

only been attained by the second solution of the problem—that is to say, by increasing the power of propulsion by means of special apparatus.

The contrivances for hurling missiles may be divided into three categories, according to the three forces which set them in motion: direct application of the muscular force of man, elasticity of certain solid bodies, and lastly, the pressure of gases. Of the first of these forces but little use is made. The *amentum* of classic antiquity had only a restricted use. The throwing-stick,[1] or stick provided with a notch which serves to increase the force of the impulse given by the arm to a javelin, is only used in some very circumscribed regions of the globe, especially on the borders of the Pacific Ocean, in Australia, where it bears the name of *Woomera*, in Melanesia (Fig. 76), in the north-west of America, among the Eskimo and Chukchis. It was also known in pre-Columban times in Mexico and Peru, whence, perhaps, it passed into Brazil. Another similar weapon, *the sling*, in former times much used by Semitic peoples, and still surviving as a common toy of our children, is scarcely used as a weapon of any importance, except by some Polynesian or American tribes (Hupa Indians, Araucans, Fuegians).

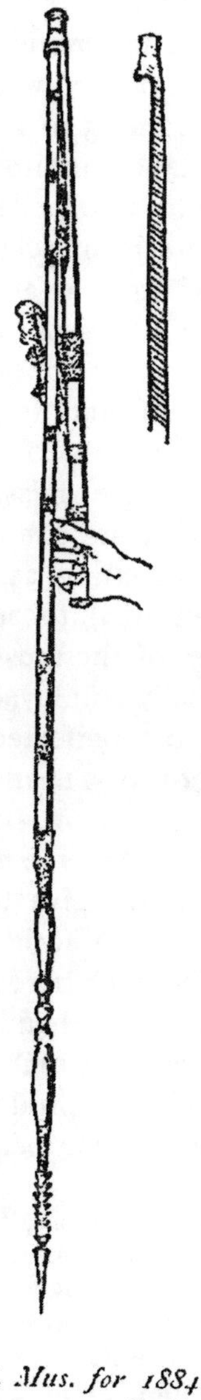

FIG. 76.—Throwing-stick of the Papuans of German New Guinea, and the manner of using it in order to hurl a javelin; below, longitudinal section of a throwing-stick. (*Partly after Von Luschan.*)

Missile weapons which make use of the pressure of gases are very little known among uncivilised peoples. We can only mention the blow-tube, the *Sarbacan*, or more correctly speaking the *Zarabatana*, of the South American Indians, and its homologue the *Sumpitan* of the Malays, in common use among the Indonesians of the Asiatic Archipelago and Indo-China.

This weapon is known in Europe from

[1] O. Mason, "Throwing-sticks," *Rep. U.S. N. Mus. for 1884;* F. v. Luschan, "Wurfholz, etc.," *Festschr. . . . Bastian* p. 131, Berlin, 1896.

the circumstance of a child's toy bearing the first of these names. It is a long tube from which a little arrow is expelled by the breath, resembling in size and appearance a knitting-needle, and provided at its unpointed end with a ball of elderpith or tow, which serves as wadding. The range of this arm is from 75 to 100 feet. The sumpitan may be considered as a weapon indirectly set in motion by muscular force, for the arrow is expelled from it as the result of contractions of the thoracic muscles, but it is better to regard it as the prototype of the fire-arm, as the arrow may be discharged by utilising the expansion of gas, and thus transformed into a fire-arm. As to true fire-arms, known to the Chinese and peoples of antiquity, they have only made real headway in Europe, and that from the fifteenth century.

But if the missile weapons in the two categories which I have just enumerated are little known to uncivilised peoples (setting aside, of course, the fire-arms imported by civilised man), those of the third category, in which advantage is taken of the muscular force of an elastic body (the bow), is universally employed by them, as it was formerly in Europe. The most perfected arm of this kind was the complicated cross-bow of our ancestors and the Chinese.

The Bow and Arrow.[1]—The origin of the bow is unknown; certain authors consider that a flexible twig arranged as a snare would give the first idea of it. This may be so, for among the Maoris of New Zealand there used to be a hand-weapon which bore a striking resemblance to this snare: a whip with a flexible handle, by means of which an arrow held in the hand was shot off.[2] Among several Eurasian peoples there is a toy which reproduces this weapon as a survival; among the Votiaks it even bears the name of *n'el*, which means arrow in

[1] See H. Balfour, "On the Structure and Affinities of the Composite Bow," *Journ. Anthr. Inst.*, London, 1889, vol. xix., p. 220; Anuchin, *Look i Strely* (Bow and Arrows), Moscow, 1889 (in Russian); O. Mason, "Bows, Arrows, and Quivers of the North American Aborigines," *Smithsonian Report*, Washington, 1893.

[2] Phillips, *Trans. N. Zeal. Inst.*, vol. x., p. 97, Wellington, 1877.

several Finnish languages.[1] However that may be, we may divide the infinite variety of bows into two groups: the *plain* bow—that is to say, the bow formed of a single piece of wood, and the *composite* bow, made of various materials—wood, horn, ivory, sinews, leather, etc., glued solidly together.

The least complicated type of the composite bow is that of the eastern Eskimo, of wood and horn, or of wood and bone, the weapon being strengthened by a cord of sinews applied along the "back" or the *outer side* (opposed to the "belly," *inner side*, which is nearest the archer when he bends the bow).[2]

Among simple bows we must mention that of the Melanesians, having a groove sometimes on the outer, sometimes on the inner side; that of the Monbuttus, provided with a "grip"; lastly, that of the Andamanese, in the form of an **S**, resembling in its general appearance on the one hand certain bows of the Eskimo, and on the other, those of certain Bantu Negroes of Eastern Africa (according to Foa).[3]

[1] M. Buch, *Die Wotiaken*, p. 78, Helsingfors, 1882; Extract from *Acta Soc. Scient. Fennicæ*, vol. xii.

[2] The prototype of the *true composite bow*, characterised by the addition to it of a mass of moistened sinews which, on drying, make the bow curve up, must have had another form; it bore a resemblance probably to the bow of the Indian tribes of the north-west of America and of California, in which the sinew covering often goes beyond the body of the bow and hangs down at its two extremities.

The improved forms of the composite bow are only found on the Asiatic continent. The so-called "Tatar" or Mongolian bow, the Chinese "kung," is chiefly composed of a piece of wood to which is fixed with bird-lime on the inner side a piece of horn, and on the outer side two layers of sinews covered with two layers of birch-bark. All other composite bows, Persian, Hindu, etc., are only complicated forms of this type, to which we may also refer the exceptional types of bow of the Lapp and Javanese, etc.

Accepting the view of General Pitt Rivers, *loc. cit.*, we may say that the composite bow is not a more perfect weapon than the simple bow, and that it could only have had its origin in countries where the absence of very elastic varieties of wood make it necessary to seek in the superposition of various materials the elasticity required to augment the force of the weapon.

[3] The substance used in the manufacture of the bow-string varies with the region; thus in the west of Africa it is always of rattan, as far as Butembo (country of the Ponondas), where strings of *Crotalaria* and bamboo begin to be used. (Weule, *Ethnol. Notizblatt. Mus. Berlin*, vol. i., No. 2, p. 39, 1895-96.)

Arrows cut wholly from one piece of wood are rare. Most of them are composed of three distinct parts fitted together: head, shaft, and feather. The head is of hard wood (sometimes hardened in the fire) or of human bone among the Melanesians; of chipped stone among certain American Indians and our quaternary ancestors; of bone, wood, and iron among various Siberian peoples; of iron among most of the other peoples. The form of the head varies infinitely; but the varieties turn around two types: sagittal (as a classic or conventional arrow) and lanceolate (as a laurel leaf). There are likewise arrow-heads with transverse or hollowed edges in the form of the fruit of the maple (Turks and Tunguses of Siberia, Negroes of the Congo). Lastly, there are arrows of which the head has nothing pointed about it, for it is shaped like a ball, an olive or cone upside down, etc. These arrows are used by several Siberian peoples (Ostiaks, Tunguses), by Negroes of the Congo, Indians of Western Brazil, etc., as a blunt weapon for killing animals whose fur, being valuable, might be spoilt by the blood flowing from a wound. The Buriats of old used whistling arrows, probably to frighten their enemies, etc. The feather is wanting in several forms of Melanesian arrows very complicated as regards the head, in certain African arrows, etc. Among the Monbuttus it consists of the hair of animals; everywhere else, however, of birds' feathers.

The mode of shooting the arrow and bending the bow vary too with different countries. The Veddahs draw the cord lying on the back, holding the bow between the feet; the Andamanese and the Eskimo hold the bow vertically, the Omahas and the Siouans, horizontally, etc. To bend the immense Mongolian or Scythian bow it was necessary to hold it by the knees, etc. Morse[1] distinguishes five special methods of releasing the arrow. The most primitive (*primary release*) is that which is naturally adopted by children of every race when they attempt for the first time to draw the bow (Fig. 77, top): the arrow and the cord are held between the stretched-

[1] E. Morse, "Ancient and Modern Methods of Arrow-release," *Essex Inst. Bull.*, Salem, Oct.-Dec., 1885.

out thumb and the second joint of the bent forefinger (Ainus, Chippewas, Assyrians, etc.). The second method is only a variant of the first, and is widespread like the first, especially among the North American Indians. Both give but a moderate propelling power to the arrow. The third method consists in holding the arrow between the thumb and the second joint of the scarcely bent forefinger, whilst the first joint of this finger draws the string, with the help of the third finger. In this method of release it is necessary to hold the bow horizontally (Omahas, Siamese, the natives of the greater Andaman Island, the Egyptians and the Greeks of antiquity). The fourth, so-called Mediterranean, method (Fig. 77, bottom) consists in drawing the string by the first joints of all the fingers except the thumb and the little finger, the arrow being nipped between the fore and middle fingers and placed on the left of the bow; this is the method practised by European archers of all ages, as well as that of the Hindus, Arabs, Eskimo, and

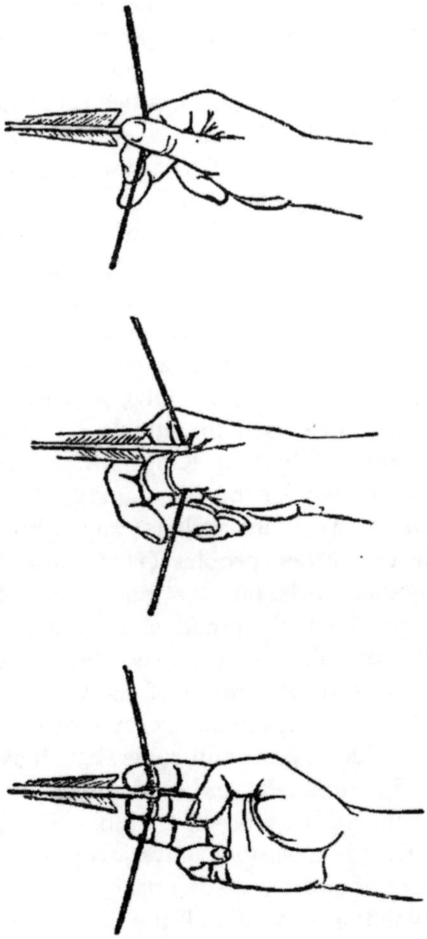

Fig. 77.—Different methods of arrow release. Top, primitive release. Middle, Mongolian release. Bottom, Mediterranean release. (*After E. Morse.*)

Veddahs. Lastly, the fifth method, known as the Mongolian method (Fig. 77, middle), is quite different from the others. The string in this case is drawn by the bent thumb, kept in this position by the forefinger; the arrow, taken in the hollow at the base of these two fingers, is placed on the right of the bow. This method has been practised from the most remote antiquity by Asiatic peoples: Mongols, Manchus, Chinese, Japanese, Turks, Persians, and was likewise practised by the ancient Scythians; in order that the hand may be protected from the recoil of the string, it is necessary to wear a special kind of ring, either of bone, horn, ivory, or metal, on the thumb, or a peculiar three-fingered glove.

Defensive Weapons.—Originally, in their simplest forms, they would not differ appreciably from offensive weapons such as tree-branches, or clubs, perhaps a little broader and flatter than those used for attack. The inhabitants of Drummond Island (Gilbert or Kingsmill archipelago, Micronesia), as well as the natives of the Samoan Islands, can ward off hostile arrows in a marvellous way with only cudgels and clubs; several other peoples (Hawaiians, Tahitians) are acquainted neither with buckler nor cuirasse, and defend themselves with clubs, their native weapons. The Dinkas of the upper White Nile, the Mundas, their neighbours on the south, as well as the Baghirmis of the Central Sudan, can turn aside the arrows of their enemies by means of sticks, either straight or bent like a bow, and somewhat thicker in the middle.

The different forms of shield are only derivatives from the primitive weapon, the club. The evolution must have been effected in various ways, according to local conditions. We may, however, distinguish two principal lines, two types, of evolution to which all the others can be referred. The first is only the development in breadth and the flattening out of the club; this is the origin of most of the long shields. The second is characterised by the presence of a piece of wood, skin, etc., applied to the club around the place where it is held by the hand; this hand-guard was the origin of the round shields and some of the long ones.

The most striking example of the first type is furnished by the shields of the Australians. Certain of them (the *Tamarangs*) are only clubs a little flattened out and enlarged in the middle; others (the *Mulabakas*) are very narrow little boards rounded towards both ends with a hilt formed by the slit made in the hinder side, which is a little bulging or ridge-like (Fig. 78); others take the form of boards somewhat broad,

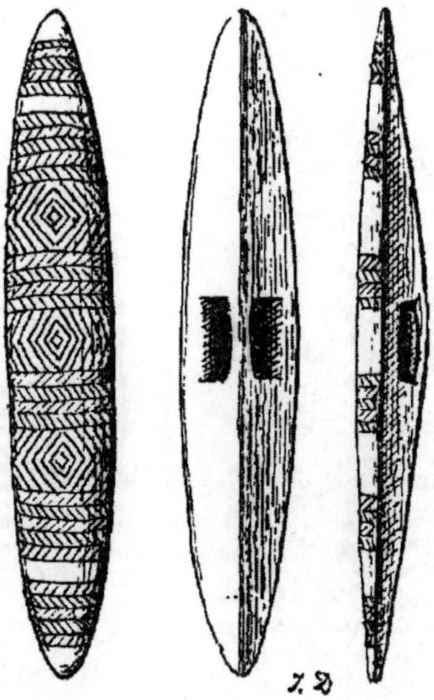

FIG. 78 —Australian shield in wood; three sides shown.

oval, and sometimes ridge-like. Shields of a similar kind, with the ridge a little enlarged at both ends, are used by the Alfurus of the Southern Moluccas (Fig. 79, *b*). The characteristic shield of the Dyaks and other Indonesians (including those of lower Burma, see Frontispiece) is also derived from a type analogous to the *Mulabaka*. It is a ridge-like wooden board, sometimes adorned with human hair (Fig. 79, *f*).

The second mode of development of the shield is marked by the placing on the club some sort of wooden, metal, or skin guard. The clubs or primitive shields of the Monudus are surrounded in the middle by a band of buffalo skin, under which the hand is passed to hold them. Let us suppose that some day this annular band, becoming half-detached, formed in front of the hand a bulwark, the

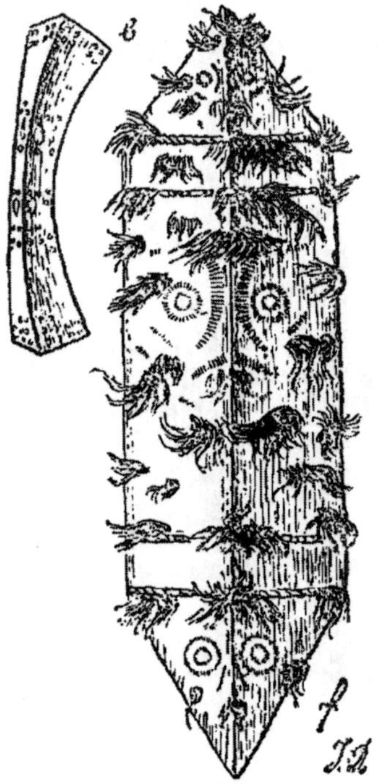

FIG 79.—Indonesian shields—*b*, of the Alfurus of the Moluccas (wood and inlayings); *f*, of the Dyaks (painted wood, tufts of human hair).

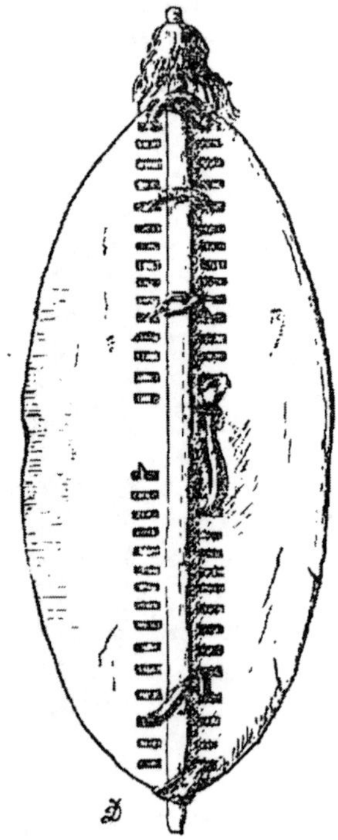

FIG. 80.—Shield of Zulu-Kafirs, in ox skin, with medial club.

somewhat large surface of which protected it more effectually than the primitive ring, and we understand the origin of shields formed of bits of animal skin fixed on a club, at first very small, like those of the Hottentots, then becoming enormous, like those of the Zulus (Fig. 80). Similar, but quadrangular bucklers are found among the Shulis of the upper White Nile, the Fans of the Ogowé, etc. Among other equestrian and nomadic peoples the frequent changes of place that were rendered necessary decided the rounded, lighter form of the leather shield, the club of which has disappeared, the hand-grip being made of a thong. Such are the shields of the Bejas, the Abyssinians, the Somalis, and also those of the North American Indians.

In countries where cattle are scarce, shields similar to those of the Zulus are made with rattan twigs or reeds, or palm-leaves artistically plaited; such are the large shields of the Niam-Niams, of certain Dyak and Nagă tribes (Frontispiece), etc. These shields are not very strong, but there is this to be said for them, that the arrows striking them instead of rebounding, pierce them, and remain fixed, to the benefit of the owner of the defensive weapon.

The space which we have given to the description of shields hardly permits us to dwell longer on *protective armour*, breast-plates, coats of mail, helmets, vantbraces, greaves,[1] etc. It may, however, be said that there exist peculiar kinds of armour among certain peoples and in certain regions of the world: the dress of the natives of the Kingsmill Islands, woven from cocoa-nut fibres, which affords an admirable protection against their wood-handled weapons with sharks' teeth fixed in their edges; breast-plates of buffalo skin, in use among the Indians of America; the padded breast-plates of the Baghirmi warriors and Chinese soldiers, ancient Japanese and ancient Mexicans. Among the latter, armour consisting of little boards of lacquered wood was further affixed to the breast-plate, similar kinds being found all around the shores of the North Pacific, among the Eskimo, the Chukchi, the Koriaks (little ivory or bone plates), and among the Tlinkit Indians of the north-west of America (wooden plates sewn on stuffs), etc.[2]

[1] With regard to greaves, see the note on p. 257.

[2] W. Hough, "Prim. Am. Armour," *Rep. U.S. Nat. Mus. for 1893*, p. 625, Washington, 1895.

But it would require a volume to describe all the inventions which have resulted from the hostile relations of peoples. Let us pass on to a more peaceful subject, to *neutral relations*, which are more profitable to men.

Commerce is almost unknown among uncivilised hunters. It could only develop in societies already numerous, inhabiting various territories, their products differing to such an extent that they might be exchanged with advantage. The progress of industry, with the division of labour and the specialisation which it involves, also had something to do with it. Thus, in Guiana, each tribe has its special industry and visits even a hostile tribe to effect exchanges.[1] This is the primitive form of commerce, originating probably in the custom of exchanging presents.

Primitive commerce is not infrequently conducted in such a way that the treating parties do not see each other. According to Humboldt, at the beginning of this century the modern Mexicans traded with savage tribes, wandering on their northern frontier, in this way. The barterers did not see each other; the goods were fastened to posts devoted to this use and then left. The purchaser came for them, replacing them by objects having an equal value. It is thus that the Sakai still traffic with the Malays, the Veddahs with the Singhalese. The Veddahs even order things in this silent way; they deposit, for example, side by side with the goods which they offer, cut leaves representing the form of the spear-head which they desire to acquire from the Singhalese blacksmiths.

Commerce, indispensable to societies at all complex, developed everywhere as soon as man emerged from savagery, and it has been a powerful agent in the diffusion of ideas, and often even an agent of civilisation. It has profoundly modified societies in which it has developed, opening out before them new horizons and making them learn foreign tongues and the manners of other societies.

It was a step towards broader solidarity, but at the same

[1] O. Mason, *loc. cit.*, p. 364.

time it opened the door to the spirit of lucre, to monopoly of wealth, to mercantile egoism, to greed of gain. This explains why in most primitive societies merchants were but little esteemed.[1]

Money.—In the primitive forms of commerce exchanges were made directly; object was bartered for object, as we see it still done to-day sporadically in many countries. But soon the need for values was felt—standards which would render exchanges more rapid, easy, and equitable. For this purpose objects coveted by the greatest number of persons were chosen. These objects were either ornaments (on which primitive commerce especially depends) or things which everybody wanted. It is thus that jewels, objects of adornment (feathers, pearls, shells, etc.), stuffs, furs (Siberian peoples, Alaska), salt (Laos), cattle (Africa, "Pecunia" of the Romans), slaves (Africa, New Guinea), became the first current money of primitive commerce. Later, certain objects were chosen which by their rarity are of great value. It is thus that the Pelew islanders treasure up as current money (Andou) a certain number of obsidian or porcelain beads (Fig. 81, 1 and 8) and terra-cotta prisms, imported no one knows when and how into the country, which have a very great value; a certain tribe possesses *one* single clay prism (called *Baran*) and regards it as a public treasure, etc. In the island of Yap, in the neighbourhood of the Pelews, the place of money is taken by blocks of aragonite, a rock which, being unknown on the island, has to be sought for in the Pelews. The greater the block the greater its value. Fifty pound bank-notes are replaced here by enormous mill-stones, so heavy that two men can hardly carry them; they serve rather to flatter the vanity of the rich people of the country, who exhibit them before their huts, than to facilitate exchanges.[2] It is clear from this example that the rarity of a substance is not sufficient to make it into good money. The second condition is that it may be easily handled, and though small in bulk, may represent a high value, either real or fiduciary.

[1] Letourneau, *L'évolution du commerce*, Paris, 1897.

[2] Kubary, *Ethn. Beitr. Karolinen-Archipel.*, p. 1, Leyden, 1889-95.

Such are the teeth of the Wapiti deer (*Cervus canadensis*), which the Shoshone Indians and the Bannocks of Idaho and Montana[1] still make use of in their transactions. Such, again,

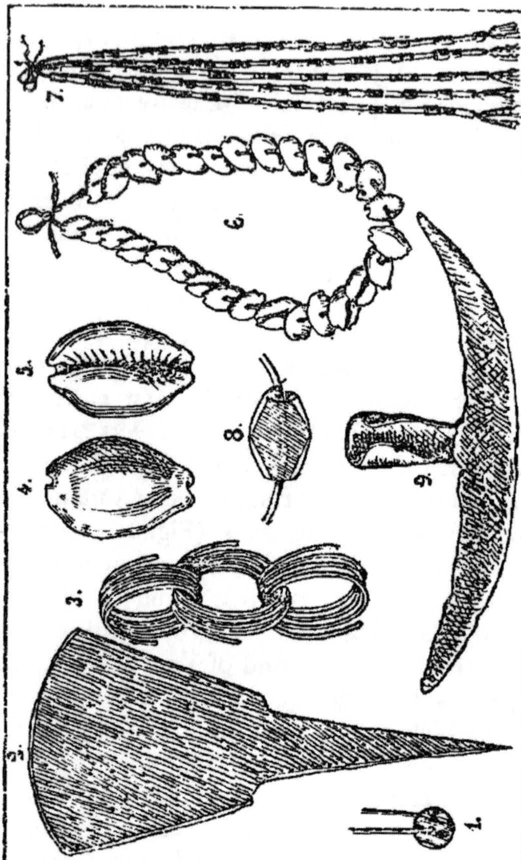

FIG. 81.—Money of uncivilised peoples: 1, 8, pearls (Pelew Islands); 2, iron plates (Ubangi): 3. rings of copper (Central Africa); 4, 5, cowries; 6, string of cowries; 7, "wampum" (N. Am. Indians); 9, money pick-axe (Negroes of the Upper Nile). Figs. 1, 4, 5, and 8 are two-thirds, the others one-eighth of actual size.

is the skin-money of the ancient Carthaginians and Scandinavians,[2] the cocoa-seed money of the ancient Mexicans, the

[1] Balfour, *Journ. Anthro. Inst.*, vol xix., 1889, p. 54.

[2] Nillsson, *Ureinwohner Skand. Nordens*, p. 37, Hamburg, 1866, i. Nachtr.

use of which is kept up to the present day; the animal skull-money of the Mishmee, etc.[1]

Let us give a glance at eatables employed as money: rice-grains by the ancient Coreans and the modern natives of the Philippines; grains of salt in Abyssinia and at Laos; "cakes of tea," which serve as the monetary unit in Mongolia. Let us also make but a passing reference to the pieces of stuff of a fixed length, which have a current value in China, Thibet, Mongolia, Africa, etc., and come to the subject of shells. Several species are employed as money: the *Dentalum entalis* by the Indians of the north-west of America, the *Venus mercenaria*, transformed into beads (wampum) by the Indians of the Atlantic coast of the United States (Fig. 81, 7), etc. But of all shells, the cowry is the best known. Two species are specially utilised as money, *Monetaria (cyprea) moneta, L.* (Fig. 81, 4, 5, 6), and *Monetaria annulus, L.* The first-mentioned seems to be most commonly used in Asia, the second in Africa.[2] Both are known all over the Indian Ocean, but they are gathered in great quantities only at two points, the Maldive Islands (to the west of Ceylon) and the Sooloo Islands (between the Philippines and Borneo). On the Asiatic continent the use of them was widespread, especially in Siam and in Laos. Twenty years ago 100 to 150 of these shells were worth a halfpenny. In Bengal, in the middle of last century, 2,400 to 2,560 cowries were worth a rupee, 100 a penny.

The true zone in which the cowry circulates is, however, tropical Africa; the fact is explained by its rarity, for the shell not being known in the Atlantic, it is only by commercial relations that it could have been propagated from east to west across the continent, from Zanzibar to the Senegal, and these

[1] Cooper, *The Mishmee Hills*, London, 1873.

[2] It is the English who have given to this porcelain the name of *cauri* or cowry, which appears to be a corruption of the Sanscrit word *Kaparda*, *Kapardika*, whence *Kavari* in the Mahratta dialect; the Portuguese call it *Bouji* or *Boughi;* the inhabitants of the Maldives, *boli;* the Siamese, *bios* (which means shell in general in their language); the Arabs, *wadda* or *vadaat*.

commercial relations must have existed for a long period, for Cadamosto and other Portuguese travellers of the fifteenth century mention the use of the cowry as money among the "Moors" of the Senegal. The rate of exchange of the cowry is much higher in Africa than in Asia, which shows that this shell is an imported object. It was probably by the Arabs that the cowry was introduced to the east coast of Africa. Later on the Europeans also got hold of this trade.[1]

The cowry is still current to day along all the west coast of Africa as far as the Cuanza River in Angola; farther south, as far as Walfisch Bay, another kind of "shell-money" is found, chaplets formed of fragments of a great land shell, the *Achatina monetaria*, strung on cord; they are principally made in the interior of the country of Benguela, in the district of "Selles," and are despatched along the whole coast, and as far as London. These chaplets, about eighteen inches long, were worth fifteen years ago from fivepence to one shilling and threepence.[2]

But it is to metals especially that we may trace the origin of true money. Iron or bronze plates of fixed size or weight served as money in Assyria, among the Mycenians, and the inhabitants of Great Britain at the time of Julius Cæsar. Metal plates of varying form are in general use in Africa as money, as for example the "loggos" of the Bongos and other negroes of the Upper Nile (Fig. 81, 9), the spear-heads of the Jurs, the iron plates of the peoples of the basin of the Ubangi (Fig. 81, 2), the X-shaped bronze objects made in Lunda, which are current all over the Congo. Thirty years ago, in Cambodia, iron money, in the form of

[1] Martens, "Über verschiedene Verwendungen von Conchylien," *Zeit. für Ethn.*, Berlin, 1872, vol. iv., p. 65; Andree, *Ethnol. Parall.*, p. 233; Stearns, "Ethno-conchology," *Report U.S. Nat. Mus. for 1887*.

[2] In 1858, 2,938 piculs of cowry-shells (about 177 tons) were exported from Manilla, for the most part to England. In 1848, 59½ tons of cowries were imported into Liverpool. At the time of the Dutch dominion of Ceylon, Amsterdam was the principal market of this trade; there were sold there in 1689 192,951 pounds (Dutch) of these shells; and in 1780 133,229 pounds (Johnston).

thin rings, from five and a half to six inches long, and weighing about seven ounces, was used.

A general fact to be noted in regard to primitive money is that it may be transformed without much trouble into an object of use (lance-iron, shovel, hoe, arrow-head, sword). In China the first bronze money had the form of a knife, the handle of which terminated in a ring; in time the blade became shorter and shorter, and at last disappeared, leaving only the ring, which was transformed into that Chinese money, pierced with a square hole, called "sapec," or "cash." Brass or copper wire, of which pieces are cut up (Fig. 81, 3), represents money in Central Africa. Silver bars, pieces of which are cut according to need, are also current money in China, as they were in Russia in the fifteenth century, as well as skins.

The question of *transport* and *means of communication* is closely allied to that of commerce. There is little to say about trade-routes, which most frequently are tracks made by chance in savage countries, and sometimes horrible neck-breaking roads in half-civilised countries. The means of transport are very varied, and may furnish matter for an interesting monograph, as O. Mason has shown.[1] The simplest mode of transport is that on men's backs, with or without the aid of special apparatus, like the *ski* and snow-shoes in cold countries (Figs. 115 and 116). To be noted apart are the attachments for climbing trees, used from Spain to New Caledonia, passing through Africa and India (Fig. 82). We come next to the utilisation of animals, the ass, horse, mule, camel, ox, zebra, dog, etc., which at first carried the loads on their backs, and were afterwards employed as draught animals.

Primitive Vehicles.—Most uncivilised peoples are unacquainted with any form of vehicle. This is so among the Australians, Melanesians, and most of the natives of Africa and America. But there are also a number of populations pretty well advanced in civilisation whom their special circumstances do not permit the use of chariots or other vehicles on wheels; such are the

[1] O. Mason, *loc. cit.*, p. 327, and "Prim. Travel and Transport," *Smithsonian Report U.S. Nat. Mus. for 1894*, p. 239, Washington, 1896.

Eskimo and other Hyperboreans, the Polynesians, etc. The sledges of the former, the canoes of the latter, fitly take the place of the carriage. Nomadic peoples have a kind of aversion to every sort of vehicle; they prefer to carry things on the backs of camel, ass, or horse. The earliest vehicle must have been something of the same description as that seen among the Prairie Indians of the present day—two tree branches

FIG. 82.—Method of tree-climbing in India. (*After B. Hurst.*)

attached to the sides of a horse, that is to say, inclined shafts, the ends of which drag on the ground; on them is laden the luggage, which is used by these Indians as a seat. Let us suppose that one day this primitive vehicle happens to break, but incompletely, so that one portion of the branch drags horizontally on the ground, and we shall understand the advantage which men must have taken of this mishap. He must have understood at once that traction is made easier by joining at an obtuse angle one pair of horizontal branches to another serving as shafts. From this point to placing pieces of wood transversely on horizontal branches there is only a step, and the sledge, as we see it still among the Finns and Russian peasants, was invented. Primitive as is this vehicle, it is admirably adapted to primitive roads, and still remains to-day the sole means of locomotion, winter as well as summer, in the forest regions of northern Russia, where no wheeled carriage would be able to pass, the pathways being scarcely visible across the dense virgin forest, when the ground is covered with a thick bed of moss and grass. It is only later, and in less wooded countries, that man thought of putting rollers under the horizontal branches of the sledge, contrivances which afterwards became transformed into true wheels. If this genesis of the vehicle be accepted, the appearance of sledges in funeral rites, even at the time when wheeled carriages were already invented, is explained quite simply as the survival of a custom the more venerated the greater its antiquity.[1]

The two-wheeled chariot was known in Asia from the most remote antiquity; it was used either in war (Assyrians, Chaldeans, Persians) or for purposes of transport. Even at the present day in India, Ceylon, Indo-China, the light waggon drawn by zebras or asses is much more common than the four-wheeled cart drawn by buffaloes. In the far East, where man is employed for draught purposes, the wheel-barrow takes the place of the car, and the Japanese *jinrickshaw*, as well as the Indo-Chinese *pousse-pousse*, are only adaptations of modern carriages to this mode of transport by men. It is only to the north of the Yang-tse-Kiang that one comes across Chinese cars with two cogged wheels, and heavy waggons, a sort of tumbrel without springs, with massive and sometimes solid wheels, drawn by buffaloes. It is perhaps such vehicles

[1] D. Anuchin, "Sani, etc" (The sledge, the canoe, and horses in funeral rites, in Russian), *Drévnosti* (*Antiquities*), vol. xiv., Moscow, 1890.

that served as the type for the Russian *tarantass*, a box fixed on long parallel shafts which rest on the axles. It was likewise from Asia that the Greeks and Romans, and perhaps the Egyptians, brought back the models of their elegant and light war-chariots. As to four-wheeled waggons, the populations of Europe must have known them at least from the bronze age, to judge from the remains found in the lake-dwellings of Italy and the tombs of Scandinavia. The waggons of the ancient Germanic peoples, also employed in war, resembled those which are still met with at the present day among the peasants of central and western Europe. The same kind of conveyances have been transported by the Dutch Boers as far as South Africa, and by the colonists of the Latin race even into the solitudes of the Pampas.

Navigation.—Transport by water has undergone more important transformations than vehicular transport. From the air-filled leather bottle, on which, after the manner of the ancient Assyrians, rivers are still crossed in Turkestan and Persia,[1] to elegant sailing yachts; from the primitive reed rafts of the Egyptians and the natives of lake Lob-Nor (Chinese Turkestan) to the great ocean liners, there are numberless intermediate forms. Australian canoes made from a hollowed-out tree-trunk, Fuegian canoes made of pieces of bark joined together by cords of seal's sinews, the effective Eskimo "kayaks" made with seal skins, the elegant skiffs of the Polynesians with their outriggers or balancing beams which defy the tempests of the ocean (Fig. 83), heavy Chinese junks, etc. We cannot enter into the details of this subject; let us merely observe that there is a great difference in the aptitude of various peoples for navigation. It is not enough to live by the sea-shore to become a good sailor; take for example the case of the Negroes who have never been able to go far away from their coasts, and who often have not even an elementary knowledge of navigation, while the Polynesians and the

[1] See the Assyrian bas-reliefs, Maspero, *Hist. anc. de l'Orient*, vol. ii., p. 628, Paris, 1897; O. Mason, *Origins of Invention*, p. 334; and Moser, *A travers l'Asie Centrale*, p. 220, Paris, 1885.

Malays make bold and perilous voyages of several thousand miles across the Pacific and Indian oceans; canoes of the Malay type are seen from Honolulu and Easter Island to

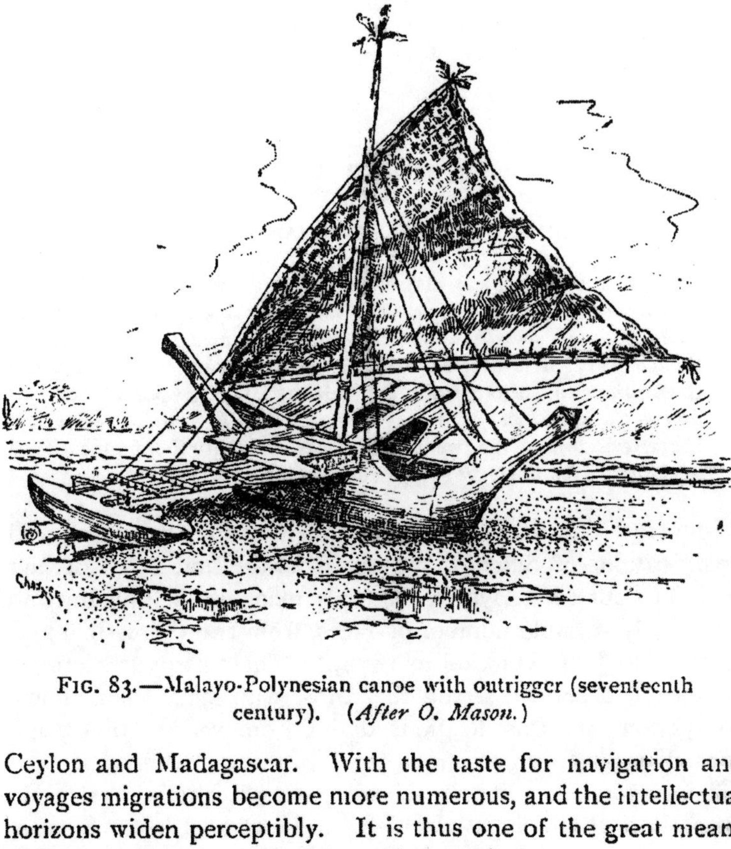

FIG. 83.—Malayo-Polynesian canoe with outrigger (seventeenth century). (*After O. Mason.*)

Ceylon and Madagascar. With the taste for navigation and voyages migrations become more numerous, and the intellectual horizons widen perceptibly. It is thus one of the great means of bringing peoples into closer relationship.

CHAPTER VIII.

CLASSIFICATION OF RACES AND PEOPLES.

Criticism of anthropological classifications—Frequent confusion of the *classing of races* and *of peoples*—The determining of races can be based only on *somatic characters*—For the classing of peoples, on the contrary, it is necessary to take into account *ethnic characters* (linguistic and sociological), and above all *geographical distribution*—*Classification of races proposed by the author*—Succinct characterisation of the twenty-nine races which are therein mentioned—*Classification of ethnic groups* adopted in this work.

EXCEPTION has frequently been taken to the anthropological classifications of different authors, from the time of F. Bernier (1672) to our own days, in that they recognise in humanity an excessively variable number of races, from two (Virey in 1775) up to thirty-four (Haeckel in 1879).[1] These strictures are by no means deserved, seeing that those who make them almost always compare classifications dating from various times, and consequently drawn up from facts and documents which are not comparable. In all sciences, classifications change in proportion as the facts or objects to be classed become better known.

Besides, if we go to the root of the matter we perceive that the diversity in the classifications of the genus *Homo* is often only apparent, for most classifications confuse ethnic groups and races. If my readers refer back to what I said in the

[1] See for the history of classifications, Topinard, *L'Anthr. gén.*, pp. 28-107, 264-349; Giglioli, *Viaggio . . . della Magenta*, p. xxvii., Milan, 1875; and Keane, *Ethnology*, p. 162, Cambridge, 1896.

introduction on "races" and "ethnic groups," they will understand all the difficulties this causes.

In order to class peoples, nations, tribes, in a word, "ethnic groups," we ought to take into consideration linguistic differences, ethnic characters, and especially, in my opinion, geographical distribution. It is thus that I shall describe the different peoples in the subsequent chapters, while classing them geographically. But for a classification of "races" (using the word in the sense given to it in the introduction), it is only necessary to take into account physical characters. We must try to determine by the anthropological analysis of each of the ethnic groups the races which constitute it; then compare these races one with another, unite those which possess most similarities in common, and separate those which exhibit most dissimilarities.

On making these methodic groupings we arrive at a small number of races, combinations of which, in various proportions, are met with in the multitude of ethnic groups.

Let us take for example the Negrito race, of which the Aetas of the Philippines, the Andamanese, and the black Sakai are the almost pure representatives. This race is found again here and there among the Melanesians, the Malays, the Dravidians, etc. In all these populations the type of the Negrito race is revealed on one side by the presence of a certain number of individuals who manifest it almost in its primitive purity, and on the other by the existence of a great number of individuals, whose traits likewise reproduce this type, but in a modified form, half hidden by characters borrowed from other races. Characteristics of various origin may thus be *amalgamated*, or merely exist in *juxtaposition*.

Race-characters appear with a remarkable persistency, in spite of all intermixtures, all modifications due to civilisation, change of language, etc. What varies is the *proportion* in which such and such a race enters into the constitution of the ethnic group. A race may form the preponderating portion in a given ethnic group, or it may form a half, a quarter, or a very trifling fraction of it; the remaining portion consisting of others. Rarely is an ethnic group composed almost exclusively of a single race; in this case the notion of race is confused with that of *people*. We may say, for example, that the tribes called Bushmen, Aetas, Mincopies, Australians, are formed of a race still almost pure; but these cases are rare. Already it is difficult to admit that there is but one race, for example, among the Mongols; and if we pass to the Negroes we find among them at least three races which, while being connected one with another by a certain number of common characteristics, present, nevertheless, appreciable differences. Now, each of these races may be combined, in an ethnic group, not only with a kindred race, but also with other races, and it is easy to imagine how very numerous may be these combinations.

I have just said that the number of human *races* is not very considerable; however, reviewing the different classifications proposed, in chronological order, it will be seen that this number increases as the physical characters of the populations of the earth become better known. Confining ourselves to the most recent and purely somatological classifications, we find the increase to be as follows:—In 1860, Isid. Geoffroy Saint-Hilaire admitted four principal races or "types," and thirteen secondary ones.[1] In 1870, Huxley proposed five principal races or types, and fourteen secondary ones or

[1]

Principal Races.	*Secondary Races.*
(1) Caucasian.	(1) Caucasian, (2) Alleghanian (Red Indian).
(2) Mongolian.	(3) Hyperborean (Lapps), (4) Malay, (5) American (except the Red Indian), (6) Mongolian, (7) Paraborean (Eskimo), (8) Australian.
(3) Ethiopian.	(9) Kafir, (10) Ethiopian, (11) Negro, (12) Melanesian.
(4) Hottentot.	(13) Hottentot.

—Isid. Geoffroy Saint-Hilaire, "Classif. Anthropologique," *Mem. Soc. Anthr. Paris*, vol. i., p. 125, 1861.

"modifications."[1] Finally, in 1878, Topinard enumerated sixteen races, and increased this number in 1885 to nineteen.[2] In mixed classifications, based on both somatic and ethnic characters, a very much greater number of sub-divisions is found, but the reason of that is that "ethnic groups" are included.

Putting these aside, we see in the most complete mixed

[1] *Principal Races.*	*Secondary Races or "Modifications."*
(1) Negroid.	(1) Bushmen, (2) Negro, (3) Papuan.
(2) Australoid.	(4) Australians, (5) Black race of Deccan (Dravidians), (6) Ethiopian (Hamite).
(3) Mongoloid.	(7) Mongol, (8) Polynesian, (9) American, (10) Eskimo, (11) Malay.
(4) Xanthochroid.	(12) Xanthochroid of Northern Europe.
(5) Melanochroid.	(13) Melanochroid of Southern Europe, (14) Melanochroid of Asia (Arabs, Afghans, Hindus, etc.).

—T. Huxley, "Geogr. Distrib. of Mankind," *Journ. Ethnol. Soc. London*, N.S., vol. ii., p. 404, map, 1870. The classification of Flower (*Jl. Anthro. Inst.*, vol. xiv., 1885, p. 378) differs from that of Huxley in a few details only. This eminent anatomist grouped his eleven races and three sub-races under three "types"—Negro, Mongolian, and Caucasian.

[2] In the first edition of his classification (*Rev. d'Anthr.*, 2nd series, vol. i., p. 509, Paris, 1878), Topinard admits sixteen races in three groups:—

(*a*) *Straight-haired Races.*—Eskimo, Red Indians, Mexico-Peruvians, Guarani-Caribs, Mongols.

(*b*) *Wavy or Frizzy-haired Races.*—Fair-haired people of Europe (Xanthochroids of Huxley), dark-haired people of Europe and Semites (Melanochroids of Huxley), Australians and Indo-Abyssinians (Australoids of Huxley), Fulbé, Finns, Celto-Slavs, Turanians.

(*c*) *Woolly-haired Races.*—Bushmen, Papuans, Kafirs, Negritoes.

In the second edition, dating from 1885 (*Elém. Anthr. gén.*, p. 502, we find nineteen races grouped under three heads:—

(*a*) *White Leptorhine Races.*—Anglo-Scandinavians, Finns (first type, Western), Mediterraneans, Semito-Egyptians, Lapono-Ligurians, Celto-Slavs.

(*b*) *Yellow Mesorhine Races.*—Eskimo, Tehuelches, Polynesians, Red Indians, yellow peoples of Asia (including Finns of the second type), Guaranis (or South Americans, except the Tehuelches), Peruvians.

(*c*) *Black Platyrhine Races.*—Australians, Bushmen, Melanesians, Negroes, Tasmanians, Negritoes.

classifications only four or five principal races, and twelve to eighteen secondary races. Thus Haeckel and Fr. Mueller admit four principal races (called "tribes" by Haeckel, "sub-divisions" by Mueller), and twelve secondary races (called "species" and sub-divided into thirty-four "races" by Haeckel, called "races" and sub-divided into numerous "peoples" by Fr. Mueller).[1] On the other hand, De Quatrefages sub-divides his five "trunks" into eighteen "branches," each containing several ethnic groups, which he distinguishes under the names of "minor branches" and "families."[2]

Some years ago I proposed a classification of the human races, based solely on physical characters.[3] Taking into account all the new data of anthropological science, I endeavoured, as do the botanists, to form natural groups by combining the different characters (colour of the skin, nature of the hair, stature, form of the head, of the nose, etc.), and I thus managed to separate mankind into thirteen races. Continuing the analysis further, I was able to give a detailed description of the thirty sub-divisions of these races, which I called *types*, and which it would have been better to call secondary races, or briefly "races." A mass of new material,

[1] Tribes (sub-divisions): (1) *Lophocomi* (woolly hair, tufted), comprising the following species (races): Papuans, Hottentots; (2) *Eriocomi* (woolly hair, growing uniformly and not in tufts): Kafirs and Negroes; (3) *Euthycomi* (straight hair): Australians, Malays, Mongols, Arctic people (Hyperboreans), Americans; (4) *Euplocomi* (curly hair): Dravidians, Nubians (Ethiopians), Mediterraneans (Aryans). (Haeckel, *Natürl. Schöpfungsgesch.*, 7th ed., pp. 628 and 647, 1879; Fr. Mueller, *Allg. Ethnogr.*, 2nd ed., pp. 17 and 19, Vienna, 1879.)

[2] "Trunks": (1) *Negro*, with its "branches," Indo-Melanesian, Australian, African, and Austro-African; (2) *Yellow*, with its "branches," Siberian, Thibetan, Indo-Chinese, and American (Eskimo-Brazilian); (3) *White*, with its "branches," Allophyle (Ainu, Miao-tse, Caucasian, Indonesian-Polynesian, etc.), Finnish, Semetic, and Aryan. "Mixed Races": (1) *Oceanians* (Japanese, Polynesian, Malay); (2) *Americans* (of North, Central, and South America). (A. de Quatrefages, *Hist. Gen. Races Hum.*, pp. 343 *et seq.*, Paris, 1889.)

[3] Deniker, "Essai d'une classification des races hum., etc.," Paris, 1889 (*Extr. du Bull. Soc. Anthr.*, vol. xii., p. 320). Cf. O Mason, *Smithson. Report for 1889*, p. 602.

and my own researches, have compelled me since then to modify this classification. This is how it may be summarised in the form of a table, giving to my former "types" the title of race or sub-races, and grouping them under six heads—

Characters			Races and Sub-races.	
A. Woolly Hair, Broad Nose.				
Yellow skin, steatopygous, short stature, dolichocephalic			*Bushmen* (s. r. Hottentots and Bushmen)	1
Dark skin	Reddish-brown, very short stature, sub-brachycephalic or sub-dolichocephalic		*Negrito* (s. r. Negrillo and Negrito)	2
Dark skin	Black, stature tall, dolichocephalic		*Negro* (s. r. Nigritian and Bantu)	3
Dark skin	Brownish-black, medium stature, dolichocephalic		*Melanesian* (s. r. Papuan and Melanesian)	4
B. Curly or Wavy Hair.				
Dark skin	Reddish-brown, narrow nose, tall stature, dolichocephalic		*Ethiopian*	5
Dark skin	Chocolate-brown, broad nose, medinm stature, dolichocephalic		*Australian*	6
Dark skin	Brownish-black, broad or narrow nose, short stature, dolichocephalic		*Dravidian* (s. r. Platyrhine and Leptorhine)	7
Skin of a tawny white, nose narrow, hooked, with thick top, brachycephalic			*Assyroid*	8
C. Wavy Brown or Black Hair, Dark Eyes.				
Clear brown skin, black hair, narrow, straight or convex nose, tall stature, dolichocephalic			*Indo-Afghan*	9
Tawny white skin, black hair	Tall stature, elongated face	Aquiline nose, prominent occiput, dolichocephalic, elliptical form of face	*Arab* or *Semite*	10
Tawny white skin, black hair	Tall stature, elongated face	Straight coarse nose, dolichocephalic, square face	*Berber* (4 sub-races)	11
Tawny white skin, black hair	Tall stature, elongated face	Straight fine nose, mesocephalic, oval face	*Littoral European*	12
Tawny white skin, black hair	Short stature, dolichocephalic		*Ibero-insular*	13
Dull white skin, brown hair	Short stature, strongly brachycephalic, round face		*Western European*	14
Dull white skin, brown hair	Tall stature, brachycephalic, elongated face		*Adriatic*	15

D. Fair, Wavy or Straight Hair, Light Eyes.

Reddish white skin, hair	Somewhat wavy, reddish; tall stature, dolichocephalic	*Northern European*	16
	Somewhat straight, flaxen-haired, short stature, sub-brachycephalic	*Eastern European*	17

E. Straight or Wavy Hair, Dark, Black Eyes.

Light brown skin, very hairy body, broad and concave nose, dolichocephalic		*Ainu*	18
Yellow skin, smooth body	Prominent nose, sometimes convex, tall stature, elliptical form of face, brachy- or meso-cephalic	*Polynesian*	19
	Short stature, flattened, sometimes concave nose, projecting cheek-bones, lozenge-shaped face, dolichocephalic	*Indonesian*	20
	Short stature, prominent straight or concave nose, meso- or dolicho-cephalic	*South American* (s. r. Palæo-Am. & S. Amer.)	21

F. Straight Hair.

Warm yellow skin	Straight or aquiline nose	Tall stature, mesocephalic	*North American* (s. r. Atlantic and Pacific)	22
		Short stature, brachycephalic	*Central American*	23
	Straight nose, tall stature, brachycephalic, square face		*Patagonian*	24
Brownish-yellow skin, short stature, round flattened face, dolichocephalic			*Eskimo*	25
Yellowish-white skin	Turned-up nose, short stature, brachycephalic		*Lapp*	26
	Straight or concave nose, short stature, meso- or dolicho-cephalic, projecting cheek-bones		*Ugrian* (s. r. Ugrian and Yeniseian)	27
	Straight nose, medium stature, strongly brachycephalic		*Turkish* or *Turco-Tatar*	28
Pale yellow skin, projecting cheek-bones, Mongoloid eye, slightly brachycephalic			*Mongol* (s. r. Northern and Southern)	29

My table contains the enumeration of the principal somatic characters for each race. Arranged dichotomically for convenience of research, it does not represent the exact grouping of the races according to their true affinities. It would be vain to attempt to exhibit these affinities in the lineal arrangement of a table; each race, in fact, manifests some points of resemblance, not only with its neighbours in the upper or lower part of the table, but also with others which are remote from it, in view of the technical necessities of construction of such a table. In order to exhibit the affinities in question, it would be necessary to arrange the groups according to the three dimensions of space, or at least on a surface where we can avail ourselves of two dimensions. In the ensuing table (p. 289) are included twenty-nine races, combined into seventeen groups, arranged in such a way that races having greatest affinities one with another are brought near together. Seven of these groups only are composed of more than one race. They may be called as follows (see the table):—XIII., American group; XII., Oceanian; II., Negroid; VIII., North African; XVI., Eurasian; X., Melanochroid; IX., Xanthochroid. This table shows us clearly that the Bushman race, for example, has affinities with the Negritoes (short stature) and the Negroes (nature of the hair, form of nose); that the Dravidian race is connected both with the Indonesian and the Australian; that the place of the Turkish race is, by its natural affinities, between the Ugrians and the Mongols; that the Eskimo have Mongoloid and American features; that the Assyroids are closely related to the Adriatics and the Indo-Afghans; that the latter, by the dark colour of their skin, recall the Ethiopians, and the Arabs by the shape of the face, etc. Here are, moreover, some details of the twenty-nine races (marked by their numbers of order) of the first table, and of the seventeen groups of the second (marked in Roman figures).

I. 1. The *Bushman* race is found in a relative state of purity among the people called Bushmen (Fig. 24), and less pure among the Hottentots (Fig. 143). The presence of the Bushman type may be detected among a great number of Negro peoples to the south of the equator (for example, among the Bechuana and Kiokos, etc.).

II. The *Negroid* group comprises three races: Negrito, Negro, and Melanesian.

2. The *Negrito* race may be split up into two sub races: *a*, the *Negrilloes* of Africa, of which the pure representatives are the Akkas, the Batuas, and other sub-dolichocephalic pigmies; and *b*, the *Negritoes* of Asia (Andamanese, Fig. 124, black Sakai, Fig. 123, Aetas, etc.), mesocephalic or sub-brachycephalic, of a little taller stature than the Negrilloes. The presence of Negrito elements has been noticed among different Bantu negroes (for example, among the Adumas). As to the influence of the Negrito type on that of the Malays, the Jakuns, certain Indonesians, etc, it is perfectly well recognised.

3. The *Negroes* may likewise be sub-divided into two sub-races: *a*, the *Nigritians*, of the Sudan (Fig. 140) and of Guinea (Fig. 9), more prognathous (more "negroid," if we may thus express it) than *b*, the *Bantus* of sub-equatorial and southern Africa (Figs. 47, 141, and 142). The Negro element is strongly represented in the mixed populations of Africa (certain Berbers and Ethiopians, islanders of Madagascar). The majority of the Negroes of America belong to the Negritic sub-race.

4. The *Melanesian* race differs from the Negro race especially in having less woolly hair with broader spirals (see p. 39), and the skin a lighter colour. It comprises two variations or sub-races: one with elongated ovoid face, hooked nose, especially prevalent in New Guinea (*Papuan sub-race*, Figs. 53 and 152), and the other with squarer and heavier face, which occupies the rest of Melanesia (*Melanesian sub-race* properly so called, Fig. 153).[1] The first of these sub-races enters into the composition of several mixed tribes of Celebes, Gilolo, Flores (Figs. 146 to 148), Timur, and other islands of the Asiatic Archipelago situated farther to the east.

III. 5. The *Ethiopian* race forms by itself the third group. It is preserved fairly pure among certain Bejas (Fig. 138) and the Gallas, but is modified by the admixture of Arab blood

[1] Fig. 153 represents individuals of one tribe only, but belonging to the two sub-races mentioned. Fig. 151 represents the blending of the two types with Polynesian admixture.

GROUPING OF THE HUMAN RACES ACCORDING TO THEIR AFFINITIES.

XIII.
Patagonian.
North American.
Central American.
South American.

XII.
Polynesian.
Indonesian.

XI.
Ainu.

V.
Dravidian.

IV.
Australian.

II.
Melanesian.
Negrito.
Negro.

XIV.
Eskimo.

XVII.
Mongolian.

I.
Bushmen.

VI.
Assyroid.

XV.
Lapponic.

XVI.
Ugrian.
Turkish.

VII.
Indo-Afghan.

III.
Ethiopian.

IX.
Eastern European.
Northern European.

X.
Western European.
Ibero-Insular.
Adriatic.
Littoral.

VIII.
Arab.
Berber.

among the Somalis, Abyssinians, etc., and by Negro blood among the Zandehs (Niam-Niams, etc.), and especially among the Fulbé or Peuls, though among the latter fine Ethiopian types, almost pure, are still met with (Fig. 139).

IV. 6. The *Australian* race (Figs. 14, 15, 149, and 150) is remarkable for its unity and its isolation on the Australian continent, and even the *Tasmanians* (see Chapter XII.), the nearest neighbours to the Australians, at the present day extinct, had a different type.

V. 7. The *Dravidian* race, which it would have been better to call *South-Indian*, is prevalent among the peoples of Southern India speaking Dravidian tongues, and also among the Kols and other peoples of India; it presents two varieties or sub-races, according to Schmidt:[1] *a*, *leptorhinean*, thin nose, very elongated head (Nairs, etc.); *b*, *platyrhinean*, with very broad nose and a somewhat shorter head (Dravidians properly so called, Figs. 8, 126, and 127). The Veddahs (Figs. 5, 6, and 133) come much nearer to the Dravidian type, which moreover penetrates also among the populations of India, even into the middle valley of the Ganges.

VI. 8. The *Assyroid* race, so named because it is represented in a very clear manner on the Assyrian monuments, is not found pure in any population, but it counts a sufficient number of representatives to give a character to entire populations, such as the Hadjemi-Persians (Fig. 22), the Ayssores, certain Kurdish tribes, and some Armenians and Jews. The characteristic Jewish nose of caricature, in the form of the figure *6*, is an Assyroid nose; it is almost always associated with united eyebrows and thick lower lip. The Todas (Fig. 130) partly belong, perhaps, to this type.

VII. 9. The *Indo-Afghan* race (see Chapter X.) has its typical representatives among the Afghans, the Rajputs, and in the caste of the Brahmins, but it has undergone numerous alterations as a consequence of crosses with Assyroid, Dravidian, Mongol, Turkish, Arab, and other elements (Figs. 125 and 134).

[1] E. Schmidt, "Die Anthropologie Indiens," *Globus*, vol. 61, 1892, Nos. 2 and 3.

VIII. The *North African* group is composed, 10, of the Arab or Semite race, represented by typical individuals among the Arabs and certain Jews (Fig. 21), the features of which are often found in most of the populations of Syria, Mesopotamia, Beloochistan (Fig. 134), Egypt, and the Caucasus; 11, of the *Berber* race (Fig. 136), which admits four varieties or "types," according to Collignon (see Chapter XI.).

IX. The *Melanochroid* group comprises the four dark-complexioned races of Europe (12 to 15), *Littoral, Ibero-insular, Western* (Fig. 98), and *Adriatic.*

X. The *Xanthochroid* group contains the two fair races of Europe (16 and 17), *Northern* (Figs. 88 to 90) and *Eastern.* (For further details respecting groups IX. and X. see Chapter IX.)

XI. 18. The *Ainu* race is preserved fairly pure among the people of this name (Figs. 49 and 117); it forms one of the constituent elements of the population of Northern Japan (see Chapter X.).

XII. The *Oceanian* group is formed of two races, the relations of which are somewhat vague. 19. The *Polynesian* race (Figs. 154 to 156), found more or less pure from the Hawaiian Islands to New Zealand, undergoes changes in the west of Polynesia owing to intermixture with the Melanesians (Fiji, New Guinea). It furnishes perhaps a more hirsute sub-race in Micronesia. 20. The *Indonesian* race is represented by the Dyaks, the Battas, and other populations of the Malay Archipelago (Nias, Kubus), or of Indo-China (Nicobariese, Nagas, Fig. 17 and Frontispiece). It is modified by intermixture with Negrito elements (White Sakai of the Malay peninsula), Hindus (Javanese, Fig. 145), Mongoloids (Malays, Khamtis, Fig. 22), or Papuans (Natives of Flores, Figs. 146 to 148).

XIII. The American group comprises the four races numbered in my table 21 to 24, which will be dealt with in the chapter devoted to America. Let me merely say that the type of *Central Americans,* brachycephalic, short, with straight or aquiline nose (Figs. 163 and 164), is frequently met with on the Pacific slope of the two Americas, as well as on several points of the Atlantic slope of South America. In the former of these two regions the population is principally formed of a blending of this type with the *North American* race; in the latter, with the *South American* race (Fig. 171).

Two sub-races may be distinguished in the North American race: *a*, *Atlantic*, mesocephalic, of very tall stature, good representatives of which, for example, are the Siouans (Figs. 158 and 159); and *b*, the *Pacific*, of which the Tlinkit Indians may give an approximate idea, differing from the former by shorter stature, more rounded head, and better developed pilous system. Further, in the *South American* race we most probably admit two sub-races: *a*, the *dolichocephalic* race, with hair often wavy, or even frizzy (Figs. 48, 165, 172, and 175),[1] which is perhaps derived from the oldest inhabitants of the continent, and which I called *Palæo-American* type in my first attempt at a classification of the human races (1889), and another (*b*), which would be the present type of South American *mesocephalic* race with straight hair (Figs. 167 to 170). The tall *Patagonian* race, brachycephalic, of deep brown colour, has its representatives among the Patagonians and among certain peoples of Chaco and the Pampas.[2]

XIV. 25. The *Eskimo* race (Fig. 157) has kept fairly pure on the east coast of Greenland, as well as in the north of Canada; but it is modified by intermixtures with the North American race in Labrador, in Alaska, on the west coast of Greenland (where there is, further, intermixture with the Northern European race), and with the Mongolic races (Chukchi, Aleuts, etc.) on the shores of Behring's Sea.

[1] Ehrenreich, *loc. cit.* (*Urbewohner Brasil.*), and Von den Steinen, *loc. cit.*, describe numerous individuals with wavy or frizzy hair among the Bakairis, the Karayas, the Arawaks, etc. I myself have noticed Fuegians with frizzy or wavy hair (Hyades and Deniker, *loc. cit.*). See also Fig. 171, which represents the blending of the Central American and South American types, and portraits of the *Goajires* in *Le Tour du Monde*, 1898, 1st half year.

[2] A. Barcena, "Arte . . . lengua Toba," *Rev. Mus. de la Plata*, vol. v., 1894, p. 142.

XV. 26. The *Lapp* race is fairly pure among some tribes of Scandinavian Lapps; elsewhere it is blended with the northern and eastern races (Scandinavians, Finns, Russians).

XVI. The two races which compose the *Eurasian* group (so named because its representatives inhabit Europe as well as Asia) have only a few common characters (yellowish-white skin, modified Mongolian features, etc.). 27. The *Ugrian* race predominates among the eastern Finns (Ostiaks, Permiaks, Cheremiss, Fig. 106), and perhaps as a variety among the Yeniseians. It is found again interblended with the Samoyeds, and perhaps with the Yakuts. 28. The *Turkish* race, which I would willingly call *Turanian*, if this term were not too much abused, enters into the composition of the peoples called Turco-Tatars, who speak Turkish idioms. The type, fairly pure, is common among the Kirghiz and the Tatars of Astrakhan (Figs. 107, 108), but in other ethnic groups it is weakened by intermixture with such races as the Mongolo-Tunguse (Yakuts), Ugrian (Shuvashes), Assyroid (Turkomans, Osmanli Turks, etc.).

XVII. The *Mongol* race admits two varieties or sub-races: *Tunguse* or *Northern Mongolian*, with oval or round faces and prominent cheek-bones, spread over Manchuria, Corea, Northern China, Mongolia (Figs. 20, 115, 116, and 118); and *Southern Mongolia*, with lozenge-shaped or square faces and cheek-bones laterally enlarged, which may be observed especially in Southern China (Fig. 119) and in Indo-China (Fig. 121).

We have now sketched out the classing of *races*, that is to say of the somatological units. It remains for us to deal with the "ethnic groups" or sociological units.

In these the grouping must rest on linguistic, sociological, and especially geographical affinities, for sociological difference, are very often the product of differences in the immediate environment.

I have already spoken of the classing of languages (p. 127) and social states (p. 124). In subordinating them to considerations of habitat, I shall give the table of mixed classification, geographico-lingustic, which I have adopted in the descriptive part of this work. But first, a few words on the relations of the different classifications of ethnic groups one with another.

The purely linguistic grouping does not correspond with the geographical grouping of peoples: thus in the Balkan peninsula, which forms a unit from the geographical point of view, we find at least four to six different linguistic families; in the British Isles, two or three, etc. Neither does this grouping coincide with the somatological grouping: thus, the Aderbaidjani of the Caucasus and Persia, who speak a Turkish language, have the same physical type as the Hadjemi-Persians, who speak an Iranian tongue; the Negroes of North America speak English; several Indians of Mexico and South America speak Spanish as their mother-tongue; different Ugrian tribes (Zyrians, Votiaks, Permiaks) make use of Russian, etc. In European countries cases of changes of language in any given population are known to every one. The limits of the Breton language in France, of the Irish in Ireland in the sixteenth century, were at least 60 miles to the east of their present frontier. The limits of Flemish in France, of Lithuanian in Prussia, have perceptibly receded to the east during the last hundred years; it is the same with so many other linguistic limits in Europe, the only continent where accurate data on this subject exist.

But similar, though isolated facts may be adduced from other parts of the world. Thus in India the Irulas, who differ physically from the Tamils, yet speak their language; many of the Kol, Dravidian, and other tribes at the present time speak Hindustani instead of their primitive tongues. According to the last census,[1] out of 2,897,591 Gonds, only 1,379,580, less than half, speak the language of their fathers.

However, in certain regions where there is little intermixture due to conquest, in South America for example, language may give valuable indications for the classification of ethnic groups. As to "states of civilisation," it is very difficult to make clear

[1] Bain, *Census of India, 1891.* Calcutta, 1896.

sub-divisions, seeing that frequently one and the same people may be at the same time shepherds and fishers (Chukchi), hunters and tillers of the soil (Tlinkits), hunters, shepherds, and tillers of the soil (Tunguses), etc. Certain characters of civilisation, especially of material culture, are of clearly defined extent, and form what Bastian calls "ethnographic provinces." I have spoken of them in connection with the geographical distribution of plate-armour, the throwing-stick, pile dwellings, etc. But similarity of manners and customs, and identity of objects in common use, do not yet give us the right to infer an affinity of race or language, and still less a common origin. At the very most, they may indicate frequent communication, whether pacific or not, between two peoples and "adoption" of customs and material culture. Sometimes even two distinct peoples, having never communicated with each other, may happen to produce almost identical objects and adopt almost similar manners and customs, as I have previously shown.

Having said this much I shall proceed to give the classification of the "ethnic groups" adopted in this work.

I adopt in the first place the best known geographical division, into five parts, of the world (including Malaysia or the Asiatic Archipelago with Oceania).[1] I afterwards divide each part of the world into great linguistic or geographical regions, each comprising several populations or groups of populations, according to the following arrangement:—

I. Europe.—We may distinguish here two linguistic groups: Aryan and Anaryan, and a geographical group, that of the Caucasians.

The *Aryans* are sub-divided into six groups: the Latins or Romans (examples: Spaniards, French, etc.), the Germans or Teutons (Germans, English, etc.), the Slavs (Russians, Poles,

[1] Each continent in fact contains distinct populations, with the exception, however, of Asia, to which belongs half a score of peoples, of whom part live outside its borders: in America (Eskimo), Oceania (Malays and Negritoes), Africa (Arabs), Europe (Samoyeds, Vogulc-Ostiaks, Tatars, Kirghiz, Kalmuks, Caucasians, Armenians, and Russians), or in other parts of the world (Greeks, Jews, Gypsies).

etc.), the Helleno-Illyrians (Greeks and Albanians), the Celts (Bretons, Gaels, etc.), and the Letto-Lithuanians (Letts and Lithuanians). The *Anaryans* are represented in Europe by the Basques (whose language is not classified), and by peoples of Finno-Ugrian languages (Lapps, Western Finns, Hungarians, and Eastern Finns; the latter partly in Asia). The *Caucasians* are the native peoples of the Caucasus; they form four groups: Lesgian, Georgian or Kartvel, Cherkess, and Ossets. The language of the last is Iranian; the idioms of the three others form a group apart, not classified.

II. Asia.—We include in this continent six great geographical regions. *Northern Asia* comprises three groups of populations: *Yenisians* (Samoyeds, Toubas, etc.), the *Palæo-asiatics* (Chukchis, Giliaks, Ainus), and the *Tunguses* (Manchu, Orochons, etc.). *Central Asia* likewise contains three groups of populations: *Turkish* (Yakuts, Kirghiz, Osmanlis, etc.), *Mongol* (Buriats, Kalmuks, etc.), and *Thibetan* (Lepchas, Bods, etc.). *Eastern Asia* is occupied by three "nations": *Japanese*, *Coreans*, and *Chinese*. *Indo-China*, or the Transgangetic peninsula, includes five ethnic divisions: the *Aborigines* (Negritoes, Tsiam, Mois, Mossos, Naga), the *Cambodians*, the *Burmese*, the *Annamese*, and the *Thaï* (Shans, Kakhyens, Siamese, Miao-tse, etc.). The Cisgangetic peninsula, or India, includes four linguistic divisions: the *Dravidians* (Tamils, Khonds, etc.), the *Kols* (Santals, etc.), the *Indo-Aryans* (Hindus, Kafirs, etc.), and *the peoples whose languages are not classified* (*Veddahs*, *Singhalese*, *Nairs*, etc.). *Anterior Asia* is divided between two great linguistic groups: *Eranian* or *Iranian* (Persians, Afghans, Kurds, etc.) and *Semite* (Syrians and Arabs, the latter partly in Africa), and further comprises some other peoples *not classified* (Brahuis, Takhtajis), or *cosmopolites* (Gypsies and Jews).

III. Africa.—In this continent there are three great divisions: one linguistic in the north, the Semito-Hamites; and two ethnic or even somatological ones in the south, the Negroes and the Bushmen-Hottentots. The peoples speaking *Semitic* or *Hamitic* languages may be united into three groups: the

Arabo-Berbers (Touaregs, Fellahs, etc.), the *Ethiopians* (Gallas, Bejas, Abyssinians), and the *Fulah-Zandehs* (Fulahs, Niam-Niams, Masai, etc.). The *Bushmen-Hottentots* form an ethno-somatological group quite apart. As to the *Negroes*, they may be divided as follows:—the *Negrilloes* or Pygmies (Akkas, Batuas, etc.), the *Nigritians* or *Negroes properly so called* (Dinkas, Hausas, Wolofs, Krus, Tshis, etc.), and the *Bantus* (Dwalas, Batekes, Balubas, Swaheli, Kafirs, Bechuanas, etc.). The populations of the *Island of Madagascar* also form a *linguistic and geographical* group apart.

IV. OCEANIA.—Four ethnic regions are here well defined: Malaysia, Australia, Melanesia, and Polynesia. Malaysia (to which, strictly speaking, should be joined a portion of the populations of Madagascar, Indo-China, and the Sino-Japanese islands) comprises four great groups of populations: the *Negritoes* (Aeta, etc.), the *Indonesians* (Battas, Tagals, etc.), and mixed peoples like the Javanese, the Bugis, the Malays, etc. *Australia* is peopled, over and above the white or yellow colonists, by only one race-people, the *Australians;* the *Tasmanians* who lived near them no longer exist. *Melanesia* is peopled by Papuans (of New Guinea), and by *Melanesians properly so called* (of New Caledonia, Solomon Islands, etc.). Lastly, *Polynesia* comprises the *Polynesians properly so called* (Samoans, Tahitians), and the *Micronesians* (natives of the Carolines, the Marshall Islands, etc.).

V. AMERICA.—For *North America* we may adopt three ethno-geographical groups: the *Eskimo*, with the Aleuts; the *American Indians* (Athapascans, Yumas, Tlinkits, etc.); and the *Indians of Mexico and of Central America* (Aztecs, Pimas, Miztecs, Mayas, Isthmians, Ulvas, etc.).

South America has four geographical groupings: the *Andeans* (Chibchas, Quechua-Aymara, etc.); the *Amazonians* (Caribs, Arawak, Pano, Miranha, etc.); the Indians of *East Brazil*, and of the *central region* (Tupi-Guarani, Ges or Botocudo-Kayapo, etc.); and, finally, the *Patagonians*, tribes of Chaco, of the Pampas, etc., with the *Fuegians*.

It is likewise well, as regards the New World, to take into

account the imported Negroes, and the descendants of colonists: Anglo-Saxon in the north, Hispano-Lusitanians in the south. These settlers form the nucleus of the different civilised nations of the two Americas, around which are grouped other elements from Europe or originating on the spot (Half-breeds of various degrees, Quadroons, Creoles, etc.).

CHAPTER IX.

RACES AND PEOPLES OF EUROPE.

Problem of European ethnogeny—I. ANCIENT INHABITANTS OF EUROPE—*Prehistoric races*—Quaternary period—Glacial and interglacial periods—Quaternary skulls—Spy and Chancelade races or types—Races of the neolithic period—Races of the age of metals—*Aryan question*—Position of the problem—*Migration* of European peoples in the *historic period*—II. EUROPEAN RACES OF THE PRESENT DAY—Characteristics of the six principal races and the four secondary races—III. PRESENT PEOPLES OF EUROPE—A. *Aryan peoples:* Latins, Germans, Slavs, Letto-Lithuanians, Celts, Illyro-Hellenes—B. *Anaryan peoples:* Basques, Finns, etc.—C. *Caucasian peoples:* Lesgians, Georgians, etc.

OF all parts of the world Europe presents the most favourable conditions for the interblending of peoples. Easy of access, a mere peninsula of Asia, from which the Ural mountains and straits a few miles wide hardly separate it, Europe has a totally different configuration from the continental colossus, heavy and vague in outline, to which it is attached. Indented by numberless gulfs, bays, and creeks, provided with several secondary peninsulas, crossed by rivers having no cataracts, and for the most part navigable, it offers every facility for communication and change of place to ethnic groups. Thus from the dawn of history, and even from prehistoric times, a perpetual eddying has taken place there, a coming and going of peoples in search of fortune and better settlements.

These migrations, combined with innumerable wars and active commerce, have produced such a blending of races, such successive changes in the manners and customs and languages spoken, that it is very difficult to separate from this chaos the elements of European ethnogeny, and that in spite of the great number of historical and linguistic works published on the subject. We may, however, thanks to the progress in prehistoric, anthropological, and ethnographical studies, obtain a glimpse of the main outlines of this ethnogeny, in which history and linguistics give us often but vague, and in any case very slight information.

The better to understand the distribution of races at the present day, we must cast a glance at those which are extinct, going back to geological times removed from us by several hundreds or even thousands of centuries.

I.—ANCIENT INHABITANTS OF EUROPE.

Geological Times.—The portions of Europe emerging towards the end of the tertiary period of the geological history of our globe have been inhabited by man, probably from this very time, and assuredly from the quaternary period which succeeded it—the predecessor of the present geological period. The existence of *tertiary man* in Europe has not, however, been directly proved. The finds of artificially chipped flints in the miocene and pliocene beds in France (at Thenay, Puy-Courny, and Saint-Prest), in England (the uplands of Kent, Cromer), and in Portugal (Otta, near Lisbon); the discovery made in Italy (Monte Aperto) of bones with rude carvings on them, asserted to be the work of pliocene man, and so many other interesting facts, are now called in question by leading men of science, and have few supporters at the present day.[1] In every case in these finds we have to deal only with objects supposed to be worked by man, or by some

[1] See for details, De Mortillet, *Le Préhistorique*, chap. iii., Paris, 1883; Stirrup, "So-called Worked Flints of Thenay," *Journ. Anthr. Inst.*, vol. xiv., 1885, p. 289, and *Rev. d'Anthr.*, 1885; Cartailhac, *La France Préhistorique*, p. 35, Paris, 1889; Newton, "The Evidence for the Existence of Man in the Tertiary Period," *Proceed. Geolog. Assoc.*, vol. xv., London, 1897; Salomon Reinach, *Antiquités Nationales, Descrip. Musée St.-Germain*, vol. i., p. 96, Paris, 1889,—this work contains a mass of prehistoric information and a copious bibliography.

hypothetical being, for no remains of human bones have been found up to the present time in the tertiary beds of Europe.[1]

It is only in quaternary beds that the presence of human bones has been ascertained beyond question. The *quaternary age* in Europe is characterised, as we know, by the succession of "glacial periods," each of which comprises a greater or less extension of glaciers, followed by their withdrawal ("interglacial periods"), with accompanying changes of climate. The well-known geologist Geikie[2] claims, from the end of the pliocene age to proto-historic times, the existence in Europe of six glacial periods; but most other geologists (Penck, Boule) reduce this number to two or three, considering the movements of the glaciers of some of Geikie's periods as purely local phenomena, having exercised no influence on the continent as a whole.

At the beginning of quaternary times the climate of Europe was not the same as that of the present day; hot and moist, it was favourable to the growth of a sub-tropical flora. Dense forests gave shelter to animals which no longer exist in our latitudes—the *Elephas meridionalis*, a survival of the pliocene age, the *Rhinoceros Etruscus*, etc.

But soon, from causes still imperfectly known, ice began to accumulate around *certain elevated points of Northern Europe;* a veritable "mer de glace" covered all Scandinavia, almost the whole of Great Britain, the emerged lands which were between these two countries, as well as the north of Germany and half of Russia.[3] This is the *first glacial period*, or the period of the

[1] The so-called tertiary skeleton of Castenedolo, near Brescia, discovered by Ragazonni, is an "odd fact," an "incomplete observation," to use the happy phrase of Marcellin Boule, and cannot be taken into account.

[2] J. Geikie, *Great Ice Age*, London, 1894; Marcellin Boule, "Paléontol. stratigr. de l'Homme," *Rev. d'Anthr.*, Paris, 1888.

[3] The extreme limit of the spread of glaciers to the south at that period may be indicated by a line which would pass near to Bristol, London, Rotterdam, Cologne, Hanover, Dresden, Cracow, Lemberg; then would go round Kief on the south, Orel on the north, and rise again (on the south of Saratov) up to Nijni-Novgorod, Viatka, the upper valley of the Kama, to blend with the line of the watershed of this river and the Pechora (see Map I.).

great spread of glaciers (Map 1). Such an accumulation of ice, combined with a change of climate, which had become cold and moist, was not very favourable to the peopling of the country. Besides, if we consider that all the great mountain chains, the Alps, the Pyrenees, the Caucasian range, with their advanced peaks, were covered entirely with ice, and that the Aralo-Caspian depression was filled with water as far as the vicinity of Kazan on the north (Map 1), we shall easily understand that the habitable space thus available for man at this period in Europe was very restricted.

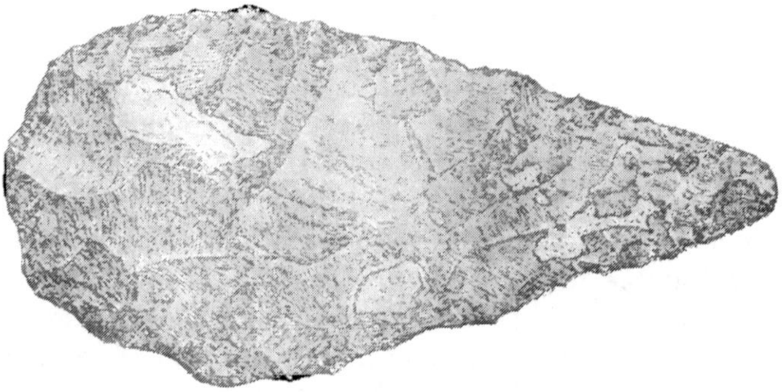

FIG. 84.—Chellean flint implement, Saint-Acheul (Somme); half natural size. (*After G. and A. de Mortillet.*)

France with Belgium, the south of England, the three southern peninsulas (Iberian, Appenine, and Balkan), the south of Germany, Austria-Hungary, the plains of Southern Russia as far as the Volga, and the basin of the Kama, communicating on the south of the Ural by a narrow isthmus with the Siberian steppes—these were the only countries which quaternary man could occupy. These conditions only changed at the time that the glaciers began to withdraw (*first interglacial period*). The climate became milder again, and the Arctic flora gave place to the flora of the forests of the Temperate Zone. It is to this period that the most undoubtedly ancient vestiges of mankind in Europe are to be attributed.

The men of that period have handed down to us imple-

MAP I.—Europe in the first glacial period. Light grey, glaciers; medium grey, sea; dark grey, land; white points, floating ice. (*After De Geer.*)

ments of a very rude type: fragments of flint of pointed form, the sinuous edges of which are scarcely trimmed by the removal of some flakes.[1] These implements are called "knuckle-dusters" (G. de Mortillet), or "Chellean axes" (Fig. 84), from the Chelles bed in the valley of the Seine; but such implements are found *in sitû* in numerous places—in France (especially in the valley of the Somme), in England (valleys of the Ouse and the Thames), in Spain, Portugal, Austria, Belgium, etc.[2]

The first interglacial period, characterised, as we have just seen, by a mild and moist climate, was followed by a new glacier invasion (*second glacial period*). This time the sea of ice did not extend as far as in the first period: it covered Ireland, Scotland, the north of England (as far as Yorkshire), Scandinavia, Finland, and stopped in Germany and Russia at a line passing nearly through the present site of Hamburg, Berlin, Warsaw, Vilna, Novgorod, Lake Onega, Archangel.

To this period succeeded, after the withdrawal of the glaciers, a period called "post-glacial" (or *second interglacial period*), characterised at first by a continental climate, dry, with a very cold winter, and a short but hot summer, and by flora of the Tundras and steppes. At the end of this epoch, the climate becoming milder, there appeared the flora of the meadows and forests, which has remained to the present day.[3] The harsh

[1] See G. and A. de Mortillet, *Musée préhistorique*, Paris, pl. vi. to ix.; J. Evans, *Ancient Stone Implements*, 2nd ed., chap. xxiii., London, 1897.

[2] Frequently these implements have been found, in sufficiently deep beds, beside bones of the straight-tusked elephant (*Elephas antiquus*), the smooth-skinned, two-horned rhinoceros (*Rhinoceros Merckii*), the great hippopotamus—that is to say, of animals characteristic of the first interglacial period. As these species are allied to the elephant, the rhinoceros, and the hippopotamus of Africa of the present day, the hypothesis has been propounded that they came from this continent, utilising the numerous isthmuses then existing (between Gibraltar and Morocco, between Sicily, Maltà and Tunis, etc.). Man, the maker of the Chellean implements, followed, it is supposed, in their steps. One might argue with equal force that the migration took place in the opposite direction.

[3] Woldrich (after Nehring), *Mit. Anthr. Gesell.*, vol. xi., p. 187, Vienna.

climate of the beginning of this period could only be favourable to the preservation and growth of thick-furred animals: the mammoth or elephant with curved tusks (*Elephas primigenius*), the rhinoceros with divided nostrils (*R. tichorinus*), the reindeer (*Cervus tarandus*), the saiga, the lemming, etc.

The man who inhabited Europe during the two overflows of the glaciers and the two interglacial periods is known to us chiefly by the stone implements which are found in the strata of these periods, along with the bones of animals which are now extinct or which have migrated into other regions. It must not be inferred from this that palæolithic man used no other but stone tools or weapons. The finds of objects made out of bone, horn, stag's horn, shell, and wood belonging to these periods are there to bear witness to the contrary. Only these finds are much more rare, on account of the ease with which bone, horn, and especially wood, decompose after a more or less prolonged stay in the ground. Basing their conclusions on the variety of the forms of the stone implements and partly on the frequent occurrence of bone objects, palæethnologists have divided the two interglacial periods which form their *stone age* or *palæolithic period* into two or three periods, according to country. It would have been better, in my opinion, to have replaced in the present instance the word "period" by the term "state of civilisation," for these periods are far from being synchronous throughout the whole of Europe; the Vogules and the Samoyeds were in the "stone age" hardly a century ago.

Nevertheless, for certain defined regions, we may consider it settled that the first so-called *Chellean* "period," characterised by the "knuckle-duster," belongs, as we have seen (p. 302), to the first interglacial period, and that the others coincide with the second (Boule). In a general way, we may distinguish in the latter a more ancient period, characterised by the abundance of mammoth bones and by smaller and more varied implements than the Chellean tool; and a more recent period characterised by the presence of the reindeer in Central and Western Europe, by the frequent occurrence of bone tools, and by the appearance of the graphic arts, at least in certain regions.

The first of these "periods" is known as the *Mousterian;* it is well represented in France, Belgium, southern Germany, Bohemia, and England.[1]

Instead of a single flint implement, the "knuckle-duster," which was used variously in the Chellean period, with or without a handle, as an axe, hammer, and dagger, a variety of implements make their appearance in the Mousterian period, and, among others, tools needed in the manufacture of garments, blades to open and skin animals, scrapers to make their hides supple, sharp-edged awls for cutting the skin and when necessary making cords or straps from it, for piercing it and making button-holes.[2] On the other hand, the use of the bow does not seem to have been known, for in the Mousterian deposits there have not been found any arrow-heads either in flint or bone. These arrow-heads appear only in the next period, generally called the *reindeer age;* in France styled, according to the classification of G. de Mortillet, the *Magdalenian period.*[3] The man of this period was still in the hunting stage,

[1] In England it is sometimes designated the "cave period" to distinguish it from the Chellean, called "River-drift" period, but this term is open to objection; thus, for example, in the celebrated Kent cavern there have been found at the bottom implements of the Chellean type identical with certain objects of the River-drift. (See the works already quoted, as well as Windle, *Life in Early Britain*, p. 26, London, 1897.)

[2] According to G. de Mortillet, Mousterian industry also differs from the Chellean in regard to technique. In the Chellean period what is utilised is the core or nucleus of the stone cut right round on both sides; while in the Mousterian period what are fashioned are the splinters struck off from this core, which are trimmed especially on one face, the inner face remaining smooth and showing the trace of its origin under the form of a "cone" or "bulb of percussion," which corresponds to a hollow in the block from which the splinter has been dislodged. However, implements recalling at first sight the "knuckle-duster," but which differ from it by their amygdaloidal form and their straight edges (Saint-Acheul type), are still to be found at this period.

[3] In G. de Mortillet's classification a yet additional period is inserted between the Mousterian and the Magdalenian. This is the *Solutrian*, characterised by finely cut heads (spear or arrow?) in the shape of a

but had more perfect hunting weapons than in the Mousterian period; he was also occasionally a fisher, and probably reared the reindeer. But his especial characteristic in certain regions, as in the south-west of France, is that he was a consummate artist. He has left us admirable carvings (Fig. 85, B), and engravings on bone most expressive in design (Fig. 85, A).[1]

After the second glacial period, the era of great overflows and withdrawals of the glaciers came to a definite close for Central Europe; but it continued in the north, in Scotland, and especially around the Baltic, even as it is still prolonged to our own day in Greenland and Iceland.

According to Geikie and De Geer, the glaciers advanced and withdrew thrice again in Scandinavia and Scotland after continental Europe was almost entirely rid of them (Geikie's fourth to sixth glacial periods).[2]

laurel leaf. But the zone in which these implements are met with is limited to certain regions of the south and west of France only. For many palæethnographers this is a "facies local" of the Magdalenian period.

[1] There may be added to the masterpieces here reproduced the famous representation of the mammoth carved on the tusk of this animal itself by a man of La Madeleine (Dordogne), discovered and described by Lartet; and by Boyd Dawkins, *Early Man in Brit.*, p. 105, London, 1880. See Cartailhac, *loc. cit.*, p. 72.

[2] After the second interglacial period the "Great Baltic Glacier" still covered the Scandinavian peninsula, with the exception of its southern part (Gothland), extended over the emerged bottom of the Baltic, over nearly the whole of Finland, and spreading round Gothland invaded the east coast of Denmark and the littoral of Germany to the east of Jutland. After the retreat of this glacier and a series of changes in the surface of the ground (a sinking which brought the Baltic into communication with the North Sea by means of the Strait of Svealand, followed by the upheaval which cut off that communication and made of the Baltic the *Ancylus Lake* of the geologists), the climate became milder in these parts, and the trees of Central Europe, first the pines, then the oaks and birches, penetrated into Denmark and Gothland, while in the north of Sweden there were two other new glacier movements. (Gerard de Geer, *Om Skandinavens Geografiska Utveckling*, Stockholm, 1897; G. Andersson, *Geschichte Végétat. Schwed.*, Leipzig, 1896.)

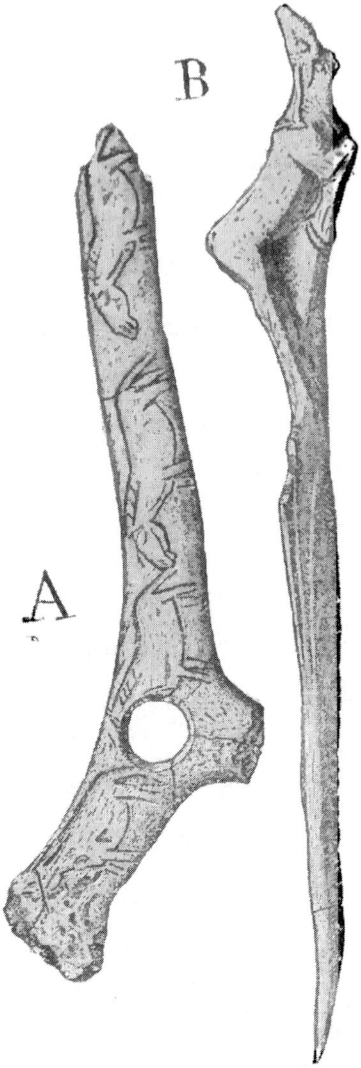

FIG. 85.—Quaternary art (Magdalenian period): B, dagger of reindeer horn with sculptured haft, Laugerie-Haute (Dordogne); A, "Baton of command" with carving (La Madeleine, Dord.); two-thirds natural size. (*After G. and A. de Mortillet.*)

A slow sinking of the land, which submerged beneath the ocean all the countries to the north and north-east of Europe, marks the end of the quaternary period, and the beginning of the present era in the geological sense of the word. This era is characterised, from the archæological point of view, by the substitution for the "earlier stone age" (*palæolithic period*) of another "age," or, better, of another stage of civilisation, that of the *later stone age* (*neolithic*).

However, this "age" did not come in abruptly, after a lapse of time, the *hiatus* of ancient palæethnologists, during which man retired, it was supposed, from Central Europe and emigrated towards the north after the reindeer.[1] There must have been a transitional or *mesolithic* period.[2] Nor was neolithic civilisation established everywhere at the same time. Thus the Scandinavian peninsula, from

[1] This supposition is invalidated by this fact among others, that, in the neolithic "shell heaps" of Scandinavia no remains of the reindeer are found.

[2] As witnessed by the diggings of Piette at Mas d'Azil, see p. 163.

which the glaciers have not yet altogether withdrawn, was in course of formation during this period.[1] The "neolithic folk," settling at first in Denmark, then in Gothland, have left us in the kitchen-middens (kitchen refuse, accumulations of shells) certain chipped stone implements, a sort of hatchet of a special form, contemporaneous with the neolithic tools of the rest of Europe.

These tools are associated in the geological beds and prehistoric stations with other objects which denote among the Europeans of this period a fairly advanced civilisation: knowledge of agriculture, pottery, the weaving of stuffs, the rearing of cattle.

The "neolithic people" constructed pile-dwellings near lakesides, in Switzerland, France, Italy, Ireland; they buried their dead under dolmens, and raised other megalithic monuments (upright stones, the rows at Carnac, etc.), of which the meaning has not yet been cleared up.

As may have been seen from this brief account, it is almost perfectly well known what were the stages of civilisation of the Europeans in the quaternary and neolithic periods. It is different with regard to the physical type of these Europeans. In fact, of interglacial man, contemporary of the *Elephas antiquus*, the maker of those flint implements exhumed from the lowest beds of the oldest quaternary alluvia, we have no remains, except perhaps two molar teeth, found by Nehring in the Taubach station (near Weimar), and some other disputed fragments (Neanderthal, Brux, and Tilbury skulls). This statement, made for the first time by Boule in 1888, is now admitted by many palæethnologists.[2] As far as man contemporary

[1] There was yet to take place another sinking of the ground which established a communication, by means of the Sound, between the "Ancylus Lake" of the preceding period with the North Sea, transforming it thus into a very salt and warm sea called, from the principal fossil which reveals to us its existence, the Littorina Sea.

[2] Nehring, *Zeitschr. f. Ethnol.*, 1895, No. 6 (Verh., pp. 425 and 573); Salomon Reinach, *L'Anthropologie*, 1897, p. 53; P. Salmon, *Races hum. préhist.*, p. 9, Paris, 1888; Cartailhac, *loc. cit.*, p. 327; M. Boule, *loc. cit.*, p. 679; G. de Mortillet, *La Format. de la Nat. Franc.*, p. 289.

with the mammoth (*Elephas primigenius*) and the reindeer is concerned, we possess a certain number of skulls and bones from the river drifts and caves. But a doubt exists as to the beds in which many of these specimens were found, and consequently as to their date. Eliminating all those of unknown or uncertain age, we have at the most, for the whole of Europe, but a dozen skulls or fragments of skulls and a score of other bones genuinely quaternary.[1] Evidently that is insufficient for the forming of an opinion on the physical type of quaternary Europeans. However, one significant fact is elicited from an examination of this small series, and it is this: that all the skulls composing it are very long, very dolichocephalic. The exceptions put forward, like the skulls of upper Grenelle (Seine), Furfooz (Belgium), La Truchère (Saône-et-Loire), Valle do Areciro

[1] Out of forty-six skulls to which the title "quaternary" has been applied, I have only been able, after a careful examination of all evidence, to recognise as such the ten to fifteen following skulls. For the age of the mammoth or "Mousterian" period, seven skulls certainly quaternary: two skulls from Spy (Belgium), and those from Egisheim (Alsace), Olmo (Val d'Arno, Italy), Bury St. Edmunds (England), Podbaba (Bohemia), and Predmost (Moravia). Perhaps we should refer to this period the skulls which cannot be definitely traced to a certain alluvial bed, like those of Neanderthal (Rhenish Prussia), Denise (Auvergne), Marcilly-sur-Eure (Eure), La Truchère (Saône), and Tilbury (near London). As to the skulls of the "reindeer" age (Magdalenian period), three only are known which are not called in question: these are the skulls of Laugerie-Basse, Chancelade (Dordogne), and Sordes (Landes). Perhaps we should include among them the skulls of uncertain date, like those of Bruniquel, Engis, Sargels (near Larzac), and perhaps others which certain authorities classify as belonging to mesolithic and even neolithic times: the three skulls of Cro-Magnon (Dordogne); the six so-called Mentone skulls (Baoussé-Roussé, Maritime Alps); the skulls of the *Trou de Frontal* at Furfooz (Belgium), of Solutré (Valley of the Saône), Bohuslan (near Stangenas, Sweden), Clichy and Grenelle (Paris). And, lastly, we have no data on which to form an opinion as to the date of the skulls of Canstatt (Wurtemberg), Maëstricht (Holland), Gibraltar, Brux (Bohemia), Lhar, Nagy-Sap (Hungary), Schebichowitz (Bohemia), Valle do Areciro (Portugal), etc. Cf. S. Reinach, *loc. cit.* (*Antiquités Nation.*), p. 134; and Hervé, *Rev. École Anthr.*, p. 208, Paris, 1892.

(Portugal), do not conflict with this assertion; there are reasons for believing that certain of these skulls belong to the neolithic period, and that others date from the mesolithic period, or, at the very outside, from the end of the quaternary period. These then, even admitting the authenticity of their date, would only be isolated precursors of the neolithic brachycephals with whom we shall deal further on.

Let us return to our palæolithic dolichocephals. These appear to belong to two distinct types, the so-called Neanderthal or Spy type, referred to the Mousterian period, very well

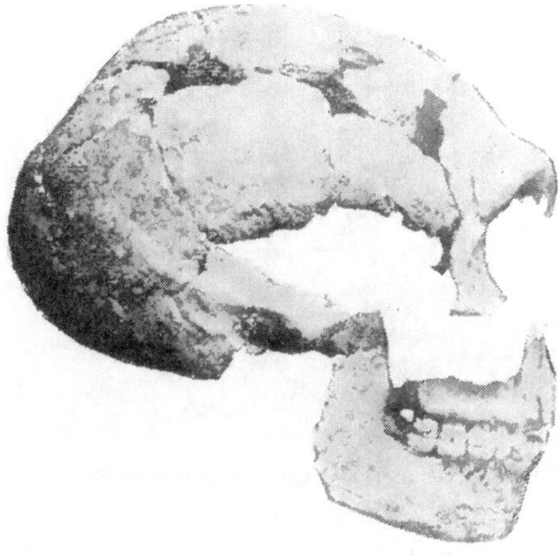

FIG. 86.—Spy skull, first quaternary race.
(*After Fraipont and Jacques.*)

represented by the skulls and bones found at Spy, near Namur in Belgium; then the type of the Magdalenian period, represented by the skulls exhumed at Laugerie-Basse and Chancelade (Dordogne). The first of these types is characterised by marked dolichocephaly (ceph. ind. from 70 to 75.3), by the exceedingly low and retreating forehead, by the prominent brow ridges (Fig. 86), and probably by a low stature (about 1 m. 59). Several pithecoid characters are observable on the skull and bones of this type, the presence of which has been noted, from England (skull from Bury St. Edmunds, in Suffolk), Belgium (Spy skull, La Naulette jaw), and perhaps the

Rhenish province (Neanderthal skull), to the Pyrenees (jaw found at Malarnau, Ariège), Bohemia, Moravia (Predmost and Podbaba skulls), and Italy (Olmo skull). Like all the other prehistoric races, that of Neanderthal or Spy has not entirely disappeared; Neanderthaloid skulls are found, few in number it is true, in several prehistoric or historic burial-places (at Furfooz in Belgium, in the dolmens of France, England, Ireland, etc.). Scattered here and there, some rare individuals may still be observed in the populations of the present day showing the characters of this race, according to the statements of Roujoux, Quatrefages, Virchow, Kollmann, and

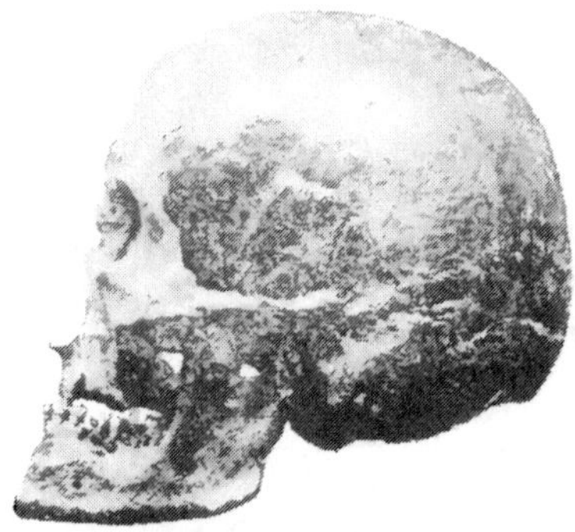

FIG. 87.—Chancelade skull, second quaternary race. (*After Testut.*)

other anthropologists.[1] The second so-called Laugerie-Chancelade race (Hervé) is represented at the present day by only three or four skulls and some other bones found at Laugerie-Basse, Chancelade (Dordogne), and Sordes (Landes). It is characterised by a dolichocephaly almost equal to that of the preceding race, but it differs from it in the high and broad forehead, the capacious skull, the absence of the brow ridges, the high orbits, and especially the face with projecting cheek-bones, high and broad at the same time (Fig. 87). Its stature

[1] The instances of the skull of Saint Mensuy, an Irish bishop, and others, are universally known. See on this subject, Godron, *Mem. Acad. Stanislas*, p. 50, Nancy, 1884; Worthington Smith, *Man, the Primeval Savage*, p. 38, London, 1893; and W. Borlase, *The Dolmens of Ireland*, vol. iii., p. 922, London, 1897.

is rather low. This is the type to which approximates the race of the *Baumes-Chaudes* of Hervé or the true race of *Cro-Magnon*, which appeared quite at the end of the Magdalenian, if not at the transitional or mesolithic period. The latter race differs from the former in its very pronounced dolichocephaly (ceph. ind. from 63 to 74.8), its lower face and orbits, its very lofty stature (from 1m. 71 to 1m. 80), and many other characters.[1] We see then, at the beginning of the neolithic period, the second quaternary dolichocephalic race still existing slightly modified, but we also see the earliest brachycephals appearing along with it.

Several hundred skulls, found in neolithic burial-places in France, Switzerland, Austria, and Germany, exhibit an intermixture of brachycephals and dolichocephals. According to the more or less frequent occurrence of the former in relation to the latter in each burial, we may, with Hervé,[2] trace the route followed by these brachycephals of Central Europe, from the plains of Hungary, by the valley of the Danube, into Belgium and Switzerland; from these last-named countries they flung themselves on the dolichocephalic populations of France and modified the primitive type, especially in the plains of the north-east and in the Alpine region.

But if the "neolithic" people of France and Central Europe belonged to at least two distinct races, the same has not been the case with the other countries of our continent. In the British Isles we find ourselves, on the contrary, as regards this period, in presence of a remarkable homogeneity of type; it is without exception dolichocephalic (cephal. ind. from 65 to 75 for the men), with elongated faces, such as are found in the long-barrows. Did they come from the Continent in neolithic times, or are they the descendants of the palæolithic men of Great Britain, the physical type of which is unknown to us? This is a question which still awaits solution. In Russia also,

[1] De Quatrefages and Hamy, *Cr. Ethn.*, p. 44; De Quatrefages, *Hist. Gén. Races Hum.*, vol. i., p. 67; Hervé, *Rev. Ecole. Anthr.*, Paris, 1893, p. 173; 1894, p. 105; 1896, p. 97.

[2] Hervé, "Les brachycéphales néolith.," *Rev. École. Anthr.*, Paris, 1894, p. 393; and 1895, p. 18.

we only meet with dolichocephals during the later stone age (certain "Kourganes" and the neolithic station of Lake Ladoga).[1] In Spain, in Portugal, in Sweden, dolichocephalic skulls are found in conjunction with some brachycephalic ones, the latter somewhat rare however.[2]

It is impossible for us to enter into details while treating of the period which followed the neolithic, that is to say the "age" of metals (copper, bronze, and iron). The metal which first took the place of stone was probably copper. In fact, the copper weapons are hammered or cast after the pattern of the stone axes and daggers, and in certain stations in Spain have been found ornaments in bronze (precious metal rarely) by the side of tools and arms in copper (ordinary metal). The existence of a "copper age" is, however, admitted to-day by almost all authorities, who regard it as an experimental period; it supplies one of the arguments in favour of the theory that the bronze industry did not come from the East (from the shores of the Euxine, Egypt, Mesopotamia, India, or Indo-China, according to different authors), as was thought until recent times, but sprang up locally in Europe itself.

The complete absence of oriental objects, for instance Assyrian cylinders or Egyptian sculptured scarabæi in the finds of the bronze age in Europe, is an argument in favour of the new theory, maintained chiefly by Salomon Reinach in France and Much in Austria. The Scandinavian authors, Sophus Müller and Montelius, admit the local development of the industry in metallic objects, but with materials supplied by the merchants of the Archipelago and Cyprus. The great trade-route for amber, and perhaps tin, between Denmark and the Archipelago is well known at the present day; it passes through

[1] J. Beddoe, *The Races of Britain*, Bristol-London, 1885, and "Hist. de l'indice ceph. dans les îles Britan.," *L'Anthropol.*, 1894, p. 513; Windle, *loc. cit.*, p. 9; Inostrantsev, *Doïstoritcheskiï, etc.* (*Prehistor. Man of Ladoga*), St. Petersburg, 1882, fig. and pl.

[2] Montelius, *Temps. préhist. en Suède*, p. 41, Paris, 1895; Cartailhac, *Ages préhist. Esp. et Portug.*, p. 305, Paris, 1886; H. and S. Siret, *Prem. âges du métal dans le sud-est de l'Esp.*, 3rd part (by V. Jacques), Antwerp, 1887.

the valley of the Elbe, the Moldau, and the Danube. The commercial relations between the north and south explain the similarities which archæologists find between Scandinavian bronze objects and those of the Ægean district (Schliemann's excavations at Mycenæ, Troy, Tiryns, etc.).[1]

It is generally admitted that the ancient bronze age corresponds with the "Ægean civilisation" which flourished among the peoples inhabiting, between the thirtieth and twentieth centuries B.C., Switzerland, the north of Italy, the basin of the Danube, the Balkan peninsula, a part of Anatolia, and, lastly, Cyprus. It gave rise (between 1700 and 1100 B.C.) to the "Mycenian" civilisation, of which the favourite ornamental design is the spiral.[2]

In Sweden the bronze age began later, in the seventeenth or eighteenth century B.C., but it continued longer there than in Southern Europe.

So also, according to Montelius, the introduction of iron dates only from the fifth or third century B.C. in Sweden, while Italy was acquainted with this metal as far back as the twelfth century B.C. The civilisation of the "iron age" distributed over two periods, according to the excavations made in the stations of Hallstatt (Austria) and La Tène (Switzerland), must have been imported from Central Europe into Greece through Illyria. This importation corresponds perhaps with the Dorian invasion of the Peloponnesus. The so-called "Hallstattian" period lasted in Central Europe, France, and Northern Italy from the tenth or ninth to the sixth century B.C. The Hallstattian civilisation flourished chiefly in Carinthia, Southern Germany, Switzerland, Bohemia, Silesia, Bosnia, the south-east of France, and Southern Italy (the pre-Etruscan iron

[1] S. Reinach, "Mirage oriental," *L'Anthropologie*, 1894, pp. 539 and 699; A. Evans, "Eastern Question," *Rep. Brit. Assoc.*, 1896, p. 911; Montelius, *loc. cit.*; Much, "Die Kupferzeit in Europa," Jena, 1893.

[2] A. Evans, *loc. cit.*, "Eastern Question"; Sal. Reinach, *L'Anthropol.*, 1893, p. 731; Montelius, "The Tyrrhenians, etc.," *Jour. Anthr. Inst.*, vol. xxvi., 1897, p. 254, pl.; and "Pre-classic Chronology in Greece," *ibid.*, p. 261.

age of Montelius). The period which followed, called the second or iron age, or the La Tène period,[1] was prolonged until the first century B.C. in France, Bohemia, and England. In Scandinavian countries the *first iron age* lasted till the sixth century, and the *second iron age* till the tenth century A.D.

The physical type of the inhabitants of Europe during the bronze age varies according to country. In England they were sub-brachycephals (ceph. ind. 81), of whom the remains found in the "round barrows" have been described by Thurnam and Beddoe. In Sweden and Denmark they were dolichocephals or mesocephals, tall and fair-haired, as far as one can gather from the remains of hair found in the burial-places (Montelius and S. Hansen). In the valley of the Rhine and Southern Germany they were typical dolichocephals, above the medium stature (type of the "Reihengräber" or row-graves, established by Holder and studied by Ranke, Lehmann-Nietsche, and others). In Switzerland, in the pile-dwellings, the neolithic brachycephals, of whom we have spoken, were succeeded in the bronze age by dolichocephals similar to those of Germany. During the Hallstattian period of the "iron age," we notice the persistence of the dolichocephalic and tall type in the row-graves of the Rhine and Mein valleys; while during the following period of the same age (that of La Tène or the Marnian), we find in the forms of the skulls exhumed from the burial-places a diversity almost as great as that which is seen in the populations of the present day.

The ages of bronze and iron, as we have seen, overlapped, in certain regions, the historic period, the period of the Phœnician voyages, the development of Egypt, the origin of Greek civilisation; and yet it is very difficult to say to what peoples known to history must be attributed the characteristic civilisations of each of the periods of the age of metals, and

[1] This term, used first in Germany, is accepted by almost all men of science. The La Tène period corresponds pretty nearly with the "*Age Marnien*" of French archæologists and the *late Celtic* of English archæologists. Cf. M. Hoernes, *Urgesch. d. Mensch.*, chaps. viii. and ix., Vienna, 1892.

what were the languages spoken by these peoples. Most historians believed until quite recently that the Euscarians, and perhaps the Ligurians or Lygians of Western Europe, as well as the Iberians, the Pelasgian Tursans or Turses[1] of the three southern peninsulas of our continent, were the "autochthones," or rather the oldest European peoples known to history. These would then be the probable descendants of the palæolithic Europeans, the races of Neanderthal, Spy, and Chancelade. Further, according to the philologists and historians, these peoples spoke *non-Aryan* languages, and at a certain period, which D'Arbois de Jubainville[2] places vaguely at twenty or twenty-five centuries B.C., Europe was invaded by the *Aryans*, coming from Asia, who imposed their languages on the autochthones. The Basque language of the present day, derived from the Euscarian, is the only dialect surviving this transformation. The central point for the ethnographic history of Europe is, according to the philologists, the arrival of the Aryans.

But who were these Aryans? Nobody quite knows. It is no part of my plan to write the history of the Aryan controversy.[3] It is enough to say that men of acknowledged authority in science (Pott, Grimm, Max Müller) have maintained for a long time, without any solid proof, the existence not only of a primitive Aryan language, which gave birth to the dialects of nearly every people of Europe, but also of an "Aryan race," supposed to have sprung up "somewhere" in Asia, one part migrating towards India and Persia, while the remainder made its way by slow stages to Europe. Generations of scientific men have accepted this hypothesis, which, after all, had no other foundation than such aphorisms as "ex oriente lux" put forward by Pott, or "the irresistible impulse towards the west" invented by

[1] Together with the Sards, the Turses are the only European peoples of which the Egyptian inscriptions anterior to the thirteenth century B.C. make mention, under the name of *Shordana* and *Thursana* (W. Max Müller, *Europa und Asien*, 1894).

[2] D'Arbois de Jubainville, *Les Anciens Habitants de l'Europe*, new ed., vol. i., p. 201, Paris.

[3] See for this history, Isaac Taylor, *The Origin of the Aryans*, chap. i., London, 1890, and S. Reinach, *L'origine des Aryens*, Paris, 1892.

Grimm. It must, however, be mentioned that objections against this hypothesis by recognised authorities were raised as soon as it was promulgated; they came from philologists like Latham (1855), ethnographers like d'Omalius d'Halloy, anthropologists like Broca (1864); but it was only about 1880 that a somewhat lively reaction took place against the current ideas, and it originated in the camp of the philologists themselves. De Saussure, Sayce, and others, returning to the ideas expressed long before by Benfey, rightly observed that the assumed close relationship between Sanscrit and Zend and the primitive Aryan language rests solely on the fact of the archaic forms of these two dialects being preserved to the present time in written monuments, while the Aryan languages of Europe do not possess documents so ancient. They said further, that the European languages of the present day, such as Lithuanian, for example, are much nearer the primitive Aryan forms than the Asiatic dialects, Hindu for example. As to the Asiatic origin of the Aryans, a somewhat rude blow was struck at this second hypothesis by Poesche and Penka, who, taking up the ideas of Linné and d'Omalius d'Halloy on the exclusive existence in Europe of fair-haired populations, identified these populations, without any proof, it is true, with the Aryans.[1] In reality, the hypothesis of the fair-haired "Aryan race," tall and dolichocephalic (Fig. 88), indigenous to Europe, does not rest on a firmer foundation than that of the "Aryan race" coming from Asia.

Anthropology is powerless to say if the ancient owners of the dolichocephalic skulls in Southern Europe spoke an Aryan language or not. Moreover, the works of modern philologists, with Oscar Schrader[2] at their head, show that we can no longer speak to-day of an "Aryan race," but solely of a *family of*

[1] Th. Poesche, *Die Arier*, Jena, 1878; Penka, *Die Herkunft der Arier*, Vienna, 1886. This identification has been turned to account by several men of science, especially by O. Ammon (*loc. cit.*) in Germany and V. de Lapouge (*Sélections sociales*, Paris, 1895) in France, in the construction of somewhat bold sociological theories.

[2] Osc. Schrader, *Sprachvergl. u. Urgesch.*, 2nd ed., Jena, 1890.

Aryan languages, and perhaps of a primitive *Aryan civilisation* which had preceded the separation of the different Aryan dialects from their common stock.

This civilisation, as reconstituted by O. Schrader, differs much from that which Pictet had sketched out in his essay on "Linguistic Palæontology." This was something analogous to the neolithic civilisation; metals were unknown in it (with the exception, perhaps, of copper), but agriculture and the breeding

FIG. 88.—Islander of Lewis (Hebrides), Northern Race. (*Phot. Beddoe.*)

of cattle had already reached a fair stage of development. However, there is nothing to prove that peoples speaking non-Aryan languages had not been in possession of the same civilisation, which with them would be developed in an independent manner. Hence we see the uselessness of looking for a centre from which this Aryan culture might have proceeded. The only question which we may still ask ourselves is, what was the point from which diffusion of the Aryan *languages* in

Europe began. This point no one at the present time seeks any longer in Asia. It is in Europe, and what we have to do is to define it (S. Reinach). Latham and d'Omalius d'Halloy located the habitat of the primitive Aryans in the south or south-east of Russia. Penka had placed it in Scandinavia. Other learned authorities have selected intermediate points between these extremes.[1]

On the whole, the Aryan question to-day has no longer the importance which was formerly given to it. All that we can legitimately suppose is that, in the period touching the neolithic age, the inhabitants of Europe were *Aryanised* from the point of view of language, without any notable change in the constitution of their physical type, or, probably, of their civilisation.

Migrations of European Peoples during the Historic Period.—It would require volumes to relate even succinctly all the movements and dislocations of European peoples. We can only recall here the more salient facts.

The confirmation afforded by history respecting European populations does not go farther back than the eighth or ninth century B.C. for the Mediterranean district, and than the second or third century B.C. for the rest of Europe. But proto-historic archæology makes us acquainted with a movement of peoples between the tenth and the eleventh century B.C. The Dorians

[1] According to Hirt, "Die Urheimat . . . d. Indogermanen," *Geogr. Zeitsch.*, vol. i., p. 649, Leipzig, 1895, the home of dispersion of the primitive Aryan language would be found to the north of the Carpathians, in the Letto-Lithuanian region. From this point two linguistic streams would start, flowing round the mountains to the west and east; the western stream, after spreading over Germany (Teutonic languages), left behind them the Celtic languages in the upper valley of the Danube, and filtered through on the one side into Italy (Latin languages), on the other side into Illyria, Albania, and Greece (Helleno-Illyrian languages). The eastern stream formed the Slav languages in the plains traversed by the Dnieper, then spread by way of the Caucasus into Asia (Iranian languages and Sanscrit). In this way we can account, on the one hand, for the less and less marked relationship between the different Aryan languages of the present day and the common primitive dialect, and, on the other hand, the diversity between the two groups of Aryan languages, western and eastern.

and the inhabitants of Thessaly penetrated at this date into Greece and forced a portion of the inhabitants of this country (the Achæans, the Eolians) to seek refuge on the nearest coast of Asia Minor. About the same period the Tyrrhenians or Turses (a small section of the Pelasgians) moved into Central Italy, taking with them the Mycenian civilisation, somewhat debased, and founding there the Etruscan "nation." This nation drove back the *Ombro-Latins* or *Italiotes*, who, in their turn, expelled the *Sicules* (a branch of the *Ligurians*, according to D'Arbois de Jubainville) in Sicily.

The *Venetes* and the *Illyrians* made their appearance at nearly the same period on the coasts of the Adriatic, and the *Thracians* in present Bosnia.

Central Europe was occupied, probably from this period, by Celtic populations who, from their primitive country between the upper Danube and the Rhine, spread into the valley of the Po (bronze age of the "terramare," sites or foundations of prehistoric huts), in the middle valley of the Danube (Hallstatt), and later (seventh century B.C.?) into the north of Gaul, whence they reached the British Isles ("ancient Celts" of the English archæologists, "Gaelic Celts" of the philologists).[1] It was also about the tenth century B.C. that the Scythians, established in Southern Russia some time before, spread themselves towards the mid-Danube.

About the fifth century B.C. there evidently occurred another movement of peoples. The *Trans-Alpine Celts* or *Galatians* invaded, under the name of *Celto-Belgæ*, Jutland, Northern Germany, the Low Countries, England (the "new Celts" or Britons of English authors). They also spread over a large part of Gaul, and into Spain (*Celtiberians*), and then in 392 B.C.,[2] they penetrated into Italy, where they found their kinsmen, who had been settled there for three centuries, and were under the subjugation of the Etruscans; these they overturned, and only halted after having taken Rome (390). A

[1] A. Bertrand and S. Reinach, *Les Celtes dans la vallée du Pô, etc.*, Paris, 1894.

[2] D'Arbois de Jubainville, *loc. cit.*, vol. ii., p. 297.

little later (about 300), other waves of Celts, the Galatians, occupied the valley of the Danube, whence they chased the Illyrians and the Thracians. The more audacious of them continued their course across Thrace and penetrated into Asia Minor, where they established themselves in the country, since known as Galatia (279).

During this period (from the fifth to the third century), which may be called Celtic, by analogy with that which followed,

FIG. 89.—Norwegian of South Osterdalen. Ceph. ind., 70.2. Northern race. (*After Arbo.*)

styled the Roman period, history mentions the *Germans* as a people similar to the Celts, and dwelling to the north-east of the latter.

The Roman conquest of transalpine Europe, effected in the first centuries B.C. and A.D., imposed the language of Latium on the majority of Celts, Iberians, and Italo-Celts, and maintained the populations within almost the same bounds during three centuries.

The period extending from the second to the sixth century

of the Christian era comprises the great historic epoch of the "migrations of peoples." In this period we see the *Slavs* spreading in all directions: towards the Baltic, beyond the Elbe, into the basin of the Danube and beyond, into the Balkan peninsula; this movement determined that of the *Germans*, who invaded the south-east of England (Angles, Saxons, Jutes), Belgium, the north-east of France (Franks), Switzerland, and Alsace (Alemanni), the south of Germany

FIG. 90.—Same subject as Fig. 89, seen in profile.

(Bavarians), and spread even beyond the Alps (Longobards). The Celts in their turn pushed the Iberians farther and farther into the south-west of France and Spain, while the Italo-Celts absorbed little by little the rest of the Etruscans and Ligurians. Towards the end of this period a final wave of invasion, that of the Huns (fifth century), the Avars (sixth), and other allied tribes, once more threw Europe into a state of perturbation; they spread out into the plains of Champagne, then drew back, severed the Slavs into two groups (northern and southern), and subsided in the plains of Hungary, already partly occupied for several centuries by the Dacians. Almost at the same time the Bulgarians removed from the banks of the Volga to both sides of the Danube. After the sixth century other ethnic movements, less general, but not less important, occurred in every part of Europe. In the eighth or ninth century the invasion of the Varecks (Scandinavians or Letts?) took place in the north-west of Russia. In the ninth century the Hungarians, pushed by the tribes of the Pechenecks and the Polovtsis who invaded the south of Russia, crossed the Carpathians and settled in the valley of the Tissa. From the ninth or tenth century, the Normans or Northmen (Danes, Scandinavians) established themselves in the north and east of the British Isles as well as the north of France, a part of which still bears their name. Almost at the same time (tenth to eleventh century) the Arabs made themselves masters of the Iberian peninsula, of Southern Italy and Sicily; they maintained their position to the south of the Guadalquivir until the fifteenth century. In the twelfth century the Germans drove back the western Slavs to the banks of the Vistula, which led to the expansion of the eastern Slavs towards the north-east at the expense of the Finnish tribes. In the thirteenth century came the Mongols, or rather the Turco-Mongolian hordes; they occupied the whole of Russia (as far as Novgorod in the north), and penetrated into Europe as far as Liegnitz in Silesia. They soon withdrew from Western Europe, but remained until the fifteenth century in the east of Russia, and even until the eighteenth century in the Crimea and the steppes of southern Russia. Finally, the fourteenth and fifteenth centuries witnessed the invasion of the Osmanli Turks into the Balkan peninsula, Hungary, and even into lower Austria, as well as the migrations of the Little Russians into the upper basin of the Dnieper. About the sixteenth century began the definite movement of the Little Russians towards the steppes of Southern Russia, and the slow but sure march of the Great Russians beyond the Volga, the Ural mountains, and farther, into Siberia—a movement which continues in our own time.

We can only mention other migrations or colonisations of a more limited range, that of the Illyrians and Albanians into Southern Italy, that of the Germans in Hungary and Russia, etc., as well as the arrival of non-European peoples, *Gypsies* and *Jews*, who are scattered at the present day among all the nations of our continent.

II.—EUROPEAN RACES OF THE PRESENT DAY.

Setting out from the fact that the peoples or nations of Europe, like those of the rest of the earth for the matter of that, are formed of the intermixture in varying proportions of different races or varieties (see the *Introduction*), I have endeavoured, by grouping the exact characters, carefully abstracted from many million individuals, relating to stature, form of head, pigmentation, and other somatic particulars, to determine the constituent elements of these intermixtures. I have thus succeeded in distinguishing the existence of six principal and of four secondary races, the combinations of which, in various proportions, constitute the different "European peoples" properly so called, distinct from the peoples of other races, Lapp, Ugrian, Turkish, Mongolian, etc., which are likewise met with in Europe.[1]

Here, in short, are the characters and geographical distribution of those races which, in order to avoid every interpretation drawn from linguistic, historical, or nationalist considerations, I describe according to their principal physical characters, or for the sake of brevity, according to the geographical names of the regions in which these races are best represented or least crossed.

We have in Europe, to begin with, two *fair-haired races*, one dolichocephalic, of very tall stature (Northern race), and another, sub-brachycephalic, comparatively short (Eastern race). Then

[1] For particulars see J. Deniker, "Les Races de l'Europe," *Bull. Soc. d'Anthropol.*, 1897, pp. 189 and 291; *L'Anthropologie*, 1898, p. 113 (with map); and "Les Races de l'Europe," first part, *L'indice Céphal.*, Paris, 1899 (coloured map). Cf. Ripley, "Racial Geography of Europe," *Appleton's Popular Science Monthly*, New York, for the years 1897, 1898, and 1899.

four dark-haired races: two of short stature, one of which (Ibero-insular) is dolichocephalic, the other (Cevenole or Western) brachycephalic; and two of high stature, of which one is sub-dolichocephalic (Littoral), the other brachycephalic (Adriatic). Among the four secondary races two have a relation to the fair-haired race, while the two others may be con-

FIG. 91.—Young Sussex farmer. Dolichocephalic, fair. Northern race. (*After Beddoe.*)

sidered as intermediate between the fair and dark-haired races (see Map 2). I now give a few details respecting these races.

1. *Fair, dolichocephalic race of very high stature*, which may be called the *Northern Race*, because its representatives are grouped together almost exclusively in the north of Europe. Principal characters: very lofty stature (1 m. 73 on an average);[1]

[1] See in Appendices I. to III. the figures relative to the different populations of Europe, taken from the works referred to by me in the previous note.

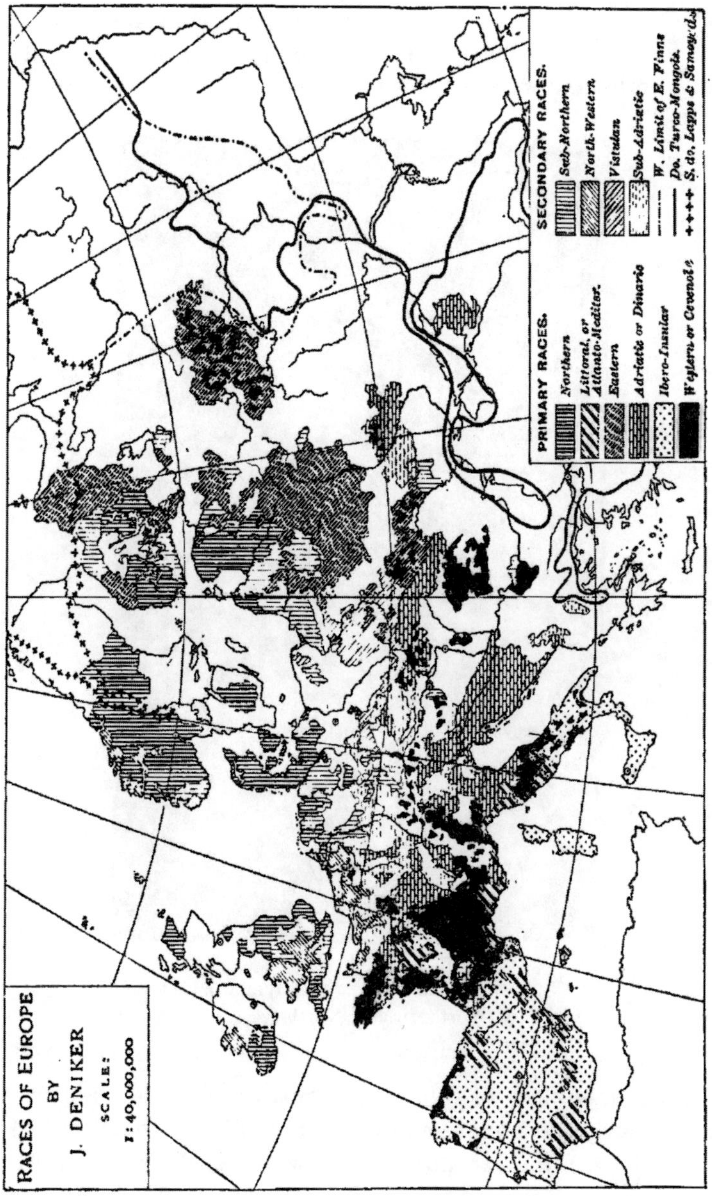
RACES OF EUROPE
BY
J. DENIKER
SCALE:
1:40,000,000
PRIMARY RACES.
Northern
Littoral, or Atlanto-Mediter.
Eastern
Adriatic or Dinaric
Ibero-Insular
Western or Cevenole
SECONDARY RACES.
Sub-Northern
North-Western
Vistulan
Sub-Adriatic
W. Limit of E. Finns
Do. Turco-Mongols.
S. do. Lapps & Samoy

fair, sometimes reddish, wavy hair; light eyes, for the most part blue; elongated, dolichocephalic head (cephalic index on the living subject from 76 to 79); ruddy white skin, elongated face, prominent straight nose. The race of this type, pure or

FIG. 92.—Englishwoman of Plymouth (Devon). Mixed Northern and North-western races (?). (*Phot. Beddoe.*)

slightly modified, of whose principal traits Figs. 88 to 92 give a fairly good representation, is found in Sweden, Denmark, Norway (with the exception of the west coast); in the north of Scotland; on the east coast and in the north of England, in Ireland (with the exception of the north-west), in the northern Faroe Isles, in Holland (north of the Rhine); in the Frisian countries, in Oldenburg, Schleswig-Holstein, Mecklenburg; lastly, in the Baltic provinces of Russia, and among the Tavasts of Finland. It is the *Cymric race* of Broca, the *Germanic* race (*the race of the row-graves*) of German authors, or, in fine, the *Homo Europeus* of Lapouge.

To this race is related a secondary race, *fair*, *mesocephalic*, *of tall stature*, called *Sub-northern*, with angular face, turned-up nose, straight hair; it is found more especially in Northern Germany, among the Letto-Lithuanians, in Finland, and on the west coast of Norway (in part Figs. 89 and 90).

2. *Fair*, *sub-brachycephalic*, *short race*, or *Eastern race*, so styled because its representatives are almost exclusively grouped together in the east of Europe. Principal characters: stature somewhat short (1m. 63 or 1m. 64 on an average), moderately rounded head (cephalic index, 82 to 83 on the living subject), straight, light yellow or flaxen hair, square-cut face, nose frequently turned up, blue or grey eyes. The representatives of this race are the White Russians, the Polieshchooki of the Pinsk marshes, and certain Lithuanians. Blended with others this type is frequent among the Vielkorousses or Great Russians of Northern and Central Russia, as well as in Finland and Eastern Prussia (Figs. 104 and 105, modified type).

With this race we have to connect a secondary race, *fair*, *mesocephalic*, *of very short stature* (*Vistulian* race), the characters of which are frequently met with among the Poles, the Kashoobs, and probably in Saxony and Silesia.

3. *Dark*, *dolichocephalic*, *short race*, called *Ibero-insular*, because it is chiefly found in the Iberian peninsula and the islands of the western Mediterranean. It is found, however, somewhat softened, in France (in Angoumois, Limousin, and Perigord) and in Italy (to the south of the Rome-Ascoli line). Principal characters: very short stature (1m. 61 to 1m. 62 on an average), very elongated head (cephalic index averaging 73 to 76 on the living subject), black, often curled, hair, very dark eyes, tawny skin, straight or turned-up nose, etc. It forms, partly,

the "*Mediterranean race*" of Sergi,[1] or the *Homo meridionalis* of certain authors (Ripley, Lapouge). Figures 99 and 100 represent traits of this race, but modified by intermixtures.

4. *Dark, very brachycephalic, short race*, named the *Western* or *Cevenole race*, because of the localisation of its most characteristic type in the extreme west of Europe, in the Cévennes, on the central table-land of France, and also in the western Alps. But it is met with, a little modified, in Brittany

FIG. 93.—Fisher people of Island of Aran (Ireland). North-western race (?). (*Phot. Haddon.*)

(with the exception of Morbihan), in Poitou, Quercy, the middle valley of the Po, in Umbria, in part of Tuscany, in Transylvania, and probably the middle of Hungary. Blended with other races, it is found again at a number of points in Europe, from the basin of the middle Loire to that of the Dnieper, passing through Piedmont, Central and Eastern Switzerland, Carinthia, Moravia, Galicia, and Podolia. In Southern Italy it is blended

[1] Sergi, *Origine . . . Stirpe Mediterranea*, Rome, 1895.

with the Ibero-insular race. It is the *Celtic* or *Rhetian* race, the *Celto-Slav*, *Ligurian*, or *Celto-Ligurian* race of some anthropologists, the *Homo Alpinus* of others. It is characterised by a very rounded skull (average ceph. ind. on the living subject from 85 to 87); by shortness of stature (1m. 63 or 1m. 64 on an average); by brown or black hair, light or

FIG. 94.—Young woman of Arles. Mixed Littoral race (?). (*Phot. lent by School of Anthropology, Paris.*)

dark brown eyes, rounded face, thick-set figure (Fig. 98, perceptibly softened type of this race).

5. *Dark, mesocephalic, tall race, Littoral* or *Atlanto-Mediterranean race*, so styled because it is found in a pure or mixed state along the shores of the Mediterranean from Gibraltar to the mouth of the Tiber, and on several points of

the Atlantic coast, from the straits of Gibraltar to the mouth of the Guadalquivir, on the Bay of Biscay, in the lower valley of the Loire, etc. It is not met with anywhere at a greater distance than 120 or 150 miles from the sea. This Littoral race is still little studied; it is distinguished by its moderate dolichocephaly or mesocephaly (ceph. ind. on living subject 79 to 80), by its stature above the average (1m. 66), and very deep colouring of the hair and eyes. It corresponds pretty well

FIG. 95.—Pure type of Highlander (clan Chattan); grey eyes, hair dark brown. (*Phot. Beddoe.*)

with the "*Mediterranean race*" of Houzé,[1] and with the Cro-Magnon race of certain authors.

It is probably with this Littoral race that we must connect a *secondary* so-called *North-Western race, tall, sub-dolichocephalic*, with *chestnut hair*, often almost brown. It is found chiefly in

[1] Houzé, "Caract. phys. des races européennes," *Bull. Soc. Anthro.*, Brussels, vol. ii., 1883, 1st part.

the north-west of Ireland (Fig. 93), in Wales (Fig. 19), and the east of Belgium.

6. *Dark, brachycephalic, tall race*, called *Adriatic* or *Dinaric*, because its purest representatives are met with along the coast of the Northern Adriatic and especially in Bosnia, Dalmatia, and Croatia. They are also found in Rumania, Venetia, among the Slovenes, the Ladinos of the Tyrol, the Romansch of Switzerland, as well as in the populations of the

FIG. 96.—The same, seen in profile.

tract of country which extends south to north from Lyons to Liège, at first between the Loire and the Saône, then on to the table-land of Langres, in the upper valleys of the Saône and the Moselle, and into the Ardennes. In all these parts the Adriatic race appears with its essential characters: lofty stature (1m. 68 to 1m. 72 on an average), extreme brachycephaly (ceph. ind. 85-86), brown or black wavy hair; dark eyes, straight eyebrows; elongated face, delicate straight or aquiline nose; slightly tawny skin. The same characters, somewhat softened, are met with among the populations of the lower valley of the Po, of the north-west of Bohemia, in Roman Switzerland, in Alsace, in the middle basin of the Loire, among the Polish and Ruthenian mountaineers of the Carpathians, and lastly among the Malorousses or Little Russians, and probably among the Albanians and the inhabitants of Servia.

We may connect with this principal race a *secondary race, not quite so tall* (medium stature 1 m. 66) and less brachycephalic (average ceph. ind. from 82 to 85), but having lighter hair and eyes. This race, which we might call Sub-Adriatic, springing probably from the blending of the principal race with the tall, fair mesocephals (secondary Sub-northern race), is found in Perche, Champagne, Alsace-Lorraine, the Vosges, Franche-comté, Luxemburg, Zealand (Holland), the Rhenish provinces, Bavaria, the south-east of Bohemia, German Austria, the central district of the Tyrol, and a part of Lombardy and Venetia. It partly corresponds with the *Lorraine Race* of Collignon.[1]

III.—PRESENT PEOPLES OF EUROPE.

Linguistic study being older than anthropological study, the classing of the best known peoples in Europe is that which is based on difference of language. Nearly every one knows that the ethnic groups of our continent are as a consequence distributed into "Aryan" and an-Aryan peoples. The former are divided (1) into three great linguistic families, *Latin or Roman* in the south-west of Europe, *Teutonic* in the centre and north, *Slav* in the south-east and east; and (2) into three smaller ones: *Celtic* in the extreme north-west of the continent, *Helleno-Illyrian* in the extreme south-east, and *Letto-Lithuanian* in the centre. As to the non-Aryan group, it comprises the *Basques*, the *Finno-Ugrians*, the *Turks*, the *Mongols*, the *Semites*, and the *Caucasian* peoples.

These groups are heterogeneous enough in physical type

[1] R. Collignon, *Bull. Soc. Anthro.*, Paris, 1883, p. 463, and *L'Anthropologie*, 1890, No. 2.

and civilisation. What, for example, have the two *Latin* peoples, the Portuguese and Romans, in common? or the two *Slav* peoples, like the Kashoobs, fair, short, thick-set, peaceful cultivators of the plain, and the Montenegrins, dark, tall, slender, warlike shepherds of the mountain? What more striking contrast can we imagine than that between a Norwegian, tall and fair, a bold sailor, whose flag floats in every port of the world, and a Tyrolese of the north, dark and short, a sedentary cultivator of the soil, whose horizon is bounded by the summits of his mountains? However, both these are included in the "Germanic" group.

Nevertheless, and only to bring out better the differences between linguistic divisions and those of ethnography and ethnology, I shall rapidly pass in review the "peoples" of Europe, according to the linguistic grouping as outlined above.

A.—ETHNIC "ARYAN" GROUPS.

I. *Latin or Roman Peoples*, that is to say speaking languages derived from the Latin. The majority of philologists divide them into seven distinct groups, viz., French of the north, Languedocian-Catalan, Spanish, Portuguese-Galego, Italian, Romansch-Ladino, and Rumanian.

1. *The French group of the north*, or the Langue d'oil, comprises the populations (Fig. 98) on the north of the line which, starting from the Gironde, passes by Angoulême, Montmorillon, Montlucon, Lyons, and the crests of the Jura, to terminate in the neighbourhood of Berne in Switzerland.[1] Among the numerous dialects recognisable in it, we must make special mention of *Wallon*, spoken in the southern part of the department of the north in France, and in the southern half of Belgium,[2] in the commune of Malmedy in Prussia, and in

[1] Ch. de Tourtoulon and Bringuier, "Limite . . de la langue d'oc, etc.," *Arch. Miss. Sc. Paris*, 1876. Cf. *Rev. École Anthr. Paris*, 1891, p. 218.

[2] Province of Namur, nearly the whole of the provinces of Hainault, Liège, and Luxemburg, as well as the southern part of Brabant. Cf. Bremer, *Nationalit. und Sprache in Belgien* (with map), Stuttgart, 1887.

several places in the grand duchy of Luxemburg. Northern French is likewise spoken in the west part of Lorraine and lower Alsace annexed to Germany, as well as in several places in upper Alsace.

2. *The Languedocian-Catalan group*, or the *Langue d'oc*, situated south of the line referred to above, comprises four great dialectal divisions which make a distinction between

FIG. 97.—Anglian type, common in north and north-east of England. (*After Beddoe.*)

the *Gascons* (south of the Garonne) (Figs. 99 and 100) and the *Languedocians* and *Provençals* (Fig. 94), while admitting the mixed so-called *Rhodanian* group (basin of the upper Rhone, Roman Switzerland, Savoy, and the French valleys of Piedmont)[1] and the *Catalan* group (Roussillon in France,

[1] H. Gaidoz, "Die französisch. Thäler Piemonts," *Globus*, p. 59, 1891, with map; Sachier, *Le Français et le Provençal* (Fr. trans. by Monet, Paris, 1891).

Catalonia and Valencia in Spain, the Balearic Islands, and a point on the west coast of Sardinia).

3rd and 4th. The *Spanish* group comprises the peoples of *Castillian* language, that is to say, the whole population of Spain, with the exception of the Catalans and the inhabitants of Galicia; the latter speak *Galego*, an idiom allied to Portuguese, and form with the population of Portugal our fourth linguistic group, *Galego-Portuguese.*

FIG. 98.—Frenchman of Ouroux (Morvan). Mixed western race. (*Phot. School of Anthropology, Paris.*)

5. The *Italian group* comprises the *Italians* [1] of the peninsula, of Sicily, Sardinia, and the inhabitants of Corsica, of southern Tyrol (south of Botzen), of the Swiss canton of Tessin, and of the coast of Istria and Dalmatia. The Italian dialect enters also into the constitution of the *Maltese* jargon, derived for the most part from the Arabic.

6. The *Romansch-Ladino* or *Rheto-Roman* group is formed

[1] F. Pullé, "Profilo antr. dell' Italia," *Archivo. p. Antr.*, 1898 (with maps).

by the *Romansches* of the southern part of the canton of Grisons (German Switzerland) and by the Ladinos of the south-

FIG. 99.—Dolichocephalic Frenchmen of Dordogne. Ibero-insular race (?). (*Phot. Collignon.*)

FIG. 100.—The same subjects as in Fig. 99, seen in profile.

east of Tyrol (Groedner Thal, etc.). These are probably the remnants of the old Alpine population, having adopted the language of the Roman legionaries of the time of the conquest.

They are, moreover, in process of extinction as a linguistic unit; their language gives place to Italian in the Tyrol, to German in Switzerland. It is the same with the Friulans who are related to this group, and who inhabit the basin of the Tagliamento in Venetia.

7. The *Rumanian group* comprises the *Rumanians* who are found, beyond Moldo-Wallachia, again in Transylvania (Austria), the south-east of Hungary, the north-east of Servia, Bessarabia, and in the lower valley of the Dniester (south-west of Russia). To the Rumanians are related the *Aromunes* or *Kutzo-Vlakhs*, or *Zinzars* of Epirus and Macedonia, speaking a dialect allied to Rumanian, but modified by contact with Turks, Greeks, and Albanians.[1]

There is no unity of type in any of these seven Latin linguistic families. Among the Languedocian-Catalans we distinguish the presence of at least three races: Western or Cevenole, which prevails on the central table-lands of France, Littoral or Atlanto-Mediterranean, predominant in Provence and Catalonia; Ibero-insular, which we find in Angoumois as in Catalonia (see p. 329, and Map 2). In the same way we may perceive in the Italian group the existence of representatives of almost all the European races (except the Northern); we have only to recall the striking contrast between the Venetian, tall, chestnut coloured, brachycephalic, and the inhabitant of Southern Italy, short, dark, and dolichocephalic. It is among the Portuguese, perhaps, that we find the greatest unity of type; the majority of them belong to the Ibero-insular race, except in the north of the country, where we find intermixtures with the Western race, as among the Galicians of Spain.

II. The *Germanic or Teutonic peoples* are usually divided into three great linguistic groups: Anglo-Frisian, Scandinavian, and German.

1. The languages of the *Anglo-Frisian* group, derived probably from the ancient Gothic, are spoken by the *Frisians*

[1] Dr. N. Manolescu, *Igiena Teranului* (Hygiene of the Rumanian peasant, an ethnographical inquiry), Bucharest, 1895; S. Weigand, *Die Aromunen*, vol. i., Leipzig, 1895 (with plates and maps).

of the north of Holland and the extreme north-west of Germany, by the inhabitants of England (Figs. 91, 92, 97, and 101), and a considerable part of Scotland (Figs. 88, 95, and 96), Ireland (Fig. 93), and Wales (Fig. 19), where English encroaches more and more on the domain of the ancient Celtic languages.

The English language, which comprises many dialects,[1] is, in the main, the Anglo-Saxon dialect, a branch of low German imported into the island in the fifth century and modified in the eleventh century by the language of gallicised Normans.

2. The *Scandinavian* group comprises the *Swedes*, *Norwegians* (Figs. 89 and 90), and *Danes*, the two last speaking almost the same language. The Swedish language is also found in Finland (especially on the coast), as Danish is in Schleswig. The *Icelanders*, descended for the most part from Danish colonists, speak a special dialect, which approaches most nearly to the old Norse.

3. The *German* or *Teutonic* group. The Germans of the north (Saxons, Hanoverians, etc.) speak low German (*platt-Deutsch*, *nieder-Deutsch*). One of the dialects of this idiom is transformed into the *Flemish* or *Dutch* tongue, employed by the Netherlanders, as well as the Flemings of the north of Belgium,[2] and several cantons of the department of the north in France. The southern Germans (the *Alemanni* of German Switzerland, of Alsace and Baden; the *Swabians* of this last province, Wurtemberg, and of Bavaria; the *Bavarians* of eastern Bavaria and of Austria) speak high German (*hoch-Deutsch*). The inhabitants of middle Germany (Thuringians, Franconians, etc.) speak middle German (*mittel-Deutsch*). This is also the language of the *Prussians*, a people formed in part from the Slavo-Lithuanian elements germanised but a few centuries ago. The boundary-line between low and high German passes, from the Flemish zone in France and Belgium,

[1] A. J. Ellis, *English Dialects*, London, 1890, two maps; and other publications of the English Dialect Society (1873-98).

[2] Almost all the two Flanders, the half to the north of Brabant, the provinces of Antwerp and of Limbourg. Cf. Bremer, *loc. cit.*

almost by Dusseldorf, Cassel, Dessau, and curving round Berlin in the north reaches the confluence of the Oder and of the Warta, following the course of this last.[1] There exist further in Europe several German colonies: in upper Italy (Sette-Communi, etc.), in Bohemia, in Hungary, and in the south and south-east of Russia. The German tongue is

FIG. 101.—Englishman (Gloucestershire), Saxon type. (*After Beddoe.*)

much spoken in the Baltic provinces of Russia, as well as in Poland and Austria-Hungary.[2]

[1] R. Andree, "Gränzen Niederd. Sprache," *Globus*, 1891, vol. lix., No. 2.

[2] See Langhans, *Deutsch. Kolon. Atlas*, maps Nos. 3 to 7. For a comprehensive view of the Germans generally, see Ranke, *Der Mensch.*, vol. ii. Somat., Archeol.), and E. H. Meyer, "Deutsche Volkskunde" (Ethnography, Folk-lore), Strassburg, 1898; for the Austrians: *Oester.-Ung. Monarchie*, vols. iv. and vi., Vienna, 1886-89; and for the Bavarians, *Beiträge z. Anthr., etc., Bayerns*, Munich (1876-99).

From the somatological point of view, the Germanic group is no more homogeneous than the "Latin." Let us take, for example, the Anglo-Frisians. We find among them at least three races in manifold combinations. The Northern race (see p. 328, and Map 2) is prevalent in the Frisian countries of

FIG. 102.—Russian carpenter, 47 years old, district of Pokrovsk (gov. Vladimir). (*Phot. Bogdanoff, Coll. Museum of Nat. Hist., Paris.*)

Germany and Holland, as well as in that part of England situated north of the line from Manchester to Hull, and on the east coast, south of this line (Figs. 88, 91, and 97). The secondary North-west race preponderates in the centre of England (counties of Oxford, Hertford, and Gloucester, Fig. 101, etc.), while the influence of the secondary Sub-northern race is especially felt in the counties of Leicester and Nottingham, and on the south coast, with the exception of Cornwall and Devon, where the Northern and North-western races are counter-balanced (Fig. 92). In Scotland the Northern type is often disguised by the dark colouring of the

FIG. 103.—Same subject as Fig. 102, seen in profile. (*Phot. Bogdanoff, Coll. Museum of Nat. Hist., Paris.*)

hair (Figs. 95 and 96). The Scandinavian group is fairly homogeneous, especially formed as it is of the Northern race (Figs. 88 to 90). But in the German group diversities reappear, and we find in it elements of almost all the races of Europe except the Littoral and Ibero-insular ones.

III. The *Slav peoples* may be divided into three great

linguistic groups—eastern, western, and southern.[1] The eastern group comprises the *Great Russians* or *Vielkorousses* (Figs. 102 to 105), the *Little Russians* or *Malorousses*, otherwise called *Ukrainians* or *Ruthenians*, and the *Bielorousses* or *White Russians*. The latter inhabit the upper basins of the Dnieper, the Dwina, and the Vistula as far as the river Pripet (a tributary of the Dnieper), which separates them from the Little Russians. As to the boundary between these and the Great Russians, it follows an undulating line from the town of Souraj towards the Don, then a little to the north of the province of Kharkov, and thence to the south as far as the shores of the Sea of Azov. The Little Russians of eastern Galicia and Bukovina are known by the collective name of *Ruthenians*, or the local names of *Gorales* (mountaineers), *Huzules*, *Boïki*, *Tukholtsi*, etc. The colonisers of eastern and northern Russia have been Great Russians; the Little Russians have founded colonies in the south-east of Russia.

The *western* Slav *group* is composed of *Poles* of Russian Poland, western Galicia, Posen, and eastern Prussia (*Mazours*, *Kashoobs*), whose language is somewhat common in Lithuania; of *Wends* or *Lujichanes* or *Sorobes*, of the kingdom of Saxony and the Prussian province of Saxony (several thousands are in process of being germanised), of *Czechs* or *Bohemians* of Bohemia, and of a part of Moravia, of *Slovaks*, of Moravia and Hungary.

As to the *southern group*, it comprises the *Slovenes* or *Slovintsi* of Carniola and the interior of Istria (Austria-Hungary), and the *Serbo-Croats*, known by the name of *Khorvates* in Hungary, of *Serbs* in Servia, of *Morlaks*,

[1] See for the Slav languages: A. Pypine and Spassovitch, *Istoria, etc.* (Hist. of Slavonic Literatures), St. Petersburg, 1879, 2 vols., of which there is a translation of the first in French by S. Denis (1881); for a slight general view: F. von Hellwand, *Die Welt der Slaven*, Berlin, 1890; Zograf, *Les peuples de la Russie*, Moscow (1895); and *Oester-Hung. Monarch.*, vols. ix., xi., xiv., xv. (1891-96); for ethnogeny and archæology: Lubor Niederle, *O Puvodu Slovanu* (Origin of the Slavs), Prague, 1897 (in Czech); and *Cheloviechestvo, etc.* (Prehistoric Man), Russian translation, St. Petersburg, 1898.

Uskoks, etc., in Dalmatia, of *Herzogovinians*, *Bosnians*, *Montenegrins*, or *Tsrnagortsi* in other parts of the Balkan peninsula. The Servian tongue is also spoken in a portion of Macedonia. The Slav colonies which still existed some centuries ago in Greece and Thessaly must have been formed largely of Serbo-Croats. We must, lastly, include in this group the *Bulgarians*, a people of Turco-Finnish origin, slavonised for at least ten centuries; their habitat is in Bulgaria, Rumelia, a part of Macedonia, and several localities of Turkey. There exist several Bulgarian colonies in Russia (Crimea, northern shore of the Sea of Azov).

No greater homogeneity is shown by the Slav group than by the two great preceding ones, from the point of view of corporeal structure, and it is useless to look for a "Slav type." Among the Slav peoples there is an interblending, as far as is known at present, of three principal and three secondary races, without taking into account the Turco-Ugrian elements. The traits of the secondary Vistulian race appear especially among the Poles of Prussia and Russia; the Eastern race is most marked in the White Russians, but is also met with among the Great Russians, the Mazours, and the Wends; the Adriatic race characterises the Serbo-Croats, as well as certain Czechs and Ruthenians; the sub-Adriatic race is well represented by a section of the Czechs, while numerous elements of the Western race are met with among the Slovaks, the Little Russians, and certain Great Russians.

Joined to the three great linguistic groups of Aryan peoples which we have just characterised are three others, less considerable but not less interesting, their manner of speech perhaps being nearer to the primitive Aryan tongue. These are the Letto-Lithuanian, Helleno-Illyrian, and Celtic groups.

The peoples of the *first group* are the *Letts* of Livonia and Kurland (Russia), and the *Lithuanians* peopling the provinces of Vilna, Grodno, the north of Russian Poland, as well as western Prussia, where they are germanised for the most part.

The majority of the Letts belong to the Northern or Sub-northern race, while the Lithuanians exhibit elements of the Sub-northern and Eastern race.

Among the peoples of the Helleno-Illyrian group the *Greeks* are distributed outside the political frontiers of the kingdom of Greece, in Epirus, and on the coast of Macedonia and the Propontis. Greek colonies are found in the rest of

FIG. 104.—Russian woman of the district of Veréïa (gov. Moscow), 20 years old, Eastern race (?). (*Phot. Bogdanoff, Coll. Museum of Nat. Hist., Paris.*)

Turkey, in southern Russia, and in the south-east of Italy (province of Lecce, Terra d'Otranto). The *Albanians* or *Skiptars* form a people whose linguistic affinities are little known. Two sub-divisions are recognised, formed of very distinct elements from the physical point of view: the *Gegs* and the *Mirdites* on the north, the *Tosks* on the south.

Albanian colonies are found in Greece, in the south of Italy (Basilicata, Calabria, and Sicily), and Corsica (in *Cardevole*).

The physical types are very diversified among the Greeks, and still require to be studied. The Albanians of the north appear to be connected with the Adriatic or sub-Adriatic race, but nothing is known about the southern Albanians. The

FIG. 105.—Same subject as Fig. 104, seen in profile. (*Phot. Bogdanoff, Coll. Mus. of Nat. Hist., Paris.*)

Albanian colonists in Italy and Corsica have the same physical traits as the surrounding population.

The peoples speaking Celtic languages are divided into two sections according to dialect: the Gaelic section comprises the Celts of the north-west of Scotland, the west of Ireland, and the Isle of Man. The second or Cymric section is composed of the inhabitants of Wales (*Welsh* language) and of Brittany (*Bas Breton*). The Cornish language, spoken two centuries ago in Cornwall, is now a dead language. The other Celtic dialects are also destined to disappear owing to the spread of such highly developed and widely known languages as English and French. There is no "Celtic" type or race. The Gaels of Scotland, as well as the Irish of Munster, appear to be connected with the Northern race; the Irish of Connaught present two or three types, variants of the secondary North-western race, which is predominant among the Welsh, and which is found again modified in Cornwall and in Devon (Fig. 92), by side, perhaps, of the remnants of Neolithic types; and lastly, the Low Bretons belong to the Western race, more or less intermixed, like the French of the central table-land.[1]

B.—AN-ARYAN PEOPLES.

As we have already said, peoples speaking Aryan tongues are not the only ones to inhabit Europe. We find in it the representatives of other linguistic families: Basque, Finno-Ugrian, Turkish, Mongolian, Semitic, etc.

The *Basques* inhabit the extreme south-west corner of France (in the department of the Basses Pyrenées) and the adjoining part of Spain, provinces of Guipuzcoa and Biscay (as far as Bilbao on the west), and the north of the provinces of Navarre and Alava. The affinities of their agglutinous language have not yet been clearly determined. As to their physical type, it is also quite peculiar. Its chief characteristics, according to Collignon, are its mesocephaly "with a peculiar swelling in the parietal regions," conical torso, elongated and pointed face, etc. In the main this type approaches most nearly to the Littoral race, and is met with, in a pure state, especially among the French Basques.[2]

[1] Beddoe, "The Kelts of Ireland," *Journ. of Anthropol.*, 1871, p. 117 (map); Broca, "La Question Celtique," *Bull. Soc. Anthro. Paris*, 1873, pp. 313 and 247; Havelock Ellis, "The Men of Cornwall," *New Century Review*, 1897, Nos. 4 and 5.

[2] T. Aranzadi, *El pueblo Escalduna*, San Sebastian, 1889 (maps); R. Collignon, "La Race Basque," *L'Anthropologie*, vol. v., 1894, p. 276.

Peoples speaking the Finno-Ugrian dialects.—The *Magyars* or *Hungarians*[1] occupy in a compact mass, four millions and a half in number, the plain of Hungary. They represent 43 per cent. of the population of this State. There may still be distinguished among them traces of the ancient divisions into various tribes (*Haiduks, Yazigs, Kumans*, etc.). The eastern portion of Transylvania is also inhabited by a division of the Magyars, the *Szeklers*, who differ by their meso-cephalic skull from the other Hungarians, who are brachycephalic for the most part. The *western Finns* are divided into Finns properly so called or Suomi, Baltic Finns, and Karelians. The Suomi (in the singular Suomalaiset) occupy Finland, with the exception of certain points on the coast, taken by the Swedes; they are sub-divided into several small sections, according to their dialects: *Savolaks, Tavasts, Kvènes* or *Kvanes*. The latter inhabit the north of Sweden. The *Baltic Finns*, formerly very numerous, are reduced to two peoples, the *Esthonians* or *Esths* of the Russian provinces of Esthonia and Livonia, with the adjacent islands (Ösel, Dago, etc.); and the *Livonians*, quartered to the number of 2000 at the extremity of the north coast of Kurland; they have entirely disappeared from Livonia, from which they derive their name. The *Karelians* are scattered in groups, more or less important, over the south-east of Finland, in the Russian province ("government") of Olonetsk, and in the north-west of the province of Archangel. Isolated groups of this population found on the plateau of Valdai and almost in the heart of Russia (in the north of the province of Tver) are indications of the ancient expansion of the western Finns towards the east. We must connect with the Karelians the *Veps* (to the south of Lake Onega) and the *Chukhontsi*, Finns of the province of St. Petersburg, descendants of the ancient Ingrians and Chudes whose name recurs often in Russian chronicles and legends.[2]

The 42nd degree of longitude east of Greenwich seems to

[1] *Oester.-Ung. Monarchie*, vols. v., ix., and xii., 1888-93.

[2] Retzius, *Finska Kranier*, Stockholm, 1878, pl. (with French summary); see also publications of the Finno-Ugrian Society of Helsingfors, etc.

mark the boundary between the western Finns and the following group, that of the *eastern Finns* or *Ugrians*. These are tribes dispersed in the north-east of Russia, for the most part mixed with the Russians, and Russianised in language, religion, and customs. We may distinguish among them three principal divisions. The northern division comprises the *Zyrians*, re-

FIG. 106.—Cheremiss of Ural Mountains.
(*Phot. Sommier.*)

duced to some thousand families, buried in the midst of the Russian population, in the eastern part of the provinces of Archangel and Vologda (between the 60th degree of latitude north and the polar circle). The middle division is composed of two neighbouring peoples, *Votiaks* and *Permiaks*, dwelling among the Russians, in more or less considerable islets in the space comprised between the Vetluga and the Kama, tributaries of the Volga. More to the south, in the middle basin of the Volga, as far as about the 50th degree of north latitude, we find the southern group of the Ugrians composed of *Cheremiss* (Fig. 106) on the left bank of the upper Volga and of *Mordva* or *Mordvinians* on both banks of the middle Volga in numerous islets between the 42nd and 54th degree east longitude.[1]

We may class among the Finns, for linguistic reasons, three peoples differing from each other as much as they are distinguished from the groups I have just mentioned. These are the Lapps, the Samoyeds, and the Ostiaks. The Lapps occupy the most northern region of Sweden and Norway (*Scandinavian Lapps*), as well as the north of Finland and the Kola peninsula in the north of Russia (*Russian Lapps or Lopari*). They appear to have been formerly spread much more to the south of their present habitat. They are the shortest in stature of all Europeans, and almost the most brachycephalic (see Appendices I. and II.). One portion only of the *Samoyeds* inhabits Europe, on the east of the river Mezen and to the north of the polar circle; the rest wander about Siberia between the Arctic Ocean and the lower Obi. Their neighbours on the south, the *Ostiaks*, extend from the middle Obi to the Ural mountains, over which they pass to occupy several points in Europe. The Ostiaks of both slopes of the Urals bear also the name of *Vogules* or *Manz*.[2]

As regards physical type there is a great difference between

[1] S. Sommier, *Un Estate in Siberia*, Florence, 1885; and *Archivo p. l'Antro.*, vols. xvii. and xix. (1887-89); Maïnof, *Resooltaty*, etc. (*Anthr. and Jurid. Studies of the Mordva*); "Zapiski," Russian Geog. Socy. (Ethnog. Sec.), vols. xi. and xiv. (1883-85); works of Smirnov on the Mordva, Cheremiss, etc., Fr. trans. by Boyer (Paris, 1897-98).

[2] P. Mantegazza and Sommier, *Studii antr. sui Lapponi*, Turin, 1880 (phot. pl.); "Notes on the Lapps," by Prince R. Bonaparte, Keane, and Garson, *Jour. Anthr. Inst.*, vol. xv., 1885, pp. 210 *et seq.;* Montefiore, "The Samoyeds," *Jour. Anthr. Inst.*, vol. xxiv., 1895, p. 396; Zograf, "Esquisse des Samoyedes," *Izviestia* (*Bull.*) *Soc. Friends. Nat. Sc.*, Moscow, vol. xxxi., 1878-79, supl. (analysed in the *Rev. d'Anthr.*, 1881); Sommier, *loc. cit.* (analysed *Rev. d'Ethnogr.*), Paris, 1889.

the western and the eastern Finns. The former are the offspring of the union of the Northern or Sub-northern race with the Eastern race, somewhat tall, mesocephalic, and light-com-

FIG. 107.—Kundrof Tatar (Turkoman) of Astrakhan, with cap. (*Phot. Sommier.*)

plexioned, while the latter belong for the most part to a special Ugrian race, short, dolichocephalic, dark, with slightly Mongoloid face.

For the other Eurasian peoples (*Turks*, *Armenians*, *Gypsies*, *Jews*, etc.), see the following chapter.

c. CAUCASIAN PEOPLES.[1] — All who have seen the ethnographical maps of the Caucasus must have been struck by the motley appearance which they present; fifty various

FIG. 108.—The same in profile, with skull-cap, which is never removed, worn under the cap. (*Phot. Sommier.*)

tribes may in fact be counted in this isthmus, the area of which is less than that of Spain. I shall speak here only of

[1] R. Erckert, *Der Kaukasus u. Seine. Völker*, Leipzig, 1885 (with map); E. Chantre, *Rech. Anthropol., dans le Caucase*, Lyons, 1885-87, 4th vol., and atlas; Pantiukhof, "Obser. Anthr. au Caucase," *Zapiski Caucasian Sec. of Russ. Geog. Soc.*, vol. xv., Tiflis, 1893, phot.

the *Caucasians properly so called*—that is to say, of the peoples who dwell only in the Caucasus, putting on one side all others (Iranians, Europeans, Turks, Mongols, Semites, etc.) who have overflowed into this country from the adjacent regions.

The *Caucasians* are sub-divided into four linguistic or ethnic groups: the Cherkess (on the north-west of the Caucasian range), the Lesgian Chechen (on the north-east of the range), the Kartvels or Georgians (on the south-west of the range), and the Ossets (in the centre of the range on both slopes). The last, by their language, are the nearest to the Iranians and the Armenians, but the three other groups form a perfect linguistic unit. The dialects which they speak preserve the impress of a common origin and form a family apart which has nothing in common with any other.

The *Cherkess* or *Circassians*, until the middle of this century, inhabited all the western part of Ciscaucasia; but, since the conquest of their country by the Russians, they have emigrated *en masse* into the Ottoman empire. At the present day there are only a few remnants of them in the Caucasus. Principal tribes, *Abkhazians*, *Adighé* or *Cherkess* (Circassians) properly so called, *Kabards of the plain*, *Abadzeh*, *Chapsugh*, etc.

The *Chechen-Lesgians* are divided, as the name implies, into two groups: the Chechen (with the *Ingushes*, the *Kists*, etc.) of the upper basin of the Terek, who have long been considered as a population apart (Figs. 110 and 111), and the *Lesgians* of Daghestan. These last are sub-divided into five great sections, according to their dialects: (1) The *Avars-Andi*, with the *Dido*, whose language tends to preponderate owing to the historic part played by the tribe of the Avars, to which belonged the famous Shamil, the hero of the Caucasus, whose memory still lives. (2) The *Dargha* in the centre of *Daghestan*, the best known tribe of which is that of the Kubachi, living in little houses piled one above the other on the sides of the mountains. (3) The *Kurines* of the Samur basin, with the *Tsakhurs* (Tabassaurans, etc.). (4) The *Laks* or *Kazi-Kumyks*, with which are connected lesser known tribes, like the *Agul*, the *Budukh*, and the *Khinalugh*, whose language is distinct from all the other dialects of Daghestan. (5) The *Udes*, an ancient Christian tribe converted to Islamism, of which there remain but 750 individuals still acquainted with their mother-tongue (district of Nukha, province of Elisabetpol).

The *Kartvels, Karthli* or *Georgians*, who alone of the

FIG. 109.—Georgian Imer of Kutais.
(*Phot. from Coll. of Author.*)

Caucasians possess a special mode of writing, and a literature, are divided into three linguistic sections: (1) *Gruzin*, which comprises the *Georgians properly so called* of the plains of the province of Tiflis, *Georgians of the mountains* (*Khevsurs, Pshavs*, and *Toushs*, 21,300 in all), and the *Imers* (Fig. 109) with the *Gurians*. (2) The *Mingrelian* section of people living more to the west, composed of the *Mingrelians* of the Kutais country and the *Lazes* of the Batum circle. (3) The *Swan* section, comprising the tribe of *Swanet* or Swanetians, driven back into the unhealthy regions of the province of Kutais, where the race degenerates; cretins and those afflicted with goitre form a third part of the population.

The *Ossets*, while speaking a language which (in the *Digorian* dialect) is nearly allied to Iranian, have nevertheless

FIG. 110.—Chechen of Daghestan.
(*Phot. Chantre.*)

much in common with the other Caucasians, from whom they are distinguished perhaps by the frequent occurrence of fair hair (10 per cent.) and light eyes (29 per cent.); more frequent than among all the other Caucasian peoples, the Imers, the Lesgi-Dido, and the Chechen excepted. But figures are still too inadequate in regard to the number of subjects with dark hair and eyes (51 and 53 per cent.) to enable us to affirm, as all authors from Am. Marcellinus to our own days have done, that the Ossets are a people of fair race. They are above the average in stature (1m. 68), and sub-brachycephalic (ceph. ind. on the liv. sub. 82.6).

As to the somatic characters of the other Caucasians, we know little of those of the Cherkess (sub-brachycephalic, of medium height), but we are better informed in regard to the Lesgians and the Kartvel. The contrast between the two groups is striking. The Lesgians are very brachycephalic (see Appendix II.), especially the tribes of the east; their stature is

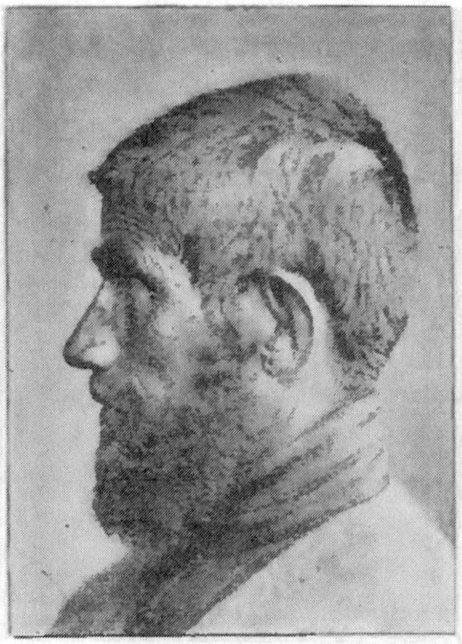

FIG. 111.—Same as Fig. 110, seen in profile.
(*Phot. Chantre.*)

fairly high. To these characters are united others which, in their totality, produce the most singular effect; the prominent nose, straight or curved, recalls the Semites, while the projecting cheek-bones, broad face, and angles of the lower jaw directed outward, suggest the Mongols; lastly, the whole aspect becomes still more odd, owing to the light grey or greenish eyes, and fair or chestnut hair, so common among the Lesgians (Figs. 110 and 111).

Quite different are the characters of the Kartvel. In the first place, they form a less homogeneous group; we must distinguish in it between the eastern and the western Georgians. The former (Gruzins) are true brachycephals, though in a lesser degree than the Lesgians, while the latter (Mingrelians, Imers) are distinguished from all the other Caucasians by the elongated form of the head (see Appendix II.). The stature varies in harmony with the cranial forms; the Kartvel tribes with rounded heads have the shortest stature, and the dolichocephalic tribes the highest; light hair is less common in the two groups than among the Lesgians, but we find among the Georgians in general a great number of subjects in whom the iris has a particular yellow colour, a grey or greenish yellow. The Gruzins have a rather rounded face and broad nose, while the Imers have an elongated visage, thin nose, tight lips, pointed chin (Fig. 109); their physiognomy reminds one of a goat's head, according to Pantiukhof, who considers the Imers to be the purest representatives of the primitive Kartvels.[1]

[1] For particulars see Deniker, *loc. cit.* (*Races de l'Europe*).

CHAPTER X.

RACES AND PEOPLES OF ASIA.

ANCIENT INHABITANTS OF ASIA. — Prehistoric times — *Pithecanthropus erectus* (Dub.)—Ages of stone and metals.—PRESENT INHABITANTS OF ASIA.—Races of Asia—I. *Peoples of Northern Asia*—Yeniseian, Palæasiatic and Tunguse groups.—II. *Peoples of Central Asia*—Turkish, Mongolian, and Thibetan groups—Peoples of the south-west of Thibet and of South China (Lolo, Miao-tsé, Lu-tsé, etc).—III. *Peoples of Eastern Asia*—Chinese, Coreans, and Japanese.—IV. *Peoples of Indo-China*—Aborigines, Mois, Kuis, Siam, Naga, etc.—More recent mixed populations: Annamese, Cambodians, Thai, etc.—V. *Peoples of India*—Castes — Dravidians and Kolarians—Indo-Aryans and unclassified populations—VI. *Peoples of Anterior Asia*—Iranians and Semites.

ANCIENT INHABITANTS OF ASIA.

Prehistoric Times.—It is a common practice to call Asia, or at least certain regions of Asia, "the cradle of mankind," the "officina gentium." The migrations and invasions of the Asiatic peoples into Europe, which took place from the most remote times, gave birth, naturally enough, to this idea among the western peoples (p. 317 *et seq.*). However, no serious data authorise us to say that the first man was born rather in Asia than Europe. Nowhere do we find there any traces of tertiary man.[1] Eugène Dubois discovered, it is true, quite close to the

[1] The flint flakes resembling palæolithic tools, found by F. Noetling (*Records Geol. Survey, India*, vol. xxvii., p. 101, Calcutta, 1894) in Miocene or lower Pliocene beds, at Yenang-Yung (Central Burma), are considered by Oldham and other scholars as natural products. However, Noetling has since (in 1897) described an animal bone, artificially polished (?), of the same beds.—*Nat. Science*, London-New York, 1894, p. 345; 1895, 1st half-year, p. 367; 2nd, pp. 199 and 294; and 1887, 1st half-year, p. 233.

Asiatic continent in the very uppermost tertiary beds (upper pliocene) of the Island of Java, the bones of a being which he considers as intermediate between man and the anthropoid apes, and which he has called *Pithecanthropus erectus* (Figs. 112 and 113). But Java belongs to-day as much to the Oceanian world as to Asia, and the Pithecanthropus is not altogether a man, either according to his discoverer or many other authorities.

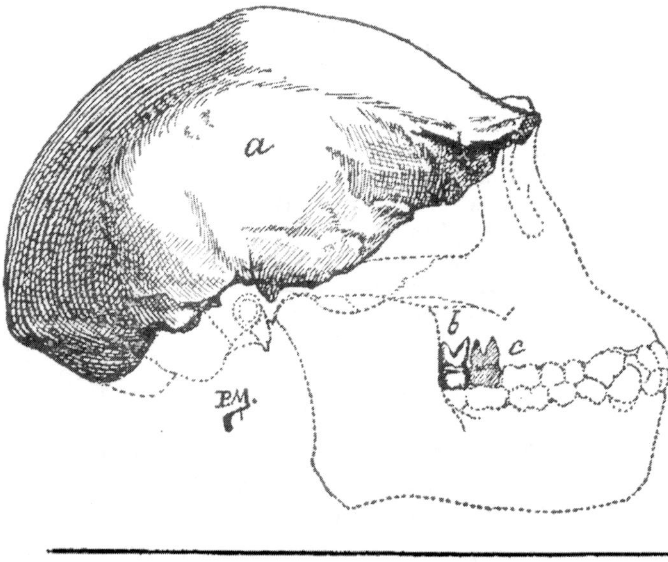

FIG. 112.—Skull of the *Pithecanthropus erectus*, Dub. The calvaria (*a*) and the teeth (*b c*) *are designed by P. Moutet after the casts* and photographs of E. Dubois. The reconstruction of the rest is made *after Dubois and Manouvrier.*

Some regard this being simply as a gigantic gibbon, while others (myself among the number) hold that he is a being more closely related to man than to the anthropoid apes, or even a man of a race inferior to all existing ones. If this last hypothesis be correct we must admit the existence of tertiary man in Asia, since it is highly probable that even at the end of the tertiary period the islands of Sumatra and

Java were connected with the great continent by the Malay peninsula.[1]

As to quaternary man, if no bones have yet been found, tools absolutely similar to those of Europe have been noted almost everywhere in Asia; in Siberia, around Lake Baikal (Tchersky and Poliakof), and near to Tomsk in the loess, beside a dismembered and calcined skeleton of a mammoth, the remains of a pantagruelic repast of quaternary Siberians (Kuznétzof); in Japan, in the ancient province of Jenchiou, now Osaka, the Ivate and Miaghi province, northern Nippon (S. Fuse), western Nippon (Vidal) in the country of Rikuzen, now in the province of Etzigo or Teshigo (Inuzuka); then in anterior Asia, in the grottos at the mouth of the Nahr-el-Kelb, near Beirut (Lortet); at Hannauch to the east of Tyre (Lortet and Pelagaud), in Galilee (Cazalis of Fondouce and Moretain), in Phœnicia (Zumoffen), etc.[2] In India, attention has been drawn to several palæo-

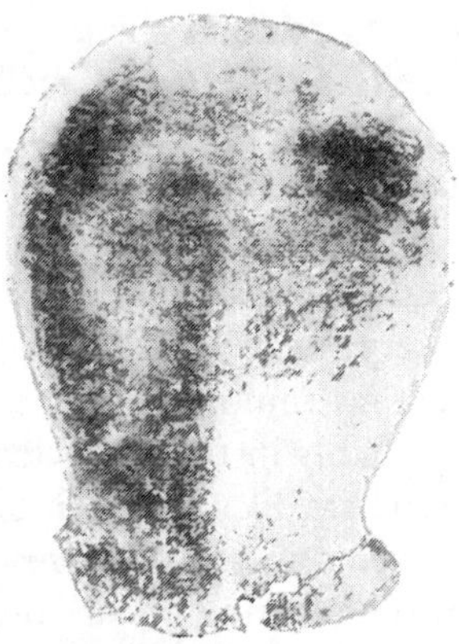

FIG. 113.—Calvaria of *Pithecanthropus*, seen from above. (*Phot. Dubois.*)

[1] The bones of the *Pithecanthropus*, a thigh-bone, a calvaria (Figs. 112 and 113), and two molar teeth (Fig. 112), were found by Dr. Dubois at Trinil (province of Madioun), on the bank of the river Bengavan, in a layer of lava, by the side of bones of animals of the Pliocene period. The calvaria, indicating a cranial capacity of about 900 cubic centimetres, recalls rather the Neanderthal-Spy skull (Fig. 86) than that of a gibbon; the thigh-bone is entirely human; the teeth are of a form intermediate between those of Man and of the Anthropoids.—For particulars see E. Dubois, *Pithecanthropus . . . aus Java*, Batavia, 1894; and his articles in the *Anat. Anzeig.*, 1896, No. 1, and the *Jour. Anthr. Inst.*, London, vol. 25, p. 240 (1896); Manouvrier, *Bull. Soc. Anthr.*, Paris, 1895, pp. 12 and 553; 1896, pp. 396 and 467; G. Schwalbe, *Zeitsch. Morph. u. Anthr.*, vol. i., p. 16, Stuttgart, 1899.

[2] Uvarof, *Arkheologia*, etc. (*Archeol. of Russia*, vol. i., Moscow, 1881, p. 162, in Russian); Kuznétzof, *Mittheil. Anthr. Gesell.*, Vienna, 1896, Nos. 4 and 5; "Age de la pierre au Japon," *Mater. hist. . . . homme*, Toulouse-

lithic stations in the midst of the ancient alluvia of the rivers Nerbadda, Krishna, and Godaveri (Wynn); in certain places there quartzite implements were associated with the bones of extinct animals (*Equus nomadicus, Hippopotamus palæindicus*) or animals which have since emigrated into other regions (*Bos palæindicus*, etc.). Single tools have been found in the beds of laterite near Madras, in Scinde, at Banda, in the central provinces (Rivett-Carnac), in the south-east of Bengal.[1]

Monuments and objects of the *polished stone* and *bronze* periods, often confounded in Asia, have been found almost everywhere. They are connected with peoples who presented at that remote date great differences in their civilisation and probably in their physical type. The excavations of Schliemann at Hissarlik (Asia Minor) have brought to light a civilisation which appears to correspond with the end of the stone age and the beginning of the bronze epoch (2,500 years B.C.?). Prehistoric objects in polished stone and bronze have been found at other points of Asia Minor (A. Martin), in Lycaonia (Spiegelthal), in the Sinai peninsula (Bauermann and Richard), on the shores of Lake Issik-koul (Russian Turkestan). Southern Siberia, the Kirghiz steppes, north and north-western Mongolia are covered with stone circles (*Kereksur*), barrows, tumuli, menhirs (*Kishachilo*) of every form, with burial-places in which are found objects in wood, bone, bronze, copper, iron (Radloff, Potanin, Klementz). The skulls which have been taken from some of these burial-places, in the upper valley of the Yenisei, are dolichocephalic; the plaster mortuary masks

Paris, 1879, p. 31; S. Fuse, *Journ. Anthr. Soc. Tokyo*, vol. xi., 1895, No. 122 (in Japanese); Inuzuka, *ibid.*, No. 119; E. Cartailhac, "L'âge de la pierre en Asie," *Congr. Orientalistes*, 3rd ser., 1, p. 315, Lyons, 1880; G. Chauvet, "Age de la pierre en Asie," *Congr. intern. arch. prehis.*, 11th session, vol. i., p. 57, Moscow, 1892. The arrows picked up by Abbé A. David in Mongolia, and supposed to be palæolithic, belong to the historic period (Hamy, *Bull. Mus. Hist. Nat.*, 1896, p. 46).

[1] Medlicot and Blandford, *Manual of Geol. of India*, Calcutta, 1879, 2 vols.; Cartailhac, *loc. cit.*; Rivett-Carnac, *Journ. Anthr. Inst.*, vol. xiii., 1884, p. 119.

found in the same region by Adrianof present a type somewhat European.[1]

It must not be forgotten that many of these monuments date from the historic epoch and belong, as proved by the runiform inscriptions of Mongolia discovered by Yadrintsef and deciphered by Thomson, to the seventh and eighth centuries of the Christian era.[2]

The kitchen-middens of Omori, near Tokio, and of several other localities in Japan examined by Morse, Milne, and Tsuboi, afford evidence of the existence in this country of a fairly civilised race which was acquainted with pottery, but employed only bone and partly polished stone implements. The excavations of ancient underground dwellings in the islands of Yezo (Morse, Tsuboi) and Saghalien (Poliakoff) lead us to believe that this race extended much farther to the north. It is possible that it was related to the men whose polished flint implements have been found in Siberia in the valley of the Tunka, in that of the Patcha, one of the tributaries of the river Amur (Uvarof), and in the shell-heaps of the Pacific coast near Vladivostok (Margaritof).[3] Polished stone hatchets

[1] Potanin, *Otcherki*, etc. (*North-West Mong. Sketches*), St. Petersburg, 1881-83, 4 vols. (in Russian); Adrianof, "Zapiski, etc.," *Mem. Russ. Geog. Soc.*, Sect. Gen. Geog., vol. xi., 1888, p. 149; Radloff, *Aus Sibirien*, Leipzig, 1884, 2 vols., and *Arbeit. Orkhon. Exped.*, St. Petersburg, 1893-97 (in course of publication). For summary of the question and bibliography, see Deniker, *Nouvelles Geogr.*, p. 54, Paris, 1892 (with map).

[2] Radloff, *loc. cit.* (*Arbeit.*, etc.); Thomson, *Mem. Soc. Finno-Ougrienne* vol. v., Helsingfors, 1896. We cannot admit as a general rule an exact synchronism between the prehistoric periods of Europe and those of Northern Asia. If, as Uvarof says, the age of the mammoth was earlier in Siberia than in Europe, it is none the less true that many peoples of Eastern Siberia were still in the midst of the "stone age" at the time when the Russians penetrated into this country (seventeenth century). As to the peoples of Western Siberia and the Kirghiz Steppes, the beginning of their bronze age goes back at the furthest to the beginning of the Christian era.

[3] Margaritof, *Memoirs Amurian Soc. of Naturalists*, vol. i., Vladivostok, 1887. The only skull found in these heaps is dolichocephalic and reminds one of the Ainu skull. Thus one might suppose, as Milne had done (*Trans. As. Soc. Jap.*, Tokio, 1899, vol. vii., p. 61), in connection with

have been found in the north-east of China in the vicinity of tumuli resembling the American "mounds" (Williamson); others have been picked up in the Yunnan (Sladen), and in Burma (Theobald); Moura, Jammes, and Morel exhumed in Cambodia, between Lake Tonlé-Sap and the Mekong, side by side with objects of bronze, several polished stone implements of a peculiar type (Fig. 114), a kind of square-tongued axe (shouldered celt), which has since been found again in several other places in Indo-China as far as the upper Laos (Lefèvre-Pontalis) and Burma.[1] In the district of Somron-Sen (Cambodia), previously explored by Jammes, as well as in the neighbourhood of Saigon, Corre discovered similar implements close to shell-heaps containing, besides pottery and stone tools, human bones, but no skulls.

FIG. 114.—Polished stone axe found in Cambodia. Prehistoric type peculiar to Indo-China.

Lastly, in India, the "cromlechs," "mounds," and finds of stone objects similar to those which are found in Europe, may be counted in hundreds. It is certain that the stone "circles" of the central provinces and the "Kouroumbarings" of Southern India date from a period anterior to the Aryan immigration. As in Europe, so in Asia the age of metals borders very closely on the historic period of which the

the similar kitchen refuse found in Japan, that they are the work of the Ainus; however, the presence of pottery, unknown to the Ainus even to recent times, militates against this view.

[1] The Nagas have still at the present day axes of precisely the same form, which they use as hoes. (S. Peal, *Journ. As. Soc. Bengal*, vol. lxv., Part III., p. 9, Calcutta, 1896.) Cf. Noulet, "Age de la pierre . . . au Cambodge d'après Moura," *Mus. Nat. Hist.*, vol. i., p. 3, Toulouse, 1879; and *Mater. Hist. Nat. Homme*, vol. xiv., p. 315, Toulouse, 1879; Cartaillac, *L'Anthropol.*, p. 64, 1890 (a summary of Jammes's discoveries).

Chinese annals have preserved for us a record. The monuments of Chaldea, Assyria, Asia Minor, India, and Cambodia, also reveal ethnographical facts of great interest (see, for instance, note 2, p. 419).

PRESENT INHABITANTS AND RACES OF ASIA.—It is impossible in the present state of our knowledge to draw up a complete table of the *migrations* which have taken place on the Asiatic continent in *historic* times. I shall mention those in connection with some peoples whose history is partially known (Chinese, Turks, Mongols, Thai).

So also, in the present state of anthropological knowledge, we can only discern in the midst of the numerous Asiatic populations, in a quite general way, the elements furnished by the following eleven races:—Five races peculiar to Asia (*Dravidian*, *Assyroid*, *Indo-Afghan*, *Ainu*, *Mongolian*), and six races which are also met with in other parts of the world: *Negrito*, *Indonesian*, *Arab*, *Ugrian*, *Turkish*, and *Eskimo* (leaving out of account the Assyroid and Indo-Afghan races, which are found again among the Jews and the European Gypsies). I have already given (p. 285 *et seq.*) the principal characters of these races; it only remains to say a few words as to their geographical distribution in Asia.

The *Eskimo* race is quartered in the north-east of the continent; that of the *Ainus* in Saghalien, Yezo, and perhaps in northern Japan; while the *Ugrian* race is represented by its *Yeniseian* variant. The *Mongolian* race (with its two secondary races, *northern* and *southern*) is found almost all over Asia. The *Turkish* race is limited more particularly to the inland regions of Central Asia. The *Indonesians* are numerous in Indo-China, and in the islands from Japan to the Asiatic Archipelago, while the *Dravidians* and *Indo-Afghans* abound in India. The latter are also met with in anterior Asia, side by side with the *Assyroids* and *Arabs*. Some representatives of the *Negrito* race inhabit the Malay peninsula and the Andaman Islands; the elements of this race are also found among the inhabitants of Indo-China and perhaps India.

As to existing populations of the Asiatic continent, I shall rapidly pass them in review, grouping them, according to geographical region, under six heads: peoples of Northern Asia; of Central Asia; of Eastern Asia; of Indo-China; of India; and lastly, of Anterior or Western Asia.

I. NORTHERN ASIA, consisting almost exclusively of Siberia, a cold country covered with dense virgin forests (*taïga*) or marshy, frozen plains (*tundra*), harbours, in addition to Russian or Chinese colonists, only a few somewhat wretched tribes, mainly hunters, but depending partly on fishing and hoe-culture.

We may group them thus:—(1) tribes of Western Siberia, having some affinities with the Samoyeds and the eastern Finns, which I shall call *Yeniseians* or *Tubas;* (2) peoples of the extreme north-east of the Asiatic continent, whom Schrenck [1] describes as *Palæasiatics;* (3) the Tunguses of Eastern Siberia and Manchuria.

1. *Yeniseians* or *Tubas.*—Besides the *Samoyeds of Asia*, who differ from their kinsfolk in Europe only by their more Mongoloid features, the *Yeniseians* comprise two distinct groups of populations. In the first place the so-called *Ostiaks of the Yenisei*, on the right bank of this river (between Yeniseisk and Touroukhansk), probable descendants of the *Kien-Kouen* and the *Ting-ling* of the Chinese annals. It is a tribe in process of extinction, whose language differs from the Samoyed tongue and the Finnish dialects properly so called (Castren). Then come the tribes who formerly formed the Tuba nation, mentioned until the seventh century A.D. by the name of *Tu-po* by the Chinese annalists; they inhabited the basin of the upper Yenisei, the Altai region, and north-western Mongolia, and bore the local names of *Matores*, *Arines*, *Kottes*, *Assan*, *Tuba*, etc.

These peoples have disappeared as linguistic units,[2] but

[1] Schrenck, *Reisen in Amur-Lande*, vol. iii., Parts I. and II., St. Petersburg, 1881-91.

[2] Müller and Gmelin saw in 1753 the last surviving Arines, and in 1855 Castren was still able to find five individuals speaking the Kotte tongue.

their physical type, some of their characteristic manners, as well as a few words of their language, are preserved among certain populations speaking a Turkish dialect. The Russians call these populations "Tatars"; they might more suitably be called by the name of *Altaians*. This ethnic group, whose physical type has been altered by intermixtures with peoples of Turkish or Mongolian race, comprises the "*Tatars*" of *Abakan*, that is to say, *Katchines*, *Koibals* (eight hundred individuals), *Sagai*, and *Kizils;* the "*Tatars*" of *Altai* and those of *Chulim*, among whom must be noted the "Tatars of the black forests" (*Cherniewyié Tatary* in Russian), called "Tubas" by their neighbours. The latter are mesocephalic, of medium height; they have abandoned little by little the hunting state, and become primitive cultivators of the soil; they break up the ground with the hoe, which was used by them until not very long ago to dig up edible roots, and they cut their corn with hunting-knives.[1] The Soiots or Soyons of North-western Mongolia, who call themselves *Tubas*, are probably the descendants of the ancient Uigurs (Turkish nation) commingled with aboriginal Yeniseians of this country and partly Mongolised about the seventeenth century.

2. The *Palæasiatic* group should comprise, according to Schrenck, all the ancient peoples of Asia driven back at the present day towards the north-eastern extremity of the Continent. The more important of these peoples are the following:—The *Chuchi* (or *Chukchi*), numbering about 8000, are the most typical representatives of the group; they inhabit the north-east of Siberia, and the occupation of some is the breeding of reindeer, and fishing of others; however, the distinction between the nomadic and fishing Chukchi is both of an economic and ethnic order.[2] The *Koriaks* dwell to the south of the Chukchi, as far as Kamtchatka; they bear a close resemblance to them and speak the same language. The

[1] Yadrintsef, "Ob Altaïtsakh, etc." (On the Altaians and Tatars of Chern), *Izviestia of the Russ. Geogr. Soc.*, St. Petersb., 1881.

[2] Nordenskiold, *Voyage de la Vega*, vol. ii., chap. xii., Paris, 1883-84; Deniker, *loc. cit.* (*Rev. Anthr.*, p. 309, 1882).

FIG. 115.—Tunguse hunter (Siberia) with ski and staff.
(*Phot. Shimkiévich.*)

FIG. 116.—Same subject as Fig. 115, full face. (*Phot. Shimkiêvich.*)

Eskimo of Asia, *Namuollo*, or *Yu-Ite* formerly occupied the coast of the Chukchi country, as shown by their ancient habitations excavated by Wrangel and Nordenskiold. At the present day they are not found except in isolated camps on the coast and in the islands of the Behring Sea. They differ but very little from the Eskimo of Alaska; their ornaments, however, recall rather those of the Aleuts. The *Kamtchadals* of the centre and west of Kamtchatka differ from the peoples just mentioned. They number 4,250 at the present day, and are becoming Russianised very rapidly. They have completely given up their language, which has no relation to any linguistic family now known, and they speak a very corrupt form of Russian. Nominally orthodox Christians, they are at bottom animists, and the anthropomorphic element, often under obscene forms, occupies a large place in their myths and legends. They are fishers and hunters.

The *Yukaghirs* are the last remnants of a somewhat powerful people who formerly occupied all that part of Siberia situated to the east of the Lena, and who were composed of several tribes: *Omoks*, *Anauls*, *Cheliags*, etc.[1] It was believed until the last few years that even the Yukaghirs had disappeared, but quite recently Iokhelson[2] ascertained that there are at least 700 individuals, and that their language, which has no affinities with any of the Uralo-Altaic dialects, is spoken by a certain number of Tunguse-Lamuts (see p. 373), their neighbours. On the other hand, the Yukaghirs of Verkhoiansk, have adopted the Lamut dialect, and those of the

[1] The disappearance of these tribes is more apparent than real. The Anauls, in the neighbourhood of the Gulf of Anadyr, exterminated by the Cossacks in 1649, were only a fraction of the Yukaghirs, as is indicated by the termination "ul" which is found again in the name "Odul," which the Yukaghirs use to describe themselves. The word "Omok" means simply people, "tribe" in Yukaghir language. As to the Cheliags, who, according to the Cossack Amossof, occupied at the end of the last century the Siberian coast between the Gulf of Chaun and the mouth of the Kolima—they were probably one of the Chukchi tribes.

[2] Iokhelson, "Izviestia, etc.," *Bull. East-Siberian Sect. of the Russ. Geogr. Soc.*, vol. xxix., p. 8, Irkutsk, 1898.

banks of the Iana the Yakut tongue. By several peculiar manners and customs (classificatory system of relationship, pictography, etc.) they approach very closely certain North American Indians. Physically they resemble the Tunguse-Lamuts, though more brachycephalic and somewhat less dark-haired as a rule.

The Ainus (Figs. 49 and 117), who are classed among

FIG. 117.—Ainu of Yezo (Japan) with crown of shavings. (*Phot. lent by Collignon.*)

the Palæasiatics, inhabit the north and east parts of the island of Yezo, the south of Saghalien, and the three most southern islands of the Kuriles. They form a group by themselves, different from all the other peoples of Asia. Their elongated heads (ceph. index on the liv. sub. 77.8), their prominent supraciliary ridges, the development of the pilous system, the form of the nose, give to them some resemblance to the Russians, the Todas, and the Australians; but other characters (coloration of the skin, prominent cheek-bones, short stature, frequent occurrence of the *os japonicum*, etc.) distinguish them from these peoples and afford grounds for classing them as a separate race (see Chap. VIII.). According to Japanese historians, the Ainus or *Asuma Yebissu* occupied the whole of Nippon from the seventh century B.C. until the second century of the Christian era. In the seventh century A.D. they still occupied all that portion of this island situated to the north of the 38th degree of north latitude, and even in the ninth century the chronicles speak of the incursions of these "barbarians." Thus the Ainu element enters very largely into the composition of one of the types of the Japanese people, not only at Yezo but in the north of Nippon (province of Aomori), where several Ainu words still survive in current speech. In the Kurile islands the Ainus are intermixed with the Kamtchadals and the Aleuts introduced by the Russo-American Company about the middle of the present century.

It is calculated that there are about 18,500 Ainus (of whom 1,300 are in the island of Saghalien) at the present time; their number at Yezo has remained stationary for several years. The dress of the Ainus is a sort of greatcoat with broad sleeves, fastened with a girdle so that the right lappel covers the left lappel as among Turkish peoples, and contrary to the way it is done among the Chinese and Mongols. The chief occupation of the Ainus is hunting and fishing; they engage but little in agriculture. Their religion is pure animism; the word *Kamui*, which means spirit (like the *Kami* of the Japanese Shintoists), also serves to indicate everything incomprehensible, in the same way as the word "shif," the literal meaning of which is "animal" (may this be a word corresponding to totem?).

The Ainus, like most Asiatic peoples, such as the Giliaks, Tunguses, etc., have a special veneration for the bear; they organise festivals in its honour, during which a bear is killed, after having received the homage of many *inaou* (staffs decorated with shavings).

The Ainu language is agglutinative, and has no analogy with any known language.[1]

The Giliaks, who inhabit the north of Saghalien, and the mainland to the north of the mouth of the Amur, suggest by their traits sometimes the Ainus, sometimes the Tunguses, but they are brachycephalic. They are a people of fishers, living on the banks of rivers and the sea, in the winter in huts half buried in the ground, in the summer in little houses on piles. The Giliaks are readily disposed to trade, and are distinguished by their taste for ornaments. Their number hardly exceeds 5000 individuals.[2]

The *Tunguses*, while speaking a particular language, exhibit the Mongol type, softened by intermixtures with the primitive inhabitants (Palæasiatics?) of their territory, which extends from the Arctic Ocean to the 40th degree of north latitude, and from the Yenisei to the Pacific Ocean. Their number can hardly exceed 50,000 individuals over this immense stretch of country. They are divided into *southern* and *northern* Tunguses and *maritime* Tunguses or *Lamuts*. The river Amur forms the approximate boundary between the first two sections of Tunguses. The *Lamuts* occupy the shores of the sea of Okhotsk, the north-west of Kamtchatka, and extend more to the west to the river Iana. The *Northern Tunguses* are split up into several tribes, of which the following are the principal, going from east to west:—The *Olchas* or *Mangoon*, at the mouth of the Amur; their congeners the

[1] Anuchin, "Izviestia" *Soc. Friends Sc. Moscow*, suppl. to vol. xx., 1876 (analysed *Rev. d'Anthr.*, 1878, p. 148); Scheube, *Mitt. Deut. Gesell. Natur. u. Volkenk*, vol. iii., pp. 44 and 220, Yokohama-Tokio, 1880-82; G. Batchelor, *Trans. As. Soc. Japan*, vol. x., part 2, Tokio, 1882, and *The Ainu of Japan*, London, 1892; Chamberlain, *Mem. Imper. Univ. Japan*, Litter. coll. No. 1, Tokio, 1887 (analysed *Rev. d'Anthr.*, 1888, p. 81); Tarenetsky, *Mem. Ac. Sc. St. Petersburg*, 1890, vol. xxxvii., No. 13; Hitchcock, *Rep. U.S. Nat. Mus. for 1890*, pp. 408 and 429; S. Landor, *Alone with the Hairy Ainu*, 1893; Koganeï, *Beitr. z. Phys. Anthr. Aino* (extr. from *Mit. Med. Fakult.*, vols. i. and ii., Tokio, 1893-94).

[2] Schrenck, *loc. cit.*; Seeland, *Russiche Rev.*, vol. xi., St. Petersburg, 1882; Deniker, *Les Ghiliaks*, Paris, 1884 (extr. from *Rev. d'Ethnogr.*).

Oroks, in the north of the island of Saghalien; the *Orochons*, of a very pure Tunguse type; the *Manegres* (Fig. 43), and the "Olennyié" *Tunguses*, or the *Tunguses with reindeer* (Figs. 115 and 116). As to the *southern Tunguses*, they comprise the *Goldes* of the lower Amur and Ussuri, of a very pure type, and having a fairly well developed ornamental art; the *Oroches* of the coast; and lastly the *Solon-Daurs*, very much intermixed with the Mongols, of which colonies exist in the Kuldja.

The *Manchus*, reduced to a small number, belong by their dialect as well as by their physical type to the Tunguse group. They are being absorbed more and more by the Chinese, and hardly form a tenth part of the population of the country which bears their name (Pozdniéef). It is probable that the *Niu-chi* or *Yu-chi* of Shan-alin and Sien-pi on the northern border of Corea, mentioned in the Chinese annals, were Tunguse tribes.

The type which predominates among the Tunguses represents the secondary race called North Mongolian and characterised by mesocephaly or a slight sub-dolichocephaly, and by a rather elongated face. The stature varies; the Orochons are of average stature and the Manchus very tall, etc.[1]

II. Peoples of Central Asia.—The immense central Asiatic region, whose waters have no outlet towards the sea, is formed principally of denuded table-lands (Thibet) or of plains, sometimes grassy, sometimes desert (Mongolia, Turkestan). It is inhabited for the most part by populations which may be grouped from the linguistic point of view under three heads, Turks, Mongols, Thibetans.[2]

[1] C. Hiekisch, *Die Tungusen*, St. Petersburg, 1879; L. Schrenck, *loc. cit.*; H. James, "A Journey in Manchuria," *Proc. Geogr. Soc. London*, 1886, p. 779; D. Pozdniéef, *Opissanie*, etc. (*Description of Manchuria*, in Russian), vol. i., chap. vi., St. Petersburg, 1897. For measurements, see Appendices II. and III.

[2] This classification is not at all absolute. Turks and Mongols inhabit the wooded regions of Northern Asia (Yakuts, Buriats); they are also to be found in Europe and Asia Minor. The table-land of Iran, belonging to the region without outlet, assimilated since the works of Richthofen to Central

The peoples speaking the different *Turkish* dialects who are called *Turco-Tatars* or *Turanians* are scattered over an immense area comprising half of Asia and a large portion of Eastern Europe, from the Arctic Ocean (Yakuts) to Kuen-lun (Polus) and Ispahan (Turkomans of Persia), from the banks of the Kolima and the Hoang-ho (Yegurs) to Central Russia (Tatars of Kasimov) and Macedonia (Osmanli Turks). All these peoples may be gathered together into three great groups: eastern, central, and western.[1]

The *eastern group* comprises the Yakuts, who have preserved in its purity the ancient Turco-Uigurian language, but who in type, manners, and customs show the influence of contiguity with the Palæasiatics; then the various tribes of non-Yeniseian "Tatars" (see p. 366) of Siberia, like the Altaians (called *Kalmuks of Altai*, although they have nothing in common with the true Kalmuks), nomads who have recently adopted settled habits, like the *Teleuts* (or *Kara-Kalmuks*), likewise nomads, or the *Tatars of Siberia*, divided, according to their habitat, into *Tatars of the Baraba steppes*, *Tatars of Irtish*, of *Tobol*, etc.[2]

To this group must be added the *Taranchi* and other "Turks" of East Turkestan, as well as the Polus of the northern slope of the Kuen-lun, more or less mingled with Indo-

Asia, is mostly inhabited by Iranian peoples having a connection with those of anterior Asia. The Thibetans chiefly occupy the upper valley of the Yaro-tsanpo, which is now in the line of communication between Central and peripheral Asia, etc.

[1] See my articles "Turks" and "Tatars" in the *Dict. Univ. de Geogr.* of Vivien de Saint-Martin and Rousselet, vol. vi., Paris, 1894; and for details the works of Radloff and Vambery, to which reference is therein made.

[2] These "Tatars" have sprung from the intermixture of three elements: the primitive Tatars, the probable descendants of the *Tu-Kiue* of Chinese authors, the founders of the kingdom of Sibir destroyed by the Russians in the sixteenth century; the Sartes and the Uzbegs, coming especially from Bokhara; lastly, the Tatars of the Volga, immigrating in the wake of the Russians. In the west of Siberia there are also Ostiak tribes which bear the name of Tatars (such as the *Zabolotnyé Tatary*), because they have adopted the customs and religion of their neighbours the Tatars.

Afghan elements; the *Yegurs* of the province of Kan-su in China, etc.[1]

The *central group* comprises, in the first place, the *Kirghiz-Kazak* of the plains between the Irtish and the Caspian, with the *Kara-Kirghiz* of the Tian-chan mountains, typical nomads who under a Mussulman veneer have preserved many ancient Turkish animist customs;[2] then the *Uzbegs* and *Sartes*, villagers or citizens, more or less mingled with Iranian elements, of Russian Turkestan; and finally the *Tatars of the Volga*, or *of European Russia*. Among these last, the so-called *Kazan Tatars*, descendants of the Kipchaks, must be specially mentioned. Arriving on the banks of the Volga in the thirteenth century, they intermingled there with the Bulgarians. They differ from the *Astrakhan Tatars* (Figs. 107 and 108), descendants of the Turco-Mongols of the Gold horde, mixed with the Khazars, as well as from the Nogai of the Crimea,[3] representatives of whom we find also in the Caucasus, near Astrakhan, and in Lithuania, where, while remaining Mussulmans, they have adopted the language and the garb of Poles. With this group we must connect the *Bashkir-Mesthcheriaks*, a tribe intermixed with Turkish, Mongol, and Ugrian elements; and their congeners the *Shuvashes*, as well as the *Kumyks*, the *Karachai*, the *Kabards*, or *Tatars of the Caucasus mountains*, distinct from the true *Kabards*.

The *western group* is composed of *Turkomans* of Persia (*Khojars*, *Afshars*) and Russian (*Turkmen*) or Afghan Turkestan (*Jemshids*, etc.), of *Aderbaijani*, Turkish-speaking Iranians

[1] Dutreuil de Rhins and Grenard, *Miss. Sc. Haute Asie*, vol. ii., Paris, 1898.

[2] See bibliography in the monograph on the Kirghiz-Bukei by Kharouzin, "*Izviestia*" *Soc. Friends of Nat. Sc.*, Moscow, vol. 72, 1891.

[3] We must distinguish among the "Tatars of the Crimea" two ethnic groups, speaking the same Turkish dialect: the *Tatars of the Steppes* (Nogai), and the *Tatars of the Mountains* and *of the Coast*, or *Tauridians* (*Krimchaki* in Russian). These are the Islamised descendants of the ancient populations of the Taurus (Kipchaks, Genoese, Greeks, Goths). The Nogai belong to the Turkish race, more or less crossed, while the Tauridians have many traits of the Adriatic and Indo-Afghan races.

of the Caucasus and Persia, and lastly the *Osmanli Turks.* Included under this name are subjects of the Sultan speaking the Turkish language and professing Islamism. We must distinguish among them the settled Osmanli, much intermixed, and the nomadic tribes (*Turkomans*, *Yuruks*, etc.), who exhibit several characteristics of the Turkish race.

The *Turkish race*, so far as can be gathered from recent anthropological works, is preserved in a comparatively pure state among the Turks of the central group, but in the eastern group it has been profoundly modified in consequence of intermixtures with the Mongolian, Tunguse, and Ugrian races; as also in the western group, in which we have to take into account elements of the Assyroid, Indo-Afghan, and Arab races, and certain European races (Adriatic chiefly). The Turkish race may be thus described: Stature, above the average (1m. 67—1m. 68); head, hyper-brachycephalic (ceph. ind. on the liv. sub., 85 to 87), elongated oval face, non-Mongoloid eyes, but often with the external fold of eyelid (p. 78); the pilous system moderately developed; broad cheek-bones, thick lips; straight, somewhat prominent nose; tendency to obesity.[1]

The Turks are essentially nomadic, and when they change their mode of life it is rather towards the chase, commerce, or trade that their efforts are directed; the true cultivators of the soil (Taranchi, Sartes, Osmanli, Volga Tatars) are Turks already powerfully affected by intermixtures. The Turkish tent is the most highly finished of transportable habitations (p. 164-166). Meat and milk products form the staple foods, as they do among all nomads. With the exception of the Christian Chuvashes and the Shaman Yakuts, all the Turks are Mussulmans; but often they are only nominally such, at bottom remain-

[1] For statistics as to stature, ceph. index, etc., see Appendices I. to III.; these figures are borrowed from the works of Benzengre, Bogdanof, Chantre, Elissiéef, Erckert, Hecker, Kharuzin, Lygin, Malief, Merejkovsky, Nazarof, Païssel, Pantiukhof, Sommier, Ujfalvy, Vyrubof, Weisbach, Weissenberg, Yadrintzef, etc. (Cf. Deniker, *Les Races de l'Europe*, I. Ind. ceph., Paris, 1899.)

ing Shamans. The veneer of Islamism becomes thinner and thinner among the Turkish peoples as we go from west to east. The Osmanlis, the most fanatical of all the Turks, are the most mixed as regards type, language, manners, and customs. It is perhaps to this mixed origin that they owe the relative stability of the state which they have founded, for no nomadic Turkish tribe has been able to create a political organism of long duration, and the vast empires of the Hiungnu, the Uigurs, the Kipchaks, have had only an ephemeral existence.

2. The *Mongols*[1] form an ethnic group more homogeneous as regards manners and customs and physical type than the Turks. Their name is chiefly known on account of the great empire founded by Genghis Khan, but it must be observed that the nomadic hordes united into a single body, and led to victory by this conqueror, were only very partially composed of Mongols, other nomadic peoples, and especially Turks, formed more than half of them. Hence the practice among Europeans, as among the Chinese,—a practice which is kept up to the present time,—of giving the name of one of the Turkish tribes, Ta-ta or Tatar, transformed into *Tartar*, to the Mongols, and extending it to many of the Mongoloid peoples, like the Tunguses for example.

Three principal divisions are recognised in this group: Western Mongols or Kalmuks, the Eastern Mongols, and the Buriats.[2] The *Western Mongols*, who style themselves

[1] Pallas, *Samml. Hist. Nachricht.*, St. Petersburg, 1776-1801, 2 vols.; Bergmann, *Nomad. Streifereien. u. d. Kalmuk*, Riga, 1804, 4 vols.; Howorth, *History of Mong.*, London, 1877, 4 vols.; Deniker, *loc. cit.* (*Rev. Anthr.*, 1883-84); Ivanovsky, *loc. cit.* (Mongols-Torg.); Potanin, *loc. cit.*; A. Pozdniéef, *Mongolia, etc.* (Mongolia and the Mongols, in Russian), St. Petersburg, 1896, vol. i., and other publications of this learned writer.

[2] In many works to these three divisions of Mongols are also added the so-called *Hezare* or *Hazara* and the *Aimaks*, tribes styled Mongolian, left by Tamerlane in Afghanistan. It appears that at the present time these tribes have only preserved of their origin a few physiognomical features; they speak a Turkish dialect and have intermixed with the Jemchids, whose mode of life and religion they have adopted.

Eleuts, and whom the neighbouring peoples call *Kalmuks*, are scattered, owing to wars and migrations, over the immense tract lying between Siberia and Lassa, from the banks of the Hoang-ho to those of the Manich (a tributary of the Don). The more compact groups are found in European Russia (Kalmuks of Astrakhan, Figs. 20 and 44, and the Caucasus); in Dzungaria (the *Torgoots*) and north-western Mongolia, between Altai and Thian-Shan; lastly, in Alashan and farther to the west in the Chinese province of Kuku-Nor and northern Thibet. They number about a million.

The *Eastern Mongols* occupy almost the whole of the region known by the name of Mongolia properly so called. In the south of this country they are broken up into a multitude of tribes (*Tumets*, *Shakars* or *Tsakhar*, etc.); while in the north they form a single nation, that of the *Khalkhas*, which has still preserved, in spite of its submission to China, some traces of its ancient political organisation. The Khalkhas number about 200,000, and the southern Mongols 500,000.

The *Buriats* form a population sprung from the Khalkhas, intermixed at several points with various Siberian elements, Tunguse, Yakut, Russian; they occupy the steppes and forests of the province of Irkutsk, but their central seat is Transbaikal, whence they spread out even into Mongolia, into the valleys of the Orkhon and the Argun. They number about 250,000.

The type of the *Mongolian race* is very strongly marked among most of the Kalmuks and Khalkhas; it is less distinct among the Buriats, etc. It may thus be described: Nearly average stature (1m. 63-64); head, sub-brachycephalic (ceph. ind. on the liv. sub. 83); black straight hair, pilous system little developed; the skin of a pale-yellow or brownish hue, prominent cheek-bones, thin straight flattened nose, Mongoloid eyes (p. 77), etc.

With the exception of some Buriat tribes the Mongols are typical nomadic shepherds. Their live-stock, camels, sheep, and horses supply them not only with food, the raw material for the manufacture of tents and garments, but also means of transport and fuel (camel excrement or dried dung). Unlike the nomadic Turks, who are fond of fighting, the Mongols of the present day are gentle and peaceable folk. Can this be the effect of the influence of Lama-Buddhism, which they all profess except a few small Buriat tribes, who have remained Shamans? We are inclined to believe this when we consider the important part which this religion plays in the daily life of the Mongols.

3. *Thibetans.*[1]—We may include under this name the non-Mongolian populations of Thibet and the surrounding countries, known by the name of *Bod*, or *Thibetans properly so called* in southern Thibet, by the name of *Tanguts* in the Chinese province of Kuku-Nor, of *Si-fan* in western Sechuen, by that of *Ladaki* and *Champa* in eastern Cashmere (province of Leh), of *Gurong*, *Limbu*, *Mangar* and *Murmi* in Nepal, of *Lepchas* or *Rongs* in Sikkin, of *Bhutani* in Bhotan, etc. The *Abors*, *Mishmee*, etc., of the Himalayan country who dominate Assam are also included among the Thibetans, but they approach the Indonesians in type. It is the same with the *Garro* and their neighbours on the east, the *Khasia* or *Djainthia*, whose language, however, differs from the Thibetan.[2]

Most Thibetans are cultivators of the soil or shepherds, pillagers in case of need, and fervent votaries of numerous Lamaite-Buddhist sects, of which that of the Geluk-pa (yellow caps) represents the ruling church. Its chief, the Dalai-Lama, residing at Lassa, is at the same time the sovereign of Thibet.

[1] Cf. Prjevalsky, *Trétie, etc.* (Third Journey in Central Asia), St. Petersburg, 1883; and *Jour. Geog. Soc.*, 1886-87; Rockhill, *The Land of the Lamas*, London, 1891; *Ethnol. of Tibet*, Washington, 1895; and *Rep. U.S. Nat. Mus. for 1893*, p. 665; Desgodins, *Le Tibet*, 2nd ed., Paris, 1885; Waddell, *Buddhism of Thibet*, London, 1895; and *Among the Himalayas*, London, 1899.

[2] See Dalton, *Descrip. Ethnol. of Bengal*, p. 13 *et seq.*, Calcutta, 1872. We leave untouched the peoples sprung from the intermixture of the Thibetans with the Mongols (*Kara-Tanguts* of the Kuku-Nor), with the Iranians and the Hindus (*Balti*, of Cashmere, etc.), with the Punjabi Hindus (*Gurkhas*, *Nepalese*), with the Assam peoples (*Dophlas*, *Miris*, etc.).

From the somatological point of view the Thibetans exhibit certain sufficiently marked variations. The Bothia are below the average stature (1m. 62 or 1m. 63); the Lepchas are short (1m. 57); and the Thibetans of Nepal vary as regards average stature from 1m. 59 (Mangars) to 1m. 67 (Murmis). The head is mesocephalic (ceph. ind. 80.7 on the liv. sub.), but sub-dolichocephalic or sub-brachycephalic forms are frequently met with. As a general rule, side by side with the Mongoloid type may be seen among the Thibetans, singly or united, the traits of another type, a somewhat slender figure, thin, prominent, often aquiline nose, straight eyes with undrooping eyelids, long and sometimes wavy hair, reminding one, in short, of the Gypsy type.[1] This type, moreover, is found beyond Thibet. The *Lo-lo* or *Nèsus*, as they call themselves, of western Sechuen and the north-east of Yunnan, with whom we must connect the *Kolo* or *Golyk* of the country of Amdo (east of Thibet), perhaps represent it in its purest form, if the portrait of them drawn by Thorel is correct. With slight figure, brownish complexion, they have a straight profile, oval face, high forehead, straight and arched nose, thick beard even on the sides of the face and always frizzy or wavy hair.[2] Their language, however, fixed by a hieroglyphic mode of writing, appears to belong to the Burmese family.[3] The Lo-lo not under Chinese rule are of a gay disposition; they love dancing and singing. Woman is held among them in great respect; there are some tribes even whose chiefs belong to the weaker sex.

We must connect with the Lo-lo a multitude of other tribes, less pure in type: the various *Miao-tsè*, mountaineers of the southern part of the province of Hunnan, of Kwei-chow, of

[1] Prjevalsky, *loc. cit.*; Risley, "Tribes and Castes of Bengal," *Anthr. Data*, Calcutta, 1891, 2 vols.; Rockhill, *loc. cit.*; Dutreuil de Rhins, *loc. cit.*

[2] Fr. Garnier, *Voyage . . . en Indo-Chine*, Paris, 1873, vol. i., p. 519, and vol. ii., p. 32 (*Memoir of Thorel*).

[3] Colb. Baber, "Travels . . . in West China," *Supp. Pap. Geogr. Soc.*, vol. i., London, 1882; Colquhoun, *Across Chryse*, London, 1883, vol. ii., Appendix.

the northern part of the Kwang-si, the north-west district of Kwang-tung, more or less intermixed with the Chinese; the *Lissus* of the Lu-tse-Kiang (Upper Salwen) and the Lantsan-Kiang (Upper Mekong), near to the new boundary of China and British India; the *Mosso* or *Nashis* of the district of Li-Kiang to the east of the Lissus, related to the latter and having an iconomatic writing; lastly, the *Lu-tse* or *Kew-tse*, who call themselves *Melams* or *Anoogs*, to the west of the Lissus and separated by an inhabited tract from the *Mishmee*, the *Sarong* and other Thibeto-Indonesian tribes. The language of the Lu-tse differs from that of any of the neighbouring peoples, and their physical type places them between the Lissus and the Indonesians, such as the Naga for example; they are short (1m. 56 according to Roux), but strong and vigorous; their hair is frizzy.[1] The *Mu-tse* mentioned by Terrien de Lacouperie, the *Lawa* or *Does* described by Holt Hallet, the *Muzours* of T. de Lacouperie or the *Musos* of Archer, the *Kas-Khuis* of Garnier, scattered between the Mekong and the Salwen from the twentieth to the twenty-fifth degree of north latitude, are probably akin to the Lo-lo and the Mossos.[2]

III. Populations of Eastern Asia.—The far east of Asia is inhabited by three nations of mixed origin: Chinese, Coreans, Japanese.

1. The *Chinese* form by themselves alone more than the third, if not the half of the population of Asia. They occupy in a solid mass the whole of China properly so called, and

[1] Roux, *Le Tour du Monde*, 1897, 1st half, p. 254. The adorning of the body and limbs with rings, so characteristic of the Dyaks and other Indonesians, is also found among the Lu-tse; they wear around the loins and limbs numerous iron wire rings coated with black wax and fastened together in two places with metal rings. Great phalanstery-like houses, 40 metres long, similar to those of certain Indonesians and Polynesians, and used by several families, in which men and women sleep promiscuously, are met with among the western *Kew-tse* on the boundary of their country with the *Khamti* (see p. 40).

[2] Terrien de Lacouperie, *The Languages of China before the Chinese*, p. 92, London, 1887; Fr. Garnier, *loc. cit.*; H. Hallet, *Proc. Geogr. Soc.*, p. 1, London, 1886 (with map).

stretch in isolated groups far beyond the political limits of the "eighteen provinces." Manchuria, Southern Mongolia, Dzungaria, a portion of Eastern Turkestan and Thibet have been invaded by Chinese colonists; and outside of the Empire it is estimated there are not less than three millions of "Celestials" who have emigrated to Indo-China, Malaysia, the two Americas, and even to the islands of the Pacific Ocean and Africa.

The Chinese people have sprung from manifold intermixtures, and indeed there are several types to discover in this nation, the anthropological study of which is scarcely more than outlined; as it is, however, according to historical data we may presume that five or six various elements enter into its composition.

We know from the books of Shu-King that the primitive country of the Chinese was the north of the present province of Kan-su. Thence the agricultural colonists moved (about the year 2200 B.C., according to a doubtful chronology) into the fertile valley of the Houng-ho and its tributary the Wei or Hwei. Little by little, the Chinese colonists spread along other valleys, but it took them centuries to conquer the aboriginal tribes (the *Djoong*, the *Man*, the *Pa*, the *Miao-tse*). Again in the seventh century B.C. (when exact chronology commences) the territory occupied by the Chinese scarcely extended beyond the valley of the lower Yang-tsi on the south and that of the Pei-ho on the north, and comprised within these limits several aboriginal tribes like the *Hoai*, of the valley of the same name, or the *Lai* of the Shantung peninsula, who maintained their independence. However that may be, the Chinese succeeded, little by little, in driving back the first occupiers of the soil into the mountains of the west and south, where they are still found under the names of *Man-tse*, *Miao-tse*, *I-gen*, *Mans*, *Thos*, etc.[1]

While this work of driving back was carried on in the south, the Turkish tribes, the Tunguses, the Mongols, the Manchus,

[1] See the summary of the data in this respect in Richthofen, *China*, vol. i., Berlin, 1875, and in Reclus, *Geogr. Univ.*, vol. vi., Paris, 1882.

invaded in turn the north of the country. Thence resulted a marked difference between the northern and the southern Chinese, while the Chinese of the central parts have perhaps best preserved the original type (Fig. 119). The Chinese of the south belong very largely to the southern Mongolian race (p. 293); they are short, sub-brachycephalic, except in Kwang-si, where mesocephaly predominates, in consequence,

FIG. 118.—Educated Chinaman of Manchu origin, interpreter to Embassy, twenty-one years old, height 1m. 75. (*Coll. Mus. Nat. Hist. Paris.*)

probably, of intermixtures with the aborigines of Indonesian race (H. Girard); while the Chinese of the north are on the contrary almost tall of stature; the head is sub-brachycephalic with a tendency towards mesocephaly in the north, towards brachycephaly in the south (Fig. 118). The skin is lighter among the former than among the latter, the face more elongated, etc. One of the peculiarities of the Chinese skull is the retreating forehead, and the contraction at the level of the temples.[1]

The multiplicity of dialects is equally great. The Chinese of the various provinces would have long since ceased to understand one another had they not possessed as a medium of communication the common signs of the written language (p. 141), which the mandarins read in their own dialects and

FIG. 119. — Leao-yu-chow, Chinese woman, born at Foo-chow, eighteen years old, height 1m. 52. (*Coll. Mus. Nat. Hist. Paris.*)

languages not only in China but also in Corea, in Japan, and Indo China. We distinguish the *Mandarin*, or *northern*, *dialect* (with which we connect the Hakka speech employed in Kwang-tung) and that of the *south*, then the dialects of Fu-

[1] See in the appendices the statistics of stature, ceph. index, etc., from the works of Girard, Hagen, Janka, Poyarkof, Ten Kate, Weisbach, Zaborowski and my own observations.

Kian, of Che-Kiang, etc. The peculiarities of the Chinese character—filial love, attachment to the soil, aptitude for agriculture and commerce, peaceful disposition, love of routine, respect for letters, observance of form, etc.—are sufficiently known.[1] Most of them are the corollaries of ancestor-worship, of the very rigorous patriarchal régime and the constitution of the commune (p. 248), the basis of the whole social fabric of the Chinese Empire, which, let it be said by the way, exhibits less organic cohesion than is generally supposed. The frequent co-existence of belief in three religions, Taoism, Confucianism, and Buddhism or Foism, in one and the same individual is one of the remarkable facts of Chinese sociology. Another fact, not less interesting, is the administrative and political mechanism inspired theoretically by very wise and moral ideas, but leading in practice to peculation and carelessness on the part of public officials of which we find it difficult to form any idea in Europe.

2. The *Coreans*, who by their civilisation are connected with China, have in all probability sprung from the intermixture of Tunguse, Indonesian, and Japanese elements. The men are of tall stature,[2] strong, with sub-brachycephalic head (ceph. ind. on the liv. sub. 82.3, according to Elissiéef, Koganei, and Bogdanof). The women are more puny, and are not conspicuous for beauty; they have a yellowish complexion, small eyes, prominent brow, and very small feet, but not deformed like those of the Chinese (p. 175). The Corean values only one physical charm in woman, and that is her abundant head of hair and eyebrows, "fine as a thread" (Mme. Koïke). Besides, woman is of no account in Corean society; she

[1] Note also the inferior position of woman, her ability to move about limited by deformation of the feet (p. 175).

[2] The exact figures for the height of Coreans are contradictory: Dr. Koïke (*Internat. Arch. Ethnogr.*, vol. iv., Leyden, 1891, Parts I. and II.) gives the excessively high stature of 1m. 79 as the average of seventy-five men measured; while Elissiéef ("*Izviestia*" *Russ. Geogr. Soc.*, St. Petersburg, 1890) found 1m. 62 the average height, but according to the measurements of ten men only.

is an instrument of pleasure or work; she is kept strictly apart from men, rarely leaves the house, and must veil her face.

The Corean language belongs to the Uralo-Altaic family, and is closely related to the Southern Tunguse dialects. Its mode of writing, called *wen-mun*, differs from the Chinese, and appears either to have been invented or derived from the Sanscrit by the Buddhist monks (M. Courant).

The Coreans have no state religion. Buddhism, introduced towards the close of the fourth century, has not taken root among them, and is more and more in danger of extinction. Most Coreans live in a sort of irreligion tempered with some animistic practices: sacrifices to the spirits of the forests and mountains, etc. The Corean civilisation was borrowed entire from China of the fifth or sixth century. The associative tendency, and regard for form and ceremony, are perhaps stronger in Corea than in China. Further, enslavement for debt, crime, etc., exists as a regular thing in the country.[1]

3. The *Japanese* exhibit, like so many other peoples, a certain diversity in their physical type; the variations fluctuate between two principal forms. The *fine* type (Figs. 16 and 120), which may chiefly be observed in the upper classes of society, is characterised by a tall, slim figure; a relative dolichocephaly, elongated face, straight eyes in the men, more or less oblique and Mongoloid in the women, thin, convex or straight nose, etc. The *coarse* type, common to the mass of the people, is marked by the following characters: a thick-set body, rounded skull, broad face with prominent cheek-bones, slightly oblique eyes, flattish nose, wide mouth (Bälz).[2] These

[1] W. Carles, *Life in Corea*, London, 1888; Gottsche, "Land. u. Leute in Korea," *Verh. Ges. Erdk.*, p. 245, Berlin, 1886; A. Cavendish and Goold-Adams, *Korea*, London, 1894; Pogio, *Korea*, trans. from the Russian, Vienna and Leipzig, 1895; L. Chastaing, "Les Coréens," *Rev. Scientif.*, p. 494, 1896, second half-year; Maurice Courant, *Bibliogr. Coréenne*, Introduc., vol. i., Paris, 1895; and *Transact. As. Soc. Japan*, vol. xxiii., p. 5.

[2] See Appendices I. and III. for the measurements given from Miss Ayrton, Bälz, Koganei, etc.

FIG. 120.—Young Japanese women taking tea; *fine* type. (*Phot. lent by Collignon.*)

two types may have been the result of crossings between Mongol sub-races (northern and southern) and Indonesian or even Polynesian elements. The influence of the Ainu blood is shown only in Northern Nippon.[1]

In a general way the Japanese are of short stature (1m. 59 for men, 1m. 47 for women), rather robust and well proportioned. The colour of the skin varies from pale yellow, almost white, to brownish yellow. The Japanese have no colour in their cheeks, even when their skin is almost white; at birth there is an accumulation of pigments on the median line of the belly and pigmental spots (see p. 51). The pilous system is scantily developed, except in cases where an admixture of Ainu blood may be suspected. The head is mesaticephalic as a rule (ceph. ind. on the liv. sub. 78.2), with a tendency to brachycephaly in the gross type, to dolichocephaly in the fine type. The skull, which is capacious, exhibits two peculiarities: the *os japonicum* (p. 68) and the particular conformation of the upper jaw, which is very low and broad, without the canine fossa. With regard to Japanese writing, see p. 141.

The most striking traits of the Japanese character are politeness and aptness in concealing the emotions; it must not be inferred from this that their nature is bad; on the contrary, they are honest, hard-working, cheerful, kind, and courageous (Mohnike, Mechnikof).[2] European civilisation and the re-

[1] It might be supposed that the representatives of the first type were the descendants of tribes who had come by way of Corea and the Tsu-shima and Iki-shima islands in the south-west of Nippon at some period unknown, but at any rate very remote. As to the coarse type, its representatives are perhaps descended from the warriors who invaded about the seventh century B.C. (according to a doubtful chronology) the west coast of the island of Kiu-siu and then Nippon. These invaders, intermixing with the aborigines of unknown stock, founded the kingdom of Yamato, and drove back the Ainus towards the north (see p. 372).

[2] The ancient practice of suicide in case of injury (*Harakiri*), now abolished, also denoted great courage; sometimes it was a disguised form of vendetta, for the relatives of the suicide were bound in honour to exterminate the offender.

forms introduced into Japan since 1868 have appreciably modified the manners and customs, but the essential traits of the national character remain unaltered, as they were previously unmodified by the introduction of the Chinese civilisation. The ancient chivalrous spirit of the aristocracy, holding trade

FIG. 121.—Tong King artisan of Son-tai, twenty-three years old. (*Phot. Pr. Rd. Bonaparte.*)

in contempt, still survives at the present day, and partly explains the ardour with which persons of this class have flung themselves into political life, since Japan obtained a parliamentary administration (1889). The Japanese have two religions, *Shintoism*, or the national worship of the *Kami* (native divinities), and Buddhism; but they are fundamentally very sceptical on the subject of religion.[1]

The *islanders* of the *Liu-Kiu* or *Loo-choo* archipelago resemble the Japanese (Chamberlain), but they have a thicker beard and a darker complexion (Bälz); they are of short stature (1m. 58, according to Dr. Furukawa), and Wirth has even noted among them a tribe of pigmies 1m. 30 in height in the island of Okinava.

As to the *natives of Formosa*, the Chinese, who have colonised half of the island, divide them into *Pepo-hoan* ("mellowed" or tamed savages) and *Sek-kuan* or *Che-hoan* (raw or uncivilised savages). The former are met with almost everywhere, but chiefly in the north and west of the island, the latter have been driven back into the mountains of the interior and to the south coast. The Che-hoan are split up into several tribes (*Atayal*, *Vonum* in the north, *Pai-wan*, *Sarisen*, *Butan* in the south, *Amia* on the east coast, etc.), and remind us of the Indonesians by their type as well as by several customs (skull-hunting, tattooing, ear-ornaments, house in common or "Palankan"). Some of these "savages" are acquainted with agriculture, others live by the product of the chase. The languages of all these Formosans belong to the Malay family, especially approximating to the Tagal.[2]

IV. Populations of Indo-China.—We must distinguish in the transgangetic peninsula the probable *Aborigines* and the peoples sprung from the interminglings of these aborigines with the invaders coming from the adjoining countries, and whose migrations are at least partly known to history. These

[1] Mohnike, *Die Japaner*, Münster, 1872; Bälz, *loc. cit.*; J. J. Rein, *Japan*, Leipzig, 1881-86, 2 vols.; Mechnikof, *L'empire Japonais*, Paris-Geneva, 1882; B. Chamberlain, *Things Japanese*, Yokohama, 1891; "Tokyo Jinruigaku," etc. (*Journ. Anthr. Soc. Tokio*, in Japanese), 1888-98.

[2] Dodd, *Jour. Str. Br. As. Soc.*, No. 15, p. 69, Singapore, 1885; I. Ino, "Distrib. géog. tribu. Formose," *Tokyo Jinruigaku*, p. 301, 1898 (analysed in *l'Anthropologie*, 1899); Imbault-Huart, *L'île de Formose*, Paris, 1893; A. Wirth, "Eingeborn. Stämme auf Formosa u. Liu-Kiu," *Peterm. Mitt.*, p. 33, 1898.

mixed populations are the *Annamese*, the *Thais*, the *Khmers* or *Cambodians*, the *Burmese*, and the *Malays*.

(1) *The Aborigines.*—The numerous populations scattered almost all over Indo-China having a right to this name may be mustered into eight groups, of which I proceed to give a short account.

a. The Mois.—We designate by this name the numerous so-called "savage tribes" dispersed over the table-lands and mountains between the Mekong and the Annamese coast, from the frontiers of Yun-nan to Cochin-China (district of Baria). In spite of the various names given to the Mois by the adjoining nations (they are called *Mois* in Annam, *Pennongs* in Cambodia, *Khas* in Laos, etc.), and of the multitude of tribes into which they are divided (the *Mo*, the *Sas*, the *Bruns*, the *Bolovens*, the *Lové*, the *Bannars*, the *Rdé*, the *Laté*, the *Thioma*, the *Trao*, etc.), the Mois exhibit a remarkable uniformity in physical type and manners (Neïs). They are as a rule short (1m. 57), and dolichocephalic (ceph. ind. on the liv. sub. 77); their skin is tan-like white in colour, reddish; their hair is more or less wavy, they have straight eyes, etc. In short, they differ as much from the Annamese as the Thai, and in all probability belong for the most part to the Indonesian race. Hunters or primitive husbandmen (the crop is gathered by picking with the hand the rice from the stalk; the cooking of the rice is effected in bamboos, which roast on the fire, etc.), they go almost naked and use only primitive arms, spears, poisoned arrows, etc. They are of fairly peaceful habits.[1]

b. The Kuis.—This name distinguishes two ethnic groups of Indo-China: one in the south-east of Siam and the north-west of Cambodia, the other in the country of Kieng-Tung or Xieng-Tong (Shan States, under British protection). The former appear to be aborigines like the Mois; the latter are simply a

[1] Dourisboure, *Les Sauv. Ba-Hnars*, Paris, 1873; Neïs, *Excurs. et Reconn.*, Saigon, Nos. 6 (1880), 10 (1881), and *Bull. Soc. Géogr.*, p. 372, Paris, 1884; Harmand, *loc. cit.*, and *Tour du Monde*, 1879 and 1880; Pinabel, *Bull. Soc. Géogr.*, p. 417, Paris, 1884.

branch of the *Lo-lo* or *Mosso* (see p. 381). The Kuis of Cambodia are in stature under the average (1m. 63), sub-brachycephalic (ceph. ind. on the liv. sub. 82), and have a darker skin than the Laotians (Harmand). Nearly all of them can

FIG. 122.—Khamti of Lower Burma, Assam frontier. (*Coll. Ind. Mus., London.*)

speak Cambodian and are forgetting their mother-tongue; they have the reputation of being skilful smiths.[1]

c. The *Mons* or *Talaing* are the remnants of a population which formerly occupied the whole of lower Burma, and have been driven back into the unhealthy region of the deltas of

[1] Aymonier, "Voyage dans le Laos," *Ann. Mus. Guimet.* (Bibl. d'Étude, vol. v.), vol. i., p. 38, Paris, 1895; Harmand, *loc. cit.*

the Irrawaddy, Sittong, and Salwen rivers; their territory has mostly been taken by a population sprung from the intermingling of the Mons with the Burmese.

The three groups of tribes which we have just enumerated speak monosyllabic dialects correlated as regards their vocabularies, at least so far as the words indicating numbers, the parts of the body, trades, etc., are concerned. These dialects further present analogies with the Khmer (p. 398) and Khasia languages (p. 380).[1]

d. The *Tziam* or *Chiam*, on the other hand, are closely allied to the Malaysian linguistic family. Their language, fixed by writing of Indian origin, reminds us of the dialects of the Philippines. About 130,000 in number, they inhabit the province of Binh-Tuan and several other points of Southern Annam, as well as Cochin-China (province of Baria, etc.) and Cambodia. They represent all that remains of a once powerful people, the founders of the empire of *Champa*, which extended over the whole of Annam, as it now is, and the southern part of Tong King. A section of the Tziam are Mussulmans, but the majority are animist. The physical type is handsome; nose almost aquiline, eyes without the Mongoloid fold, wavy or frizzy hair, dark skin. Contrary to what exists among other peoples of Indo-China, among the Tziams it is the woman who asks the hand in marriage.[2]

e. The *Karens*, who inhabit the upper valley of the Me Ping and the mountainous districts of Arakan, Pegu, and Tenasserim, the country between the Sittong and the Salwen (*red Karens*), probably came into Burma at a later date than the Mons; they maintain that they came thither from Yunnan about the fifth century of the present era. In stature they are under the average (1m. 64, according to Mason), and they exhibit traits

[1] E. Kuhn, *Sitzungsberichte, Phil.-hist. Kl. Bayer. Akad. Wiss.*, p. 289, Munich, 1889.

[2] Aymonier, *Excurs. et Reconn.*, Saigon, Nos. 8 and 10 (1881), 24 (1885), chap. viii., No. 32 (1890), and *Rev. d'Ethnogr.*, 1885, p. 158; Bergaigne, *Journ. Asiat.*, 8th series, vol. xi., 1888; Maurel, *Mem. Soc. Anthr.*, 1893, vol. iv., p. 486.

intermediate between those of the Malays and the Thai (see below). Numbering about a million, they are speedily becoming civilised while striving at the same time to preserve their independence.[1]

The *Khyens* or *Chin* of the mountains of Arakan and the *Tung-tu* of Tenasserim are Karens crossed with Burmese and Shans (p. 401). The *Lemets*, the *Does*, and the *Khmus* of Fr. Garnier (*Kamu* and *Kamet* of MacLeod) who inhabit the east of Luang-Prabang (French Laos), and perhaps the *Lavas* or *Does* of H. Hallet, mountaineers of West Siam, are related to the Karens or Khyens.

f. The *Nagas* of Manipur and the mountains extending to the north (Patkoi, Barai) of this country are Indonesians more or less pure both in physical type (Frontispiece and Fig. 17) and manners and customs. They may be sub-divided into *Angami*, *Kanpui*, etc., wearing the petticoat or apron, of the west; into *Lhota*, *Ho*, etc., wearing the plaid, of the centre; and into *Nangta*, or naked, of the east. Various ethnic peculiarities, skull-hunting and multicoloured hair or feather ornaments, long shields (Frontispiece), breast-plates, method of weaving, and houses in common (*Morong*), connect them with the Dyaks and other Indonesians. Tattooing prevails only among the tribes with a monarchical organisation (Klemm). The *Lushai*, who live at the south of Manipur, are Nagas mixed with Kyens and Burmese of Arakan. They may be sub-divided into several tribes: the *Kuki*, subject to the English, very short (medium height 1m. 57); the *Lushai* properly so called, partly in subjection (41,600 in Assam), somewhat slender (1m. 63), with brown skin, flat nose, prominent cheek-bones, husbandmen;[2] the *Saks*, *Kamis*, and *Shendons* or *Shaws*. West of the

[1] Mrs. Mason, *Civilising Mountain Men*, etc., London, 1862, and other works of this author. Smeaton, *The Loyal Karen*, etc., London, 1886.

[2] There exists among them a strange custom: the men experience great pleasure in putting into their mouths and then spitting out the juice from the narghiles smoked by the wives. The offer of *tobacco juice* is one of the first duties of hospitality.

Lushai dwell the *Tippera* and the *Mrows*, tribes of short stature (1m. 59), still more pronouncedly intermingled with the Burmese.[1]

g. The *Selungs* are also regarded as Indonesians; numbering but a thousand in all, they live in their canoes in the *Mergui* archipelago, wandering from island to island like veritable gypsies of the sea, after the manner of the *Orang-Sletar* of the

FIG. 123.—Black Sakai of Gunong-Inas (Perak, Malay Peninsula). (*Phot. Lapicque.*)

Straits of Singapore, now quite disappeared. In the same category we may also place the natives of the *Nicobar* islands,

[1] J. Butler, "Angami Nagas," *Jour. As. Soc. Bengal*, vol. xliv., p. 216, Calcutta, 1875; Woodthorpe, "Notes . . . Naga Hills," *Jour. Anthro. Inst.*, vols. ix. (1882) and xix. (1890); Reid, *Chin-Lushai Land*, Calcutta, 1893; Peal, "Naga," *Jour. Anthr. Inst.*, vol. iii., 1874, p. 476; *Nature*, 20th May 1897; *Jour. As. Soc. Bengal*, vol. lxv., part 3, p. 17, Calcutta, 1897; and "Ein Ausflug, etc.," *Zeit. f. Ethn.*, 1898, p. 281 (trans. by Klemm, with notes and bibliog.); Miss Godden, "Naga, etc.," *Jour. Anthr. Inst.*, vols. xxvi. and xxvii. (1896-97).

though among the latter we must distinguish (1) the *Nicobarese* of the small islands and the coasts of Great Nicobar who have intermixed with the Malays, and (2) the *Shom-Pen* of the interior of the latter island, savages of a somewhat pure Indonesian type.[1]

h. We must also include in this long list of the aboriginal peoples of Indo-China the *Negritoes*,[2] belonging to a distinct race, chiefly characterised by short stature, black skin, and frizzy or woolly hair (see p. 288). As genuine representatives of this race, only three tribes are known: the *Aeta*, who inhabit the Philippine islands (p. 483); the *Sakai* of the interior of the Malay peninsula; and the *Minkopis* of the Andaman islands.

The *Minkopis* or *Andamanese* (Fig. 124), of very short stature (1m. 49), sub-brachycephalic (ceph. ind 82.6 average on the skull and on the liv. sub.), are in the lowest scale of civilisation. They live in "chongs"—small roofs on four stakes (p. 160), go naked, and procure the strict necessaries of life by hunting, making use of a peculiar kind of bow (p. 263). In number they scarcely exceed five thousand (E. Reclus).

i. The pure *Sakai*, *Semangs* or *Menik* (as for example those of Gunong-Inas, Fig. 123) are the same height as the Minkopis (1m. 49), but their head is less round and their face more angular than those of the latter; they live likewise by hunting and by the gathering of honey, camphor, india-rubber, and other products of tropical forests, which they exchange with the Malays for tools, arms, etc. Several populations of the Malay peninsula, particularly the *Mintra*, the *Jakhuns* of Jokol, are Sakai-Malay half-breeds, as is shown by the light colour of their skin, their stature, higher than that of the Sakai, but still very short (1m. 54), their frizzy hair, etc.

[1] J. Anderson, *The Selungs*, Lond., 1890; Lapicque, *Bull. Soc. Anthr.*, 1894, p. 221, and "A la rech. des Negritos," *Le Tour du Monde*, 1895, 2nd half-year, and 1896, 1st half-year; Man, *Journ. Anthr. Inst.*, vol. xiv., 1886, p. 428; Roepstorff, *Zeitschr. f. Ethnol.*, 1882, p. 51.

[2] Man, "Aborig. Andam. Isl.," *Jour. Anthr. Inst*, vol. xi., 1882; De Quatrefages, *Les Pygmées*, Paris, 1887; Lapicque, *loc. cit.*, and "La race Negrito," *Ann. de Geogr.*, No. 22, Paris, 1896.

2. Let us pass on to the *mixed populations* of Indo-China, springing from the probable cross-breeds of the autochthones and the invaders.

The *Cambodians* or *Khmers* have the first place by seniority. At the present day they inhabit Cambodia, the adjoining parts of Siam, and the south of Cochin-China, but they formerly extended much farther. Two centuries ago, before the arrival of the Annamese, they occupied the whole of Cochin-China,

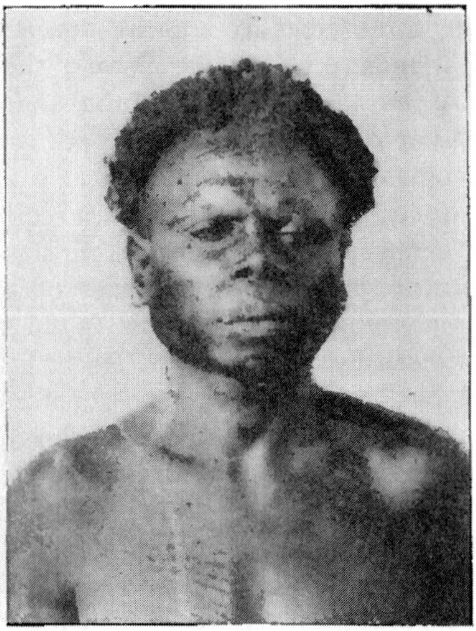

FIG. 124.—Negrito chief of Middle Andaman, height 1m. 49; cephalic ind. 83.4. (*Phot. Lapicque.*)

while to-day they are found in any considerable number only in the unhealthy and marshy regions of the Rach-gia, Soktrang, and Tra-Vinh districts, where their number equals or exceeds that of the Annamese. It may be conjectured that the Khmers have sprung from the intermixing of the Malays and Kuis, with an infusion of Hindu blood at least in the higher classes of society. The Cambodians are taller (1m. 65) than the Annamese and the Thai, but almost as brachycephalic (ceph. ind. on the liv. sub. 83.6); their eyes are rarely oblique, their hair is often wavy, etc. This population has preserved much of its primitive savagery in spite of the influence of several successive civilisations, of which remain the splendid monuments of Angkor-Vat, Angkor-Tom, etc.[1]

The population which chronologically succeeds the Cambodians is that of the *Annamese* (Fig. 121), the inhabitants of the delta in Tong King, of the coast in Annam, and most of Cochin-China. Some Annamese colonies are also found in Cambodia, in Laos, and among the Mois. The Annamese people, fifteen to seventeen millions strong at the present time, is the outcome of numerous interminglings. Of western origin, according to its traditions, that is to say akin to the Thai peoples, it came at an early period into the country which it now occupies. It found already installed there the Mois, the Khmers, and the Malays, which it succeeded in assimilating or pushing back into the mountains and the unhealthy regions; but it has had to support in its turn the continual immigrations of the Chinese who brought their civilisation to it. In spite of these complex interminglings the Annamese type is very uniform (Harmand). The men are short in stature (1m. 58), with slender limbs, brachycephalic head (ceph. ind. 82.8), of angular visage with prominent cheek-bones, and Mongoloid eyes.

The Annamese of Tong King are a little taller (1m. 59) and darker than those of Cochin-China and Annam (height 1m. 57); they have also a broader and flatter nose, the result perhaps of intermixture with the Thos mountaineers (p. 401) who live near them.[2] The social life of the Annamese is modelled on that of the Chinese; the village community and the patriarchal family form the base of it, in the same way as ancestor-worship is the religious foundation. Annamese Buddhism is only a colourless copy of Chinese Foism and has no great hold of the

[1] Moura, *Royaume de Cambodge*, Paris, 1883, 2 vols.; Aymonier, *Géographie du Cambodge*, Saigon-Paris, 1876; L. Fournereau and Porcher, *Les Ruins d'Angkor*, etc., Paris, 1890; Morel, *Mém. Soc. Anthr.*, vol. iv., Paris, 1893.

[2] Deniker and Laloy, "Races exot.," *L'Anthropologie*, 1890, p. 523.

people. Very docile, the Annamese are intelligent, cheerful, and well gifted, without being exempt from certain defects of character, common to all Asiatics of the far East, such as dissimulation, hypocrisy, and perfidy.

The *Burmese* or *Mramma* made a descent on Indo-China perhaps at the same time as the Annamese, from their original country, which is supposed to be the mountains of the south-east of Thibet. To-day they occupy Upper Burma, Pegu, and Arakan. In the last-mentioned country they bear the name of *Mag* or *Arakanese*, and differ a little from the true Burmese of Upper Burma, who are the purest representatives of the Burmese people. Like the Annamese, they have attained a certain degree of civilisation, mainly due to the influence of India. We find existing among them monogamy, the order of castes, and Buddhism of the south but slightly altered. The Mag are mesocephalic (ceph. ind. 81.8) and of short stature (1m. 61).[1]

The Thai.—The numerous peoples speaking different Thai dialects were the last arrivals in Indo-China. Their migrations may be followed from the first century B.C., when the *Pa-y* tribes came from Sechuen into Western Yunnan to found there the kingdom of Luh-Tchao. Another kingdom, that of Muang-ling, was founded more to the south-west in Upper Burma, etc. The recent researches of Terrien de Lacouperie, Colquhoun, Baber, Hosie, Labarth, Billet, H. Hollet, Bourne, Deblenne, and of so many others besides, enable us to show the relations which existed between these various Thai peoples and to assign the limits with sufficient exactitude to their habitat, which extends from Kwei-chow to Cambodia, between the 14th and the 26th degrees of N. latitude.[2]

[1] Risley, *loc. cit.*

[2] Terrien de Lacouperie, *loc. cit.*; Colquhoun, *loc. cit.*, Appendix and Preface by T. de Lacouperie; Bourne, *Parliam. Pap.*, C., 5371, London, 1888; C. Baber, *loc. cit.*; Hosie, *Three Years' Jour. in Western China*, London, 1890; Labarth, "Les Muongs," *Bul. Soc. Géogr. hist. et descr.*, Paris, 1886, p. 127; H. Hollet, *loc. cit.*; Aymonier, *loc. cit.*, ch. vii; Billet, "Deux ans dans le Haut Tonkin," *Bull. Scient. de la France et de la Belgique*, vol. xxviii., Paris, 1896-98; Deblenne, *Mission Lyonnaise en Chine*, p. 34, Lyons, 1898.

Four principal Thai peoples may be distinguished in this territory: the *Thos-Muong* in the north-east (Tong King and China), the *Shans* in the north-west (Upper Burma), the *Laotians* in the south-east (French Laos), and the *Siamese* in the south-west (Siam).

We put together, under the name of *Thos-Muong*, all the natives of Upper Tong King and the Tong King hinterland (except the mountain summits occupied by the *Mans*, allied probably to the Lo-lo), as well as the primitive inhabitants of Kwang-si, Southern Kwei-chow, and Eastern Yunnan, now driven back to the mountains. The Thos inhabiting Tong King to the east of the Red River (basin of the Claire River), are sub-brachycephalic (ceph. ind. 82.5), of lofty stature (1m. 67),[1] having elongated face, straight non-Mongoloid eyes, and brownish complexion. They partly recall the Indonesians, and partly the still mysterious race to which the Lo-lo belong (p. 381). They are husbandmen, living in houses on piles, and wearing a very picturesque costume different from that of their ancient masters the Annamese. The *Muongs* of Tong King to the west of the Red River (basin of the Black River), the *Pueun* and the *Pu-Thai* of Annamese Laos resemble them both in type and in language, which is a Thai dialect very much altered by Chinese and Annamese. The *Tu-jen*, the *Pe-miao*, the *Pa-i*, forming two-thirds of the population of Kwang-si, and found in the south of Kwei-chow and the north-west of Kwangtung, as well as the *Pe-jen* or *Minkia* of Yunnan, are Thos slightly crossed with Chinese blood in the same way as the *Nongs* of Tong King, the neighbours of the Thos. Most of these peoples have a special kind of writing, recalling that of the *Laotians*. The latter, as well as the *Shans*, differ somewhat from the Thos in regard to type, in which we may discern interminglings with the Indonesians, Malays, Mois, and Burmese. Among the Shans we must distinguish the *Khamti* (Fig. 122), a very pure race, and the *Sing-po* with the *Kackyen* or *Katchin*, somewhat

[1] From Dr. Girard, quoted by Billet, *loc. cit.*, p. 69.

intermixed with the Burmese, both of them races of mountaineers of the northern parts of Upper Burma, between the Lu-Kiang (upper Salwen) and the Lohit-Brahmaputra. The upper valley of the latter river is inhabited by the *Assamese* or *Ahoms*, cross-breeds between the Shans and Hindus, speaking a particular dialect of the Hindi language. The *Laotians* are sub-brachycephalic (83.6) and of short stature (1m. 59); those of the north tattoo their bodies like the Shans. They are husbandmen, shepherds, and hunters.[1]

It is perhaps among the *Siamese* that the primitive Thai type has been most changed by intermixture with the Khmers, Kuis, Hindus, and Malays. In stature above the average (1m. 61), very brachycephalic (ceph. ind. 85.5) with olive complexion, they have prominent cheek-bones, lozenge-shaped face, and short flattish nose. They are fervent votaries of southern Buddhism, and are the most civilised of the Thai. They have succeeded in preserving their relative independence and forming a state in which several reforms of European character have been attempted in recent times.

V. THE POPULATION OF INDIA represents about a third of the inhabitants of Asia (287,223,431 inhabitants according to the census of 1891). It is sub-divided into a hundred tribes or distinct peoples, but this multiplicity of ethnic groups is rather apparent than real, and they may easily be incorporated into a small number of somatic races or linguistic families; these groups frequently represent castes alone.

Caste is indeed an institution peculiar to India. Of ancient origin, this institution has developed very considerably, assuming the most varied forms. Springing from a Hindu or Brahman source, it penetrated little by little the other ethnic and religious groups of the peninsula, and one might say that it is the basis of the social organisation for four-fifths of the population of India, despite of the fact that its power is declining at the present day beneath the strong hand of British rule. About 2000 castes may be enumerated at the present

[1] Harmand, *loc. cit.*; Aymonier, *loc. cit.* (Voyage au Laos).

day, but year by year new ones are being called into existence as a certain number disappear.[1]

The names of these castes are derived either from hereditary occupations (tanners, husbandmen, etc.); from a geographical source (Pathani, etc.), or a genealogical one—from a supposed common ancestor; or, especially among the Dravidians, from

FIG. 125.—Gurkha of the Kus or Khas tribe, Nepal; mixed Indo-Thibetan type. (*Coll. Ind. Mus., London.*)

objects or animals singled out as *totems* (p. 247). The essential characteristics of all castes, persisting amid every change

[1] The so-called primitive division into four castes: Brahmans (priests), Kshatriya (soldiers), Vaisyas (husbandmen and merchants), and Sudra (common people, outcasts, subject peoples ?), mentioned in the later texts of the *Vedas*, is rather an indication of the division into three principal classes of the ruling race as opposed, in a homogeneous whole, to the conquered aboriginal race (fourth caste).

of form, are endogamy within themselves and the regulation forbidding them to come into contact one with another and partake of food together (Sénart). Endogamy within the limits of the caste implics, as a corollay, exogamy among the sections of the caste. The typical form of these sections is the "gotra," an eponymous group reputed to be descended from a common ancestor, usually from a *rishi*, a priest or legendary saint.

Outside of this endogamic rule marriage is forbidden in all castes between relatives to the sixth degree on the paternal side and to the fourth degree on the maternal side. Caste has no religious character; men of different creeds may belong to it. It is ruled by a chief and a council (*panchâyet*), and has not limits as rigid as is commonly supposed; the way is smoothed by compromises and liberal interpretations of rules for rich and clever people to pass from a lower to a higher caste.

In this way or some other a man may rise from one caste to another: in Mirzapur many Ghonds and Korvars have become Rajputs, etc. (Crooke). Employment is by no means the criterion of caste, as is very often supposed. "Those who have seen Brahmans," says Sénart, "girdled with the sacred cord, offer water to travellers in the railway stations of India, who have seen them drilling among the sepoys of the Anglo-Indian army, are prepared for surprises of this kind."[1] And in conclusion the castes do not always agree with ethnic and somatic divisions.[2]

Side by side with caste another characteristic institution of

[1] Senart, "Les Castes dans l'Inde," *Ann. Mus. Guimet.*, *Bibl. de Vulgar*, Paris, 1896 (sums up the question). To the bibliographic references to castes which are found in this excellent book must be added the "Introduction" to the work of W. Crooke, already quoted; it appeared subsequently.

[2] The ingenious deductions of Risley (*loc. cit.*, *Ethnogr. Glossary*, vol. i., Preface, p. 34, Calcutta, 1892), which may be summed up in the aphorism, "The nasal index increases in a direct ratio to the social inferiority of the caste," have been criticised by Crooke (*loc. cit.*, p. 119), who however is too absolute in his statements, and does not take any account of the seriation of anthropometric measurements.

FIG. 126.—Group of Paniyan men and children of Malabar. (*Phot. Thurston.*)

the Cisgangetic Aryan or Aryanised peoples must be noted; it is the village (*grama*) with common proprietorship of the

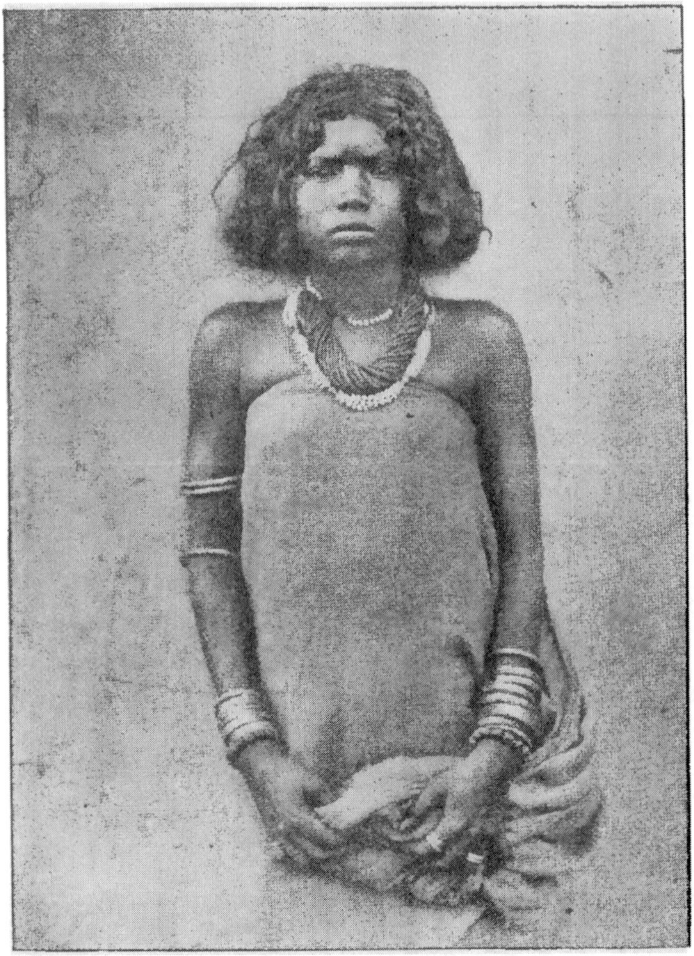

FIG. 127.—Young Irula girl. (*Phot. Thurston.*)

soil and family communities, on which I cannot dilate for want of space (see p. 247).

India was the cradle of two great religions which have

become international, Brahmanism and Buddhism. This fact deserves to be borne in mind on account of the impress left on these two religions by the national Hindu character. The foundation of both is formed of those characteristically Hindu beliefs,—the ideas of metempsychosis, final deliverance, and the doctrine of the moral world, which form a contrast with the Semitic religions. Brahmanism is professed by about three-fourths (72 per cent.) of the inhabitants of India, while

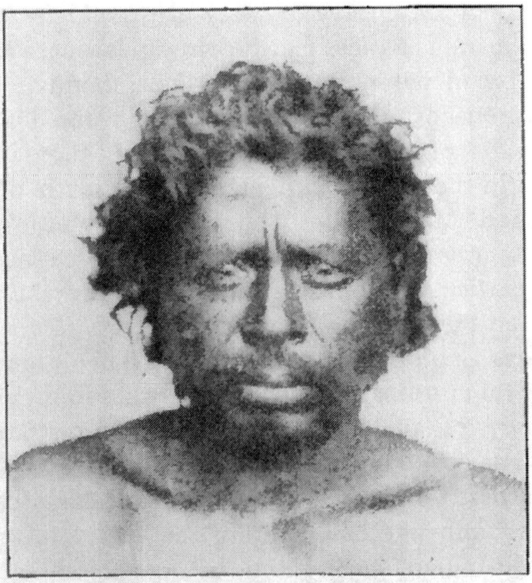

FIG. 128.—Santal of the Bhagalpur hills.
(*Coll. India Museum, London.*)

Buddhism and its derivative Jainism only number, apart from the island of Ceylon, three per cent. of the total population of the peninsula. The most widespread religion after Brahmanism is Islamism (20 per cent. of the whole population of India).

From the somatological point of view it may be affirmed to-day, after the excellent works of Risley, Crooke, Thurston, Sarasin, Schmidt, Jagor, Mantegazza, etc., that the variety of types found in the country is due to the crossing of two indigenous races, Indo-Afghan and Melano-Indian or Dravidian, with the admixture here and there of foreign elements: Turkish and Mongol in the north, Indonesian in the east, Arab and Assyroid in the west, and perhaps the Negritoid element in the centre. The Indo-Afghan race, of high stature, with light brown or tanned complexion, long face, wavy or straight hair, prominent and thin nose, dolichocephalic head, predominates in the north-west of India; the Melano-Indian or Dravidian race, also dolichocephalic but of short stature, with dark brown or black complexion, wavy or frizzy hair, is chiefly found in the south. In it two sub-races may be distinguished: a *platyrhinian* one, with broad flat nose, rounded face, found in the mountainous regions of Western Bengal, Oudh and Orissa, also at several points of Rajputana and Gujarat, then in Southern India, and in the central provinces to the south of the rivers Narbada and Mahanadi. The other sub-race, *leptorhinian*, with narrow prominent nose, and elongated face may be noted in some particular groups, especially among the Nairs, the Telugus, and the Tamils.[1]

1. *Melano-Indians or Dravidians.*—This group, at once somatological and linguistic, includes two sub-divisions, based on differences of language: the division of Kolarians, and that of Dravidians properly so called.

a. Kolarians.[2]—The numerous tribes speaking the languages of the Kol family and belonging to the platyrhinian variety of the Melano-Indian race, more or less modified by interminglings, occupy the mountainous regions of Bengal and the provinces of the north-west. Certain of these tribes, of the purest type, like the *Juang* or *Patua* of Keunjhar and Dhenkanal (Orissa), are distinguished by very short stature (1m. 57),

[1] E. Schmidt, "Die Anthrop. Indiens," *Globus*, vol. lxi. (1892), Nos. 2 and 3. For the measurements of the different peoples of India see Appendices I. to III.; the figures are chiefly borrowed from Risley, *loc. cit.*, Crooke, *loc. cit.*, Jagor, Thurston, *loc. cit.*, Sarasin, *loc. cit.*, E. Schmidt, *loc. cit.*, Deschamps, *Au pays des Veddas*, Paris, 1892, with pl.

[2] Jellinghaus, "Sagen, Sitten . . . der Munda-Kolhs," *Zeit. f. Ethn.*, vol. iii., 1872, p. 328; Dalton, *loc. cit.*, p. 150; Risley, *loc. cit.*, *Ethnogr. Glossary*; Crooke, *loc. cit.*

zygomatic arches projecting outwards, and flat face, as well as by certain ethnic characters; they go nearly naked, live on the products of the chase and the fruits and roots gathered; they also practise a little primitive cultivation by burning the forests, etc. The *Kharia* of Lohardaga (Chota Nagpur), who resemble the Juang in type, language, and tattooings (three lines above the nose, etc.), are partly civilised; some cultivate the ground with a plough, have a rudimentary social constitution, etc. The other Kols are, for the most part, still further advanced. Such are the *Santals* or *Sonthals* (Fig. 128) of Western Bengal, of Northern Orissa, and of Bhagalpur, who call themselves "Hor"; the *Munda* or *Horo-hu* of Chota Nagpur; the *Ho* or *Lurka-Kols* of the district of Singbhum (Bengal); lastly, the *Bhumij* of Western Bengal, all probably sections of one and the same people, formerly much more numerous.[1] The Kols of the north-west provinces (height 1m. 64; ceph. ind. 73.2, according to Risley and Crooke) are closely allied to the groups which I have just mentioned. The *Savaras* or *Saoras*, scattered over Orissa, Chota Nagpur, Western Bengal, and as far as the province of Madras, speak a language which Cunningham, Cust, and Fr. Müller consider Kolarian, while, according to Dalton, it belongs to the Dravidian family properly so called. Physically, they resemble the Malé Dravidians, and exhibit the tolerably pure type of the platyrhinian sub-race of the Melano-Indians.[2] The same

[1] The word Ho (Hor or Horo), which recurs in the name of all these tribes, signifies everywhere "man," and indicates their close linguistic relationship; their manners and customs are also alike, especially in regard to the constitution of the community. Religion among them all is an animism blended with very vague polytheism. In their physical characters there are some differences; the Munda and the Bhumij are short (1m. 59) and very dolichocephalic (ceph. ind. on the liv. sub. 74.5 and 75), the Santals are below the average height (1m. 61) and a little less dolichocephalic (76.1). The *Ho*, among whom we may assume a greater infusion of Indo-Afghan blood, are of somewhat high stature (1m. 68). The number of these four tribes, united under the name of Santals in the census of 1891, amounted to a million and a half.

[2] Ball, *Jungle Life in India*, p. 267; Fawcet, "The Saoras of Madras," *Journ. Ant. Soc. Bombay*, vol. i., 1888, p. 206; E. Dalton, *loc. cit.*, p. 149.

doubt exists in regard to the linguistic affinities of the *Bhils* of Central India and the north-west provinces.

b. Dravidians properly so called.—They may be divided into two groups, those of the north and those of the south.

Dravidians of the North.—These are in the first place the *Malé* (plural *Maler*) or *Asal Paharia* of the Rajmahal hills (Bengal), probably one of the sections of the Savara people (see above);[1] the *Oraons* (523,000 in 1891), several tribes of which are also found in the north-west of Chota Nagpur; lastly, the *Gonds* (three millions) of the Mahadeo mountains and part of the central provinces situated farther south, between the rivers Indravati and Seleru, tributaries of the Godavari. To the east of the Gonds dwell the *Khands* and the *Khonds* (600,000), who have spread into Orissa.

All these tribes have scarcely got beyond the stage of hunters or primitive husbandmen, who set their forests on fire in order to sow among the ashes. In this respect the *Korwa* of Sarguja, of Jashpur (Bengal), and Mirzapur (north-west province) resemble them, if they are not even more uncivilised. They are unacquainted with clothes of any kind, obtain fire by sawing one piece of wood with another, and have an animistic religion much less developed than that of the Gonds or Oraons.[2]

Dravidians of the South.—To the south of the Godavari dwell five black, half-civilised peoples, having a particular form of writing, professing Brahmanism, and showing an intermingling of two varieties of the Melano-Indian race. Side by side with them, and among them, are found a number of small

[1] They must not be confused with the *Mal-Paharia*, who dwell farther to the south in the same district of Santhal Parganos (Bengal), and whose affinities are still obscure; from the somatic point of view there is, however, hardly any difference between the two groups.

[2] They must not be confounded with the *Kharwar* or *Kharvar*, Dravidians of Chota Nagpur, the southern parts of Behar and Mirzapur; these are half-civilised husbandmen, having a particular social organisation. Their higher castes have an infusion of Hindu blood, while the type of the lower castes recalls that of the Santals. The *Kûrs* of the Mahadeva hills are closely allied to the Kharwar.

tribes more or less uncivilised and animistic, having somatic types of considerable variety.

The five half-civilised Dravidian peoples are the *Telingas* or *Telugus* of the Coromandel coast, of Nizam and Jarpur (some twenty millions); the *Kanaras* of the Mysore table-land (about ten millions); the *Malayalim* of the Malabar coast (nearly six millions); the *Tulus* of Mangalore (350,000); lastly, the Tamils, occupying the rest of Southern India and the north of Ceylon (about fifteen millions).

As to the uncivilised tribes, some occupy the Anamalli hills (the *Kader*, the *Madavars*), others inhabit Travancore (*Pulaya*, *Paligars*, *Tir*, *Shanar*, etc.). Also to be noted are the *Choligha*, at the foot of the Mysore hills, the *Paniyans* (Fig. 126) of Vaïnad or Vinad (Malabar coast), very short (1m. 57), dolichocephalic (ceph. ind. on the liv. sub. 74), and very platyrhine (nas. ind. 95 1); lastly, the very interesting *tribes* of the *Nilgiri hills*; the *Irulas* (Fig. 127) and, above these, the *Kurumbas* (Fig. 8), on the southern and northern slopes; the *Badagas*, the *Kotas*, and the *Todas* on the plateau crowning these heights.[1]

The *Kurumbas* and the *Irulas* (58,503 in 1891) are of short stature (1m. 58 and 1m. 60), dolichocephalic (ceph. ind. on the liv. sub. 75.8), and platyrhine (nas. ind. 87 and 85). They are the half-savage tribes of the jungles.

As to the tribes of the plateau, they are distinguished according to their occupation and type. The *Badagas* (29,613 in 1891) are husbandmen, the *Kotas* (1,201) are artisans, and the *Todas* (Figs. 7, 129, and 130) shepherds. The two former approximate to the other Dravidians in type; they are of average height (1m. 64 and 1m. 63), hyper-dolichocephalic (ceph. ind. on the liv. sub. 71.7 and 74.1), and mesorhine (nas. ind. 75.6). But the Todas present a particular type:

[1] Cf. Shortt, *Account of the Tribes of the Nilghiris*, 1868; Marshall, *A Phrenologist among the Toda*, London, 1873; Elie Reclus, *Primitive Folk*, ch. v.; Thurston, *Madras Gov. Museum Bullet.*, vol. i., No. 1, and vol. ii., No. 4; G. Oppert, *The Original Inhabitants of India*, London, 1894, and *Zeit. f. Ethnol.*, 1896, pt. 5.

high stature (1m. 70), associated with dolichocephaly (ceph. ind. on the liv. sub. 73.1) and mesorhiny (nas. ind. 74.9), somewhat light tint of skin, and the pilous system very developed (Figs. 129 and 130). In short, they appear to belong to the Indo-Afghan race, with perhaps an admixture of the Assyroid race. Besides, a number of customs and manners (group marriage, aversion to milk, rude polytheism,

FIG. 129.—An old Toda man of Nilgiri hills. (*Phot. Thurston.*)

etc) differentiate them from the other populations of India. They are a very small tribe, which, however, increases from year to year (693 individuals in 1871, 736 in 1891).

2. The *Aryans of India* form the greatest portion of the population to the north of the Nerbada and Mahanadi; they speak different dialects of the neo-Hindu language (ancient Bracha language, branch of the *Prakrit* or corrupt vulgar Sanscrit). The following are the principal dialects: the

Hindi, *Bengali*, *Punjabi*, *Kashmiri*, *Guzrati*, and *Sindi*. We distinguish several ethnic groups by these dialects, or the generic names designating aggregations of castes: *Brahmans*, *Rajputs* (10½ millions), *Jats* and *Gujars* (9 millions altogether), *Katis* (42,000); or by their religion, as the *Sikhs*, renowned for their warlike disposition, and recognising, at least theoretically, no castes.[1]

The root-stock of all these populations is formed by the Indo-Afghan race. This race we find again in almost a pure state among the Sikhs (stature 1m. 71, ceph. ind. in the liv. sub. 72.7, nas. ind. on the liv. sub. 68.8), and a little weakened among the Punjabi (height, 1m. 68, ceph. ind. 74.9, nas. ind. 70.2). Among the Hindus of Behar, of the north-west provinces and Oudh, among the Mahratis between the river Tapti and Goa, the type is still more changed in consequence of interminglings with the Dravidians; the stature becomes shorter (1m. 63 and 1m. 64), the head rounder (ceph. ind. 75.7), the nose broader (nas. ind. 80.5 and 74), the complexion darker, etc.[2] With the Indo-Aryans are grouped, according to their type and language, the Kafirs or Siahposh of Kafiristan, and the *Dardi* or *Dardu*, occupying the countries situated more to the east, between the Pamirs on the north, Kashmir on the south, Kafiristan to the west, and Baltistan to the east—that is to say, Chitral, Dardistan (Yassin, Hunza, Nagar), Gilghit, Chilas, Kohistan. The Dardis are divided into four castes or tribes (Biddulph); that of the *Chins*, forming the majority of the people, is distinguished by its short stature and its dark complexion, and recalls the Hindus of the north-west provinces (Ujfalvy); while another tribe, called *Yeshkhun*, speaks a language which, according to Biddulph, has affinities with the Turkish languages, and, according to Leitner, is a

[1] The name *Rajputs* is only honorary, and is attached to a crowd of tribes and castes varying in origin, in mode of life, and in dress. The Jats of the Punjab, of which the Sikhs are only a section, are constituted of a mixture of strongly differentiated populations.

[2] Risley, *loc. cit.*; Crooke, *loc. cit.*; Fonseca Cardoso, "O indigena de Satory," *Revista de Scien. Naturæs*, vol. iv., No. 16, Oporto, 1896.

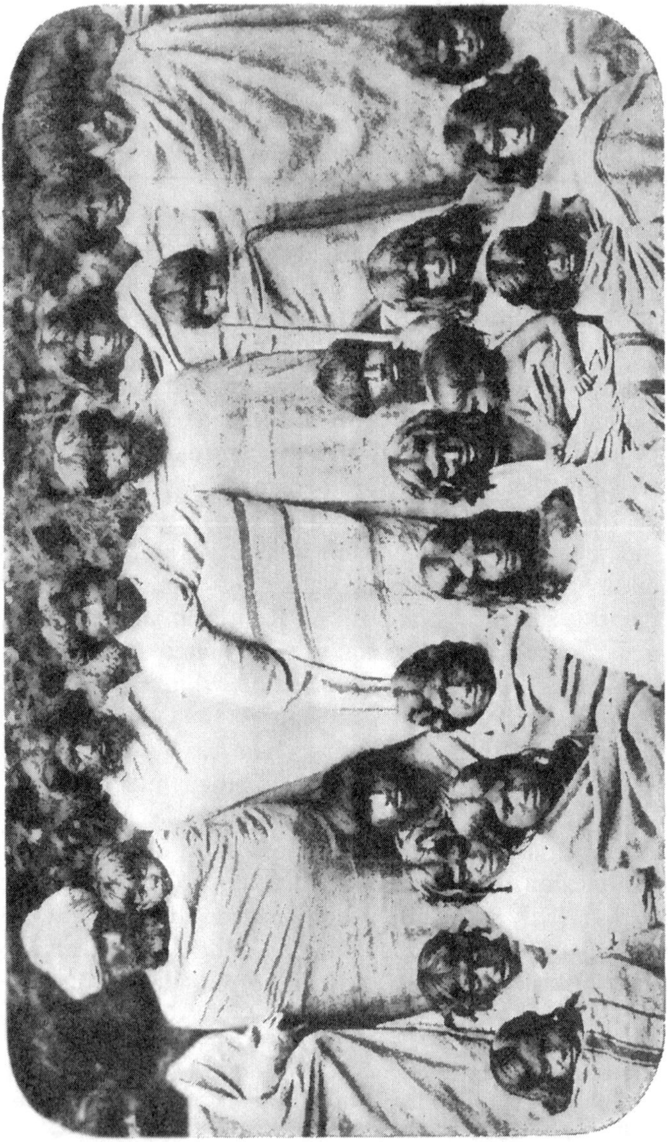

FIG. 130.—Group of Todas of Nilgiri Hills. (*Phot. lent by Deyrolle.*)

non-Aryan agglutinative language presenting analogies with Dravidian dialects. The Yeshkhuns inhabit Dardistan. Biddulph affirms that one may often encounter among them individuals with light and especially red hair. The forty-four Yeshkhuns and Chins measured by Ujfalvy were below the average height (1m. 61), dolichocephalic (ceph. ind. 75.8), with black wavy hair, fine shaped nose, and rather dark skin; while nineteen "*Turki-Dardi*" of Hunza-Nagar and Yassin measured by Risley and Capus give a stature above the average (1m. 69), and the cephalic index almost mesocephalic (77). They are thus closely allied to the *Chitrali* (stature 1m. 67, ceph. ind. 76.9 from six subjects only, measured by Risley).[1] Most of the Dardu tribes are endogamous; polygamy is general. In certain tribes there are to be found survivals of polyandry and of the matriarchate.[2]

The *Baltis*, neighbours of the Dardus on the east, speaking a Thibetan dialect, and the *Pakhpuluk* of the other side of the Kara-Korum (upper valley of the Karakash), speaking a Turkish tongue (Forsyth), are a mixture of Indo-Aryan and Turkish races. On the other hand, in the Himalayan region, the *Nepalese* (the *Kulu-Lahuli* and *Paharias* on the west, the *Khas*, the *Mangars* and other *Gurkhas*, Fig. 125, on the east), speaking a neo-Hindu language, have sprung from the intermingling of Indo-Afghan and Mongolic races (by the Thibetans). There are in India other peoples among whom linguistic or somatological affinities with the Indo-Aryans are found. Such are the *Nairs* of Malabar, a conglomerate of various castes and tribes, well known by their marriage customs (p. 232), many of these tribes forming a

[1] Biddulph, *Tribes of the Hindoo-Koosh*, Calcutta, 1880; De Ujfalvy, *Aus dem Westl. Himalaya*, Leipzig, 1884; Leitner, *The Hunza and Nagar Handbook*, London, 1893; Capus, *Manuscript Notes;* Risley, *loc. cit.*

[2] The brother of the dead husband may marry all the latter's widows, and none of them has the right to marry again without the consent of her brother-in-law. There is no term in the Chin and Yeshkhun languages to denote nephews and nieces—they are called "sons or daughters"; aunts on the maternal side are called "mothers."

contrast with the Dravidians by their fine type, their light complexion, their thin and prominent nose.[1]

FIG. 131.—Singhalese of Candy, Ceylon, twenty-seven years old; ceph. ind. 72.4. (*Phot. Delisle.*)

The *Singhalese* (Figs. 131 and 132) of the south of Ceylon speak a fundamentally Aryan language. They have certain

[1] De Ujfalvy, "Les Koulou," *Bull. Soc. Anthr.*, 1882, p. 217; Forsyth, *Yarkand Mission*, Calcutta, 1875; S. Mateer, *Native Life in Travancore*, London, 1883; Elie Reclus, *loc. cit*, p. 143 (Nairs); E. Schmidt, "Die Naïrs," *Globus*, vol. lxviii. (1895), No. 22; Waddell, *loc. cit.* (*Am. Himal.*), chap. ix.

traits in common with the Indo-Afghans and the Assyroids, but their type has been affected by the neighbourhood of a

FIG. 132.—Same subject as Fig. 131, seen in profile.
(*Phot. Delisle.*)

small mysterious tribe, that of the *Veddahs* (Figs. 5, 6, and 133), driven back into the mountains of the south-west of Ceylon. This is the remnant of a very primitive population whose physical type approximates nearest to the platyrhine variety of the Dravidian race, at the same time presenting certain peculiarities. The Veddahs are monogamous; they live in caves or under shelters of boughs (p. 160), hiding themselves even from the Singhalese.[1]

VI. PEOPLES OF ANTERIOR ASIA.—The multitude of peoples, tribes, castes, colonies, and religious brotherhoods of Iran, Arabia, Syria, and Asia Minor, this crossing-place of ethnic migrations, are chiefly composed in various degrees of the

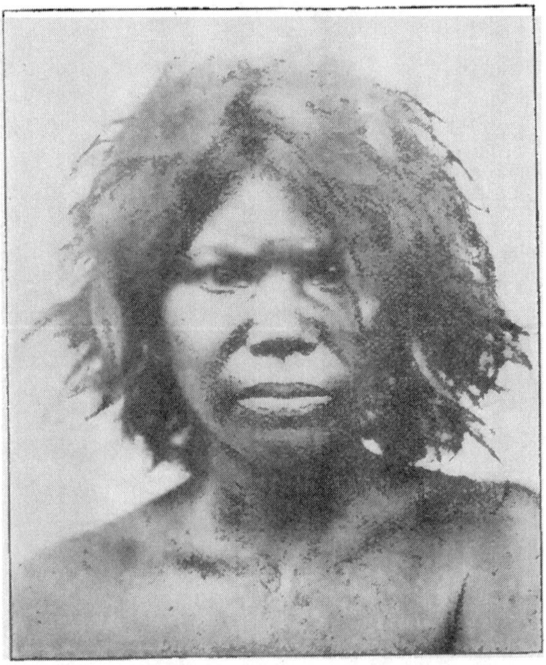

FIG. 133.—Tutti, Veddah woman of the village of Kolonggala, Ceylon; twenty-eight years old, height 1m. 39. (*Phot. Brothers Sarasin.*)

three races—Indo-Afghan, Assyroid, and Arab, with the addition of some other foreign races, Turkish, Negro, Adriatic, Mongolic, etc.

From the linguistic point of view, this multitude may perhaps be reduced to two great groups: the Eranians or Iranians and

[1] Sarasin, *loc. cit.*, gives bibliog.; Deschamps, *Ceylan*, *loc. cit.* For the measurements of these peoples, see the Appendices I. and II.

the Semites, if we exclude some peoples whose linguistic affinities have not yet been established.

1. The *Iranians* or *Eranians* occupy the Iranian plateau and the adjoining regions, especially to the east. They speak different languages of the Eranian branch of the Aryan linguistic family. In physical composition the main characters are supplied by the Assyroid race (Fig. 22) with admixture of Turkish elements in Persia and Turkey, Indo-Afghan elements in Afghanistan, and Arab and Negroid elements in the south of Persia and Baluchistan.

Among Iranian peoples the first place, as regards number and the part played in history, belongs to the *Persians*. They may be divided into three geographical groups. If within the approximate limits of Persia of the present day a line be drawn running from Astrabad to Yezd and thence towards Kerman, we shall have on the east the habitat of the *Tajiks*, on the west that of the *Hajemis* (between Teheran and Ispahan[1]), and that of the *Parsis* or *Pharsis* (between Ispahan and the Persian Gulf). The *Tajiks*, moreover, spread beyond the frontiers of Persia into Western Afghanistan, the north-west of Baluchistan, Afghan Turkestan and Russian Turkestan, as far as the Pamirs (*Galcha*), and perhaps even beyond. In fact, the *Polu* and other "Turanians" of the northern slope of the Kuen Lun, while speaking a Turkish language, bear a physical resemblance to the Tajiks (Prjevalsky). Like the *Sartes*, settled inhabitants of Russian Turkestan, and the *Tats* of the south-west shore of the Caspian, and the *Aderbaijani* of the Caucasus, they are Persians more or less crossed with Turks, whose language they speak.

The *Tajiks* are brachycephalic (ceph. ind. 84.9), above the average height (1m. 69), and show traces of intermixture with the Turkish race,[2] while the *Hajemis* (Fig. 22), and in

[1] The Hajemis of the Caspian littoral are called more particularly *Talych* and *Mazandarani*.

[2] The interminglings with the Turks must be of recent date; for if we may still discuss the "Turanian" characters of the Sumero-Acadian *language*, there is no indication of the existence of the *Turkish race* in

some measure the *Parsis*, who are dolichocephalic (77·9), and of average height (1m. 65), are of the Assyroid or Indo-Afghan type.

The *Parsis* are not very numerous in Persia. Most of them emigrated into India after the destruction of the empire of the Sassanides (in 634); they form there an important and very rich community (89,900 individuals in 1891), having still preserved their ancient Zoroastrian religion. This community, if chiefly composed of bankers, has also many men of letters. The education of women in it is specially looked after, the first woman to obtain the diploma of Doctor in Medicine in India being a Parsi.[1] Physically they are of the mixed Indo-Assyroid type, the head sub-brachycephalic (ceph. ind. 82, according to Ujfalvy).

After the Persians come the Pathan Afghans[2] or *Pashtu.* They form the agricultural population of Afghanistan, and are divided into *Duranis* (in the west and south of the country), *Ghilzis* (in the east), and into several other less important tribes: the *Swatis*, the *Khostis*, the *Waziris*, the *Kakars*, etc. The Afghans of India and the Indo-Afghan frontier are divided into several tribes, of which the principal ones are the *Afridis* near the Khyber pass and the Yusafzais near Peshawar.[3]

The *Baluchis* or *Biloch* of Baluchistan and Western India speak an Eranian dialect akin to Persian; physically they belong to the Indo-Afghan race, but mixed with the Arabs on the south and the Jats and the Hindus on the east, with the Turks

Asia Minor in ancient times. The famous sculptured head of Tello (in the Louvre) has a false Turkish air, owing to the head-dress and the broken nose; three other statuettes from the same locality, preserved at Paris, have a fine and prominent nose and meeting eyebrows: Assyroid characters (see De Clercq, *Album des Antiq. de la Chaldée*, Paris, 1889-91; Maspero, *Hist. des peupl. Orient. Class.*, vol. i., p. 613, Paris, 1895; and E. de Sarzec, *Découvertes en Chaldée*, published by Heuzey, Paris, 1885-97).

[1] D. Menant, "Les Parsis," *Ann. Mus. Guin.*, *Bibl. Et.*, vol. vii., Paris.

[2] E. Oliver, *Across the Border*, *Pathan and Biloch*, London, 1890.

[3] For the measurements of the Iranians see Appendices I. to III. (from Danilof, Houssey, Ujfalvy, Bogdanof, Chantre, Troll, Risley).

on the north and the Negroes on the south-west. The *Mekrani* of the coast of Baluchistan and partly of Persia are a mixture of Indo-Afghan, Assyroid, and Negro races (Fig. 134). The *Rinds* ("Braves") of the same coast of Mekran, who claim to be pure Baluchis, are only Arabs of the Kahtan tribe.[1] The nomadic *Brahuis* of Eastern Baluchistan, especially those of the environs of Kelat, resemble the Iranians. It is said that

FIG. 134.—Natives of Mekran (Baluchistan): on the right, Afghan type; on the left, the same with Negro intermixture. (*Phot. Lapicque.*)

their language has some affinities with the Dravidian dialect. In reality, the ethnic place of this population, predominant in Beluchistan, is yet to be determined.

With the Iranian group it is customary to connect, especially from linguistic considerations, the Kurds, the Armenians, and the Ossets (p. 356). The first-mentioned people, influenced here and there by interminglings with the Turks,

[1] Möckler, "Origin of Baluch," *Proc. As. Soc. Bengal*, 1893, p. 159.

physically resemble the Hajemis: sub-dolichocephalic head, 78.5 when it is not deformed (p. 176), height above the average (1m. 68), aquiline nose, etc. They occupy in a more or less compact mass the border-lands between Persia and Asia Minor; but they are found in isolated groups from the Turkmenian steppes (to the north of Persia) to the centre of Asia Minor (to the north-west of Lake Túz-gól). As to the *Armenians* or *Hai*, they are found in a compact body only around Lake Van and Mount Ararat, the rest being scattered over all the towns of the south-west of Asia, the Caucasus, the south of Russia, and even Galicia and Transylvania. It is a very mixed and heterogeneous ethnic group as regards physical type. The stature varies from 1m. 63 to 1m. 69 according to different localities, but the cephalic index is nearly uniformly brachycephalic (85 to 87). The predominant features are however formed by the Indo-Afghan, Assyroid, and perhaps Turkish and Adriatic races. Their language differs appreciably from the other Eranian tongues.[1]

2. The *Semite* linguistic group is represented by Arabs, Syrians, and Jews.

The *Arabs* occupy, besides Arabia, a portion of Mesopotamia, the shores of the Red Sea, the eastern coast of the Persian Gulf, and the north of Africa. The pure type, characterised by dolichocephaly (ceph. ind. 70), prominence of the occiput, elongated face, aquiline nose, slim body, etc., is still preserved in the south of Arabia among the *Ariba Arabs*, among the mountaineers of Hadramaout and Yemen (country of the ancient *Himyarites* or *Sabeans*), and among the *Bedouins*,

[1] Chantre, *Rech. Anthr. As. Occid. Transcaucasie, Asie Min. et Syrie*, Lyons, 1895 (with pl. and fig.); and "Les Kurdes," *Bull. Soc. Anthr. Lyons*, 1897. The Lurs of Western Persia living south of the Kurds are akin to the latter; they may be divided into Luri-Kuchucks (250,000) or little Lurs in Luristan, and into Luri-Buzury, farther south, in Hazistan, a part of Fars. Their best known tribes are those of the *Bakhtyari* and *Maamaseni*. The Lurs are above the average height (1m. 68), and sub-brachycephalic (ceph. ind. 84.5), according to Houssay, Duhousset, and Gautier. Cf. Houssay, "Les Peuples de la Perse," *Bull. Soc. Anthr. Lyons*, 1887, p. 101; and Pantiukhof, *loc. cit.*

descendants of the *Ismaelites* of the interior of Central and Northern Arabia; but the tribes which have drawn nearer the coast or the valleys of Mesopotamia show signs of inter-minglings with populations of a predominant Assyroid or Turkish type, without taking into account, as at Haza and on the coast of Yemen, the Negro and Ethiopic influence. Typical nomads, having in the religion founded by Mahomet a national bond of union, the Arabs make their influence widely felt over the world. Traces of the Arab type are met with not only over the whole of Northern Africa (see p. 432), but also in Asia Minor, the Caucasus, Western Persia, in India; while numerous traces of the Arab language[1] and civilisation are found in Europe (Malta, Spain), in China, Central Asia, and in the Asiatic Archipelago. The *Melkits* and the *Wahabits* are two religious sects of Arabs.

The people of Syria and Palestine, known by the name of Syrians in the towns, of *Kufar* in the country, is the product of the interminglings of Arabs with descendants of Phœnicians and with Jews. It also forms the basis of numerous ethnic groups connected solely by religion, and of constituent elements often very heterogeneous: such are the *Maronites* of Western Lebanon, the *Nestorians*, the *Druzes* of Hermon and Djebel Hauran (Kurdish elements), among whom woman occupies a higher position than among other Asiatics; the *Metouali* (Shiah sect) of Tyre; the *Nazareans* or *Ansarieh*, who perhaps represent, along with the *Takhtaji* (Gypsy elements), the *Kizilbashes* and the *Yezides* or *Yezdi* (Kurdish elements) of Mesopotamia, the remains of the primitive population of Asia Minor, akin, according to Luschan, to the Armenians.[2]

The *Jews* are not very numerous (250,000) in Asia, and are found scattered in small groups throughout the world.

[1] The Arab tongue of the present day includes three dialects: *Western*, extending from Morocco to Tunis; *Central*, spoken in Egypt; and *Eastern*, spoken in Arabia and Syria.

[2] Petersen and Von Luschan, *Reisen in Lykien, etc.*, chap. xiii., Vienna, 1889; Chantre, *loc. cit.*

Even in the country which was formerly a Jewish State, Palestine, they scarcely exceed 75,000 in number at the present day. They are found in compact groups only in the neighbourhood of Damascus, at Jerusalem, and at the foot of the mountain-chain of Safed.

It is well known that to-day the Jews are scattered over the whole earth. Their total number is estimated at eight millions, of which the half is in Russia and Rumania, a third in Germany and Austria, and a sixth in the rest of the world, even as far as Australia. The great majority of Jews are unacquainted with *Hebrew*, which is a dead language; they speak, according to the country they inhabit, particular kinds of jargon, the most common of which is the Judeo-German. Physically the Jews present two different types, one of which approximates to the Arab race (Fig. 21), the other to the Assyroid. Sometimes these types are modified by the addition of elements of the populations in the midst of which they dwell;[1] but, even in these cases, many traits, such as the convex nose, vivacity of eye, frequency of erythrism (p. 50), frizzy hair, thick under lip, inferiority of the thoracic perimeter, etc., show a remarkable persistence. The Arab type is common among the Spanish Jews who practise the Sefardi rite, among the native Jews of the Caucasus, very brachycephalic however (85.5 ceph. ind., according to Erckert and Chantre),[2] and among those of Palestine, while the Assyroid type dominates among the Jews of Asia Minor, Bosnia, and Germany. These last, like the Jews of Slav countries, practise the Askenazi rite. The Jews of

[1] It is known, in fact, that the isolation of the Jews from the rest of the population is not always absolutely complete. There have been peoples of other races converted to Judaism: the Khasars in the seventh century, the Abyssinians (present *Falacha*), the Tamuls or "black Jews" (p. 115, note), the Tauridians of the *Karaite* sect, etc. (p. 222). Cf. J. Jacobs, "Racial Charact. . . . Jews," *Journ. Anth. Inst.*, vol. xv. (1885-86), p. 24; and Jacobs and Spielmann, *ibid.*, vol. xix. (1889-90).

[2] The Aissors or Chaldeans who migrated to the Caucasus are probably allied to these "Jews of the mountains"; they are also very brachycephalic (ceph. ind. 88) and of rather high stature (1m. 67) (Erckert, Chantre).

Bosnia, called Spaniols, coming from Spain by Constantinople, are under average height (1m. 63) and mesocephalic (ceph. ind. 80.1, Gluck); those of Galicia, Western Russia, and Russian Poland are shorter (1m. 61 and 62) and sub-brachycephalic (ceph. ind. 82); those of England are of the same stature (1m. 62), but mesocephalic (ceph. ind. 80).[1]

Along with the Jews we must put another people, also dispersed over nearly the whole earth, and of Asiatic origin, probably from India, to judge by the affinities of its language with the Hindu dialects—the *Gypsies*. They are found in India (*Banjars*, *Nats*, etc.), Persia and Russian Turkestan (*Luli*, *Mazang*, *Kara-Luli*, etc.), in Asia Minor (where are also found their congeners, the *Yuruks*); then in Syria (*Chingane*), in Egypt (*Phagari*, *Nuri*, etc.), and all over Europe, with the exception, it is said, of Sweden and Norway; they are found in considerable numbers in Rumania (200,000), Turkey, Hungary, and the south-west of Russia. In all they number nearly a million. The pure so-called "Black Gypsies" are of the Indo-Afghan race (stature 1m. 72, ceph. ind. on the liv. sub. 76.8), but very often they have intermingled with the populations in the midst of which they dwell.[2]

[1] See the art. "Juifs" in the *Dict. Géog. Univers.* of Vivien de Saint-Martin and Rousselet, vol. ii., Paris, 1884 (with bibliog.); Andree, *Zur Völkerkunde der Juden*, Bielefeld, 1881, with map; and publications of the *Soc. des Études Juives*, Paris. The measurements given in the Appendices are after Ikof, Chantre, Jacobs and Spielmann, Gluck, Kopenicki, Weissenberg, Weisbach, etc.

[2] See my art. "Tsiganes," in the *Dict. Géog. Univ.*, quoted above, vol. vi., 1893; Paspati, *Étude sur les Tchinghianê*, Constantinople, 1870; A. Colocci, *Gli Zingari*, Turin, 1889, with map; H. von Wlislocki, *Vom . . . Zigeuner-Volke*, Hamburg, 1890; and the publications of the Gypsy-Lore Society, London (1886-96).

CHAPTER XI.

RACES AND PEOPLES OF AFRICA.

ANCIENT INHABITANTS OF AFRICA—Succession of races on the "dark continent"—PRESENT INHABITANTS OF AFRICA—I. *Arabo-Berber or Semito-Hamite Group:* Populations of Mediterranean Africa and Egypt—II. *Ethiopian or Kushito-Hamite Group:* Bejas, Gallas, Abyssinians, etc.—III. *Fulah-Zandeh Group:* The Zandeh, Masai, Niam-Niam populations of the Ubangi-Shari, etc., Fulbé or Fulahs—IV. *Nigritian Group:* Nilotic Negroes or Negroes of eastern Sudan—Negroes of central Sudan—Negroes of western Sudan and the Senegal—Negroes of the coast or Guinean Negroes, Kru, Agni, Tshi, Vei, Yoruba, etc.—V. *Negrillo Group:* Differences of the Pygmies and the Bushmen—VI. *Bantu Group:* Western Bantus of French, German, Portuguese, and Belgian equatorial Africa—Eastern Bantus of German, English, and Portuguese equatorial Africa—Southern Bantus: Zulus, etc.—VII. *Hottentot-Bushman Group:* The Namans and the Sans—VIII. *Populations of Madagascar:* Hovas, Malagasi, Sakalavas.

THE term "Black Continent" is often applied to Africa, but it must not therefore be supposed that it is peopled solely by Negroes. Without taking into account the white Arabo-Berbers and the yellow Bushmen-Hottentots, which have long been known, it may now be shown, after a half-century of discovery, that the population of Africa presents a very much greater variety of types and races than was formerly imagined.

ANCIENT INHABITANTS OF AFRICA.—We are only just beginning to know something about prehistoric Africa. Egypt, that classic land of the oldest historic monuments of the earth, has yielded in late years, thanks to the excavations of Flinders Petrie, D'Amelineau, and above all, of De Morgan, a large quantity of wrought stone objects, similar in character to those of Europe, and if certain objections may still be raised in regard to the palæolithic period of Egypt, which is not dated by a fauna, we can scarcely deny the existence of the *neolithic* period in this country, the period which preceded or was contemporaneous with the earliest dynasties of which monuments have yet been discovered.[1]

Hatchets, knives, and scrapers of very rude palæolithic and neolithic types have been discovered in Cape Colony (W. Gooch, J. Sanderson); flint arrow-heads and implements of the Chellean type in the country of the Somalis, in the Congo Free State;[2] ironstone arrow-heads in the country of the Monbuttus (Emin Pacha). Numerous stone implements and weapons of various palæolithic types, much finer than the preceding, as well as neolithic hatchets, have been found in Algeria (at Tlemcen), in South Algeria (at El-Golea, etc.), and as far as Timbuctoo (Weisgerber, Lenz, Collignon, etc.). Lastly, Tunis presents a progressive series of palæolithic implements absolutely similar to those of Europe in several stations (at Gafsa and, in a general way, west from the Gulf of Gabes).[3] But all these finds are very isolated and too far removed one from another to enable us to

[1] Fl. Petrie and Quibell, *Nagada and Ballas*, London, 1896; De Morgan, *Recherches sur les Origines de l'Egypte*, Paris, 1897-98, 2 vols. See for summary of the question: S. Reinach, *L'Anthropol.*, 1897, p. 322; and J. Capart, *Rev. Université*, Brussels, 4th year (1898-99), p. 105. Let us remember while on this point that at the quaternary period lower Egypt was still covered by the sea, and that the climate of Egypt and the Sahara was much more humid than to-day (Shirmer, *Le Sahara*, p. 136, Paris, 1893). Most of the prehistoric finds in Egypt have been made on the table-lands, not covered by the alluvial soils of the Nile.

[2] W. Gooch, *Journ. Anthr. Inst.*, vol. xi. (1882), p. 124; Seton Karr, "Discov. of Evid. Paleolith. Age in Somaliland," *Journ. Anthr. Inst.*, vol. xxv. (1896), p. 271; X. Stainier, "L'âge de la pierre au Congo," *Annales Mus. du Congo*, 3rd series (Anthr.), vol. i., part 1, Brussels, 1899 (with plates).

[3] R. Collignon, "Les âges de la pierre en Tunisie," *Mater. Hist. Nat. Homme*, 3rd series, vol. iv., Toulouse, 1887; Couillault, "Station préhist. Gafsa," *L'Anthropologie*, vol. v., 1894, p. 530; Zaborowski, "Period néolith. Afr. du nord," *Rev. Ec. Anthr.*, Paris, 1899, p. 41.

infer from them the existence of one and the same primitive industry over the whole continent.[1] Numerous facts on the contrary, particularly the absence of stone implements among the most primitive of the existing tribes of Africa (with the exception of the perforated round stone with which the digging-stick is weighted, as well as the stone pestles met with among some Negro tribes), and the rarity of superstitions associated with stone implements, lead us to suppose that the stone age only existed on the dark continent in a sporadic state and in virtue of local and isolated civilisations. Further, the absence of bronze implements, outside of Egypt, leads us to suppose that the majority of the peoples of Africa, with the exception of the inhabitants of Egypt and the Mediterranean coast, passed from the age of bone and wood to that of iron almost without transition.

Several palæethnologists go so far as to think that the iron industry was imported into Europe from Africa. At all events skilful smiths (Fig. 135) are found in the centre of Africa among Negro tribes somewhat backward in other respects.

Historic data are lacking in regard to most of the peoples of Africa, especially for remote periods, except in Egypt. However, combining the various historic facts known to us with the recent data of philology and those, still more recent, of anthropology, we may assume with sufficient probability the following superposition of races and peoples in Africa.

The primitive substratum of the population is formed of Negroes, very tall and very black, in the north; of Negrilloes, brown-skinned dwarfs, in the centre; of Bushmen, short, yellow, and steatopygous, in the south. On this substratum was deposited at a distant but indefinite period the so-called Hamitic element of European or Asiatic origin, the supposed continuators of the Cro-Magnon race.[2] This element has been preserved in a comparatively pure state among the

[1] See for details, R. Andree, "Steinzeit Afrikas," *Globus*, vol. xli. (1882), p. 169; and X. Stainier, *loc. cit.*, p. 18.

[2] Recent discoveries of stone objects in Egypt have revived the question of Asiatic or European influence in Africa. While Flinders Petrie, De

Berbers, and perhaps has been transformed by interminglings with the Negroes, into a new race, analogous to the Ethiopian, with which we must probably connect the ancient Egyptians. The Berbers drove back the Negroes towards the south, while the Ethiopians, a little later, filtered through the Negroid mass from east to west. This infiltration continues at the present day.

A new wave of migration followed that of the Hamites. These were the southern Semites or Himyarites who crossed from the other side of the Red Sea. Probably as far back as the Egyptian neolithic period they began the slow but sure process of modifying the Berbers, Ethiopians, and Negroes of the north-east of Africa.

The Negro populations driven back towards the south were obliged to intermingle with the Negrillo pygmies, the Ethiopians, and Hottentot-Bushmen, and gave birth to the Negro tribes composing to-day the great linguistic family called *Bantu*. Bantu migrations, at first from the north to the south, then in the opposite direction and towards the west, have been authenticated.[1] As a consequence of the interminglings due to these migrations, the Negrilloes and the Hottentots have been absorbed to a great extent by the Bantus, and the rare representatives of these races, still existing in a state of relative purity, are to-day driven back into the

Morgan, and others suppose that Petrie's "new race" of the neolithic period which preceded Egyptian civilisation in the Nile valley is related to the Libyans coming from the north-west of Africa, and perhaps from Europe, Schweinfurth (*Zeitsh. f. Ethnol.*, 1897; *Verhandl.*, p. 263) thinks that these neolithic people were immigrants from Arabia (Semites?), who had come into the Nile valley from the south, through Nubia. The recent discovery of chipped flints in the country of the Somalis, as well as considerations of a botanic character, confirm this supposition, without excluding, however, the possibility of the arrival of the Libyans of the north-west in the palæolithic period, and the tribes of Syria and Mesopotamia in historic times. (Evidence: the "Hyksos" of the Egyptian annals, the presence of cuneiform tablets at Tel-el-Amarna, upper Egypt, to which attention was drawn by Sayce, etc.)

[1] Barthel, "Völkerbewegungen . . . Afrikan. Kontin.," *Mittheil. Verein Erdkunde*, Leipzig, 1893, with map.

FIG. 135.—Arts and crafts among the Kafirs. To the left, pottery making (coiling method); to the right, smiths and

most unhealthy and inhospitable regions of Central and Southern Africa. The last important invasion of alien peoples into Africa was that of the Northern Semites or Arabs. It was, rather, a series of invasions, ranging from the first century B.C. to the fifteenth century, when the climax was reached. The Arab tribes have profoundly modified certain Berber and Ethiopian populations from the somatic point of view as well as the ethnic. Moreover, the Arab influence under the form of Islamism continues to the present time its cnward march over the dark continent, making from the north-east to the south-west. The Guinea coast, the basin of the Congo, and Southern Africa alone have as yet remained untouched by this influence. Let us note in conclusion the Malay-Indonesian migration towards Madagascar, and the European colonisation begun in the seventeenth century.

EXISTING POPULATIONS OF AFRICA.—Putting on one side the Madagascar islanders and the European and other colonists,[1] the thousands of peoples and tribes of the "dark continent" may be grouped, going from north to south, into six great geographical, linguistic, and, in part, anthropological units: 1st, the Arabo-Berbers or Semito-Hamites; 2nd, the Ethiopians or Kushito-Hamites; 3rd, the Fulah-Zandeh; 4th, the Negrilloes or Pygmies; 5th, the Nigritians or Sudanese-Guinea Negroes; 6th, the Bantus; 7th, the Hottentot-Bushmen.[2]

[1] Jews and Maltese on the coast of the Mediterranean; Persians and Hindus on the east coast and the islands off it; a few hundred Chinese introduced into the Congo State and the Mauritius and Réunion islands. Among the Europeans, the *Boers* of Cape Colony, of the basin of the Orange river, and the Transvaal, as well as the Portuguese of Angola and Mozambique, are more or less intermingled with the natives. The English of the Cape, and the French of Algeria-Tunis, and the "Creoles" of the island of Réunion have kept themselves more free from intermixture. Finally, let us note the Spanish of Algeria-Morocco and the Canary Isles, the latter the hybrid descendants of the prehistoric Guanches, which are perhaps connected with the European Cro-Magnon race. (See S. Berthelot, "Les Guanches," *Mem. Soc. Ethnol.*, Paris, vols. i. and ii., 1841-45; Verneau, *Iles Canaries*, Paris, 1891.)

[2] Hartmann, "Les Peuples de l'Afrique," Paris, 1880 (*Bibl. Internat.*), a work written from a different standpoint from the present chapter.

I. The *Arabo-Berber* or *Semito-Hamitic* group occupies the north of Africa as far as about the 15th degree of lat. N., and is composed, as its name indicates, of peoples having as a base the Arab and Berber races. Under the name of *Berbers* are included populations varying very much in type and manners and customs, speaking either Arabic (Semitic language) or Berberese (Hamitic language). Three-fourths of the "Arabs" of Northern Africa are only Berbers speaking Arabic, and are the more "Arabised" in regard to manners and customs as they are nearer to Asia. The nomads of the Libyan desert and Tripoli have preserved fairly well the Berber type, but they have become Arabs in language and usages. In Tunis and Algeria the Arab influence is still very much felt in the south; in Morocco it is very trifling. From the social point of view, the contrast is great between the settled Berber and the nomadic Arab. To give but one example, the democratic *régime* of the former, based on private property, bears no resemblance whatever to the autocratic *régime* of the latter, founded on collective property. But all the Berbers are not of settled habits (example: the Tuaregs), and several tribes have adopted the Arab mode of life.[1]

Physically, the Algero-Tunisian Berber also differs from the Arab. His height is scarcely above the average (1m. 67), while the Arab is distinguished by his lofty stature. The Berber head is, generally speaking, not so long as the Arab, although both are dolichocephalic. The face is a regular oval in the Arab, almost quadrangular in the pure Berber. The nose is aquiline in the former, straight or concave in the latter, and moreover, the Berbers have a sort of transverse depression on the brow, above the glabella, which is not seen in the Arabs; on the other hand, they have not so prominent an occiput as the latter. This characterisation is quite general; in reality,

[1] See for details, Hanoteau and Letourneux, *La Kabylie*, etc., Paris, 1872-73; Quedenfeld, "Berberbevölkerung in Marokko," *Zeits. f. Ethn.*, vol. xx.-xxi., 1888-89; Topinard, "Les types de . . . l'Algérie," *Bull. Soc. Anthr. Paris*, 1881; Villot, *Mœurs, coutumes . . . des indig. de l'Algérie*, Algiers, 1888; Ch. Amat, "Les Beni-Mzab," *Rev. Anthr.*, 1884, p. 644.

among the Arabs, and especially among the Berbers, there is a very great variety of type. According to Collignon,[1] four Berber sub-races or types must be recognised. (1) The *Djerba* sub-race, characterised by short stature, globular head (ceph. ind. on the living sub. 78 to 81.7), is well represented in the populations of the south-east and the east Tunisian coast, as well as by certain *Kabyles*, by the *Mzabs*,[2] and the *Shawias* of the Aures. (2) The *Elles type*, dolichocephalic, with broad face, occupies the centre of Tunis and the east of Kabylia.

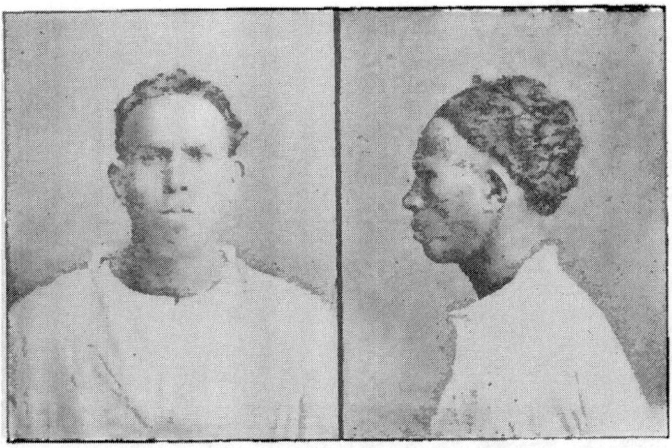

FIG. 136.—Tunisian Berber, Oasis type. Ceph. ind. 70. (*After Collignon.*)

(3) The *dolichocephalic Berber sub-race*, with narrow face and stature above the average, forms the present type in Algeria-Tunisia. (4) The *Jerid* or *Oasis type* (Fig. 136), of somewhat lofty stature and dark complexion, is well represented around the Tunisian "Shotts."

Among the nomadic Berbers we must mention separately

[1] Collignon, "Ethn. gén. de la Tunisie," *Bull. Géogr. hist. et descr.*, Paris, 1887. Cf. Bertholon, "La population de la Tunisie," *Rev. gén. des Sc.*, Paris, 1896, p. 972 (with fig.).

[2] It is to be noted that these last belong, like the islanders of Djerba, to the *Ibadite* sect, an offshoot of orthodox Islamism.

the *Tuaregs* or *Imoshagh*, as they call themselves,[1] with their manifold divisions (*Azjars*, *Haggars*, etc.) spread over the western Sahara. Very characteristic of their costume is the black veil which covers the head leaving only the eyes free, the stone rings on the arms forming also a very national ornament. They employ certain characters in writing peculiar to themselves. In the *Maghrebi*, who roam over the plateaus situated to the west of the Nile, the Arab strain is very

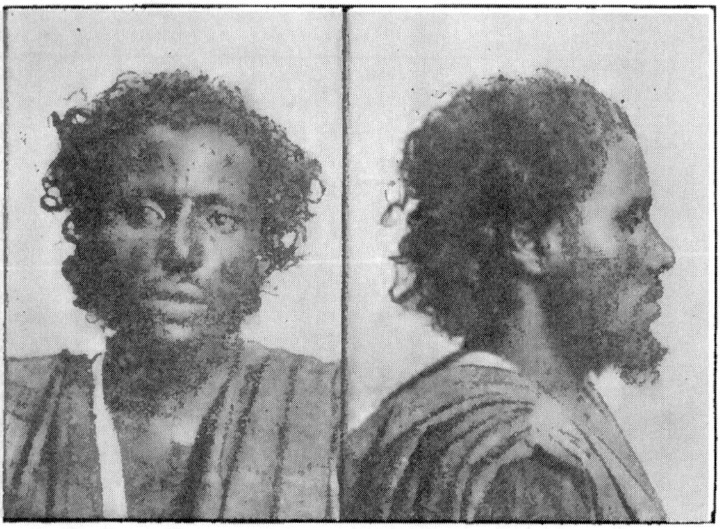

FIG. 137.—Trarza-Moor of the Senegal. (*Phot. Collignon.*)

strongly marked.[2] On the other side of the great African river, towards the Red Sea, the Berbers have entirely disappeared and the population is formed of Arabs more or less unmixed. The Bedouins of Egypt (237,000 in 1894) are Berber-Arabs divided into numerous tribes (*Aulad-Ali*, *Gavazi*, *Eleikat*, etc.).

The nomadic or settled *Moors* (Fig. 137) of the western Sahara, extending from Morocco to the Senegal (the *Trarza*,

[1] Duveyrier, *Les Touareg du Nord*, Paris, 1864; Schirmer, *loc. cit.*

[2] Rohlfs, *Quer durch Africa*, vol. i., Leipzig, 1888.

the *Brakna*, etc.), speak Arabic and "Zenagha," which is a Berber dialect. These are Berbers more or less crossed with Negro blood. It must further be observed that the name of Moors is very wrongly applied to the Mussulman inhabitants of the towns of Algeria and Tunis and to the *Riffians* of Morocco.[1]

The *Fellaheen*, Mussulmans (635,600 in 1894) of the lower valley of the Nile (as far as the first cataract), mixed descendants of the ancient Egyptians, must be included among the Arabo-Berbers because they have abandoned the speech of their ancestors, adopting that of the Arabs, but many of them have preserved intact the type of the primitive Egyptians, fundamentally Ethiopian, so well represented on various monuments in the valley of the Nile.[2] The ancient Egyptian language is preserved, however, under the form of the *Coptic* dialect which, until quite recent times, served as the liturgical language to the Christian section of the inhabitants of Lower Egypt, known by the name of *Copts* (500,000 in 1894; cephalic index 76, according to Chantre).

We must likewise add to the Arabo-Berber group the *Barabra* (in the singular *Berberi*) inhabiting to the number of about 180,000 the part of the Nile valley situated between the first and the fourth cataract. It is a people sprung from the inter-

[1] Faidherbe, "Les Berbers . . . du Sénégal," *Bull. Soc. Anthr. Paris*, 1864, p. 89; R. Collignon and Deniker, "Les Maures du Sénégal," *L'Anthropologie*, 1895, p. 287.

[2] According to the best preserved monuments, the ancient Egyptians had a brownish-reddish complexion of skin, long face, pointed chin, scant beard, straight or aquiline nose like the Ethiopian race (see p. 288). The hair of the mummies makes us think of the black and frizzy hair of the Ethiopians themselves. Lastly, the few ancient Egyptian skulls examined are meso- or dolicho-cephalic. See Pruner-Bey, *Mem. Soc. Anthr. Paris*, vol. i., 1863; Hartman, *Zeits. für Ethnol.*, vols. i. and ii., 1869-70, and *Die Nigritier*, Berlin, 1876; E. Schmidt, *Arch. f. Anthr.*, vol. xvii., 1888; S. Poole, *Journ. Anthr. Inst.*, vol. xvi., 1886, p. 371; S. Bertin, *ibid.*, 1889, vol. xviii., p. 104; *Phot. Coll.*, Flinders-Petrie (Brit. Assoc. 1887); Sergi, *Africa Antropol. della stirpe camitica*, Turin, 1897. Virchow (*Sitzungsb. Preuss Akad. Wiss.*, 1888) has endeavoured to show that the most ancient type of the Egyptians was brachycephalic, but his deductions are disputable, being based on measurements of statues.

mingling of Ethiopians, Egyptian Fellaheen, and Arabs (ceph. ind. 76). One of the most commercial tribes of this ethnic group is that of the *Danagla* inhabiting the country of Dongola.

II. The *Ethiopians* or *Kushito-Hamites*, who are sometimes called *Nuba* or *Nubians*,[1] inhabit the north-east of Africa, from the 25th degree lat. N. to the 4th degree lat. S. They occupy almost all the coast land of the Red Sea, and that of the Indian Ocean from the Gulf of Aden to Port Durnford or Wubashi. Their territory is bounded on the west by the Nile, the Bahr-el-Azrek, the western edge of the Abyssinian plateau, Lake Rudolf and Mount Kenia.[2]

In the northern part of this territory dwell the *Bejas* or *Nubians*, the different tribes of which, *Bejas* or *Bisharin*, *Hamrans* (Fig. 138), *Hadendowas*, *Hallengas*, etc., are stationed one after another between the Red Sea and the Nile, from the first cataract to the Abyssinian plateau. Certain Beja tribes, like the *Ababdeh* (19,500), to the north in Upper Egypt, partly of settled habits, the *Beni-Amer* to the east, the *Jalin* to the west, are in a large measure Arabised, but still speak a Hamitic language, while side by side with them dwell Semitised Ethiopian tribes, speaking only Arabic like the *Habab* and the *Hassanieh* of the Bayuda steppe or the *Abu-Rof* and *Shukrieh* of the lower basin of the Blue Nile.[3]

[1] Sometimes the Barabras are also similarly designated, in my opinion wrongly, for this leads to a triple confusion, "Nuba" being still the name of a Negro tribe (see p. 444). It would be more correct to employ this term as a synonym of *Northern Ethiopian*; besides, according to Strabo (Book XVII.), Eratosthenes refers to the "Nubians" in his time as a people distinct from the Negroes and Egyptians. The Barabras are not so dark, have not such frizzy hair, and are not so tall as the Bejas, the Hamrans, and other Ethiopians their neighbours, and consequently belong, not only by their language, but also by their physical type, to the Arabo-Berber group.

[2] For general works see Paulitschke, *Beiträge Ethnogr. u. Anthr. d. Somâl. Galla*, Leipzig, 1886, and *Ethnogr. Nordost Africas*, Berlin, 1893-96, 2 vols.; Sergi, *loc. cit.* (*Africa*).

[3] Hartmann, "Die Bedjah," *Zeit. f. Ethnol.*, vol. xi., 1879, p. 117; Virchow, *Zeit. f. Ethn.*, vol. x., 1878 (Verh. p. 333, etc.), and vol. xi., 1879 (Verh. p. 389); Deniker, *Bull. Soc. Anthr. Paris*, 1880, p. 594.

It is in the same category of Semitised Ethiopians, but speaking the *Amharinga* and *Tigrenga* dialects, etc., which have sprung from a different Semitic language, *Ghéez*, that we must place the inhabitants of the north and east of Abyssinia, as well as the natives of Kaffa and the east of Shoa, who have sprung from the intermingling of the *Gallas* (see below) with the Arabs.

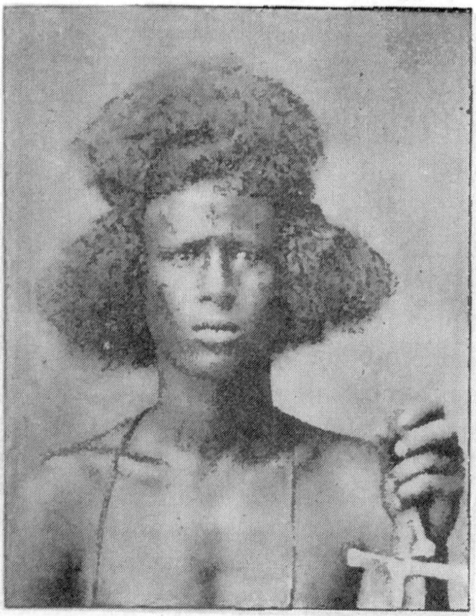

FIG. 138.—Hamran Beja of Daghil tribe; height, 1m. 79, 25 years old. Hair arrangement characteristic of Ethiopians. (*Author's coll.*)

The *Amharinga* language is spoken in Amhara and Godjam; the *Tigrenga* farther to the north, in Tigre; the *Curagheh*, derived from the ancient Amharinga, to the west of Lake Zuwai and to the south of Shoa, and the sources of the Hawash. The term "Abyssinian" has only a political signification, like that of "Austrian" for example; it is a corruption of the word "Habeshi" ("mixed"), which the Arabs formerly gave in derision to the inhabitants of the Abyssinian plateau united together into a Christian state. The substratum of the population of the Abyssinian plateau is formed by the *Agaw*, Ethiopian in type, Hamitic in language, but the Abyssinians of the higher classes are strongly Semitised. The national religion of the Abyssinians is monophysite Christianity, closely allied to the Coptic religion, but impregnated with Mussulman, Judaic, and indigenous animist elements.

To the south of the Abyssinian plateau, from the neighbourhood of Lake Tsana to the extreme limits of the extension of the Ethiopian peoples to the south and west is the territory of the *Gallas* or *Oroma*, representing the purest Ethiopian type. To the east of the Gallas, from about the 42nd degree long. east of Greenwich, dwell the *Somalis*, probably only Gallas more or less intermingled with the Arabs, who for several centuries have overrun the country. They occupy the whole of the seaboard from Cape Jibuti (at the southern extremity of Obok) to the mouth of the Jeb, or Jubba, and the plain of Aji-Fiddah, which extends below the equator, but in the interior of their country, especially in the north, numerous Galla tribes are found.

To the north of the Gallas, between Abyssinia and the coast (from Cape Jibuti to Hamfila Bay), are the *Afar* (in the plural *Afara*) or *Danakil* (*Dankali* is in the singular), who form the bulk of the population of the French colony of Obok-Tajura. Physically they resemble the Somalis, but they are less Arabised. To the north of the Danakil there is a population akin, it is said, to the Agaw, or aborigines of Abyssinia, and known by the name of *Saho* or *Shaho*. It occupies the southern part of the country of Massowah, the northern being taken by the Ethiopian tribes known by the collective name of Massowans.[1]

From the somatological point of view, the Ethiopians are characterised by a rather high stature (1m. 67 on the average), a brownish or chocolate-coloured complexion with a reddish tinge, by an elongated head (average ceph. ind., 75.7 to 78.1

[1] Révoil, *La Vallée du Darrar*, Paris, 1882; Paulitschke, *loc. cit.*; Sergi, *loc. cit.*, p. 178; Santelli, *Bull. Soc. Anthr. Paris*, 1893, p. 479.

on the living subject, according to Chantre), frizzy hair, intermediate between the curly hair of the Arabs and the woolly hair of the Negroes, and lastly by the face elongated to a perfect oval, and the prominent, straight or convex, very narrow nose.[1] Thin and slender, the Ethiopians have fine ankles and wrists, long and very sinewy limbs (especially the fore-arm), broad shoulders, and conical-shaped trunk like the ancient statues of Egypt. In short, they are good representatives of the Ethiopian race.

III. *Fulah-Zandeh Group.*—Under this term we include the whole series of populations resulting from the intermingling of the Ethiopians and the Nigritians (or Sudanese Negroes), and extending from east to west across the whole of Africa, over a belt of 5 to 6 degrees in width. This belt passes through the following regions, starting from the east: The country of the Masai (between Lake Rudolf and the 6th degree of latitude S.); the region comprised between the upper valleys of the right-hand tributaries of the Bahr-el-Arab on the one hand and the basin of the Ubangi-Welle on the other; Darfur, Dar-Runga, Wadai, Baghirmi, and Bornu; Dar Banda and the upper basin of the Shari; a good part of the basin of the Niger-Benue and the whole of the basin of the Senegal. This territorial zone may be divided from the ethnographical point of view into two distinct portions by the line of the watershed between the basins of the Nile and Congo on the one hand and the basins of the Chad, Niger, and Senegal on the other. To the east of this line dwell, in compact groups, the Zandeh or Niam-Niam, Masai, and other populations who have sprung from the intermingling of the Ethiopians with the Negroes of the eastern Sudan (Nilotic Negroes), and in some rarer cases with the Negrilloes and Bantus. To the west, on the contrary, we find, scattered over an immense tract, isolated groups of one population only, that of the *Fulahs* or *Peuls*, sprung from the crossings of

[1] See Appendices I. to III. for the measurements given from the works already quoted of Deniker, Paulitschke, Santelli, Sergi, and Virchow.

Ethiopians with the Negroes of the central and western Sudan, and further impregnated with a strain of Arabo-Berber blood.

In the eastern group, which I propose to call provisionally the Zandeh group, we find the *Masai* and the *Wakuafi* peoples of an Ethiopian type modified by intermingling with the Nilotic Negroes of the north, with the Bantus and perhaps with the Bushmen of the south, to judge by the photographs published by Luschan. The Masai speak a Nilotic-Negro language. On the north-east they touch the habitat of the Gallas, and are surrounded on every other side by Bantu tribes, except on the north-west, where, between Lake Rudolf and the upper Bahr-el-Jebel, exist populations still imperfectly known, the *Latukas*, the *Turkan*, the *Lurems*, who are probably half-breeds in various degrees of Ethiopians and Nilotic Negroes,[1] as are the *Drugu* and the *Lendu* of the region of the sources of the Ituri, the *Loggos* and the *Momvus* or *Mombuttus* (who must not be confounded with the *Mangbattus*) of the upper valley of the Kibali.[2]

To the west of these tribes, in the basin of the Ubangi-Welle, we find a compact group of several peoples who, under various names, have however a certain family likeness in their physical type, manners and customs, and language. These are, in the first place, the *Niam-Niam* or *Zandeh*, who with their congeners the *Banja* dwell to the north of the Welle. They extend beyond the ridge which divides this river from the White Nile, in the upper valleys of the Sere, the Jubé, and other tributaries of the great river. We also find a few isolated Zandeh groups to the south of the Welle, but the greater part of the country watered by the left tributaries of this waterway is the domain of the *Ababuas*, the *Abarmbos*, and the *Mangbattus* or *Monbuttus*, remarkable for their light

[1] J. Thomson, *Through Masai Land*, 2nd ed., London, 1887; Stuhlmann, *Mit Emin Pascha ins Herz von Afrika*, Berlin, 1894; F. von Luschan, *Beitr. zur Völkerk. d. Deutsch. Schutzgebiet*, Berlin, 1897, with meas. and phot.

[2] W. Junker, *Reisen in Afrika*, Vienna and Olmütz, 1889-91; and *Ergänzungsh. Peter. Mit.*, Nos. 92 and 93, Gotha, 1888-89.

skin, as well as the lighter shade of their hair compared with that of the other Zandehs (fair hair in five per cent.). The Niam-Niam extend to the eastward to the country of the Makaraka (tribes of *Bombeh*, *Idio*, etc.), where they intermingle with the *Mundus* and the *Babukurs*. On the north-west the Zandeh are in contact with tribes still little known, like the *Krej* (basin of the upper Bahr-el-Arab), the *Bandas*, and the *N'Sakkaras*, who, however, seem to be closely related.[1]

The Niam-Niam and the Mangbattus, who may be taken as types of Zandeh populations, suggest physically the Ethiopians; however, strains of Nilotic-Nègro blood are manifest among them. They have a civilisation well characterised by several traits in their material life: anthropophagy (see p. 147), garments of bast (p. 183), ornaments worn in the nostrils and in the lips perforated for the purpose, spiral-shaped bracelets, weapons of a particular kind (pp. 259 and 269), partly borrowed from the Egyptians, as were perhaps their harp, bolster, and so many other objects. They are cultivators using the hoe (p. 192), fetichists partly converted to Islamism and forming little despotic states.[2]

The populations encountered by the travellers Crampel, Dybowski, and Maistre westward of the countries peopled by the Zandeh, between the Ubangi and the Grinbingi (one of the principal branches of the Shari), must also be connected with the Zandeh group. These are, going from south to north, the *Bandziri*, the *Ndris*, the *Togbo*, the *Languassi*, the *Dakoa*, the *Ngapu*, the *Wia-Wia*, the *Mandjo*, the *Awaka*, and the *Akunga*. The physical type of these tribes suggests that of the Niam-Niam, except the stature, which is higher, (1m. 73, according to Maistre). The language common to all these peoples, *Ndris*, differs from the Bantu dialects spoken on the Congo, and appears to approximate to the Zandeh

[1] Schweinfurth, "Die Monbuttu," *Zeits. f. Ethn.*, 1873, p. 1, and *Artes Africanæ*, Leipzig, 1875; Junker, *loc. cit.*; P. Comte, *Les N'Sakkaras*, Bar-le-Duc, 1895.

[2] See Schweinfurth, *loc. cit.* (*Artes Africanæ*), and *The Heart of Africa*, 2nd ed., London, 1878; Junker, *loc. cit.*

language. As to their material culture and civilisation, these are almost the same as among the Zandeh tribes.[1]

The *western group* of the great Fulah-Zandeh division, of which I have spoken above, is formed of a population more homogeneous in type and language than the Zandeh, but dispersed in isolated groups in the midst of the Negroes. These

FIG. 139.—Yoro Combo, fairly pure Fulah of Kayor (Futa-Jallon); height, 1m. 72; ceph. ind., 68.3; nas. ind., 81.2. (*Phot. Collignon.*)

are the *Fulbés* or *Fulahs*[2] speaking the Fulah tongue, their true name being Pul-bé (in the singular *Pul-o*, which means "red"

[1] Crampel, *Le Tour du Monde*, 1890, 2nd half-year, p. 1; Dybowski, *La Route du Tchad*, Paris, 1893; Maistre, *De l'Oubanghi à la Bénoué*, Paris, 1895.

[2] Béranger-Féraud, *Peuples de la Senagambie*, chap. iii., Paris, 1879; and the works of Faidherbe, Binger, Tautin, P. C. Meyer, quoted later.

or "light-brown" in the Fulah tongue). The Mandingans call them *Fulbé*, the Hausas *Fellani*, the Kanuri *Fellata*. It is a mixed population, the substratum of which is Ethiopian but with a predominance either of Arab and Berber, or Negro elements.[1]

The favourite occupations of the Fulahs, stock-breeding and war, lead them away on more or less distant migratory journeys and expeditions; thus it happens that they are found dispersed among the Nigritian populations over a large tract of country comprised between the lower Senegal and 10° latitude N. on the one part, and from Darfur to the hinterland of the Cameroons on the other part. A fact to be noted in regard to their geographical distribution is that they have not yet reached any point on the coast of the Atlantic. They are especially numerous in the valleys of the Senegal and the Niger-Benue, as well as in Futa-Jallon and Darfur. The latter country is probably the primitive country of the Fulahs, whence they set out towards the west and the south; their migrations from the Senegal towards the east are of recent date and continue to the present day.

IV. *The Nigritians.*—We include under this name all the Negro populations who do not speak the Bantu dialects; these populations exhibit as a rule the classic traits of the Negro: lofty stature (from 1m. 70 among the Mandingans to 1m. 73 among the Furs and the Wolofs, according to Collignon, Deniker, Felkin, Verneau, etc.), very marked dolichocephaly (ceph. ind. on the liv. sub. reaching from 73.8 among the Toucouleurs to 76.9 among the Ashantis, according to the same authors), black skin, woolly hair in a continuous mat, large and flat nose (nas. ind. varying from 96.3 among the Negroes of Tunis to 107.5 among the Ashantis), forehead bulging on the median line and often retreating, thick lips projecting outward, frequent prognathism. The territory of the various peoples composing the Nigritian group may be defined as

[1] Stature, 1m. 75; ceph. ind., 74.3; nas. ind., 95.3 (Collignon and Deniker on 32 subjects).

follows: on the north, a wavy line which at first, going from the mouth of the Senegal to the great bend of the Niger, then deviates little from the fourteenth parallel going to the Bahr-el-Ghazal and the Nile; on the south, the coast of the Gulf of Guinea to the Cameroons, then the mountain ranges of Adamawa and the seventh degree of latitude N., to the countries occupied by the peoples of the Fulah-Zandeh group, and farther to the east to the basin of the upper Nile. The latter constitutes the eastern limit, while to the west this limit is clearly indicated by the Atlantic Ocean.[1]

Among the Nigritians we also class the *Tibus* or *Tejas* of the country of Tibesti, which extends in the midst of the Sahara between the encampments of the Tuareg on the west and the Libyan desert on the east. But it is a population already much mixed with Berber and Arab elements.[2]

The Nigritian group may be divided into four great sections: *a*, the Nigritians of the Eastern Sudan (Anglo-Egyptian) or Nilotic Negroes; *b*, those of the Central Sudan (French), that is to say the Hausa-Wadai group, with the Tibu already mentioned; *c*, the Nigritians of the Western Sudan (French) and the Senegal; lastly, *d*, the Nigritians of the coast or *Negroes of Guinea*.

a. The *Nigritians of the Eastern Sudan* or *Nilotic Negroes* speak various dialects having a certain relationship, and brought together under the name of "Nilotic" languages. These populations are Negroes in every acceptation of the word, except the not uncommon instances where they are intermingled with the Ethiopians (chiefly in the east) or with the Arabo-Berbers (principally in the north). Thus the *Nuba* and the *Funje of Fazokl* are connected by several facial characteristics to the Ethiopians; they have besides even adopted a Hamitic dialect, just as the Negroes of Kordofan, intermixed

[1] It follows from what has been said previously that in many places the northern portion of the Negro territory is invaded by the Ethiopians, the Fulah-Zandeh, and the Arabo-Berbers.

[2] Nachtigal, *Sahara et Soudan*, vol. i. (trans. into French), p. 245, Paris, 1881.

with the Arabs, have exchanged their language for the Semitic mode of speech. The Negroes of Darfur (the *Furs* or *Furava* and the *Dajo*), of high stature, and very black (Nachtigal), are much purer; they speak a Nilotic-Negro dialect. In the west of the country they are mixed with the Fulahs, and Arab tribes surround them on all sides. The predominant race is descended from pure Arabs established first in Tunis, who achieved the conquest of Darfur only in the nineteenth century.[1] To the south-east of Darfur, separated from this country by the encampments of the *Bahr-el-Huer* or *Bagarra*, Arabised Nilotes, dwell other Nilotics of a well-marked negro type. These are, first, the *Nuers* of the right bank, and the *Shilluks* (about a million) of the left bank of the Bahr-el-Ghazal from Mechra-et-Reg to Fashoda; then the *Dinka*, *Denka*, or *Jangha* (about a million) of the low country watered by the right-hand tributaries of the Bahr-el-Ghazal, and by the Bahr-el-Jebel or Upper Nile. All these tribes are shepherds, sometimes also fishers or husbandmen.

The upper valleys of the right-hand tributaries of the Bahr-el-Ghazal are occupied by the *Bongo* Negroes, divided into several tribes: *Moru*, *Mittu*, *Bongo* (said to be steatopygous). Slightly blent with the Ethiopians, they have an almost red skin, of the colour of the soil of their country, impregnated with ore. They are accomplished smiths and good agriculturists. Between the Bongo of the west, the Dinkas of the north, and the Niloto-Ethiopian tribes like the *Latuka* of the east, there are established in the country traversed by the Bahr-el-Jebel the Nilotic Negroes called *Bari*. As to the upper basin of the Bahr-el-Jebel, it is occupied by the *Madi* (not to be confounded with the *A-Madi* of the Welle), the *Shueli* or *Shuli* (whose speech connects them with the Shilluks), and the *Luri*, who are, like the Dinka and Shilluks, true representatives of the Negro race. Very tall and slim, they resemble, with their long limbs, the wading birds of the marshes whose approaches they inhabit; for the most part their head is elongated and com-

[1] Nachtigal, *Sahara und Sudan*, Berlin-Leipzig, 1879-89, 3 vols.

pressed, the forehead retreating, their skin is black, and they are blubber-lipped; the face is the prognathous face of the Negroes, such as, in accordance with convention, they used generally to be represented. They are settled cattle-breeders and tillers of the soil.[1]

b. The *Nigritians of Central Sudan* present almost the same type as the Nilotes. Such, for instance, are the Negroes of Wadai (the Tama, the Massalits) and of Baghirmi (the Barmaghé), or at least those among them who have remained free from intermixture, either with the Fulahs or the Arabs. As much cannot be said of the nomadic Tibu or Teda of Tibesti (p. 444), nor of their neighbours the Kanem, to the north of Lake Chad, and the Kanuri of Bornu and of the north of Adamawa, who closely resemble them, but who are tillers of the soil. The great nation of the Hausas prevails in the region situated between the Benue, Bornu, the middle course of the Niger, and Sahara (Sokoto, etc.); it extends even farther, into Adamawa. Their language has become the language of commerce in those parts of the country limited by the bend of the Niger, into which Fulah has not yet penetrated; it extends also into Bornu and Adamawa to the east, and into the country of the Mossi and the Kong to the west. The Hausa nation comprises a large number of peoples and tribes, with a greater or lesser Arab and Fulah intermixture, among whom also should probably be classed the Sara and their near relatives the Tumok between the Shari and the Logone. The Sara are distinguished by tall stature (average 1m. 77, according to Maistre), very dark colour, and globular head (average cephalic index on the living subject, 82).[2]

c. The Nigritians of Western Sudan and of Senegal.—This

[1] Schweinfurth, *loc. cit.*, vol. i., chaps. vii. and lciv.; Stuhlmann, *loc. cit.*, chap. xxii.; Frobenius, *Die Heiden-Neger*, Berlin, 1893; E. de Martonne, *Annales de Géogr.*, Paris, 1896, p. 506, and 1897, p. 57.

[2] Nachtigal, *loc. cit.*; Barth, *Reisen . . . in Nord u. Centr. Afr.*, Gotha, 1857-58, 5 vols.; Monteil, *De Saint-Louis à Tripoli*, Paris, 1895; Maistre, *loc. cit.*; Staudinger, *Im Herzen der Haussaländer*, Berlin, 1889, 2 vols.

group, going from east to west, comprises: 1st, various mixed tribes, dwelling between the Niger and the basin of the upper Black Volta; 2nd, the Mandé or Mandingan peoples; 3rd, the Toucouleur; and, 4th, the Wolofs.

1st. The peoples living between the Hausa on the east and the Mandingans on the west are still little known, and seem to be much mixed. Quite to the north, in the bend of the Niger, below Timbuctoo, are found the Songhai or Sonrhays, who speak a language apart, and in the north are mixed with the Ruma "Moors," emigrants from Morocco, and in the south with the Fulahs. To the south of their territory live the Tombo, partly speaking Mandé, and the Mossi, whose language also has affinities with Mandé. To the north of Wagadugu, the Mossi, interblent with the Fulahs, speak their language, while south of this town, they are of purer type and have a knowledge of the Hausa dialect. To the east of the Mossi, in the region of the sources of the White Volta, live the Gurma; while the upper basin of this river, as well as that of the Red Volta, is occupied by the Gurunga who previously formed the Grussi (or Gurunssi?)[1] state. Farther to the south, in the territory made neutral by a treaty between Germany and England, are found the Dagomba, the Mampursi, and their congeners the Gonja; these last, whose centre is at Salaga, have exchanged their primitive language for "Guang," which appears to be a dialect of the Ashanti tongue (Binger). In commercial relations they employ also the Hausa and sometimes the Mandé and Fulah languages, just as do the Dagomba and the Gurunga. The *Bariba*, natives of Borgu, the hinterland of Dahomey, have affinities with peoples we have just enumerated.

2nd. The Mandé, Mandingan,[2] or better Mandénké (the word

[1] The Diumma or Diammo, to the north-east of the bend of the Black Volta, are probably a branch of the Gurunga; only having for long been subject to the Ashantis they have adopted their language, which is the only one they use in addressing strangers. (Binger, *Du Niger au golfe de Guinée*, Paris, 1892.)

[2] Béranger-Féraud, *loc. cit.*, ch. v., and *Rev. Anthr.*, 1874, p. 444; Binger, *loc. cit.*

nké signifying "people" in the Mandé language) form a compact linguistic group whose domain extends from the Senegal and Upper Niger to that portion of the West African coast comprised between Saint Louis and Monrovia. The domain of the Mandé language extends much farther to the east than the territory of the Mandénké peoples properly so called; it encircles Timbuctoo, the countries of the Gurma and the Diumma, where it competes with the dialect of the Fulahs, and encroaches even on the domain of the Dogomba and the

FIG. 140.—Bonna M'Bané, Mandingan-Sossé; height, 1m. 74; ceph. ind., 74.7; nasal index, 102. (*Phot. Collignon.*)

Gonja (to the north of Salaga), where the Hausa speech prevails. The Mandénké properly so called includes a large number of tribes, which may be divided into two great clans: the Bamma or Bambara, whose "tenné" or totem is the crocodile, and the Malinké (hippopotamus totem). The Mandénké are Mussulmans, except the clan Bamma or Bambara of the basin of the upper Niger, which has remained fetichist. Related to the Mandénké, according to their dialects, are the *Soninké* of the interior and many other populations of the coast of Senegal. The Soninké or Sarakolés [1] inhabit the right bank of the Senegal, above Matam and the margins of the Niger, and below the Bamako as far as the vicinity of Timbuctoo; they are crossed with the Torodo, Bambaras, and Fulahs. As to the populations of the coasts, the following, proceeding from north to south, are the chief.[2] First, the Diola,[3] between Casamanze and the Gambia, who have remained fetichist. They are tall (1m. 70) and dolichocephalic (cephalic index, 74.5 according to Collignon and Deniker). The principal tribe, that of the Felups, has imposed its dialect on all the others. To the south of the Diola are the Balantes and the Bagnoris, a bellicose and turbulent people; the Papels, one of the tribes of which, the Mandjacks, is the most in harmony with its masters, the Portuguese; the Bujagos of the Bissagos islands; the Biafares, the Nalus, the Landumans, fetichists of Rio Nunez, having affinities with the Hausa; finally, the Baga of the Compong delta, half-savage fishers, fetichist like the two preceding, but of much fairer skin and more pacific.[4] To the south of the Pongo river are met the Sussus or Sossé (Fig. 140), driven from Futa-Jallon by the Fulahs. Their language is spoken fluently in French Guinea, and even among the Nalus and Landumans. To the south of Mellacory, in Sierra Leone, the Timni take the place of the Sussus; then come the Vei or Way, who extend as far as Monrovia; alone among Negroes, they appear to possess a special mode of writing. All the Mandé peoples bear a strong likeness to each other in physical type (high stature, 1m. 70, dolichocephalic, colour black, etc.), and the different tribes are only to be distinguished by tattooings and other signs of an ethnographic kind, and by their dialects.[5]

[1] Faidherbe, "Les Sarakolés," *Rev. de Linguist.*, 1881, p. 80.

[2] For details see C. Madrolle, *En Guinée*, Paris, 1895.

[3] They must not be confounded with the Diula of the regions of Kong and the upper Niger, one of the first Mandénké tribes converted to Islamism, at the same time one of the least fanatic, perhaps because the most given to trade. (See M. Monnier, *loc. cit.*)

[4] Coffinières de Nordeck, *Tour du Monde*, vol. li., p. 273, 1886.

[5] Binger, *loc. cit.*; Tautin, "Les Castes des Mandingues," *Rev. Ethnogr.*, vol. iii., Paris, 1884.

3rd. The Toucouleur or Torodo, regarded by some as Fulahs intermixed with Wolofs (see below), inhabit the left bank of the Senegal, from Dagana to Medine. They are to be found also in the Segu Sikoro country and in the basin of the upper Niger, in the midst of the Soninké and Fulah shepherds, to whom these agricultural populations are subject. The Toucouleur are tall (1m. 73), and very dolichocephalic (ceph. ind. on living subject, 73.8).

4th. The Yolofs, Wolofs, or Jolofs of Lower Senegal, with their congeners the Leybu and the Serers of Lower Gambia, are perhaps the most black of all Negroes; these are distinguished by tall stature (1m. 73, according to Collignon, Deniker, and Verneau), and by moderate dolichocephaly (index on the living sub. 75.2). Their language is very widespread in Senegal and Guinea, for they are good merchants as well as tillers of the soil.[1]

d. The Littoral Nigritians or Guineans occupy all the coast of Guinea from Monrovia to the Cameroons, and exhibit a great uniformity of physical type. Less tall, in general, than the Senegalese and the western Sudanese, the head is more elongated and the complexion fairer. Notwithstanding this uniformity, they are divided into several tribes, which, according to their linguistic affinities, may be grouped into five great sections.

1. First, the tribes speaking the various dialects of the Kru language—that is to say, Kru properly so called or Krumen, Bassa in Liberia, and Grebo in French Guinea (to the east of Cape Palmas).

The Kru are less tall (1m. 69), less dark, but more hairy than the Senegalese; the head barely dolichocephalic (75.1 ceph. index on living subject).[2] Of all Negroes these are the

[1] For details in regard to the Wolofs, the Toucouleur, etc., see Béranger-Féraud, *loc. cit.*, chap. i., and *Rev. Anthr.*, 1875; Tautin, "Études . . . ethnol. peuples Senegal," *Rev. Ethnogr.*, 1885; Deniker and Laloy, *loc. cit.*, p. 259; Collignon and Deniker, unpublished notes; Verneau, "Serer, Leybou, Ouolofs," *L'Anthropol.*, 1895, p. 510.

[2] Deniker and Laloy, *loc. cit.*; Ten Kate and Serrurier, *Musée Ethnogr. Leyden, Notices Anth.*, No. I., undated (1891 ?), in fol.

best factory workers, the best man-of-war's men and ordinary seamen. They are obedient, faithful, and courageous; they enter readily into engagements, and make a fair bargain. They retain in their hands a good part of the trade of their country.[1]

2. To the east of the Grebo, between San Pedro and Apollonia, live people speaking different dialects of the Agni language. These are the Assinians or Okin (stature, 1m. 75), the Agni of Krinjabo or Sanwy (Fig. 9), the Apollonians or Zemma, the handsomest of the Negroes, who formerly furnished to Brazil its thousands of slaves; finally, the Pai-pi-bri, between San Pedro and Lahu, whom Admiral Fleuriot de Langle took for a white race. These Negroes are really of a bronzed tint, much fairer than, for example, the Okin. Other somatic traits (projecting nose, lips not thrust out, etc.), as well as ethnic traits (bark clothing, etc.), together with the recent arrival in the country of the Pai-pi-bri, have led it to be thought that they have a kinship with the Zandeh peoples.[2] Their neighbours to the east, the Jack-Jack or Jacks, live opposite Dabu, on a narrow tongue of land separating the lagoon from the sea; they call themselves Awekwom, and speak, like their Ebrié and Attié neighbours, a dialect of the Tshi language. They are excellent traders, nearly all knowing English.

3. But the Awekwom and their congeners form only a linguistic parish in the Agni country. The true domain of the populations speaking the languages of the Tshi or Ochi family begins only on the east of Apollonia. In the interior are encountered the Ashanti and Ton shepherds and tillers—that is to say in the ancient kingdom of Ashanti (now an English possession),—and the Fanti traders on the coast, in the region of Elmina.[3]

[1] Buttikofer, *Reisebilder aus Liberia*, vol. ii., Leyden, 1890.

[2] Fleuriot de Langle, *Le Tour du Monde*, 1873, 2nd half-year; Binger, *loc. cit.*, 2nd vol.; Delafosse, "Les Agni," *L'Anthropologie*, 1893, p. 403.

[3] Ellis, *The Tshi-speaking Peoples, etc.*, London, 1887, and *The Ewe-speaking Peoples, etc.*, London, 1890; Foa, *Le Dahomey*, Paris, 1895; D'Albecca, *Le Tour du Monde*, Feb. 1896; F. von Luschan, *loc. cit.* (*Beitr. Deutsch. Schützg. . . .*).

The Accredians of the coast, between the town of Accra and the mouth of the Volta, formed a mixed population whose language is not yet classed.

4. The Volta provides the approximate limit between the Tshi tongues and the Evé or Ewe dialects. The bulk of the people speaking Ewe occupy the German colony of Togo and the west of the French colony of Dahomey. In this group are distinguished six dialectic families: The Anlo or Anglo of the coast between the Volta and Togo, whose dialect is the best known; the Krépis, mountaineers of the Akposso, to the north of the preceding, who speak the Anfueh language; the Ana, of Atakpamé; the Fon or Fawins, better known as Dahomese, to the east of the Anlo and Krépis, who speak the Jeji or Jege dialect; the Ewe properly so called, or Henhué, to the north of the preceding, especially around the town of Wida (Glé-ewé, "land of the Ewes"); lastly, the Mahi or Maki, entirely to the north, speaking the purest Ewe dialect, and coming, as they say, from the banks of the Niger.[1]

e. The River Wami separates in the east the Ewes from the peoples speaking the Yoruba tongues, and who are, from west to east: the Egba or Ikba of the Abeokuta country, the Nago of Porto Novo, the Ikelu and the Jebu of Lagos. The Yoruba originally occupied all the region comprised between the Slave Coast and to about the ninth latitude N.; but they have been driven back towards the coast and into the east by the Ewe peoples, who, towards the beginning of the eighteenth century, invaded the present country of the Dahomese, and later (in 1772), the Togo and the ancient kingdoms of Porto Novo and Wida (formerly Juida). In this last the Jege or Fon (of Ewe stock) have imposed their dominion on the Nagos (of Yoruba stock). Most of the Nagos have been reduced to slavery; they, together with the Mina, emigrants from Ashanti, formed, while the slave-trade flourished, the bulk of the black cargoes consigned to Brazil.[2]

[1] Rev. Dennis Kemp, *Nine Years on the Gold Coast*, London, 1898.

[2] The name Mina was applied in Brazil without distinction to all Negroes imported from the Slave Coast, while those from the Gold Coast

The Ewes and the Yorubas are shorter in stature (1m. 64 and 1m. 65) than Nigritians in general, and are often brachycephalic or mesocephalic. These two characters, combined with the comparatively fair colour of the skin, observed by all travellers, and the great development of the pilous system, are, I consider, sufficiently indicative of the presence in these people of Negrillo elements, of which I shall presently speak.[1]

The Protectorate of the Niger coast and the delta of this river are occupied by populations related to the Yorubas, but much intermixed. The Benin, in the interior, whose kingdom, where human sacrifices were much in vogue, has lately been destroyed by the English; then on the coast the active-trading Jakris tribe, the Bonky and the Calabaris, who formerly furnished so many slaves; finally, the Idzo or Ijos, of the delta of the Niger, divided into several tribes—Brass, Patani, etc., good ship-builders, but very turbulent,—who have attacked time after time the settlements of the Niger Company.[2] In the interior of the territory of this Company are found the Igbera, mountaineers, forming several independent little states (about a million and a half individuals) between Adimpa on the lower Niger and Sakun on the middle Niger, as well as on the Benue, and sub-divided into "Sima" of the towns and "Panda" of the forests. Their neighbours the Igara, speaking Yoruba, occupy the left bank of the Niger and lower Benue, where they are more or less subdued, while in the interior they remain wild hunters. In the Cameroons, the Bantu, like the Dualas and the Bakokos, have driven into hinterland the Bobondi, Buyala, and other Nigritian tribes.

were called Apollonians. Batty, "Yorouba Country," *Journ. Anthro. Inst.*, vol. ix. (1890), p. 160; Moloney, *ibid.*, p. 213; Ellis, *The Yoruba-speaking Peoples*, London, 1894

[1] Deniker, "Les Dahoméens," *Rev. gén. Sciences*, 1891, p. 174; Deniker and Laloy, *loc. cit.*

[2] See, about these populations, the 1st Appendix, by Comte de Cardi, in *West Afric. Stud.*, by Miss M. Kingsley, London, 1899.

V. *The Negrilloes.*[1]—The pigmy black populations are dispersed over a large zone extending from three degrees north and south of the equator, across the entire African continent, from Uganda to the Gabun. The Akkas or Tiky-Tiky of the upper Nile and of the country of the Niam-Niam, the Afiffi of the country of the Momfu (between Kibali and Ituri), the Wambutti of the Ituri, the Watwa or Batua living to the south of the great curve of the Congo and the valleys of its tributaries on the right, the Chuapa-Bussera and the Lomami, the O-Bongo (plural Ba-Bongo), the Akua, the Achango of the French Congo, the Boyaeli and Bayago of the Cameroons, the Ba-Bengaye of Sanga, are the principal rings of this chain of dwarf peoples stretched between the region of the great lakes and the Atlantic ocean. But Negrilloes have also been noted outside these limits. Without stopping to consider the evidence of the traveller Mollien (1818), who speaks of dwarfs in the Tenda-Maië country, near the sources of the Niger, where modern explorers have never met with anything of the kind, we may, however, bring together a certain amount of serious testimony to the existence of dwarfs in the basin of the upper Kasai, as well as more to the east, as far as Lake Tanganyika, and lastly to the north of the Lakes Stefanie and Rudolf (English East Africa), near the borders of Kaffa, 7° latitude north, where pigmies have been described by older travellers under the name

[1] Schweinfurth, *loc. cit.*; Stanley, *In Darkest Africa*, London, 1890; Wolff, *Zeit. f. Ethn.*, 1886 (Verh., p. 25); De Quatrefages, *loc. cit.* (*Les Pygmées*), p. 253; De Quatrefages and Hamy, *Cran. Ethn.*, p. 334; Falkenstein, *Zeit. f. Ethn.*, 1877 (Verh., p. 194 and pl. xii.-xiv.); W. Flower, *Journ. Anthr. Inst.*, vol. xviii. (1889), p. 3; Deniker and Laloy, *loc. cit.*, p. 288; Emin Bey (afterwards Pasha), "Sür les Akka, etc.," *Zeit. f. Ethn.*, 1886, p. 145; Junker, *loc. cit.*; Nebout, *Tour du Monde*, 1892, vol. i., p. 64; Crampel, "Les Bayagas," *Compte rend. Soc. Geogr.*, Paris, 1890, p. 548; O Lenz, *Ueber Zwergvölker Afr.*, Vienna, 1894; Deniker, *Bull. Soc. Anthr.*, 1894, p. 440; Dybowski, *La Nature*, 1894, 2nd half-year; Stuhlmann, *loc. cit.*, pl. xvi.-xvii., p. 436; Schlichter, "Pygmy of Africa," *Scot. Geog. Mag.*, 1892, p. 289, and *Peterm. Mitteil.*, 1896, p. 235; Donaldson Smith, *Geog. Journ.*, London, 1896, pp. 225 and 235; Burrows, *loc. cit.*

of Dogbo, and where, in 1896, they were indeed discovered by D. Smith. They call themselves Dumes, are about 1m. 50 (4 ft. 11 in.) in height, and resemble other pigmy tribes. According to Schlichter, other tribes of short stature live more to the north, in Kaffa and Shoa: the Bonno, the Aro, and the Mala; these last two are probably the same tribes as those spoken of by the old explorers, D'Abadie and L. des Avranches, under the name of Areya and Maléa.

According to Stuhlmann, the populations of the upper basin of the Ituri are a blend of Pigmies with Bantus (the Vambuba, the Vallessi), or with Nilotes (the Momfu).

Several authors confound in one group of Pigmies the Negrilloes and the Bushmen. Nothing, however, justifies their unification. The colour of the skin in Bushmen is a fawn yellow, while in Negrilloes it is that of a chocolate tablet or of coffee slightly roasted; the hair of the former is black and tufted, while the hair of the latter is like extended fleece and often of a more or less light brown. The face of the Bushman is lozenge-shaped, the cheeks are prominent, and the eyes are often narrowed and oblique, which traits are not met with at all in Pigmies. Steatopygy (see p. 40-41), a special trait of the Bushman race, has not been noted among Negrilloes, except in individual cases among the women, and to a less degree than among Bushmen, as, for example, is proved by the two portraits of Akka women published by Stuhlmann. At the same time the profile of the sub-nasal space, always convex in the Akkas according to Stuhlmann, is often to be observed among Bushmen. Thus, therefore, a slight degree of steatopygy in individual cases and the profile of the sub-nasal space would be the sole characters connecting the two races. In support of this connection, shortness of stature has also been adduced.

At first sight this last appears feasible, but rigorous measurements on a sufficient number of subjects are still lacking. In the various series of Bushmen the figures vary from 1m. 37 to 1m. 57, and in those of Negrilloes from 1m. 36 to 1m. 51. These figures, however, are based on only from 3 to 6 individuals, except in three cases: a series of 50 Bushmen of Kalahari, measured by Schinz, which gives the average height as 1m. 57—that is to say, the same as the Japanese or Annamese; another series of 30 Akkas (by Emin Pasha) giving an average height of 1m. 36; and a third series of 98 Watwas (by Wolff) giving an average of 1m. 42.[1] On comparing these three large series, the only ones deserving attention, a difference of 0m. 18 (7 inches) in height in favour of Bushmen is shown. As to the cranial form, it varies also. Notwithstanding the paucity of documents, it may be said that the Negrilloes are, in general, sub-dolichocephalic or mesocephalic (average index of 9 living subjects, 79.7); while Bushmen are undoubtedly dolichocephalic (average index of 11 living men, 75.8). Let me add in conclusion that the Negrilloes are covered with a fairly thick down over the entire body (Emin Pasha, Yunker, Stanley, Stuhlmann), and that nothing analogous has been noted in Bushmen.

The Negrilloes live in the midst of other peoples (Bantus, Nilotes, etc.), either as isolated individuals (for the most part slaves) or in little groups (up to about 800 individuals), hidden in the deepest thickets. These little hunters have established a sort of *modus vivendi* with the agricultural populations surrounding them: they exchange with them the produce of their chase, or of their gathering, for foods and objects in metal; they also pay for the protection of their powerful neighbours by doing service, for the benefit of the latter, as clearers of the forest, where it is a critical matter to meet them on account of their arrows, poisoned with the juice of a certain *Aroidea*, or with certain putrid animal matters derived especially from the ant. The bow and arrows which they use are the same as those of their protectors, only proportioned to their stature.

VI. The *Bantu group* comprises the numerous peoples of Central and Southern Africa whose dialects form the Bantu

[1] Schinz, *loc. cit.*; Emin, *loc. cit.*; Wissmann, Wolff, Von François, and Müller, *Im Innern. Afrik.*, Leipzig, 1888, Appendix IV., and *Zeit. f. Ethn.*, 1884, Verh , p. 725.

linguistic family, without having any analogy with the Nigritian languages. They have all an agglutinative structure, and are especially characterised by the exclusive use of prefixes. Each principal prefix indicates an entire category of objects or ideas; such a prefix is *M'*, *Um*, or *Umon* (according to dialect), denoting the singular; *Ba*, *Wa*, or *Va*, denoting the plural. Thus the root *Ntu* (man) united to the prefix *Umon* means

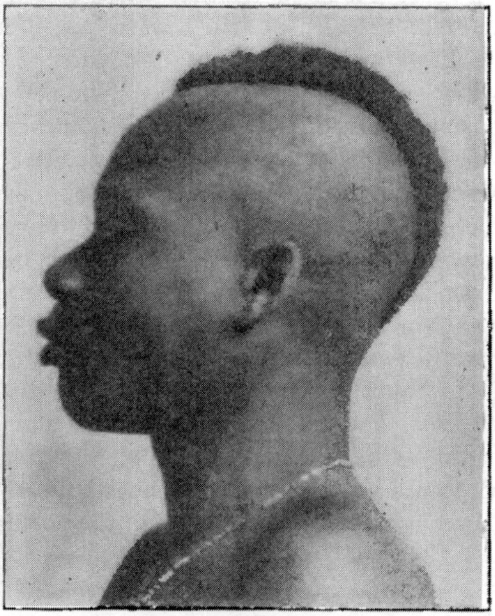

FIG. 141.—Catrai, Ganguela-Bantu; height, 1m. 73; ceph. ind., 75.8; nasal index, 107. (*Phot. Prince Roland Bonaparte.*)

"a man" (*Umon-Ntu*), and with the prefix *Ba* "men" (*Ba-Ntu*). It is superfluous to say that physically the Bantus present a great variety of types. This is due especially to intermixture with the Negrilloes and Ethiopians to the north, and with the Bushmen-Hottentots to the south. Nevertheless, there may be discerned a probably primitive type, which, while being fundamentally Negro, yet is distinguishable from the Nigritian type. In this type the stature is generally not so high, the head less elongated, and prognathism also less; the median convexity of the brow often disappears, and the nose is more prominent and narrower.

We may divide the Bantus, according to their ethnographic and linguistic characters, into three large sections: western, eastern, and southern.

1. The territory occupied by the *Western Group*[1] covers almost exactly the south-east of the Cameroons, French Congo, Angola, and Belgian Congo, except those parts of these states situated to the north of the Congo. The Dwala (28,000 individuals, stature 1m. 69; ceph. ind. 76.2, according to Zintgraff) and the Bakunda of the Cameroons, relatively civilised, are found up to the point of junction of the Bantu and Nigritian peoples, where the African coast changes its westerly direction and becomes nearly north by south. Like their neighbours of the south, the Mungos or Minihé of the north-west, and the Balongs, who live in large phalansteries, they are intermixed with Nigritian elements. East of the Dwala are found the Basas and the Bakoris; these last are notable for their spirit of solidarity, for the practice of the taboo and worship of ancestors. From the somatic point of view, a great difference is to be observed among them in the stature of men and women. Like the *Dwala*, they use the drum language (see p. 134). The *M'Fan* or *Fang*, called *Pahuins*[2] by the

[1] Dybowski, *loc. cit.*; Maistre, *loc. cit.*; Clozel, *Tour du Monde*, 1896, vol. ii.; Guiral, *Le Congo Français*, Paris, 1889; Deniker and Laloy, *loc. cit.*, p. 274; Buchner, *Kamerun*, Leipzig, 1887; Morgen, *Durch Kamerun*, Leipzig, 1893; Zintgraff, *Nord-Kamerun*, Berlin, 1895, and "Congo-Völk.," *Z. f. Ethn.*, 1886, Verh., p. 27, and 1889, p. 90; F. von Luschan, *loc. cit.* (*Beitr.*, etc.); V. Jacques, "Le Congolais de l'expos. d'Anvers," *Bull. Soc. Anthr.*, p. 284, Brussels, 1894; J. Wauters, *L'État Indép. du Congo*, Brussels, 1899; Mensé, "Völk. Mittl. Kongo," *Z. f. Ethn.*, 1897, Verh., p. 624.

[2] The Oshyeba are a section of the Fan people; they may be divided into *Makima* (in the Upper Ogowe) and into *Mazuna* (of the Gabun). They are a people of famous warriors, composed of 200,000 individuals, which number is increasing with extraordinary rapidity.

Negroes of the Gabun, occupy the country situated between the 3rd degree of N. latitude and the Ogowe, and its right tributary the Ivindo. But it is probable that their habitat extends farther to the east, for the *Botu*, whom Mizon had met with in the basin of the Sanga, appeared to be of the same race. The Fans touch the sea-board of the Atlantic only at a few points. With the *Gabunese* (*Benga*, *Kumbé*, etc.) and the *M'Pongwes* of the coast (whose language, which is very rich, has been adopted by other tribes), they form almost the whole of the population of French Congo to the north of the Ogowe. It is supposed that the Fans, certain traits and manners and customs of whom recall the Zandeh, have immigrated quite recently, perhaps at the end of the last century, into their present region, coming from Upper Ubangi, where the Zandeh tribes live (see p. 441).

In the valley itself of Low Ogowe are found the *Baloa* or *Galois*, and, farther to the south, between the Muni and Sette Camma, the *Bakalai* or *Bahèlè* (about 100,000 according to Wilson), former nomads, who have become carriers and merchants. Ascending the Ogowe are met successively the *Apingi*, the *Okanda*, the *Aduma*, the *Okota*, etc. All these tribes speak the same language as the islanders of Corisco, and are for the most part very tall and dolichocephalic (average stature of the Okandas 1m. 70, and ceph. ind. on the living sub., 74.2, according to Deniker and Laloy). But there are met with also among them tribes like the Aduma, who on the contrary are short (1m. 59) and sub-brachycephalic (ceph. ind. 80.8, according to the same authorities), which indicates inter-mixtures with the Negrillo race, represented in the vicinity by the Obongos or Ashangos to the east (Du Chaillu), and by the Akoas to the west (Touchard and Dybowski). The Adumas, who are slave merchants (Guiral), are good boatmen. To the south of Bakel, in the basins of the coast rivers, Rembo, Nyanga, etc., are found the *Balumbo*, the *Bavili*, on the coast, and the *Ashira* in the interior. The basin of the lower Kuilu or Niari is occupied partly by *Mayombé* and the *Loango* (height 1m. 65, ceph. ind. 77.5), mixed tribes, who are dispersed equally over the coast from the river Nyanga to the north to Landana to the south.

As to the upper basin of the Niari, it is inhabited by the *Bakuni* or *Bakunghé* to the north, and by the *Bakamba* (height 1m. 69, according to Maistre) to the south. These populations resemble the Loangos and somewhat also the *Kacongo* (height 1m. 65, ceph. ind. 75.6, according to Zintgraff). Farther to the south are the *Basundo*, savages with, it is said, red hair, and the *Babembé* (height 1m. 72, according to Maistre) and the *Babuendi*, recognisable by the tattoo of a crocodile on the breast, who people the right bank of the Congo from the mouth to Brazzaville. Among their neighbours the *Bacongo* or *Bafyot*, who thickly populate the opposite bank, the influence of the old Portuguese Christians is still to be recognised in many spots by processions with the crucifix, but the supreme god has become feminine, having relation both to the Virgin Mary and to the "Earth-mother of All."[1] This goddess, called Nzambi, is the principal personage of a trinity, the other members of which are a son, and a third spirit, Deisos. The Bacongo have also as an institution popular guardians of justice (p. 253), whom they call *pagasarios*. Above Brazzaville, on the right bank of the Congo, as far as Bolobo, are met various *Bateke* tribes, distinguished by their short stature (1m. 64), marked dolichocephaly (73.6, according to Mense), powerful trunk, and tattoo marks of several rows of parallel strokes on the cheeks. They extend to the west as far as 10° long. E, and occupy to the north all the basin of the upper Alima. The *Batekes*, who, with their neighbours the *Baboma* and the anthropophagous *Ballali*, were the first to submit to French dominion, are travellers and, though practising anthropophagy, a temperate people. The *Ashikuya* of the region of the sources of the Nkheni, neighbours of the *Batekes*, are celebrated as the best weavers of the Congo. The lower valley of the Alima,

[1] A. Bastian, *Zeitschr. f. Ethnol.*, vol. vi., 1874; E. Reclus, *Geogr. Univers.*, vol. xiii., p. 125, Paris, 1888.

as well as the right bank of the Congo as far as the mouth of the Ubangi and even above, are occupied by the *Bangi*, *Bubangis*, or *Bapfuru* (height, 1m. 73, according to Maistre), differing from other tribes by their mode of head-dress and their tattoo: a large swelling of flesh on each temple and on the middle of the brow. Their number is estimated at about a million.[1] North of the Bangis, between the Congo and the Ubangi, live their congeners the *Baloi* and the *Bonjos*, veritable athletes and proved to be cannibals (Dybowski). The river M'Poko, which enters the Congo opposite the town of Bangi, marks to the north the limit of the Bonjos, as of the Bantus generally of this part of Africa. Their immediate neighbours to the north, the Bandziris, are more like the Zandeh than the Bantus.

To the south of the Congo the various Bantu tribes are still little known.[2] On the coast, between the mouth of the Congo and the Kunene, the collective name of Angolese is given to various much-intermingled tribes: *Mushikongo* (1m. 66, ceph. ind. 72.5), *Kiamba*, *Kissama*, *Mondombé* (plural, *Bandombé*; 1m. 67, ceph. ind. 76.8), *Bakissé* (1.66, 75.5), etc. The mountainous region situated more to the east—that is to say, Bangala, the basin of the Kulu, the left tributaries of the Kasai (ancient kingdom of Muata-Yamvo), the region of the source of the Zambesi — is inhabited by populations who have preserved the Bantu type in purer form. These are, starting from the south, the *Ganguela*, occupying the table-land bordered on the east by the upper valley of the Kwando, on the south by the right tributaries of the

[1] It is supposed that the Bubangis arrived at the north of French Congo about the eighteenth century, and their migration towards the south, stayed for the time being by the Batekes, has gone on to the present day.

[2] Pogge, *Im Reiche d. Muata Jamwo*, Berlin, 1880, and *Mittheil. Afrik. Gesell.*, vol. iv., 1883-85, p. 179; Wolff, *Verh. Gesell. Erdkunde*, Berlin, 1887, No. 2; A. J. Wauters, *L'État independant du Congo*, Brussels, 1899, p. 257 *et seq.*; Serpa Pinto, *How I Crossed Africa*, 2 vols., London, 1881, with figs.; Wissmann, Wolff, Von François, and Müller, *Im Inneren Afrikas*, Leipzig, 1888, with figs.; Jacques, *Les Congolais.*

Zambesī, and on the west by the Mubungo tributary of Lake Ngami; they are excellent smiths, supplying articles in iron to their neighbours, who are the *Amboella*, the *Kimbandé*, and the *Kioko* or *Akioko*. These last, scarcely thirty-five years ago, taking up a position to the east of the Ganguelas, have to-day advanced to the 10th degree of S. latitude, into the western part of Muata-Yamvo. But the basis of the population of this ancient kingdom is constituted by the *Lunda* tribes, whose territory extends from the Kwango (affluent of the Kasai) to lakes Bangweolo and Moero. They occupy the basin of the Kasai (*Kalunda*), the swampy plains to the east of the upper Zambesi (the *Balunda*, the *Lobalé*), and are distinguished by their peaceable habits and hospitality. Their women enjoy a certain freedom.

The *Baluba*, who form an important nation, occupy the territory between the Kasai, the chain of the Mitumba mountains and the 6th degree of S. latitude. They appear to have many analogies with the Lunda. Of tall stature (1m. 70), their head is more globular and complexion less dark than with most Negroes (ceph. ind. 79, according to Wolff). The original country of these tribes is the upper basin of the Congo. Many of the Baluba are mixed with the *Bashilange* aborigines who dwell between the middle valley of the Kasai and that of its right affluent, the Lulua, and form a separate population, relatively civilised, who emigrate as far as the Congo, where they become engaged as carriers. These are a lively people; the head is slightly elongated (stature, 1m. 68, cephalic index 76.9, according to Maistre). About 1870 they underwent a politico-religious revolution and introduced the hemp or "Riamba" cult, in accordance with which all the smokers of Riamba declare themselves friends, the duty of mutual hospitality is acknowledged, the sale of girls interdicted, etc. Crimes are punished by excessive administrations of the drug, which in the end stupefy the criminal (Pogge, Wolff). Their neighbours to the north, the Bakuba of the great bend of the Sankuru, who speak a different language, are more sedentary and busy themselves in trade and the cultivation of their fields, with the assistance of Negrilloes who live among them. The Basongo, their neighbours to the north, are redoubtable man-eaters.

All these populations, who, as we have seen, are characterised by stature above the average and by moderate dolichocephaly, are distinguished also by fairer complexion than their neighbours the Bantus of the Congo (Maistie, Serpa Pinto, Deniker and Laloy). The region they hold has frequently (from the sixteenth to the eighteenth century) been invaded by the "Djaga," armed bands in the service of certain families of the Balunda people. The invaders intermingled with the aboriginal race, which is probably allied to the Bushmen and Hottentots; at least, there are till now to be met with in the country individuals of very pure Bushman type, above all among the Kiokos.

The populations to be found between the great bend of the Congo and the 5th degree of south latitude, known collectively as the Mongo or Balolo, and Bayombe, seem to possess traits intermediate between the Lunda and the natives of French Congo. They are degenerate tribes. Such cannot be said of the Bayanzi of the right bank of the Congo, between Bolobo and Lake Tumba, nor of the Banga, between the Congo and the Ubangi, who are very alert, active, and intelligent. Their mode of head-dress, in which the hair is plaited into horns, is entirely characteristic.

Most of the western Bantu of French Congo and Congo Free State wear ornaments in the lips, file or pull out the incisor teeth, tattoo, and build small square dwellings.[1]

b. The group of *Eastern Bantus* includes numerous tribes often having an intermixture of Ethiopian blood, and ranging from the region of the sources of the Nile to 15° S. latitude, between the east coast of Africa and the

[1] L. Frobenius (*Der Ursprung der Afrik. Kulturen*, Berlin, 1898) sees in this last-cited fact a proof of the supposed influence of the Malays; E. Reclus (*Geogr. Univers.*, vol. xiii., p. 271) regards it as the result of imitation of the European factories which have been established for three centuries on the coast.

great lakes. German ethnographers distinguish among them the *ancient* and *modern* Bantus, according to their immigration from the south or north (see p. 429). On the coast, between Cape Delgado and Port Durnford, the Bantus are interblent with the Arabs and form a compound population speaking the Kiswahili language.[1] This Bantu dialect has, owing to the simplicity of its structure, become the *lingua franca* of almost the entire region occupied by the eastern Bantus. To the west of the Swahili live, in Unyamwesi and the surrounding countries, the Usambara and the Unyamwesi, belonging to the "ancient Bantus," and having, like them, migratory tendencies towards the north.

As to the *Bantus of the Lake Region*, the tribes of which are dispersed between the south of Unyoro and Lake Tanganyika, they are not more free from intermixture. But they speak the dialect derived from that primitive Bantu language, "Kirundi," or "Kikonjo," which to-day is preserved in its original purity only in a narrow tract of some fifty kilometres, extending from the foot of Mount Ruwenzori to the northern extremity of Lake Tanganyika. Mixed with Nilotes in Unyoro, with Wahuma Hamites elsewhere, the language of these "ancient Bantus" was adopted by their conquerors. The most southern tribe of this group is that of the Makua, who extend to 16° S. latitude. The tribes who people Uganda (to the north-west of Lake Victoria Nyanza) have probably sprung from the same stock, but speak a different language.

The peoples speaking Bantu to be met with south of Kilima Njaro, on the Iramba table-land, the Wakamba, Wataita, Wakaguru, and Wagogo, are Hamito-Bantus who have adopted the manners and customs of the Masai. These "Bantus of recent immigration" have come from the north-east, from the country of the Gallas, where their remaining fellows are still to be found under the name of Wapokompo in the upper valley

[1] The prefix *Ki* means "language," as *U* means "country," and *Va-Ua*, or *Ba*, "people," or "men."

of the Tsana, and Watakosho, speaking Galla, near Lake Rudolf. Among the eastern Bantus are provisionally classed the Wavira, who perforate the lips like the western Bantus; the Wahuma, who are of Ethiopian type; and the other tribes who dwell between the middle Congo and the lakes, from the equator to 5° lat. S., who are also called Waregga (People of the Forest). These are cannibals who have come from the south-west; their language differs from that of their neighbours, the Manyuema, who are of Ethiopian type. The tribes living to the south of the Ituri valley, the Wambuba, the Wallessi, etc., appear to be a hybrid of Negrilloes and Bantus.

The group of *Southern Bantus*[1] is composed of Kafir-Zulus to the east, of Bechuana to the centre, and of Herrero to the west. The Zulus (Fig. 47), of which the most southern tribe or "Ama," the Amaxosa or Kafirs (Fig. 135), live in the eastern part of Cape Colony, and have of recent times advanced towards the north, far from the country of their origin, up to the region of Usagara. Among the chief Zulu tribes should be noted the Banyai, the Bakalaka, the Baronga, the Swazi (Fig. 142), and the Tonga, between Delagoa Bay and the Transvaal; the "Ama" Mpondo of Pondo, the "Ama" Tembu of Kafirland; the Makong, neighbours of the Shinia (Foa) on the banks of the middle Zambesi, etc. Except these Kafirs, who have a special language, all the other Zulus speak the Takesa tongue.

The Bechuana, separated from the Zulus by the chain of the Drakensberg Mountains, are infused more or less with Hottentot blood; they are divided into *Eastern Bechuana* or *Basuto*, among whom Bantu traits predominate, and the *Western Bechuana* or *Bakalahari*, who show a more marked

[1] Fritsch, *Die Eingeborenen Sud-Afrikas*, Breslau, 1872, with atlas; Holub, *Sieben Jahre in Sud-Afrika*, Vienna, 1881, vol. ii., figs. and maps, and "Die Matabele," *Zeitschr. f. Ethnol.*, vol. xx., 1893; Kropf, *Das Volk d. Xosa-Kaffern*, Berlin, 1889; Wood, *loc. cit.*, vol. i.; Macdonald, "Manners . . . South-African Tribes," *Journ. Anth. Inst.*, vol. xix., p. 264, and vol. xx., p. 123 (1889-90); Johnston, *British Central Africa*, London, 1897; Junod, "Les Ba-Ronga," *Bull. Soc. Neuchateloise de Géogr.*, vol. x., 1898.

intermixture of Hottentot elements. To the north of the Bechuanas, in the upper basin of the Zambesi, live the Barotsé, a people related to the Zulus, of which one tribe is known as the Mashona. Finally, two other Bantu tribes extend to the south of the Kunene, surrounding the table-land inhabited by the Hill Damaras or Haw-Koïn (see below); these are the

FIG. 142.—Swazi-Bantu woman and girl. (*Coll. Anthr. Inst. Great Britain.*)

Ovambo or Ovampo, tillers of the soil (over 100,000), to the north between 16.30° and 20° lat. S., and the Ova-Herrero or Damara shepherds, of a fine Bantu type, to the west and south.

Physically the Zulus are of high stature (1m. 72, according to Fritsch) and dolichocephalic (average ceph. ind. of 86 skulls 73.2, according to Fritsch, Hamy, and Shrubsall). They have these traits in common with the

Nigritians,[1] but they are not so dark as the latter, and are less prognathous. The face also is square and the nose prominent, although somewhat coarse.

VII. The Bushmen-Hottentots[2] probably occupied formerly the whole of South Africa from the 15th degree of south latitude to the Cape of Good Hope. Hardly pressed for three centuries by Bantus in the east and north, and for a century by Europeans in the south, they are reduced to-day to a few thousands of families, wandering or sedentary, in the uncultivated country of Namaqualand, in the desert of Kalahari, and in some points of the hinterland of the Cape. To the north of 18° S. latitude are found only a few islets of

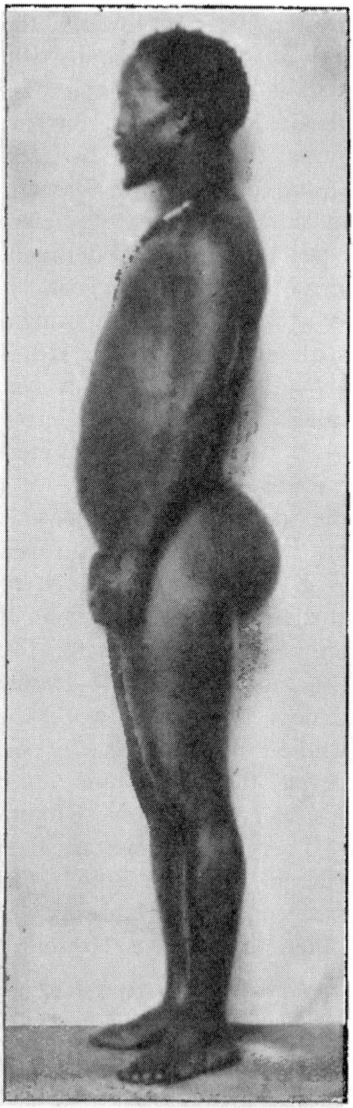

FIG. 143.—N'Kon-yui, Bushman of the region of Lake Ngami; 40 years old; height, 1m. 44; ceph. ind., 77.2; nas. ind., 97.5. (*Phot. Coll. Anthr. Soc., Paris.*)

[1] The Bechuana are a little shorter (1m. 68, according to Fritsch) and more dolichocephalic (ceph. ind. of four skulls, 70.9, according to Hamy, "Documents Cafrerie," *Arch. Mus. Hist. Nat.*, p. 357, Paris, 1882). Shrubsall (*Journ. Anth. Inst*, N.S, vol. i., 1898) gives the ceph. index as 71.3 for the Basuto skulls. The Herrero and Damara skulls have the indices, 71 and 72.

[2] Fritsch, *loc. cit.*; Schinz, *loc. cit.*; Von Luschan, *loc. cit.*

Hottentots, and towards the south they are no longer met with in compact groups within sixty miles from the coast. To the east, their habitat is limited at about 23° longitude E. of Greenwich. And further, we must gather within these limits the territory between the Herrero country and 18° S. lat. of the Hill Damaras or Haw-Koin, who, although speaking a Hottentot dialect, possess a quite special physical type; they are notably much darker than the Hottentots, and recall rather the Negroes of Guinea. They are miserable savages who live by hunting and plunder.

In addition to the Hill Damaras there are to be noted in the group of which we are treating: 1st, the Naman, called Hottentots by Europeans (modification of the Dutch word "hüttentüt," meaning of little sense, stupid), inhabiting the west of the territory we have just defined (Fig. 24); 2nd, the San ("Sab" in the masculine singular), called "Bosjesmen" or "Bushmen" by Europeans, in the east of this territory (Fig. 143). It should be remarked, however, that the word Bosjesman (in Dutch, "man of the bush") is often applied to Hottentot populations, or to Hottentot-Bushmen like, for instance, the mixed breeds of Namaqualand who speak a Hottentot dialect. In certain works the name Koi-Koin is applied to the whole group before us. This is incorrect, for the Koi-Koin, or better, the Hau-Khoin, are no other than a Hottentot tribe, just as are the Nama, Gorana, and others (about 20,000).

There are numerous likenesses between the San and the Naman, who are both representatives of the Bushman race[1] (see pp. 287 and 455), but there are also numerous differences. The Hottentot language is of the same stock

[1] The Bushmen represent the race almost in its purity, while the Hottentots show the traits of this race somewhat modified. The stature of the latter is higher, the head more dolichocephalic, the complexion darker, and the hands are not so small as is the case with Bushmen. Their features are more negroid, and it has been suggested that contact with the neighbouring Bantu tribes has had something to do with this. (See Deniker, "Les Hottentots," *Rev. d'Anthrop.*, 1889, p. 1.) The skin of the Hottentots, however, is still of a hue of yellow, and their steatopygy is almost as pronounced as with the Bushmen.

as that of the Bushmen; and both are characterised by the presence of certain articulations known as "clicks." But the Hottentot dialects, which closely resemble each other, possess four palato-dental clicks, while the Bushmen dialects, differing much from each other, have besides these four clicks another guttural click, as well as a certain articulation which is not effected by inhalation as are the clicks proper, but by rapid and repeated expirations made between the two half-opened rows of teeth.

The two peoples differ equally in manners and customs. Let it suffice to recall that the Bushmen live in the woods and are nomadic hunters, who do not practise circumcision, but whose custom it is to cut the finger-joints in sign of mourning. (See pp. 181, 204, 211, and 228 for other particulars.) The Hottentots, on the contrary, are nomadic shepherds; they live in the steppes, practise circumcision, and are unacquainted with the custom of ablation of the phalanges. Besides, they have lost all ethnic individuality; they dress in the European fashion, speak Dutch or English, and live like the white colonists. Children born of marriages between Hottentots and Europeans are called "Bastards," a title which in Africa is not regarded as discreditable.

VIII. The population of the island of Madagascar[1] may be divided into three great groups: the Hovas in the middle, the Malagasies of the east coast, and the Sakalavas of the rest of the island. There is further to be noted the Arab infusion, especially on the north-east and south-east coast.

The Hovas, or better, Huves, who occupy the high tableland of Imerina (from which comes their true name, "Anta-

[1] For particulars see Sibree, *Great Afric. Island . . . Madagascar*, 1880; M. Leclerc, "Les peuplades de Madagascar," *Rev. d'Ethnogr.*, vol. v., 1886, p. 397, and vol. vi., 1887, p. 1; Catat, *Voyage à Madagascar*, Paris, 1895, in quarto; Grandidier, "Les Hovas," *Rev. gén. des Sciences*, No. for 1st June, 1895; A. Jolly, *L'Anthropologie*, 1894, p. 385; Besson, *ibid.*, p. 674; "Le Madagascar," *Rev. gén. des Sciences*, Paris, No. for 15th Aug., 1895, fig.; Last, *Journ. Anthr. Inst.*, 1896, p. 47; Bouchereau, *L'Anthr.*, 1897, p. 149; J. Carol, *Chez les Hovas*, Paris, 1898.

Imerina"[1]) are Indonesians more or less intermixed with Malay stock; their skin is olive-yellow, their hair straight or slightly wavy, their eyes sometimes narrow; their stature is short, their head globular, the nose prominent and somewhat sharp (Fig. 144).[2] They preserve many manners and customs Indonesian in character—their square houses on piles, sarong, instruments of music, *fadi* or *taboo* for diet, infanticide, polygamy, canoe with balance-pole, cylindrical forge bellows, form of sepulture, etc. A half-civilised people, they are tillers of the soil, shepherds, and traders. The Sakalavas, on the contrary, are almost pure Bantu Negroes, black, dolichocephalic, of high stature, with frizzy hair and flat noses. They have preserved some features of Negro life (palavers, fetichism, etc.), but are adopting more and more the mode of life of the Hovas or the Malagasies. These last present traits intermediate between the two groups; of chocolate-brown complexion, with frizzy hair, of medium height, they have other features so modified as to recall sometimes the Hovas, sometimes the Sakalavas.

The Hovas arrived in Madagascar only seven or eight centuries ago (Grandidier), and succeeded in subjugating the Sakalavas and the mixed populations. Up to the period of the French occupation (1896) they were masters of the island, with the exception of the west coast and some points in the south. They have imposed their language on the subjugated populations, and all the peoples of the island, notwithstanding their diversity of origin, of type, and of manners and customs, speak Malagasy, which is a dialect of the Maleo-Polynesian linguistic family with some intermixture of Bantu elements.

It is supposed that before the advent of the Hovas other Malay and Indonesian incursions took place in the island,

[1] The prefix *Antan* or *Anta* (in some dialects *Ta*) in Malagasy language means "people of," and is found in the nomenclature of all the tribes and people of the island.

[2] See the measurements given in Appendices I. to III., according to Bouchereau, *loc. cit.*, and my own unpublished observations made in conjunction with Dr. Collignon.

though nothing certain is known in regard to this; that the arrival of the Negroes was due to their own action is problematical, notwithstanding the relative nearness (250 miles) of the coast of Mozambique, the notorious incapacity of the Negroes as navigators being taken into account. It is possible that the Negroes were introduced into the island entirely by the Maleo-Indonesians, who have always been good seamen. The Arab invasions date back hardly five or six centuries.

The constitution of Hova society up till recently was divided into nobles (*Andriana*), freemen (*Hovas*), and slaves (*Andevo*). The abolition of Royalty and slavery, after the French occupation, have to a certain extent modified this hierarchy. For thirty years converts to Protestantism, at bottom the Hovas are very indifferent in religious matters, but cling to their ancient animistic beliefs. To the Hovas should be joined the Betsileo, who live to the south of the Imerina table-land; they are not of such pure race as the Hovas, while they are less intermixed than are the Malagasies.

Among these last must first be distinguished the populations of the coast: the Betsimasaraka and the Antambahoaka to the north of the 20th degree of S. latitude; the Antaimoro, the Antaifasina, the Antaisaka, and the Antanosi to the south of this latitude; then the population of the interior: the Antsihanaka to the north of Imerina, the Bezanozano in the centre of the island, the Antanala or Tanala, and the Bara and Antaisara to the south.

The Betsimasaraka are dolichocephalic (ceph. ind. 76.3, according to Collignon and Deniker), and of stature below the average (1m. 64). The Antambahoaka and the Antaimoro claim an Arab origin, but they hardly differ from the other Malagasies; they are rather backward in culture and emigrate from their country readily, but with the idea of returning. The Antaifasina (who number about 200,000) have close affinities with the Antaisaka, their warlike neighbours on the coast, in closer proximity to Vangaindrano; both have many customs of Arab-Mussulman origin, and are connected, according to all probability, with the Bara tribe. This last lives inland, to the south of Betsileo, side by side with the Antaisara, said to be true savages, but among whom are nevertheless observed signs of Arab blood (Scott Eliott). The Antanosi are grouped round Fort Dauphin, but some of this tribe has emigrated to the interior, extending as far as the neighbourhood of the west coast, where it has assimilated the customs of the Bara people. As a race the Antanosi are less negroid than the other Malagasies, and recall rather the

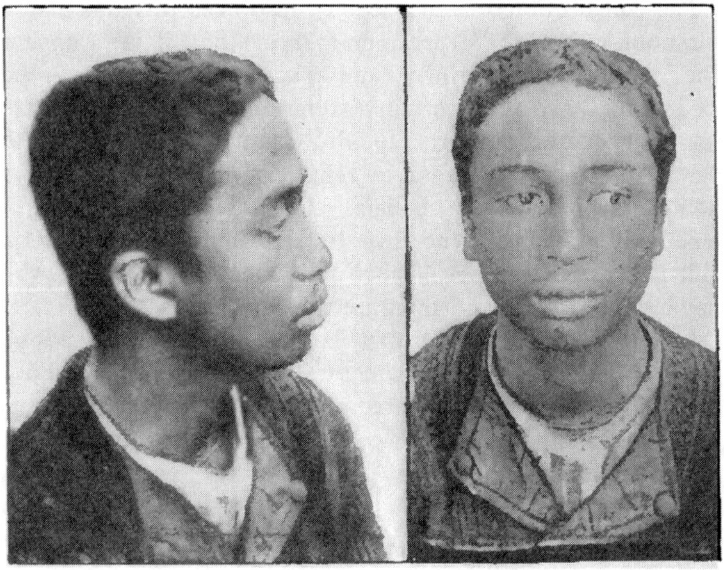

FIG. 144.—Hova of Tananarivo; 21 years old; height, 1m. 62; ceph. ind., 79.3. (*Phot. Collignon.*)

Betsimasaraka. They have curly or almost smooth hair (Catat), and complexion of light chestnut. They are a peaceable and intelligent people, of cleaner habits than the other Malagasies. Like most of the tribes of the south of Madagascar, even the Sakalavas (as, for example, the Antavandroi), they wear garments of matting plaited with straw, except on the coast, where European fabrics have now replaced the native garments.

The Sakalava tribes are numerous. The best known are the Menabe, Milaka, Ronondra, and Mahafali. In the north of the island the Sakalavas are mixed with the Betsimasaraka, and form the Antankar or Antankara people, wild shepherds and tillers of the soil, recalling the Bantus; their centre is at Diego-Suarez. In the south, blended with the Bara, they enter into the composition of the Antandroy population (about 20,000), almost savage, who depend largely for sustenance on the cactus berries of their sterile country, live by cattle-raising, and have many manners and customs borrowed from the Bara.

CHAPTER XII.

RACES AND PEOPLES OF OCEANIA.

The Stone Age in Oceania—I. *Australians:* Uniformity of the Australian race—Language and manners and customs of the Australians—Extinct *Tasmanians*—II. *Populations of the Asiatic or Malay Archipelago:* Papuan and Negrito elements in the Archipelago—Indonesians and Malays of Sumatra, Borneo, Celebes, etc.—III. *Melanesians:* Papuans of New Guinea—Melanesians properly so called of the Salomon and Admiralty Islands, New Hebrides, New Caledonia, etc.—IV. *Polynesians:* Polynesians properly so called of Samoa, Tahiti, and Sandwich Islands, New Zealand, etc.—Micronesians of the Caroline and Marianne Islands, etc.—Peopling of the Pacific Islands and of the Indian Ocean.

"OCEANIA" appears to me the term best adapted to designate comprehensively all the insular lands scattered in the immensity of the Pacific and Indian Oceans. These in their entirety are, from the ethnographic point of view, divided into a continent, Australia, which shelters a distinct race, the Australians, and into two groups of islands. The western group, that of the Asiatic Archipelago, formed especially of large islands, is peopled principally by Indonesians, pure and mixed. As to the eastern group, it falls into two regions: one region consisting of New Guinea (which, after Greenland, is the largest island of the world), together with the neighbouring archipelagoes peopled by the Melanesian race; and the other region formed of the innumerable islands, islets, rocks, and atolls situated farther east, and occupied by the Polynesian race. I shall describe separately the populations of these four regions, but I must say a few words in advance in regard to the *prehistoric periods of Oceania.*

With the exception of Sumatra, Java, and perhaps Borneo, still connected with Asia at the end of the tertiary period, the rest of Oceania formed an insular world apart, of ancient geological origin. Except the discovery of the *Pithecanthropus* in Java (see p. 360), hardly any finds relating to quaternary man can be pointed to in this part of the world. The objects in chipped or polished flint noted here and there in Malaysia, Australia, or New Zealand, as having been found at a certain depth of earth, have no fixed date, and, seeing that all Oceania, except West Malaysia, was up to the end of the last century still in the "stone age," and remains in that age yet at several places, it will be understood that these finds may hardly be dated back further than some tens or hundreds of years, and have no connection with geological periods.[1] As to the megalithic monuments,—the ruins of "Morai" and other erections in Oceania, of which the best known are those of Easter Island, but which exist also in the Marquesas, Tahiti, Pitcairn, and Caroline Islands,—a precise date can with no greater certitude be assigned to them.[2]

The long duration of the stone age in Oceania may be explained especially by the absence of metallic deposits in Polynesia, and by the relative difficulty of working the iron and copper ores of New Zealand and of the rest of Oceania.[3]

The contemporary stone age, together with the affinity of the Malay, Polynesian, and Melanesian languages (Von

[1] For particulars see C. Pleyte, "De prähist. steenen wapenen . . . Oost-Indish. Archipel.," *Bijdr. t. d. Taal-Land-en Volkenk. van Nederl. Ind.*, Batavia, 5th series, vol. ii., p. 586; Wilken, *loc. cit.*, p. 83; Etheridge, "Has Man a Geological History in Australia?" *Proc. Linn. Soc. N. S. Wales*, 1890, p. 259; B. Smyth, *loc. cit.*, vol. i., p. 239, and vol. ii., p. 234; R. Chapmann, *Trans. N. Zeal. Inst.*, 1891, p. 479.

[2] See W. Thomson Smith, *loc. cit.*; Tautain, "Monuments des Marquises," *L'Anthropol.*, 1897, p. 4; F. Christian, "On Micronesian Weapons," *Journ. Anthr. Inst.*, N.S., 1899, vol. i., p. 288, pl. xx. and xxiv.

[3] Besides, the Maoris of New Zealand know nothing of pottery, notwithstanding their clay deposits, nor of weaving, notwithstanding the presence in their island of *Formium* and other textile plants.

Gabelentz), are perhaps the most characteristic traits of Oceanic ethnography.

I. AUSTRALIA.—The Australians form a distinct ethnic group, even a race apart from the rest of mankind. Notwithstanding some local differences, they exhibit great unity, not only from the somatic point of view, but also from the point of view of manners, customs, and speech. Up to a certain point

FIG. 145.—Ambit, Sundanese of Java (Preanger prov.), 30 years old; height, 1m. 67; ceph. ind., 85 7; nas. ind., 88.6. (*Phot. Pr. Roland Bonaparte.*)

this unity may be explained by the fact that the nature and surface of the soil, as well as the climate, the fauna and flora, vary to a relatively slight degree throughout the whole extent of the continent.[1]

[1] The division, based on physical characters, of tribes of the interior, composed of a strong people of high stature and regular features, and of tribes of the coast, formed of a little, ugly, and puny people, a division proposed by Topinard (*Bull. Soc. Anthro.*, 1872), has not been confirmed by later investigations.

Formerly owners of the entire face of their country, the Australians are now driven back farther and farther into poor, sterile, and unhealthy regions. Those who remain in contact with the invading European colonists are debased and degenerate, and disappear rapidly. The tribes of purest type, those of the mid-region and of the north coast, have recently been well studied by Stirling, Baldwin Spencer and Gillen, and W. Roth.[1]

The census of 1851 included 55,000 natives in Australia; that of 1881 declared only 31,700; and that of 1891, no doubt better compiled and including newly-discovered districts, gives a return of only 59,464 natives and cross-breeds.[2]

Between 1836 and 1881 the number of natives in Victoria fell from 5000 to 770; the tribe of the Narrinyeri in South Australia, which in 1842 was composed of 3,200 members, was by 1875 reduced to only 511 individuals. But no positive proof has been obtained of diminution in the number of the natives of the interior, nor of those of the west and north coasts.

Most Australians exhibit the sufficiently pure type of the *Australian race* as I have already described it (p. 285): dark chocolate-brown skin, stature above the average (1m. 67); frizzy or wavy hair, very elongated dolichocephalic head (av. ceph. ind., 71.2 in skulls, and 74.5 on the living subject),

[1] "Report . . . Horn Scientif. Exped. Centr. Austr.," Part IV., *Anthropology*, by E. Stirling, London-Melbourne, 1896; Baldwin Spencer and F. Gillen, *The Native Tribes of Central Australia*, London, 1899, pl.; W. E. Roth, *Ethnol. Stud. . . . N.-W. Centr. Queensl. Aborig.*, Brisbane-London, 1897. For tribes of the east and south, see E. Curr, *The Australian Race*, Melbourne, 1886, 3 vols. with atlas; Lumholtz, *Among Cannibals*, London, 1890; and the works already quoted of Howitt, Fison, and B. Smyth. The measurements given in the Appendices are obtained from the works of Stirling and Gillen, Houzé (*Bull. Soc. Anthr. Bruxelles*, vol. iii., 1884-85); Cauvin, "Les Races de l'Océanie," *Arch. Miss. Scient.*, 3rd series, vol. iii., Paris, 1882; Topinard, *loc. cit.*; Turner, *loc. cit.*, etc.

[2] These natives and mixed breeds are apportioned by colonies, thus:—Victoria, 565; New South Wales, 8,280; South Australia, 23,789; West Australia, 6,245; Queensland, 20,585 (of which 12,000 are pure aborigines).

prominent superciliary arches, nose flat and often convex, sunken at the root, where it is very thin, but much enlarged on the level of the nostrils, thick and sometimes protruding lips, etc. The cranial capacity is rather low (see p. 99). The pilous system is well developed over the whole body (Figs. 14, 15, 149, 150). Some of these characters, the dolichocephaly and crooked nose, are common both to the Australians and the Melanesians of the archipelagoes extending north-east of the continent; while other traits (wavy or frizzy hair, etc.) differentiate these two races, and connect the Australians with the Veddahs of Ceylon and with certain of the Dravidian populations of India.

Deviations from the type just described are very slight, and have been attributed, without, I think, much justice, to intermixtures with Malays and Papuans on the coasts; elsewhere deviations are quite limited.

The Australians have great powers of endurance, are temperate and fairly agile; they climb trees readily with the aid of a rattan rope, in the style of natives of India, of the Canacks and the Negroes (p. 275 and Fig. 81).

Most travellers agree in regard to the low intellectual development of the Australians. However, they have sufficiently complex social customs, an extensive folk-lore,[1] and their children have been known, in the missionary schools, to learn to read and write more quickly than European children; arithmetic only appearing to be outside the limits of their intelligence. It should be remarked in regard to all Australian dialects that they have special words only for the figures one and two, occasionally for three and four; but most frequently "two and one" is used for "three," and "two and two" for "four" (see p. 223).

The Australian languages present great resemblances to each other; they all belong to a single family, having no affinity with any other linguistic group. All these languages are

[1] See L. Parker, *Australian Legendary Tales*, London and Melbourne, 1897, and *More Australian Tales*, *ib.*, 1898; Spencer and Gillen, *loc. cit.*

agglutinative. The various forms of the words are produced by the addition of suffixes, while in the Malay and Papuan

FIG. 146.—Natives of Livuliri (near Larantuka, Floris). Indonesian race with intermixture in varying degrees of Papuan blood. Height from 1m. 55 to 1m. 64; ceph. ind., 76.6 to 86.9. (*Phot. and particulars, Lapicque.*)

languages they are produced by means of prefixes. Abbreviations, slovenliness of pronunciation, and neologisms are very constant, and rapidly lead to changes in these dialects.

Gesture language is fairly developed, especially as an ideographic mode of communication between tribe and tribe. Very often a gesture completes the phrase, even in a colloquy between two members of the same tribe; certain of these gestures recall those of European children, such as lightly

FIG. 147.—Buri, a Solorian of Adanara Island (close to Floris); Mussulman. Height, 1m. 64; ceph. ind., 85.1. (*Phot. and particulars, Lapicque.*)

rubbing the stomach to signify "I have had enough" (W. Roth).

The Australians are typical hunters (for their weapons, see pp. 259 and 267, and Figs. 75 and 78). They know nothing of cattle-raising; their only domestic animal, the dingo, is half wild. Fruit gathering and the digging up of roots of wild plants are the principal occupations of the women. Intoxicating drinks, apart from the regions penetrated by colonists, are unknown; the custom of chewing "pituri" leaves (*Duboisia*) as a narcotic is fairly widespread.

Most of the tribes live under such shelters as nature affords, or in huts made of leafy branches, hemispherical or semi-ovoid in shape, and very low (p. 161); even these they do not take the trouble to put up if they have other means of protecting themselves from cold, such as the woollen blankets distributed by the Colonial Governments.

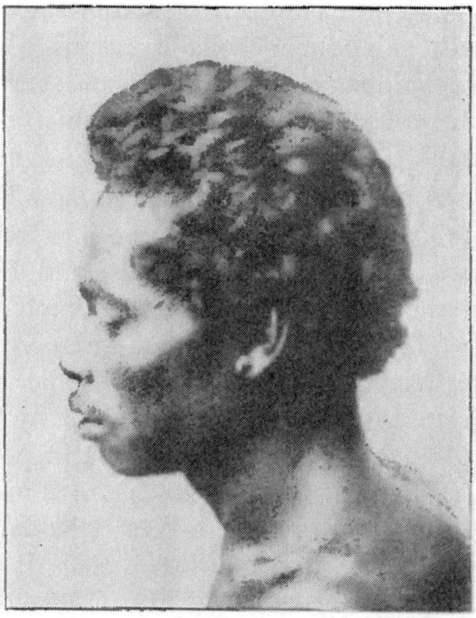

FIG. 148.—Same subject as Fig. 147, seen in profile; a striking blend of Melanesian and Indonesian traits. (*Phot. Lapicque.*)

Sundry particulars have already been given in regard to the ornaments of the Australians (p. 178, and Figs. 59, 149, and 150), in regard to their marriage customs (p. 232), their system of affiliation (p. 234), the "corroborees," and their ceremonies of *initiation* (p. 241), at which time are practised the circumcision and urethral sub-incision (*mika* operation, p. 239) of the young people. On p. 210, *et seq.*, I have already given some details in regard to the music, poetry, and arts of these people.

In most ethnographical works, the extinct *Tasmanian*[1] people are described side by side with the Australian. The only reason of this lies in the proximity of their habitat, for really the Tasmanians recall rather the Melanesians, both in somatic traits and in mode of life. The language of the Tasmanians, which is agglutinative with prefixes and suffixes, presents no analogy either with Australian or Melanesian tongues. The Tasmanians appear to have been of stature below the average (1m. 66); head, sub-dolichocephalic (ceph. ind., 76 to 77); broad and prognathous face; flattened and very broad nose; frizzy hair (which last constituted their chief difference from the Australians).[2]

II. Asiatic Archipelago or Malaysia.—The population of this part of Oceania may be separated into four great ethnic groups: Malays, Indonesians, Negritoes, and Papuans. The first two form the basis of most of the ethnic groups of the Archipelago, while the Negrito element is represented only in the Malay peninsula (which from the ethnic point of view may be associated with the Archipelago), in the Andaman Islands (see p. 397), in the Philippines, and perhaps in Riu-Linga; and the Papuan element in the Aru and Ke Islands, and in a lesser degree in the South-West Islands, Ceram, Buru, Timur, Floris, and the neighbouring islets. It has long been supposed that the interior of the Malay Islands is occupied by negroid races akin to the Negritoes or Papuans; but no

[1] Estimated at 1000 in 1817, the Tasmanians numbered 340 in 1824 (first census). The number fell to 111 in 1834, to 51 in 1842, to 16 in 1854, to 4 in 1865 (H. Hull, *Statist. Summary of Tasmanians*, 1866). The last representative of the Tasmanian people, a woman called Truganina, died in 1876. Miss F. C. Smith, still living, and described as a Tasmanian, in 1889, is a Tasmano-European half-breed (Ling Roth, *Journ. Anthr. Inst.*, vol. xxvii., p. 451, 1897-98).

[2] In his work, *The Aborigines of Tasmania*, 2nd ed., London, 1899, with figs., Ling Roth has conscientiously summarised all that has been published about the Tasmanians.

explorer of Sumatra, Borneo, Java,[1] or Celebes has yet encountered Negritoes there, although the centres of these islands have repeatedly been traversed; hence there is little hope of discovering negroid races in them. Besides, the assumed Negritoes of the Mergui Archipelago, of Nicobar and of Engano, described by Anderson, Lapicque, Man, Sherborn and Modigliani, have been shown to be simply Indonesians. The existence of true Negritoes has been affirmed only in the extreme north of the Archipelago, in the spots named above, the Andaman Islands, etc. If there be any trace whatever of intermixture with these races, it should not be necessary to search beyond the north parts of Sumatra and Borneo—in other words, beyond the equator going south.

I have already given some particulars in regard to the Negritoes of Malacca and the Andamanese (p. 397). As to the people of the Philippines,[2] known under the name of *Aeta* or *Aita* (a corruption of the Malay word "hitam," meaning black), they occupy the interior of Luzon Island in little groups, and are to be met with also in the Mindoro, Panay, and Negros islands, and in the north-east part of Mindanao. They are shorter (1m. 47) than the Andamanese and the Sakai, but are very like them generally. They are uncivilised hunters; in certain districts where they are crossed with Tagals they have begun to till the soil.

The Papuans (see p. 493) are still less numerous than the Negritoes in the Asiatic Archipelago. They are to be found, more or less pure, only in the Aru, Salawatti, and Waigiu Islands, etc. All these islands form part of the Archipelago only from the political point of view; they belong by their climate, their flora and fauna, to the New Guinea and Australian

[1] There is no justification for supposing that the Kalangs of Java are Negritoes, as A. R. Meyer has assumed in his memoir (*Leopoldina*, part xiii., Nos. 13-14, 1877). See on this point, Kohlbrugge, "L'Anthr. des Tenggerois," *L'Anthropologie*, p. 4, 1898.

[2] See Montano, "Mission aux Philippines," *Arch. Miss. Scient.*, 3rd series, vol. xi., with figs., Paris, 1885; De Quatrefages, *loc. cit.* (*Les Pygmées*); Schadenberg, *Zeitschr. f. Ethnol.*, 1880.

world. There are also tribes which recall the Papuans in Ceram and Buru, in the Ke and Tenimber islands; but in the remainder of the Moluccas, and in Floris and Timur islands,

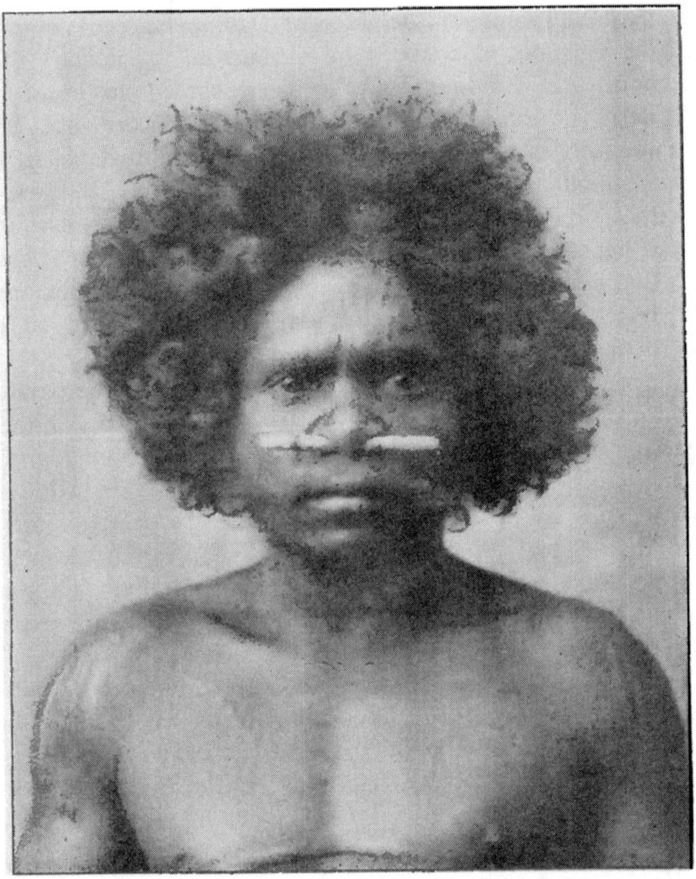

FIG. 149.—"Billy," Queensland Australian; height, 1m. 51; ceph. ind., 70.4; nas. ind., 107.5. (*Phot. Prince Roland Bonaparte.*)

only traces of Papuan or Melanesian blood can be discovered, generally in the form of intermixture with or modification of the Malay or Indonesian type (see p. 491, and Figs. 46 to 48). Such at least is the conclusion to which lead the researches of

Ten Kate and Lapicque,[1] the only anthropologists who have studied the question on the spot.

There remain the two principal groups of the population of

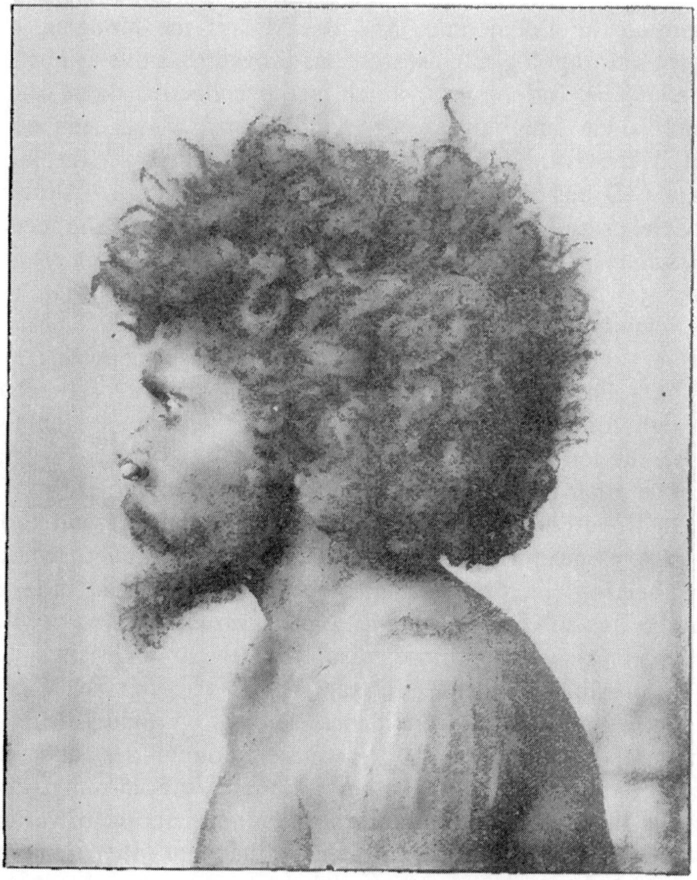

FIG. 150.—Same subject as Fig. 149, in profile. Tattooing by cicatrisation. (*Phot. Prince Roland Bonaparte.*)

[1] Ten Kate, "L'Anthropologie d'Oceanie," *L'Anthropologie*, vol. iv., 1893, p. 279; "Verslag eener Reis in Timorgrœp," *Tijdschr. Nederl. Aardrijk. sk. Genoot.*, Amsterdam, vol. xi., 1894, with summary in French; and *Anthropol. Problem in Insulindie . . . Festbundel . . . Dr. P. Veth aangeboden*, p. 212, Leyden, 1894; Lapicque, *loc. cit.* (*Tour du Monde*).

the Archipelago: the *Indonesians* and *Malays*, who differ from each other much less than till recently was supposed.

It has been said and frequently repeated, though without precise documents to warrant the assertion, that the Indonesians resemble the Polynesians, and the Malays the Mongols, but recent anthropological research has proved that this is not the case.[1] The Indonesians, which is the collective name under which, since Junghuhn, Logan, and Hamy,[2] have been comprised the little intermixed inland populations of the large islands (Dyaks of Bornea, Battas of Sumatra, various "Alfurus" of Celebes and certain Moluccas, etc.), have none of the special characters of Polynesians. They are of very short stature (1m. 57 on the average), mesocephalic or dolichocephalic (av. ceph. ind., 78.5 on the liv. sub.), while the Polynesians are very tall (1m. 72 on the average) and brachycephalic; and if the yellow colour of the skin and the nature of the hair (straight or slightly curled) are almost the same in the two races, the form of the nose, of the lips, of the face, as well as various other traits, present notable differences.

On the other hand, the Indonesians singularly resemble the Malays. Speaking generally, the Malays are somewhat taller (av. height, 1m. 61) and brachycephalic (av. ceph. ind., 85 on the liv. sub.), but there is a great variety of type in this group, which is much more mixed than the Indonesian. It is even possible that the Malays (that is to say, the Malays properly so called of Malacca and of Menangkabau in Sumatra, as well as the Javanese, Sundanese, and the riverine "Malays" of the other islands) are a mixed nation, sprung from the intermixture of Indonesians with various Burmese, Negrito, Hindu, Chinese, Papuan and other elements.

[1] Modigliani, *loc. cit.*, and *L'isola delle Donne . . . Engano*, Milan, 1894; Danielli, "Cranii di Engano," *Archiv. p. l'anthr.*, vol. xxiv. See also the works already quoted of Montano, Hagen (as well as his *Anthropolog. Atlas Ostasiat . . . Völk.*, Wiesbaden, 1898), Ten Kate, Deniker and Laloy, Lapicque, Kohlbrugge, etc.

[2] Junghuhn, *Battaländer auf Sumatra*, vol. ii., p. 375; Hamy, "Les Alfourous de Gilolo," *Bull. Soc. Geogr. Paris*, 6th ser., vol. xiii., p. 490.

In this case, the Indonesians would be of the pure Malay type, the real Protomalays. Intermixtures of Indonesians and Chinese are especially pronounced in Java, in the north of Bornea, and in the Philippines of the north; while in Mindanao, in Sulu and Palawan islands, Arab elements (*Moros*) dominate, and Hindu elements in certain parts of Java, Sumatra, Bali, and of the south of Borneo. As to intermixtures with Negrito blood they are, as I have already said, specially notable in the north of the Archipelago, while Papuan influence predominates in the south-east.

Apart from some savage tribes like the Olo-ot, the Punañ of Borneo, and the Kubus of Sumatra, all the Indonesians and Malays are tillers of the soil, using the hoe. The plant most extensively cultivated is rice, a foreign importation; it has replaced the indigenous plant, millet (*Panicum italicum*), which only some backward Dyak tribes, the Alfurus of Buru, and the natives of Timur continue to cultivate. Mention has already been made of the use of *siri* or *betel* (p. 158), and of geophagy and anthropophagy (p. 145, *et seq.*) in the Archipelago. The characteristic dress of the Indonesians and Malays is the *kaïn*, a piece of stuff passed round the loins and between the legs; also the "sarong," which appears to have been imported from India —a piece of stuff enveloping the body (Figs. 126 and 146), worn by both sexes; the women wear besides the *javat* or chastity belt. Among other ethnic characters special to the Malay-Indonesians should be mentioned the quadrangular houses on piles,[1] the use of the "sumpitan" (p. 261), the bow being of foreign importation, either from India (in Java and Bali) or from Melanesia (in the islands of the south-east and south-west, in Timur, and the east of Floris); the national weapon, the "kris," an inlaid dagger with slightly bent handle and sheath in the form of an axe; the large quadrangular or hexagonal shield (Fig. 79); tattooing, practised among the Dyaks, the Igorrotes of the Philippines, the inhabitants of Ceram, of Timur Laut, the Tenimber Islands, etc.

[1] The dwellings in trees at Sumbawa, among the Mandayas of Mindanao (Philippines), among the Lubu of Sumatra, should also be noted.

Among the customs of the family life should be noted the alterations of names (the father at the birth of a son takes the name of "the father of so-and-so"); exogamy in relation to the clan (the "saku" of the Malays of Sumatra, the "marga" of the Battas), practised everywhere in Malaysia except by the Dyaks and the Alfurus to the north of Celebes; the patriarchate, existing everywhere except in the "Padangshe Bovenlanden" (upper Padang district, Sumatra), among the Nias and the Alfurus of Baru and Ceram; the universal custom of carrying off the bride and the indemnity paid at once to the relatives ("halaku" of the Dyaks, the "sompo" of the Bugis). The barbarous practice of head-hunting, either to be assured of servitors in the other world, or to lend importance there (see p. 251), is in vogue with the Dyaks, the Nias, the Alfurus of Minahassa (north Celebes), the Toradja (mid Celebes), as well as in Ceram and Timur islands.[1] Family property exists almost throughout the Archipelago, side by side with individual property.

The Malay languages, which form part of the Malayo-Polynesian family, are of agglutinative structure, with prefixes and suffixes; by the introduction of *infixes* they have a tendency towards flexion. Many words, however, do not change at all, and represent at the same time noun, verb, adjective, etc. Among the dialects, Tagal is the richest in affixes and gives to its words the finest shades; then comes the Batta dialect, the dialect of the Alfurus of Minahassa, and lastly, Javanese (see also p. 133). The dialect least complicated grammatically is the Malay properly so called; it has become the *lingua franca* and official language of the Mussulmans throughout the Archipelago. Among other dialects may be mentioned Mangkassarese and the "Behasa tanat" of the Moluccas.

The Javanese make use of a special alphabet; the inhabitants of the south of Sumatra have a hooked mode of writing, different from the rounded writing of the Battas; finally, the

[1] Pleytte, "De Geogr. Otbreiding v. h. Koppensnellen, etc.," *Tijdschr. v. h. Aardrijksk. Genoots*, p. 908, Amsterdam, 1891.

Bugis and Mangkassars of Celebes, as well as the Bisayans and Tagals of the Philippines, have special forms of writing derived probably from the Devanagari. The Malays employ the Arabo-Persian alphabet.

I will now add some particulars of the population of each of the large islands of Malaysia.[1]

The interior of the island of Sumatra is inhabited by independent populations, known in the north under the name of Battas (with whom should probably be associated the Ala and the Gaja of the interior of Achin), and under the name of Kubu and Lubu in the south. All these tribes, who are primitive tillers of the soil, are famous as man-eaters and head hunters. As to the regions contiguous to the east and west coasts, they are inhabited (as well as in part the middle of the island, between the Kubu and the Batta) by the so-called Menangkabau Malays (the name of the ancient native kingdom). The north coast is taken up by the Achinese, a mixed Arabo-Indonesian people; while the south part of the great island is occupied by other compound populations, the Palenbangs or Javanese of Sumatra, the Rejangs (Malayo-Javanese), the Passumahs (Indonesians intermixed with Javanese blood), and finally the Lampongs, cross-breeds of Passumahs with Sundanese (see below) and the natives of the south, such as the Orang-Abong, who have to-day almost disappeared. The islands skirting west Sumatra are peopled with tribes resembling the Battas, like the islanders of Nias, of Engano (p. 486, note), etc. The islands to the east are peopled by Malays, except Riu and the middle of Biliton, which are occupied by the Baju, a tribe perhaps of Negrito race. The island of Bangka is occupied mostly by a branch of the Passumahs.

In Java are to be noted the Sundanese in the west, the Javanese in the east, the former being less affected by Hindu

[1] For the anthropometry of some of the peoples enumerated below, see Appendices I. to III. The figures there given are derived from the works of Hagan, Ten Kate, Lapicque, Deniker and Laloy, Kohlbrugge, Jacobs, Weisbach, Lubbers and Langen.

elements. The Madurese of Madura and Bavean islands, as well as the Balinese of Bali, are like the Javanese. In the less accessible mountains of the province of Bantam (west of the island) live the Baduj, and in those of the east (province of Pasuruan) the Tenggerese. These are two fairly pure Indonesian tribes, who have preserved their heathen customs in the midst of the Mussulman population of Java. There are people like them in Bali, Lombok, and Sumbawa.[1]

In Borneo, the coast is occupied by Malays, except the north-east part, where are found Suluans (Arabised Indonesians from the Sulu Islands), Bugis, and the Bajaus or Sea Gypsies, analogous to those of Riu and Mergui (p. 396).

The interior of the large island is, however, the exclusive domain of the Dyaks, the numerous tribes of which may be divided into two great groups, the one of stationary, the other of nomadic habits. The sedentary tribes, more or less intermixed with immigrant elements, Chinese, Malay, and Bugi, are more or less civilised. First come the Kayans, the Bahau, and the Segai; then the Tagans, among whom, it is said, the practice obtains of girls being deflowered by their fathers; and, lastly, the Dusuns or Sun Dyaks, the Baludupis, the Land Dyaks, and the Sea Dyaks of Sarawak, etc. Second, the nomads, who are purer than the fixed tribes, and sometimes half savage, as, for example, the Punan and Olo-ot of the middle of the island, are still little known.[2]

The Philippine archipelago[3] contains, besides Negritoes (p. 483), a crowd of Indonesian tribes, which, from the lin-

[1] See J. Jacobs, *De Badoejs*, S'Gravenhage, 1891, and Kohlbrugge, *loc. cit.*, and "De heilige bekers d. Tenegerezen," *Tijdschr. v. Ind. Taal-Land-in Volkenk*, vol. xxxiv., 1896. Among the Tenggerese some vestiges of Buddhism may be discovered.

[2] See Ling Roth, *The Natives of Sarawak*, 2 vols., London, 1896, and *Jour. Anthr. Inst.*, vols. xxi. and xxii. (1892-93).

[3] Blumentritt, "Versuch. einer Ethnographie der Philip.," *Ergänzungsheft*, *Peterm. Mitteil.*, No. 67, Gotha, 1887, with map; Montano, *loc. cit.*; Virchow, "Die Bevölker. d. Philip.," *Sitzungsber. Berlin Acad. Wiss.*, 1897, p. 279, and 1899, p. 14; Brinton, "The Peoples of Philip." (short summary), *Amer. Anthropologist*, October, 1898.

guistic and ethnic point of view, may be grouped as follows:—Starting in the north-east we meet first the Cagayanes or Ibangs around Lake Cagayan in the island of Luzon, and their neighbours the Ifugaos, who are hunters of skulls; then farther south we find the Igorrotes and their congeners; then the Tagals; then, still farther south, in the interior, on all the east coast of Luzon, as well as on the coast of Mindoro, are found the savage Mangianes. At many points these peoples are intermixed with Chinese blood. The west coast of Luzon is occupied by the Ilocanos, who are bold colonists, and, farther south, towards Manilla, tribes of the Zambales and Pangasinanes. The quite southern extremity of Luzon is occupied by the Bicols, nearly related to the Tagals, whom one finds again also scattered over the islands (Catanduanes Islands, north Masbate Island, etc.). West Mindanao is taken up by the mixed population (Arabo-Negrito-Indonesian) of pirates, Mussulman fanatics, known by the name of Moros; the east of this island being inhabited by several tribes as yet little known, such as Mandayas in the south, Bogobos in the north, etc., and the Caragas tribe of Bisaya or Vissaya. Most of these last people occupy the rest of the archipelago north of Mindanao, as far as and including the south of Masbate and Samar and Tablas islands. They are met again beside the Moros in Palawan Island between the Philippines and Borneo. The Tagaloc language is largely superseding other dialects in the archipelago; it has already displaced Bicol in the north of the province of Camarine, Bisayan on Marinduque Island, etc. Besides, Tagals emigrate to the other parts of the archipelago and even to Marianne Islands. Most of the Tagals are Christians; many can read and write Spanish, and not a few have received a superior education.

Celebes Island is peopled in the north (Minahassa province) by the Alfurus; in the south by Mangkassars and Bugis, and by various tribes (Toraja, Gorontolo, etc.), who as yet have been little studied, in the middle. The Moluccas are inhabited by other "Alfurus," with a greater strain of Papuan blood. Timur, apart from its Malay or Indonesian coast populations, contains also tribes imbued with Papuan blood; such are the Emabelo of the middle of the island; the Timur-Atuli of the east coast; the Helong-Atuli in Samu Island opposite Kupang, the capital of Timur; and lastly, the Rottinese of Rotti Island, south-west of Timur, etc.

In Floris Island, the Sikanese of the central isthmus and

Fig. 151.—Young Papuan woman of the Samarai people (Dinner Island, Moresby group, south of the south-east extremity of New Guinea). Mixed type (Papuan-Melano-Polynesian). (*Phot. Haddon.*)

the east part possess traits intermediate between Papuans and Indonesians, while the Ata-Krowé of Koting and the Hokar mountaineers are almost pure Papuans. The Lios to the west of the Sikanese present again a mixed type, as do also the inhabitants of the region of Larantuka (Fig. 146), among whom may be found all the degrees between Indonesian and almost pure Papuan. This applies also to the Solorese of the Solor Archipelago, east of Floris (Figs. 197 and 198).[1]

III. MELANESIA.—The Melanesians are a well-characterised race. However, they exhibit in somatic type differences sufficiently marked to separate the Melanesian race into two sub-races. The one, Papuan, with elongated face and hooked nose, is especially spread over New Guinea; the other, or Melanesian properly so called, with broader face, straight or concave nose, has a geographical area which covers (from north-west to south-east) the Admiralty Islands, New Britain (Bismarck Archipelago), Solomon, Santa-Cruz, and Banks Islands, the New Hebrides, Loyalty Islands, and the Fiji Archipelago. Further, there are a certain number of ethnic characters which also justify the separation of the Papuans from the Melanesians properly so called. (See pp. 494-495.)

The Papuans[2] are found in the large island of New Guinea and the coast islets; for the most part they present the more or less uniform type of the Papuan sub-race (long face, convex nose, etc.), but the Melanesian type properly so called is also

[1] For the populations of Celebes, Timur, Floris, etc., see Max Weber, *Tijdsch. Aardrijksk. Genoots.*, 2nd ser., vol. vii., Amsterdam, 1890, and *Inter. Arch. Ethnogr.*, suppl. to vol. iii., Leyden, 1890, pl.; Brothers Sarasin, *Verh. Ges. Erdk. Berlin*, 1894, 1895, and 1896; Ten Kate, "Reis in de Timor groep," *Tijd. Aardr. Genoot.*, 2nd ser., vol. xi., p. 199, Amsterdam, 1894, and *L'Anthropologie*, 1893, p. 279; Lapicque, *loc. cit.*

[2] See my summary of what was known of the Papuans in 1882 in the *Rev. d'Anthr.*, 1883, p. 484, and the following works which have since appeared: Chalmers, *Pioneering in New Guinea*, London, 1887, and other works; De Clercq and Schmeltz, *Ethnogr. Beschrijving van de W. en N. Nederl. New Guin.*, Leyden, 1893; Finsch, *Samoafahrten*, Leipzig, 1888, and his articles in the *Ann. naturh. Hofmus.*, Vienna, 1888 and 1891, in the *Rev. d'Ethnogr.*, 1886, etc.; Haddon, "Decorat. art Brit. N. Guin.," *Cunningham Memoirs*, vol. x., *Roy. Irish Acad.*, 1894; and "The Ethnography of Brit. New Guinea," *Science Progress*, vol. ii., 1894, pp. 83 and 227, London, with map and bibliog.; Macgregor, *Proc. R. Geogr. Soc.*, 1890, p. 191, and his official reports; Thomson, *Brit. New Guinea*, London, 1892.

to be found among them. The frequency of individuals with a skin relatively fair, chocolate colour, especially in the south-east of the island (British New Guinea), joined to the frequency of wavy and straight hair, which, in the case of the children, is sometimes chestnut or sandy at the ends and black at the roots, has given the impression that there was a strong infusion of Polynesian blood in the veins of the Papuans; but this idea has been refuted by all ethnologists who have studied the populations on the spot—Miklukho-Maclay, Finsch, Haddon. According to the last, the evidence is in favour of some intermixture with the Melanesians, who, in general, are fairer than the Papuans, and have often wavy hair.[1] Some anthropologists (Miklukho-Maclay, Meyer, Hamy, Mantegazza) have also pointed out the presence of Negritoes or Negrito Papuan cross-breeds in New Guinea, basing their opinion on the study of skulls. These Negrito-Papuans appear to be localised at a single spot on the island, at the mouth of the river Fly.[2]

It should also be said that some Polynesian customs, kava drinking, tattoo by pricking, the possession of outrigger

[1] It is also to be noted that the supposed Papuan-Polynesian cross-breeds of the south-east of New Guinea neither drink kava nor know the art of pottery, unlike true Polynesians. Besides, their language approximates more nearly to the Melanesian dialects and presents no affinities with Polynesian languages (Ray, "Languages of Brit. N. Guinea," *Journ. Anthr. Inst.*, vol. xxiv., p. 15, 1894).

[2] Papuan skulls are generally very dolichocephalic (av. ceph. ind. 73), and the presence of brachycephalic skulls in the series of New Guinea origin is certainly of significance, only their proportion is very slight. Out of 500 New Guinea skulls described I have been able to find only 36 brachycephalic, or seven per cent. More than half of these skulls come from one and the same locality, the Kiwai and Canoe Islands in the delta of the Fly. Either a Malay colony may therefore be assumed there, a remnant of Negritoes, or that it was a centre of the custom of deforming the head, a custom which in fact obtains in the neighbourhood of the mouth of the Fly. On this question see my summary of 1882 cited above, and Haddon, *loc. cit.*; Schellong, "Anthr. d. Papus," *Zeit. f. Ethn.*, p. 156, 1891; J. Chalmers, "Anthropometr. observ., etc.," *Journ. Anthr. Inst.*, vol. xxvii. (1897).

canoes, etc., to be met with at certain points of New Guinea, are equally to be found in Melanesia (New Hebrides, Fiji, etc.). Many ethnic characters may be brought forward which are proper to the Papuans, or in which either Indonesians or Australians resemble them—large phalanstery-houses (up to 300 feet) on piles with roofs of the shape of a reversed boat; the ceremony of initiation for the young of both sexes; the use of the bull-roarer and of very elaborate masks in religious ceremonies, the seated attitude of limbs crossed tailor-fashion, in which last they differ from the Melanesians, who rest squatting.

The Papuans (perhaps a million in all) are divided into a great number of tribes. In the west (Dutch) portion are the Mafors or Nofurs; the Varopen or Vandamenes in Geelvink Bay and the islands lying within it; the Arfaks, their neighbours of the interior; then, on the north coast, the Amberbaki, the Karons, one of the tribes practising anthropophagy (tolerably rare among Papuans); lastly, the Talandjang, near Humboldt Gulf; the Onimes in the neighbourhood of McClure Gulf, and the Kovai farther to the south. The Papuans of German New Guinea present linguistic differences: those of Astrolabe Bay do not understand the natives of Finsch Haven, etc. In British New Guinea the following tribes are known: the Daudai to the west of the mouth of the Fly, the Kiwai in the mouth of this river; the Orokolo and the Motu-Motu or Toaripi in the Gulf of Papua; the Motu or Kerepunu (Fig. 152) of Port Moresby;[1] the Koitapu and the Kupele more in the interior of the country, near the Owen Stanley range; the Loyalupu and the Aroma to the south of the foot of Moresby; finally, the Massim of the extremity of the peninsula, the Samarai (Fig. 151) and their congeners of the Entrecasteaux Islands and the Louisiade archipelago.[2]

[1] The Kerepunu are good agriculturists; their mode of working is quite remarkable (Fig. 152). The soil is turned up at the word of command by a row of men, each of whom thrusts into the earth two pointed sticks, then using these sticks as levers a layer of earth is raised and a furrow is thus made.

[2] Hamy, "Papous de la mer d'Entrecasteaux," *Rev. Ethnog.*, 1889.

FIG. 152.—Papuans of the Kerepunu tribe at Tamain-Hula (New Guinea), ready to turn up the soil

The Papuans are tillers of the soil, and especially cultivate sago, maize, and tobacco; occasionally they are hunters and fishers, and are then very adroit in laying snares and poisoning waters; their favourite weapons are the bow and arrow with flint heads. Excellent boat-builders, they merely do a coasting trade, and while understanding well how to handle a sail, rarely ever venture into the open sea. Graphic arts are developed among them (see p. 202, and Figs. 60 to 62). The practice of chewing betel is universal. The dress of the men is a belt of beaten bark (Fig. 60); that of the women an apron made of dry grasses. Funeral rites vary with the tribe: burial, exposure on trees, embalmment. Very superstitious, living in dread of "spirits" at the merest whispering of leaves in the forest, of a bad augury at the least cry of a bird, the Papuans have no religion properly so called any more than they have "chiefs"; all public matters are discussed at meetings where, however, individual influences are always predominant. Among their principal customs may be noted the vendetta and the head-hunt.

The inhabitants of Torres Straits very much recall the Papuans; they have nothing in common with the Australians.[1]

The Melanesians properly so called[2] are for the most part of the variety with large square or lozenge-shaped face, with the straight or *retroussé* nose of the Melanesian race

[1] Haddon, *Journ. Anthr. Inst.*, vol. xix., p. 297; S. Ray and Haddon, "Languages of Torres Straits," *Proceed. R. Irish Acad.*, 3rd ser., vol. iv., 1897; Rev. Hunt, *Journ. Anthr. . . . Inst.*, N.S., vol. i., p. 5, 1898-99.

[2] R. Codrington, *The Melanesians*, Oxford, 1891, fig.; Finsch, *loc. cit.*, *Rev. Ethnogr.*, 1883, p. 49, and *Anthrop. Ergeb. einer Reise in der Sudsee*, Berlin, 1884, with fig.; Flower, "Cran. caract. Fiji Islanders," *Journ. Anthr. Inst.*, vol. x., 1881, p. 153; Hagen and Pineau, "Les Nouvelles-Hébrides," *Rev. Ethnogr.*, 1888, p. 302; Guppy, *The Solomon Islands and their Natives*, London, 1887; Hagen, "Les Indigènes des Salomon," *L'Anthropol.*, 1893, pp. 1 and 192; Aug. Bernard, *La Nouvelle Caledonie* (thesis), p. 249 *et seq.*, Paris, 1894; Luschan, *loc. cit.*; Schellong, *loc. cit.*

(Fig. 153). In general they are taller and more dolichocephalic than the Papuans. (See Appendices I. and II.) All tillers of the soil, cultivating especially the yam and taro,

FIG. 153.—Woman of the Fualu clan (east coast of New Caledonia), of pure Melanesian race. (*Phot. E. Robin.*)

they practise hunting and fishing only at times; the pig is their only domestic animal. Most of the Melanesians still live in the stone age, but the former fine axes of polished serpentine, artistically hafted, are disappearing more and more. They also make many weapons and tools of wood, of shells, and of human humerus bones. The favourite weapons are the club, bow, and spear, this last being used only in war (except in New Caledonia, where the bow is little employed).

The arrow and spear heads are most often of human bone, barbed, and sometimes poisoned with juices of plants or microbes from the ooze of ponds or lagunes.

The Melanesians build outrigger and twin canoes, but they do not sail far from the coasts. Pottery in certain islands is unknown; the dwellings are little houses on piles, except in New Caledonia, where circular huts are met with. Communal houses ("Gamal") exist everywhere. Tattooing, little practised, is most often done by cicatrices. The habit of chewing betel is general, except in New Caledonia; but kava is almost unknown. Anthropophagy is now indulged in only on the Solomon Islands and in some islands of New Britain and New Hebrides, although the custom of preserving the skulls of the dead, and of hanging them near the hut side by side with those derived from head-hunting, is general. As in New Guinea, there exists a mob of dialects and tongues in each of the Melanesian Islands, and even in different parts of the same island. Melanesian women are very chaste and virtuous, and that notwithstanding the absence of the sense of modesty, at least in New Britain, where they go completely naked, as also do the men. The men, in certain islands, wear only antipudic garments (see p. 170). Taboo in Melanesia assumes a less clear form than in Polynesia, where it amounts to simple interdiction without the intervention of mysterious forces. As in Australia there are no "tribes" among the Melanesians (except perhaps in New Caledonia), but in each island there exists two or more exogamous "classes" or clans (as in Australia), and the regulations of group marriage (p. 231) are observed as strictly in the Solomon Islands as in Viti-Levu (the largest of the Fiji Islands). Secret societies (Duk-Duk, etc., p. 253) flourish especially in Banks Islands, but are met with also in the rest of Melanesia and even in the Fijis, where, especially in the west islands, the population is already intermixed with Polynesian elements.[1]

IV. Polynesians.[2]—Seeing that the Polynesians are distributed over a number of islands, and exist under the most varied conditions, we might expect to find a multitude of types. This is not the case; the Polynesian race shows almost the same traits from the Hawaii Islands to New Zealand. This fact is due to the constant migrations from island to island, and the active trading conducted by all the Polynesians with each other, the effect of which is to efface, by process of intermixture, differences arising from insular isolation.

From the physical point of view the Polynesian is tall (1m. 74, average of 254 measurements), sub-brachycephalic (ceph. ind., 82.6 according to 178 measurements on the living subject, 79 according to 328 skulls), of a fair complexion (warm yellow or brownish), with straight or curly hair, most often straight nose, the cheek-bones fairly projecting, the superciliary arches little marked, and, especially among the women, something languorous in the look (Figs. 154 to 156). The Polynesian therefore differs completely from the Melanesian, whose stature is below the average (1m. 62 according to 295 measurements), and who is dolichocephalic (ceph. ind., 77 according to 223 measurements on living subject); he has dark skin, woolly or frizzy hair, concave or convex nose, and, lastly, prominent superciliary arches,

[1] The number of Polynesians (2,310 in 1897) has diminished by half in the Fijis since 1881, while that of the natives (100,321 in 1897) has hardly varied. The Polynesian element is appreciable in the Aoba, Tanna, and Espiritu Santo islands of the New Hebrides, but its importance has been exaggerated so far as the Loyalty Islands and New Caledonia are concerned (see my note in the *Bull. Soc. Anthr.*, p. 791, 1893).

[2] Ellis, *Polynesian Researches*, 4 vols., London, 1853; Tautain, "Les Marquisiens," *L'Anthropologie*, 1894, 1895, and 1898; Meinecke, *Die Inselen des stillen Oceans*, 2 vols., Leipzig, 1875; Markuse, *Die Hawaischen Inselen*, Berlin, 1894; Lister, "Natives of Fakaofu (Bowditch Island)," *Journ. Anthr. Inst.*, vol. xxi., 1892, p. 43; Ch. Hedley, "The Atoll of Fanafuti, Ellice group," *Australian Museum, Memoir III.*, Sydney, 1897; H. Gros, "Les populations de la Polynesie française en 1891," *Bull. Soc. Anthr. Paris*, 1896, p. 144; Ten Kate, *loc. cit.*

which, combined with the pigmentation of the cornea, give a fierce and suspicious look. The Polynesian is more subject to obesity than the Melanesian. He is more lively, more imaginative and intelligent, but also more dissolute in his habits than the Melanesian.

Before the advent of Europeans, the Polynesians of the upper volcanic islands were expert tillers of the soil (as witness the ruins of irrigation works in Tahiti, New Zealand, and elsewhere), and in the lower coral islands lived on the produce of the cocoa-nut and bread-fruit trees. Everywhere they were accustomed to fish. They cooked their foods by means of heated stones (p. 153), having (except in Micronesia, in the Tonga and Easter Islands) no knowledge of pottery; they excelled in the art of plaiting, in the preparation of *tapa* (p. 183), and especially in navigation. Their light canoes with outriggers (Fig. 82), or their large twin canoes connected by a platform and always carrying a single triangular sail of mat, furrowed the ocean in all directions. For weapons they had short javelins, slings, and wooden clubs, but neither bow nor shield. They made tools of shell and polished stone, and were proficient in the art of wood-sculpture (Fig. 71). Pictography appears to have been known only in Easter Island (p. 140). Kava (p. 158) was their national drink; tattooing had reached the condition of an art in New Zealand only. The custom of taboo (p. 252) probably originated in Polynesia, where also two or three social classes are to be met with. After the arrival of Europeans the Polynesians, adopting the customs of the new-comers, underwent rapid changes. For the most part Christians, especially Protestants, they have modified their very rich old mythology by the incorporation of Christian legends. In several islands, in Hawaii, Samoa, and New Zealand, the Polynesians have even risen to the height of having parliamentary institutions, in the management of which they themselves take part. On the other hand, civilisation, in ensuring peace, has had the effect of making the Polynesians unenterprising and lazy, and more inclined to dissipation than they were formerly. And the population is diminishing, owing either to imported epidemic diseases (particularly syphilis and tuberculosis), or to cross-breeding.

In the Sandwich Islands, now subject to the United States, the Hawaiians do not number more than 31,019 out of the 109,020 inhabitants registered by the last census (1896), or 28

FIG. 154.—Tahitian woman of Papeete, twenty-six years old. Pure Polynesian race. (*Phot. Prince Roland Bonaparte.*)

per cent. of the population; while in 1890 there were 34,436, constituting 38 per cent. of the total population. The chief causes of this reduction are phthisis and leprosy, as well as the Sino-Japanese and European immigration. In the Marquesas Islands, belonging to France, the native Polynesians numbered only 4,304 at the census of 1894, while in 1887 there were still 5,246; the principal cause of this diminution being tuberculosis (Tautain). The Moriori of Chatham Island (east of New Zealand) are reduced to fifty in number; and the Maoris of New Zealand, so celebrated for their tattooings, their legends,

FIG. 155.—Same subject as Fig. 154, seen in profile. (*Phot. Prince Roland Bonaparte.*)

and their ornamental art, do not count more than 41,933 (census of 1891), distributed over the northern island and over the northern part of the southern island. They are also losing their native originality, are growing civilised, and intermix with the Europeans.

The Samoans (35,000), and their neighbours the Tongans (25,000), who have frequent relations with the Fijians, seem to remain stationary in number. The native population (1,600) of Tahiti has not varied since the establishment of the French dominion. The Hervey or Cook Islands shelter 8000

FIG. 156.—Tahitian of Papeete; pure Polynesian race. (*Phot. Prince Roland Bonaparte.*)

Polynesians, the Tuamota Islands 7000, and the remaining islands less than 2000 each.

The Polynesians of the western islands situated north of the equator (Gilbert, 35,000; Marshall, 12,000; Caroline, 22,000; Marianne) are called Micronesians. They differ slightly in type from the Polynesians; they are more hairy, are shorter, their head is more elongated, and they possess some ethnic characters apart: rope armour, weapons of shark's teeth, special money (p. 271), etc.[1]

The peopling of the innumerable islands of the Pacific and Indian oceans by three distinct races whose languages have affinities with Malay dialects, forms one of the most interesting problems of ethnology. Anthropologists have largely discussed the point of departure of these races.[2] According to common opinion it is from the south-east of Asia, from Indo-China, that the peoples now scattered from Madagascar to Easter Island originally set out; on the one hand driven by the monsoons of the Indian Ocean, and on the other by the monsoons of the Pacific, both of which, during a period of the year, are contrary to the directions of the prevailing winds. The peopling of Melanesia and Polynesia from west to east becomes very probable if, as Bernard[3] has justly remarked, the distribution of lands and islands, the disappearance of continents in proportion as we proceed eastward, is taken into account. It is in fact evident that migrations were effected more easily across large islands fairly near each other, like those of the Indian Ocean or the western Pacific, even granted contrary winds and currents, than across very small and very distant islands like those of the western Pacific, even granted favourable currents. If it is a question of involuntary migrations, the cyclones and tempests which drive canoes afar amount to an inversion of normal winds, and migrations of this kind are effected in all directions.[4] As to voluntary migrations, they are also deliberately made in a direction opposite to that of the prevailing winds. It was in order to ensure their safe return that primitive peoples noted the regular winds and currents, merely taking advantage of

[1] Kubary, *loc. cit.*, and *Journ. Mus. Godeffroy*, parts 2 and 4, 1873.

[2] De Quatrefages, *Les Polynesiens et leurs migrations*, Paris, 1866, with maps.

[3] A. Bernard, *loc. cit.*, p. 272.

[4] Sittig, "Unfreiwillige Wanderungen . . .," *Peterm. Mittheil.*, p. 61, 1890.

some chance breeze in setting off. Legends afford little help to determine these migrations in detail, and, apart from some historic facts, it is difficult to state precisely the origin of the populations of each of the Oceanian islands.

CHAPTER XIII.

RACES AND PEOPLES OF AMERICA.

The four ethnic elements of the New World—*Origin of the Americans*—ANCIENT INHABITANTS OF AMERICA—Problem of palæolithic man in the United States—Palæolithic man in Mexico and South America—Lagoa Santa race; Sambaquis and Paraderos—Problem of the Mound-Builders and Cliff-Dwellers—Ancient civilisation of Mexico and Peru—*Present American Races*—*American languages.*

PEOPLES OF NORTH AMERICA—I. *Eskimo*—II. *Indians of Canada and United States: a.* Arctic—Athapascan group; *b.* Antarctic—Algonquian-Iroquois, Chata-Muskhogi, and Siouan groups; *c.* Pacific—North-west Indians, Oregon-California and Pueblo groups—III. *Indians of Mexico and Central America: a.* Sonorian-Aztecs; *b.* Central Americans (Mayas, Isthmians, etc.)—Half-breeds in Mexico and the Antilles.

PEOPLES OF SOUTH AMERICA—I. *Andeans:* Chibcha, Quechua, and other linguistic families; the Araucans—II. *Amazonians:* Carib, Arawak, Miranha, and Panos families; unclassed tribes—III. *Indians of East Brazil and the Central Region:* Ges linguistic family; unclassed tribes (Puri, Karaya, Bororo, etc.); Tupi-Guarani family—IV. *South Argentine:* Chaco and Pampas Indians, etc.; Patagonians, Fuegians.

AT the present day about six-sevenths of the population of the two Americas are composed of Whites and Half-breeds of all sorts. The remainder is made up almost equally of Negroes and natives, the latter improperly called Indians.[1] Notwithstanding the relatively small number of these last (about 10 millions), I shall deal almost exclusively with them

[1] A. von Humboldt, in his *Évaluation numérique de la population du Nouveau Continent*, Paris, 1825, reckoned that in the Americas there were 13 millions of Whites, 6 millions of Half-breeds, 6 millions of Negroes, and 9 millions of Indians; three-quarters of a century later (in 1895-97) it was computed that there were 80 millions of Whites, 37 millions of Half-breeds, 10 millions of Negroes and 10 millions of Indians in a total population of 137 millions (1897).

in this chapter, as they are especially interesting from the ethnological point of view, besides having been the best studied from this point of view. A few words will suffice in regard to the Whites and Negroes. The white colonists and their uncrossed descendants belong for the most part to Anglo-Saxon or Germanic peoples in North America, and to Neo-Latin peoples in South America. Nine-tenths of the population of the United States owe their origin to the Anglo-Scotch, to the Irish, Germans, and Scandinavians, the fusion of which with other European types and with half-breeds tends to produce the *Yankee* type, which, if not a physical, is at least a social type. In Canada two-thirds of the white population are Anglophones, and the rest Francophones. In Mexico, in the Antilles, and in South America, nearly all the "white" population is made up of Neo-Latins—in Brazil descendants of the Portuguese, in Argentine of Italo-Spaniards, and elsewhere of Spaniards. The Latins have also contributed to form the half-breeds of America, of which several varieties exist. Half-breeds are especially numerous in Mexico and in the countries where the three elements, White, Indian, and Negro come together, as in the Antilles, in Columbia, Venezuela, and in Brazil. I shall give some particulars of the Half-breeds in connection with the populations of these lands (pp. 542 and 545). As to the Negroes of America, they are the descendants of slaves imported, during more than three centuries, almost exclusively from the West African coast, and particularly from Guinea. (See p. 452.) The Negroes are especially numerous in the south of the United States and in the Antilles, as well as in the north and on the east coast of South America, as far as Buenos Ayres.[1]

Origin of the Americans.—To-day the existence of an *American race*, or rather a *group of American races* (p. 291), is generally conceded, a group to which all the native populations of the New World belong; but as to the origins of these races unanimity of opinion is far from being reached. According to

[1] Williams, *Hist. of the Negro Race in America*, 2 vols., New York, 1885; B. A. Gould, *loc. cit.*

some authorities, the New World is a special centre of the manifestation of species, the *Homo Americanus* having developed on the spot; according to others, the ancestors of the present Indians came from neighbouring countries—a few from everywhere: from Siberia and China (by Behring's Straits), from Polynesia (driven by currents), from Europe (failing Atlantis, by the table-land which in the quaternary period probably stretched between England and Greenland). Unfortunately, almost all these hypotheses are based on a confusion both of time and space. It may without difficulty be conceded that occasional Chinese and Japanese junks may have been driven towards America, although the existence of this continent remained unknown both to China and Japan till quite recent times. We know positively that the Northmen visited the shores of North America long before Christopher Columbus. And there is reason to suppose that the Polynesians, who are excellent navigators, may have ventured, urged forward by currents, as far as the South American coast. But all these occurrences would be too recent, and such migrations would be in fact both too insignificant and too isolated, to account for the peopling of a vast continent. The origins of American man are much more distant in the past, and the migrations, if migrations there were, must have taken place in the quaternary epoch, and probably as much from the coast of Europe as from the coast of Asia.

Ancient Inhabitants of America.—Just as is the case with Europe, it is not certain that man existed in America during the tertiary period,[1] but it is certain that he appeared

[1] The celebrated skull discovered by Whitney in the auriferous sands of Calaveras (California), which has been said to belong to the pliocene age, has been disputed both as regards its authenticity and the supposed date of its bed; and it is the same with the pestles and mortars discovered in the same neighbourhood by such geologists as Skertchly and C. King (cf. W. Holmes, "Prelim. Revis. Evidence to Aurif. Gravel Man in Calif.," *Am. Anthropologist*, N.S., vol. i., Nos. 1 and 2, New York, 1899). The imprints of human feet, or rather of moccasins, discovered at Carson (Nevada), even granted that they are authentic, have in any case been found in beds whose period is by no means tertiary.

there during the quaternary age. This period, in the New World as in the Old, had its glacial epochs. According to Dawson, Wright, and Chamberlin, there were two or three great movements of invasion and withdrawal of the American glaciers. It is not known if these movements were synchronous with those of Europe, but it is established that, as in Europe, the first invasion of glaciers was also the more widespread.[1]

Chipped argilite tools, similar to the quaternary quartz tools of sub-Pyrennean countries, have been found by Abbott in the gravels of the Delaware, near Trenton (New Jersey), side by side with quaternary animals (probably of the second glacial period, notably the fragment of a jaw-bone). Other implements have been gathered on the spot by Haynes in New Hampshire; by Dr. Metz in the gravels of Little Falls (Minnesota), regarded by W. Upham as more recent than those of Trenton; by Cresson at Medora (Indiana), and at Claymont (mouth of the Delaware), in a more ancient deposit than the Trenton one; by Wright and Volk at Trenton (in 1895); without reckoning the thousands of finds either on the surface or in lesser-known beds, which have been enumerated in a special memoir by Wilson. If I dwell on these details, it is because all these finds have latterly been vigorously attacked in the United States, since Holmes, who had studied the ancient quarries of the Indians, pointed out the great resemblances between the spoiled or waste argilite axes and arrowheads which he had found in these quarries, and the supposed palæolithic implements, particularly those of Trenton. Several authorities, such as Chamberlin, MacGee, Brinton, have, like

[1] At this period Greenland, all Canada, a corner of Alaska, and a good part of the United States were covered with glaciers almost uninterruptedly. The limit of the moraine to the south may be indicated by a line which, leaving New York, for Lake Erie, would follow the course of the Ohio as far as the region of its junction with the Mississippi, and would be continued along or a little to the west and to the south of the Missouri to coincide then with the Canadian frontier. The fauna of the American quaternary period differed somewhat from that of Europe: the *Rhinoceros tichorhinus*, for instance, was missing, while the *Mastodon ohioticus* and several large edentata, such as the *Megatherium*, *Mylodon*, etc., are met with.

Holmes himself, come to the conclusion that all the so-called palæolithic tools of America, and perhaps even those of Europe, are only spoiled or waste tools of the same kind, and relatively modern. This conclusion seems to overshoot the mark, seeing that specialists like Wilson, Boule, etc., are almost unable to distinguish undoubted quaternary tools of Europe from those of Trenton, and that the beds of many American prehistoric tools have been perfectly well ascertained not to have undergone any rehandling, and have been established as quaternary by competent geologists.[1]

Outside the United States palæolithic finds in the New World are not very numerous, and often are questionable.

Palæolithic tools of the Chellean and Mousterian type have been found in Mexico by Franco and Pinart;[2] other quaternary tools, together with a fragment of a human jaw-bone, have been described in the valley of Mexico by S. Herrera.[3]

In Brazil, on the shores of Lake Lagoa-do-Sumidoro (province of Minas Geraes), Lund exhumed human skeletons

[1] See for details, Abbott, *Primitive Industry*, Cambridge (Mass.), 1881, and *Evidence . . . Antiquity of Man in East N. America*, 1888; F. Wright, *The Ice Age in North America*, New York, 1889, chaps. xxi. and xxii., and *Meet. Amer. Assoc. Adv. Sc. of Buffalo*, 1896; Geikie, *loc. cit.* (chap. li., written by T. Chamberlin); Metz, *Proceed. Boston Soc. Nat. Hist.*, vol. xxiii., p. 242; W. Upham, *ibid.*, p. 436; Hille-Cresson, *Proceed. Bost. Soc. Nat. Hist.*, 1889; Holmes, *loc. cit.* (*Fifteenth Rep. Bur. Ethn.*); Th. Wilson, *A Study of Prehist. Anthrop.*, Washington, 1890 (Extract from *Rep. U.S. Nat. Mus.*, 1887-88, p. 597). For the discussion, see *Science* for 1892 and 1898. Marcellin Boule has summarised most of the works quoted, and shows the present state of the question in *Revue d'Anthropologie*, 1888, p. 647, and in *L'Anthropologie*, 1890 and 1892; see also Nadaillac, *L'Anthropologie*, 1897 and 1898. I will merely note that the tendency of surface objects to sink towards deep beds, brought forward by the opponents of Abbott, Wright, etc., altogether fails to explain why *other* implements (in flint, jade, etc.) or pieces of pottery have not similarly been carried down, and that only argilite tools are found *flat* in deep beds.

[2] Hamy, "Anthropologie du Mexique," *Miss. scientifique du Mexique* (*Rech. zool.*, 1st part), p. 11, Paris, 1884.

[3] S. Herrera, *Proceed. Am. Ass. Adv. Sc.*, Madison, 1893, pp. 42 and 312; Th. Wilson, *loc. cit.*; De Nadaillac, *L'Amerique préhistorique*, Paris, 1883, and *Revue d'Anthropol.*, 1879 and 1880.

and flint objects, together with remains of animals which, if not quaternary, at least exist no longer in the country. Ameghino[1] also has collected in quaternary layers of the Pampas of the Argentine Republic remains of primitive human industries. I will only mention the numerous neolithic objects found almost everywhere in America. Among these objects it is necessary to give special attention to the "grooved axes" which are entirely characteristic of the New World (Wilson).

As to prehistoric human bones, investigation reduces them to little. I have already said that the tertiary or quaternary skull of Calaveras (brachycephalic) is classed as doubtful. The skeleton of Pontimelo (with dolichocephalic skull), found by Roth under the carapace of the glyptodon, an enormous armadillo of the Pampas regions of the Rio Arrecifes, a tributary of Rio de la Plata, also inspires but a limited confidence in many authorities. Lastly, the skulls and bones of Lagoa Santa, if not quaternary, at least very ancient, afford special characters (dolichocephaly, short stature, third trochanter), on the strength of which De Quatrefages has established a special race,[2] whose probable descendants constitute my *Palæ-American sub-race.* (See p. 292.)

Side by side with finds of stone objects and bones in very ancient strata, it is necessary to note also the shell-heaps and kitchen-middens scattered along all the coast of both Americas, from Newfoundland, Nova Scotia, and Louisiana to Brazil, to Patagonia and Tierra del Fuego. In this last country the present inhabitants, who subsist especially on molluscs, contribute to the piling up of these heaps or to the formation of new ones. This is enough to indicate that all the kitchen-middens are not synchronous; and if there be some

[1] Ameghino, *La Antiguedad del hombre en El Plata*, Paris-Buenos-Ayres, 1880, 2 vols.

[2] De Quatrefages, "L'homme foss. de Lagoa-Santa," *Izviestia Soc. of Friends of Nat. Sc.*, Moscow, vol. xxxv., 1879; Sören Hansen and Lutken, *Lagoa Santa Racen*, Copenhagen, 1889, extract from *E Museo Lundii*, vol. iv.; Hyades and Deniker, *loc. cit.*, p. 163.

which go far back into antiquity, on the other hand there are some which are quite modern. The "Sambaquis," for instance, of the mouth of the Amazon and of the province of Parana must be very ancient; some of the skulls which have been found in them recall the Palæ-American or Lagoa Santa race.[1] The *paraderos*, or elongated hillock graves, discovered in the province of Entre Rios, in the valley of the Rio Negro (Argentine Republic), by Moreno and R. Lista, enclose flint tools (neolithic?) and numerous skulls, among which a certain number also exhibit likenesses to those of Lagoa Santa.[2]

In North America, the *Mounds*, fortified enclosures or tumuli of the most varied appearance, round, conical, and in the shape of animals, have also for long attracted the attention of archæologists. But if the discoveries and excavations made in these monuments have been many, an exact explanation of their meaning was lacking till recent times. The groups of mounds are scattered over an immense tract of country, from the great lakes to the Gulf of Mexico, from the Rocky Mountains to the Atlantic Ocean; but they abound particularly in the valley of the Mississippi, along its left tributaries, in Arkansas, Kansas, etc., as well as in the basin of the Ohio. Farther west, towards the Rocky Mountains, as well as towards the Atlantic coast, they become less frequent. Till recently, the construction of these hillocks was attributed to one and the same people, called by the not very compromising name of "Mound-Builders." This people, tillers of the soil and relatively civilised, must have lived from the most remote antiquity in the region planted with these mounds, and must have been destroyed by the nomadic and wild hordes

[1] Lacerda and Peixoto, "Contribuições . . . raças indig. do Brasil," *Archiv. do Mus. nac.*, Rio-de-Janeiro, vol. i., 1876, and *Mem. Soc. Anthrop.*, Paris, 2nd ser., vol. ii., 1875-82, p. 535; H. von Ihering, "A civilisaçao prehist. de Brazil merid.," *Revista do Museu-Paulista*, vol. i., p. 95, S. Paulo, 1895.

[2] Moreno, "Cimet. et paraderos prehist., etc.," *Rev. Anthrop.*, 1874, p. 72; Verneau, "Crânes préhist. de Patagonie," *L'Anthropol.*, 1894, p. 420.

represented by the present Indians. Such, at least, was the prevailing hypothesis. However, an attentive study of these mounds and the objects they covered has led little by little the most competent authorities (Cyrus Thomas, Carr, H. Hale, Shepherd, and the numerous members of the "Mound Exploring Division") to distinguish several "types" of mounds, the geographical distribution of which would serve to indicate the settlements of diverse tribes. E. Schmidt, in a comprehensive work, has brought together all these investigations, and, by the light of linguistic data furnished by Hale, Brinton and others, has been able to state precisely who these various tribes were.[1]

It may be said at once that these investigations have by no means confirmed the great antiquity of the mounds; on the contrary, objects of European origin (iron swords, etc.), found in certain mounds, the tales of the early explorers which tell us that the Indians raised these mounds, and the traditions of the natives themselves, all force us to the conclusion that the builders of these funereal monuments or fortified enclosures were no other than the various Indian tribes whose remaining descendants exist to-day in the reservations. These tribes were tillers of the soil at the period of the discovery of America, as indeed the tales of contemporary explorers bear witness, as do also the traces of irrigation canals and other agricultural operations around these mounds. But the invasion of the country by Europeans from the seventeenth century onward, and the introduction of the horse, hitherto unknown, brought so much confusion into the existence of these tribes, that such of the Indians as survived the wars of extermination changed

[1] E. Schmidt, *Die Vorgeschichte Nord-Amerikas*, Brunswick, 1894; cf. *Arch. f. Anthrop.*, vol. xxiii., 1894. For details see Cyrus Thomas, "Burial Mounds," *Fifth Ann. Rep. Bur. Ethn.*, Washington, 1887 and "Rep. Mound Explorat., *Twelfth Rep. Bur. Ethn. for 1890-91*, Washington, 1894; Carr, "Crania from Stone Graves, etc.," *Eleventh Rep. Peabody Mus.*; Hale, "Indian Migration, etc.," *Amer. Antiquar.*, 1883; Shepherd, *Antiquities of State Ohio*, Cincinnati, 1890; Brinton, *Essays of an Americanist*, p. 90, Philadelphia, 1890.

their mode of life and became hunters or nomadic shepherds. If the distribution of the mounds be studied, three parallel archæological zones may be distinguished, extending from west to east, between the Mississippi and the Atlantic Ocean, each such zone presenting great differences in regard to the type of mound it circumscribes.[1] On comparing this distribution with the ancient settlements of the tribes the following result is arrived at: the mounds of the north have been built by the Iroquois and Algonquians, except the mounds of animal shape, which are due to Dakota-Siouan tribes; the mounds of the south may be attributed to tribes of the Muskoki or Muskhogi family; and, as regards the numerous monuments of the basin of the Ohio, there is a strong presumption in favour of their having been raised by the Shawnies and the Leni-Lenaps in the south, and by the Cherokis in the north. The study of these mounds, in connection with historic data, suffices to determine very satisfactorily the migrations of all these tribes, to which I shall refer later.

West of the Rocky Mountains no more mounds are met with. Their place is taken by other monuments, structures of stone erected among the rocks and along the cañons. A large number of these are found in the valley of San Juan, in that of Rio Grande do Norte, of the Colorado Chiquito, etc. These monuments are still more modern than the mounds. The peoples who erected these structures, the "Cliff-Dwellers," are still represented by the Moqui, Zuñi, and other tribes who inhabit the high table-lands of Arizona and New Mexico.

Tribes probably related to the Cliff-Dwellers erected in Central America those immense phalansteries in stone or adobe of several storeys, constructed to shelter the whole clan,

[1] The northern zone, circumscribing the great lakes, is characterised by monuments of rude form; the southern zone, between the Gulf of Mexico and the basin of the Ohio, is distinguished by mounds in the form of a truncated pyramid; while the middle zone, that of the basin of the Ohio, presents a large number of mounds of peculiar and very perfected types. In each of these zones special regions may be distinguished, characterised by the shape of the mounds and by the nature of the objects immured in them.

which the conquering Spaniards called pueblos.[1] Adobe pueblos are still occupied by Zuñi people, descendants of the Cliff-Dwellers.

While in North America among the Mound-Builders only rude attempts at civilisation are found, in Central America and Mexico there flourished up to the period of the conquest a relatively advanced civilisation. Various peoples, whom many authors have sought to identify with the Mound-Builders, formed more or less well-organised states in Mexico. Such were the Mayas in the Yukatan peninsula; the Olmecs, and, later, the Aztecs, on the high table-land. And on the west of South America there developed a corresponding civilisation, that of the Incas of Peru. The Incas were none other than one of the tribes of the Quechua people, who, after having brought into subjection the Aymara aborigines founded in Peru a sort of communist-autocratic state. To the north, in present Columbia, lived the Chibchas, who have equally attained a certain degree of civilisation. Lastly, to the south flourished the civilisation of the Calchaquis.

Existing American Races.—The natives of America, cut off from the rest of the world probably since the end of the quaternary period, form, as we have already seen, a group of races which may be considered by themselves, in the same way as the Xanthochroid or Melanochroid groups of races (see Chap. VIII.). It must be borne in mind that there exists but a single character common to these American races, that is the colour of the skin, the ground of which is yellow. This appears to conflict with the current opinion that the Americans

[1] Cushing, *C. R. Congr. Internat. des Americanistes*, p. 150, Berlin, 1888; V. Mindeleff, "Pueblo Architecture," *Eighth Report Bur. Ethnol. for 1886-87*, p. 1, Washington, 1891-93; C. Mindeleff, "Casa Grande Ruin," *Thirteenth Report Bur. Ethn. for 1891-92*, Washington, 1894; Nordenskiold and Retzius, *The Cliff-Dwellers*, etc., Stockholm, 1893, in fol. L. Morgan has sought to show in his monograph, "Houses and House Life of Am. Aborigines," *Contrib. N. Amer. Ethn.*, vol. iv, Washington, 1881, that the phalanstery-houses were the typical form of dwelling-place all of the North, and some of the South Americans, in association with the communal organisation of the tribes.

are a *red race*, and yet it is the statement of a fact. None of the tribes of the New World have a red-coloured skin, unless they are painted, which often is the case. Even the reddish complexion of the skin, similar, for example, to that of the Ethiopians, is met with only among half-breeds. All the populations of America exhibit various shades of yellow colouring; these shades may vary from dark-brownish yellow to olive pale yellow.[1] By the yellow colour of the skin, as well as the straight hair common to most, but not to all, Americans, they have affinities with the Ugrian and Mongol races; but other characters, such as the prominent, frequently convex nose, and the straight eyes, separate them widely from these races.

As to the characters peculiar to the five races which I adopt provisionally for the New World: Eskimo, North American, Central American, South American, and Patagonian, with their sub-races, they have been given in Chapter VIII., to which I refer the reader.

American Languages.—Several authors are of opinion that, as regards America, a more satisfactory classification of the peoples may be obtained from linguistic than from ethnic and somatological characters; they even think that these linguistic characters afford indications as to the *races* of the New World.[2] But opinions are divided on this point, as well as on the question whether all the American dialects belong to one and the same family. Brinton affirms that there exists, in spite of diversity of vocabulary and superficial differences of morphology, a common bond of union among all the American languages. This bond is to be looked for in

[1] I have always maintained this opinion, which is amply confirmed to-day by the investigations made by Ten Kate ("Somatol. Observ. Ind. South-west," *Journ. Amer. Ethnol.*, vol. iii., p. 122, Cambridge, Mass., and *Rev. d'Anthrop.*, 1887, p. 48), from Canada to the Pampas. As to South America, the prevalent yellow colouring has been further noticed by A. von Humboldt, and recently confirmed by Ranke (*Zeitsch. f. Ethnol.*, 1898, p. 61).

[2] Gatschet, "Klamath Indians," *Contrib. N. A. Ethnol.*, vol. ii., Part I., p. 43, Washington, 1890; D. Brinton, *The American Race*, p. 57, New York, 1891; Ehrenreich, *loc. cit.*

the inner structure of the dialects, a structure characterised especially by the development of pronominal forms, the abundance of generic particles, the more frequent use of ideas based on actions (verbs) than of ideas of existence

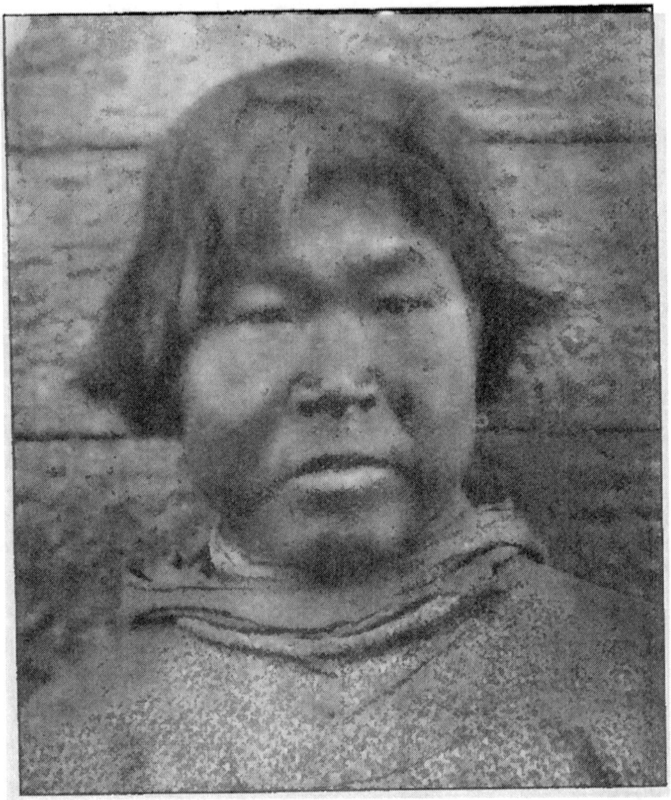

FIG. 157.—West Greenland Eskimo. (*Phot. Sören Hansen.*)

(nouns), and as a consequence the subordination of the latter to the former in the proposition.[1] The latter feature characterises the process called *incorporation,* all American languages being polysynthetic (see p. 131) Does the simi-

[1] D. Brinton, "Certain Morph. Traits of Am. Languages," *Amer. Antiquarian*, November, 1894.

larity of structure of the American languages (which might further extend to other groups of agglutinative languages) warrant the opinion that they all have sprung from a single stock? Competent philologists like Fr. Müller and L. Adam think it does not, and Powell,[1] attributing much more importance to similarity of vocabulary than to similarities of grammatical form, arrives at the conclusion that the tribes of North America do not speak languages related to each other and springing from a single original stock; on the contrary, they speak several languages belonging to distinct families, which do not appear to have a common origin.

The number of languages spoken by the natives of both Americas certainly exceeds a hundred, even without counting the secondary dialects. Brinton estimates the number of linguistic families known in the New World at 150 to 160; this figure is probably not far short of the truth, for Powell admits, merely for that part of the continent north of Mexico, 59 linguistic families, some of which comprise several dialects.[2]

PEOPLES OF NORTH AMERICA.

The greater part of the native population of North America is composed of tribes called *Indians* or *Red-skins* of the United States and Canada. They touch on the north the Eskimo and Aleuts, and on the south the Mexican and Central American Indians. I shall briefly review these three great divisions, going from north to south.

[1] Powell, "Indian Linguist. Families, etc.," *Seventh Rep. Bur. Ethn. for 1885-86*, Washington, 1891 (92), p. 1 (with map).

[2] A curious fact is brought out by the study of the linguistic chart published by Powell: that most of the families of different languages are grouped in the western, mountainous part of North America. Thus, out of 59 linguistic families, 40 are found in the limited area between the Pacific and the Rocky Mountains, while all the rest of the continent is divided among 19 linguistic families only. The same fact is observed in South America. We can reduce to a dozen groups the languages of the Atlantic slope of this continent, while in the Andes and on the Pacific slope an enormous number of linguistic families have been noted without any apparent common connection.

I. The *Eskimo*,[1] or *Innuit* as they call themselves (about 360,000 in number), afford the remarkable example of a people occupying almost without a break more than 5000 miles of sea-board, from the 71st degree N. lat. (north-east of Greenland) to the mouth of the Copper river or Atna (west of Alaska). A section of this people has even crossed Behring's Strait and inhabits the extreme north-east of Asia (see p. 370). Over the whole of this extent of country nowhere do the Eskimo wander farther than thirty miles from the coast. It is supposed that their original home was the district around Hudson's Bay (Boas) or the southern part of Alaska (Rink), and that from these regions they migrated eastward and westward, arriving in Greenland a thousand years ago, and in Asia barely three centuries ago. Their migrations northward led them as far as the Arctic Archipelago.[2]

Physically, the pure Eskimo—that is to say, those of the northern coast of America, and perhaps of the eastern coast of Greenland—may form a special race, allied with the American races, but exhibiting some characteristics of the

[1] E. Petitot, *Monogr. Esquim. Tchiglit du Mackenzie*, Paris, 1876, 4to; Dall, "Tribes of . . . extr. North-West," *Contrib. to North Amer. Ethnol.*, vol. i, p. 1, Washington, 1877; Ray, *Intern. Polar Exped. Point Barrow*, Washington, 1888; Sören Hansen, *loc. cit.*, and "Ost Grönl. Anthropol.," *Meddel om Groenland*, vol. x.; Boas, "The Central Eskimo," *Sixth Ann. Rep. Bur. Ethn.*, 1888, p. 409; G. Holm, *loc. cit.*; Rink, "The Eskimo Tribes," *Meddelel. om Grönl.*, vol. xi., and other works by this author in Danish, quoted by Bahnson, *Ethnographien*, vol. i., p. 223, Copenhagen, 1894; F. Nansen, *Eskimo Life*, London, 2nd edit., 1894, figs.; Dix Bolles, *Catal. Eskimo Collect. Rep. U.S. Nation. Mus. for 1887*, p. 335; R. Peary, *Northward over the Great Ice*, 2 vols., New York, 1898.

[2] The most northern point now inhabited by the Eskimo is situated on the Greenland side of Smith's Sound, 78° 8′ N. lat. (see the description of this tribe of 2,344 persons in Peary, *loc. cit.*, vol. i., p. 479); but Greely found traces of the permanent settlement of this people near Fort Conger, in Greenland, 81° 44′ N. lat. The most southern point occupied by the Eskimo is Hamilton Inlet (55° N. lat.) in Labrador, but it is not long since they reached as far as the straits of Belle-Isle in Newfoundland and even farther south, to the estuary of the St. Lawrence (50° N. lat.).

Ugrian race (short stature, dolichocephaly, shape of the eyes, etc.). They are above average stature (1m. 62), whilst the Eskimo of Labrador and Greenland are shorter, and those of southern Alaska a little taller (1m. 66), in consequence perhaps of interminglings, which would also explain their cranial configuration (ceph. ind. on the living subject, 79 in Alaska, against 76.8 in Greenland), which is less elongated than among the northern tribes (average cephalic index of the skull, 70 and 72). Their complexion is yellow, their eyes straight, and black (except among certain Greenland half-breeds); their cheek-bones are projecting, the nose is somewhat prominent, the face round, and the mouth rather thick-lipped. The Eskimo language differs little from tribe to tribe. Fishers and peaceful hunters, the Eskimo have no chiefs, and know nothing of war; they cultivate the graphic arts, are always cheerful, and love dancing, singing, story-telling, etc.

I have already given, however, in the preceding pages (see especially pp. 137, 151, 160, 245, 263 *et seq.*) several characteristics of Eskimo life.[1]

The Aleuts, about 2000 in number, inhabiting the insular mountain-chain which bears their name, speak an Eskimo dialect, but differ from the true Eskimo in some respects, having brachycephalic heads and several peculiarities of manners and customs. Besides, the majority of them have adopted the habits and religion of the Russians.[2]

II. The *Indians*, improperly called *Red-skins*,[3] occupy a territory of such vast extent that, in spite of a certain common like-

A great change in the habits of the Eskimo of Alaska will be effected by the introduction of reindeer, through the agency of the United States Government (see Jackson, *Rep. Introd. Reindeer in Alaska*, Washington, 1894 and 1895).

[2] Erman, "Ethnol. Wahrnem Behring Meeres," *Zeitsch. für Ethnol.*, vol. iii., pp. 159 and 205; Dall, *Alaska, etc.*, London, 1870; Bancroft, *Native Races Pacif. St. of America*, Washington, vol. i., 1875-76, pp. 87 and 111, and 1882, p. 562.

[3] Brinton, *loc. cit.* (*Amer. Race*); Schoolcraft, *loc. cit.*; Powell, *loc. cit.* (*Ind. Ling. Fam.*); Catlin, *Letters and Notes N. Amer. Ind.*, London, 1844 (cf. *Report U.S. Nation. Mus.*, 1885).

FIG. 158.—Gahhigué-Vatake (chief), a Dakota-Siouan Indian with tomahawk, 38 years old. (*Phot. Prince Roland Bonaparte.*)

FIG. 159.—Siouan chief of Fig. 158, front face. (*Phot. Prince Roland Bonaparte.*)

ness, considerable differences are noticeable among them, according to the countries they occupy, the climate, configuration, and fauna of which vary in a marked degree. We can in the first place distinguish the *Indians of the Arctic and Atlantic slopes* of Canada and the United States, belonging to a taller and less brachycephalic race than that which predominates among the *Indians* in the northern part of the Pacific slope. In the southern part of the Pacific slope we note the appearance of the Central American race, short and brachycephalic, and in the Californian peninsula perhaps the Palæ-American sub-race.[1] Each of the slopes in turn afford several "ethnographic provinces,"[2] the boundaries of which approximately coincide with those of the linguistic families now about to be rapidly passed in review.

a. The Indians of the Arctic slope—that is to say, of the low-lying country watered by the Mackenzie and the Yukon—belong to one and the same linguistic family, called Athapascan.

The best known tribes are the *Kenai* in Alaska, the *Loucheux* on the lower Mackenzie, the *Chippewas*, the numerous Tinné clans between Hudson's Bay and the Rocky Mountains, the *Takullies* to the west of these mountains, etc. All these *Athapascans*, of medium height (1m. 66), and mesocephalic, are skilful hunters; they traverse the immense forests of their country hunting fur-bearing animals in winter on their snow shoes, in summer in their light beech-bark canoes. The Athapascan linguistic family is not, however, confined to the wooded region of Alaska and western Canada. Members of this tribe have migrated to a far distant part of the Pacific slope, where they have settled in two

[1] Ten Kate, *Bull. Soc. Anthrop.*, Paris, 1884, p. 551, and 1885, p. 241.

[2] According to Powell, *Smiths. Rep.*, 1895, p. 658, the Atlantic slope may be divided into four provinces: *Algonquian, Iroquian*, that of the *southern part of the United States* (Muskhogean), and that of the *plains of the Great West*. The Pacific slope is split up in its turn into five provinces: North Pacific, Columbia, Interior Basin, California-Oregon, and the Pueblos region which encroaches upon Mexico.

different districts. The Athapascans of the West, or the Hupas who dwell in southern Oregon and northern California, differ but little physically from the Athapascans properly so called, but they are already Californians in ethnic character. The *Athapascans of the south*—that is to say, the *Navajos* or *Nodehs*

FIG. 160.—Woman of Wichita tribe, Pawnee Nation, Indian Territory, U.S.

and the *Apaches* (Fig. 161), taller (1m. 69), more brachycephalic (ceph. ind. 84) than their northern kinsfolk[1]—live in the open country of the Pueblo Indians (Arizona, New

[1] The "Pueblos," Zuñis, Moquis, etc., from whom these Athapascans have conquered their territory, are short and brachycephalic. Interminglings have modified only the form of the head of the Southern Athapascans; but it must be remembered that the practice of deforming the skull prevails among them.

Mexico), from whom, however, they differ in regard to manners and usages. They are husbandmen relatively civilised, fierce warriors and bold robbers, whose name has been popularised by the novels of Gustave Aimard and Gabriel Ferry. They are more numerous (23,500 in the United States)[1] than the Athapascans of the north (8,500) and the Hupas (scarcely 900).[2]

b. The Indians of the Atlantic slope are divided into three great linguistic families: Algonquian-Iroquoian, Muskhogean-Choctaw, and Siouan or Dakota.

1. The *Algonquians* and *Iroquoians* occupy the "ethnographical province" which bears their name and extends over the east of Canada and the north-east of the United States, between the Mississippi and about the 36th degree of N. latitude. This province is characterised by a temperate climate, abundance of prairies, and broad water-ways; it affords facilities for the chase and the gathering of wild rice and tobacco; certain usages are common to all the tribes inhabiting it (tattooing, colouring the body, moccasins similar to those of the Athapascans, etc.).

The original home of the Algonquians was the region around Hudson's Bay, where the *Cree* tribe, which speaks the purest Algonquian language, still exists. Leaving this region, they spread as far as the Atlantic, the Mississippi, and the Alleghany Mountains, driving back the Dakotas into the prairies of the right bank of the Mississippi. The *Abnakis* of Lower Canada, the *Micmacs* of Acadia and Newfoundland, the *Leni-Lenapé* of the Delaware, who fought so valiantly against the European immigrants; the *Mohicans*, idealised by Cooper; the warlike *Shawnees*, the *Ojibwas* or *Chippewas* (Fig. 30), who, to-

[1] There are some Apache tribes in Mexico, the *Lipans*, the *Jarros*, but their numerical force is not known.

[2] See J. Stevenson, "Navajo Ceremonial," *Eighth Rep. Bur. Ethnol.*, and articles by Matthews on the Navajos in the 2nd, 3rd, and 5th Reports of the *Bur. Ethnol.*; Ten Kate, *Reizen en Ondezokongei in N. Amer.*, Leyden, 1885; cf. *Bull. Soc. Anthropol.*, 1883, and "Somatol. Observ. Ind. South-west," *Journ. Amer. Ethnol*, vol. iii., Cambridge, 1891.

gether with the Lenapé, are alone among the Red-skins in possessing a rudimentary writing; the *Ottawas*, the *Black Feet*, the *Cheyennes*, and so many other tribes besides belonged to this great Algonquian people. It has left traces of its existence in the "mounds" as well as in a great number of the geographical names of the region which it formerly occupied. It is estimated that at the present day there are not more than 95,000 Algonquians, of whom two-thirds inhabit Canada. The most numerous tribe is that of the Chippewas (31,000), while the "last" of the Mohicans were only 121 in the census of 1890. Among the Algonquians ought probably to be included a tribe which became extinct in 1827, that of the Beothucs of Newfoundland, whose affinities with other tribes have not yet been definitely established.[1]

At the time when the Algonquians held a large part of modern Canada and the United States, an isolated portion of their territory was peopled with Iroquoians around Lakes Erie and Ontario, as well as on the lower St. Lawrence. The Iroquoians, sprung from the same common stock as the Cherokis, the ancient mound-builders of the Ohio basin, have dwindled down to a few thousand families in the upper valley of the Tennessee (H. Hale). They are divided into *Hurons* (between Lakes Ontario and Huron) and *Iroquois* or *Iroquoians properly so called*. The latter formerly comprised five nations: *Mohawks*, *Oneidas*, *Onondagas*, *Senecas*, and *Cayugas*, united into a democratic confederacy by the famous chief Hiawatha, of whom Longfellow has sung. At a later date the *Tuscaroras*, who dwelt farther to the south-west in Virginia, were also admitted into the confederacy.[2]

[1] Lloyd, "On the Beothucs," *Journ. Anthropol. Inst. Great Britain*, vols. iv. and v. (1874-75); and Gatschet, *Proc. Am. Philos. Soc.*, 1885-86, and 1890.

[2] H. Hale, "The Iroquois Book of Rites," No. 2 of the *Library of Aborig. Amer. Lit.* of Brinton, Philad., 1883, chaps. i. and ii. (history of the confederation summarised from the standard works of Morgan, Colden, etc.); C. Royce, "The Cherokee Nation, etc.," *Fifth Rep. Bur. Ethn. for 1883-84;* Mooney, "Sacred Formulæ of Cherokee," *Seventh Rep. Bur. Ethn. for 1885-86.*

The wars in which the Iroquoians have been engaged have singularly reduced their number; to-day there are only about 43,000, of whom 9000 are in Canada.

2. The *Muskhogean group* comprises several tribes: *Apalachi*, *Chata-Choctaw*, *Chicasaws*, *Creeks* or *Muskhogis*, who formerly dwelt between the lower Mississippi, the Atlantic, the Tennessee River, and the Gulf of Mexico. To these we must add the *Seminoles* who formerly occupied the Florida peninsula.[1] The habits of the Muskhogean tribes, of which Hernando de Soto drew so vivid a picture in 1540, were those of husbandmen somewhat advanced in civilisation; they had a hieroglyphic writing (Brinton), but were unacquainted with the use of metals, gold excepted. The southern portion of the United States which these tribes occupied is a region with a sub-tropical climate, favourable to the cultivation of the sugar-cane, maize, and tobacco. The ancient Muskhogis wore garments of special texture, and daubed their bodies like the Algonquians, but were unacquainted with tattooing. At the present day they have dwindled down to 25,500 individuals. Certain tribes, like the *Yamasis*, have completely disappeared; in 1886 there were only three *Apalachi* women left. We include among the Muskhogis the tribes who formerly lived in the lower valley of the Mississippi, and whose dialects have not been classified: the *Natchez*, idealised by Chateaubriand, a score of whom still dwell among the Creeks and Cherokis; the *Atacapas*, reduced in number to a dozen individuals, in the Calcasieu Pass (Louisiana), etc.

3. The *Siouans* or *Dakotas* (Figs. 158 and 159) occupied at the time of the discovery of America the whole country extending to the west of the Mississippi, between the river Arkansas on the south and the Saskatchewan on the north, as far as the Rocky Mountains. For a long time this was believed to be their original home; but it has been found

[1] The primitive population of Florida, the *Timuquanans*, appear to have been exterminated in the eighteenth century. See MacCauley, "The Seminol Ind.," *Fifth Rep. Bur. Ethn. for 1883-84*, p. 467, Washington, 1887.

necessary to modify this opinion since the discovery by Hale and Gatschet of tribes speaking a Siouan tongue with archaic forms east of the Mississippi. These tribes are the *Tutelos* of Virginia, of whom but a score of individuals are left; the *Biloxis* of Louisiana, and the *Winnebagos*. It is now admitted

FIG. 161.—Christian Apache Indian.

that the original home of the Siouans was the Alleghany Mountains and the surrounding country; thence they were doubtless forced back by the Algonquians into the prairies to the west of the Mississippi, where they became buffalo-hunters.

The principal Siouan tribes are: the *Assinaboins* on the Saskatchewan, the *Minnetaris* on the Yellowstone river, the

Ponkas and the *Omahas* in Nebraska, the *Osages* of the borders of Arkansas, the *Hidatsas* of Dakota, the *Crows* of Montana, the *Siouans* or *Dakotas* properly so called (Figs. 26, 158, and 159) in the upper basin of the Missouri, etc. The total number of the Siouans is estimated at 43,400 individuals, of whom 2,200 are in Canada.[1]

The Indians of the four groups just enumerated all resemble each other in physical type: stature very high (from 1m. 68 among the Cherokis of the east, to 1m. 75 among the Cheyennes and Crows), head sub-dolichocephalic or mesocephalic (ceph. ind. on the liv. sub., from 79.3 among the Iroquoians to 80.5 among the Cheyennes), face, oval.[2] Near the Siouans, in the same ethnographic region of the plains of the Great West, dwelt the *Pawnees* or *Caddoes*, one of the tribes of which, the *Aricaras* or *Rikaris* (450 individuals at the present day), emigrated north towards the sources of the Mississippi. As to the *Pawnees properly so called* they were established in the valley of the Plata, whence they were transferred in 1878 into the Indian Territory; they numbered 820 individuals in the census of 1890. The rest of the nation, the *Wichitas* (Fig. 160), the *Caddoes*, etc., have abandoned the predatory habits of the true Pawnees and become good husbandmen distributed over different reservations.

The *Kiowas* form a small linguistic group by themselves. The neighbours formerly of the Comanches and the Shoshones, these ex-robbers are at the present day installed, to the number of 1,500, in the Indian Territory.

The Pawnees and Kiowas are tall and mesocephalic, with a tendency towards brachycephaly.

[1] R. Rigges, "Dictionary . . . and Ethnogr. of Dakota," *Contrib. N. Amer. Ethn.*, vol. viii.; Dorsey, "Furniture and Implements of Omaha," *Thirteenth Rep. Bur. Ethn.*; "Omaha Sociology," *Third Rep. Bur. Ethn.*; Mooney, "Siouan Tribes of the East," *Bull. Bur. of Ethn.*, No. 24, Washington, 1894.

[2] See Appendices I. to III.; the measurements there given are principally taken from Boas, Ten Kate, the American military commission, and my own observations with Laloy.

c. Indians of the Pacific slope.—The coast tribes of the Pacific might be united into a single group in spite of the great diversity of language existing among them.[1] In fact, most of these Indians belong to one and the same sub-division of the North American race, the *Pacific sub-race.* They are above medium height (from 1m. 66 among the *Utes* to 1m. 69 among the *Chahaptes*), sub-brachycephalic (mean ceph. ind. from 82.7 to 84.7, except the Utes, whose index is 79.5), with rounded face (Tsimshians and Haidas), or elongated (Kwakiutls); they have straight eyes and their pilous system is well developed (Boas). It is only in the region of the Pueblos that we can detect the admixture of the short, brachycephalic Central American race.[2] Ethnic characters enable us to divide the Indians of the Pacific into three groups: Indians of the north-west, Indians of Oregon-California, and Pueblo Indians.[3]

1. *The Indians of the north-west*[4] are divided into two slightly

[1] Not less than 39 linguistic families may be enumerated on that long but narrow strip of land which extends from Alaska to California, between the Rocky Mountains and the ocean. (Powell, *loc. cit.*)

[2] The Moquis and Zuñis are in fact 1m. 62 in height, and have a ceph. ind. of 83.3 and 84.9. We must, however, notice some exceptions in regard to the somatic type of the Indians of the Pacific slopes: the *Salishans* of the coast (with the exception of the Bilcoolas) are almost short and brachycephalic, while those of the interior are almost tall and brachycephalic, like the *Bilcoolas*, the *Maricopas*, the *Mohares* (Fig. 4).

[3] The first of these groups occupies Powell's North Pacific and Columbian "ethnographic provinces" (*loc. cit.*); the second, the province of Oregon-California; the third, the Interior Basin and the region of the Pueblos.

[4] Gibbs, "Tribes of W. Washington and N.-W. Oregon," *Contrib. N. Am. Ethn.*, vol. i., p. 157, Washington, 1887; Dall, "Tribes N.W. Washington," *ibid.*; Petroff, *Rep. on Populat. . . . of Alaska*, Washington, 1884; *Amerikas Nordweskiiste* (Publ. Ethn. Mus.), Berlin, 1883-84, 2 vols., fol.; Krause, *Die Tlinkit Indianer*, Jena, 1885; "Reports . . . Committee, North-West Tribes . . . Canada" (in the *Rep. Brit. Assoc.* from 1885 to 1898; especially the reports by H. Hale and Wilson on the Black-Feet in 1885 and 1887, and the full reports of Boas, 1888 to 1890, and in 1898, partly summarised in *Peterm. Mittheil.*, 1887 and 1896, and in the *Transact. Roy. Soc. Canada*, 1888, 2nd sect.); Boas, "Die Tsimshian," *Zeitsch. f. Ethn.*, 1888, p. 231; Niblack, "Coast Ind. South Alaska and N. Brit. Colomb.," *Rep. U.S. Nat. Mus. for 1898.*

distinct groups by their ethnic characters. In the north, on the indented coast of Alaska and British Columbia, as well as in the innumerable rocky islands lying off it, dwell tribes of fishers and hunters who form a very characteristic group by their ethnic traits, of which the following are the principal: garments of woven wool or of bark (before the arrival of the Whites); communal barracks, near which are raised "totem posts," usually of slate, ornamented with anthropomorphic sculptures, grotesque or horrible, representing totems; plated armour, composite bow of wood and bone, tattooing, etc. The Pacific coast to the south of Vancouver and the Columbia drainage area is occupied by another group of populations, which, while having some traits in common with the former (communal barracks but without "totem post," cooking by means of heated stones, zoomorph masks, etc.), exhibits a multitude of characters (garments of raw hides, cranial deformations, absence of tattooings, plain bow, etc.) which keep them widely separate.

The first group comprises the following tribes, beginning at Cape St. Elias and going towards the south: the *Tlinkits* or *Kolushes* as far as the 55th degree of N. lat. (6,437 individuals in 1880, according to Petroff); the *Haidas* or *Skittagets* of the Queen Charlotte Islands (2,500), skilful carvers in wood; the *Tsimshians* of the coast situated opposite to these islands; the *Wakashes*, sub-divided into *Nootkas* of Vancouver Island and *Kwakiutls* of the adjacent coast. The second group is composed of the remnants of the *Salishans*, *Selish*, or Flat-heads (12,000 in Canada, 5,500 in the "reservations" of the United States); of the *Shahapts* or "*Nez-percés*" (300), to the south of these; and lastly, the *Chenooks*, well known for their cranial deformations (p. 176).

2. *The seaboard of Oregon and California* is a succession of short, isolated valleys, abounding in fibrous plants, fruit, and fish. These are excellent conditions for the formation of little isolated ethnic groups; thus it happens that the Indians of this coast are divided into twenty-four or twenty-six distinct linguistic families.

Of these the principal, as we go from north to south, are: the *Copehs* of the right bank of the Sacramento; the *Pujunnas* or *Pooyoonas* of the left bank of the same water-way; the *Kulanapans* to the north of San Francisco; the *Costanos* to the south of that town; the *Salinas*, who formerly inhabited the valley bearing the same name, but of whom there remain but a dozen individuals; the *Maripos* or *Yokuts* (145 individuals) to the east of the last-named tribe; the *Chumashes* around the mission of Santa-Barbara, 35° N. latitude, of whom scarcely two score individuals still speak the language of their fathers; the *Hupas*, very primitive in their habits. Among most of these populations are found vestiges of the ancient custom of tattooing and the use of garments fashioned from vegetable fibres.

It is probably in this group that we must include the *Yumas* of the lower valley of the Colorado (Arizona) and of the Californian peninsula, of whom the principal tribes are as follow: the *Mohaves* (Fig. 4) and the *Yumas* properly so called, in the valley of the Colorado; the *Maricopas* of the valley of the Gila; the *Soris* or *Seris* in Mexico, opposite to the Californian peninsula; lastly, in this peninsula itself the *Cochimis* in the north and the *Periquès*, now extinct, at the southern extremity of the peninsula; there is not, however, any direct evidence that these last spoke a *Yuma* tongue; further, they burnt their dead while all the other Yumas buried theirs. The population of lower California was very scattered (10,000 individuals in all); they gained a miserable existence from hunting and fishing, and could not even make canoes. To-day but few are left. To judge from the bones gathered at the extreme end of the Californian peninsula, the Indians who dwelt there (the ancestors of the Periquès?) were if anything of short stature; by this characteristic, as well as by their dolichocephaly, they would appear then to be allied to the Palæo-American sub-race.[1]

[1] Bancroft, *loc. cit.*, vol. iii.; Ten Kate, *Bull. Soc. Anthrop.*, Paris, 1884, and *loc. cit.*; Deniker, *Bull. du Museum d'Hist. Nat.*, 1895, No. 2.

3. The name *Pueblo Indians* is sometimes given to the populations inhabiting the caves hollowed out of the sides of the deep cañons and the "pueblos" of the warm and arid table-lands of Arizona, New Mexico, and the adjacent parts of Utah, California, and Mexico.

Some of these populations, the *Moquis* (2000) for example, belong to the Shoshone linguistic family,[1] others perhaps to the *Pima* stock (see p. 535); but there are three small groups of these cliff-dwellers whose languages present no analogy with one another nor with any other dialect. These are the *Keres* (3,560 individuals) and the *Tanos* (3,200 individuals), both in the upper basin of the Rio Grande, and the *Zuñis*, who to the number of 1,600 occupy the "pueblo" of the same name in the west of New Mexico.

In spite of the diversity of their dialects all the cliff-dwellers have certain physical characters in common, such as stature above the average, brachycephaly, etc.[2] It must not be forgotten that the cliff-dwellers are surrounded on all sides by immigrant populations of the Athapascan stock (see p. 524).

[1] The Shoshones, who inhabited by themselves the *interior basin* between the Rocky Mountains and the Sierra-Nevada, have now dwindled to 17,000 individuals, just managing to subsist by fishing and gathering roots on infertile soil. They are composed of twelve tribes, of which the more important are those of the *Shoshones*, the *Utes* (Fig. 40), the *Piutes* or *Pai-Utes*, and the *Comanches*. Buschmann (*Die Spuren d. Aztek Sprache, etc.*, Berlin, 1859) was the first to draw attention to the affinity of their dialect with the Sonoran-Aztec linguistic group (see p. 535), while Gibbs (*loc. cit.*, p. 224) was the first to point out their probable migration from the region situated between the Rocky Mountains and the Great Lakes towards the deserts of the Great Basin. Brinton (*Amer. Race*, p. 119) confirms this observation, arriving at his conclusion from new facts.

[2] It should be mentioned that this brachycephaly is also found, even a little more accentuated, in the skulls which Mr. Cushing and the members of the Hemenway expedition discovered in the ancient habitations of the Salado valley and in the Hanolawan pueblo, attributed to the not very remote ancestors of the Pueblos of the present day. These skulls are hyper-brachycephalic (mean ceph. ind. of 94 skulls, 89); they also exhibited an extraordinary frequency of the "Inca bone" (p. 67), and several other osteological peculiarities, as, for instance, in the structure of the hyoid bone (p. 96).

III. *The Indians of Mexico*[1] *and Central America* may be divided, from the ethnographical point of view, into two great groups: the Sonoran-Aztecs, inhabiting the north of Mexico or what is improperly called the Anahuac plateau; and the Central Americans of Southern Mexico and the states situated more to the south as far as the Costa Rica republic.[2]

a. The *Sonoran-Aztecs* are allied by language to the Shoshones, and by manners and customs to the true Pueblo Indians of the United States, while they exhibit some divergences as regards physical type. Physically the Sonorans are allied to the North Americans of the Atlantic slope, while the peoples of the Aztec group show a great infusion of Central American blood.

The *Pimas* and their congeners the *Papajos* constitute one of the principal tribes of the Sonorans. They dwell in pueblos or "casas grandes," and expend a prodigious amount of labour in drawing their subsistence from the infertile soil of the Gila valley. However, they are fine tall men (mean height 1m. 71, according to Ten Kate), slim and nimble, having the head a trifle elongated (ceph. ind. on the liv. sub., 78.6), the nose prominent, etc. Their neighbours the *Yakis* and the *Mayas*, included in the *Cahita* linguistic group, 20,000 strong, have the same type as the Pimas. They inhabit the sterile regions through which flow the rivers Yaki and Mayo, and have preserved their racial purity almost intact,[3] unlike their kinsmen

[1] Orozco y Berra, *Geografia de las lenguas . . . de Mexico*, Mexico, 1864, with ethn. chart (which may still be profitably consulted).

[2] According to Brinton, the great Uto-Aztecan linguistic family is composed of three branches: Shoshonean (or Ute), Sonoran, and Nahuatlan (Aztec).

[3] It is the same with the *Coras* (3000), and especially with the *Huicholes* (4000) of the Nayarit Sierra (north of Jalisco), who are tillers of the soil, and the last remnants of a formerly numerous and warlike population. The Huicholes worship the sun and various plant divinities, more particularly the "peyote" (a cactus, *Anhalonium Lewinii*), the fruit of which has stimulative and anaphrodisiac properties. (Hamy, *Bull. Mus. Hist. Nat.*, 1898, p. 197; Lumholtz, *Bull. Amer. Mus. Nat. Hist.*, 1898, p. 1, with plates; L. Diguet, *Nouv. Arch. Miss. Scientif.*, vol. ix., p. 571, plates, Paris, 1899.)

the *Opatas* and the *Tarahumaras* of Chihuahua and Sonora, in whom there is a powerful strain of Spanish blood.[1]

Under the collective name of *Aztecs* or *Nahua* are comprised several peoples and tribes who formerly occupied the Pacific slope from Rio de Fuerte (26th degree of N. lat.) to the frontiers of Guatemala, with the exception of the Isthmus of Tehuantepec; their colonies even extended farther into Guatemala and Salvador (example, the *Pipils*). On the other side, on the Atlantic slope the Nuhua tribes inhabited the regions around Mexico. There they had formed, probably two or three centuries before the arrival of the Europeans, three confederate states: *Tezcuco*, *Tlacopan* and *Tenochtitlan*, under whose dominion were ranged tribes of the same origin scattered along the coast, among the *Totonac* people in the existing province of Vera Cruz; one of these tribes, the *Nicaraos* or *Niquirans*, migrated into Nicaragua.[2]

[1] Hamy, "Distrib. geogr. des Opatus, Tarahumars, etc.," *Bull. Soc. Anthrop.*, Paris, 1883, p. 785; Ten Kate, "Sur les Pimas, etc.," *Bull. Soc. Anthr.*, 1883; Lumholtz, "Tarahumara," *Bull. Amer. Geogr. Soc.*, 1894, p. 219.

[2] It is impossible to enter here into details on the ancient Aztec society. Let us simply bear in mind that from the economic point of view it was based on "hoe-culture" (see p. 192) of maize, tobacco, and cocoa, as well as on a well-developed industry: the weaving of stuffs, pottery, manufacture of paper, malleation and melting (a somewhat rare case in pre-Columbian America) of gold, silver, copper, and bronze. Architecture and sculpture had attained there a great perfection, as well as ideographic and iconomatic writing (see p. 140). It was politically a confederacy of democratic states, often under the dominion of a dictator on whom the Spaniards bestowed the title of king. It was thought until recent times that there had been several invasions of different peoples into Mexico, the *Toltecs* in the first instance, then the *Chichimecs*, lastly the *Nahuatlans;* but from the recent works by Morgan, *loc. cit.* (*The House-life, etc.*), Bandelier (*Report Peabody Mus.*, vol. ii., Cambridge, Mass., 1888), Brinton (*Essays of an Americanist*, Philadelphia, 1890, and *Am. Race*), and Bruhl (*Die Culturvolker Alt-Amerikas*, Cincinnati, 1875-87), we may conclude that the name *Toltec* has only relation to a small clan or even perhaps to an imaginary mythical people. As to that of *Chichimec*, it was employed by the Nahuas to denote all those peoples outside of their own civilisation; they used this term as the Romans did that of "barbarian."

At the present day the Aztecs, about 150,000 in number, are dispersed over the whole Mexican coast from Sinaloa in the south to Tepic, Jalisco, Michoacan on the west. Very peaceful, sedentary, with a veneer of civilisation, they are nominally Catholics, though at bottom they are animists, and full of superstition. In many of the Aztec villages the ancient Nahua language is still spoken.[1]

Side by side with the Aztecs there exist in Mexico three other ethnic groups which may be designated by the name of *Mexicans properly so called.* These are:—

1st. The *Otomis*, presumably the aboriginal inhabitants of the Mexican table-lands, now settled in the state of Guanajuato, and the basin of the upper Moctezuma between Mexico and San Luis de Potosi. They afford a unique example of an American people speaking an almost monosyllabic language. They are below the average height, brachycephalic as a general rule, with a tendency towards mesocephaly.[2]

2nd. The *Tarascos*, formerly spread over the whole of the state of Michoacan, in Guanajuato and Queretaro,[3] have been absorbed by the half-breed population. Lumholtz, however, states that nearly 200,000 uncrossed Tarascos are still living (1896) in the mountains of Michoacan. They had a form of pictography peculiar to themselves, and must have come, according to their traditions, from the northern regions, like the Nahuatlans.

3rd. The *Totonacs* of the province of Vera Cruz, formerly very civilised, resemble physically their neighbours on the north-east, the *Huaxtecs;* the latter, however, belong to the Maya linguistic group (see below).

b. The Central Americans.—They may be divided into three geographical groups, the Indians of Southern Mexico, the Mayas, and the Isthmians.

I. Among the numerous aboriginal peoples of Southern Mexico the *Zapotecs* of the state of Oajaca are the most

[1] L. Biart, *Les Aztèques, histoire, mœurs*, Paris, 1885.

[2] E. Hamy, *loc. cit.* (*Anthr. Mex.*); Brinton, *loc. cit.* (*Am. Race*).

[3] E. Hamy, *loc. cit.*, *Bull. Soc. Anthrop.*, Paris, 1883, p. 787, chart.

numerous (about 265,000 individuals). These are the descendants of a once powerful people who had attained to nearly the same degree of civilisation as the Aztecs.

The *Miztecs* (Figs. 163 and 164), who occupy the eastern part of the state of Oajaca and the adjacent regions of Guerrero, have dwindled to a few thousand individuals. They appear to be of fairly pure Central American race, are very short,

FIG. 162.—Young Creole woman of Martinique.
(*Phot. Coll. Anthr. Soc. Paris.*)

brachycephalic, and have a dark brown skin and projecting cheek-bones.[1]

In the east of Oajaca and in Chiapa, on the frontier of Guatemala, are found the *Zoques*, the *Mixes*, and the *Chapanecs*, with whom it is customary to connect the *Chontals* and the *Popolucas*. But these two vocables signify in Nahuatlan merely "stranger" and "one who speaks badly or stammers."[2] Among

[1] D. Charnay, quoted by Hamy, *loc. cit.* (*Anthr. Mex.*).

[2] Berendt, *Bull. Amer. Geogr. Soc.*, New York, 1875-76, No. 2; Brinton, *loc. cit.* (*Am. R.*), p. 117.

the tribes of Oajaca and Tabasco, described under the name of Chontals, some speak a dialect peculiar to themselves, the Tequistlatecan, allied to the Yuma language (Brinton), while others speak the Maya dialects.[1]

II. The peoples composing the *Maya group* appear to have come in post-quaternary times (by sea?), and in a state of

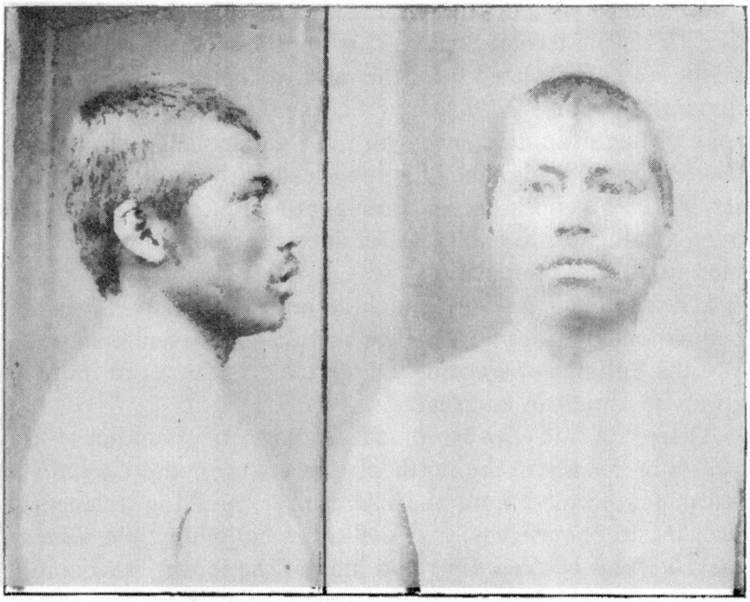

FIG. 163.—Miztec Indian (Mexico), Central American race. (*Phot. D. Charney, Coll. Mus. Nat. Hist. Paris.*)

civilisation already well advanced,[2] into the Yucatan peninsula. Thence they spread into Guatemala and the surrounding regions of Salvador and Honduras, where at the present day they form the bulk of the population. The ancient Maya

[1] The Chontals of Nicaragua are the *Lenkas* (see p. 540). The "*Popolucas*" of Puebla speak a *Miztec* dialect; those of Vera Cruz the *Mixe* dialect; those of Guatemala the *Cakchiquel*, one of the Maya dialects adopted as the official language by the Catholic Church, etc.

[2] Mercer, *Hill-Caves of Yucatan*, Philad., 1896.

civilisation resembled that of Mexico, the sanguinary creeds of the latter excepted; their writing was of a perfect hieroglyphic type. Besides the *Mayas properly so called* of Yucatan, the principal tribes of this group are: the *Tsendals* or *Chontals* of Mexico, already mentioned above; the *Mopans* of Northern Guatemala; the *Koïtches* or *Quichés* farther south, the only Indian people possessing an aboriginal written literature; the *Pokomams* of the district around the town of Guatemala; the *Chortis* on the territory where the ruins of Copan stand; and a long way off, isolated from the rest of their kinsmen, in the Mexican province of Tamaulipas, the *Huaxtecs* (p. 537). In spite of linguistic differences, all the Guatemalans or Indians of Guatemala resemble each other physically; they are short, thick-set, with high cheek-bones, prominent and often convex nose.[1] Some characteristic habits, as for instance geophagy, are common to all these populations.

III. *The Isthmians.*—We include under this name the native populations of Central America, scattered between Guatemala and the Isthmus of Panama, whose dialects do not fit into any group of American languages.[2]

These are the *Lenkas* of the interior of Honduras; the *Xicaks* or *Sihahv* in the north of this country; the *Chontals* of Nicaragua, formed from the *Matagalpes*, speaking a language peculiar to themselves; and the tribes adjoining the *Lenkas*, the *Guatusos* or *Huatusos*, who inhabit the forests surrounding San Juan. The latter were formerly classed, without adequate reason, with the Nahua, and they were represented as having dark complexions, whereas they are as yellow as the rest of Americans. In number they scarcely exceed 600 individuals.[3]

[1] A. Stoll, *Zur Ethnogr. d. Rep. Gutemala*, Zurich, 1884; K. Sapper, "Ethnogr. von S.-E. Mexico und Brit. Honduras," *Peterm. Mittheil.*, 1895, p. 177, chart, and "Die unabhängige Indianerstaaten von Yucatan," *Globus*, vol. 67, 1893, p. 196.

[2] See for the geographical distribution of these peoples in pre-Columbian times, D. Pector, *Arch. Soc. Americaine*, new series, vol. vi., Paris, 1888, pp. 97 and 145.

[3] Fernandez and Bramford, *Rep. Smiths. Inst.*, 1882, p. 675; Brinton, *loc. cit.* (*Am. R.*), p. 163.

To all these peoples there must be added certain uncivilised tribes of the *Ulva* group (Soumoo of the English),[1] on the coast of Mosquito, who are sometimes called Caribs, although they have nothing in common with the true Caribs (p. 552); then the *Micas*, the *Siquias* of the Rio Mico, the *Subironas* of

FIG. 164.—Miztec women (Mexico). (*Phot. D. Charney, Coll. Mus. Nat. Hist. Paris.*)

the Rio Coco, etc., who are all distinguished by the colour of their skin, which is darker than that of Indians in general.

The *Moscos* or *Mosquitos* who inhabit the neighbourhood of the Blewfields lagoon (Mosquito reservation) are still darker, indeed, almost black like Negroes, without, however, exhibiting other points of resemblance with the latter. They are

[1] Wickham, "Soumoo or Woolwa Indians," *Journ. Anthr. Inst.*, vol. xxiv., 1894-95, p. 198.

short in stature, having a fine, prominent nose, etc., and it is not difficult to distinguish those who are the offspring of Mosquitos crossed with true Negro blood. About 6000 in number, the Mosquitos are relatively civilised, and make use of the Latin alphabet, introduced by missionaries, for writing their mother-tongue. In an island of the Blewfields lagoon, between the Rio Mico and the Rio San Juan, have been found the *Rumas*, of very high stature, but their language is as yet unknown.

Half-breeds of North America.—In the United States and Canada the half-breeds of Indians and Whites, as well as Mulattos, form but a very slight portion of the population. This is not the case in Central America and Mexico. The aboriginal populations of Central America are reduced to a few thousand individuals; on the other hand, the half-breeds, produced by the crossings between them and the Europeans, form almost the whole of the population.

In Mexico the half-breeds form a little less than the half of the population, and in a general way they increase in number as we go from north to south and from west to east. Their nomenclature is somewhat complicated.[1] On the other hand, Negroes and Mulattos are not very numerous in Mexico and Central America. The Negro element exhibits a marked predominance only in the Antilles. The population of the

[1] The name half-breed (Mestizo) is given in Mexico only to a child born of the union of a Spaniard with an Indian woman. By being crossed with a Spaniard a "Mestizo" may give birth to a "Castiza"; the scion of the latter and a Spaniard reverts, it is said, to the race of the father, and is set down as Spanish. A Mulatto woman, the offspring of a Spaniard and a negress, may give birth to a "Morisco" by uniting with a Spaniard; this Morisco will produce with a Spaniard what is called an "Albino," and it is only to her son, the offspring of a Spanish father, who should revert to his father's race, that the name of "Tornatro" will be applied. An Indian marrying a negress produces a "Sobo," and the latter engenders with a negress a "Chino." The progeny of a Chino and an Indian is called "Cambujo," and that of an Indian and a half-breed, "Cayote." (Hamy, following Ignacio de Castro, quoted by de Quatrefages, *Hist. Gén. Races Hum.*, p. 605.)

island of Haiti is almost wholly Negro or Mulatto; that of the other islands has sprung from the manifold crossings between the ancient Carib or Arawak aborigines (see p. 552), and between Negroes and Europeans. The children of a white man and a mulatto woman are called Quadroons in the Antilles, but most of the half-breeds among whom European blood predominates prefer the name of *Creoles*. The Creole type of the Antilles is indeed very fine, especially among the women (Fig. 162), who sometimes have a vivacious look and a bewitching smile unique of their kind.

PEOPLES OF SOUTH AMERICA.

Accepting, with Brinton, the northern political frontier of Costa Rica as the ethnological limit of South America, I propose to pass in review the native populations of the continent, grouping them according to the four great natural regions: the Cordillera of the Andes; the plains of the Amazon and the Orinoco, with Guiana; the table-lands of eastern and southern Brazil; lastly, the Pampas of the southern part of the continent, with Tierra del Fuego.

This division corresponds pretty well with the distribution of races, languages, and ethnographic provinces.[1] In fact, the substratum of the Andean populations is formed of the Central American race, while that of the Amazonians and Guianas is composed of the South American race with its two sub-races, South American properly so called, and Palæo-American; the latter predominates also in east Brazil and Tierra del Fuego, while there are mingled with it Patagonian and other elements in the south of Brazil and among the Pampeans.

[1] I think that it corresponds better with the facts themselves than the mixed and chronological classification of the South Americans into four groups (Eskimoid and Ugroid peoples of the early stone age; Caribs of the later stone age; Mongoloid semi-civilised brachycephals of the stone and bronze ages; hunting and warlike tribes of the bronze age) proposed by Siemiradzki, *Mittheil. Anthrop. Gesellsch.*, vol. xxviii., p. 127, Vienna, 1898.

As regards language there is the same difference. In the Andean dialects the pronominal particles are suffixes, while in the Amazonian dialects these particles are prefixes, but both groups allow of a limitative form of the personal pronoun in the plural. As to the Pampean dialects, they are without the limitative form in most cases, and sometimes make use of prefixes, sometimes of suffixes.[1]

The ethnological differences of the three groups are manifold. This subject will be briefly dealt with further on. For the present let us observe that, in a general way, the Andeans are husbandmen, and have had a highly-developed native civilisation, while the Amazonians and the Brazilians of the east are for the most part fishers or hunters, often in the lowest scale of civilisation. As to the Pampeans, they are typical pastoral nomads. Before the arrival of the Europeans, the Andeans were acquainted with the weaving of stuffs; they worked in gold, silver, and bronze, manufactured fine pottery, had houses of stone and fortified towns, and employed as their chief weapons clubs and slings. The Amazonians and their congeners, on the other hand, still go almost naked, and adorn themselves with feathers; they were unacquainted with metals on the arrival of the Europeans, and some are ignorant even now of the art of pottery; they dwell in shelters or huts of branches and leaves, and their weapons are the blow-pipe and poisoned arrows. The Pampeans, before being influenced by the Andean or European civilisation, clothed themselves with skins, were acquainted neither with metals nor pottery, dwelt in huts, and used the *bollas* as their principal weapon.

Before beginning a rapid review of the South American tribes, it must again be remarked that their nomenclature often leads to confusion. A great number of terms are only qualifications applied by Europeans to the most different peoples, in no way akin one to the other. Such, for example,

[1] Lafone Quevedo, Preface to the "Arte de la lengua Toba" of Barcena, *Revista Mus. La Plata*, vol. v., p. 143, 1894. This distinction is criticised by Brinton, *Proc. Am. Philos. Soc.*, vol. xxxvii., p. 179, Philad., 1898.

is the term "Bougres," which is given in the east of Brazil to savages in general; or that of "Jivaros," employed in the same sense in Peru; such also are the appellations of *Coroados* (crowned or tonsured), of *Orejones* (pierced ears), of *Cherentes*, *Caribs*, etc., without taking into account those relating to the half-breeds.[1]

I. *The Andeans.*[2]—By this name we shall describe the principal populations which are stationed in the Cordilleras, and on the high table-lands shut in by these mountains from Costa Rica to the 45th degree of S. latitude. Most of them belong to the Chibcha and Quechua linguistic families; but there are also several whose linguistic affinities have yet to be determined.

1. *Chibcha Linguistic Family.*—The *Talamancas* of Costa Rica, sub-divided into several tribes (*Chirripos*, *Bribris*, etc.), form the most northern tribe of this group; they dwell partly on the Atlantic slope, partly on the Pacific. By certain ethnic characters (feather ornaments, use of the blow-pipe) they are related to the Amazonians.[3] Farther away the *Guaymis* inhabit the region of Chiriqui (Panama), where such beautifully ornamented ancient pottery (Figs. 63 and 64) has been found in the tombs of a still mysterious population. They are short, thick-set, and flat-faced, resembling the Otomis of Mexico. There may be about 4000 of them, according to Pinart; but some of their tribes had dwindled to such an extent, that of the *Muoi*, for example, there were only three individuals in 1882. They organise feasts among the tribes, to which invitations are sent by means of a staff sent round (a portion of a liana-stem, having as many knots as there are days remaining before the feast). With their bodies daubed with red or blue, the Guaymis give themselves up during these feasts to drinking

[1] The "*Mamelucos*" or *Paulists* of the province of Sao Paulo (Brazil), European and Indian half-breeds; the *Gauchos* of Chaco, offspring of Whites and Indians of the Pampas; the *Curibocos*, Indo-negro half-breeds in Brazil, etc.

[2] D'Orbigny, *L'homme Americain*, Paris, 1859, 2 vols.

[3] G. Bovalius, "En reza . . . Talamanca-Land," *Ymer*, p. 183, map, Stockholm, 1885.

and the game of *balza*, which consists in throwing a sort of club at the legs of their adversaries. There are also lesser feasts, feasts of initiation called here *urotes*.[1] The *Chibchas* of Columbia, whose civilisation is no whit behind that of the *Nahuas*,[2] have been under Spanish influence since the conquest, and to-day but a few tribes are met with who still speak their mother-tongue or who have preserved their ancient customs.

Such are the *Chimilas* of the Sierra-Perija; the *Tunebos*, true cliff-dwellers, eastward of Bogota; the *Arahuacos*, dwelling to the number of 3000 in the Sierra-Nevada of Santa Marta. The latter have nothing in common with the true Arawaks, unless it be their name, which, however, they repudiate as an insult; the name they give to themselves is *Cöggaba*, that is to say, "Men."[3] As to the *Chibcha* or *Muisca* Indians of the Rio Magdalena, who were the most civilised of all the peoples speaking the Chibcha tongue, no survivors are to be found.

2. *The Quechua Linguistic Family* is one of the most far-reaching of South America. The Quechua dialects are still spoken to-day on the coast, and along the chain of the Andes from Quito to the 30th degree S. latitude. This is practically the extent of the ancient empire of the *Incas*, the best known nation among the Quechua peoples. But the influence of the Inca civilisation and the Quechua language extended even farther, to Columbia, the borders of Ucayale, and the Bolivian table-land on the north, to the edge of the Pampas on the south (among the Calchaquis). For the western part of South America the Quechua tongue was the *lengua general*, as the Tupi-Guarani tongue was the *lingua geral* for the east

[1] Pinart, "Chiriqui," *Bull. Soc. Géogr.*, Paris, 1885, p. 433.

[2] The Chibchas were husbandmen, manufacturers, and merchants, but unacquainted with the use of metals, except gold. They too have not left any great monuments of architecture (see for further information the works already quoted of Bruhl, Brinton, etc.).

[3] Are they not related to the *Cayapas* of Ecuador, described by Santjago Basurco? (*Tour du Monde*, 1894, p. 401.)

(Brazil, Paraguay, etc.). This language is not at all superseded by Spanish; on the contrary, the Whites learn it, and several Quechua words: *guano*, *pampa*, *condor*, *quina*, have found their way into the languages of all civilised nations.[1] The principal tribes are: the *Huancas* to the north-east of Lima, the *Lamanas* near Trujillo, the *Incas* in the vicinity of the Rio Apurimac, the *Aymaras* of the high table-lands of Bolivia (600,000 individuals, of whom two-thirds are of pure blood).

In spite of the diversity of dialects all the Quechuas and Aymaras present a remarkable uniformity of physical type. They are of low stature (1 m. 60 according to D'Orbigny, 1 m. 57 according to Forbes), thick-set, and very strong. The chest is broad, the head massive and globular, the nose aquiline, forehead retreating. This last peculiarity should however be attributed to the custom of deforming the head, very widespread among all the Quechuas and neighbouring peoples; this deformation is still practised in the same way as in the days of the Inca civilisation. It is very unlikely that the frequent occurrence of the "Inca bone" (p. 67) in Peruvian skulls has any connection with this deformation. The greatest part of the population of Peru is composed of Quechuas and Aymaras, or of Quechua-Spanish half-breeds.[2]

The *Calchaquis*,[3] the ancient inhabitants of the modern

[1] I shall not deal further with the important part which the Quechua civilisation played in all the western regions of South America. Let me observe, however, that this civilisation differed in many respects from that of the Nahuas; the Incas lived under a despotic communistic régime, they had no art of writing, and were content with mnemonic means to communicate with one another, they reared the llama, their religious rites were less sanguinary than those of the Nahua, etc. (Seler, *Peruanische Alterthüm*, Berlin, 1893; Brinton, *loc. cit.*; Bruhl, *loc. cit.*; Uhle, *Kultur Sud-Amerik. Völker*, vol. ii., Berlin, 1889-90.)

[2] Middendorf (E.), *Peru*, Berlin, 1893, 3 vols.

[3] Ten Kate, "Excursion Archæol. . . Catamarca, etc.," *Rev. Mus. La Plata*, vol. v., 1893, p. 329; *Intern. Arch. für Ethnog.*, vol. vii., 1894, p. 142; Ambrozetti, "Archeol. Calchaqui," *Bol. Inst. Geog. Arg.*, 1896, p. 117; Brinton, *Amer. Anthropologist*, N.S., vol. i., No. 1, New York, 1899.

south-west provinces, Argenton, Catamarca, Rioja, Santiago, etc., probably also spoke a Quechua dialect. It was a very civilised population; the only one in the South American

FIG. 165.—Guaraunos chief (Mouth of the Orinoco) with his two wives. (*Phot. Crevaux, Coll. Mus. Nat. Hist. Paris.*)

continent which knew how to construct buildings of freestone. Although partly borrowed from the Peruvians, the Calchaqui civilisation has a character of its own, and in several respects recalls that of the Pueblo Indians, particularly the Zuñis (arrangement of their cities in a series of seven, copper tools and weapons, etc.).

The last Calchaqui tribe, the *Quilmes*, was transported in 1670 by the Spaniards near to Buenos Ayres, where it forms the village of this name.

3. *Unclassified Tribes.*—In Columbia let us note the following tribes:—

The *Cuna* Indians, also called *Tula Dariens*, etc., of southern Panama. They are people of low stature (1m. 50, according to Brinton), thick-set, of light yellow complexion, very brachycephalic (ceph. ind. 88.6, according to Catat), with broad faces, somewhat resembling the Guaymis, their neighbours in the east (p. 545). It is asserted that individuals with grey eyes and chestnut or reddish hair are not rare among them. They are not numerous; the tribe of the *Changuina Dorasks*, which formerly numbered 5000, had dwindled down in 1883 to a dozen individuals, still speaking their mother-tongue; the *Sambu Chocos*, who occupied the whole of the lower valley of the Atrato, and extended westward to the Pacific coast, are now scarcely 600 in number in southern Darien. They are short (1m. 55), brachycephalic (ceph. ind. on the liv. sub., 84.1), very broad-faced.[1]

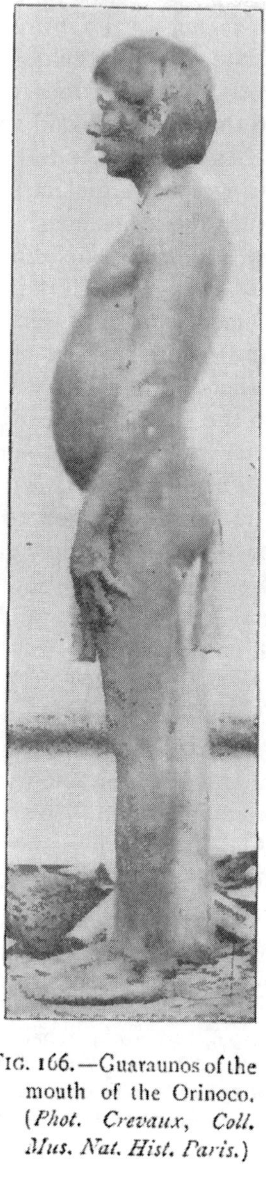

FIG. 166.—Guaraunos of the mouth of the Orinoco. (*Phot. Crevaux, Coll. Mus. Nat. Hist. Paris.*)

[1] L. Catat, "Les Habitants du Darien Merid.," *Rev. Ethnogr.*, 1888, p. 397; Pinart, "Les Indiens de Panama," *Rev. Ethnogr.*, No. 33, 1887, p. 117.

To the eastward of the *Chibchas* (p. 545) dwelt several families of the *Paniquitas* and *Paezes*, included in a distinct linguistic group, of which the other representatives, *Colimas* and *Manipos*, have entirely disappeared. In central Columbia (state of Antioquia) dwell the last remnants of the *Nutabehs* and *Tahamis*, tribes resembling the Muisca Indians (p. 546) in their customs and social state.

As to the Ando-Peruvian region, several ethnic groups, using special dialects, are also found there, having no relation with the Quechuas. Such as the small tribe of the *Puquinas* in the neighbourhood of Lake Titicaca, the *Yuncas* or *Cuna-Yuncas* ("inhabitants of the hot lands" in the Quechua tongue), settled on the Pacific coast between the 5th and 10th degrees of S. latitude); finally, the *Atacameños*, fishers of the Loa valley, and the *Shangos* or *Changos*, more to the south, in the desert of Atacama. These two tribes are characterised by their low stature (1m. 60, according to D'Orbigny).

It may be as well to class with the Andeans the *Araucans*, or *Mapu-che* as they call themselves, whose linguistic affinities are still obscure, but whom we must connect with the Central American race by their physical characters; stature almost low (1m. 61), sub-brachycephalic (ceph. ind. on the liv. sub., 82, skull 81), elongated face, with slightly projecting cheek-bones, straight or convex nose, etc., the general appearance recalling the Aymaras and the Quechuas;[1] certain ethnic characters (perfected weaving of stuffs, irrigation, hoe-culture, metallurgy, etc.) place them in the same category as the Andeans, and point to Peruvian influence. They are only found, in fact, to the north of the Bio-Bio river (37°–38° S. lat.)

[1] Siemiradzki, *loc. cit.*, p. 160. The figures here given from Oldendorf, Manouvrier, Hamy, Virchow, and derived from my own observations, relate to the Chilian Araucans. The Araucans of the Pampas are shorter (1m. 57, according to De la Vaulx, *Compt. rend. Soc. Geogr.*, Paris, 1898, p. 99), and brachycephalic, to judge from the measurements of Ten Kate (*Rev. Mus. La Plata*, vol. iv., p. 209), who finds the mean cephalic index of 53 skulls to be 83.92 in a series in which, however, several skulls of the Palæo-American type are met with.

—that is to say, only in those places reached by the Inca civilisation. South of this line, with the exception of the coast, where European influence makes itself felt, the Araucans have remained until recent times hunters or nomadic shepherds, almost uncivilised. It is estimated that there are 40,000 Chilian Araucans. At a comparatively recent period some Araucan tribes migrated to the eastern slope of the Cordilleras (the Manzanieros)[1] and into the Argentine pampas, as far as the neighbourhood of Buenos Ayres. In these parts they have been pushed back, firstly by the European colonists, then by the Argentine soldiers, farther and farther south, beyond the Rio Negro. This population is a very mixed one; we find in it Patagonian, Quechua, Chaco, and even European elements (see p. 574).

From the social point of view, all the Araucans have preserved their ancient organisation of hordes governed by a hereditary chief. Little is known about their religious ideas; it is understood that they hold in the highest reverence an evil spirit called "Pilgan" by the Andean Araucans, "Nervelu" ("bird with metal beak and claws") by the Araucans of the Pampas. Formerly, the Araucan warriors were buried with their weapons, their horse was felled on the grave and consumed.[2]

[1] The Manzanieros, so named from the country of crab-apple-tree forests which they inhabit, have preserved better than the Araucans of the Pampas their physical type; but they have adopted for the most part, like the latter, the manners and customs of the Indians of the Pampas and the *Gauchos* Euro-Indian half-breeds, similar to the *Cow-boys* of the western parts of the United States. They live as nomadic shepherds in tents of guanaco skins, and wear garments of tanned skin, after the manner of the Gauchos; they have no pottery, subsist almost exclusively on meat, etc. Excellent horsemen, they hunt the guanaco with bolas, exactly like the Patagonians and the Gauchos.

[2] The Archipelagoes of *Chiloé* and *Chonos*, which lie off the Chilian coast in the neighbourhood of Cape Peñas, were peopled by Araucan tribes of *Gauchos*, *Payos* and *Chonos*, of whom there remain only a few descendants, with a strain of Spanish blood. These Gauchos must not be confounded with the half-breeds of the same name (see above, note 1), nor the Chonos with the tribe of the same name living farther to the south between Cape Peñas and the Straits of Magellan; the latter tribe appears to be related rather to the Fuegians.

Among the Andean populations we must also mention the *Yurucares,* to the west of the Rio Mamoré, of very high stature, their skin being, it is said, almost as white as that of Europeans.

II. *The Amazonians.*—The vast plains and impenetrable forests, rich in birds and arboreal mammalia, watered by the great tropical streams, the Amazon and the Orinoco, are peopled by a large number of tribes who may be grouped to-day—thanks to the recent works of philologists—into four families. Two of these, the Carib and Arawak, or Maypure families, comprise the tribes of the eastern part of the country;[1] the two others, which are less important, the *Miranha* and *Pano* families, are composed of the tribes of the western part of the country.

1. *The Carib Family.*—It was thought until recently that the peoples of this linguistic group had settlements only in the Guianas and the Antilles, but recent studies have shown that they extended much farther over the South American continent, as far as the source of the Yapura on the west, and the 14th degree of S. latitude on the south. As the speech of the southern Caribs is purer, less sprinkled with Arawak words than that of their northern brethren, philologists suppose that the original home of the Caribs in general should be found somewhere in the centre of Brazil, to the south of the Amazon. It is from there that they must have migrated into Guiana, whence their hordes moved towards the Antilles probably two centuries

[1] For the philology of the Caribs and the Arawaks, see L. Adam, "Trois fam. linguist. . . . de l'Amazone, de l'Orénoque, etc.," *Congrès Intern. Americanistes*, Berlin, 1888, p. 489, and *Biblioth. linguist. Americaine*, vol. xviii., Paris, 1893; Von den Steinen, *loc. cit.*, and *Centr. Brasil*, Leipzig, 1886; Ehrenreich, *loc. cit.*, and *Peterm. Mitth.*, 1897, No. 4. For the ethnography, see the works already quoted of Ehrenreich, of Von den Steinen, and the following works: Schomburgh, *Reisen in Brit. Guyana*, Leipzig, 1847, 2 vols.; Coudreau, "Note sur 54 trib. Guyane," *Bull. Soc. Geogr.*, Paris, 1891, and "Dix ans de Guyane," *ibid.*, p. 447, map; E. Im Thurn, *Among the Indians of Guiana*, London, 1883; Crevaux, *Voyages dans l'Amer. du Sud*, Paris, 1883; Stoddard, *Cruising among the Caribbees*, London, 1895.

before the arrival of Columbus. There they found already the Arawak tribes (see p. 557), whom they supplanted in the lesser Antilles, and against whom they directed their maritime expeditions as far as the east coast of the island of Haiti. These *Antillian Caribs* have been exterminated by the European colonists, and except in the islands in the vicinity of the Guianas, like Trinidad, there remain to-day but 192 individuals in the island of St. Vincent (census of 1881) and 200 individuals, of whom there are barely a dozen unhybridised, in the island of Dominica. Most of the Caribs of the island of St. Vincent were transported by the English in 1796 to Ruatan Island and Trujillo, on the north coast of Honduras. Their descendants, crossed with Negro blood, numbering about 6000, live in these places as well as in British Honduras, where they are known by the name of "Black Caribs."

The most southerly tribes of the Caribs are the *Bakairis* (Fig. 172), and the *Nahuquas* of the upper Xingu, as well as the *Palmellas* of the lower Guapore, a sub-tributary of the right of the Rio Madeira. The *Apiacas* of the lower Tocantins, who must not be confounded with the Tupi tribe of the same name (p. 569), form the link between this distant branch and the bulk of the Caribs peopling Guiana. The latter are known as *Apotos* and *Waywai* in Brazilian Guiana; as *Roucouyennes* and *Galibis* in French Guiana; as *Kalinas* in Dutch Guiana (Figs. 167 and 168). The Caribs of British Guiana belong chiefly to the *Macusi* tribe, those of Venezuela are represented by the *Makirifares* in the east, and farther away to the west, by the *Motilones*, who keep to the borders of Colombia (Ernst). The ancient Carib tribes of Venezuela called *Chaimas* and *Kumanas* are represented at the present day by the Indians of *Aguasai* (87 miles north of Bolivar), who speak Spanish, but who have preserved the Carib type (Ten Kate). It is the same with the *Aborigines of Oruba Island*, to the north-east of the Gulf of Venezuela (Pinart). Lastly, in the upper basin of the Yapura, outside of Brazilian territory, there are likewise known members of the Carib family, particularly the *Uitotos* or *Carijonas*, who live side by side with the Miranhas (p. 560) (Crevaux). To judge from some ethnographical analogies (similarity of tattooing, etc.), the *Araras* or *Yumas*, who wander on the right bank of the Amazon, in the neighbourhood of the mouths of the Xingu, Tapajos, Madeira and Purus, belong also to the Carib family, but as yet nothing is known about their language.[1]

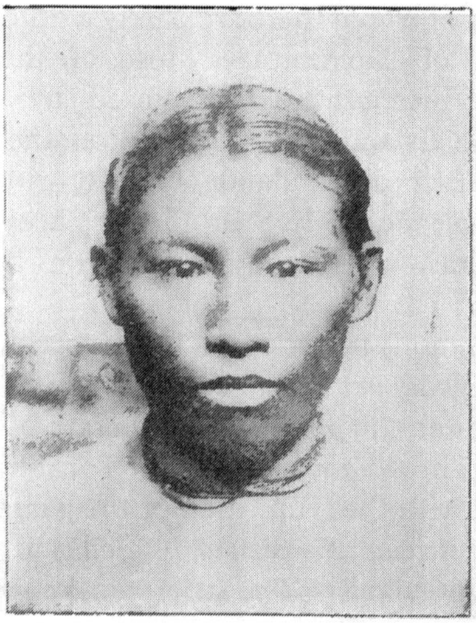

FIG. 167.—Kalina or Carib of Dutch Guiana. (*Coll. Mus. Nat. Hist., Paris.*)

The physical type of the Caribs of Guiana and Venezuela differs slightly from that of the Caribs of the upper Xingu. The former are of low stature (1m. 58 for men, 1m. 45 for women), and mesocephalic (mean ceph. ind. in the liv. sub, 81.3), while the Caribs of the upper Xingu are below the

[1] According to Siemiradzki, *loc. cit.*, p. 147, the *Guancavelica* and *Montubio* Indians of the coast of Ecuador, who are completely Hispanified, as well as the *Payaguas* (see p 572), bear a strong resemblance in physical type to the Caribs.

average height and sub-dolichocephalic (1m. 61 for men, 1m. 52 for women: mean ceph. ind. on the liv. sub., 79.6).[1] What is characteristic of certain Carib tribes of the south (Bakáiris, etc.) is the frequent occurrence of individuals with wavy or frizzy hair and convex nose, in the midst of the common type having straight hair, short and somewhat broad nose, etc. The ancient Caribs of the Antilles were short,

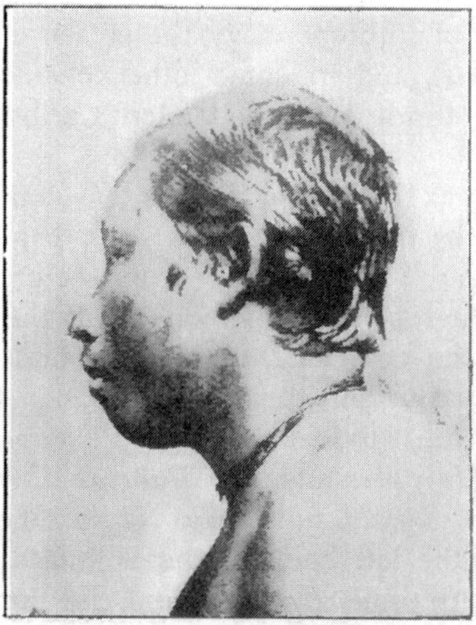

FIG. 168.—Same subject as Fig. 167, in profile. (*Coll. Mus. Nat. Hist., Paris.*)

somewhat light-skinned, and had the custom of deforming the head by flattening the frontal region of the skull.

From the ethnic point of view, the Caribs are distinguished by their acquaintance with the hammock; a plaited (not woven) texture; and a particular kind of cassava squeezer (p. 188);

[1] These figures are given from the measurements of Manouvrier and Deniker (*Bull. Soc. Anthrop.*, Paris, 1893), of Maurel (*Mem. Soc. Anthrop.*, Paris, 2nd ser., vol. ii., 1875-85), Ten Kate (*Rev. d'Anthr.*, Paris), and Prince Roland Bonaparte (*Les Habitants de Surinam*, Paris, 1884), for the Caribs of the north; from Ehrenreich, *loc. cit.* (*Anthrop. Stud.*), for the Caribs of the south.

by their fondness for painting the body; by the practice of the "couvade" (p. 240), etc. The blow-pipe and poisoned arrows are not their "national weapons," as has sometimes been said; the Caribs of the south are unacquainted with them, and, on the other hand, several non-Carib tribes of the Amazon basin make use of them. Their favourite weapon is or was the battle-axe of polished stone (basalt, diabase). The slight difference between the mode of life of the Caribs of the Antilles and that of the Caribs of the present day was due to the existence of anthropophagy, the presence of "communal houses" (*Carbets*), and to some other characteristics which denote their superiority over the modern Caribs from the social point of view.[1]

2. The Arawak linguistic family, as constituted by L. Adam, at first by the name of *Maypure*, has been called by Von den Steinen "*Nu-Arawak*," from the prenominal prefix "nu" for the first person, common to all the Arawak tribes, scattered from the coast of Dutch Guiana and British Guiana to the upper basins of the Amazon and Orinoco. The principal tribes are: the *Aturai* and the *Vapisiana* of British Guiana; the *Maypures* and the *Banivas* of Venezuela; the *Manaos* and the *Aruacos* of the Rio Negro; the *Yumanas* and the *Passehs* of the left bank of the Solimães; the *Marauas* more to the south; the *Paumary* and the numerous *Ipurina* tribes of the *Purus* basin; lastly the half-civilised *Moxos* or *Mohos* of the upper Mamoré, and the *Canopos* or *Antis* of the forests of the upper basin of the Ucayale (Peru), of average stature, brown-coloured skin, skilful hunters.[2] The tribes of the upper Xingu are the *Vaura* and the *Mehinacu*. Let us also note the *Parecis* of the region of the sources of the Tapajos, among whom we observe the influences of the Quechua civilisation (Pandean pipes) or the Peruvian (a particular head-dress of birds' feathers and porcupine quills,

[1] See, for example, the summary of the data of ancient authors in J. Ballet's *La Guadeloupe*, vol. i., 2nd pt., p. 220, Basse-Terre, 1894.

[2] O. Ordinaire, "Les Sauvages du Perou," *Rev. Ethnogr.*, 1887, p. 264.

cotton textiles, plaited hats, etc.). In upper Paraguay, as far as the 21st degree of S. latitude, are also found tribes speaking the Arawak tongue; the *Quinquinaos*, the *Layanas*, etc. (This is the Moho-Mbaure group of L. Quevedo) On the other hand, in the marshy island of Marajos, in the middle of the estuary of the Amazon, there dwelt a few decades ago the *Aruan* people, who spoke an Arawak dialect, while in the north of Venezeula, the peninsula of *Goajira* is occupied by the *Goajires* tribe, which also belongs to the same linguistic family. De Brette estimates its numerical force at 30,000 individuals (1890-95).[1]

The pre-Columbian aborigines of Porto Rico, Haiti, Jamaica, and Cuba were Arawaks, to judge from the toponymy of these islands. The authors of the eighteenth century speak of the *Ciboneys* in Cuba, Bahama, and the west of Haiti, and of the "Aravagues" in the east of this latter island and in Porto Rico. These aborigines, although in a state of constant warfare with the Caribs, resembled them in certain characteristic customs (cranial deformation, colouring of the body, etc.). They were exterminated by the Whites, being reduced to 4000 in Cuba as far back as 1554. In 1848 there remained of these tribes but a few hybrid families in the Sierra Maestra of Cuba and the village of Boya to the north of the town of San Domingo.[2]

Physically the Arawaks present several types, as might have been expected from the wide diffusion of this group. Those of the Guianas, as well as the Ipurinas and their congeners are

[1] This traveller also mentions a tribe very different from the *Goajires*, inhabiting the mountains of the north, now completely unknown. These Indians call themselves *Piecer* (?). They might possibly have some slight relation with the Arawaks inhabiting the upper valleys of Sierra Nevada. De Brette, *loc. cit.*; H. Candelier, *Rio Hacha et les . . . Goajires*, Paris, 1893.

[2] Particulars concerning the archæological and osteological remains of the aborigines of the Greater Antilles will be found in J. Duerden's "Aborig. Ind. Remains in Jamaica," *Journ. of the Instit. of Jamaica* (with "note on the craniology," by Haddon), Kingston, 1897, vol. ii., No. 4; and in Brinton's "The Archæology of Cuba," *Amer. Archæologist*, vol. ii., No. 10, Columbus, 1898.

a little lower in stature (1m. 55 and 1m. 59 according to Ten Kate and Ehrenreich) and a little more brachycephalic (ceph. ind. 83.4) than the Caribs of the same regions. Those of the upper Xingu, on the contrary, are a little taller (1m. 64) and more dolichocephalic (ceph. ind. 78.2) than their Carib-speaking neighbours. Their face is somewhat broader and

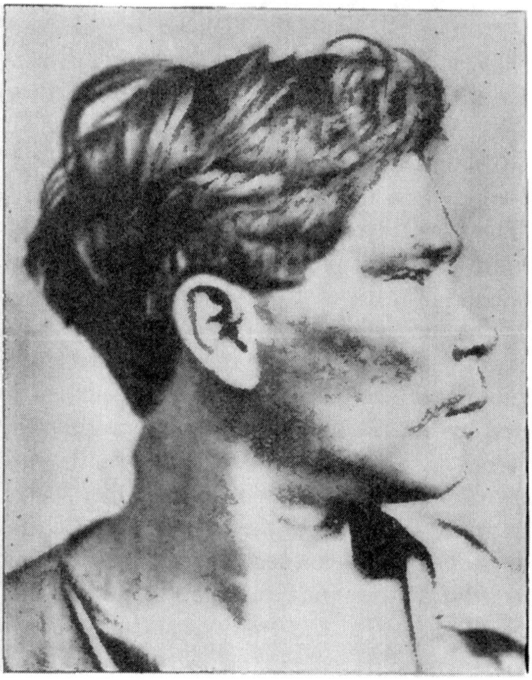

FIG. 169.—Miranha Indian of Rio Yapura. (*Phot. Crevaux, Coll. Soc. Anthr. Paris.*)

their eyes often oblique. The difference between the tribes of the north and those of the south is thus more pronounced among the Arawaks than among the Caribs. The Ciboneys, to judge from the skulls found in Cuba and Jamaica, were hyper-brachycephalic in consequence of deformations (Haddon). The occurrence of individuals with wavy or frizzy hair is also as frequent among the Arawaks as among the Caribs. From the ethnographical point of view there are some differences between the Arawaks of the north and the south. The use of the blowpipe is very general among the Arawak tribes of the upper Amazon and its tributaries, but it is unknown among others. With the exception of tribes influenced by the Quechua-

FIG. 170.—Same subject as Fig 169, seen full face. (*Phot. Crevaux, Coll. Soc. Anthr. Paris.*)

Peruvian or European civilisation, the Arawaks are unacquainted with the weaving of cotton, and are still in the stone, and especially the wood age. Their scanty garments are made with plaited fibres or with beaten bark; their ornaments are birds' feathers and the teeth of mammalia.

3. The tribes composing the *Pano* linguistic group, as

established by R. de la Grasserie,[1] chiefly inhabited the north-west of eastern Peru, but they are likewise met with in the west of Brazil (the *Karipunas* of the banks of the Madeira), and in the north of Bolivia (the *Pacaguara*), separated from their racial brothers by a series of tribes speaking the Arawak dialects. The principal Pano tribes in Peru are: the *Kassivo*, cannibals of the upper Ucayle who resemble the Fuegians; the *Conibos* of the same river, very low in stature;[2] the *Panos*, of whom there remain but a few families.[3] The *Araunos*, of the region comprised between the two principal branches of the Madeira (Madre de Dios and Beni) speak a Pano language, but with a considerable admixture of Quechua elements.

4. The tribes of the banks of the Iça and the Yapura have received from their neighbours the name of *Miranhas*, which, it appears, means "rovers." Ehrenreich employed this name to designate various tribes whose dialects presented a certain family likeness. Of these tribes, which are rarely visited by the Brazilian-Portuguese merchants, the following are the chief: the *Miranhas* properly so called (Figs. 169 and 170), between the Iça and the lower Yapura, mentioned long ago by Martius; the *Kœrunas* on the left bank of the Yapura; the *Tucanos* and the *Jupuas* to the east of the last-named, in the vicinity of the river Uaupes. The Miranhas have maintained their primitive condition. Of a very warlike disposition, they use as their principal weapon a particular kind of club, a sort of broadsword of hard wood. They employ the *drum language* (see p. 134). Though living on the banks of fish-yielding rivers, they do not fish, but confine themselves to hunting, like the ancient

[1] R. de la Grasserie, *Congr. Internat. Americanistes*, Berlin, 1888, p. 438.

[2] Barboza Rodriguez (*Revista da Exposiçao Anthrop. brazileira*, Rio de Janeiro, 1882) has measured four specimens, which have given him the mean height of 1m. 47.

[3] Ordinaire (*loc. cit.*) also describes together with these populations the wholly savage tribe of the *Lorenzos* living completely in the stone age on the banks of the Palcazu.

Quechuas, by means of nets stretched out between trees, into which they drive, with cries and gestures, the terrified animals (Crevaux).

In addition to the tribes forming the four families just described, several others, *whose languages have not yet been classified*, should be mentioned.

It is in the basin of the Orinoco that we meet with most of these tribes who have as yet been little studied; the *Otomacs* between the Apure and Meta rivers, geophagous and monogamous; the *Guamos* of the Rio Apure, reduced to a few families; the *Piaroas*, whose sub-brachycephalic heads are often deformed; the *Chiricoas* and the *Guahibos*, veritable "gypsies" of South America, who are encountered between the Meta, the Orinoco, and the Rio Branco; lastly, the *Guaraunos* or *Warraus* of the coast between the mouths of the Orinoco and the Corentin (Figs. 165 and 166), probably allied to the *Guayqueris* of the country around Cumana in Venezuela. The latter, however, are sub-dolichocephalic (ceph. ind. on five liv. subjects, 78.5 according to Ten Kate), while the Guaraunos are all mesocephalic (ceph. ind. 81.5 according to the same author). In the upper valleys of the numerous rivers which combine to form the Amazon, there are likewise dwelling tribes of undetermined linguistic affinities, whose names only are known. The most important, that of the *Zaparos* or *Jeberos* (about 15,000 individuals), is stationed between the Pastaza and Napo rivers, as well as along the Maranon from the mouth of the Zamora to that of the Morona. Farther north in the Cordilleras, in a state of complete independence, dwell the *Jebaros* or *Jevaros* (*Civaros*), fierce warriors, celebrated for their skill in preparing the heads of their vanquished enemies; these are hideous mummified and shrivelled objects with their long hair left on them.[1] To the east of the Jevaros are the *Maynas*, and on the Rio Javary, the *Yameos* or *Lamas*. Farther east again, near the Rio Napo, wander the hunting tribes, the *Tecunas* or *Triconnas*, and the *Orejones*, so named from their

[1] Hamy, *Rev. d'Anthr.*, 1873, p. 385; Colini, *Atti. Acc. Lincei.*, Rome, 1883.

habit of inserting wooden plugs into the lobe of the ear, a practice which, however, is also found among several other peoples.

III. *The Indians of East Brazil and the Central Region of South America* belong on the one side to the Ges or Ghes linguistic family (formerly called *Tapuyas*, *Botocudos*, etc.), and on the other form several tribes whose affinities are yet to be determined. Lastly, the *Tupi-Guarani* linguistic family (see p. 567) is also represented in this region. From the ethnological point of view these three groups of population have felt the influence of environment and habitat; we must therefore

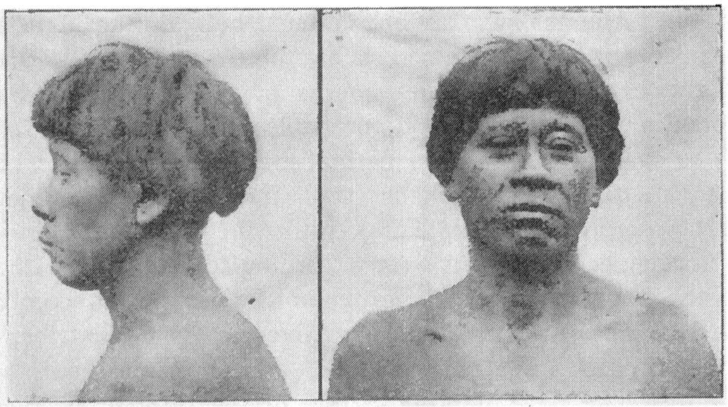

FIG. 171.—Bakairi, Carib tribe of upper Xingu. (*Phot. Ehrenreich.*)

consider separately the Indians of east Brazil and those of the central region, and lastly the *Tupi-Guarani* family.

1. *East Brazil* is composed of plateaux formed of friable rocks rising to the east of the Tocantins between the wooded *Sierras*. These plateaux do not afford so many resources as the Amazon region; thus it is that the tribes inhabiting them are more uncivilised, often more wretched than the Amazonians. The rarity of hard rocks suitable for the manufacture of tools causes many of them to be still in the wood age. The greater part belong to the *Ges* or *Ghes* linguistic family. This term, which comes from the syllable "ges" placed at the end of most of the tribal

names, was adopted by Martius to designate the Botocudos and some neighbouring tribes. But of recent years Von den Steinen and Ehrenreich have widened the meaning of this word.[1] Henceforth it denotes a collection of tribes which, besides linguistic character, exhibit many other common features in their habits and mode of life (great phalansterial houses with private hearths for each family, absence of hammocks, ignorance of navigation,[2] use of "botocs" or ear and lip plugs, arrows barbed on one side, etc.). Among the tribes of the Ges tongue we must distinguish those which dwell on the right bank of the Tocantins in east Brazil and those who have migrated to the west of this river into the centre of Southern America. The former have retained much better their individual character, but they have been partly decimated by the European colonists, and are not very numerous at the present day. Of the ancient *Kamakans*, of the *Patacho*, and so many other tribes, there remain but the memory or a few hybrid descendants, but three tribes have yet preserved themselves more or less intact in the midst of their forests: the *Botocudos*, the *Kayapos*, and the *Cainguas*. The *Botocudos* or *Aymoros*,[3] who call themselves *Burus*, dwell between the Rio Doce and the Rio Pardo (Minas Geraes Prov.). They are men of low stature (1 m. 59 according to Ehrenreich), dolichocephalic (mean ceph. ind. 74.1 on the skull, according to Rey, Peixoto, etc.; 78.2 on the liv. sub.), and their skulls recall very strongly

[1] Both these authors prefer the term "*Ges*" to that of *Tapuyas*, by which the aborigines in question are known to the Brazilians. In fact, the word "Tapuya," which in the Tupi tongue means "barbarian," is not only applied to the Ges, but also to a host of other backward tribes, as, for instance, the *Puris* (p. 565).

[2] Probably on account of the numerous cataracts on the rivers.

[3] Maxim Pr. von Wied Newied, *Reise nach Brasil.*, Frankfort-a-M., 1820, 2 vols.; Martius, *Beitr. zur Ethnogr. . . . Amerikas*, Erlangen-Leipzig, 1863-67; Lacerda and Peixolo, "Contrib. estudo. Anthrop. das racas Indig. do Brazil," *Archiv. de Mus. Nacion.*, Rio de Janeiro, vol. i., 1876, p. 47; Ph. Rey, *Étud. Anthrop. sur les Botocudos*, Paris, 1880 (thesis); Peixoto, "Novos estudos. craniol. sobra Botocudos," *Arch. Mus. Nac.*, Rio de Janeiro, vol. vi., 1884, p. 205; Ehrenreich, "Ueber die Botocudos," *Zeitschr. für Ethnol.*, 1887, pp. 1 and 49.

those of the prehistoric race of Lagoa Santa and the "Sambaquis," while the living subjects are closely allied to the Fuegians, as much by the size and form of the head as by the lines of the face, the prominent supraciliary ridges, the sunk nose narrow at the root, etc. I have given (pp. 160, 210, etc.) several characteristics of the ethnography of the Botocudos. The Kayapos,[1] who were believed to be an extinct race, and who, on the contrary, are one of the most important and warlike tribes of Brazil, are divided into three sections. The *Northern Kayapos* occupy the middle Tocantins, and overflow on one side into the sterile "Sertaos" of the province of Maranon, and on the other into central Brazil, on the left bank of the lower Araguaya; the *Western Kayapos*, who keep in the upper valley of the Xingu, have been described by Ehrenreich and Von den Steinen under the names of *Suya* and *Akua* (the *Chavantes-Cherentes* of the Brazilians). They differ from the Botocudos in physique, being brachycephalic, tall, and very light-skinned. As to ethnical characteristics, these are for the most part borrowed from their Carib and Arawak neighbours. The *Southern Kayapos* (near the river Parana, 20° S. lat.) are merely known by name. The *Kaingans* or *Kame*, wrongly called *Coroados* (see p. 545), inhabit the mountains of the Brazilian provinces of São Paulo, S. Catharina, and Rio Grande do Sul; they are tribes of uncivilised and nomadic hunters.

Besides the clans of the Ges family, we must also mention in the eastern region of Brazil the following tribes *whose languages have not been classified*, and whose affinities with the Ges are not very clear. The more important of these tribes are the *Puris* or *Pouris* and the *Kiriris*, wrongly called "Tapuyas" or "Coroados" (see p. 545). At the beginning of the century the *Puris* in fairly large numbers still inhabited—together with the *Koropos*—the mountains between Rio de Janeiro and Uro Preto. There is but a small remnant left at the present day, consisting of a few individuals living together in the hamlet of

[1] Castelnau, *Expedition parties Centr. Am. du Sud. Hist. des vog.*, Paris, 1852-57, 6 vols.; Martius, *loc. cit.*; Ehrenreich, *loc. cit.* (*Peterm. Mitt.*).

San Laurenço and in the "aldeamento" of Etueto, near to the boundary line of the Minas Geraes and Spiritu Santo provinces. Formerly the *Puris* comprised several tribes, hunters and fishers. They plaited their hammocks, had special ceremonies when their daughters arrived at the age of puberty, believed in a superior spirit, "Tupan," having the form of a white bird, etc.

The *Kiriris* or *Sabuyas* of the province of Pernambuco formed, two centuries ago, a powerful and semi-civilised nation; there are now only 600 left, living under wretched conditions in the lower valley of the São Francisco.

2. *The central region of South America* is formed of table-lands and wooded chains which cover the south-east of Bolivia and the Brazilian province of Matto Grosso (twice as big as France). Corresponding to the diversity of the elevations and climates there is a diversity of peoples inhabiting the country. We have already observed in this region tribes of Carib speech (Bakairi, etc.), of Arawak (Paressi, etc.), of Ges (western and southern Kayapos), and we may further notice tribes of Tupi speech (the Chiquitos, etc.). But outside of these classified peoples there are other ethnic groups occupying the table-lands of Matto Grosso, whose affinities are not yet well known, the more important of them being the Karayas, the Trumaï, and Bororos.[1]

The *Karayas* are divided into two sections which know nothing of each other. It was the northern Kayapos of Ges speech who thus separated the Karayas, driving them, on the one side, into the valley of the Xingu, and on the other, into the valley of the Araguaya. Like the Ges, the Karayas are unacquainted with the use of the hammock, but, unlike them, are good boatmen and draughtsmen. It has been observed that they have a special language for the women, which appears to be the ancient form of the present language of the men. They are fairly tall (1m. 69) and dolichocephalic (ceph. ind. 73), their nose is convex, and their hair sometimes curly.

[1] See the works of Castelnau, Von den Steinen, and Ehrenreich, already quoted.

The Trumai of the sources of the Xingu are, on the contrary, short (1m. 59) and mesocephalic (ceph. ind. 81.1), and they have convex noses and retreating foreheads.

The *Bororos* (Fig. 173), scattered from the upper Paraguay to the upper Parana, are hunters; they have great bows and arrows of bamboo or bone. Polygamy exists among them, and there are also cases of polyandry. They are tall (1m. 74) and mesocephalic (ceph. ind. 81.5).[1]

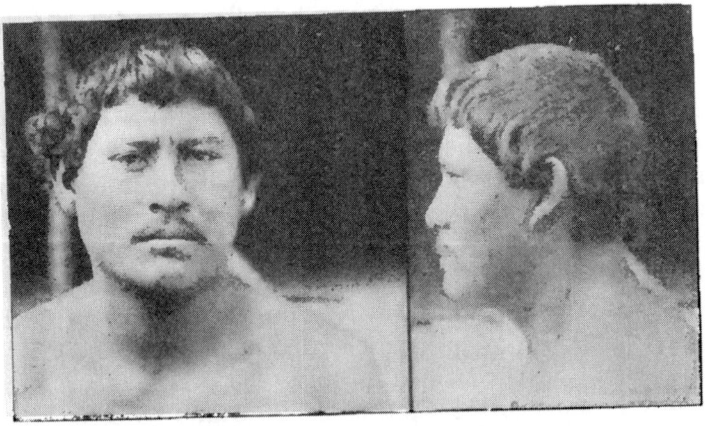

FIG. 172.—Aramichau Indian (Tupi or Carib tribe of French Guiana). (*Coll. Mus. Nat. Hist., Paris.*)

In spite of the diversity of language and race, several of the tribes of the central region, living side by side, have the same manners and customs, and the same kind of existence, as a result of mutual borrowings.[2] The best example of this is furnished by the Caribs, Arawaks, Ges, Tupis, and Trumai of the upper Xingu. They all go naked, the women sometimes wearing the triangular palm-leaf which plays the part of the fig-

[1] J. Koslowsky, "Algun. datos sobre los Bororos," *Bol. Inst. Geogr. Argent.*, vol. vi., 1895; Ehrenreich, *loc. cit.* (*Anthr. Unter.*).

[2] See on this point the suggestive monograph of H. Meyer, "Bows and Arrows in Centr. Brazil," *Smiths. Rep. for 1896*, p. 549, pl., Washington, 1898.

leaf; their huts are grouped around the "house of flutes," or the dwelling of the young men—a Carib importation—in which are preserved symbolic masks, which, like the pottery, are of Arawak invention. The tools are primitive, frequently of stone.[1] One might almost say that these tribes in ploughing imitate the movements of burrowing animals, for in this operation they make use of the long claws of the front paws of a great armadillo (*Dasipus gigas*), two of them attached together. The throwing-stick and blunt arrows are used by the Trumai, as by the Tupi tribes. They have no domestic animals, but keep some wild animals in captivity—parrots, lizards (to hunt insects), etc. The custom of the couvade and the existence of witch medicine-men are common to all these tribes.

3. *The Tupi-Guarani.*—In South America there exist a great number of tribes scattered from Guiana to Paraguay, from the Brazilian coast to the eastern slope of the Andes, who speak the different dialects of the Tupi linguistic family.[2] They may be divided into two groups: on one side, to the east, the tribes speaking the ancient Tupi language, which, in imitation of Quechua, was a "lingua geral," and on the other, the numerous tribes to the west, speaking different dialects which have only a vague resemblance to Tupi, according to L. Adam. At the time of the conquest the Tupi tribes, called *Tupi-namba Tanuyo*, who were cannibals, occupied not only the whole of the Brazilian coast from Para to Santos, but also the valley of the Amazon as far as Manaos. These primitive Tupis have mostly been exterminated by the Portuguese, but their language, which has become that of the converted Indians,

[1] The way in which the aborigines cut trees with their stone hatchets is remarkable; they make in the first place a great number of holes all around the trunk, then enlarge them till they touch, and so form a continuous incision. Similarly, in order to cut a thin piece of wood from a tree branch they make notches in the latter at equal distances, then they remove the portions of wood between the notches, making use of the same stone hatchet like a wedge. (Ehrenreich, "Mittheil . . . Xingu Exped.," *Zeitschrift für Ethnol.*, 1890, p. 61.)

[2] L. Adam, *Bibliothèque Linguist. Amer.*, vol. xviii., Paris, 1896.

has spread as far as the valley of the Rio Negro, a tributary of the Amazon, where there have never been any Tupi tribes.

The Eastern or Guarani Tupis, formerly so numerous in the Brazilian provinces of São Paulo and the Rio Grande do Sul, are reduced at the present time to a few families; on the other hand, they still form the bulk of the population

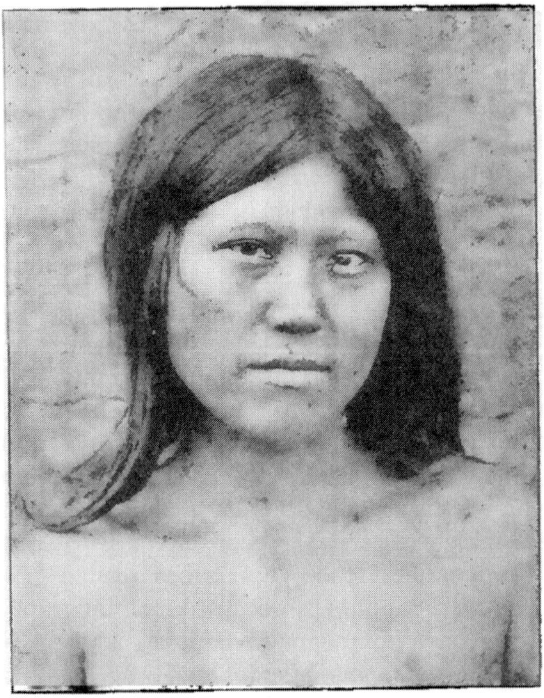

FIG. 173.—Bororo woman (unclassified tribe of Matto Grosso). (*Phot. Ehrenreich.*)

of Paraguay, and the territory of Missiones in the Argentine Republic. The Guarani of Paraguay, "tamed" in the commanderies by the Jesuits, have intermingled their blood with that of the Spaniards, and adopted their mode of life. However, there still remain in the depths of the forest some tribes who have kept intact their type and manners. Among the more interesting of these we must note the *Cainguas* or

Kaigguas[1] of south-east Paraguay and Missiones (Argentine), scattered in little groups, obeying one cacique or chief. They are short (1m. 60), mesocephalic (mean ceph. ind. of 12 men, 80.4), of bronzed complexion; their hair is lank or wavy, often reddish in the children; the nose is straight, the cheek-bones are prominent. From ten to twenty thousand Cainguas are estimated to be in Paraguay alone. Extremely fond of dancing and music, they like drawing as well, and possess as a rule a quick understanding. They are husbandmen, going almost naked, obtain fire by friction, are acquainted with weaving and pottery, have barbed and sometimes blunt-pointed arrows.[2] Other tribes, the *Jacunda*, the *Pacajas*, the *Tacunas*, keep to the lower valley of the Xingu. The *Mauhès*, stationed between this latter river and the Madeira, are at the extreme limit of the expansion towards the west of the pure Tupis. On turning again towards the south we come across the *Apiacas* of Tapajos (who must not be confounded with the similarly named tribe of the Carib family), the *Camayuras* of the upper Xingu, the *Chiquitos* and the *Chiriguanos* of Bolivia, now Hispanified.

The migrations of the Tupis from the south to the north,

[1] I. Ambrosetti, "Los Indios Caingua," *Bol. Inst. Geogr. Argentino*, vol. xv., Buenos Ayres, 1895.

[2] It is in the vicinity of the Cainguas, between the Parana and the central chain of Paraguay, south of the sources of the Acaray, that the five or six hundred *Guayakis* dwell, primitive hunters, still in the stone age, of whom Bove (*Bull. Soc. Geogr. Ital.*, 1884, p. 939) had caught a glimpse, and whom La Hitte and Ten Kate have quite recently described (*Ann. Mus. La Plata*, vol. ii., *Anthrop.*, 1897). Armed with their enormous bows and their polished stone hatchets, with their caps of jaguar skin, they have rather a grotesque appearance, and their low stature (the only adult subject measured was 1m. 52, and the skeleton of a woman, 1m. 42), as well as their legs wide apart, are not such as to improve their appearance. They are sub-brachycephalic, and nevertheless in type remind us of the Fuegians and the Botocudos. Their habitations are tree shelters, sometimes eighty feet long; their principal tool consists of a tooth of the agôuti fastened to the thigh-bone of a monkey. Their household vessels are plaited baskets rendered impermeable by the addition of a layer of wax, etc. The Cainguas are perhaps hybridised Guayakis.

conjectured in D'Orbigny's day, have now been absolutely demonstrated. Paraguay and the east of Bolivia were the starting-points of these migrations. The exodus of the Tupis took place at first towards the coast, then along the seaboard to the mouth of the Para, and thence further northward into French Guiana, where some Tupi tribes are still to be found, the *Emerillons* of the valley of the Saï, a left tributary of the Inini, the *Ovampis* of the upper Oyapoc, etc. The *Aramichaux* (Fig. 172), who were believed to be extinct, and who dwell between the Uaqui and the Arua,[1] seem to be also of the Tupi stock. Another stream of migration may be traced straight towards the north-east; it passes through the upper basin of the Xingu, to terminate eastward of the Tocantins (the tribe of the *Guajajaza*). An isolated Tupi group exists far to the north-west of the territory occupied by the bulk of this family. It consists of the *Omaguas* and the *Cocomas*, half-civilised tribes of the upper valley of the Maranon (Peru), to the eastward of the Jivaros. Individuals with wavy or frizzy[2] hair are not rare among these hybrid peoples.

The family of the *Western Tupis*, whose linguistic affinities are less clear, comprises, provisionally, the *Mundrucus*, or *Mundurukus*, of the middle Tapajoz, the *Yurunas* of the lower Xingu, the *Anetö* of the upper course of this river, etc.

Physically, the Tupis differ but little from the Caribs; those of the north, the Mauhés and the Mundurukus for example, studied by Barboza Rodriguez, are 1m. 58 and 1m. 60 in stature, whilst the *Kamayuras* and the *Anetö* of the upper Xingu are taller (1m. 62 on an average); the cephalic index of the latter is 79 (Ehrenreich). The Guarani should be, according to D'Orbigny, more than 1m. 66 in height.[3] But the anthropological study of the Tupis is still to be made.

[1] Coudreau, *loc. cit.*, pp. 123 and 131.

[2] Köppig, quoted by Brinton (*Am. R.*, p. 231). We must not confound these Cocomas with the tribe of the same name living between the upper Burus and the Jurua, and which appears to belong to the Pano family.

[3] Barboza Rodriguez, *loc. cit.*; Ehrenreich, *loc. cit.* (*Anthrop. Stud.*); D'Orbigny, *loc. cit.*, vol. ii., p. 324.

If we consider the accounts of the different dialects of the four great linguistic families which we have just described: Carib, Arawak, Ges, and Tupi, we are bound to admit the following hypothesis as to the migrations of the peoples belonging to these families. There have been two movements, centrifugal and centripetal. From the centre of the continent the *Tupis* have spread radially in all directions, and the *Caribs* towards the north-east, reaching as far as the Antilles. On the other hand, towards this centre converge the migrations of the *Arawaks* arriving from the north, perhaps from Columbia and the Antilles, and the migrations of the *Ges* coming from the east. Did the centrifugal movement of the Tupis and the Caribs and the centripetal movement of the Arawaks and the Ges take place simultaneously or in some order of succession? We have not sufficient information as yet to solve this problem, but the first supposition appears to be more probable, for we still see in our own day both movements going on simultaneously.

IV. *The Pampeans and the Fuegians.*—That portion of the American continent situated beyond the 30th degree of S. lat., between the Andes, the Atlantic, and the Strait of Magellan, is a vast plain which passes imperceptibly from the rich pasturage of Chaco to the monotonous Pampas, and from the latter to the bare plateaux of Patagonia.

This plain is occupied by various tribes who have nothing in common but the nomadic and pastoral mode of life determined by the environment since the introduction of the horse. Of the ancient peoples who occupied these regions as well as Uruguay at the time of the conquest, there remain but the *débris*, or descendants hybridised to the furthest extent possible.

The *Charruas* and their congeners the *Minuanes* and the *Yaros*, who fought so valiantly during the centuries of the Spanish domination, at first with their clubs and bows, then, becoming horsemen, with "bolas" and the lasso, were exterminated only in 1832. The four last representatives of the race were exhibited as curiosities in Paris in 1830. The *Charruas* had a very dark-coloured skin and were of somewhat high stature (1m. 68), like their neighbours on the other side of the Rio de la Plata, the *Chanases*, and especially the *Querandis*, whose bands were decimated at the end of the sixteenth century, after their last attack on Buenos Ayres.[1]

Their hybrid descendants, called *Talhuets*, were still fairly numerous in 1860 between Buenos Ayres and Rio Negro. The *Abipones* to the west of the Paraguay, so well described by Dobrizhoffer,[2] were destroyed at the end of the eighteenth century, partly through conflicts with their congeners the *Mocovis*, of whom there are no survivors.

All these tribes probably belonged to the *Guaycuru linguistic family*, established by L. Quevedo, whose most numerous representatives are now the *Tobas* of southern Choco to the north of Pilcomayo, and the *Matacos* who wander about between the latter river and the Vermejo.[3] We must further add to this group the *Caduves* or *Caduvei* of the Brazilian bank of the Paraguay, between 20° and 23° S. lat., a hundred or so of unhybridised individuals, all that remain of the ancient *Mbaya* people, and the *Payaguas*, an ancient warlike and plundering tribe thought to have disappeared, but of which there remain between two and three score representatives in the

[1] Martin de Moussy, *Descrip. Confed. Argent.*, vol. ii., p. 141, Paris, 1861, and *Industr. des Indiens La Plata*, Paris, 1866; Lafone Quevedo, "La Razza Americana de Brinton, etc.," *Bol. Inst. Geogr. Argent.*, vol. xiv., 1894, p. 524 (on the disappearance of the Charruas), and *Bol. Inst. Geogr. Argent.*, vol. xviii., 1897, pp. 124 and 127; *Arrivée en France de quatre sauvages Charrua*, Paris, 1830, and Flourens, *Ann. Sc. Nat.*, 2nd ser., Zool., vol. viii., p. 156; F. Outes, *Los Querandies*, Buenos Ayres, 1897, and *Ethnogr. Argent.*, *Seconda Contrib. al Ethnog. Querandi*, Buenos Ayres, 1899; Ambrozetti, "Alfarerias Minuanes," *Bol. I. G. Argent.*, vol. xiv., 1893, p. 212; L. Quevedo, *Bol. Inst. Geogr. Argent.*, vol. xviii., 1897, pp. 117 and 130.

[2] Dobrizhoffer, *An Account of the Abipones*, London, 1822, 2 vols.

[3] L. Quevedo, *loc. cit.*, *La Razza*, etc., p. 519, *Arte Toba*, etc; Massei and L. Quevedo, "Grupo Mataco-Mataguayo," *Bol. Inst. Geogr. Arg.*, 1895 and 1896; Pelleschi, "Los Indios Matacos," *Bol. Inst. Geogr. Arg.*, 1897, p. 173.

immediate neighbourhood of Assumption, peaceful basket-makers, potters, or fishers.[1]

The *Lenguas* of the ancient authors (a term used by them to describe very different tribes), who lived side by side with the Tobas, and of whom there remain but a few individuals, seem to form, with the *Guanes* of southern Chaco, the *Sanapanas*, the *Angaites*, and other tribes between the Salado and the Yababeri (tributaries on the left of the Paraguay), a separate linguistic family, which Boggiani proposes to call *Ennema*. Their neighbours, the *Samucos* or *Chamococos* of the Bolivian Chaco also constitute a special linguistic group, but their manners and customs approximate to those of the southern Arawaks.[2]

The *Guatos* of the marshes which extend from the Paraguay to the Sao Laurenço also speak a special language. They are excellent boatmen, who fish with their great bows and bone-pointed arrows. They are also renowned as hunters of jaguars.[3]

Most of the *Guaycurus* and their neighbours seem to be of high stature and to have a brownish-yellow skin; but almost nothing is known either as to the shape of their head or their other somatic characters.

To the south of the Choco, between the Rio Salado de Santa Fe and the Rio Chubut, in the Pampas and the north of the Patagonian table-land, the primitive population which spoke the Guaycuru language in the north and the Patagonian language in the south, has disappeared. It has been absorbed or

[1] Certain authorities (Ameghino, Brinton, etc.) place the Charruas, the Chanases, and the Querandis in the Tupi-Guaranian family, and make a separate group of the Matacos.

[2] Boggiani, *Viaggi d' un artista in Amer. Merid.*, I. Caduvei, II. Ciamococo, Rome, 1894-95 (preface and note by Colino); and "Ethnografia del Alto Paraguay," *Bol. Inst. Geog. Arg.*, vol. xviii., 1897, p. 613, ethn. chart. According to Brinton ("Ling. Cartogr. of Chaco," *Proc. Am. Phil. Soc.*, vol. 37, p. 178, Philad., 1898), the dialect of the *Samucos* should belong to the Arawak family.

[3] Koslowsky, "Tres semanas entre . . . Guatos," *Bol. Inst. Geog. Arg.*, vol. vi., p. 221, Buenos Ayres, 1895.

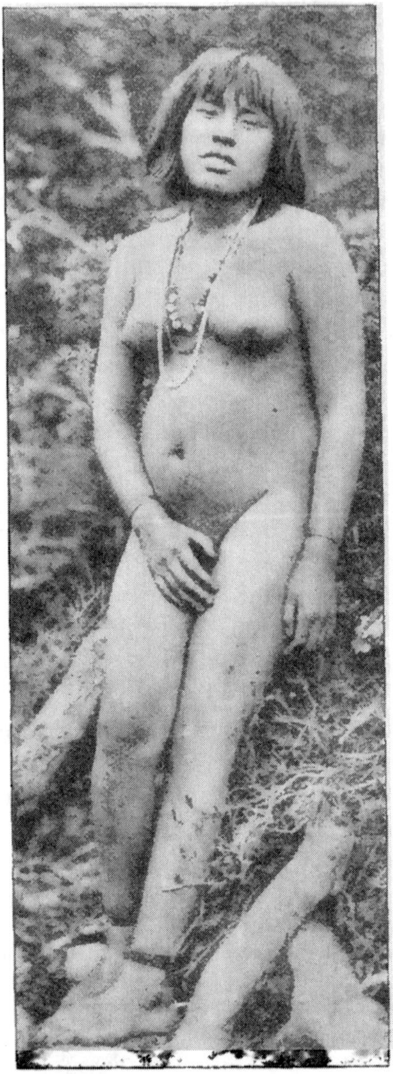

FIG. 174.—Kamanakar Kipa; young Yahgan Fuegian girl; height, 1m. 40; ceph. ind., 79.7. (*Phot. Cape Horn Scient. Mission.*)

modified by the invasions of the Araucans coming from the west, and by the encroachments of the Europeans coming from the east. The interminglings have given birth to new tribes like the *Puelches*, sprung from the Patagonians and the Araucans (p. 551), with a strain of Guaycuru blood, and the *Gauchos*, Guaycuru-European hybrids. The invasion of the Europeans increasing, the Puelches and the Araucans (*Pehuenches, Rankels, Huilitches*) have been pushed back farther and farther to the south. After the war of extermination waged by General Roca in 1881, the "Pampeans" migrated in a mass to the south of the Rio Negro, where they absorbed a portion of the Patagonians, driving away the remainder to the south of the Rio Santa Cruz.[1]

Cramped between this river and the Strait of Magellan, the *Patagonians* or *Tehuelches*, who call themselves by the name of *Tsoon-ké*, are now reduced to 2000 individuals.

[1] Siemiradzki, *loc. cit.*; De la Vaulx, *C. R. Soc. Geog. Paris*, 1898.

Those dwelling far from the coasts, as well as the *Onas* of Tierra del Fuego (the only Patagonian tribe that does not possess horses), have perhaps better preserved the characteristics of the Patagonian race. They are very tall (from 1m. 73 to 1m. 83 according to different authors), very brachycephalic (average ceph. ind. on the living sub., 85), have an elongated face, thinnish nose, eyes slightly oblique, projecting cheek-bones.[1]

The Fuegians (Figs. 48, 174, and 175) inhabit the southern

FIG. 175.—Tualanpintsis, Yahgan Fuegian (height 1m. 59, ceph. ind. 81.6); and his wife Ticoacli (height 1m. 40, ceph. ind. 80.1). (*Phot. Cape Horn Scient. Mission.*)

and western coasts of Tierra del Fuego, as well as the archipelagoes which lie to the west and south of this great island. They form a population by themselves, divided into two tribes,

[1] Ch. Musters, *At Home with the Patagonians*, London, 1871, and "The Races of Patagonia," *Journ. Anthrop. Inst.*, vol. i., 1875, p. 193; F. Moreno, *Viage à la Patagon. settentr.* . . . Buenos Ayres, 1876, and *Viage Pat. Austral.*, Buenos Ayres, 1879; R. Lista, *Viage al païs de Tehuelches*, Buenos Ayres, 1878, and *Explorat. de la Pampa, etc.*, Buenos Ayres, 1883. As regards the Onas, see R. Lista, "La Tierra del Fuego," *Bol. Inst. Geog. Arg.*, vol. ii., 1881, and *Viage al païs . . . Ona*, Buenos Ayres, Darapsky, "Patagonia," *Bol. Inst. Geog. Arg.*, vol. x., 1889, p. 368; J. Hultkrantz, "Nagra Bidrag, etc.," *Ymer*, pt. i., Stockholm, 1898, with figs. The three Ona skulls described by Hultkrantz are dolichocephalic (ceph. ind. 74.7).

the *Yahgans* to the south of the chain running from Sarmiento to Mount Darwin, and the *Alakalufs* to the north of this chain. I have mentioned several facts concerning the somatic characters (pp. 89, 108, etc.) and the ethnic ones (p. 146, note 2, pp. 181, 189, 214, etc.) of the Fuegians. Let me further add that the predominant type among them is that of the Palæo-American sub-race. Their language is not yet classified. The Alakalufs are at the present day reduced to 200 individuals. The Yahgans, who numbered about a thousand individuals in 1884, no longer exist to-day as an independent tribe. The last survivors of ravages caused by epidemics are gathered together in the two missionary stations called Ushuaia (Beagle Channel) and Tekenika; numbering about 90, they are dressed in the European fashion, speak English, and are employed in the various works at the mission.[1]

[1] For measurements see the Appendices. The bibliography of the Fuegians will be found in the work of Hyades and Deniker already quoted. To these must be added the following selection from important works omitted or recently published: L. Darapski, "Fuegians," *Bol. Inst. Geog. Arg.*, vol. x., 1889, p. 276; Bridges, "La Tierra del Fuego, etc.," *Bol. Inst. Geog. Arg.*, vol. xiv., 1893; and O. Nordenskjold, "Das Feuerland," *Geog. Zeitsch.*, vol. ii., p. 663, Leipzig, 1896.

APPENDIX I.

AVERAGE HEIGHT OF MEN, 288 SERIES

(see p. 29).

Number of Subjects.	ETHNIC GROUPS.	Height in Millimetres.
	LOW STATURES (UNDER 1M. 60, OR 63 INCHES).	
	Africans.	
38	Akka Negrilloes of the country of the Monbuttus	1,378
64	Kalahari Bushmen of Angra Pequena, etc.	1,529
	Asiatics.	
42	Aeta-Negritoes of the Philippines	1,465
115	Andamanese	1,485
28	Black Sakais or Menings of Gunong-Inas	1,490
36	Jakuns and Mantras of Johor	1,535
25	Ostiaks of the Yenisei (Turukhansk)	1,540
33	Pure Veddahs of Central Ceylon	1,554
99	Samoyeds (of Asia and Europe)	1,555
75	Kurumbas of Wynaad (India)	1,556
58	Irulas (Nilgiri plains)	1,560
33	Malé (Nayar and Arrayan) of Southern India	1,564
32	Japanese (workmen and coolies)	1,570
95	Annamese of Cochin-China	1,571
29	Paniyans of Malabar	1,574
26	Cherumas of Calicut	1,574
200	Mal-Paharias (Dravidians of Bengal)	1,577
100	Dravidian Bhuiyas of Chota Nagpur	1,577
155	Veddahs of Ceylon generally	1,578
300	Trao Mois of French Indo-China	1,579
210	Ostiaks	1,581
45	Solorese of Flores and Solor	1,582
359	Annamese in general	1,583
457	Mois in general (French Indo-China)	1,585
2,500	Japanese (1,260 of them soldiers)	1,585
125	Islanders of Bavean (between Java and Borneo)	1,587
100	Munda Kols of Chota Nagpur	1,589
1,100	Japanese of the upper and middle classes	1,590
76	Annamese of Tonkin	1,590
56	Laotians of Lower Laos	1,590

Number of Subjects.	ETHNIC GROUPS.	Height in Millimetres.
76	Sundanese of Java	1,591
90	Bhumij (Bils of Chota Nagpur)	1,592
100	Chakamas (Araknese-Bengali half-breeds)	1,596
29	Timurians (of the western part of the Island)	1,597
	Americans.	
28	Caribs of the three Guianas and Venezuela	1,572
26	Eskimo of Labrador	1,575
139	Yahgan and Alakaluf Fuegians	1,577
50	Mauhe and Mundurucus (probably Tupis)	1,588
	Europeans.	
259	Lapps of Scandinavia	1,529
25	Lapps of Russian Lapland	1,555
126	Vogules	1,591
	STATURES BELOW THE AVERAGE (1600-1649M., OR 63-65 INCHES).	
	Asiatics.	
105	Tenggerese of Eastern Java	1,604
58	Battas of Lake Toba (Sumatra)	1,605
27	Rotti Islanders (south-west of Timur)	1,605
30	Siamese	1,607
100	Kurmis (Kols of Chota Nagpur)	1,608
90	Maghs or Arakanese of Chittagong	1,608
45	Sumba Islanders (south of Flores)	1,609
31	Bugis of Celebes	1,609
27	Kulu-Lahulis of Nepal	1,610
45	Dards of Ghuraiz, Hunza and Ghilgit	1,611
58	Tipperahs of Chittagong (Lushai-Kumis)	1,611
83	Baltis	1,612
100	Santals	1,614
25	Southern Chinese of Long-Chow (Kwang-si)	1,615
80	Javanese	1,616
100	Kharvars (Dravidians of Chota Nagpur)	1,617
149	Malays of Sumatra and Malacca	1,617
500	Oraons of Chota Nagpur	1,621
15,582	Southern Chinese (principally Hakkas)	1,622
45	Singhalese of Colombo and Candy	1,625
80	Kling Tamils born at Sumatra	1,629
25	Kothas of the Nilgiris	1,629
296	Kalmuks or Mongol Torgots of Dzungaria	1,629
695	Hindus of the province of Behar	1,630
82	Brahmans of Southern India	1,631
26	Nicobarese	1,631
685	Dravidians N.W. prov. and Oudh (Chero, etc)	1,634
1,443	Dravido-Hindu castes, N.W. prov. and Oudh	1,634
1,616	Malayalim of Southern India	1,634

Number of Subjects.	ETHNIC GROUPS.	Height in Millimetres.
142	Hindus of various castes, N.W. prov.	1,635
40	Singhalese in general	1,635
387	Kirghiz-Kazaks of the three Hordes	1,638
25	Uru-Kurubas of Southern India	1,639
100	Karens of Lower Burma	1,640
92	Derbete-Kalmuks of Astrakhan	1,646
117	Cambodians (Khmers)	1,648
64	Tamils of Ceylon	1,649
37	Chukchis	1,649
231	Burmese	1,649
	Europeans.	
4,220	Jews of Russian Poland	1,612
3,313	Chuvashes (3,076 of them conscripts)	1,612
100	Permiaks	1,618
119	Votiaks	1,619
6,607	Sardinians (soldiers)	1,619
1,200	Magyars of West Hungaria (conscripts)	1,619
247	Jews of Kuba and Kutais (Caucasus)	1,621
167,677	Poles of Russian Poland (conscripts)	1,624
6,517	Volga Tatars (principally conscripts)	1,627
1,210	Cheremisses (1,141 of them conscripts)	1,627
31,707	Conscripts of German Switzerland	1,629
500	Corsicans	1,633
132	Austrian Jews of Hungary	1,634
25	Lesgian Údes of Elizabetopol	1,634
32,024	Sicilians (soldiers)	1,635
2,532	Conscripts of Italian Switzerland	1,635
382	Rumanians of Hungary	1,635
61	Jews (Spaniol) of Bosnia	1,636
961	Bielorousses or White Russians	1,636
800	Portuguese	1,637
292	Hungarians (conscripts)	1,637
4,894	Spanish Basques	1,638
1,955	Bulgarians of Western Bulgaria	1,638
2,252	Mordvinians	1,639
890	Lithuanians of Russian Poland	1,639
1,355	Ruthenes of the Plains (Galicia)	1,640
1,771,948	Russians of European Russia (conscripts)	1,642
437	Karelians of Russia (conscripts)	1,642
100	Esthonians	1,642
2,000	Jews of the Ukraine	1,642
4,701	Lithuanians of Lithuania (conscripts)	1,643
1,831	Gruzin Georgians (mostly conscripts)	1,644
344,371	Italians in general (soldiers)	1,645
7,396	Spaniards	1,645
77,579	Magyars of Hungary (soldiers in 1868)	1,646

Number of Subjects.	ETHNIC GROUPS.	Height in Millimetres.
447,172	French in general (conscripts)	1,646
9,456	Conscripts of French Switzerland	1,646
1,483	Mingrelian Georgians	1,646
33,541	Piedmontese (soldiers)	1,649
	Americans.	
90	Salishans (Harrison Lake, British Columbia)	1,613
30	Salishans of the Frazer River delta (British Col.)	1,618
28	Guaranis (Kamayuras and Anetos)	1,620
614	Eskimo of Greenland	1,621
73	Zuñis of New Mexico	1,623
54	Moquis	1,629
85	Eskimo of Alaska	1,630
55	Kwakiutl Indians (British Columbia)	1,639
	Africans.	
50	Mzabites (Berbers of M'Zab, Algeria)	1,620
36	Batekes of the Congo	1,641
	Oceanians.	
31	Aborigines of the island of New Britain	1,602
67	Papuans of German New Guinea	1,608
156	Natives of the Solomon Islands	1,616
38	Melanesians of the archipelago of New Britain	1,620
40	Australians of Southern New South Wales	1,630
142	Papuans of New Guinea in general	1,640
	STATURES ABOVE THE AVERAGE (1650-1699M., OR 65-67 INCHES).	
	Asiatics.	
32	Kols (of the N.W. provinces and Oudh)	1,650
108	Hajemi Persians (principally of Teheran)	1,651
792	Armenians of the province of Tiflis (conscripts)	1,652
40	Badagas of the Nilgiri plains	1,658
362	Osmanli Turks (288 of them in Asia Minor)	1,660
60	Baluchis of Baluchistan	1,662
60	Khatris (Punjab caste)	1,662
72	Chuhras (do.)	1,666
979	Brahmans and other higher castes of the N.W. provinces and Oudh	1,666
56	Tamils of Southern India	1,667
54	Sartes of Russian Turkestan	1,668
33	Aissores of neighbourhood of Lake Urmia (Cauc.	1,668
74	Kara-Kirghiz of Russian Turkestan	1,668
53	Turkomans of the Transcaspian	1,670
54	Chinese of the north (Che-Fu and Kuldja provinces)	1,674
38	Sibos (Manchu Tunguses)	1,675
120	Uzbegs of Russian Turkestan	1,683

Number of Subjects.	ETHNIC GROUPS.	Height in Millimetres.
444	Punjabi in general	1,684
140	Kurds of the Caucasus	1,686
80	Pathans (Punjab caste)	1,687
155	Tajiks and Galchas of Russian Turkestan	1,692
192	Armenians of Transcaucasia	1,694
239	Aderbaijanis of Persia and Transcaucasia	1,698
	Europeans.	
59,761	Rumanians of the kingdom of Rumania (soldiers)	1,650
226	Abkhasians of the Caucasus	1,650
71	Greeks of the kingdom of Greece	1,651
140	Meshtcheriaks of Perm and Orenburg	1,652
2,012	Saxons of the Halle-Mansfeld district (Prussia)	1,653
61	Gypsies of Hungary (soldiers)	1,654
1,838	Gruzin Georgians	1,654
100	Jews of Bukovina	1,654
84,141	Russians of Asiatic Russia	1,654
35,416	Belgians in general	1,655
493	Dutch of the province of Zeeland (conscripts)	1,655
1,481	Mingrelians	1,656
2,865	Imer Georgians	1,656
1,003	Lithuanian Jmudins (conscripts)	1,656
31	Gypsies of Crimea	1,657
142	Svane Georgian highlanders	1,658
370	Bashkirs of Orenburg and Ufa	1,658
1,305	French Basques	1,658
231	Crimeans of the south coast	1,664
187	Ruthenian highlanders (Galicia)	1,666
20,509	Venetians	1,666
6,909	Thuringians of the Saxon prov., Prussia (conscripts)	1,667
60	Slovens	1,668
200	Ukrainians or Little Russians of Kief	1,669
200	Ruthenes of the Bukovine (soldiers)	1,670
200	Rumanians of the Bukovine (soldiers)	1,673
28	Lesgians (Avars and Kazi Kumyks)	1,676
22,979	Karelians of Finland	1,680
458	Ossets	1,680
1,220	Swedes of the province of Kalmar (conscripts)	1,681
80	Tavastians or Western Finns	1,682
44	Kabards (Cherkesses) of the Caucasus	1,684
9,345	Dutch (conscripts)	1,685
3,000	Danes	1,685
4,964	Sleswickians (soldiers)	1,692
89,021	German emigrants to the United States	1,693
741	Inhabitants of Wales	1,695
41	Gypsies of Bosnia	1,695
176	Tatar (Kabard) highlanders (Caucasus)	1,697

Number of Subjects.	ETHNIC GROUPS.	Height in Millimetres.
	Africans.	
32	Arabs of Algeria	1,656
28	Mushikongos of the Congo	1,658
1,103	Berbers of Tunis	1,663
29	Abyssinians	1,669
35	Danakils of Tajura	1,670
52	Berbers of Biskra (Chauia tribe?)	1,673
244	Kabyles of Great Kabylia	1,677
180	Berbers of Algeria	1,680
27	Bashilange of the Kasai	1,680
2,020	Negroes of the United States	1,681
863	Mulattos of the United States	1,682
28	Bechuanas	1,684
25,828	Negroes and Mulattos of the United States (conscripts)	1,693
	Oceanians.	
50	Aborigines of Southern Australia	1,657
65	Australians in general	1,667
233	Australians of Central Australia	1,670
52	New Caledonians (Melanesians)	1,673
72	Papuans of British New Guinea	1,674
58	Australians of Victoria	1,677
50	Maoris of New Zealand	1,680
	Americans.	
61	Tinné of the S.W. (interior of British Columbia)	1,658
32	Hupa Indians (Tinné of Oregon)	1,661
121	Ute Indians	1,661
26	Bilkula Indians	1,661
37	Tsimshian Indians (Brit. Columbia)	1,666
165	Shushwap Indians (Salish)	1,670
104	Cherokis of the East	1,677
74	Comanches	1,678
30	Klamath Indians	1,679
59	Chicasaw Indians	1,679
68	Piute Indians	1,683
57	Cree Indians	1,685
147	Apaches and Navajos	1,686
37	Flathead Indians (Salishan Têtes plates)	1,687
32	Papagos of California	1,695
71	Sahaptin Indians (Nez percés)	1,697
28	Ottawa Indians	1,699

Number of Subjects.	ETHNIC GROUPS.	Height in Millimetres.
	HIGH STATURES (1M. 70, OR 67 INCHES AND UPWARDS).	
	Americans.	
111	Indians of the south of the State of California (Yuma?)	1,700
260	Choctaws	1,700
100	Pimas	1,703
21,645	Canadian soldiers (chiefly descendants of French)	1,703
76	Cherokis of the west	1,712
198	Ojibwas of the south	1,712
41	Pawnees	1,713
92	Delawares and Blackfeet	1,715
79	Micmacs and Abenakis	1,717
315,620	Citizens of the United States born in the country	1,719
29	Maricopas of California	1,722
1,413	Ojibwas of the east	1,723
612	Siouans	1,726
94	Iroquoians or Iroquois	1,727
517	Indians of the United States (chiefly Iroquois)	1,730
91	Omahas and Winnebagos	1,732
213	Crow Indians	1,732
53	Creek Indians	1,735
35	Mohaves of California	1,740
50	Cheyennes	1,745
	Africans.	
31	Mandingans in general	1,700
25	Bejas (called Nubians)	1,708
72	Kafirs (Ama-Xosa and Ama-Zulu)	1,715
56	Western Zandehs (Mandjas, Akungs, Awakas, etc.)	1,717
56	Somalis (Eyssa, Habis, Awals, etc.)	1,723
30	Toucouleurs or Torodos	1,725
62	Wolofs, Serers and Leybus	1,730
25	For Negroes of Darfur	1,730
35	Fulahs or Fulbés of French Sudan	1,741
	Asiatics.	
33	Awan (Ghazikhan tribe, Punjab)	1,706
97	Sikhs of the Punjab	1,709
29	Gypsies of Russian Turkestan (Lulis, etc.)	1,719
	Oceanians.	
25	Polynesians of the Samoan Islands	1,726
414	Polynesians in general	1,730
32	Polynesians of Tahiti, Pomotu, Tubuai	1,733
202	Polynesians of the Marquesas Islands	1,743

Number of Subjects.	ETHNIC GROUPS.	Height in Millimetres.
	Europeans.	
605	Dutch of the province of Overijssel (conscripts) -	1,701
61	Cossacks of Kuban (Little Russians) - - - -	1,701
68	Letts of Esthonia - - - - - - - -	1,704
232,367	Swedes in general (soldiers) - - - - -	1,705
1,107	Serbs of the Kingdom of Servia (conscripts) -	1,709
763	Bosnian-Herzogovinians (soldiers) - - -	1,710
6,194	English in general - - - - - - -	1,712
1,489	Finns of Finland in general (682 of them soldiers)	1,713
325	Dalmatians - - - - - - - -	1,715
9,979	Swedes of the province of Helsinghe (soldiers) -	1,716
8,585	Inhabitants of the United Kingdom of Great Britain and Ireland - - - - - -	1,719
106,446	Norwegians (soldiers) - - - - - - - -	1,720
346	Irish - - - - - - - - - - -	1,725
100	Livonians - - - - - - - - - -	1,736
1,304	Scotch in general - - - - - - -	1,746
134	Scotch of the north (Ayrshire, etc.) - - -	1,782
75	Scotch agriculturists of Galloway - - - -	1,792

APPENDIX II.

CEPHALIC INDEX, 336 SERIES (see p. 75).

NUMBER.		ETHNIC GROUPS.	CEPH. IND.	
Living Subjects.	Skulls.		Living Subjects.	Skulls.
		DOLICHOCEPHALS, BELOW 77 (75).		
		Oceanians.		
—	73 (S.)	Islanders of Viti-Levu (Fiji) -	—	67.2
204	—	Natives of the Caroline Archipelago	69.4	—
—	52	Natives of the smaller Fiji Islands	—	69.0
—	148	Papuans of Misore Island - -	—	70.2
—	24 (S.)	Islanders of Mallicollo (New Hebrides) - - - -	—	70.4
—	71	New Caledonians - - -	—	70 7
10	29 (S.)	Islanders of Lifu (Loyalty Islands)	72.4	70.8
—	118 (S.)	Natives of the Duke of York Islands (New Britain) - - - -	—	71.7
—	16 (S.)	Natives of Engineer Island (Louisiade Archipelago) - - -	—	71.9
27	82 (S.)	Various Australians - - -	74.2	71.2
—	10	Australians of Queensland - -	—	72.2
—	20	Natives of Ruck Island (Carolines)	—	72.8
—	51	Maoris of New Zealand - -	—	73.6
20	—	Natives of the Solomon Islands -	76.3	—
—	24	Papuans of the Fly River (New Guinea) - - - - -	—	74.2
—	25	Tasmanians - - - -	—	74.9
23	30 (S.)	Natives of New Britain Archipelago	76.7	72.4
		Asiatics.		
95	—	Badagahs of the Nilgiris - -	71.8	—
40	—	Cashmerians - - - -	72.2	—
32	—	Kols of the N.W. Prov. and Oudh	72.4	—
979	—	Brahmans, Rajputs, and other high castes of the N.W. Prov. - -	72.6	—
685	—	Kolarians, N.W. Prov. - -	72.7	—
80	—	Sikhs of the Punjab - - -	72.7	—

NUMBER.		ETHNIC GROUPS.	CEPH. IND.	
Living Subjects.	Skulls.		Living Subjects.	Skulls.
1,616	—	Hindus of various castes (N.W. Prov. and Oudh)	72.8	—
103	—	Baltis	73.6	—
1,443	—	Dravido-Hindus (N.W. Pr. & Oudh)	73.8	—
45	—	Todas	74.1	—
25	—	Kotas of the Nilgiris	74.1	—
444	—	Punjabi (Hindus, Baluchis, etc.)	74.2	—
54	—	Malayalim of the Shevaroy Hills	74.3	—
27	—	Kulu-Lahuli	74.6	—
100	—	Malé or Assal (Dravid. of Bengal)	74.8	—
90	—	Bhumij of Chota Nagpur	75.0	—
55	43	Veddahs of Ceylon	75.1	71.5
58	—	Irulas of the E. slope of the Nilg.	75.1	—
15	—	Gypsies of Lycia	75.2	—
100	—	Kharvars (Dravidians of Chota Nagpur)	75.6	—
45	—	Dardi (India)	75.6	—
100	—	Kurmi of Chota Nagpur	75.7	—
695	—	Hindus of the Prov. of Behar	75.7	—
100	—	Mal-Paharia (Drav. of Beng.)	75.8	—
25	—	Urur-Kurubas of Mysore	75.8	—
100	—	Bhuiyas (Drav. of Beng.)	76.0	—
20	—	Dums of Chota Nagpur	76.0	—
100	—	Santals of Chota Nagpur	76.1	—
—	12	Alfurus of Ceram	—	74.3
—	37	Ainus of Saghalien	—	74.8
64	—	Tamils of Ceylon	76.3	—
80	—	Pathans (Afghans) of Punjab	76.5	—
33	—	Kanarese of Mysore	76.8	—
1,570	—	Bengalese	76.9	—
27	—	Islanders of Rotti (to the S. of Timur)	76.9	—
		Africans.		
14	—	Mushikongo and Bakongo	72.5	—
36	—	Bateke (Congo)	73.6	—
30	—	Toucouleurs	73.8	—
30	30	Jagga (Bantu of Kilimandjaro)	—	71.9
15	—	Hottentot-Orlans	74.3	—
37	—	Fulahs or Fulbés	74.3	—
35	—	Danakils of Tajura	74.5	—
14	—	Duala or Dwala of the Cameroons	75.1	—
27	—	Negro-Krus	75.1	—
62	13	Wolofs, Serer, and Leybus	75.2	69.8
29	10	Various Mandingans	75.5	78.8
13	—	Kakongo	75.6	—
47	—	Arabs of Algeria	76.3	—

NUMBER.		ETHNIC GROUPS.	CEPH. IND.	
Living Subjects.	Skulls.		Living Subjects.	Skulls.
—	56	Kafirs (Ama-Zulus and others)	—	72.5
184	—	Betsimisaraka (Madagascar)	76.3	—
13	—	Kabyles of Palestro	76.4	—
27	—	Bashilanges of the Kasai	76.8	—
13	—	Ashantis	76.9	—
		Americans.		
12	—	Karayas (Amazon Basin)	73.0	—
—	76	Hurons	—	74.7
614	31	Eskimo of Greenland	76.8	72.4
—	152	do. E. America	—	71.3
—	16	do. W. America	—	74.8
10	33 (S.)	Botocudos	76.8	73.9
		Europeans.		
—	417	Portuguese	—	74.3
500	—	Corsicans	76.6	—
502	—	Spaniards of Valencia	76.8	—
		SUB-DOLICHOCEPH. 77-79.6 (75-77.6).		
		Asiatics.		
12	—	Ladaki	77.0	—
17	—	Inhabitants of Nagar, Hunaza, and Yasin	77.0	—
20	—	Chinese of the North	77.0	—
75	—	Kurumbas (to the E. of the Nilgiris)	77.3	—
136	—	Tamils of the South of India and Ceylon	77.4	—
360	—	Mois of French Indo-China	77.5	—
17	—	Sikas (Central Floris)	77.7	—
11	92	Ainus of Yezo	77.8	76.5
23	—	Turkomans of the Transcaspian	77.9	—
18	—	Lio (Central Floris)	78.1	—
208	—	Aderbaijanis	78.1	—
168	—	Persians in general	78.4	—
11	—	Disfulis of Susa	78.4	—
332	—	Kurds	78.5	—
78	64	Japanese of all classes	78.5	80.2
68	—	White and Yellow Sakais (Malay P.)	78.7	—
30	—	Atoni of the west of Timur	78.8	—
142	—	Singhalese	78.8	—
20	—	Yuruks of Lycia	78.9	—
28	—	Black Sakais of Gunong Inas (Malay Peninsula)	79.5	—
29	—	Tates of the Transcaucasus	79.0	—

NUMBER.		ETHNIC GROUPS.	CEPH. IND.	
Living Subjects.	Skulls.		Living Subjects.	Skulls.
106	—	Moormen of Ceylon	79.1	—
45	44	Sumbawa Islanders	79.1	—
—	37	Nias Islanders	—	77.6
106	37	Ostiaks	79.3	74.3
16	—	Tatar-Tchern (Altaians)	79.5	—
25	—	South Chinese of Lang-Choo	79.5	—
		Africans.		
50	—	M'Zabits of Algeria	77.3	—
56	—	Western Zandeh (Mandja, etc.)	77.9	—
—	14	Bushmen	—	75.9
—	139	Negroes of Fernand-Vaz	—	75.9
—	13	Hausas	—	77.3
		Americans.		
—	62	Half-caste Algonquians	—	76.2
—	315	Natives of Santa Barbara Archip.	—	76.9
14	—	Arawaks of the Rio Xingu (Mehinaku, etc.)	78.2	—
31	—	Indians of Arizona	78.6	—
419	—	Pimas of New Mexico	78.4	—
123	—	Ute Indians	79.5	—
28	—	Tupis of the Xingu (Kamayuras and Anetos)	79.1	—
114	37	Eskimo of Alaska	79.2	77.0
—	103	Indians of the Californian coast	—	77.3
135	—	Iroquoians	79.3	—
26	27	Yahgan Fuegians	79.5	76.8
570	42	Indians: Algonquians, Abenaki, Cree, etc.	79.8	77.4
261	136	Siouans	79.8	78.9
		Oceanians.		
163	—	Natives of Solomon Islands	77.6	—
—	12 (S.)	Morioris of the Chatham Islands	—	76.2
—	30	Natives of the Marquesas Islands	—	76.4
22 (S.)	22 (S.)	Natives of the Gilbert Islands (Kingsmill)	78.4	73.8
59	—	Various Polynesians	79.7	—
		Europeans.		
122	—	Catalans of the Balearic Islands	77.7	—
6,579	—	Sardinians	77.5	—
1,410	—	Castillians	78.5	—
574	—	Catalans of Spain	78.1	—
8,368	—	Spaniards in general	78.2	—

NUMBER.		ETHNIC GROUPS.	CEPH. IND.	
Living Subjects.	Skulls.		Living Subjects.	Skulls.
—	48	Swedes of the central provinces -	78.2	76.0
50	—	French Catalans of Roussillon -	78.6	—
—	59	Chuvashes - - - - - -	—	77.2
32,526	—	Sicilians - - - - - -	79.0	—
325	—	Spanish Basques - - - -	79.3	—
129	18	Cheremisses - - - - -	79.2	76.8
362	—	Belgian Flemings - - -	79.5	—
		MESOCEPHALS, 79.7-81.9 (77.7-79.9).		
		Americans.		
10	—	Bakairis of Brazil - - -	79.0	—
84	10	Pawnee Indians - - - -	80.0	78.8
16	—	Yakis - - - - - - -	79.8	—
257	38	Crow and Cheyenne Indians -	80.5	79.8
28	—	Southern Caribs of the Rio Xingu	79.8	—
20	—	Bororos of the Amazon basin -	81.2	—
15	—	Nahuquas of Brazil - - -	80.6	—
30	—	Caribs of the four Guianas - -	80.9	—
225	99 (S.)	Omahas - - - - - -	81.8	80.5
		Asiatics.		
130	—	Tenggerese of the east of Java -	79.7	—
60	—	Baluchis of Baluchistan - -	80.0	—
—	125	Chinese in general - - -	—	78.3
36	—	Nicobarese - - - - - -	80.4	—
13	—	Dungans of Kuldja - - -	80.5	—
58	—	Tipperahs of Chittagong - -	80.5	—
20	—	Achinese - - - - - -	80.5	—
58	—	Battas of Lake Toba - - -	80.6	—
22	—	Jakuns of Johor - - - -	80.9	—
61	84 (S.)	Southern Chinese (princ. of Canton) - - - - -	81.2	78.2
19	24	Andamanese - - - - -	81.4	81.6
90	—	Magh or Arakanese of Chittagong	81.8	—
11	—	Teleuts or Telenghits (Siberia) -	81.8	—
—	14	Eskimo of Asia - - - -	—	79.0
		Europeans.		
35	—	Gypsies of Hungary - - -	79.9	—
37	—	Tatars of the Crimea - - -	80.0	—
55	—	Jews of Bosnia - - - -	80.1	—
171	—	French of the dep. du Nord - -	80.4	—
60	—	Letts of the Baltic provinces -	80.5	—
1,000	—	Limousins and Perigourdins -	80.7	—
463	—	Spaniards of the Cantabrian region	80.3	—
30 (S.)	47 (S.)	Dutch of the prov. of Gröningen -	81.0	77.6

NUMBER.		ETHNIC GROUPS.	CEPH. IND.	
Living Subjects.	Skulls.		Living Subjects.	Skulls.
1,000	—	Normans (Calvados, Seine-Inf., etc.)	81.3	—
—	87	Dutch of the province of Friesland	—	78.1
—	206	Inhabitants of the prov. of Prussia	—	79.2
—	96 (S.)	Cherkess (Abkhazians, Chapsug, etc.)	—	79.4
—	159	Franconians of N.W. of Bavaria -	—	79.8
59,165	—	Italians of the South (Abruzzi, Puglie, etc.) - - - -	81.2	—
54	—	Magyar-Szeklers - - - -	81.4	—
67	—	Georgian-Mingrelians, and Imers -	81.4	—
91	—	Provençals - - - - -	81.7	—
59	—	Meshtcheriaks - - - -	81.8	—
		Oceanians.		
14	—	Islanders of Fakaofu (Takelau Arch.) - - - - -	80.6	—
12	—	Natives of New Ireland - -	81.0	—
		SUB-BRACHYCEPHALS, 82-85.2 (80-83.2).		
		Asiatics and Eurasians.		
22	—	Parsees of Bombay - - -	82.0	—
20	—	Kouïs of Cambodia - - -	82.0	—
97 (S.)	51 (S.)	Kalmuks of the Volga - - -	82.1	81.4
11	14	Coreans - - - - - -	82.6	81.6
25	—	Man-Tien of Kaobang (Tong King)	82.5	—
182	—	Annamese in general - - -	82.8	—
49	—	Malays of Sumatra and Penang -	82.8	—
231	—	Burmese - - - - - -	83.1	—
139	—	Yakuts - - - - - -	83.1	—
14	—	Tsiams of French Indo-China -	83.2	—
—	18 (S.)	Tunguse Reindeer-holders - -	—	81.2
21	—	Solorese (E. of Flores and Solor) -	83.4	—
56	—	Laotians of Lower Laos - -	83.6	—
30	—	Cambodians - - - - -	83.6	—
76	—	Annamese of Tong King - -	83.8	—
152 (S.)	15 (S.)	Samoyeds - - - - - -	83.8	82.4
13	13	Takhtadji of Lycia - - -	84.2	—
26	—	Ansariehs of Antioch - - -	84.2	—
100	—	Chakama (Arakan-Bengali mongrels)	84.3	—
197	14	Kalmuks of Kuldja and Tarbagat.	84.5	83.3
12	30 (S.)	Bugis of Mangkassar - - -	84.6	80.6
—	12	Islanders of Madura (N. of Java) -	—	82.6
66	88 (S.)	Javanese - - - - - -	84.6	83.0
18	—	Negrito Aetas (Philippines) - -	84.7	—

NUMBER.		ETHNIC GROUPS.	CEPH. IND.	
Living Subjects.	Skulls.		Living Subjects.	Skulls.
107	27	Uzbegs of Russian Turkestan	84.8	—
74	—	Tajiks	84.8	—
		Americans.		
60	—	Arawaks of Dutch Guiana	82.6	—
63 (S.)	—	Haidas	82.7	—
77	—	Maricopas (Yuma Indians)	82.9	—
129	—	Zuñi Indians	83.0	—
16	—	Indians of S. Oregon	84.0	82.2
—	22	Navajos (deformed)	84.2	—
26 (S.)	—	Bilculas	84.5	—
74	—	Comanches	84.6	—
16	—	Yucatecs of Mexico	84.7	—
193	—	Moquis or Mokis	84.9	—
18	—	Patagonians	85.2	—
		Africans.		
20	—	Saras of Shari (Basin of Lake Chad)	82.4	—
14	—	Hovas of Madagascar	84.0	—
		Oceanians.		
10	—	Islanders of Fanafuti (Ellice group)	82.4	—
23	19	Islanders of Tonga Arch.	82.6	84.2
—	177	Hawaiians of Sandwich Islands	—	80.4
23	13 (S.)	Samoans	83.7	77.5
43	52 (S.)	Polynesians of Tahiti, Marquesas, Pomotu, and Tubuai Islands	85.1	76.0
		Europeans.		
126	—	Votiaks	82.0	—
100	—	Permiaks	82.2	—
36	—	Zyrians	82.2	—
199	—	Belgian Wallons	82.2	—
30,970	—	Italians of Liguria and Tuscany	82.3	—
290	—	Bielorousses or White Russians	82.4	—
775	—	Alsatians of Lower Alsace	82.5	—
294	—	Italians in general	82.7	—
261	—	Ossets	82.6	—
3,000	—	Bretons (France)	82.7	—
30	—	Tatars of Kassimov	82.8	—
447	421 (S.)	Great Russians of the Central and N. provinces	82.9	80.7
220	—	French Basques	83.0	—

NUMBER.		ETHNIC GROUPS.	CEPH. IND.	
Living Subjects.	Skulls.		Living Subjects.	Skulls.
98	—	Wurtembergers	83.1	—
168	—	Mordvinians	83.3	—
416	—	Jews of Galicia and Western Russia	83.4	—
1,355	—	Ruthenians of the Plain (Galicia)	83.4	—
90	—	Georgian-Gruzins	83.5	—
17	—	Veps or Chud of Olonetsk	83.5	—
187	—	Ruthenians of the Mountains (Galicia)	83.6	—
15,914	—	French in general	83.6	—
170	—	Tatars of the Mountains (Caucasus)	83.6	—
165	—	Cherkess-Kabards	83.7	—
20	—	Russian Lapps	83.8	—
19	—	Georgian-Svanes	83.9	—
6,800	—	Inhabitants of Baden	84.1	—
53,020	—	Italians (Lomb., Umbr., March.)	84.1	—
226	40 (S.)	Magyars in general	84.5	82.3
78	—	Eastern Chechen	84.5	—
200	—	Little Russians of Kiev	84.6	—
52	—	Lesghi-Didos	84.6	—
44	—	Kumyks of the Caucasus	84.7	—
52,410	—	Italians of Venetia-Emilia	85.1	—
—	134	Swiss of Untervalden	—	83.8
53	—	Jews of Akhaltsikh (Caucasus)	85.2	—
		BRACHYCEPHALS, 85.3-86.9 (83.3-84.9).		
		Asiatics.		
56	—	Galchas (Russian Turkestan)	85.5	—
—	16	Tunguse-Orochons	—	83.4
17	17	Siamese	—	83.0
341	—	Armenians in general	85.6	—
—	13	Burmese of Arakan and Talaing	—	83.7
21	18	Sundanese (West Java)	86.3	85.5
20 (S.)	35 (S.)	Giliaks	86.3	83.4
16 (S.)	—	Bicols of Luzon (Philippines)	86.6	—
333	—	Taranchi of Russian and Eastern Turkestan	86.6	—
270	—	Armenians of Transcaucasia	85.6	—
		Europeans.		
—	1000 (S.)	Bavarians of old Bavaria	—	83.2
32,790	—	Piedmontese	85.9	—
16	—	Tatar Nogai of the Caucasus	85.8	—
130	—	Lesghi-Darghis of the Caucasus	86.2	—

NUMBER.		ETHNIC GROUPS.	CEPH. IND.	
Living Subjects.	Skulls.		Living Subjects.	Skulls.
200	—	Rumanians of Bukovina	86.3	—
25	—	Lesghi-Udes	86.6	—
27	—	Georgian Lazes	86.8	—
235	—	Savoyards	86.9	—
		Oceanians and Americans.		
20	20 (S.)	Islanders of Tahiti	85 5	76.6
—	36	Aleuts	—	84.8
—	100	Araucans of Argentine Republic	—	83.9
		HYPER-BRACHYCEPHALS, 87 (85) AND ABOVE.		
		Europeans.		
—	65 (S.)	Romanches of Switzerland	—	85.0
30	—	Dalmatians	87.0	—
19	—	Jews of Daghestan (Mountaineers)	87.0	—
105 (S.)	41 (S.)	Scandinavian Lapps	87.4	85.0
69	—	Magyars of Rumania	87.8	—
140	—	French (Haute-Loire, Lozère, Cantal)	87.4	—
		Asiatics.		
384	—	Kirghiz-Kasaks and Karakirghiz	87.2	—
33	—	Aissors of Transcaucasia and Urmia	88.7	—

APPENDIX III.

NASAL INDEX OF LIVING SUBJECTS, 71 SERIES

(see p. 79).

Number of Subjects.	ETHNIC GROUPS.	Nasal Index.	Observers.
	Leptorhinians (*less than* 70).		
110	Armenians - - - -	60.4	Pantiukhof
62	Georgian Imers - - -	60.8	Pan., Chantre, Erckert
1,969	Brahmans, Rajputs and other high castes, N.W. province and Oudh - - - -	63.0	Crooke, Drake-Brocken
100	French (fair type, dolicho.) -	63.0	Collignon
41	Georgian Mingrelians - -	63.1	Pan., Chantre, Erckert
49	Georgian Gruzins - - -	64.5	Pan., Chantre, Erckert
50	Lorraines - - - -	64.6	Collignon
30	French Catalans (Eastern Pyr.) - - - -	65.1	,,
20	Anglo-Scotch - - -	65.1	Beddoe
23	Arabs of Tunis - - -	65.2	Collignon
50	French dolichoceph. of the South. - - - -	65.7	,,
184	Various Kabyles - - -	66.5	Prengruber
160	French of Normandy - -	66.5	Collignon
88	Sardinians - - - -	66.6	Gilbert d'Hercourt
27	Galchas of Turkestan - -	66.8	Ujfalvy
237	Ossets - - - - -	66.8	Ghiltchen., Ch., Erck.
168	Mordvinians - - - -	66.9	Maïnof
21	English - - - -	67.0	Beddoe
1,443	Dravido-Hindus, N.W. Prov.	67.0	——
1,000	French in general - - -	67.3	Collignon
70	Bretons - - - -	67.5	,,
80	Pathans of the Punjab - -	68.4	Risley
80	Sikhs - - - - -	68.8	,,
98	Parisians - - - -	69.1	Collignon
60	Baluchis of Baluchistan - . -	69.4	Risley
120	Tunisians (2nd Berber race) -	69.8	Collignon

Number of Subjects.	ETHNIC GROUPS.	Nasal Index.	Observers.
	Mesorhinians (70-84.9).		
10	Scotch - - - - - -	70.0	Beddoe
1,334	Tunisians in general - -	70.2	Collignon
444	Pünjabis - - - - -	70.2	Risley
865	Dravidians (Kharvars, Korwas, Cheros, Khunjas) of N.W. Prov. - - - - -	71.0	Crooke, Drake-Brock.
20	Baltis of Cashmere - -	71.4	Ujfalvy
50	Berbers (brachycephalic race)	72.5	Collignon
29	Singhalese - - - - -	74.9	Deschamps, Manouv.
36	Kalmuks of the Volga - -	74.7	Deniker, Erck., Chantre
40	Kara-Kirghiz of Semiriechie -	74.9	Seeland
27	Todas - - - - - -	74.9	Thurston
40	Badagas of Nilgiris - -	75.6	,,
23	Siouans - - - - -	75.9	Denik., Laloy, Manouv.
33	Kanarese of Mysore - -	76.8	Thurston
40	Tamil-Brahmans of Madras -	77.2	,,
22	Kotas of the Nilgiri Hills -	79.2	,,
36	Malayalim of the Chevaroy Hills - - - - -	74.4	,,
20	Dums of Chota Nagpur -	79.1	Risley
695	Hindus of Behar - - -	80.0	,,
1,616	Hindus of the N.W. Provs. and Oudh - - - - -	80.9	,,
17	Rhodias of Ceylon (both sexes) - - - - -	81.3	Deschamps
32	Kols of the N.W. Provinces and Oudh - - - - -	82.2	Risley and Oude
100	Kurmis of Chota Nagpur -	82.6	,,
90	Maghs or Arakanese of Chittagong - - - -	82.7	,,
30	Annamese of Cochin-China -	83.3	Deniker, Laloy
34	Irulas of the Nilgiris - -	83.4	Thurston
100	Chakamas (Arakanese-Bengalis) - - - - -	85.4	Risley
23	Zuñis - - - - - -	84.9	Ten Kate
	Platyrhinians (85-99.9).		
23	Annamese of Tong King -	86.2	Deniker, Laloy
90	Bhumij of Chota Nagpur -	86.5	Risley
27	Bashilanges - - - -	87.0	Maistre
21	Bubangis - - - - -	87.2	Maistre
100	Santals of Chota Nagpur -	88.8	Risley
15	Kurumbas of Wynaad - -	88.8	Thurston

Number of Subjects.	ETHNIC GROUPS.	Nasal Index.	Observers.
100	Munda-Kols of Chota Nagpur	89.0	Risley
13	Polynesians - - - -	89.8	After Collignon
11	New Caledonians and New Hebridians - - -	93.8	Collignon
17	Fulahs or Fulbés - - -	95.3	Deniker, Collignon
44	Negroes of Tunis - - -	96.3	Collignon
21	Toucouleurs - - - -	99.9	Deniker
	Ultraplatyrhinians (*over* 100).		
23	Leybus and Serers - -	100.1	Deniker, Collignon
52	Negroes of Zambesi - -	101.5	After Collignon
21	Mandingans and Bambaras -	101.6	Deniker, Collignon
13	Ashantis - - - - -	107.5	Deniker
11	Australians - - - -	107.6	After Collignon
14	Angolese Negroes (both sexes)	107.9	Deniker

INDEX OF AUTHORS.

INDEX OF SUBJECTS.

THE END.